Karl Baedeker

Italy

Handbook for travellers. First part, Northern Italy and Corsica. Vol. 4

Karl Baedeker

Italy
Handbook for travellers. First part, Northern Italy and Corsica. Vol. 4

ISBN/EAN: 9783337212162

Printed in Europe, USA, Canada, Australia, Japan

Cover: Foto ©Andreas Hilbeck / pixelio.de

More available books at **www.hansebooks.com**

HANDBOOK FOR TRAVELLERS

BY

K. BÆDEKER.

FIRST PART:
NORTHERN ITALY AND CORSICA.

With 6 Maps and 27 Plans.

Second Edition, Revised and Augmented.

COBLENZ:
KARL BÆDEKER.
1870.

PREFACE.

The object of the present Handbook, like that of the Editor's other works of the same description, is to render the traveller as independent as possible of the services of guides, valets-de-place, and others of the same class, to supply him with a few remarks on the progress of civilisation and art among the people with whom he is about to become acquainted, and to enable him to realise to the fullest extent the enjoyment and instruction of which Italy is so fruitful a source.

The Handbook is, moreover, intended to place the traveller in a position to visit the places and objects most deserving of notice with the greatest possible economy of time, money, and, it may be added, temper; for in no country is the traveller's patience more severely put to the test than in some parts of Italy. The Editor will endeavour to accompany the enlightened traveller through the streets of the Italian towns, to all the principal edifices and works of art; and to guide his steps amidst the exquisite scenery in which Italy so richly abounds.

With a few very trifling exceptions, the entire book is framed from the Editor's *personal experience*, acquired at the places described. As, however, infallibility cannot be attained the editor will highly appreciate any *bonâ fide* information with which travellers may favour him. That already received, which in many instances has been most serviceable, he gratefully acknowledges.

The Maps and Plans, the result of great care and research, will abundantly suffice for the use of the ordinary traveller. The inexperienced are strongly recommended. when steering their course with the aid of a plan, before starting, to mark with a coloured pencil the point for which they are bound. This will enable them to avoid many a circuitous route. Travellers who desire a more minute acquaintance with Northern Italy will find the following excellent maps most serviceable: *Kiepert's Special Map of N. and Central Italy*, pub. by D. Reimer, Berlin, 1860 (scale 1:800,000; price 1⅓ Thlr., or 5 fr.); Nos. IV. (S. Switzerland, Savoy and Piedmont), V. (S.E. Switzerland, S. Tyrol, Lombardy and Venice), VII. (S.E. France, Sardinia, Nice, Genoa) and VIII. (Parma, Modena, Emilia, Tuscany) of *G. Mayr's Atlas of the Alps*, mounted 2 Thlr. each, admirably executed, scale 1:450,000.

Altitudes are given in English feet (1 Engl. ft. = 0,3048 mètre = 0,938 Paris. ft.).

Distances are given in English miles. The Italian 'miglio' varies in different districts. Approximately it may be stated that 1 Engl. M. = $6/7$ Ital. migl. = $1\tfrac{1}{14}$ Roman migl.

Railway, Diligence and Steamboat Timetables. The most trustworthy are contained in the '*Guida-Orario ufficiale di tutte le strade ferrate d'Italia contenente anche le indicazioni dei Piroscafi* (steamboats), *Corrieri, Diligenze*' etc., with map, published at Milan (price 40 c.).

Hotels. In no country does the treatment which the traveller experiences at hotels vary so much as in Italy, and attempts at extortion are probably nowhere so outrageous. The asterisks are therefore to be regarded as indicating those hotels which the Editor believes to be *comparatively* respectable, clean and reasonable. The average charges stated in the handbook will at least enable the traveller to form a fair estimate of the demands which can be justly made.

CONTENTS.

		Page
I.	Travelling Expenses. Monetary System	XI
II.	Period and Plan of Tour	XII
III.	Language	XIII
IV.	Passports and Custom-houses	XIV
V.	Public Safety. Mendicity	XIV
VI.	Traffic	XIV
VII.	Locomotion	XVI
VIII.	Hotels	XVII
IX.	Restaurants and Cafés	XIX
X.	Churches, Theatres, Shops etc.	XX
XI.	Postal Arrangements	XXI
XII.	Calculation of Time	XXII
XIII.	Climate. Mode of Living	XXII

ROUTES TO ITALY.

Route		Page
1.	From Paris to Nice by Lyons and Marseilles	1
	1. From Strasbourg (Bâle) to Lyons	5
	2. From Geneva to Lyons	6
	3. From Sorgues to Carpentras	13
	4. Vaucluse	16
	5. St. Remy. Nimes	16
	6. Montpellier	18
	7. Aix	21
	8. Hyères	26
2.	From Paris *(Geneva)* to Turin by Mont Cenis	29
	1. From Geneva to Culoz	29
	2. Haute Combe	29
3.	From Lausanne to Arona on the Lago Maggiore *(and Milan)* over the Simplon	33
4.	From Lucerne to Como *(and Milan)* over the St. Gotthard	38
	1. Monte Camoghè	44
5.	From Coire to Colico *(and Milan)* over the Splügen	45
6.	From Coire to Magadino on the Lago Maggiore *(and Milan)* over the Bernardino	49
7.	From Innsbruck to Colico *(and Milan)* over the Stelvio	51
	1. Ortler	54
	2. Sta. Caterina. Mte. Confinale. Piz Umbrail	55
8.	From Innsbruck to Verona by the Brenner	57
	1. From Trent to Venice by the Val Sugana	61
	2. From Trent to Verona by Riva and the Lago di Garda	62
9.	From Vienna to Trieste. Semmering Railway	64
	1. Quicksilver Mines of Idria	67
	2. From Trieste to Pola and Fiume	70

NORTHERN ITALY.

Route	Page
10. Turin	72
1. The Superga	80
2. From Turin to Torre Luserna by Pignerol	80
11. From Turin to Aosta	80
12. From Turin to Piacenza by Alessandria	83
1. From Tortona to Novi	83
2. From Piacenza to Bobbio	85
3. Velleia	85
13. From Turin to Genoa	85
14. Genoa	86
1. Villa Pallavicini at Pegli	93
15. From Genoa to Nice by the Riviera di Ponente	94
1. The Berceau	99
2. From Mentone to Nice by the Route de la Corniche	99
16. Nice and Environs	100
17. From Nice to Turin by the Col di Tenda	106
1. Certosa di Val Pesio. Baths of Valdieri	108
2. From Savigliano to Saluzzo	109
3. From Cavaller Maggiore to Brà and Alessandria	109
4. From Villastellone to Carignano	109
18. From Turin to Milan by Novara	110
1. From Santhià to Biella	110
2. From Vercelli to Valenza	110
3. From Novara to Gozzano	111
19. Milan	111
20. From Milan to Como. The Brianza	120
1. From Seregno to Bellaggio by the Brianza	121
2. Monte S. Primo	122
3. From Como to Lecco by Erba	123
21. Lake of Como	124
1. Lake of Lecco	130
22. From the Lake of Como to the Lake of Lugano and the Lago Maggiore	131
1. From Como to Laveno direct	131
1. From Varese to Gallarate	131
2. From Como to Luino by Lugano	132
2. Monte Generoso	132
3. Monte S. Salvadore	134
4. Monte Brè. Monte Caprino	135
3. From Cadenabbia or Menaggio by Porlezza and Lugano to Laveno	136
5. Madonna del Monte	136
23. Lago Maggiore. Borromean Islands. From Arona to Milan	137
24. From Stresa to Varallo. Monte Motterone. Lake of Orta. Val di Sesia	142
1. The Sacro Monte near Orta	143
2. The Sacro Monte near Varallo	144
25. From Arona to Genoa	145
1. From Mortara to Vigevano	145
2. From Alessandria to Acqui	146

Route	Page
26. From Milan to Genoa by Pavia. Certosa di Pavia	147
1. From Pavia to Valenza	149
27. From Milan to Verona	149
1. From Bergamo to Lecco	150
28. The Lago di Garda	151
1. Fall of the Ponal. Monte Brione. Monte Baldo. Giudicaria	153
2. From Riva to Mori	154
29. From Pavia to Brescia by Cremona	154
30. Brescia	155
31. From Brescia to Tirano in the Valtellina. Lago d'Iseo. Monte Aprica	159
1. The Tonale Route	161
32. From Milan to Cremona	162
1. Soncino	163
2. From Cremona to Parma and Piacenza	163
33. Verona	163
34. From Verona to Mantua. From Mantua to Modena. Reggio, Parma, Cremona or Brescia	169
1. Pietöle	171
2. Mirandöla	171
35. From Verona to Venice. Vicenza	172
1. Baths of Recoaro	174
36. Padua	175
37. From Padua to Bologna by Ferrara	179
1. Adria	180
2. Cento	184
38. Venice	184
1. Murano	212
2. Torcello. Chioggia	213
39. From Venice to Trieste	213
a. By Land viâ Udine	213
1. From Conegliano to Belluno	214
2. Aquileia	215
b. Sea Voyage to Trieste	215
40. From Milan to Bologna	216
1. Scandiano	218
2. Correggio	218
3. Canossa	218
41. Parma	219
42. Modena	222
1. Nonantöla	225
2. Vignöla	225
3. Sassuola	225
43. Bologna	225
44. From Bologna to Ancona	234
1. S. Marino	239
2. Urbino	241
45. Ancona and its Environs. Osimo. Loreto	243
46. From Bologna to Ravenna	248
1. From Ravenna to Ferrara	256
2. From Ravenna to Rimini	256
47. From Bologna to Florence	257

CONTENTS.

Route	Page
48. From Genoa to Florence (by sea) by Leghorn, Pisa, and Empoli	258
49. From Genoa to Pisa (by land) by La Spezia	262
1. From Avenza to Carrara	264
50. Pisa	165
1. Environs of Pisa	272
51. From Pisa to Florence by Lucca and Pistoja	273
1. The Baths of Lucca	277
52. Florence	282
53. Environs of Florence	324
a. S. Miniato	324
b. Poggio Imperiale. Torre del Gallo. Villa del Galileo	325
c. Certosa in the Val d'Ema	326
d. Bello Sguardo	327
e. Monte Oliveto	327
f. The Cascine. Villa Demidoff. Villa Careggi. Villa della Petraja	328
g. Fiesole	329
h. S. Salvi	331
i. Vallombrosa	331
k. Camaldoli and Alvernia. The Casentino	333
54. Island of Corsica	335
Ajaccio	337
From Ajaccio to Bonifacio, and to Bastia by the E. Coast	339
From Ajaccio to Bastia	340
Corte and the Monte Rotondo	341
Bastia	343
From Bastia to Capo Corso, S. Fiorenzo and Calvi	343
Index	345

Maps and Plans.

1. General Map of N. Italy: before the title.
2. Map of the Environs of Nice: between pp. 104, 105.
3. Map of the Italian Lakes: between pp. 124, 125.
4. Map of the Environs of Florence: between pp. 324, 325.
5. Map of the Island of Corsica: between pp. 336, 337.
6. Railway Map of N. Italy: after the Index.

Plans of: 1. Ancona. 2. Avignon. 3. Bergamo. 4. Bologna. 5. Brescia. 6. Cremona. 7. Ferrara. 8. Florence. 9. Genoa. 10. Lucca. 11. Lyons. 12. Mantua. 13. Marseilles. 14. Milan. 15. Modena. 16. Nice. 17. Nîmes. 18. Padua. 19. Parma. 20. Pavia. 21. Pisa. 22. Ravenna. 23. Trieste. 24. Turin. 25. Venice. 26. Verona. 27. Vicenza.

Abbrevations.

M. = Engl. mile; hr. = hour; min. = minute; r. = right; l. = left; N. = north, northwards, northern; S. = south etc.; E. = east etc.; W. = west etc.; R. = room; B. = breakfast; D. = dinner; A. = attendance; L. = light.

Asterisks

denote objects deserving of special attention.

INTRODUCTION.

> "Thou art the garden of the world, the home
> Of all Art yields, and Nature can decree;
> Even in thy desert, what is like to thee?
> Thy very weeds are beautiful, thy waste
> More rich than other climes' fertility,
> Thy wreck a glory, and thy ruin graced
> With an immaculate charm which cannot be defaced."
>
> Byron.

From the earliest ages down to the present time Italy has ever exercised a powerful influence on the denizens of more northern lands, and a journey thither has often been the fondly cherished wish of many an aspiring traveller. At the present day this wish may be gratified with comparative facility. A great network of railways now overspreads the entire peninsula, and even the more remote towns may be visited with little sacrifice of time. Northern Italy, more especially, with Milan, Venice, and Genoa, is of very easy access to travellers in Switzerland and the Tyrol; and, although its attractions are doubtless inferior to those of Florence, Rome, and Naples, it is replete with interest and instruction for the ordinary traveller, as well as for those whose object is scientific research. Rapidity of locomotion is not, however, the sole advantage which has been attained since that period. A single monetary system has superseded the numerous and perplexing varieties of coinage formerly in use; the annoyances inseparable from passports and custom-houses, with which the traveller was assailed at every frontier, and even in many an insignificant town, have been greatly mitigated; and energetic measures have been adopted in order to put an end to the extortions of vetturini, facchini and other members of this irritating class.

I. Travelling Expenses. Monetary System.

The cost of a tour in Italy depends of course on the traveller's resources and habits. Generally it may be stated that the expenses need not exceed those incurred in the more frequented parts of the continent. The average expenditure of a single traveller may be estimated at 25 fr. per diem, or about half that sum when a prolonged stay is made at one place. Those who are acquainted with the language and habits of the country may succeed in reducing their expenses to still narrower limits.

In the Kingdom of Italy the French monetary system is now universal. The franc (lira or franco) contains 100 centesimi: 1 fr. 25 c. = 1 s. = 10 silbergroschen = 35 S. German kreuzer = 50 Austrian kreuzer. The silver coins in common circulation are Italian pieces of 1 and 2 fr., and Italian or French 5 fr. pieces; gold coins of the Italian or French currency of 10 and 20 fr. are the commonest (those of 5 and 40 fr. rare). The 5-centime piece, or sou, is termed soldo. Since the war of 1866 a paper-currency, at a compulsory rate of exchange, has been introduced, in consequence of which the valuable metals have entirely disappeared from ordinary circulation. Copper and banknotes down to 2 fr. are almost exclusively encountered. Besides this paper-currency issued by government, a number of towns issue notes of 50 c. and 1 fr., which are utterly worthless in other parts of the country. The change for gold or silver should always be given in silver; and paper should be declined, unless 6—7 per cent in excess of the value be proffered, a premium which the money-changers generally give. In the same way paper may be exchanged for gold or silver, at a loss of 8—10 per cent. Two points, however, should in the latter case be observed: (1) the notes of small amount (2 and 5 fr.) should be preferred, owing to the difficulty of changing those of greater value in ordinary traffic; (2) public and railway offices refuse to give change when payment is made in paper. In the latter case the precise sum should be tendered, as any amount in excess, or short of the fare is alike declined. In case of emergencies, the traveller should of course be provided with a reserve of silver. French banknotes are on a par with gold. — The traveller in Venetia, where the Austrian currency is still in common circulation, should observe that a florin = $2^1/_2$ fr. = 100 kr.; a kreuzer is therefore equivalent to $2^1/_2$ centimes.

The traveller should, before entering Italy, provide himself with *French Gold*, or *French Banknotes*, which he may procure in England, France or Germany on more advantageous terms than in Italy. *Sovereigns* are received at the full value (25 fr. in silver) by most of the principal hotel keepers, but this is not the case in the less frequented districts. For the transport of large sums the 10 *l. circular notes* issued by the London bankers will be found convenient.

II. Period and Plan of Tour.

The *season* selected, and the *duration* of the tour determined on must of course depend on the traveller himself. As a general rule the spring and autumn months are the most favourable, especially September, when the heat of summer has considerably abated. The winter in Lombardy and Piedmont is not less severe than in England and W. Europe generally. Nice and Venice are recommended as the most suitable residences for the cold season. The height of summer can hardly be recommended for travelling. The scenery, indeed, is then in perfection, and the long days are hailed with satisfaction by the active traveller; but the fierce rays of an Italian sun seldom fail to exercise a prejudicial influence upon the physical and mental energies. This result is not occasioned so much by the intensity as by the protracted duration of the heat, the sky being frequently cloudless and not a drop of rain falling for several months in succession. The first showers of autumn, which fall about the end of August, again commence to refresh the parched atmosphere.

III. Language.

The time and labour which the traveller has bestowed on the study of the Italian language at home will be amply repaid as he proceeds on his journey. It is by no means impossible to travel through Italy without an acquaintance with Italian or French, but in this case the traveller cannot conveniently deviate from the ordinary track and is moreover invariably charged *(alla Inglese)* by hotel-keepers and others, considerably in excess of the ordinary prices. A knowledge of French is of the greatest advantage, for the Italians are extremely partial to that language, and avail themselves of every opportunity of employing it. For those, however, who desire to confine their expenditure within the average limits, a slight acquaintance with the language † of the country is indispensable.

Nowhere more than in Italy is the traveller who is ignorant of the language debarred from much of the true enjoyment of travelling, and from the opportunity of forming an independent opinion of the country, its customs, history, literature and art.

---

† "*Baedeker's Manual of Conversation in four languages (English, French, German and Italian) with vocabulary etc.*" (20th edit.) will be found serviceable for this purpose. With the addition of a pocket-dictionary the traveller may safely encounter the difficulties of the situation. A few brief remarks on the pronunciation may here be made for the benefit of those unacquainted with the language. *C* before *e* and *i* is pronounced like the English ch, *g* before *e* and *i* like j. Before other vowels *c* and *g* are hard. *Ch* and *gh*, which generally precede *e* or *i*, are hard; *sc* before *e* or *i* is pronounced like sh, *gn* and *gl* between vowels like ny and ly. In other respects the pronunciation of Italian more nearly resembles that of German than that of French or English. The prosody occasionally presents difficulties, being different from what one would naturally expect: e. g. Udĭne, Vigĕvăno, Nabrĕsĭna. — In addressing persons of the educated classes 'lei' with the 3rd pers. sing. should always be employed (addressing several at once, 'loro' with the 3rd pers. pl.) 'Voi' is used in addressing waiters, drivers etc., 'tu' by those only who are proficient in the language. 'Voi' is the commonest mode of address employed by the Neapolitans, but is generally regarded as inelegant or uncourteous.

IV. Passports and Custom-houses.

On entering the kingdom of Italy, the traveller's passport is rarely demanded, but it is unwise not to be provided with one of these documents, as it may occasionally prove useful. Registered letters, for example, will not be handed over to strangers, unless they exhibit a passport to prove their identity.

The examination of luggage at the Italian Custom-houses is usually extremely lenient. Tobacco and cigars are the articles especially sought for.

V. Public Safety. Mendicity.

Italy is still frequently regarded as the land of Fra Diavolo's and Rinaldo Rinadini's — an impression fostered by tales of travellers, sensational letters to newspapers, etc. The fact, however, is, that travelling in Northern and Central Italy is hardly attended with more hazard than in any of the more northern European countries.

Mendicity, countenanced and encouraged according to the former system of Italian politics, still continues to be one of those national nuisances to which the traveller must habituate himself. The system is energetically opposed by the new regime, but in Venetia and many of the smaller towns it prevails to the same extent as formerly. Begging in Italy, to a still greater degree than in other places, is rather a trade than a genuine demand for sympathy. The best mode of liberation is to bestow a small donation, a supply of the smallest coin of the realm being provided for the purpose. A beggar, who in return for a donation of 2 c. thanked the donor with the usual benedictions, was on another occasion presented with 50 c., an act of liberality which, instead of being gratefully accepted, only called forth the remark in a half-offended tone: "ma signore è molto poco!"

VI. Traffic.

In Italy the highly pernicious custom of demanding considerably more than will ultimately be accepted is the invariable rule: but with a knowledge of the custom, as it is based entirely upon the presumed ignorance of one of the contracting parties, the evil is greatly mitigated.

Where tariffs and fixed charges exist, they should be carefully consulted. In other cases a certain average price is generally established by custom, under which circumstances the traveller should make a precise bargain with respect to the service to be rendered, and never rely on the equity of the other party.

Those individuals who appeal to the generosity of the stranger, or to their own honesty, or who, as rarely happens, are offended by the traveller's manifestation of distrust, may well be answered in the words of the proverb: *"patti chiari, amicizia lunga"*. In the following pages the prices, even of insignificant objects, are stated with all possible accuracy; and although they are liable to constant fluctuations, they will at least serve as a guide to the stranger and prove a safeguard against many gross extortions. The editor ventures to offer a homely hint, that the equanimity of the traveller's own temper will greatly assist him if involved in a dispute or a bargain, and no attention whatever should be paid to vehement gesticulations or an offensive demeanour. The less the knowledge of the Italian language, the more careful should the traveller be not to involve himself in a war of words, in which he must necessarily be at great disadvantage.

As a matter of course, no weight should be attached to the representations of drivers, guides etc., with whom even the inhabitants of the place often appear to act in concert.

Caution is everywhere desirable in Italy, but if it assumes the form of exaggerated distrust it may be construed as the result of fear or weakness on the part of the traveller, whose best safeguard is often his own self-confidence; and it must be admitted, that, the preliminaries once arranged, a trustworthiness is often exhibited of which an earlier demeanour gave no promise.

An abundant supply of copper coins should always be at the traveller's command in a country where very frequent, though trifling donations are in constant demand. Drivers, guides, porters, donkey-attendants etc. invariably expect, and often demand as their right, a gratuity *(buona mano, mancia, da bere, bottiglia, caffè, fumata)* in addition to the hire agreed on, and which varies according to circumstances from 2—3 sous to a franc or more. The traveller need feel no embarrassment in limiting his donations to the smallest possible dimensions. Liberality is frequently a source of future annoyance and embarrassment. Half-a-franc bestowed where two sous would have sufficed may be fertile in disagreeable results to the injudicious traveller; the fact speedily becomes known, and other applicants make their appearance whose demands it becomes utterly impossible to satisfy.

The demeanour of the stranger towards the natives must be somewhat modified in accordance with the various parts of the country through which he travels. Northern Italy, with the exception perhaps of Venice, may on the whole be pronounced safe in this respect. As a rule, the inhabitants of this part of the country will be found polite and obliging, whilst attempts at extortion are comparatively rare, and fixed scales of charges at the hotels and shops are now becoming more universal.

VII. Locomotion.

Railways. With regard to the rapid advance of this modern essential of civilisation the remarks already made (p. XI) may suffice. It may be added that the greatest speed attained by the trains is extremely moderate.

The most trustworthy information respecting hours of starting, fares etc. is afforded by the '*Guida orario ufficiale di tutte le strade ferrate d'Italia*' (see p. VI), containing a map, published at Milan by Edoardo Sonzogno (price 40 c.), with which the traveller should not fail to provide himself.

Steamboats. Tickets should be purchased by the traveller in person at the office of the company, and no attention paid to the proffered services of loiterers in the vicinity. Family-tickets for the first or second class for not fewer than three persons are issued by all the companies at a reduction of 20 per cent on the fare, but not on the cost of food. A child of 2—10 years pays half-fare, but in this case must share the berth of its attendant. Two children are furnished with a berth for themselves. The tickets of the Messageries Impériales are available for four months, and the voyage may be broken at the passenger's discretion.

The saloons and berths of the first class are comfortably and elegantly fitted up, those of the second tolerably.

Luggage. First-class passengers are allowed 100 kilogr. (= 2 cwt.), second-class 60 kilogr. (= 135 lbs.); but articles not intended for the passenger's private use are prohibited.

Food of good quality and ample quantity is included in the first and second-class fares. The difference between that provided for passengers of the different classes is inconsiderable. Passengers who are too ill to partake of these repasts are furnished with lemonade and minor restoratives gratuitously. Refreshments may of course be procured at other hours on payment.

Fees. The steward expects 1 fr. for a voyage of 12—24 hrs., more if the passenger has made unusual demands upon his time or patience.

Embarcation. Passengers should be on board an hour before the advertised time of starting. The charges for conveyance to the steamboat (usually 1 fr. for each pers. with luggage) are fixed by tariff at all the sea-ports, and will be found in the handbook. Passengers should therefore avoid all discussions on the subject with the boatmen, and simply direct them to row 'alla Bella Venezia', or whatever the name of the vessel may be. On arriving at the vessel, payment should not be given to the boatman until the traveller and his luggage are deposited on deck.

Diligences in Italy generally belong to private companies; where several run in competition, the more expensive are to be preferrred. The carriages are often uncomfortable, and, when ladies are of the party, the coupé (¹/₃rd dearer) should if possible be secured. Regular communication cannot be depended on, except on the principal routes. The importunities of the coachmen at the end of each stage should be disregarded.

Vetturini, by whom the sole communication between many towns was formerly maintained, are now entirely superseded by the more modern diligences and railways. The ordinary traveller will probably rarely have occasion to submit to this obsolete style of conveyance, except on the route between Savona and Mentone, and Chiavari and La Spezia. The charges of the carriages are stated in the Handbook; the traveller is, however, recommended to make a previous personal agreement with the vetturino (agents to be avoided). The contract is made 'tutto compreso', and if satisfaction is given, an additional fee may be bestowed at the termination of the journey.

A single traveller may also bargain with a vetturino for a place, the charge for which varies. The back-seats are 'i primi posti', which are generally secured by the first comers, who are first consulted with regard to the arrangement of the journey.

Besides the above-mentioned conveyances, *carriages* may everywhere be hired (one-horse about 80 c. per Engl. M.).

Prolonged *walking-tours*, such as are undertaken in more northern climates, and fatiguing excursions will be found wholly unsuitable to the Italian climate. Cool and clear weather should if possible be selected and the sirocco carefully avoided. The height of summer is totally adverse to tours of this kind.

A *horse* (cavallo) or *donkey* (sommaro), between which the difference of expense is inconsiderable, often affords a pleasant and inexpensive mode of locomotion, especially in mountainous districts, where the attendant (pedone) acts at once as a servant for the time being and as a guide.

VIII. Hotels.

The idea of cleanliness in Italy is in arrear of the age; the brilliancy of the southern climate perhaps, in the opinion of the natives, neutralizes dirt. The traveller will, however, not suffer much annoyance in this respect in hotels and lodgings of the best class. Those who quit the beaten track, on the other hand, must be prepared for privations. Insect-powder *(polvere di Persia)* or powdered camphor is some antidote to the advances of nocturnal intruders. The *zanzáre*, or gnats, are a source of great annoyance, and often suffering, during the autumn months. Windows should always be carefully closed before a light is introduced into the room. Light muslin curtains (zanzarieri) round the beds, masks for the face, and gloves are employed to ward off the attacks of these pertinacious tormentors.

In all the more frequented places, good hotels of the first class, equal in comfort to those in other parts of Europe, are always to be found, the landlords of which are frequently German and Swiss. Rooms 2½—5 fr., bougies 75 c.—1 fr., attendance 1 fr., table d'hôte 4 fr. and so on. Families, for whose reception the hotels are often specially fitted up, should make an agreement with the landlord with regard to pension (8—10 fr. each). Strangers are expected to dine at the table d'hôte, otherwise the price of the room is raised, or the inmate is given to understand that it is let over his head. French spoken everywhere. Cuisine a mixture of French and Italian.

The second-class inns are thoroughly Italian, rarely very clean or comfortable; charges about one-half the above; no table d'hôte, but a trattoria will generally be found connected with the house, where refreshments à la carte may be procured at any hour. These establishments will often be found convenient and economical by the voyageur en garçon, but are of course rarely visited by ladies.

The best hotels have fixed charges. Attendance, exclusive of boots and commissionaire, is charged in the bill. This is not the case in the smaller inns, where 1 fr. per diem is usually divided between the waiter and the facchino, or less for a prolonged stay. Copper coins are never despised by such recipients.

Hôtels Garnis are much frequented by those whose stay extends to 10—14 days and upwards, and the inmates enjoy greater quiet and independence than at a hotel. The charges are moreover considerably more moderate. Attendance about ½ fr. per diem.

Lodgings, of various degrees of comfort and accommodation, may also be procured for a prolonged residence. Here, likewise, a distinct agreement respecting the rent should be made beforehand. Where a whole suite of apartments is hired, a written contract should be drawn up with the aid of some one acquainted with the language and customs of the place (e. g. a banker). For single travellers a verbal agreement with regard to attendance, linen, stoves and carpets in winter, a receptacle for coal etc., will generally suffice.

A few hints may be here added for the benefit of the less experienced:

If a prolonged stay be made at a hotel, the bill should be demanded every three or four days, by which means errors, whether accidental or designed, are more easily detected. When the traveller contemplates departing at an early hour in the morning, the bill should be obtained on the previous evening, but not paid until the moment for starting has arrived. It is a favourite practice to withhold the bill till the last moment, when the hurry and confusion render overcharges less liable to discovery.

The mental arithmetic of waiters is apt to be exceedingly faulty, though rarely in favour of the traveller. A written enumeration of the items charged should therefore invariably be required, and accounts rejected in which, as not unfrequently happens, '*colazione, pranzo, vino, caffè* etc.' figure in the aggregate.

Information obtained from waiters and others of a similar class can seldom be implicitly relied upon. Enquiries should be addressed to the landlords or head-waiters alone, and even their statements received with caution.

IX. Restaurants and Cafés.

Restaurants *(trattorie)* are chiefly frequented by Italians, and travellers unaccompanied by ladies. Dinner may be obtained à la carte at any hour between 12 and 7 or 8 p. m., for 1½ — 3 fr. The waiters expect a gratuity of 2—4 soldi. The diner who desires to confine his expenses within reasonable limits should refrain from ordering dishes not comprised in the bill of fare. A late hour for the principal repast of the day should be selected in winter, in order that the daylight may be profitably employed. — Importunities on the part of the waiters are usually disposed of by the expression 'non seccarmi'.

The following list comprises most of the commoner Italian dishes:

Zuppa, soup.
Consumè, broth or bouillon.
Santè or *minestra*, soup with green vegetables and bread.
Gnocchi, small puddings.
Riso con piselli, rice-soup with peas.
Risotto, a species of rice pudding (rich).
Maccaroni al burro, with butter; *al pomi d'oro*, with paradise apples.
Manzo, boiled beef.
Fritti, fried meat.
Arrosti, roasted meat.
Bistecca, beefsteak.
Coscietto, loin.
Arrosto di vitello, roast veal.
Testa di vitello, calf's head.
Fegato di vitello, calf's liver.
Braccioletta di vitello, veal-cutlet.
Costoletta alla minuta, veal-cutlet with calf's ears and truffles.
Patate, potatoes.
Quaglia, quail.
Tordo, field-fare.
Lodola, lark.
Sfoglia, a species of sole.
Principi alla tavola, hot relishes.

Pollo, fowl.
Pollastro, turkey.
Umidi, meat with sauce.
Stufatino, ragout.
Erbe, vegetables.
Carciofi, artichokes.
Piselli, peas.
Lenticchie, lentils.
Cavoli fiori, cauliflower.
Fave, beans.
Fagiuolini, French beans.
Mostarda, simple mustard.
Senape, hot mustard.
Ostriche, oysters (good in winter only).
Giardinetto, fruit-desert.
Crostata di frutti, fruit-tart.
Crostata di pasta sfoglia, a species of pastry.
Fragole, strawberries.
Pera, pear.
Persiche, peaches.
Uva, bunch of grapes.
Limone, lemon.
Portogallo, orange.
Finocchio, root of fennel.
Pane francese, bread made with yeast (the Italian is made without).

Funghi, mushrooms (often too rich).
Presciutto, ham.
Salami, sausage.

Formaggio, cheese.
Vino nero, red wine; *bianco*, white; *asciutto*, dry; *dolce*, sweet; *nostrale*, table-wine.

Cafés are frequented for breakfast and lunch, and in the evening by numerous consumers of ices. Café noir *(caffè nero)* is usually drunk (20 c. per cup). *Caffè latte* is coffee mixed with milk before served (20 c.), or caffè *e* latte, i. e. with the milk served separately, may be preferred. *Mischio* is a mixture of coffee and chocolate (15—20 c.), considered wholesome and nutritious. The usual viands for lunch are ham, sausages, cutlets and eggs *(uova da bere*, soft; *toste*, hard; *uova al piatto*, fried).

Ices *(sorbetto* or *gelato)* of every possible variety are supplied at the cafés (30—90 c. per portion); a half portion *(mezzo)* may always be ordered. *Granita*, or half-frozen ice *(limonata* of lemons; *aranciata* of oranges), is especially in vogue in the forenoon. The waiter *(bottega)* expects a sou or more according to the amount of the payment; he occasionally makes mistakes in changing money, if not narrowly watched.

The principal Parisian newspapers are to be found at all the larger cafés, English rarely.

Valets de Place *(servitori di piazza)* may be hired at 5 fr. per diem, the employer previously distinctly specifying the services to be rendered. They are generally trustworthy and respectable, but implicit reliance should not be placed on their statements respecting the places most worthy of a visit, which the traveller should ascertain from the guide-book or other source. Their services may always be dispensed with, unless time is very limited. Travellers are cautioned against employing the *sensali*, or commissionaires of an inferior class, who pester the stranger with offers of every description. Contracts with vetturini, and similar negociations should never be concluded through such a medium, or indeed any other. Interventions of this description invariably tend to increase prices, and are often productive of still more serious contretemps. This remark applies especially to villages and small towns, whether on or out of the regular track.

X. Churches, Theatres, Shops etc.

Churches are open till noon, and usually again from 4 to 7 p. m. Visitors may inspect the works of art even during the hours of divine service, provided they move about noiselessly, and keep aloof from the altar where the clergy are officiating. The verger *(sagrestano*, or *nonzolo)* receives a fee of $1/2$ fr. or upwards, if his services are required.

Theatres. The representations in the large theatres begin at 8, and terminate at midnight or later. Here operas and ballets are exclusively performed; the first act of an opera is usually succeeded by a ballet of 3 or more acts. Verdi is the most popular composer. The pit (platea) is the usual resort of the men. A box (palco) must always be secured in advance. — A visit to the smaller theatres, where dramas and comedies are acted, is especially recommended for the sake of habituating the ear to the language. Representations in summer take place in the open air, in which case smoking is allowed. The charming comedies of Goldoni are still among the most popular. — The theatre is a favourite evening-resort of the Italians, by whom during the performance of the music profound silence is never observed.

Shops rarely have fixed prices. As a rule two-thirds or three-quarters of the price demanded should be offered. The same rule applies to artizans, drivers and others. '*Non volete?*' (then you will not?) is a remark which generally has the effect of bringing the matter to a speedy termination. Purchases should never be made by the traveller when accompanied by a valet-de-place. These individuals, by tacit agreement, receive at least 10 per cent of the purchase-money, which naturally comes out of the pocket of the purchaser. This system of extortion is carried so far that, when a member of the above class observes a stranger enter a shop, he presents himself at the door and afterwards claims his percentage under the pretext that by *his* recommendation the purchase has been made. In such cases it is by no means superfluous to call the attention of the shopkeeper to the imposition ('*non conosco quest' uomo*').

Cigars in Italy, France and Austria are a monopoly of Government; those under 7—10 soldi scarcely smokable. Passers-by freely avail themselves of the light which burns in every cigar-shop, without making any purchase.

XI. Postal Arrangements.

The address of letters (whether *poste restante* or to the traveller's hotel) should, as a rule, be in the Italian or French language. Postage-stamps are sold at all the tobacco-shops. Letters to England cost 60 c., France 40 c., Germany 40 c., Switzerland 30 c., Belgium 40, Holland (viâ France) 50 c., Denmark 50 c., Norway and Sweden (viâ Austria) 75 c., Russia (viâ Austria) 70 c., America (United-States) viâ England 80 c., viâ France 1 fr. 20 c.

Letters by town-post 5 c.; throughout the kingdom of Italy 20 c. prepaid, 30 c. unpaid. Letters to Rome must be prepaid as far as the frontier (20 c.), also vice versà.

In the larger towns the post-office is open the whole day from 9 a. m. to 10 p. m. (also on Sundays and holidays).

XII. Calculation of Time.

The old Italian reckoning from 1 to 24 o'clock is now disused, except by the humbler classes. Ave Maria = 24. The hours are altered every fortnight, being regulated by the sunset. The ordinary reckoning of other nations is termed *ora francese*. The traveller will find little difficulty in employing the Italian reckoning should he have occasion to do so.

XIII. Climate. Mode of Living.

Travellers from the north must in some degree alter their mode of living whilst in Italy, without however implicitly adopting the Italian style. Strangers generally become unusually susceptible to cold in Italy, and therefore should not omit to be well supplied with warm clothing for the winter. Carpets and stoves, to the comforts of which the Italians generally appear indifferent, are indispensable in winter. A southern aspect is an absolute essential for the delicate, and highly desirable for the robust. Colds are most easily taken after sunset and in rainy weather. — Even in summer it is a wise precaution not to wear too light clothing. Flannel is strongly recommended.

Exposure to the summer-sun should as much as possible be avoided. According to a Roman proverb, dogs and foreigners (Inglesi) alone walk in the sun, Christians in the shade. Umbrellas, and spectacles of coloured glass (grey, concave glasses to protect the whole eye are best) may be used with advantage when a walk in the sun is unavoidable. Repose during the hottest hours is advisable. a siesta of moderate length refreshing. Windows should be closed at night.

English and German medical men are to be met with in the larger cities. The Italian therapeutic art does not enjoy a very high reputation in the rest of Europe. German and English chemists, where available, are recommended in preference to the Italian. It may, however, be a wise discretion in maladies arising from local causes to employ native skill.

1. From Paris to Nice by Lyons and Marseilles.

Railway to Marseilles in 24 (express in 16¹/₄) hrs.; fares 96 fr. 65, 72 fr. 50, 53 fr. 15 c. (Express from Paris to Lyons in 9, ordinary trains 12³/₄ hrs.; fares 57 fr. 35, 43 fr., 31 fr. 55 c. From Lyons to Marseilles express in 6²/₃, ordinary trains 11¹/₄ hrs.; fares 39 fr. 40, 29 fr. 55, 21 fr. 70 c.) From Marseilles to Nice in 7¹/₂ (express in 6) hrs.; fares 25 fr. 20, 18 fr. 90, 13 fr. 85 c.

Soon after quitting Paris the train crosses the *Marne* near its confluence with the Seine at the station of *Charenton* (the lunatic asylum is on an eminence to the left). To the right and left rise the forts of *Ivry* and *Charenton*, which here command the course of the Seine. Stat. *Villeneuve St. Georges* is picturesquely situated on the slope of a wooded eminence. The beautiful green dale of the *Yères* is now traversed. Picturesque country residences, small parks, and thriving mills are passed in rapid succession. Stat. *Montgeron*. The chain of hills to the left, as well as the plain, is studded with innumerable dwellings. Before *Brunoy* is reached the train crosses the Yères, and beyond the village passes over a viaduct. The valley of the Yères is now quitted, and the district becomes flatter. Stations *Combs-la-Ville*, *Lieusaint*, and *Cesson*.

The Seine is again reached and crossed by a handsome iron bridge at **Melun** *(Hôtel de France)*, capital of the department *Seine-et-Marne*, an ancient town with a population of 11,000, known to the Romans, and picturesquely situated on an eminence above the river. The Church of Notre Dame, dating from the 10th cent., and the modern Gothic Townhall are fine edifices.

After affording several picturesque glimpses of the valley of the Seine, the train reaches the forest of Fontainebleau. Stat. *Bois-le-Roi*.

Fontainebleau *(Hôtel de Londres; Aigle Noir; Hôtel de France)* is a quiet place with broad and clean streets (popul. 11,900). In the Place du Palais de Justice rises the *Statue of General Damesme*, erected in 1851. The *Palace, an extensive pile, containing five courts, is almost exclusively indebted for its present form to Francis I. (d. 1547), and abounds in interesting historical reminiscences. The interior (accessible during the absence of the Emperor, fee 1 fr.) consists of a series of sumptuous saloons and apartments. The *Jardin Anglais* in the rear of the palace contains a pond with the venerable carp of Fontainebleau. The *Forest occupies an area of 50,000 acres (60 M. in circumference) and affords a number of delightful walks. (For farther details see *Bædeker's Paris*.)

Next stat. *Thomery*, celebrated for its luscious grapes (Chasselas de Fontainebleau). The forest is quitted here. Stat. **Moret**, a venerable town on the *Loing*, which here falls into the Seine, possesses a Gothic church of the 13th cent. and a ruined château once occupied by Sully. (Railway hence to *Nemours*, *Gien*, *Nevers*, and *Roanne*.)

The line crosses the valley of the Loing by a viaduct of 30 arches. Stat. *St. Mammès;* then **Montereau** *(Grand Monarque)*, picturesquely situated at the confluence of the Seine and Yonne. Here on Feb. 18th, 1814, Napoleon gained his last victory over the Allies and the Prince of Würtemberg. (Branch line to *Flamboin*, stat. on the Paris and Troyes line.)

The train ascends the broad and well cultivated valley of the Yonne. Stat. *Villeneuve-la-Guiard, Pont-sur-Yonne*. **Sens** *(Hôtel de l'Ecu)*, the ancient capital of the Senones, who under Brennus plundered Rome (B.C. 390), the *Agedincum* of the Romans, is now a quiet and clean town with 11,000 inhab. The early Gothic *Cathedral (St. Etienne) dates from the 12th cent.; magnificent S. Portal in the Flamboyant style. The episcopal vestments and other relics of Thomas à Becket, who sought an asylum at Sens in 1164, are shown.

The following stations are *Villeneuve-sur-Yonne, St. Julien du Sault, Cézy*. **Joigny** *(Duc de Bourgogne)*, the *Joviniacum* of the Romans, is a picturesque and ancient town (6000 inhab.) on the Yonne. Next stat. *La Roche*.

From La Roche by a branch line in 52 min. to **Auxerre** *(Hôtel du Léopard)*, capital (13,000 inhab.) of the Department of the Yonne, possessing several good churches, especially the late Gothic cathedral. *Chablis*, well known for its wines, lies between Auxerre and Tonnerre (see below), 13 1/2 M. to the E. of the former.

Near La Roche the line crosses the Yonne, into which the *Armançon* here empties itself, and follows the latter river and the *Canal de Bourgogne*, connecting the Seine and Saône.

About 6 M. from *St. Florentin* is the Cistercian *Abbey of Pontigny*, where Thomas à Becket passed two years of his exile. Langton, archbishop of Canterbury, banished by John, and other English prelates have also sought a retreat within its walls.

Tonnerre *(Lion d'Or; *Rail. Restaurant)*, picturesquely situated on the Armançon, a town with 5000 inhab., possesses a monument to the minister Louvois (d. 1691). The church of *St. Pierre*, on an eminence above the town, commands a pleasing prospect.

Stat. *Tanlay* possesses a fine château in the Renaissance style, founded by the brother of Admiral Coligny, the chief victim of St. Bartholomew's Night, who with the Prince de Condé and other Huguenot leaders held meetings in one of the apartments. Then a tunnel, 540 yds. in length; bridge over the Armançon;

tunnel 1020 yds. long, and the canal and Armançon are again crossed. From stat. *Nuits-sous-Ravières* a branch-line to *Châtillon-sur-Seine* and *Chaumont*. *Montbard*, birthplace (1707) of Buffon, the great naturalist (d. at Paris in 1788), contains his château and a monument to his memory.

Beyond stat. *Blaisy-Bas* the line penetrates the culminating ridge, or watershed (1324 ft.), between the Seine and the Rhone by a long tunnel (2¹/₂ M.). Hence to Dijon a succession of viaducts, cuttings, and tunnels. Beyond stat. *Malain*, with its ruined château, the line enters the picturesque valley of the *Ouche*, bounded on the r. by the slopes of the Côte d'Or.

Dijon (Hôtel de la Cloche; du Parc; *du Jura, near the station, R. 2, D. 3¹/₂, B. 1, A. ¹/₂ fr. De la Galère; de Bourgogne; du Nord; de Genève; the last four of the second class. Rail. Restaurant; *Café adjoining the theatre. Brasserie Alsacienne, Place St. Etienne, opposite the theatre), with 39,000 inhab., the ancient capital of the Duchy of Burgundy, is now that of the Department de la Côte d'Or. For upwards of four centuries, from 1015 to the death of Charles the Bold in 1477, this was the residence of the Dukes of Burgundy. The monuments of that period impart a higher interest to this pleasant and cheerful town.

The Rue Guillaume leads from the station to the centre of the town, where the *Palais des Etats*, the ancient residence of the Dukes, is situated. After various vicissitudes the edifice was remodelled during the last century and converted into an *Hôtel de Ville*. It contains the *Museum* (principal court to the r. in the Place d'Armes; admission gratis on Sundays and holidays 12—3 o'clock, at other times for a fee of 1 fr.), with collections of engravings, statues, casts, antique vases, and smaller antiquities.

The *Salle des Gardes, formerly the Burgundian banqueting hall, contains a large old chimney-piece; *3 altar-cabinets with beautiful wood-carving (14th cent.); the *Monument of Jean sans Peur and his consort Margaret, dating from 1444, with their statues and lions at their feet; still finer the *Monument of Philip the Bold, date 1390, with frieze adorned with 40 statuettes of celebrated contemporaries. Both these monuments were destroyed during the Revolution, but restored in 1828.

The Picture Gallery contains about 500 works, most of them mediocre: 434. Portrait of Charles the Bold, master unknown; 291. *Memling* (?), Adoration of the Shepherds; 61. *Gagneraux*, Condé's passage of the Rhine; 318, 319. *Rubens*, Sketches; 159. *Prudhon*, Portrait; 399. *P. Veronese*, Finding of Moses; 410. Copy of Raphael's School of Athens; 147. *Nattier*, Portrait of Maria Lesczinska; 31. *Coypel*, Sacrifice of Jephtha; 373. *Domenichino* (?), St. Jerome; 367. *Bassano*, The Disciples at Emmaus; 306. *Meulen*, Siege of Besançon, 1674; 24. *Colson*, Sleeping girl; 265. *Champaigne*, Presentation in the Temple.

The adjacent second court contains the Musée Archéologique (fee 50 c.). 1st Room: Ancient and mediæval bronzes, weapons, keys, carronades, etc. — 2nd R.: Mediæval sculptures and tombstones. — 3rd R.: Ancient sculptures and tombstones from the Castrum Divionense (the Rom. Dijon), milestones, remains of an ancient boat found in the Loire in 1859, etc. — The concierge also shows the vast kitchen of the Dukes, erected in 1445. The doors belong to the period of the original structure.

1*

Farther E. is the church of *St. Michael*, with a façade in which the Gothic and Renaissance styles are strangely combined, consecrated in 1529. — **Notre Dame* (N. of the Palais), consecrated in 1445, possessing a peculiar unfinished portico of the 13th cent., is more purely Gothic. — The principal church is that of **St. Bénigne* (S. of the Porte Guillaume), which has undergone frequent restoration, with portal of the 10th cent. In the vicinity are *St. Philibert*, of the 12th cent., and *St. Jean*, consecrated in 1458, the latter now disfigured by modern paintings.

The *Castle* (N. of the Porte Guillaume), now in a half-ruined condition, was erected by Louis XI. (in 1478—1512), after the union of Burgundy with France. It was subsequently employed as a state-prison. — Pursuing the same direction round the town the stranger next reaches the bronze *Statue of St. Bernhard* (born in 1091 at Fontaine lez Dijon), erected in 1847; round the pedestal are celebrated contemporaries.

The town contains a number of picturesque buildings of the Renaissance period, especially interesting to architects. The old ramparts have been converted into promenades.

The line to Mâcon crosses the *Ouche* and the *Canal de Bourgogne* (p. 2), and skirts the base of the sunny vineyards of the *Côte d'Or*, which extend almost the entire distance from Dijon to Chalon and produce the choicest qualities of the Burgundy wines *(Chambertin, Clos de Bèze, Clos de Vougeot, Romanée, Tâche, Nuits, Beaune*, etc.). To the r. of stat. *Corgoloin* is the village of *Aloxe*, another well-known wine-producing place *(Corton, Charlemagne, Clos du Roi)*. Stat. **Beaune**, with 11,000 inhab., on the *Bouzoise*, contains several Gothic edifices and a monument of the mathematician Monge, who was born here in 1747 (d. 1818).

Stat. *Meursault*. From stat. *Chagny* a branch-line diverges by *Le Creuzot* to *Nevers*. The line passes under the *Canal du Centre*, which connects the Saône and the Loire, by means of a tunnel, intersects the *Col de Chagny*, and enters the valley of the *Thalie*. Stat. *Fontaines*.

Chalon-sur-Saône *(Trois Faisans; Hôtel du Chevreuil; Hôtel de l'Europe)*, with 19,000 inhab., the *Cabillonum* of the Romans, is situated at the junction of the Canal du Centre with the Saône, which is here navigated by steamboats (to Lyons in 5—6 hrs.). The town contains little to detain the traveller. The early Gothic *Cathedral*, recently restored, exhibits the transition to that style from the Romanesque. (The express trains do not touch Chalon, the branch line to which diverges from the junction *St. Côme.)*

The line follows the r. bank of the Saône; to the l. in the distance the Jura is visible; to the r. in clear weather the snowy summit of Mont Blanc, 150 M. distant. Stat. *Tournus* (5500 inhab.) possesses a fine abbey-church (St. Philibert).

Mâcon *(Hôtels du Sauvage, des Champs Elysées, de l'Europe; Rail. Restaurant)*, capital of the Department of the Saône and the Loire, with 18,000 inhab., is another great focus of the wine-trade. The remains of the early Romanesque cathedral of *St. Vincent* are interesting to architects.

The line now continues to follow the r. bank of the Saône. Scenery pleasing. The stations between Mâcon and Lyons, thirteen in number, present little to interest the traveller.

Lyons see p. 6.

From Strasbourg (Bâle) to Lyons by *Mulhouse, Besançon*, and *Bourg*, the most direct route between the S.W. of Germany and S. France. (Railway from Strasbourg to Mulhouse in 2½ hrs.; fares 12 fr. 30, 9 fr. 25 c.; from Bâle to Mulhouse in 1 hr., fares 3 fr. 70, 2 fr. 25 c.; from Mulhouse to Lyons in 12½ hrs., fares 42 fr. 80, 32 fr. 10, 23 fr. 50 c.). Mulhouse is the junction of the Bâle-Strasbourg and the Bâle-Paris lines. The first station of importance is *Belfort* (8000 inhab.), a fortress on the *Savoureuse*, erected by Vauban under Louis XIV.; the Paris line diverges here. The train now traverses a picturesque, undulating district; to the l. rise the spurs of the Jura. Stat. *Héricourt*; then *Montbéliard*, which appertained to the German Empire until 1793. Beyond stat. *Voujacourt* the line follows the course of the *Doubs*, which it crosses several times. Then stat. *L'Isle-sur-le-Doubs* beyond which several tunnels are passed through. Several unimportant stations; then

Besançon (*Hôtel du Nord, Rue Moncey, R. 1½, D. 3, A. ½ fr., omnibus to the station 60 c.; *Paris; Europe*), the ancient *Vesontio*, capital of the Sequani, was till 1654 a town of the German Empire, in 1674 conquered by Louis XIV. and united with France. It is now the capital of Franche Comté, with 46,900 inhab. Its peculiar situation in a wide basin, on the Doubs, which flows round the town and once rendered it an important miliary point, is described by Cæsar (De B. Gal. I. 38).

The substantial, old-fashioned architecture of the town is interesting, and modern innovations are comparatively rare. One of the finest structures of the 16th cent. is the *Hôtel de Ville* in the Place St. Pierre, bearing the civic motto: *Deo et Caesari fidelis perpetuo*.

The *Museum is established in a modern building in the Place de l'Abondance (admission on Sundays 1—4 o'cl. gratis, at other times by payment of a fee). The vestibule and the staircases are adorned with Roman inscriptions and antiquities. The principal saloon contains pictures: l. *92. *A. Dürer*, Christ on the Cross, at the foot of which is the Mater Dolorosa, surrounded by 6 medallions representing the principal scenes from the life of Christ, on the wings prophets; r. 116. *Gaetano*, Portrait on copper of Cardinal Granvella (born at Besançon 1517, minister of Philipp II. in the Netherlands, viceroy of Naples and president of the privy council of Spain, d. at Madrid in 1586); *46. *Bronzino*, Descent from the Cross; r. 157. *Key*, Count Palatine Frederick III.; r. 183. Girl with a dove, painted by the Empress Marie Louise. — The other saloons contain casts and antiquities, weapons and implements of the Celtic and Roman periods found in the neighbourhood, etc. — The *Library* (open to the public on Mond., Wed. and Sat. 12—5 o'clock), founded in 1694 by Boisot, contains 100,000 vols., about 1800 MSS., a collection of coins, etc.

In the principal street, the *Grande Rue*, which ascends from the Pont de la Madeleine to the citadel, is situated the *Palais Granvells*, a handsome structure in the Renaissance style (1530—40). Farther on is the *Porte Noire, a triumphal arch of the late Roman period, of very graceful proportions and adorned with sculptures and reliefs, most of which are almost obliterated. The date of its erection is unknown. The r. side has been restored. The traveller next reaches the

**Cathedral of St. Jean*, dating from several different epochs, restored for the last time during the past century. The 1st chapel on the r. near the entrance (W.) contains the monument of the archdeacon Ferrico

Carondelet (d. 1528); above it the Death of Sapphira, by *Seb. del Piombo*. In the chapel on the l. the *Virgin surrounded by angels with SS. Sebastian, John, Dominicus, and the two founders of the picture*, by *Fra Bartolommeo*, in admirable preservation, but unfortunately not favourably hung.

The street ascends hence to the *Citadel*, constructed by Vauban (permission to visit it must be obtained from the commandant in the town). The summit commands an admirable view. At the base of the citadel (8 min. walk from the Porte de Rivotte), on the river, is situated the *Porte Taillée*, originally appertaining to a Roman aqueduct, subsequently widened so as to form a gateway.

Beyond Besançon the line crosses to the r. bank of the Doubs, intersects the Dijon and Neuchâtel line, passes three small stations, and reaches stat. **Lons-le-Saulnier**, chief town of the Department of the Jura, with 9800 inhab. Near the town are celebrated saline springs; beyond it the *Château Montmorot*, birthplace of General Lecourbe.

Stat. *St. Amour*. The line then crosses the rivers *Solnan* and *Sevron*. Stat. *St. Etienne du Bois*, pleasantly situated; then

Bourg (p. 29); district hence to Lyons uninteresting.

From Geneva to Lyons Railway in 5³/₄ hrs.; fares 18 fr. 80, 14 fr. 10, 10 fr. 35 c. From Geneva to *Ambérieux* see p. 29. The Lyons line here diverges from that to Mâcon and proceeds towards the S.W. Picturesque district, presenting a series of pleasing landscapes. Beyond stat. *Leyment* the line crosses the *Ain*, commanding a beautiful glimpse of the valley of that stream. Then several unimportant places. Near Lyons the line intersects the suburbs of *La Croix Rousse* and *La Guillotière*, and soon reaches the extensive station (at Lyon-Perrache).

Lyons. Hotels. *Grand Hôtel de Lyon (Pl. a), Rue Impériale, in the Parisian style, with restaurant, café, etc., R. 3, B. 1¹/₂, A. 1 fr.; *Grand Hôtel Collet (Pl. b), Rue Impériale 60; Hôtel de l'Europe (Pl. c), Place Louis le Grand, R. 2—3, D. 4 fr.; these three hotels are of the highest class. Grand Hôtel des Beaux Arts (Pl. d); *Hôtel des Négociants (Pl. e); *Hôtel du Hâvre et du Luxembourg (Pl. f), Rue St. Dominique 3, R. 2¹/₂, L. 75 c., D. 3¹/₂, A. 1 fr.; Beauquis (Pl. g), Place Louis le Grand; Hôtel Michel (Pl. h), Hôtel d'Angleterre et des Deux Mondes (Pl. i), Hôtel de l'Univers (Pl. n), these three in the Cours Napoléon near the Perrache stat.; Hôtel de Milan (Pl. k); de la Bombarde (Pl. l); Ecu de France (Pl. m); Hôtel de France, Rue de l'Arbre Sec, near the Museum, R. 2, D. 3 fr. — *Café du Rhône*, *de la Jeune France*, Rue du Perra; *Phénix*, Place Impériale. — *Restaurants*: Maison Dorée, Place Bellecour; Bavout, Place de la Préfecture, etc.

Fiacres (2-horse carr. of the Compagnie des Petits Maîtres) per drive 1 fr. 25 c., 1st hour 1 fr. 50, each following hour 1 fr. 25, luggage free (from midnight to 7 a. m. per drive 1 fr. 65, per hour 2 fr. 50 c.; outside the town per hour 2 fr.; vehicles of other companies more expensive). — Omnibus from the station to the town 50, with luggage 75 c.; hotel-omnibus 1—1¹/₂ fr.

Bookseller: Ch. Méra, Rue Impériale 15. — *Post Office*, Place Louis le Grand (open from 7 a. m. to 8 p. m.). — *Brasserie Alsacienne*, a large establishment in the Cours Napoléon near the stat. — *Bains du Rhône*, Rue du Perra. — *English Church Service*, resident chaplain.

Railway Stations. The *Gare de Perrache* (Pl. H, 4, 5) is the principal station, where all the trains arrive and depart. The Paris trains also stop at the *Gare de Vaise* (Pl. B, 6), reached in 8 min. from the central station; and the Geneva trains at the *Gare des Broteaux* (Pl. D, 1), 19—24 min. from the central station.

Lyons, the ancient *Lugdunum*, which after the time of Augustus gave its name to one-third part of Gaul, is now the second city, and the most important manufacturing place in France, with 324,000 inhab. Silk is the great staple commodity. Lyons is an archiepiscopal see. As an episcopal residence it is

mentioned at a very early period. The first bishop St. Potinus is said to have suffered martyrdom in 177, during a fearful persecution of the Christians under Marcus Aurelius, which raged here, as well as at Vienne and Autun.

The situation of the city at the confluence of the *Rhone* and *Saône* is imposing. The Saône is crossed by 10, the Rhone by 7 bridges. Of the latter the *Pont de la Guillotière* is the most ancient; its construction is erroneously attributed to Pope Innocent IV. (1190).

Lyons is one of the best built towns in France. Grand alterations have been accomplished within the last 50 years, so that the general aspect of the city is modern. It consists of three distinct portions, the original town on the tongue of land between the Rhone and Saône, the suburbs of *Les Broteaux* and *La Guillotière* on the l. bank of the Rhone, and the suburb of *Vaise* on the r. bank of the Saône.

The city is guarded by 18 forts, which form an extensive circle of nearly 12 M., extending from *Ste. Foy* and *Fourvières* and the heights above the suburb of *La Croix Rousse* (connected with the city by means of a curious railway on an inclined plane, fares 15 and 10 c.) to *Les Broteaux* and *La Guillotière*.

The beauty of the situation and the extent of the city are best appreciated when viewed from the **** *Height of Fourvières*,** crowned by its conspicuous church, to which a number of different ways lead. The direct route is between the handsome modern *Palais de Justice* (Pl. 67) and the cathedral, through narrow and steep streets, passing the hospital of *Les Antiqualles*, which occupies the site of the ancient Roman palace where Claudius and Caligula were born. The stranger may now continue to follow the main street, or he may proceed r. by the '*Passage Abrégé*' (5 c.), which leads past gardens, vineyards, and a number of fragments of Roman masonry, with explanations attached to them, which however are not to be implicitly trusted. This footpath leads to the Observatoire on the summit, not far distant from the church of *Notre Dame de Fourvières* (Pl. 25), which contains a highly revered 'miraculous' image of the Virgin (visited by upwards of $1^1/_2$ million pilgrims annually) and numerous votive tablets. The church is a modern structure, surmounted by a gilded statue of the Madonna. The terrace adjoining it commands a noble prospect, which is still more extensive from the tower (25 c.). A more picturesque view, however, is enjoyed from the so-called '*Observatoire*' already mentioned, a small wooden tower (50 c.; adjacent is a café-restaur.) in the vicinity, the route to which is indicated by sign-posts. At the feet of the spectator lie the imposing city with its environs, the two rivers and their bridges, and the well cultivated district in the neighbourhood; E. in fine weather Mont Blanc, 85 M. distant, is sometimes visible, farther S. the Alps of Dauphiné, the Mts. of the Grande Chartreuse and Mont Pilat, W. the Mts. of Auvergne.

The *Cathedral of St. Jean Baptiste* (Pl. 41) on the r. bank of the Saône, adjoining the Palais de Justice, a structure of the 13th cent., possesses several remarkable features, a fine central tower, stained glass windows, and a curious and complicated clock of 1508, resembling that of Strasbourg. The *Bourbon* chapel (1st on the r.), erected by Cardinal Bourbon and his brother Pierre de Bourbon, son-in-law of Louis XI., contains some fine sculptures.

On the l. bank of the Saône, about $1/2$ M. lower down, is situated the church of the *Abbey d'Ainay* (Pl. 24), one of the oldest in France, dating from the 10th cent., the vaulting of which is borne by four antique columns of granite. Its Latin name was *Athenacum*, supposed to be derived from the fact that Caligula once founded an *Athenaeum*, or school of rhetoric, here. Beneath the sacristy are the former dungeons.

In the *Place des Terreaux* (Pl. 3), in which the Hôtel de Ville and the Museum are situated, Richelieu caused the youthful Marquis de Cinq-Mars, who for a brief period was the favourite of Louis XIII., and his partisan de Thou to be executed as traitors, Sept 12th, 1642. Numerous victims perished here by the guillotine in 1794, until the more wholesale system of drowning and shooting was introduced. In the *Hôtel de Ville* (Pl. 62), a handsome edifice of the 17th cent. (1647—55), the revolutionary Tribunal, under the presidency of Collot d'Herbois, held its sessions. This miscreant, who had previously been an actor, and whose performances had been hissed at Lyons, availed himself of this opportunity to wreak his revenge on the unfortunate citizens. He was subsequently banished to Cayenne, where he died in 1796. In the *Avenue des Martyrs* (in the quarter Les Broteaux) a chapel has been erected to the memory of the 2100 victims who perished here during the Revolution.

In the *Palais des Beaux Arts*, or *Museum* (Pl. 69; admission gratis, daily 9—3 o'clock), under the arcades of the spacious court, are some remarkable Roman antiquities, a taurobolium (sacrifice of oxen), altars, inscriptions, sculptures, etc.

The **Picture Gallery** is on the first floor. Salle des Anciens Maîtres: in the centre 4 Roman mosaics, representing Orpheus, Cupid and Pan, and the games of the circus. Among the pictures may be mentioned: 1. 54. *Charlet*, Episode from the Russian campaign; 171. *Ann. Caracci*, Portrait of a priest; 102. *Heem*, Breakfast; 9. *Lesueur*, Martyrdom of SS. Gervasius and Protasius; 82. *Rubens*, Intercession of the saints with Christ; 108. *School of Rembrandt*, Martyrdom of St. Stephen; 151. *Greenenbraeck*, View of Paris in 1741; 115. *Terburg*, The Message; 210. *Ryckaert*, The miser; 164. *Bordone*, Titian's mistress; 178. *Carletto Veronese*, Queen of Cyprus; 46. *Gérard*, Corinna; 89—92. *Breughel*, The four elements; 117. *Teniers* the *Y*., Liberation of St. Peter; 80. *Moreelèze*, Portrait; 257. *Sassoferrato*, Madonna. — R. (commencing again from the entrance door): 140. *Schalken*, The smokers; *169. *Palma Giovine*, Scourging of Christ; 112. *Quellyn*, St. Jerome; 105. *Ph. de Campaigne*, Finding of the relics of SS. Gervasius and Protasius; *156. *Pietro Perugino*, Ascension, one of this master's finest works, painted in 1495 for the cathedral of Perugia and carried off by the French; it was reclaimed in 1815, but presented to Lyons by Pope Pius VII.; 160. *Seb. del Piombo*, Repose of Christ; 21. *Jouvenet*, Christ expelling the money-changers; 99. *Van Dyck*, Studies; *186. *Guercino*, Circumcision; 155. *Perugino*, SS. James and Gregory; *73. *Dürer*, Madonna and the Child, bestowing bouquets of roses on the Emp. Maximilian and his consort, a celebrated picture containing numerous figures, painted by the master at Venice in 1506, originally preserved in the Imperial Gallery at Vienna, brought to Paris by Napoleon I. and presented to Lyons; 83. *Rubens*, Adoration of the Magi; 197. *Zurbaran* (?), Corpse of St. Francis; 161. *A. del Sarto*, Abraham's sacrifice. — One story higher is the Galerie des Peintres Lyonnais: *Bonnefonds*, Portrait of Jacquard, inventor of the improved loom, born at Lyons in 1752, died 1834; also busts of the celebrated Lyonnese *Philibert Delorme* (d. at Paris 1577), the botanist *Bernard Jussieu* (1699—1776), Marshal Suchet, etc.

The Musée archéologique, also in the first floor, contains in the entrance room I. the *brazen tablets (found in 1528) with the speech delivered by the Emperor Claudius before the senate at Rome in the year 48, in defence of the measure of bestowing the rights of citizenship on the Gauls; in the central saloon antique and mediæval bronzes, coins, and various curiosities; among them a treasure found in 1841 on the height of Fourvières, comprising necklaces, bracelets, and other trinkets and coins, buried during the Roman period. Life-size statue of Neptune in bronze, Head of Juno in bronze, both found in the Rhone. Gallic weapons, vases from Athens, etc. — There is also a Musée d'Histoire Naturelle here, containing zoological and mineralogical collections. — Finally a Library.

The second floor of the *Palais du Commerce et de la Bourse* contains the *Musée d'Art et d'Industrie*, founded in 1858; the specimens in illustration of the silk-culture are particularly instructive (admission daily 11—5 o'clock).

The *Civic Library* (Pl. 6), possessing 150,000 vols. and 2400 MSS., is situated on the bank of the Rhone. In the vicinity rises the bronze *Statue of Marshal Suchet* (born at Lyons in 1770, d. 1826), '*Duc d'Albufera*', who once served as a merchant's apprentice in the adjacent house.

Two new magnificent streets, the *Rue Impériale* and the *Rue de l'Impératrice*, lead from the Hôtel de Ville to the *Place Louis le Grand, or *Bellecour* (Pl. E, 3), one of the most spacious squares in Europe, which was destroyed during the Revolution in 1794, but subsequently restored, and adorned with a *Statue of Louis XIV*. in 1825.

The *Place Napoléon* (Pl. F, 4) is adorned with an *Equestrian Statue of Napoleon I.* in bronze, erected in 1822. Adjoining the E. side of this Place is the broad *Cours Napoléon*, planted with trees, situated between the Rhone and Saône, with the rail. stat. *La Perrache*. The Places Louis le Grand and Napoléon, and the streets connecting them (Rue de Bourbon etc.), are the most aristocratic quarter of Lyons. Beyond the station, occupying the entire point of the tongue of land between the rivers, is the suburb *Perrache*, named after its founder (1770) and still rapidly increasing.

The traveller may proceed as far as the point of union of the Rhone and Saône (1¼ M. from the railway-station Perrache; omnibus from the

Place de la Charité to the Pont de Mulatière 25 c.), where the rivers are separated by a breakwater. The different characters of the two streams are here distinctly observable. The Rhone, a genuine mountain-river, is clear and rapid, whilst the current of the sluggish and muddy Saône is scarcely perceptible. Steamboats ply on both rivers.

The starting-place of the Steamboats is near the Place Napoléon: to Avignon every morning in 7—10 hrs., to Arles in 13 hrs. (fares 30, 20, 10 fr.). Stations *Vienne*, *Tournon*, *Valence*, *Avignon*, *Beaucaire*, *Arles*. Those whom time permits will find the steamboat-journey more entertaining than the railway. The former distantly resembles a trip on the Rhine, but the scenery of the Rhone is less striking, and the steamers ('papins') far inferior.

The *Jardin des Plantes* at the Croix Rousse has since the construction of the railway been converted into a square (near it is the Place Sathonay with the bronze *Statue of Jacquard* by Foyatier), and is superseded by the **Parc de la Tête d'Or*, on the l. bank of the Rhone, at the N. extremity of the Quai d'Albert (1 M. from the Place des Terreaux), containing rare plants, hothouses, and pleasure-grounds in the style of the Bois de Boulogne at Paris.

The Railway to Marseilles (station see p. 6) crosses the Rhone, affording a glimpse of the imposing city, passes La Guillotière (p. 6), and traverses an attractive district surrounded by mountains. Stations *Saint-Fons*, *Feysin* with handsome château on the Rhone, *Serézin*, *Chasse*, and *Estressin*.

Vienne (*Hôtel Ombry, R. 1½—2 fr.; *du Nord*; *Table Ronde*, R. 2, D. 3, A. 1 fr.), the *Vienna Allobrogum* of the ancients, with a popul. of 24,800, lies on the l. bank of the Rhone, at the influx of the *Gère*. Several interesting mementoes of its former greatness are still extant. The so-called **Temple of Augustus*, of the Corinthian order (88 ft. long, 49 ft. wide, 56 ft. high), with 16 columns, and hexastyle portico, is approached from the ancient forum by 12 steps, in the middle of which stands an altar. The edifice was used in the middle ages as a church and seriously disfigured, but has been restored as nearly as possible to its original condition. It formerly contained a Museum of Roman antiquities which has been temporarily removed to the Hôtel de Ville and will eventually be transferred to **St. Pierre*, an ancient basilica of the 6th cent., disfigured during the past century, but now undergoing restoration. Those who contemplate a visit to the temple and church should apply to the architect *M. Quonin*, Place St. Maurice 9. The works now in progress will probably not be completed for several years. — The **Cathedral of St. Maurice* (between the temple and the bridge across the Rhone), commenced at the close of the 11th cent., but not completed till 1515, possesses a fine façade of the transition period. The interior is the most ancient part of the edifice. — On the high road, ¼ M. S. of the town, stands an archway surmounted by an obelisk termed the **Plan de l'Aiguille*, which once served as the meta (goal) of a circus. The visitor should return hence to the town by the river. — The ancient remains on *Mont Pipet* are insignificant.

Vienne is not visible from the railway, which passes through a tunnel beneath part of the town. Immediately beyond the town rises the Plan de l'Aiguille, mentioned above. The banks of the Rhone rise in gentle slopes, planted with vines and fruit-trees. On the r. bank, at some distance from the river, towers *Mont Pilat* (3689 ft.), a picturesque group of mountains, at the base of which lie the celebrated vineyards of *La Côte Rôtie*. The line continues to follow the course of the Rhone, at some distance from the river. Several small stations, then *St. Rambert* (branch-line to Grenoble, p. 31). Ruined castles and ancient watch-towers are occasionally seen on the adjacent heights. Beyond stat. *St. Vallier* rises the *Château de Vals*, near which is the *Roche Taillée*. Farther on are the pinnacles of the *Château de Ponsas*, where Pontius Pilate is said to have resided during his exile.

Stat. *Serves*; then *Tain*, where the valley of the Rhone contracts; on the l. rises the extensive vineyard of *Ermitage*, where the well known wine of that name is produced. In the distance to the l. the indented spurs of the Alps are conspicuous, above which in clear weather the gigantic Mont Blanc is visible. Tain is connected by means of a suspension-bridge with *Tournon*, on the opposite bank, a small town with picturesque old castles of the Counts of Tournon and Dukes of Soubise.

On the l. a view is now disclosed of the broad valley of the *Isère* (ascending towards the Little St. Bernard), on which *Grenoble*, the ancient *Cularo*, subsequently *Gratianopolis*, capital of the Department of the Isère, is situated. In September, B. C. 218, Hannibal ascended this valley with his army, crossed the Little St. Bernard and the Alps within 15 days, and during the same autumn gained the signal victories of the Ticinus and the Trebia over the Romans. Stat. *Roche-de-Glun*.

The train crosses the Isère and commands a view of the snowy summits of Mont Blanc to the l. To the r. lies *St. Peray* with its far-famed vineyards, on the limestone pinnacles beyond which stand the ruins of the *Château de Crussol*, once the seat of the Crussol family, Dukes of Uzès. Then, on the opposite bank,

Valence *(Lion d'Or; Tête d'Or*, both of humble pretension; **Café Armand)*, the *Valentia* of the ancients, once the capital of the Duchy of *Valentinois*, with which the infamous Cæsar Borgia was invested by Louis XII. It is now the chief town, with 20,000 inhab., of the Department of the Drôme. The situation is picturesque, but there is little else to arrest the traveller's attention. The principal curiosities are a few antiquated houses, e. g. that of the *Mistral* family, termed *Le Pendentif*, near the cathedral, date 1548; another in the Grande Rue, near the *Place aux Clercs*, with quaint decorations in the style of the 16th cent. On the ground-floor of No. 4 in the same street Napoleon once lodged when a sous-lieutenant of artillery. On Aug. 29th, 1799, Pope Pius VI. died in captivity at Valence. His bust with basrelief by *Canova* is preserved in the old Romanesque cathedral. The *Museum*, with collections of art and natural history, is insignificant. On the Rhone-promenade stands the monument of *General Championnet* (d. 1800), the conqueror of Naples, who was a native of Valence. The town is connected with the r. bank by a suspension-bridge. Branch line hence to Grenoble (see p. 31) in $3^1/_2$ hrs.

On the height above St. Peray rises the *Château de Beauregard*, erected, it is said, by Vauban in the form of a mimic fortress, now converted into a vast depôt for the highly esteemed produce of the neighbouring vineyards, the reputation of which is hardly inferior to that of Champagne itself. Stat. *L'Etoile* is picturesquely situated on the hill. Then Stat. *Livron*, where a branch line diverges r. to *Privas*. A short distance farther the influx of the Drôme is observed on the l.; the line crosses this river at stat. *Loriol* and again approaches the Rhone.

Stat. *Montélimart*. The ancient castle of the once celebrated family of the *Monteil d'Adhémar* rises on an eminence from the midst of mulberry-trees. The line here quits the Rhone, the plain on the r. expands. The silk-culture has been successfully prosecuted in this district since the campaign of Charles VIII. against Italy in 1494.

About 12 M. to the S. E. is situated the *Château de Grignan*, once the seat of the son-in-law of *Madame de Sévigné*, burned down during the Revolution. The window at which the illustrious letter-writer is said to have sat is still shown. Mad. de Sévigné died here in 1696 in her 70th year and was interred in the neighbouring church.

On the r. bank, farther on, lies the episcopal residence of *Viviers*, once capital of the Vivarais, with a conspicuous ecclesiastical seminary. The railway runs to the l. in the plain, by *Châteauneuf, Donzères* and *Pierrelatte*; opposite the latter is *Bourg St. Andéol*, with a handsome suspension-bridge. Next stat. *La Palud*; then *La Croisière*, which is also the station for *Pont St. Esprit* on the r. bank; the long stone bridge of the latter, with 26 arches, was constructed in 1265—1310. To the S.E. towers the majestic *Mont Ventoux* (6813 ft.). Stations *Mondragon, Mornas, Piolenc*, and, situated 3 M. from the Rhone, the small town of

Orange (**Hôtel des Princes* or *Poste*, R. 2, B. 1, D. 3, A. $^3/_4$ fr.), the *Arausio* of the Romans and once a prosperous place of considerable importance. In the middle ages it was the capital of a small principality, which, on the death without issue of the last reigning prince in 1531, fell to his nephew the Count of Nassau, and until the death of William III. (d. 1702), king of England, continued subject to the house of Nassau-Orange. By the Peace of Utrecht, Orange was annexed to France, and the house of Nassau retained the title only of princes of Orange. The antiquarian should if possible devote a few hours to the interesting Roman remains at Orange. On the road to Lyons, 1/4 M. N. of the town, is a *Triumphal Arch, part of which is in good preservation, with three archways and 12 columns. The sculptures are sadly defaced; their style appears to point to the latter half of the 2nd cent. as the period of their origin, not to the time of Marius or Augustus as has been conjectured. On the S. side of the town, at the foot of an eminence, lies the *Roman Theatre, 129 ft. in height, 355 ft. in length, with walls 14 ft. in thickness (the concierge lives on the spot, 1/2 fr.). The admirably preserved wall of the stage, from which an awning used to be stretched, still contains the three doors from which the actors emerged. The semicircular space for the spectators, which rises opposite, is in a much more dilapidated condition; the tiers of seats have almost entirely vanished. The acoustic arrangement of the structure is admirable. Words spoken in a loud and distinct voice on the stage are perfectly audible on the highest tier. Scanty remnants of a *Circus* adjoin the theatre. The height above the theatre, once occupied by the citadel of Orange which was destroyed by Louis XIV., affords a good survey of the neighbourhood. The promenade is adorned with a statue of the *Comte de Gasparin* (d. 1862).

Beyond Orange the line traverses a plain, in which olives begin to indicate the proximity of a warmer climate, at a considerable distance from the Rhone and the mountains. Stations *Courthézon* and *Bédarrides* (a corruption of *Biturrita*, the 'two-towered'). Stat. *Sorgues* lies on the river of that name, which descends from Vaucluse.

Branch Railway from Sorgues to Carpentras in 3/4 hr.; fares 1 fr. 90, 1 fr. 45, 1 fr. 5 c. — **Carpentras** (*Hôtel Orient; Univers; Café Alcazar*, opp. the Palais de Justice), the ancient *Carpentoracte*, is a manufacturing town with 10,918 inhab. The first conspicuous edifice, as the town is entered, is the hospital, with a statue of the founder in front. Hence in a straight direction to the *Palais de Justice*, the court of which (application should be made to the concierge) contains a small Roman *Triumphal Arch of the 3rd cent. A. D. The sculptures on the side represent two barbarians bound to a tree, on which trophies are suspended. The frieze and attic are wanting. Adjacent is the late Gothic church of *St. Séverin*, the S. portal of which merits notice. The town is encircled by ramparts with agreeable promenades, in which (1. from the station) the *Museum* containing antiquities and paintings is situated. Mont Ventoux (p. 12) bounds the horizon on the E.

To the l. on the Rhone is situated *Roquemaure*, commanded by an ancient tower, and supposed to be the locality where Hannibal accomplished the passage of the river when marching towards Italy. The train now soon affords a view of the papal palace and the towers of

Avignon [*Hôtel de l'Europe (Pl. a), R. 2, D. 3½, L. and A. 1 fr. ; Hôtel du Luxembourg (Pl. b); Louvre (Pl. c), all ¾ M. from the station, omnibus 50 c.; Hôtel du Cours Napoleon nearer to the stat.; best *Cafés* in the Place], the *Avenio* of the Romans. The old city-wall, constructed of massive blocks of stone in 1349—68, with numerous gates, admirably preserved and affording an interesting example of the fortifications of that period, testify to its ancient importance. Till the reign of Louis XIV. the popul. amounted to 80,000 (now 36,000). The town was once a Roman colony, afterwards belonged to the Burgundians, then to the Franks, became capital of the County of Venaisin, lost its independence to Louis VIII. in 1226, fell into the hands of Charles of Anjou in 1290, was the residence of the popes from 1309 to 1377, seven of whom, from Clement V. (Bertrand de Goth) to Gregory XI., reigned here (the latter transferred his seat to Rome in 1377), and continued subject to the pontifical sway until it was annexed to France by the Revolution in 1791.

The town lies on the l. bank of the Rhone, a short distance above the influx of the Durance, and is connected with *Villeneuve* on the opposite bank by a suspension-bridge. It is commanded by the abrupt *Rocher des Dons* (rupes dominorum), 300 ft. in height, which is surmounted by the *Cathedral of Notre Dame*, (Pl. 10), a structure of the 14th cent., recently restored. The portico is of considerably earlier origin. The church contains the handsome *monument of Pope John XXII. (Euse of Cahors), d. 1334, and that of Benedict XII. (d. 1342) in the l. aisle. Immediately behind the cathedral is *La Glacière*, a square tower which derives its appellation from an ice-cellar in the vicinity; it once served as the prison of the Inquisition, and during the eventful month of October, 1791, was the scene of the execution of 63 innocent victims.

Near the cathedral rises the **Papal Palace* (Pl. 3), now a barrack, a lofty and gloomy pile, erected by Clement V. and his successors, with huge towers and walls 100 ft. in height. The faded frescoes in the *Chapelle du St. Office* were executed by Simone Memmi of Siena (d. 1339). Rienzi was incarcerated here in 1351 in the *Tour des Oubliettes*, at the same time as Petrarch was entertained as a guest.

Opposite the palace stands the *Ancienne Mairie* (Pl. 2, now *Conservatoire de Musique*), the mint of the papal period. The portal bears a relief representing flowers, armorial bearings etc.

Pleasant grounds have been laid out on the hill near the cathedral. The best point of view is a rocky eminence in the centre. The **prospect, one of the most beautiful in France, embraces the course of the Rhone and its banks; *Villeneuve* on the opposite bank with its citadel and ancient towers; in the distance towards the N.W. the Cevennes; N.E. Mont Ventoux;

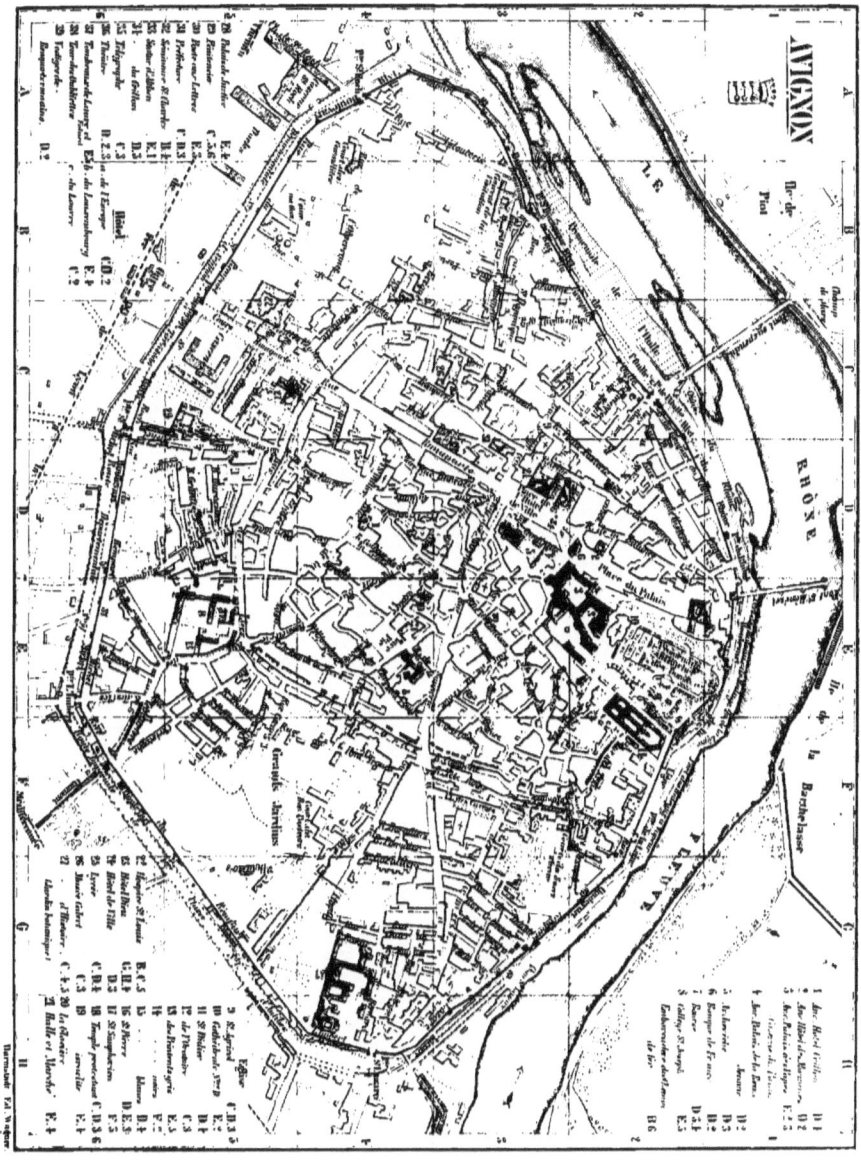

E. the Durance, resembling a silver thread, beyond it the Alps; below the spectator the tortuous and antiquated streets of Avignon. On the promenades is a statue to *Jean Althen*, erected in 1846, out of gratitude to him for having introduced the cultivation of madder, which now forms the staple commodity of the district (used extensively in dyeing the French red military trowsers).

At the base of the Rocher des Doms lies the *Grande Place*, with a number of handsome modern edifices. In front of the *Theatre* (Pl. 36) are statues of Racine and Molière; the medallions above represent John XXII. and Petrarch. The neighbouring *Hôtel de Ville* (Pl. 24) possesses a quaint clock with figures which strike the hours. In front of it stands a *Statue of Crillon* (Pl. 34), erected 1858. This hero was a scion of a Piedmontese family who settled in France in the 15th cent.; he distinguished himself at the early age of 16 under the Duke of Guise, then under Francis of Lorraine, and above all at the siege of Calais. He subsequently became a Knight of St. John and an intrepid antagonist of the Turks. He died at Avignon in 1615. His motto '*Fais ton devoir*' is inscribed on the pedestal of his statue.

In the Rue Calade is situated the **Musée Calvet* (Pl. 26) (accessible daily, custodian 1 fr.).

The Ground Floor contains a fine collection of Roman antiquities, reliefs and inscriptions; two monuments, found at Vaison near Orange, are especially remarkable for their size and excellent preservation.

On the First Floor is the Picture Gallery: 80. *Lor. di Credi*, Madonna; 101. *Eeckhout*, Crucifixion; 106. *Inn. da Imola*, Madonna; three small pictures attributed to *Holbein*. The back of the saloon is exclusively devoted to works of the *Vernet* family, natives of Avignon (*Joseph*, the painter of Madonnas, his son *Carle* and his celebrated grandson *Horace*): Madonnas and sketches by *Joseph*; a Cossack by *Carle*; *Mazeppa by *Horace*, in two copies, unfortunately retouched. — Also a collection of ancient and mediæval coins, statuettes, crystal, lamps, sculptures of the Renaissance, furniture (a collection of republican assignats), cameos, engravings, drawings, a beautiful ivory Crucifix executed in 1689 by *J. Guillermin*, etc. — The Library contains 80,000 vols. and 2000 MSS.

In the garden at the back of the Museum a monument was erected in 1823 by Mr. Charles Kensall to the memory of Petrarch's Laura. Her tomb was formerly in the Eglise des Cordeliers, but was destroyed with the church during the Revolution.

In 1326, when *Francesco Petrarca*, then 22 years of age, visited Avignon, he beheld *Laura de Noves*, who was in her 18th year, at the church of the nunnery of St. Claire. Her beauty impressed the ardent young Italian so profoundly, that, although he never received the slightest token of regard from the object of his romantic attachment, either before or after her marriage, with Hugues de Sade, he continued throughout his whole lifetime to celebrate her praises in songs and sonnets. In 1334 he quitted Avignon for Vaucluse, travelled in France, Germany, and Italy, and returned to Avignon in 1342 (with his friend Cola di Rienzi), where he found Laura the mother of a numerous family. She died in 1348, bowed down by domestic affliction. Petrarch lived till 1374, and long after Laura's death dedicated many touching lines to her memory.

The long and intimate connection of Avignon with Rome, as well as its reminiscences of Petrarch, may be said to invest the town with an almost Italian character. The whole of *Provence* indeed recals the scenery of the south more than any other district in France.

Avignon is a very windy place. The prevailing *Mistral* often blows with great violence, and has given rise to the ancient saying:

> *Avenio Ventosa,*
> *Sine vento venenosa,*
> *Cum vento fastidiosa.*

An Excursion to the Fountains of Vaucluse may easily be accomplished in the course of an afternoon with the aid of the Avignon-Cavaillon branch-railway. After several unimportant stations, the traveller arrives at *L'Isle sur Sorgue* (in 1—1½ hr.; fares 2 fr. 70, 2 fr., 1 fr. 50 c.). Thence by carr. or on foot up the valley of the Sorgue, following its sinuosities towards Mont Ventoux, to the (3 M.) village of *Vaucluse* (Hôtel de Laure). A footpath leads hence in ¼ hr. into the *Vaucluse* ravine, a rocky gorge, above which the ruined castle of the Bishops of Cavaillon rises on the r. At its extremity the sources of the Sorgue emerge from a profound grotto, at one time in precipitate haste, at another in gentle ripples. This spot is mentioned by Petrarch in his 14th Canzone: 'Chiare, fresche e dolci acque.'

Shortly after quitting Avignon the line crosses the broad bed of the often impetuous and turgid *Durance*, the Roman *Druentia*, which descends from the Cottian Alps to the Rhone. Olive-trees are abundant in this district. Stations *Barbentane*, *Graveson*, and

Tarascon (*Hôtel des Empereurs*, R. 1½, D. 3, A. ½ fr.), pop. 13,500, once the seat of King René of Anjou, the great patron of minstrelsy, whose lofty old castle, and above it the Gothic spire of the church of *St. Marthe* (14th cent.) arrest the traveller's attention. On the opposite bank, and connected with Tarascon by a bridge, is situated the busy town of *Beaucaire* (where an important annual market takes place in July), commanded by an ancient castle of the Counts of Toulouse.

From Tarascon to St. Rémy (10 M., one-horse carr. for the excursion 10 fr.). On the site of the ancient *Glanum*, ½ M. above the small town, are situated two interesting °*Roman Monuments*. One of these, 53 ft. in height, resembling the celebrated monument of Igel near Treves, was erected by the three brothers Sextus, Lucius, and Marcus Julius to the memory of their parents. It is constructed of massive blocks of stone, and consists of three different stories: the reliefs on the lowest represent battle scenes, above these are garlands and tragic masks; the next story consists of an open double arch; the third is a circular temple borne by 10 columns, with two portrait-statues. This magnificent relic belongs to the time of Cæsar. Adjacent to it is a half ruined °*Triumphal Arch*, also adorned with sculptures (Victoria with a prisoner), which appear to point to the victories of Marcus Aurelius. St. Rémy, which lies at the foot of the barren limestone rocks of the *Alpines*, was the birthplace of the celebrated physician and astrologist *Michael Nostradamus* (1503—66), who stood high in the favour of Catharine de' Medici.

Railway from Tarascon to Nimes in ¾ hr., fares 3 fr. 15, 2 fr. 25, 1 fr. 70 c.; to Montpellier in 2—3 hrs., fares 8 fr. 60, 6 fr. 45, 4 fr. 75 c. The line traverses extensive olive-plantations, passing *Beaucaire* (see above) and three other unimportant stations.

Nimes (°*Hôtel de Luxembourg* (Pl. a), in the Esplanade, R. 3, L. ½, B. 1½, D. 3½, A. ¾ fr.; *Cheval Blanc* (Pl. b), opp. the Arena; °*Hôtel et Restaurant Manivet* (Pl. c), opp. the Maison Carrée; *Hôtel de la Méditerranée*,

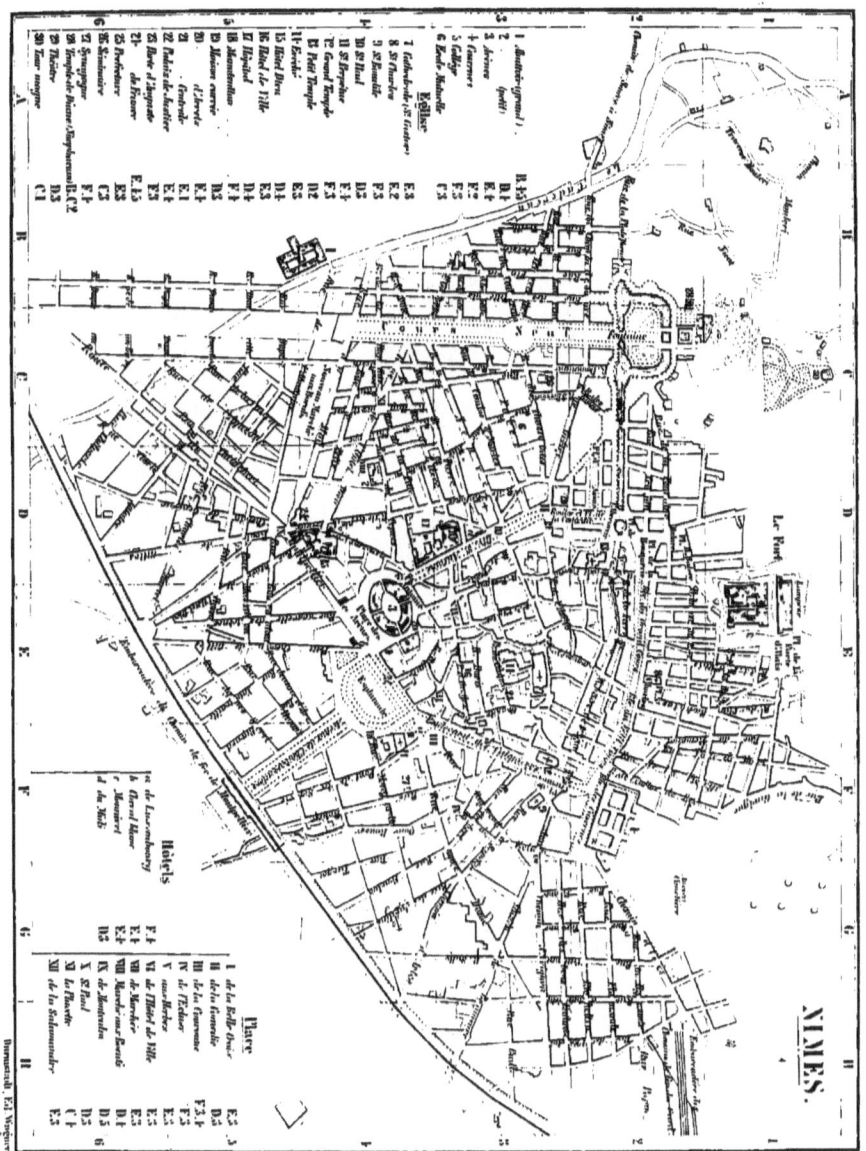

near the stat.; *Hôtel du Midi* (Pl. d), Place de la Couronne; *Café du Commerce*, opp. the Arena; *Café de l'Univers*, opp. the Maison Carrée), the ancient *Nemausus*, capital of the Gallic Arecomaci, and one of the most important places in Gallia Narbonensis, is now the chief town of the Department of the Gard.

Nimes, which numbers 42,000 Protest. among its present population of 60,200, has several times been the scene of fierce religious struggles, especially during the reign of Louis XIV. In 1704 Marshal Villars had an interview in the garden of the monastery of the *Récollets* (now the site of the theatre) with *Jean Cavalier*, the talented leader of the Camisards, who thereupon entered the service of Louis XIV., which however he soon quitted. He died in England in 1740. *Jean Nicot*, a physician of Nimes, introduced tobacco-smoking from America in 1564. *Guizot*, the celebrated statesman and historian, son of an advocate of Nimes, was born here in 1787.

The town is surrounded by agreeable Boulevards, which terminate in the *Esplanade*, adorned with a handsome modern fountain-group (representing the city of Nemausus, with 4 river-deities beneath).

The extremely interesting Roman antiquities are not far distant from the station. The stranger first reaches the *Arena*, or *Amphitheatre* (Pl. 3), consisting of two stories, each with 60 arcades, together 74 ft. in height. The exterior is in admirable preservation. The interior contains 32 tiers of seats (entrance on the W. side, where a notice indicates the dwelling of the concierge; 50 c.), and could accommodate 33,000 spectators; greater axis 148, less 112 yds., height 74 ft., inner arena 76 by 42 yds. The upper gallery is about ¹/₄ M. in circumference. The founder is unknown, but is conjectured to have been the emperor Antoninus Pius, about B.C. 140, whose ancestors were natives of Nemausus. The four original entrances are still recognised. Doors in the pavement of the arena lead to the (modern) 'souterrain', the ceiling of which is supported by beams. In the middle ages the Arena was employed by the Visigoths and afterwards by the Saracens as a fortress. Extensive works of restoration are now going on, especially in the interior and the E. side of the exterior, as the Arena is still employed for the exhibition of bull-fights (but of a bloodless character).

The next object of interest is the *Maison Carrée* (Pl. 19) (the route to which passes the modern church of *St. Paul*), a well preserved *Temple* (88 ft. long, 42 ft. wide), with 30 Corinthian columns (10 detached, 20 immured), dating from the reign of Augustus or Antoninus Pius, employed as a church in the middle ages and subsequently as a town-hall. The inscription is conjectured (from the holes made by the nails by which it was formerly attached) to have been as follows: C. CAESARI. AVGVSTI. F. COS. L. CAESARI. AVGVSTI. F. COS. DESIGNATO. PRINCIPIBVS. IVVENTVTIS., according to which the temple would appear to have been dedicated to Caius and Lucius Cæsar, the grandsons of Augustus. The edifice is, however, probably of later origin, as the style of the decorations points rather to the age of the Antonines. This temple was connected with other buildings, the foundations of which still exist, and in all probability constituted part of the ancient forum, like the similar Temple of Augustus at Vienne (p. 10). It now contains a *Museum* of antiquities and pictures, of which the following merit inspection; *1. Xaver Sigalon*, Narcissus and Locusta experimentalizing on a slave with the poison destined for Britannicus (1824); 2. *Paul Delaroche*, Cromwell at the coffin of Charles I. (painted 1831); 74. *Rigaud*, Portrait of Turenne: 38. *Rubens*, Head of a girl; 104. *Titian*, John the Baptist; 54. *Greuze*, Old woman; 27. *Van Loo*, Portrait of his mother; 112. *Caravaggio*, Portrait of a boy; 45. *Grimoux*, A young girl. Also antique mosaics, fragments of sculptures, numerous inscriptions, etc. The concierge lives opposite (1 fr.).

From the Maison Carrée the visitor should next proceed by the Boulevards and the canal to the *Jardin de la Fontaine*, where the *Nymphaeum* (Pl. 28), formerly supposed to be a *Temple of Diana*, is situated. This fine vaulted structure, with niches for the reception of statues, has partly fallen in; it contains statues, busts, architectural fragments, etc. from the excavations which have been made here. The destination of the building of which extensive ruins lie behind the Nymphæum cannot now be ascertained. Here, too, are the Roman *Baths* excavated by Louis XIV. They contain a large peristyle with low columns, a number of niches, a basin for swimming, and the spring by which Nîmes is now supplied with water. Well kept pleasure-grounds in the rococo style adjoin the baths. (The concierge at the E. entrance to the garden keeps the keys of the Nymphæum and the Baths; 1 fr.)

Beyond the spring rises a hill with promenades, surmounted by the *Tourmagne* (turris magna) (Pl. 30), a Roman structure, variously conjectured to have been a beacon-tower, a temple or a treasury (keys at a small red house, to the r. on the way from the baths, about 200 paces below the summit). It was more probably a monumental tribute to some illustrious Roman. The tower is of octagonal form and is ascended by a modern staircase of 140 steps. The °view from the summit well repays the ascent; it embraces the town and environs, as far as the vicinity of the estuary of the Rhone, and the distant Pyrenees to the W. The extent of the ancient Nemausus is distinctly recognised hence; two of the ancient gates, the *Porta Augusti* (on the E. side of the Boulevards) and the *Porte de France* are still preserved. The former, discovered in 1793, has four entrances and bears the inscription: IMPER. CAESAR. DIVI. F. AVGVSTVS. COS. XI. TRIB. POT. PORTAS. MVROS. QVE. COL. DAT., signifying that Augustus provided the colony of Nemausus with gates and walls in the year B. C. 23. The other gate is of simpler construction, and one arch of it only is preserved.

Excursion to the Pont du Gard, 14½ M., uninteresting country, by carr. in 2 hrs. One-horse carr. there and back 12 fr. (from the Hôtel du Luxembourg). Or the traveller may avail himself of one of the omnibuses which run to *Remoulins* several times daily, as far as *La Foux*, whence a road on the r. bank of the Gard leads to the far-famed 'Pont' (1½ M.), at a small house near which refreshments may be obtained.

The °°*Pont du Gard*, a bridge and aqueduct over the Gard, which descends from the Cevennes, passing the town of *Alais* with its extensive iron-works, is one of the most magnificent Roman works extant. The desolate rocky valley of the Gard is bridged over by a threefold series (the lowest 6, the next 11, and the highest 35 in number) of arches which present a most majestic appearance. Agrippa, the general of Augustus, is supposed to have been the founder. The object of this structure was to supply Nîmes with water from the springs of Airan near St. Quentin and Ure near Uzès, a distance of 14 M. Several arches are also seen N. of the Pont du Gard, and other traces of the aqueduct still exist nearer the town. The structure is now undergoing restoration and will again be used for its original purpose, as the present supply of water is defective. The bridge for carriages was added to the Roman aqueduct in 1743.

Beyond Nîmes the train traverses the broad and fertile plain on the S. of the Cevennes, passes *Lunel*, well known for its sweet wine (10½ M. to the S. lies *Aigues Mortes*, which possesses venerable towers and walls of the period of Louis IX. and Philip the Bold), and in 1½—2 hrs. reaches

Montpellier (*Hôtel Nevet*, R. 2½, B. 1½, A. ¾, Omnibus ½ fr.; *Hôtel du Midi, de Londres*), capital of the Department of the Hérault, an industrial town with 55,000 inhab., beautifully situated and frequently visited by strangers on account of the salubrity of the climate and the neighbouring baths. The village which originally stood here was converted into a town towards the close of the 10th cent., under the name of *Mons Pessulus*, and a university was founded here in 1196 by Pope Urban V. The medical faculty of Montpellier still enjoys a considerable reputation. The town suffered severely during the Huguenot wars. Here on Oct. 19th, 1622, the well-known Peace was concluded. The finest point of the town is the °*Promenade du Peyrou*, an extensive terrace planted with lime-trees, with an equestrian *Statue of Louis XIV.* and the *Château d'Eau*. Fine view hence; in clear weather the summit of the Canigou in the Pyrenees is visible. The *Jardin des Plantes* is the oldest in France. The *Musée Favre* contains a picture-gallery of some value, the gem of which is a °Portrait of Lorenzo de' Medici by *Raphael*. The public *Library* possesses a few interesting MSS. and other curiosities.

Montpellier is 1¼ hr. distant by railway from *Cette*, a sea-port founded by Louis XIV., containing salt-works and manufactories where all kinds of wines are prepared from the Spanish Benicarlo and largely exported to the north.

From Tarascon (p. 16) to Arles the railway skirts the l. bank of the Rhone. The country, which is flat, and planted with the vine and olive, presents a marked southern character. The manners and unintelligible patois of the inhabitants differ materially from those of N. France. The peculiar softness of the old Provençal language employed by the *Troubadours* may still be traced. S is here pronounced like *sh* (e. g. pershonne), *ch* like *s* (serser for chercher). These characteristics, as well as the vivacious and excitable temperament of the natives, betoken the gradual transition from France to Italy.

Arles (**Hôtel du Nord*, R. 2, B. 1½, A. 1 fr.; *Hôtel du Forum*), the *Arelate* or *Arelas* of the ancients, once one of the most important towns of Gaul, is now a somewhat dull place (popul. 25,543) on the Rhone, 24 M. from its mouth. It is connected with *Trinquetaille* on the opposite bank by a bridge of boats.

The principal sights of Arles, for which 3—4 hrs. suffice, are all within a short distance from the hotels: E. St. Trophime, the extensive Museum, and the Theatre of Augustus; N. the Amphitheatre, and S.E. the Champs-Elysées.

In the *Place* of the *Hôtel de Ville*, which was erected in 1673, rises an **Obelisk* of grey granite from the mines of Estrelle near Fréjus (p. 27), an ancient monument of unknown origin found in the Rhone in 1676 and placed here in honour of Louis XIV. It has recently been furnished with an inscription dedicated to Napoleon III., which informs the reader that under his government '*les méchants tremblent et les bons se rassurent*'.

In the vicinity stands the **Cathedral of St. Trophime* (Trophimus is said to have been a pupil of St. Paul), founded in the 6th or 7th cent., possessing an interesting **Portal* of the 12th or 13th cent., of semicircular form, supported by 12 columns resting on lions, between which are apostles and saints (St. Trophimus, St. Stephen, etc.), above it Christ as Judge of the world. The interior contains little to interest the visitor, with the exception of several sarcophagi and pictures. On the S. side (entered from the sacristy) are the **Cloisters*, with round and pointed arches and remarkable capitals, dating from various epochs. The N. side is in the half antique style of the Carlovingian period (9th cent.), the E. side dates from 1221, the W. side (which is the most beautiful) from 1389, and the S. side from the 16th cent.

The **Museum*, established in the former church of St. Anna, contains numerous antiquities found in and near Arles, most of them in the theatre, where the celebrated *Venus of Arles*, now one of the greatest treasures of the Louvre at Paris, was also discovered in 1651. The following relics deserve special mention: *head of Diana (or Venus); Augustus (found in 1834); recumbent Silenus with pipe, once used as a fountain-figure; Mithras entwined by a serpent, with the signs of the zodiac; altar of Apollo with basrelief representing the punishment of Marsyas; above the latter a relief with the 9 Muses; a number of amphorae, pipes of water-conduits, Christian tombstones and sarcophagi from the ancient burial-ground (p. 21), etc.

The *Theatre (commonly called that of 'Augustus'), a most picturesque ruin, is in a very dilapidated condition. The houses by which it is at present partially hemmed in are, however, in process of being demolished, and more of the external wall will be disengaged. The most perfect portion is the stage-wall, which according to the ancient arrangement had three doors. In front of it was a colonnade, of which two columns, one of African, the other of Carrara marble, are still standing. The opening for the letting down of the curtain is distinctly recognisable. The orchestra, paved with slabs of variegated marble, contained the seats of persons of rank. The lower tiers only of the seats of the ordinary spectators are preserved. The theatre once possessed a second story, indications of which are observed if the ruin be viewed from the Saracens' Tower (in the direction of the public promenade). The dimensions of the building when perfect were very extensive.

The *Amphitheatre is larger than that of Nimes (p. 17) but in inferior preservation. It is nearly 500 yds. in circumference; the arena is 100 yds. long and 50 yds. wide. The entrance is on the N. side. It possessed 5 corridors and tiers of seats for 25,000 spectators. The two stories of 60 arches, the lower Doric, the upper Corinthian, present a most imposing aspect. The interior was formerly occupied by a number of dwellings tenanted by poor families, but these have been almost entirely removed during the present century. After the Roman period the amphitheatre was employed by the Goths, then by the Saracens, and again by Charles Martel (who expelled the latter in 739), as a stronghold, two of the four towers of which are still standing. A staircase of 103 steps ascends the W. tower, which commands a pleasing survey of the neighbourhood. The vaults beneath the lowest tier of seats served as receptacles for the wild beasts, the gladiators, etc. They communicated with the arena by means of 6 doors. The spectators, of whom those of high rank occupied the front seats, were protected from the attacks of the wild animals by a lofty parapet. Bloodless bull-fights are now occasionally exhibited here. The concierge, who lives opposite the N. entrance, sells ancient coins and cut stones (a good specimen of the latter 5—15 fr.).

In the *Place du Forum*, the site of the ancient market-place, two granite pillars and fragments of a Corinthian pediment are still seen (near the Hôtel du Nord).

On the S.E. side of the town are the *Champs Elysées* (Aliscamps), originally a Roman burying-ground, consecrated by St. Trophimus and furnished by him with a chapel. In the middle ages this cemetery enjoyed such celebrity that bodies were conveyed hither for sepulture from vast distances. It is mentioned by Dante in his Inferno (9, 112): '*Si come ad Arli, ove Rodano stagna, ... fanno i sepolcri tutto il loco varo*'. To this day many ancient sarcophagi are still to be seen in the environs of the curious old church, although after the first Revolution great numbers were sold to relic-hunters from all parts of the world.

Branch Line from Arles in 1½ hr. to *Lunel* (p. 18) and *Montpellier*.
About 2½ M. to the N.E. of Arles, on an isolated rock, rise the grand, but now dilapidated buildings of the former abbey of *Montmajour*, founded in the 10th cent., with a church in the transition style. Beneath the latter is a spacious crypt of the 11th cent. The cloisters contain decaying monuments of the House of Anjou.

Below Arles the flat delta of the estuary of the Rhone, termed the *Ile de la Camargue*, commences. It is protected against the incursions of the sea by dykes, and is employed partly as arable and partly as pasture land, which supports numerous flocks and herds. The delta encloses the *Etang de Valcarès*, at the mouth of which, on the *Petit Rhône*, *Ste. Marie*, the only village on the Camargue, is situated near the sea. As the estuary is not accessible to vessels of heavy burden, a large canal to obviate this difficulty is projected.

After the train has quitted the station of Arles, the traveller observes the upper arches of the amphitheatre on the r., and the *Alpines Mts.* in the distance to the l. Between Arles and Salon the line intersects the stony plain of *Crau*, which the ancients mention as the scene of the contest of Hercules with the Ligures. Several small stations. Near *St. Chamas* the line skirts the long *Etang de Berre*, an extensive inland lake on the r. A rocky district, through which several cuttings lead, is next traversed. Then stat. *Rognac*.

A Branch Railway leads hence by *Roquefavour* (in a romantic valley, with an extensive modern aqueduct for the supply of Marseilles) to **Aix** (*Palais Royal*), once the Roman colony *Aquae Sextiae*, where in B. C. 102 Marius gained a bloody victory over the Teutones, in the middle ages the capital of Provence and seat of the Troubadours and their 'cours d'amour'. The church of St. Sauveur is a fine edifice. Aix also possesses a museum with numerous French and Italian pictures, warm baths, and a number of valuable private collections. The oil of Aix is in high repute.

At stat. *Vitrolles* the Etang de Berre is finally quitted. Beyond stat. *Pas-des-Lanciers* the train traverses the longest tunnel in France, nearly 3 M. in length (transit 6 min.), on emerging from which it passes some grand rocky scenery. The sea now comes in sight, and the rocky islands of Château d'If, Ratonneau, etc. are seen rising from the Gulf of Marseilles. Stat. *L'Estaque*. Groups of pines occasionally diversify the landscape, which is of a southern character and surrounded by the imposing mountains

Mont de l'Etoile, St. Cyr, Gardiole, Puget etc. In the foreground lies Marseilles.

Marseilles, the principal sea-port of France, termed *Massalia* by the Greeks, *Massilia* by the Romans, an important place even at an early period of antiquity, now a city with 300,000 inhab., is the capital of the Department of the Embouchures of the Rhone and depôt of a brisk maritime traffic with the East, Italy and Africa (Algiers).

Hôtels. °Grand Hôtel du Louvre et de la Paix (Pl. a), °Grand Hôtel de Marseille (Pl. b), °Hôtel de Noailles (Pl. c), Rue de Noailles, all in the Cannebière-Prolongée, and fitted up in the style of the great Parisian hotels, containing 250 rooms from 2 fr. upwards, table d'hôte at 6 p. m. 5 fr., B. 1½ fr., A. and L. 3 fr.; °Hôtel du Petit Louvre (Pl. d), R. 2 fr., Rue Cannebière; Hôtel du Luxembourg (Pl. e), Rue St. Ferréol 25, R. 3, L. and A. 1½ D. 4 fr.; °Hôtel des Colonies, Rue Vacon; Hôtel des Ambassadeurs (Pl. f), Rue Beauveau, R. 1½ fr.; Grand Hôtel des Princes (Pl. g), Place Royale; Hôtel d'Italie (Pl. i), at the harbour; Hôtel de Rome (Pl. h). — The atmosphere of the town in summer is hot and oppressive. Those therefore who contemplate a sojourn of several days during the warm season are recommended to select the °Hôtel des Catalans (Pl. k), in the immediate vicinity of the sea-baths and near the so-called *Résidence Impériale* (p. 24); the situation is delightful, and the house spacious and comfortable (open from May to the end of October only); omnibus to and from the station. A small establishment, somewhat more distant, is the °Hôtel Victoria (Pl. l), situated at the extremity of the Cours du Prado, at the point where it approaches the sea; there is a good bathing-place near it, and the house is recommended for a prolonged stay.

Restaurants. De la Cannebière; Hôtel de l'Orient; °Roubion (*à la Réserve*), beautifully situated on the new road La Corniche; Hôtel du Luxembourg (Parrocel). *Bouillabaisse*, good fish. Chablis, Graves, and Sauterne are the white wines usually drunk.

Cafés. De France et de l'Univers, on the E. side of the Cannebière; Bodoul, Rue St. Ferréol; Café Turc, etc., all in the handsome Parisian style. — *Beer* (Munich and Vienna) in the Café Allemand, Cannebière.

Post Office, Rue de Grignan.

Bookseller. Veuve Camoin, in the Cannebière, with reading-rooms (25 c. per diem). French newspapers, Galignani etc.

Carriages are of two descriptions. First, the *voitures du service de la gare*, destined for the conveyance of travellers to and from the railway-station and posted there only. The passenger on entering receives a detailed tariff, in which even the driver's name is stated: one-horse carr. 1 fr. 25 c. for 1 pers., for each additional pers. 25 c.; two-horse carr. 1 fr. 75 c. for 1 pers., for each additional pers. 25 c., for a drive at night 25 c. more; each article of luggage 25 c.; if the traveller fail in obtaining accommodation at the hotel, 25 c. additional for driving to another. Secondly, the *voitures de place (fiacres)*: one-horse 1 fr. 50 c. per drive, 2 fr. 25 c. for the first, and 2 fr. for each succeeding hour; two-horse 2 fr. per drive, 2 fr. 50 c. for the first, and 2 fr. for each succeeding hour. From 6 p. m. to 6 a. m. one-horse 1 fr. 75 c., two-horse 2 fr. 50 c. per drive. — *Omnibus* 30 c., each article of luggage 25 c.

Steamboats to *Ajaccio* (R. 54) once weekly in 26 hrs., fares 1st cl. 30, 2nd 20 fr.; to *Algiers* 3 times weekly in 50 hrs., 1st cl. 95, 2nd 71 fr.; to *Malta* by *Leghorn*, *Civita Vecchia*, *Naples*, and *Messina*, steamers of the Messageries Impériales once weekly (comp. *Bædeker's Central Italy*); to *Genoa* and *Leghorn*, steamers of Valery & Co. once weekly; to *Nice*, twice weekly in 14 hrs., 32 fr.

Boats in the Ancien Port at the extremity of the Rue Cannebière; 1½ fr. for the first, 1 fr. for each succeeding hour. In fine weather a de-

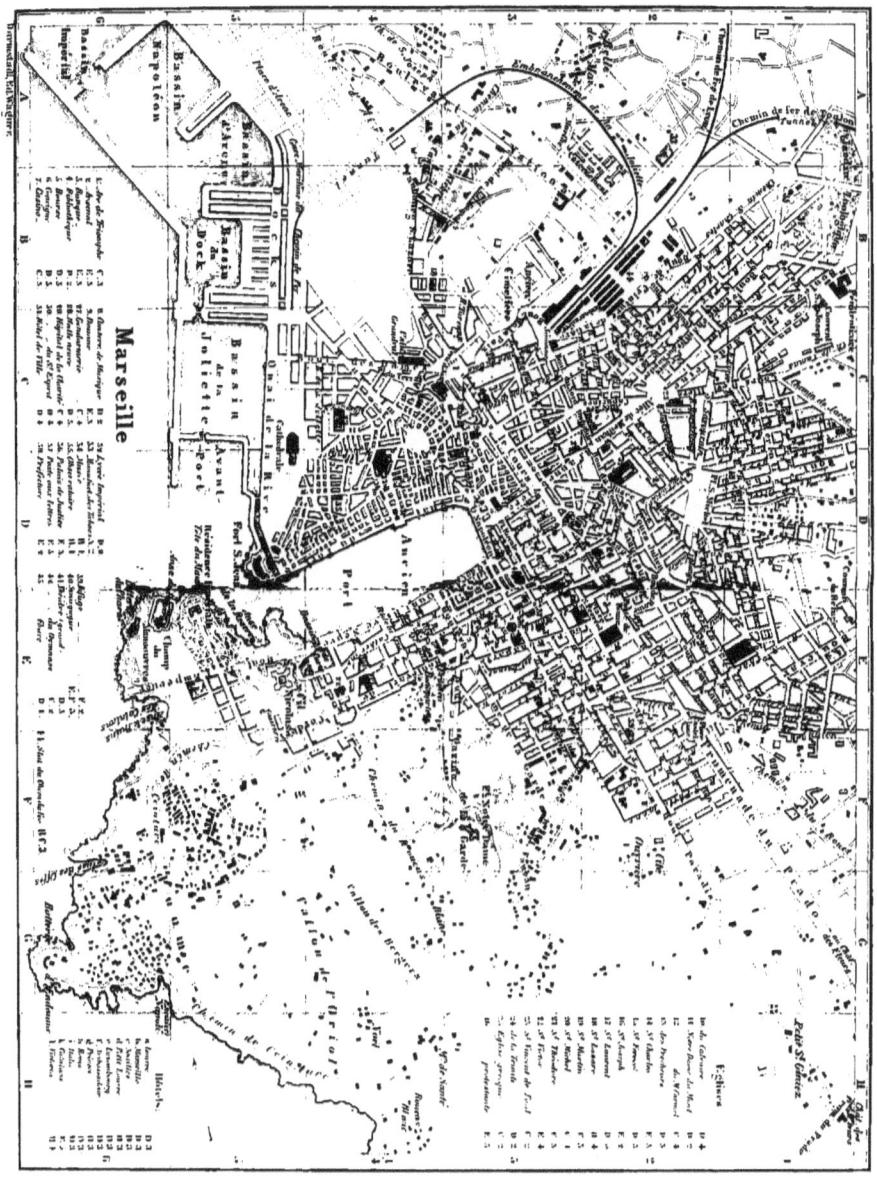

lightful excursion may be made to the islands of Ratonneau, Pomègues and the Château d'If (p. 25).

Sea-baths, handsomely fitted up, in the *Anse des Catalans*, on the E. side of the town, below the conspicuous *Résidence Impériale*; also warm seawater-baths, douche, vapour, etc. for gentlemen and ladies. Adjacent, the large *Hôtel des Catalans*, with restaurant. Omnibus to or from the baths 30 c.

English Church Service performed by a resident chaplain.

Theatres. Grand Opéra (Pl. 41), W. of the Place Royale, and Théâtre du Gymnase (pl. 42) in the Allée de Meilhan, both good. There are also two smaller theatres frequented by the humbler classes.

Massilia was a colony founded about B. C. 600 by Greeks from Phocæa in Asia Minor, who soon became masters of the sea, conquered the Carthaginians in a naval battle near Corsica, and established new colonies in their neighbourhood, such as *Tauroeis* (near Ciotat), *Olbia* (near Hyères), *Antipolis* (Antibes), and *Nicaea* (Nice), all of which, like their founders, adhered to the Greek language, customs, and culture. Massilia maintained this reputation until the imperial period of Rome, and was therefore treated with leniency and respect by Julius Cæsar when conquered by him B. C. 49. Tacitus informs us that his father-in-law Agricola, a native of the neighbouring Roman colony Forum Julii (Fréjus), even under Claudius found ample opportunities for completing his education at Massilia in the Greek manner, for which purpose Athens was usually frequented. The town possessed temples of Diana (on the site of the present cathedral), of Neptune (on the coast), of Apollo, and other gods. Its government was aristocratic. After the fall of the W. Empire Marseilles fell successively into the hands of the Visigoths, the Franks, and the Arelate; it was destroyed by the Saracens, restored in the 10th cent. and became subject to the *Vicomtes de Marseille*; in 1218 it became independent, but shortly afterwards succumbed to Charles of Anjou. In 1481 it was united to France, but still adhered to its ancient privileges, as was especially evident in the wars of the Ligue, against Henri IV. In 1660 Louis XIV., divested the town of its privileges, so that it retained its importance as a sea-port only. In 1720 and 1721 it was devastated by a fearful pestilence. During the revolution it remained unshaken in its allegiance to royalty and was therefore severely punished. In 1792 hordes of galley-slaves were sent hence to Paris, where they committed frightful excesses. It was for them that *Rouget de l'Isle*, an officer of engineers, composed the celebrated *Marseillaise:* 'Allons, enfants de la patrie', which subsequently became the battle-hymn of the republican armies.

The town contains few objects worthy of special mention. The harbour whence it derives its commercial importance, is one of the most interesting points. Since 1850 it has been extended to four times its former size, notwithstanding which there is still a demand for increased accommodation. In 1853 the *Bassin de la Joliette* was added to the *Ancien Port*, and is now the starting-point of most of the steamboats. The *Bassin du Lazaret, d'Arène,* and *Napoléon* were next constructed. It is now proposed to form two new docks and an entrance-harbour *(avant-port)*, which will render Marseilles one of the greatest sea-ports in the world. Nearly 20,000 vessels on an average, of an aggregate burden of 2,000,000 tons, enter and quit Marseilles annually. The annual amount of customs-dues exceeds 60 million francs (i. e. 2,400,000 *l.*). The old harbour is long and narrow. Its entrance is defended by the forts of *St. Jean* and *St. Nicolas*. Near the former is the *Consigne* (Pl. 6; entrance by the gate, fee 50 c.), or office of the 'Intendance Sanitaire' (quarantine authorities), the principal hall of which contains several good pictures: *Horace Vernet*, the cholera on board the frigate Melpomene; *Guérin*, the Chevalier Rose directing the sepulture of those who have died of the plague; *Puget*, the plague at Milan, a relief in marble; *Gérard*, Bishop Belsunce during the plague of 1720; *Tanneurs*, the frigate Justine returning from the East with the plague on board.

A few paces farther N. is the *Cathedral*, a new edifice constructed of alternate layers of black and white stone, in a mixed Byzantine and Romanesque style. The towers are surmounted by domes. The venerable old cathedral of *St. Lazare* has been removed. The terrace commands a pleasant survey of the Bassin de la Joliette (see p. 23).

On the S. side of the Ancien Port is the church of *St. Victor*, with crypt of the 11th cent., superstructure of 1200, towers added in 1350 by Pope Urban V. who was once abbot here. — To the E., in front of the old harbour, is the new *Résidence Impériale* (Pl. E, 5), which however is never occupied by the emperor.

La Cannebière, a broad street, intersects the town from W. to E., from the extremity of the Ancien Port to the centre of the town where the ground rises. In this street, a few paces from the harbour, stands the *Bourse*, with a portico of Corinthian columns, and adorned with the statues of (r.) Euthymenes and (l.) Pytheas, two natives of Massilia who distinguished themselves as navigators before the Christian era. To the latter we are indebted for the earliest data with respect to the length of the days in the different northern latitudes, and the ebb and flow of the tide. The opposite *Place Royale* is used as a fish-market.

A short distance further the *Cours de Belsunce* is reached on the l., a shady promenade generally thronged with foot-passengers, at the S. extremity of which stands the statue of Bishop Belsunce, 'pour perpétuer le souvenir de sa charité et de son dévouement durant la peste qui désola Marseille en 1720'. This intrepid prelate, during the appalling plague which carried off 40,000 persons, alone maintained his post and faithfully performed the solemn duties of his calling. From this point the Rue d'Aix ascends to the *Arc de Triomphe*, erected originally to commemorate the Spanish campaign of the Duke of Angoulême (1823), now decorated with sculptures by *Ramey* and *David d'Angers* of the battles of Marengo, Austerlitz, Fleurus, and Heliopolis, and bearing the inscription: '*A Louis Napoléon Marseille reconnaissante*'. The railway-station is situated to the N. of this point.

We now return to the Cannebière. Opposite to the Place Belsunce opens the *Cours St. Louis*, continued by the *Rue de Rome* and the *Cours du Prado*, which is 2½ M. in length. At the S. extremity of the latter is the *Château des Fleurs*, a small park with fish-ponds, affording various kinds of entertainments, a poor description of 'Tivoli'.

The following pleasant drive of several hours is recommended, especially for the afternoon and evening: From the Porte de Rome or the Place Castelane (both Pl. E, 2) ascend the Cours du Prado, passing the Château des Fleurs; then descend to the coast, affording charming views, and by the Chemin de Ceinture to the village of *Endoume*; hence, skirting the Anse des Catalans (baths and hotel, p. 22), to the Promenade Bonaparte. The stranger may now either return to the town, or ascend on foot to the r. to the church of Notre Dame de la Garde (see below).

To the l. in the Cours St. Louis at the entrance to the narrow Rue de la Palud, is a fountain, adorned with an insignificant bust of *Pierre Puget*, the celebrated sculptor, who was a native of Marseilles.

At the E. end of the *Boulevard de Longchamp* rises the new and handsome **Musée de Longchamp* (Pl. 34), consisting of two extensive buildings connected by a colonnade of the Ionic order, adorned with a fountain in the centre. The r. wing contains the *Musée d'Histoire Naturelle*, the other the *Musée des Beaux Arts*. The latter is approached by a vestibule embellished with two frescoes from the history of Marseilles.

Principal Saloon. R. of the entrance: *J. Vernet*, Harbour; *Murillo*, Capuchin; *Spagnoletto*, St. Peter; *Salv. Rosa*, Hermit examining a skull; *Langlois*, Bishop Belsunce. On the opp. wall: *Holbein*, Portrait (retouched); *Snyders*, Still life; *Guercino*, Hector taking leave of Priam; *Rubens*, Christ scourged; *Perugino, Madonna with saints; *Van Dyck*, Christ on the Cross; *Rubens*, Wild-boar hunt; *Schalken*, Newspaper-reader; *Flemish Sch.*, Portrait of an old man. L. of the entrance: *Ruysdael*, Landscape. — The adjoining saloon on the r. is in course of being filled with pictures of the Provençal school, that on the l. with modern works. Among the latter: *Philippoteaux, Farewell repast of Girondists on the eve of their execution; *Curzon*, Female weavers of Naples; *Ary Scheffer*, Magdalene.

The well-kept grounds at the back of the Museum extend to the *Zoolog. Garden* (adm. 1 fr.), which contains a valuable collection of animals.

The *Old Museum*, in the Boulevard du Musée, now contains nothing worthy of note.

*Point of View. The best survey of the town and environs is afforded by the church of **Notre Dame de la Garde* (Pl. F, 3), situated on an eminence to the S. of the old harbour. The old chapel, as well as the Fort Notre Dame, have been taken down, and a new chapel erected on the site of the former in the same style as the cathedral (p. 24). The interior contains an image of the Virgin and innumerable votive tablets presented by those who have been rescued from shipwreck or disease. The terrace in front of the church, and especially the gallery of the tower (154 steps), which contains a huge bell 10 tons in weight, and is to be crowned with a large figure of the Virgin, command an admirable survey of the extensive city, occupying the entire width of the valley, the innumerable white villas *(bastides)* on the surrounding hills, the harbour and the barren group of islands at its entrance, with the Château d'If, where Mirabeau was once confined (also mentioned in Dumas' 'Monte Christo'), and a portion of the Mediterranean. Several different paths ascend to this point from the old harbour, finally by steps, a somewhat fatiguing climb. Here the full force of the prevailing *Mistral*, or piercing N.W. wind, the scourge of Provence, is often felt.

The Railway to Toulon and Nice (140½ M., in 7 hrs.; fares 25 fr. 20, 18 fr. 90, 13 fr. 85 c.; to Toulon 42 M., in 1¾ hr.) runs from the station outside the Arc de Triomphe (p. 24) at some distance from the sea, passing through several rocky defiles. Several small stations; then *Aubayne*, with a statue of Abbé Barthélémy. Near *Cassis* several tunnels penetrate the rocky ridge of *Ollioule*, and stat. *La Ciotat* is reached, charmingly situated on the coast, a most agreeable retreat in winter and spring. Near stat. *St. Cyr* is situated the *Tauroeis* of the ancients. *Bandol*, with a fortified harbour, is delightfully situated in a bay. Then *Ollioules-St. Nazaire*, *La Seyne*, and

Toulon (Croix de Malte, R. 5, D. 4, A. 1 fr; *Croix d'Or, Place des Trois Dauphins; Amirauté and Victoria in the Bouvelard L. Napoléon; Cafés de Paris and de la Marine in the Champ-de-Bataille, where a military band generally plays in the evening), the war-harbour of France for the Mediterranean with 77,100 inhab., possesses a double harbour, protected by 11 forts which crown the surrounding heights. The strongest of these are *La Malgue*, *Aiguillette*, *Ballaguier*, and *Fort Napoléon*. The latter, which is sometimes termed Le Petit Gibraltar, was gallantly defended in December, 1793, by 300 English soldiers against an enemy of tenfold number, but it was at last taken by storm, whereupon the other forts also surrendered. This attack was conducted by the Lieutenant of artillery *Buonaparte*, then in his 23rd year, who six years later became Consul. In 1707 Toulon was besieged less successfully by the Austrians and Sardinians under Prince Eugene, who were obliged to retire after bombarding the town.

The town contains nothing to detain the traveller except the *War Harbour*, with the *Bagno* (prison of the forçats, or galley-convicts) and the *Arsenal*, which may be inspected daily about 2 p. m. Visitors on exhibiting their passports (or visiting-cards), are furnished with tickets of admission at the Admiralty Office 9½ a. m. (gratuities prohibited).

The *view enjoyed from the height of *La Malgue*, S.E. of Toulon, is one of the most beautiful in Provence.

Steamboats ply twice weekly from Toulon to *Corsica*, reaching *Ajaccio* in 22, *Bastia* in 24 hrs.

The *Botanical Garden* contains some fine samples of southern vegetation, such as date-palms, etc., which flourish in the open air.

Beyond Toulon the line quits the coast and winds through the *Montagnes des Maures* to the N.E.; stations *La Garde* and *Hyères*.

The small town of **Hyères** (*Hôtel des Hespérides; des Iles d'Or; de l'Europe; d'Orient; du Parc; °des Ambassadeurs*, less expensive; *de Paris*. — English Church Service in winter and spring. — *Physicians:* Drs. Duncan, Griffith) lies 3 M. from the railway (omnibus) and the same distance from the sea, on the slope of the lofty Mts. des Maures, but not sufficiently protected from the Mistral. It is much visited as a winter-residence by those suffering from pulmonary complaints, and is surrounded by a number of villas, but the town itself is uninviting. Most of the heights in the vicinity are barren. The orange and lemon-trees of which Hyères boasts are generally concealed by garden-walls. The low ground is marshy at places and exhales unwholesome vapours in summer and autumn. The *Islands of Hyères* (the *Stoechades* of the ancients; 'Lavandula Stoechas' is an aromatic flower frequently occurring here) are a group of rocky islands and cliffs near the coast. The largest of them are the *Ile du Levant* or *Titan*, *Porteros*, *Porquerolles* and *Bagneau*. Some of them are fortified and inhabited, but they do not enjoy so mild a climate as Hyères itself, being more exposed to the wind.

J. B. Massillon, the celebrated preacher, who lived during the reigns of Louis XIV. and XV., was born at Hyères in 1663 (d. 1742 as Bishop of Clermont). The *Place Royale* is adorned with his bust.

A number of unimportant places are next passed. Then stat. *Le Luc*, with the ruins of an ancient Abbey, and *Vidauban*, in a picturesque district. From the next stat. *Les Arcs* a branch-line runs to *Draguignan* (Poste), a beautifully situated town with 10,000 inhab. and enjoying a mild and salubrious climate. Next stations *Le Muy* and *Roquebrune*.

Fréjus (*Hôtel du Midi*, R. 2, B. 1, D. 3, A. 1 fr.), a small town with 2887 inhab., the ancient *Forum Julii*, founded by Julius Cæsar, contains a number of Roman remains, an amphitheatre, archway *(Porte Dorée)*, and aqueduct, none of which possess much interest. The Roman General Julius Agricola was born here; also the Abbé Sieyès, whose name is so intimately associated with the Revolution.

From Fréjus to Nice the line runs near the coast. L. rises the *Mont d'Estérel*. Stat. *St. Raphael* is delightfully situated in a ravine on the coast. At the small harbour of this place Napoleon landed in Oct., 1799, on his return from Egypt; one month later, on Nov. 9th (18th Brumaire), he overthrew the Directory at Paris and caused himself to be created First Consul. Here, too, after his abdication, he embarked for Elba, April 28th, 1814. The line traverses a romantic, rocky district, occasionally affording charming glimpses of the numerous bays of the coast. Stat. *Agay*, then four tunnels.

Cannes (more than 50 hotels; among them, near the sea, in the Boulevard de l'Impératrice, Hôtel de la Plage; Grand Hotel de Cannes, a spacious establishment in the Parisian style; Hôtel Gonnet, Gray, Beaurivage, des Princes, de la Méditerranée. In the town Grand Hôtel du Louvre, des Etrangers, du Nord, Poste, de Genève, *Pension Lérins. In the suburbs: W. Bellevue; Pavillon; N., near the stat. and in the direction towards Cannet (see below): de la Paix, de l'Europe, *Bel-Air (pension 6—10 fr.); France, Phénix, de Provence, Victoria, all fitted up for the reception of visitors making a prolonged stay. Private apartments, usually let for the whole winter, are easily procured. On the promenades: Café des Allées, de l'Univers, etc. — Physicians: *Drs. Butterby, Clark, Lee, Whiteley; Dr. de Valcourt, Dr. Frank* etc. — *English Church Service*), a small but rapidly increasing town (10,000 inhab.), picturesquely situated on the *Golfe de la Napoule*, is indebted to its sheltered situation for its repute as a wintering-place for consumptive and delicate persons. It is protected by the *Estérel Mts.* (p. 27) from the N. and N.W. winds.

The town consists of a main street, parallel with which, along the coast, runs the *Boulevard de l'Impératrice*, terminating on the W. in the *Cours*, a 'place' with promenades and fountains. The most sheltered situation is the space between the N. side of the town and the village of *Cannet*. The W. end of the town is principally occupied by English families (the English Church is situated here). The best French society is also well represented.

The old town lies at the foot of the *Mont Chevalier*, on which the parish church rises, and from which the pier closing the S.W. side of the harbour runs out. Fine view from the top.

Opposite the *Cap de la Croisette*, the promontory which separates the Golfe de la Napoule from the *Golfe de Jouan*, rise the *Iles de Lerins*. On *Sainte Marguerite*, the largest of these, is situated *Fort Monterey* (poor inn), in which 'the man with the iron mask' was kept in close confinement from 1686 to 1698. It is now occupied by Arabian prisoners. (Fine survey of Cannes and the entire coast.) On the island of *St. Honorat* rise the ruins of a fortified monastery and church (boat there and back 10—12 fr.).

The Environs of Cannes are delightful, and studded with numerous villas. Pleasant walks to the *Jardin des Hespérides*, to *Vallauris*. *Mouyins*, the monastery of *St. Cassien*, the ruin of *Napoule;* farther distant, to *Grasse* and *Bar*. The vegetation is luxuriant, but lemon-trees are not common here. Orange-trees are principally cultivated for the sake of the blossoms, which form an important article of commerce.

Beyond Cannes the line passes *Golfe Jouan;* a column marks the spot where Napoleon bivouacked on the night after his arrival from Elba, March 1st, 1815.

Antibes *(Hôtel de France)*, the ancient *Antipolis*, a colony of the Massilians, is now a small, but animated seaport (6829 inhab.), beautifully situated on a promontory and commanding a charming view of the sea, the Bay of Nice and the Alpes Maritimes. A pier constructed by Vauban connects it with several islands in the vicinity. This portion of the line traverses a remarkably rich and attractive district. It soon crosses the *Var* (Varus), an impetuous mountain-torrent, which in modern, as well as ancient times formed the boundary between France and Italy, until in 1860 Nice was ceded to France, and the frontier removed farther to the E. Stations *Vence-Cagne*, *Var*, and

Nice, see R. 16. From Nice to Genoa see R. 15.

2. From Paris *(Geneva)* to Turin by Mont Cenis.

From Paris to Culoz express in 12 hrs., to St. Michel in 16 hrs.; thence by Fell's 'chemin de fer américain' to Susa in 5½ hrs.; from Susa to Turin rail. in 2 hrs. *Through-tickets* from Paris to Turin 1st cl. 113 fr. 15, 2nd 87 fr. 5, 3rd 64 fr. 70 c.; from Paris to Bologna 1st cl. 150 fr. 10 c., to Florence 163 fr. 85 c., to Milan 129 fr. 85 c., to Venice 164 fr. 45 c.

From Paris to Macon see R. 1. The railway here quits the Lyons line and proceeds to the l., crosses the Saône, and at stat. *Pont-de-Veyle* the *Veyle*. In front and to the l. a view of the Jura is obtained. The next place of importance is

Bourg *(Hôtels de l'Europe, du Midi, du Palais)*, with 14,000 inhab., the ancient capital of Bresse, situated on the l. bank of the *Reyzousse*, ¾ M. from the station. The church of *Notre Dame de Boury*, erected from the 15th to the 17th cent., in a variety of styles, contains several pictures, sculptures, and fine wood-carving. On the promenade Le Bastion is the *Monument of Bichat (d. 1802), who once studied at Bourg, by David d'Angers. The house in which *Lalande* (d. at Paris in 1807) was born is indicated by a tablet with inscription. — Bourg is the junction of the line to Lyons, Mouchard, Besançon, and Mulhouse, which is the direct railway between Lyons and Strasbourg (comp. pp. 5, 6).

The celebrated *Church of Brou, in the florid Gothic style, erected 1511 —36 by Margaret of Austria, Regent of the Netherlands, is situated 1½ M. from the town. It contains the sumptuous *Monuments of the foundress, the Duke Philibert of Savoy her husband, and Margaret of Bourbon, her mother-in-law. Her well-known motto '*Fortune infortune forte une*', may be seen in different parts of the church.

The line intersects the forest of *Seillon*. Near Stat. **Pont d'Ain** the *Ain* is crossed.

Ambérieux, a pleasant little town on the *Albarine*, situated at the base of the Jura Mts., is the junction for Lyons (p. 8).

The train now continues to ascend the valley of the Albarine. L. lie the ruined castles of *Vieux-Mont-Ferrand* and *St. Germain*. Beyond stat. *St. Rambert de Joux* the valley becomes wilder and more imposing. The line quits the Albarine at stat. *Tenay* and enters a sequestered valley to the r., where *Les Hôpitaux* is situated. Near stat. *Rossillon* are a few fragments of a former stronghold. Beyond a tunnel, ⅓ M. in length, the lakes of *Pugieu* are observed on the r. Beyond two small stations the line now reaches the valley of the Rhone near

Stat. **Culoz** *(*Rail. Restaur.)* at the base of the *Colombier* (5000 ft.), junction of the Geneva line.

From Geneva to Culoz railway in 2½ hrs.; fares 7 fr. 50, 5 fr. 65, 4 fr. 15 c. The line follows the r. bank of the Rhone, on the slopes of the Jura Mts. Beyond *Collonges*, the fifth station, the Rhone flows through a narrow rocky valley, confined between the Jura and *Mont de Vuache*, and commanded by the *Fort de l'Ecluse*, which rises far above on the r. The line quits the defile by the long *Tunnel du Crédo* (2⅓ M.), crosses the grand *Valserine Viaduct*, and reaches stat. *Bellegarde* (Poste), at the influx of the Valserine into the Rhone. The latter here forms a species of rapid, known as the *Perte du Rhône*, where the water is occasionally lost to the view. Stations *Pyrimont*, *Seyssel*, and *Culoz*.

The line to St. Michel *(Chemin de fer Victor-Emanuel)* crosses the Rhone, and at stat. *Châtillon* reaches the *Lac du Bourget* (12 M. in length, 1½ M. in breadth), the E. bank of which it follows. Several tunnels and fine views.

Aix-les-Bains (*Hôtel Impérial*, the nearest to the station; *Venat*, with spacious garden; Globe, Europe, D. 4 fr.; Ambassadeurs; Guilland *(Poste)*; Univers, less expensive. — One-horse carr. 2 fr. per drive of 25 min.), the *Aquae Allobrogum* or *Aquae Gratianae* of the Romans, is a celebrated watering-place with 4200 inhab. (5—6000 visitors to the baths annually), possessing sulphur-springs (113° Fahr.), which are adapted for internal and external use. The large new *Etablissement Thermal* with baths and pump-room deserves inspection. In the place in front of it a Rom. triumphal Arch of the 3rd or the 4th cent.; the other scanty relics of the Roman period (fragments of a temple and of baths) are almost all within the precincts of private property and not easily accessible.

Pleasant excursion to ***Haute Combe**, a Cistercian Abbey on the N.W. bank of the *Lac du Bourget*, at the base of *Mont du Chat*. This was the burial-place of the Princes of Savoy till 1731, after which they were interred in the Superga at Turin (p. 80). The abbey was destroyed during the French Revolution, but restored in 1824 by Charles Felix, king of Sardinia. The church contains a number of magnificent monuments. The prospect from the *Phare de Gesseus*, a tower in the vicinity, has been described by Rousseau.

Branch Line from Aix-les-Bains to *Annecy* (in 1½ hr., fares 4 fr. 50, 3 fr. 35, 2 fr. 45 c.).

Near stat. *Voglans* the line quits the lake and traverses the broad valley of the *Laisse*; to the l. the beautifully wooded slopes of the *Mont d'Azi* and the *Dent de Nivolet*.

Chambéry (*Hôtel de France*, near the station; *Hôtel de l'Europe*; *Poste*, less expensive; *Hôtel des Princes*) is the capital of the Department of Savoy, with 20,000 inhab., and an archiepiscopal see. The *Cathedral*, a small, but interesting edifice of 1430, has been somewhat disfigured by a subsequent addition. A square tower and remnants of the façade of the old palace of the Dukes of Savoy, erected in 1230, still exist. On the Promenade between the station and the town is the *Monument of General de Boigne* (d. 1830), adorned with life-size figures of elephants. He was a native of Chambéry, to which he bequeathed a fortune of 3½ million francs acquired in India. *Les Charmettes*, a country-residence 1½ M. from the town, was once occupied by Rousseau and Madame de Warens.

The line traverses a picturesque district, passing the ruined castles of *Bâtie* and *Chignin*. The precipitous *Mont Granier* (6076 ft.) is indebted for its present form to a great landslip which descended from it in 1248 and overwhelmed 16 villages. Stat. *Route de Grenoble* is the junction for the branch-line to *Grenoble*, which enters the valley of the *Isère* (or *Valley of Graisivaudan*) to the r. [From Chambéry to Grenoble in 2¼ hrs.

Grenoble is connected with the Paris and Marseilles line by means of three different railways, which reach it at Lyons (p. 6), St. Rambert (p. 11) and Valence (p. 12) respectively. From Grenoble to Marseilles by railway in 13 hrs.] — The line now turns to the l. Next stat. *Montmélian*, where a good description of wine is produced. The ancient castle, of which scanty fragments now alone exist, was long the bulwark of Savoy against France. It was once defended by Goffredo Benso, an ancestor of Cavour (d. 1861). during 13 months against the army of Louis XIII. In 1705 it was destroyed by Louis XIV. Next stations *St. Pierre d'Albigny* and *Chamousset*. Picturesque view (to the l.) of the broad valley of the *Isère*, enclosed by beautifully formed mountains on both sides.

At the influx of the *Arc* into the Isère the line quits the valley of the latter and ascends the valley of the Arc, which is at first of considerable width. Beyond stat. *Aiguebelle*, which is grandly situated, the valley contracts. The Arc is now crossed. The valley expands; scenery picturesque. The district near stat. *Epierre* is rendered unhealthy by the marshy nature of the soil, and cretinism is here prevalent. Stat. *La Chambre*. Beyond *St. Jean de Maurienne* (Hôtel de l'Europe), chief place in the valley, the line crosses to the r., near *St. Julien* again to the l. bank of the Arc. The valley contracts, and the scenery assumes a bleak aspect. Several tunnels, then

St. Michel *(Hôtel de la Poste;* *Rail. *Restaurant)*, where the railway at present terminates.

Travellers are conveyed hence (unless prevented by unusually heavy falls of snow) across Mt. Cenis by *Fell's Mountain Railway*, opened in 1868, the trains of which correspond with those of the French and Italian lines (Ital. or Rom. time 47 min. in advance of that of Paris).

This Chemin de Fer du Mont-Cenis, constructed by Mr. Fell, an American engineer, in less than two years, at a comparatively trifling cost, is a most novel and interesting undertaking. The line generally follows the direction of the high road. Where the incline is great, or the curve sudden, between the ordinary rails is placed a third broad rail, against which horizontal wheels under the locomotive and carriages work. The friction is thus so greatly increased that the train is enabled to ascend even steeper inclines than the ordinary, ponderous diligence, whilst the same contrivance entirely removes the danger of sudden turns. The incline is at some points 1 : 12^1/$_2$ (Semmering and Brenner railways 1 : 40 only). Each carriage, moreover, is provided with two brakes, one for the ordinary, the other for the horizontal wheels, the united action of which is capable of stopping the vehicle effectually even on the steepest inclines. Each train usually consists of 4—5 carriages, in which about 60 passengers can be conveyed.

Beyond *La Praz*, where the locomotives are supplied with water, the new railway will quit the valley of the Arc near the village of *Fourneau*, and enter the long tunnel (8^1/$_8$ M. in length, estimated cost 38 million francs) to the S.E., penetrating the mountain beneath the *Col de Fréjus* and emerging in the valley of *Bardonnêche* (near the village and fort of that name). It will then quit the valley at *Oulx* and descend N.E. in the Dora Valley (p. 33) to Susa. The tunnel is the grandest modern undertaking of the kind. The ingenious boring machines are worked by means of compressed air. The work on the Italian side, which progressed more rapidly owing to the softer nature of the rock, was completed in Nov., 1869, whilst on the French side about 1 M. had yet to be constructed. It is expected that the tunnel will be available for public traffic about the end of 1871. Visitors are permitted to inspect the works on leaving a visiting-card at the office, but are not allowed to enter the tunnel itself. This visit may be paid during the interval between the first and second train from Modane, but this delay will (except in the height of summer) prevent the traveller from descending the beautiful valley of Susa by daylight.

Modane (Lion d'Or) is an insignificant place. On the r. bank of the Arc, a short distance farther, high above the precipice which the train here skirts, rises the *Fort Bramans d'Essillon*, which commands the road in both directions. *Bramans* and *Termignon* are the next small stations. After a steep ascent, the train now descends to

Lans-le-Bourg (*Hôtel de l'Europe; Hôtel Imperial; Rail. Restaur.*), a poor village at the N. base of Mont Cenis, the French frontier-station for travellers coming from Italy.

The *Mont Cenis Road* commences here. It was constructed by Fabbroni in 1802—5 by order of Napoleon, and is the principal channel of communication beween France and Italy. It is at the same time one of the safest of the Alpine passes. The road quits the valley of the Arc and ascends in numerous windings. The railway runs parallel with it, but avoids its sudden turns by means of longer curves. Three short tunnels; then a pleasing retrospect of the valley of Lans-le-Bourg is obtained; on the l. and r. are the huge glaciers of the *Mont de Vanoise* and the *Monte della Pricutta*. The higher parts of the line are protected from the fall of avalanches and debris by iron roofs, and at dangerous points by stone galleries. The Summit of the Pass (6848 ft., about the same height as the Great St. Bernard, Splügen, St. Gotthard, and Simplon) is reached in 55 min. from Lans-le-Bourg (descent thither in 45 min.), whilst a carriage requires 3 hrs. to accomplish the ascent (about 10 M.). Stat. *La Frontière*, boundary between France and Italy. On the summit a table-land $4^1/_2$ M. long is traversed. The *Lac du Mont Cenis*, abounding in trout, lies to the r. To the l. is the *Hospice*, founded by Charlemagne, or his son Louis the Pious, but erected in its present form by Napoleon. It is now tenanted by Benedictine monks and Italian carabinieri. At stat. *La Grand' Croix* the railway quits the road, which here descends in zigzags *(Les Echelles)*, and describes a long curve to the r., protected by numerous avalanche galleries. To the l. rises the beautiful snow-clad *Rochemelon (Roccia Melone)*, crowned by the chapel of *Notre Dame des Neiges*, where a vast concourse of the inhabitants of neighbouring districts assemble to hear mass on Aug. 5th of every year. Stat. *Bard*. The villages of *Novalesa* and *Ferrera* lie to the l. below the line. As the train descends, the views of the valley of Susa become more striking, and the vegetation more luxuriant. The first Piedmontese village is *Molaret (Il Molaretto)*, where trains do not stop. Stat. *St. Martin*. At *Giaglione* the railway and road reach the valley of the *Dora Riparia* (or *Dora Susa*) in which the road from Susa (as well as the new railway to St. Michel) ascend to the r. (S.W.) and cross the Mont Genèvre. The train soon reaches

Susa *(Hôtel de France; Soleil; *Rail. Restaur.)*, the Roman *Segusio*, seat of the Italian custom-house, a very ancient town with 2000 inhab., picturesquely situated in an amphitheatre of rocks. The garden of the Governatore contains an ancient triumphal arch, 51 ft. high, 42 ft. wide, and 26 ft. in depth, decorated with projecting Corinthian columns at the four corners, and with sacrificial scenes on the frieze. The inscription records that the prefect Cottius, son of king Donnus, and the people subject to his jurisdiction erected the arch to Augustus A. U. C. 745 (i. e. B. C. 8).

Travellers by the mountain-railway alight at the station from which the **Turin** trains start. The line follows the course of the Dora, the broad and attractive valley of which is enclosed by two mountain-ranges. Four small stations; then *S. Ambrogio;* in the vicinity, high on a rocky pinnacle to the r., stands the abbey of *S. Michele della Chiusa*, remarkable for its tombs, the corpses in which, instead of decomposing, are converted into natural mummies. At *Avigliana* the valley expands into a broad plain. Three other unimportant places are finally passed. The view is generally intercepted by the acacia plantations which skirt the railway on both sides.

Turin see p. 72.

3. From Lausanne to Arona on the Lago Maggiore *(and Milan)* over the Simplon.

Railway from Lausanne to Sierre in 4—5 hrs.; fares 12 fr. 35, 8 fr. 40, 6 fr. 20 c. Thence over the Simplon Diligence once daily in 18 hrs. Comfortable Swiss vehicles the whole way to Arona; fare (coupé) to Domo d'Ossola 35 fr. 30 c., intérieur a few fr. less. From d'Ossola to Arona 8 fr. — For the journey from Lausanne (Ouchy) to Villeneuve (or Bouveret, comp. p. 34) the steamboat is preferable to the railway. Steamers on Lago Maggiore see R. 23. — Through-tickets from Lausanne to Milan 46 fr. 30, 40 fr. 40, 37 fr. 85 c.

Lausanne (*Faucon, R. from 2½, L. ½, B. 1½, D. 3—4, A. 1 fr.; Hôtel Gibbon; *Bellevue; *Hôtel du Grand Pont, not expensive; Hôtel Riche Mont. — At *Ouchy:* °Beau Rivage, a spacious establishment opposite the steamboat-pier, R. 2 fr. and upwards, B. 1½, A. 1 fr.; Ancre), capital of the Canton de Vaud, with 20,742 inhab., is delightfully situated at the base of *Mont Jorat*, on two hills connected by the imposing *Grand Pont, a bridge constructed in 1839—44. The *Cathedral, a pure Gothic edifice erected in 1235—75, should be visited. The terrace affords a fine survey of the town, the lake, and the Alps of Savoy (still more extensive from the summit of the tower, 164 ft. in height). The *Musée Cantonal* in the Collége contains a nat. hist. cabinet and a collection of antiquities; several good pictures at the *Musée Arlaud*. — Celebrated view from the *Signal (2126 ft.), ½ hr. above the town. Mont Blanc itself is not visible from this point, but is seen from the *Grandes Roches*, 1½ M. from the town, r. of the road to Yverdon.

The railway from Lausanne to Villeneuve skirts the N.E. bank of the Lake of Geneva. The abrupt slopes between Lausanne and Vevay, termed *La Vaux*, produce excellent wine.

Vevay (°Trois Couronnes, °Grand Hôtel de Vevey, both 1st cl., R. 2—4 fr., L. ¾, B. 1½, D. 4 fr., A. 1 fr.; °Hôtel du Léman; °Hôtel Senn, and °Hôtel du Lac (smaller), both on the lake; Croix Blanche, R. 2, D. 3 fr.; Trois Rois, not far from the station, without view; °Hôtel du Pont, by the station; Hôtel de la Poste, in the town), the second town in the Canton de Vaud (popul. 6538), is celebrated for the beauty of its situation. Charming view from the small terrace in the market-place, near the *Château of M. Couvreu*. The *Church of St. Martin*, outside the town, erected 1498, used in summer only as a place of worship, is the burial-place of the regicides Ludlow and Broughton, members of the republican tribunal which condemned Charles I.

The most beautiful and imposing part of the Lake of Geneva is between Vevay and Villeneuve. The villages of *Clarens, Chernex, Vernex, Montreux, Glion, Collonges, Veytaux*, etc., which here lie scattered about, partly on the lake and partly on the mountain, all belong to the parish of **Montreux** *(*Hôtel de l' Union; Pont)*. From the lofty church a magnificent *view is enjoyed, extending from the mouth of the Rhone to a point far beyond Lausanne. Consumptive patients are frequently sent to Montreux, its sheltered situation rendering it peculiarly adapted for a winter-residence.

About midway between Montreux and Villeneuve rises the *Castle of Chillon on a rock in the lake. **Villeneuve** (1230 ft.) *(Hôtel de Ville)* lies at the mouth of the Rhone Valley, but at some distance from the river. The railway on the r. bank of the Rhone unites with that on the l. bank at St. Maurice (see below). The latter line at present terminates at *Bouveret*, where the trains correspond with the steamers. The railway along the S. (French) bank of the lake to Geneva is in process of construction.

The lower part of the Rhone Valley, 3 M. in breadth and enclosed by lofty mountains, is marshy. Stations *Aigle*, *Olton St. Triphon*, *Bex*. At St. Maurice the valley contracts. The railway of the r. bank here crosses the river and unites with that on the l. bank. Stat. **St. Maurice** (1342 ft.) *(Hôtel de la Dent du Midi; Ecu du Valais)*, the *Agaunum* of the Romans, is an ancient town with very narrow streets, on a delta between the river and the precipice. The richly endowed Abbey, founded about the end of the 4th cent., contains some curious old works of art.

To the r., 1 M. from stat. *Vernayaz* is the **Pissevache*, or waterfall of the *Sallenche*, which descends from the glaciers of the Dent du Midi and is here precipitated into the Rhone Valley from a height of 400 ft. About $3/4$ M. S. of Vernayaz, on the r., is the imposing **Gorge du Trient*, accessible for a distance of $1/2$ M. by means of a wooden gallery (admission 1 fr.).

Martigny (1387 ft.) *(*Hôtel Clerc; *Hôtel de la Tour; *Grande-Maison-Poste; Bellevue*, at the stat.), is a busy little town in summer, being the starting-point of the Simplon and Great St. Bernard routes and the bridle-paths over the Tête Noire and Col de Balme to Chamouny.

The railway runs hence in a straight direction to the *Baths of Saxon* (Hotel); beyond stat. *Riddes* it crosses the Rhone, and the *Lizerne* at stat. *Ardon*.

Sion (1732 ft.) *(*Hôtel de la Poste; Lion d'Or)*, with 4205 inhab., the chief town of the *Canton of Valais*, which in 1810—15 belonged to France under the name of *Département du Simplon*, has in the distance a handsome aspect with the picturesque castles towering above it. Two of these, the *Tourbillon* (*view) and *Majoria*, were burned down in 1788; *Valeria*, the third, erected on the site of an ancient Roman fort, now serves as an ecclesiastical seminary. The adjacent church of *St. Catherine*, founded in the 9th cent., is interesting to architects. In the town there are no objects of interest; a leisure hour is best employed in ascending to the castle of *Tourbillon* (20 min.).

The following stations are *St. Léonard* and *Granges*; the railway terminates at

Sierre (1807 ft.) *(Hôtel et Pension Baur; Soleil)*, picturesquely situated on a hill, with several ruins in the vicinity. Good wine is produced in the environs.

Diligence (comp. p. 33) hence over the Simplon. The road soon crosses the Rhone. The small village of *Pfyn* forms the boundary between the French and German languages, the latter only being spoken beyond this point.

To the l. rises the handsome old market-town of *Leuk*, or *Loëche*, with its castle and towers, high above the Rhone. On an eminence to the l., above the *Ravine of the Dala*, which here opens, glistens the church-tower of *Varen*. On the r. beyond Leuk, on a shelving pasture high above it, lies the Alpine village of *Albinen*.

The road next passes through the small village of *Susten* (*Hôtel de la Souste).

9 M. **Tourtemagne** or *Turtmann* (2208 ft.) (*Poste or *Lion; *Sonne). To the l., high above in the Lötschenthal which here opens, rise the icy slopes of the *Tschingel Glacier*; to the r. in the background is the broad Simplon group, with the imposing *Kaltwasser Glacier* (see below). L., above *Raron*, rises the snow-clad *Bietschhorn* (12,969 ft.).

8½ M. **Vispach** or *Visp*, French *Viège* (2231 ft.) (*Sonne, R. 2, B. 1½, D. 3¾, A. ½ fr.; *Post)*, a village with beautiful environs, was seriously injured by an earthquake in 1855. *View from the sluice and cemetery. The magnificent mountain visible in the background of the Visp Valley is the *Balferin* (12,401 ft.), the first peak of the *Mischabel* or *Saasgrat*, which divides the valley of Saas from that of Zermatt.

An excursion to *Zermatt* and the *Gorner Grat* may be accomplished in two days from Vispach if a horse (10 fr.) be taken to *St. Nicholas* and a char-à-bancs (12 fr.) thence to Zermatt; the Gorner Grat may then be ascended, and Vispach regained in the above manner (comp. *Bædeker's Switzerland*).

5¼ M. **Brieg** (2323 ft.) (*Trois Couronnes*; *Angleterre*, R. 2½, B. 1½, A. and L. 1 fr.), is a small town at the base of the Simplon, at the commencement of the Simplon Route, which was constructed by order of Napoleon in 1800—6, and after the Brenner (p. 57) was the first carriage-road across the Alps from Switzerland to Italy.

The road quits the valley of the Rhone and ascends by long and numerous windings on the mountains of the l. bank of the river. By means of a long circuit to the E. the *Ganterthal* is avoided.

12 M. *Berisal* (5082 ft.), the 3rd Refuge, is also a post-station and *inn. Above the 4th Refuge a retrospect is obtained in clear weather of the Bernese Alps (to the N.), from which the huge Aletsch Glacier descends. That portion of the road between the 5th Refuge and the culminating point is the most dangerous during the period of avalanches and storms. Within a distance of less than 3 M. there are no fewer than six houses of refuge and a hospice. The road passes through the *Kaltwasser Glacier Gallery*, over which the stream issuing from the glacier is precipitated into the depths below, forming a waterfall which is visible through a side opening. From the 6th Refuge a splendid final view is enjoyed of the Bernese Alps and the Aletsch Glacier; far below in the Rhone Valley lies Brieg.

The culminating point of the **Simplon Pass** (6627 ft.) is 6½ M. distant from Berisal. About ¾ M. beyond the summit is the *Hospice* (no payment demanded for hospitality, but strangers should contribute at least as much to the poor-box as they would have paid at an hotel), an extensive building founded by Napoleon, but not completed till 1825. A broad, open valley, carpeted at places with Alpine roses, here forms the highest portion of the Simplon Pass, bounded by snow-capped heights and glaciers. The imposing *Raut Glacier* is a conspicuous object on the mountains to the S. The *Old Hospice*, a lofty square tower now tenanted by herdsmen, lies far below the new road.

15 M. **Simplon** (4626 ft.), Ger. *Simpeln*, Ital. *Sempione (Post; *Hôtel du Fletschhorn*, in the lower part of the village). The road now describes a great curve to the S., which pedestrians may cut off by a rugged path and regain the road at the *Algabi Gallery*. Here the most remarkable part of the Simplon route begins. It leads through the **Ravine of Gondo*, one of the wildest and grandest in the Alps, becoming narrower and more profound at every step, until its smooth and precipitous walls of mica-slate completely overhang the road, on the other side of which rushes the impetuous Diveria. The most remarkable of the tunnels which here pierce the rocks is the *Gallery of Gondo*, 731 ft. in length, constructed in 1805 and fortified by the Swiss in 1830. At the issue of the gallery the *Fressinone* (or *Alpienbach*) dashes over the rocks from a considerable height into the gorge below. A slender bridge crosses the waterfall. On both sides the rocks tower to a dizzy height (about 2000 ft.). The dark entrance of the gallery forms a striking contrast to the white foam of the falling torrent. This magnificent Alpine *picture, especially when seen at a distance of 40—50 paces, surpasses the Via Mala (p. 46). *Gondo* (2313 ft.) is the last Swiss village; 1/2 M. beyond it is the Italian boundary-column. *S. Marco* is the first Italian village.

9 M. **Iselle** (2148 ft.) (**Posta*, R. 1 1/2 fr.) is the seat of the Italian custom-house. The wildest scenery is now quitted, but the valley continues to be extremely picturesque. It unites with the broad and fruitful valley of the *Tosa* (or *Toce*) at the lofty bridge of *Crevola*. The valley is now termed the *Val d'Ossola*. The characteristics of the scenery are thoroughly Italian.

9 M. **Domo d'Ossola** (1000 ft.) (*Grand Hôtel de la Ville*, spacious rooms; *Hôtel Albassini*, R. 2, D. 3 1/2 fr.; *Hôtel d'Espagne)* is a small town of Italian character. One-horse carr. to Stresa 12 1/2, Baveno 15, Brieg 45, three-horse carr. to Brieg 80 fr. Diligence daily (fare 6 fr.) to Pallanza on Lago Maggiore (p. 139).

At *Masone*, where the Anzasca Valley opens on the W., the Tosa is crossed.

9 M. *Vogogna* (*Corona), a small town, situated at the base of precipitous rocks. The next villages are *Premosello*, *Corciago*, and *Migiandone*, where the Tosa is crossed by a five-arched stone bridge.

7 1/2 M. **Ornavasso** *(Auberge d'Italie; Croce Bianca)*. The

marble-quarries in the vicinity yielded the material for the construction of the cathedral of Milan. To the S. a road leads through the valley of the *Strona*, which falls into the Tosa near *Gravellona* (Europa), to the beautiful **Lake of Orta* (p. 143; diligence daily between Orta, Gravellona, Pallanza, and Intra, see R. 23). *Fariolo* (Leone d'Oro), the next village, is situated in a most luxuriant district, abounding in olive-groves, maize-fields, vineyards, and plantations of chestnuts and fig-trees. The highroad passes an extensive granite quarry, of which the magnificent columns of the restored Basilica S. Paolo fuori le Mura near Rome are formed, and soon reaches the S. W. bank of *Lago Maggiore* (R. 23), from which in the distance rises *Isola Madre*, the most N. of the *Borromean Islands*.

7½ M. **Baveno** *(*Beau-Rivage; Bellevue)* is a steamboat station, at which however all the vessels do not touch (comp. p. 137). Travellers from the Simplon usually visit the Borromean Islands hence. The road, almost entirely supported by pillars of granite and solid masonry, skirts the lake and leads by **Stresa** (p. 140), *Belgirate*, *Lesa*, and *Meina*, to

12 M. **Arona** see p. 141. Railway to **Milan** see p. 141; to Genoa R. 25; to Turin RR. 25, 18.

4. From Lucerne to Como *(and Milan)* over the St. Gotthard.

Steamboat from Lucerne to Flüelen 4 times daily in $2^{3}/_{4}$ hrs. (fare 4 fr. 60 c.); from Flüelen to Camerlata Diligence in $22^{3}/_{4}$ hrs. (coupé 35 fr. 90 c., intérieur 31 fr. 90 c.). *Through-tickets* for the entire route may be procured at the Post Office, Lucerne (where coupé places are most easily secured), and also at the Steamboat Office. Luggage is weighed and charged for on board the steamers. — The diligences have three seats in the coupé (very comfortable, booking see above), and six in the interior (the two middle seats inside are of course to be avoided as affording little or no view); in addition to these, there are two very desirable seats outside, both at the disposal of the conductor, who will on application (5—6 fr.) assign one to the traveller. — The landlords of the hotels at Flüelen, Andermatt and Hospenthal, Airolo, Magadino, Faido, Bellinzona, Lugano, and Como have instituted a system of private posting, according to which a carriage for 4—5 pers. with two horses from Flüelen to Como costs 150 fr. (to which about 24 fr. for gratuities must be added; 2 fr. at least for each station). The cost therefore for four persons is but slightly in excess of the coupé fare. A written agreement (specifying fees) should be made with the proprietor of the carriage for the entire journey. Fresh horses are procured by exhibiting this at each stage. The night is spent at Airolo or Faido. Payment is made at the end of the journey. — One-horse carriage from Flüelen to Andermatt or Hospenthal 20 fr.; two-horse carr. from Flüelen to Andermatt 35, St. Gotthard 50, Airolo 65 fr.

Lucerne (*Schweizer Hof, *Luzerner Hof, *Englischer Hof, all with high charges, but excellent; *Cygne; Hôtel du Rigi; these five are opp. the steamb.-piers. *Wage, on the Reuss; Rössli, Adler, moderate; *Post, Möhren, Hirsch, all in the town and of humbler pretension), capital of the canton of that name (popul. 11,673), is situated on the *Reuss* where it emerges from the Lake of Luzerne. Its well-preserved walls and watch-towers, as well as its palatial modern hotels, impart an important appearance to the town. The view from the quay is strikingly beautiful. The celebrated *Lion of Lucerne* ($^1/_4$ M. from the Schweizerhof) was sculptured in 1821, from Thorwaldsen's design, to the memory of 26 officers and 770 soldiers of the Swiss guard, who were killed in the defence of the Tuileries, Aug. 10th, 1792. The dying lion ($28^1/_2$ ft. in length) reclines in a grotto, its body transfixed by a broken lance, its paw sheltering the Bourbon lily. — E. of the Lion, towards the lake, rises the *Hof* or *Stifts-Kirche*, dating from the 16th cent.; celebrated organ. — The extensive *Arsenal*, on the l. bank of the Reuss, contains a number of weapons and other trophies taken by the confederates from the Burgundians on different occasions.

The ***Lake of Lucerne** (1433 ft.), or *Lake of the Four Forest-Cantons* (viz. *Uri, Schwyz, Unterwalden, Lucerne*) is unsurpassed in Switzerland, and even in Europe, in the beauty and magnificence of its scenery. It is nearly cruciform in shape; length from Lucerne to Flüelen 25 M., greatest width $3^1/_2$ M.

The Steamboats start from the vicinity of the railway station and touch at the piers on the opposite bank, near the hotels, before their final departure. Strikingly picturesque retrospect of the town, shortly after the quay is quitted. As the vessel proceeds, the Rigi on the l., Pilatus on the r., and the Bürgenstock and Stanser Horn in a straight direction are the most conspicuous mountains; behind Pilatus, to the l., the majestic Bernese Alps gradually become visible: the Schreckhörner, Mönch, Eiger, Jungfrau; the Finster-Aarhorn only is hidden.

A view to the l. is soon obtained of the *Lake of Küssnacht*, and to the r. of that of Alpnach, and the central point of the cross formed by the lake is attained. In the distance to the E. *Küssnacht* is visible. Nearer the steamboat, on the l., stands the ruined tower of *Neu-Habsburg*. On the S. is the frowning, forest-clad *Bürgenstock* (3668 ft.); more to the r. tower the barren peaks of the strikingly picturesque *Pilatus*. On the l. rises the *Rigi* (5905 ft.), at the base of which gardens, orchards, and bright looking houses are situated, whilst above, it is clothed with forest and pastures to its very summit. At its base lies (l.) **Wäggis** *(Löwe; Concordia)*, in a most fertile tract, the usual landing-place for those who purpose ascending the Rigi from the S.W. side.

The next village on the l. is *Fitznau*, with the lofty red precipice of the *Rothenfluh*.

Two promontories, aptly termed the *Nasen* (noses), the one a spur of the Rigi, the other of the Bürgenstock, here extend far into the lake and appear to terminate it. Beyond this strait the lake towards the W. takes the name of the *Lake of Buochs* from the village of *Buochs* on the r., above which the *Buochser Horn* (5938 ft.) and *Stanser Horn* (6230 ft.) rise.

Beckenried (Mond; Sonne), to which the steamer now crosses, is delightfully situated on the lake. Then, on the opposite bank, *Gersau* (*Hotel Müller; *Sonne), a village in the Canton of Schwyz, situated on a narrow strip of fertile land and enclosed by rocks. On the ridge of the mountain above stands the sanitary establishment of the *Rigi-Scheideck* (5406 ft.).

To the E. rise the bald summits of the two *Mythen* (6243 ft. and 5754 ft.), at the base of which, 3 M. inland, the small town of *Schwyz* lies. On the bank of the lake, at the mouth of the *Muotta*, **Brunnen** *(Aigle d'Or; *Rössli; *Hirsch)* is situated, the port of the canton of Schwyz. R. on the height *Morschach* and *Kurhaus Axenstein*.

On the opposite bank, in the canton of Uri, is *Treib*, a small harbour. On a height above stands the village of *Seelisberg* (2490 ft.), with the two much frequented *Sanitary Establishments near the chapel of *Maria Sonnenberg* (2759 ft.). Above these rises the *Niederbauen* or *Seelisberger Kulm* (6321 ft.), commanding a noble prospect.

Near Brunnen, the S. arm of the lake, termed the **Lake of Uri**, commences. This is the grandest part of the lake, the mountains rising almost perpendicularly on both sides. At the extremity of the sharp angle which here abuts on the lake, the *Wytenstein*, or *Mythenstein*, a pyramid of rock, 80 ft. in height, rises from the water. It bears an inscription in honour of Schiller. A short distance farther, at the base of the Seelisberg, lies the *Rütli*, a meadow, memorable as the spot where on the night of Nov. 7th, 1307, the first Swiss league (between Uri, Schwyz and Unterwalden) was solemnly entered into. A short distance farther, on the opposite bank, rises the *Axenberg* (3353 ft.), at the base of which nestles the *Chapel of Tell* amid rock and wood. It stands on the '*Tells-Platte*', a ledge of rock on the verge of the lake, which is said to have been the spot where Tell sprang out of Gessler's boat when overtaken by a storm. The carriage-road above ('Axenstrasse'), leading from Brunnen to Flüelen, a distance of 8 M., hewn in many places through the solid rock, far above the level of the lake, is extremely interesting and imposing. On this road, immediately above Tell's Platte, 2½ M. from Flüelen, is situated *Tell's Platte Hotel*, also a steamboat-station. — The view of the extremity of the lake, as Flüelen is approached, is very striking.

Flüelen, Ital. *Fiora* (1433 ft.) *(*Adler; *Kreuz)*, the port of Uri, at the S. extremity of the Lake of Lucerne, is magnificently situated. A short distance to the W. the *Reuss* is conducted into the lake by an artificial channel. The St. Gotthard road leads hence to (2 M.) **Altorf** (1535 ft.) *(*Adler; Schlüssel; Löwe; Sonne)*, the capital (2430 inhab.) of the canton of Uri. A colossal *Statue of Tell* in plaster stands on the spot whence the intrepid archer is said to have aimed his arrow at the apple on his son's head. L. of the road beyond the town stands the Arsenal of the canton. Farther on, at the mouth of the *Schächenthal*, the brook descending from which is crossed by the road, lies the village of *Bürglen* (*Tell), the birthplace of Tell. The road approaches the Reuss at the *Klus*, opposite the village of *Erstfelden*. To the l. rise the abrupt *Kleine* (9846 ft.) and *Grosse Windgelle* (10,463 ft.). As the road approaches *Silinen* a fine view of the superb pyramid of the *Bristenstock* (10,085 ft.), which appears to close the valley, is obtained.

10½ M. **Amstäg** (1660 ft.) *(*Stern; *Kreuz; Hirsch; Löwe)* lies most picturesquely at the base of the Bristenstock and the Windgelle, at the mouth of the *Maderanerthal*, from which the *Kärstelenbach* descends impetuously to the Reuss.

Here the higher part of the St. Gotthard Route, constructed in 1820—32 by the cantons of Uri and Ticino, commences. The magnificence of the scenery surpasses that of all the other Alpine passes. The road at first gradually ascends on the l. bank of the Reuss, which flows in its profound bed far below and forms several waterfalls. Near

Intschi (2168 ft.), a village 1½ M. from Amstäg, a fall of the *Leutschächbach* is passed, and beyond it one of the *Intschialpbach*. The next bridge, that of the *Pfaffensprung*, affords a beautiful view in both directions. Far below, the river is precipitated through its narrow gorge. The road next crosses the impetuous *Mayenbach*, which flows from the Susten. *Wasen* (3084 ft.) (*Ochs), 6 M. from Intschi, is most picturesquely situated on a height. To the r. is a beautiful fall of the *Rohralpbach*, near *Wattingen*, where the road again crosses the Reuss. To the W. of *Göschenen* (3615 ft.) (*Rössli, unpretending), 2¼ M. from Wasen, opens the valley of the *Göschenen-Reuss*, terminated by the grand *Dammafirn*, or *Sandbalm-Glacier*. Beyond Göschenen the dark and rocky defile of the *Schöllenen commences. On both sides rise vast and almost perpendicular walls of granite, at the base of which foams the impetuous Reuss. The road winds upwards and crosses 8 bridges. Pedestrians may avoid most of the curves by following the old bridle-path. This part of the road is much exposed to avalanches; a gallery or tunnel, 80 yds. in length, carries it past the most dangerous spot.

The ***Devil's Bridge** (4629 ft.) is now reached, in the midst of a scene of wild desolation. The Reuss forms a beautiful fall, which is precipitated into the abyss 100 ft. beneath, while its spray bedews the bridge above. The old moss-grown bridge below is now disused. In 1799 this spot was the scene of fierce struggles between the French and Austrians, and a month later between French and Russians.

The road now passes through the **Urner Loch**, a tunnel

80 yds. long, cut through the solid rock in 1707, but not accessible to carriages until it was enlarged when the new road was constructed.

The *Valley of Uri* or *Urseren*, which the road enters on emerging from the tunnel, forms a striking contrast to the savage region just traversed. This peaceful dale, watered by the Reuss, and surrounded by lofty and partially snow-clad mountains, was probably a lake before the Reuss had forced a passage through the Schöllenen.

13½ M. **Andermatt** (4642 ft.) or **Urseren**, Ital. *Orsĕra (*St. Gotthard; *Drei Könige* or *Post; Krone*, moderate), 1 M. from the Devil's Bridge, is the principal village in the valley. The Oberalp route, leading to the Valley of the Vorder-Rhein and Coire, diverges here to the l.

Hospenthal (4787 ft.) (**Meyerhof; *Löwe*, moderate), 1½ M. farther, derives its name from a former hospice. The Furca road diverges here to the r. and leads to Realp and the Rhone Glacier.

The St. Gotthard Road now ascends the mountain in numerous windings through a desolate valley, on the l. bank of that branch of the Reuss which descends from the *Lake of Lucendro* (6831 ft.) (not visible from the road). The road crosses the river for the last time by the *Rodunt Bridge*, 1¼ M. from the culminating point of the **Pass of St. Gotthard** (6932 ft.). It then passes between several small lakes and traverses a lofty and dreary valley, enclosed by the highest snow-clad peaks of the St. Gotthard group.

10 M. **Hospice of St. Gotthard** (6867 ft.), for poor travellers. Adjacent is the small **Hôtel de la Prosa*. Pedestrians, by avoiding the innumerable windings of the road, may descend hence to Airolo in 1½ hr. Snow often lies on the pass throughout the summer.

About ½ M. below the hospice the road crosses the Ticino, the principal arm of which takes its rise in the *Sella Lake* to the E. (not visible from the road). A few min. farther on, near a large mass of rock lying by the road, an inscription near the old bridle-path preserves a memorial of the events of 1799. The words '*Suwarow Victor*' only are now legible. At the 1st Refuge, *Cantoniera S. Antonio*, the road enters the *Val Tremŏla*, a dismal valley 1½ M. long, into which avalanches are frequently precipitated in winter and spring. Pedestrians effect a great saving by following the telegraph-wires. Beyond the Val Tremola an extensive **view of the green valley of Airolo, as far as Quinto, is obtained. To the r. opens the *Val Bedretto*, from which the W. arm of the Ticino flows.

8 M. **Airōlo** (3868 ft.) (**Post*), the first village in which Italian is spoken. Below Airolo the *Canaria Valley* opens. The road enters the *Stretto di Stalvĕdro*, a defile which in 1799 was

defended by 600 French against 3000 Russians, and passes by means of rock-hewn galleries through four parallel ridges which descend to the Ticino. On the r. bank, 1 M. below the ravine, is the beautiful waterfall of the *Calcaccia*.

Beyond the poor inn of *Dazio Grande* (3110 ft.) the mouth of a second *ravine is reached. The Ticino has here forced a passage for itself through the *Monte Piottino*, and precipitates itself in a succession of *cataracts through the gloomy ravine. The road descends the gully close to these falls, and at one place runs for a distance of 50 paces beneath an overhanging rock. To the r., before Faïdo is reached, the *Piumegna* precipitates itself by a picturesque fall into the Ticino.

10½ M. **Faïdo** (2363 ft.) *(*Angelo; Sole)*, a village of a thoroughly Italian character, is the principal place in the *Leventina*, as the entire valley of the Ticino is termed. This district formerly belonged to the Canton of Uri, and was governed in the most despotic manner by bailiffs, who purchased their appointments from the authorities. An insurrection broke out in 1755, but was suppressed. The French effected a change in the mode of government in 1798. In 1814 the Congress of Vienna decided that the Leventina and the seven other Italian bailiwicks belonging to Switzerland should together constitute the new Canton of Tessin or Ticino.

The road passes through beautiful scenery. Numerous campanili in the Italian style peep most picturesquely from the surrounding heights. Cascades are precipitated from the cliffs on the r. and l.; that of the *Cribiaschina resembles a veil in form. Huge masses of rock lie scattered about, interspersed with fine chestnut-trees. Vines and mulberry trees now begin to appear. Where the road descends by numerous windings to the bottom of the valley, the Ticino forms another beautiful fall, spanned by a bridge over which the road passes. Beyond *Giornico* (1233 ft.) (Cervo; Corona) another picturesque waterfall on the r., termed *La Cremusina*.

9½ M. **Bodio** (1086 ft.) *(Hôtel de la Ville; Aquila)*. Beyond *Polleggio* the *Brenno* emerges from the *Val Blegno* and falls into the Ticino. The valley of the Ticino now becomes wider and takes the name of *Riviera*, or river-valley. Luxuriant vines, chestnuts, walnuts, mulberries, and fig-trees now remind the traveller of his proximity to 'the garden of the Earth, fair Italy'. The vines extend their dense foliage over wooden framework supported by stone pillars, 10—12 ft. in height. Frequent inundations render the district unhealthy. The next village, 3 M. from Bodio, is *Biasca* (Unione), with its old church on an eminence (1112 ft.).

3¾ M. *Osogna* (964 ft.). At *Cresciano* there are several picturesque waterfalls. On the l., above *Claro*, rises the monastery of *S. Maria*. On the l. the road from the Bernardino (p. 51) descends, and a short distance farther the road crosses the *Moësa* which rises on the Bernardino. *Arbedo* (comp. p. 51) lies to the l. of the road.

9½ M. **Bellinzona** (777 ft.) (**Hôtel de la Ville*, outside the S. gate; *Angelo*, in the Ital. style), one of the three capitals of the canton of Ticino and seat of the government alternately with Lugano (p. 133) and Locarno (p. 138), presents a strikingly picturesque and imposing appearance when viewed from a distance. The charm, however, is dispelled when the town is entered. The three picturesque castles, once fortified, were the residence of the bailiffs of the three ancient confederate cantons ('Ur-Cantone'). The *Castello Grande*, on an isolated hill to the W., belonged to Uri; of the others on the E. the lower, *Il Castello di Mezzo*, belonged to Schwyz, and the *Castello Corbario or Corbé* (1502 ft.), the highest, now a ruin, to Unterwalden. Each once possessed a small garrison and a few guns. The Castello Grande now serves as an arsenal and prison; visitors are admitted to the court and gardens in order to enjoy the strikingly beautiful view which they command (fee to the guide). An equally attractive prospect may be enjoyed from the loftily situated pilgrimage-chapel of *S. Maria della Salute*.

The road now descends the broad Valley of the Ticino, which expands as the Lago Maggiore is approached, and skirts the E. and S. bases of the mountains. The luxuriance of the vegetation and the beautiful forms of the mountains enhance the charms of the scenery. Near *Cadenazzo* the road to Magadino (p. 51) on the Lago Maggiore diverges to the r. The road now quits the valley and winds upwards for 4½ M. through a beautiful chestnut wood, along the slope of **Monte Cenere**, commanding a succession of *views of Bellinzona and the Ticino Valley, the influx of the latter into the Lago Maggiore, the N. portion of that lake, and Locarno (p. 138). On the summit of the pass (1814 ft.) stands a guard-house (*Corpo di Guardia*) and near it the *Osteria Nuova* (inn). The road then descends through a fertile valley to

9½ M. *Birōnico* (1483 ft.), where the *Vedeggio* is reached. This brook, usually dry in summer, rises a few miles to the E. at the base of the *Monte Camoghè*.

The **Monte Camoghè** (7306 ft.) is usually ascended (6—7 hrs.) from Bellinzona or Bironico. Magnificent view of the broad plain of Lombardy, and the entire Alpine chain from Piedmont to the Valtellina. Travellers are recommended not to spend the night in the chalets on the summit. Those who wish to avoid this fatiguing walk, may enjoy a survey of the Italian lakes by ascending from the Osteria Nuova to the summit of **Monte Cenere** (3776 ft.; 2 hrs. walk).

Beyond Bironico the scenery is picturesque and the country fertile; the double-peaked Mte. Camoghè is kept constantly on the l.; 3¾ M., *Taverne Superiori*; ¼ M., **Taverne Inferiori*;

2½ M., *Cadempino;* 1 M., *Vezia* (view from the church of Madonna di S. Martino).

Towards (1½ M.) Lugano, during the descent, the beauty and fertility of the country increase. The hill and shrine of *Monte S. Salvadore* first become visible; then the lake, in the clear green water of which the beautiful outlines of the mountains are reflected. A number of handsome villas are next passed, and the town with its flat-roofed houses is reached; in the foreground extensive *Barracks*.

9¾ M. **Lugano** (932 ft.), and thence to
19¾ M. **Como**, see R. 22, No. 2.
From Como to Milan see R. 20.

5. From Coire to Colico *(and Milan)* over the Splügen.

Diligence from Coire to Colico twice daily in summer in 16¼ hrs., comfortable vehicles (coupé 22 fr. 10 c., interior 18 fr. 20 c.).

Coire (1935 ft.) (*Steinbock; *Freieck; *Lukma'nier, near the stat.; charges in all, R. 2—3, B. 1½, A. ¾, L. ½ fr. — *Stern; Rother Löwe, near the post-office), Ger. *Chur*, capital of the Canton of the Grisons or Graubünden, situated on the *Plessur*, 1½ M. from its confluence with the Rhine, is an episcopal residence with 7560 inhab. Within the precincts of the *Episcopal Court*, which is surrounded by walls and rises above the town, stands the *Cathedral of St. Lucius*, the oldest part dating, it is said, from the 8th cent. (choir erected in 1178—1208, nave consecrated in 1282). The antiquated *Episcopal Palace* adjoins it. The *Chapel*, one of the earliest Christian structures in this district, lies within the walls of the old Roman tower of *Marsoel (Mars in oculis)*, which is connected with the Palace on the N. This tower and another named *Spinoel (Spina in oculis)* form the N. angles of the Court. Their names suggest the mode in which the Rhætians were kept in subjection by their Roman conquerors. An ancient tower to the N.W., as well as the adjacent wall, appear also to be of Roman origin.

The **High Road** from Coire (leading to the Splügen, the Bernardino, and the Vorder-Rheinthal) ascends the broad valley of the Rhine, which as far as Reichenau is nearly level. On the other side of the river (crossed by a new bridge), at the base of the *Calanda*, lies the village of *Felsberg*, partially buried by a landslip in 1850. The road passes through the thriving village of *Ems*, near the ruins of the ancient castle of *Hohenems*. A long and dark covered bridge, 85 ft. above the Rhine, now carries the road to

6 M. **Reichenau** (1922 ft.) (**Adler*), a group of houses at the confluence of the *Vorder* and *Hinter-Rhein*, the best view of

which is obtained from the terrace of the garden of M. de Planta, near the hotel. The château of M. the Planta, opposite the entrance of the garden, was at the close of the last century an educational establishment. In 1794, Louis Philippe, then Duc de Chartres, sought refuge here under the name of Chabos, and several reminiscences of his visit are still preserved.

A second covered wooden bridge (so low as to endanger the heads of outside passengers) crosses the *Vorder-Rhein*, immediately before its confluence with the Hinter-Rhein. [Through the valley of the Vorder-Rhein a post road (not crossing this bridge) leads to *Dissentis*, whence a bridle-path crosses the *Lukmänier* to *Olivone*; a high road leads from the latter to *Biasca* on the St. Gotthard route.]

The road now enters the valley of the Hinter-Rhein and ascends for a short distance. It passes the villages of (1 M.) *Bonaduz* (2146 ft.) and (³/₄ M.) *Rhäzüns*, with a castle of the Vieli family. The *Domleschg Valley*, Romanesque *Tomiliasca (vallis domestica)*, as the E. bank of the valley of the Hinter-Rhein is here termed (the W. side is called *Heinzenberg* or *Montagna*), is remarkable for its fertility and its numerous castles.

Between the *Bridge of Rothenbrunnen* and *Katzis* are the castles of *Juvalta*, *Ortenstein*, *Paspels*, *Canova*, and *Rietberg* on the l. and that of *Realta* on the r. On the l. of the road is the large *Penitentiary* of the canton of the Grisons. Near (2¹/₄ M.) **Katzis** (2188 ft.) *(Kreuz)* is a nunnery on the r.; beautiful landscape. To the S. rises the snow-clad summit of the *Piz Curver* (9761 ft.); beyond this, to the l., the Schyn Pass with the majestic *Piz St. Michēl* (10,377 ft.) in the background; to the N. the *Tinzenhorn* with the *Ringelspitz* (10,971 ft.). Near the village of *Masein* rises the castle of *Tagstein*.

11 M. **Thusis** (2326 ft.), Romanesque *Tusaun (Tuscia)* (*Via Mala*, R. 3, B. 1¹/₂ fr.; *Adler, R. and B. 3¹/₂, A. ³/₄ fr.; *Hôtel et Pension Rhaetia), lies at the confluence of the Rhine and the *Nolla*, the turbid water of which tinges the Rhine for a considerable distance. The view from the bridge by which the road crosses the Nolla is very remarkable. In the background of the valley towers the barren *Piz Beverin* (9843 ft.). The valley of the Rhine is apparently terminated by lofty mountains. The entrance of the ravine from which the Rhine issues is guarded on the r. bank by the ruined castle of *Hohen-Rhätien* or *Hoch-Realt*, on the S. side of the mountain; on the N. side stands the *Chapel of St. John*, the most ancient Christian church in the valley.

Prior to 1822 the bridle-path from Thusis ascended the valley of the Nolla on the r. bank through forest, and did not reach the gorge before *Rongellen*, r. of the present road. The path through the gorge, the celebrated ***Via Mala**, was then only 4 ft. wide, and followed the l. bank. The new road was constructed in 1822. On entering the defile the traveller will not fail to be struck by its sombre gloom. The limestone-rocks rise almost perpendicularly on both sides to a height of 1500 ft. The *Känzeli* at the entrance of the ravine commands a fine retrospective view of Hohen-Rhætien, Thusis, and the Heinzenberg. About 1½ M. from Thusis is a *Gallery*, 70 yds. in length, penetrating the solid and perpendicular rock. Beyond it the road passes beneath a huge overhanging cliff. From the point where the side-wall ceases and the wooden railings recommence, the roaring torrent is visible at the bottom of the gorge. The *retrospective view, through the narrow and gloomy defile, of the solitary tower of Hohen-Rhætien and the sunny slopes of the Heinzenberg beyond is singularly picturesque.

Near the (¾ M.) *post-house of *Rongellen* the gorge expands, but soon again contracts. The road crosses the river three times at short intervals. The scene is most imposing in the vicinity of the *Second Bridge, 1 M. from Rongellen. The Rhine, 300 ft. below the road, winds through a ravine so narrow that the precipices above almost meet. In Aug., 1834, the river rose to within a few feet of the arch of the bridge. At the upper (third) bridge, about 1 M. farther, the Via Mala ends.

The road now enters the more open *Valley of Schams* (2838 ft., *Vallis Sexamniensis*, from the six brooks which descend from the rocks; Ital. *Sessame)*, the green meadows and cheerful habitations of which present a pleasing contrast to the sombre defile just quitted. To the S. in the background is the pointed summit of the *Hirli* (5628 ft.). Above the old bridge the Rhine forms a small waterfall. The first village in the valley of Schams (6 M. from Thusis) is *Zillis*, Roman. *Ciraun* (Inn), with the most ancient church in the valley. On a height to the r. stands the ruined castle of *Fardün*, or *La Turr*. Farther down is the village of *Donat*, above which towers the *Piz Beverin* (9843 ft.).

7½ M. **Andeer** (3212 ft.) *(*Krone* or *Hôtel Fravi)* is the principal village in the valley, with 581 inhab. Near the village stands the tower of *Castellatsch*. Fine view of the valley from the church, built in 1673.

The road ascends in windings, passes the ruins of the *Bärenburg*, and enters the *Roffla Ravine*, a gorge 3 M. in length, in which the Rhine forms a series of waterfalls. Near the entrance the *Averser Rhein* descends from the *Ferrera Valley* and joins the Hinter-Rhein.

Towards the end of the gorge, the *Einshorn* with its snow-fields comes into view. An ancient bridge here crosses the Rhine; farther on, a rocky gateway *(Sasa Plana)*, 16 yds. in length, is passed. The open Alpine landscape of the *Rheinwaldthal (Val*

Rhein) is now disclosed; r. is the village of *Suvers* (4672 ft.), opposite rise the *Pizzo Uccello* (8910 ft.) and the *Einshorn* (9649 ft.); to the l. of the Splügen, near the Uccello, is the *Tambohorn* (10,748 ft.); W. the *Zapporthorn* (9803 ft.) etc.

8¼ M. **Splügen** (4757 ft.), Roman. *Speluga (*Hôtel Bodenhaus* or *Post*, R. 2, L. ½, B. 1½, D. 3 fr.), capital of the Rheinwaldthal, is a busy place, owing to its position at the junction of the Splügen and Bernardino routes. The latter (p. 49) here pursues a straight direction towards the W. The Splügen route turns to the l., crosses the Rhine, and ascends in windings, passing through a gallery 90 yds. in length, the transverse beams of which are almost touched by the top of the diligence. Retrospect of the barren *Kalkberg* rising above Splügen. The road then enters a bleak valley and ascends on the W. side by numberless zigzags, passing a solitary Refuge, to the summit of the **Splügen Pass** (6945 ft.) *(Speluga, Colmo dell' Orso)*, 3839 ft. below the precipitous *Tambohorn* or *Schneehorn* (10,784 ft.). The ice mountain on the E. is the *Surettahorn* (9925 ft.). This narrow ridge forms the boundary between Switzerland and Italy. An ancient tower stands on the summit. The pass, which was known to the Romans, was till 1819 traversed by a bridle-path only. The present road was constructed by the Austrian government in 1819—21. About ¾ M. beyond the pass the road reaches the *Dogana* (6246 ft.), the Italian custom-house, a group of houses with a poor inn, at the upper end of a bleak valley surrounded by lofty mountains.

The road now descends by numberless zigzags along the E. slope, and is protected against avalanches by three long galleries (respectively 744 ft., 682 ft., 1640 ft. in length). As the second gallery is quitted, a beautiful view is obtained of *Isola* and the old road, destroyed by an inundation in 1834. The new road avoids the dangerous *Lira* gorge between Isola and Campo Dolcino. Beyond *Pianazzo*, near the entrance to a short gallery, the *Madesimo* forms a magnificent *Waterfall, about 700 ft. in height, which is best surveyed from a small platform by the road-side.

15½ M. **Campo Dolcino** (3553 ft.) consists of two groups of houses. The first contains the church, surrounded by ash-trees, and the '*Campo Santo*'. At the second, ½ M. farther, is the Post Inn (R. 1½, B. 1 fr.). The *Lira Valley* is strewn with fragments of rock, but the wildness of the scene is somewhat modified by the luxuriant foliage of the chestnuts visible lower down, from which the slender white campanile of the church of *Madonna di Gallivaggio* gracefully rises. Near *S. Giacŏmo* there are whole forests of chestnuts, which extend far up the steep mountain slopes. The vineyards of Chiavenna now commence, and the rich luxuriance of Italian vegetation unfolds itself to the view.

CHIAVENNA. 5. *Route.* 49

8½ M. **Chiavenna** (1040 ft.) (**Hôtel Conradi*, adjoining the post-office, R. 2½, B. 1½, A. ¾ fr.; *Chiave d'Oro*. The beer of Chiavenna is the best in N. Italy), the *Clavenna* of the Romans, an ancient town with 3800 inhab., is charmingly situated on the *Maira*, at the mouth of the *Val Bregaglia*, through which the road to the Maloja Pass and the Engadine leads. Opposite the post-office are the extensive ruins of a castle, formerly the property of the *De Salis* family, frequently besieged in ancient times. Picturesque view from the castle-garden or '*paradiso*' (fee ½ fr.), which extends along an isolated rock, and is festooned with vines. — *S. Lorenzo*, the principal church, near the post-office, has an elegant slender clock-tower or campanile, which rises from the former *Campo Santo*, or burial ground, surrounded by arcades. The octagonal *Battisterio* contains an ancient font adorned with reliefs. Adjacent are two *Charnel-houses*, in which the skulls and bones are carefully arranged.

The road to Colico at first traverses vineyards; farther on, the effects of the inundations of the *Maira*, and its tributary the *Lira*, which joins it below Chiavenna, become apparent. Near

6 M. **Riva** the road reaches the *Lago di Riva* or *di Mezzola*, which, previous to the construction of the road, travellers were obliged to cross by boat. This piece of water originally formed the N. bay of the Lake of Como, but the deposits of the *Adda* have in the course of ages almost entirely separated the two lakes, which are now connected by a narrow channel only. The road skirts the E. bank of the lake, in some places supported by embankments and masonry, in others passing through galleries, and crosses the *Adda*. Before the junction of this road with that of the Stelvio (p. 56), the ruins of the castle of *Fuentes*, erected by the Spaniards in 1603, and destroyed by the French in 1796, are seen on the r. It was formerly situated on an island, and considered the key of the Val Tellina. At

9 M. **Colico** (722 ft.) (*Albergo Piazza Garibaldi*, on the lake; *Isola Bella;* both in the Italian style), the Lake of Como is reached. The Swiss diligence runs as far as *Lecco* (p. 130). *Diligence* of the Impresa Fojanini to Bormio in 14, to Sondrio 5, Tirano 9 hrs. — From Colico to **Como** and from Como to **Milan** see R. 20.

6. From Coire to Magadino on the Lago Maggiore *(and Milan)* over the Bernardino.

D i l i g e n c e (twice daily in summer) from Coire to Magadino in 18 hrs. (24 fr. 10 c.).

From *Coire* to *Splügen* see pp. 45—48.

The B e r n a r d i n o R o u t e, constructed in 1819—23 at the expense of the governments of the Grisons and Sardinia, ascends to the W. from the village of Splügen (4757 ft.) in the *Rheinwald-Thal (Val Rhein)*, on the l. bank of the *Hinter-Rhein*, and reaches

6³/₈ M. **Hinterrhein** (5315 ft.), the highest village in the valley, 4 hrs. N.E. of the source of the Hinter-Rhein (7274 ft.), which flows from the *Rheinwald* or *Zapport Glacier*. The road then crosses the highest bridge over the Rhine, ¹/₂ M. from the village, winds upwards on the steep S. slope of the valley, and soon reaches the culminating point of the **S. Bernardino Pass** (6991 ft.). The mountain, which was known to the Romans, derives its appellation from St. Bernardino of Siena, who first preached the gospel in this district, and in honour of whom a chapel was erected on the W. slope. Near the small (³/₄ M.) *Lago Moësola* stands the '*Casa di Rifugio*', an inn. From the S. extremity of the lake the *Moësa* emerges, which the road follows as far as its confluence with the Ticino, above Bellinzona. Above the handsome '*Victor Emanuel*' bridge the river forms a fine waterfall. From the foot of the bridge a view of the *Piz Moësola* (9521 ft.) is obtained through the arch. Farther on the road is protected from avalanches by a roof.

10¹/₂ M. **S. Bernardino** (5334 ft.) (*Hôtel Brocco; Hôtel Ravizza; Hôtel Motto;* pension in all 5—7 fr.), the highest village of the *Val Mesocco* or *Mesolcina*, which opens into the Riviera (p. 43) near Bellinzona, possesses a mineral spring *(Acqua Buona)* which attracts many invalids in summer. The Moësa forms a waterfall between S. Bernardino and *S. Giacomo;* the best view, however, is only to be obtained from the footpath, which runs first on the l., then on the r. bank of the stream. The road on the l. bank descends in numberless zigzags, commanding a series of charming views. From the bridge of S. Giacomo (3757 ft.) a beautiful distant prospect of the valley is obtained, with the extensive ruins of the *Castle of Mesocco* and its four towers. Then, 1¹/₂ M. farther, the village of

9 M. **Mesocco** (2592 ft.) or *Cremeo* (**Toscani*, next to the post office; *Hôtel Desteffanis)*, charmingly situated. Chestnuts, vines, and rich crops of maize indicate the Italian climate. Numerous brooklets are precipitated from the rocky slopes by which the valley is enclosed. Beyond (1¹/₂ M.) *Soazza* (2005 ft.), the bottom of the valley is attained, and the road becomes level.

Near the second bridge below Soazza the *Buffalora* forms a beautiful cascade near the road. Another waterfall near (2³/₄ M.) *Cabbiolo* (1476 ft.). In the vicinity of *Lostallo* (1562 ft.) are extensive vineyards. At

9³/₄ M. **Cama** (1260 ft.), near the Capuchin monastery, figs and mulberries are first observed. At (2 M.) *Grono* rises the massive tower of *Florentina*. The vines are here trained on trellis-work. (1¹/₄ M.) *Roveredo* (974 ft.) (Posta; Croce), with the ruined castle of the once powerful *Trivulzio* family, is the capital (1082 inhab.) of the lower Val Mesocco.

S. Vittore (882 ft.) is the last village of the Grisons, *Lumino* the first in the canton of Ticino. Before the Moesa is crossed the road joins the St. Gotthard route (p. 44). Below the confluence of the Moësa and the *Ticino* stands *Arbedo*, a village occupying a sad page in Swiss history. On July 30th, 1422, a battle took place here between 3000 Swiss and 24,000 Milanese, in which 2000 of the former fell. They were interred beneath several mounds of earth near the church of St. Paul, which is termed *Chiesa Rossa* from its red colour. Hence by

9³/₈ M. **Bellinzona** to *Cadenazzo*, see p. 44. At Cadenazzo the road to Arona diverges from that to Lugano. It descends in the broad and level valley of the Ticino, skirting the N. base of *Monte Cenere* (p. 44), to

9³/₈ M. **Magadino** (*Bellevue*, opposite the steamboat-pier), which consists of *Upper* and *Lower Magadino*, in a marshy situation on the Lago Maggiore at the mouth of the *Ticino*, the N. harbour of the lake (R. 23). Steamers see p. 137.

From Magadino to **Arona** see R. 23.
From Arona to **Milan** see p. 141.

7. From Innsbruck to Colico *(and Milan)* over the Stelvio.

206 M. Diligence from Innsbruck to Landeck daily (at 4 a. m.) in 8³/₄ hrs., from Landeck to Mals 4 times weekly in 8¹/₂ hrs. Omnibus daily from Innsbruck to Landeck, and from Landeck to Mals. — Messagerie between Bormio and Sondrio, and between Sondrio and Colico daily. In 1869 a diligence again commenced to cross the Stelvio itself (in 12¹/₂ hrs., fare 6 fl.), and during the present year open conveyances will probably run. A *vetturino* charges 10—12 fl. per day.

The road over the Stelvio, Germ. *Stilfser Joch*, the loftiest in Europe which is practicable for carriages, 9239 ft. above the sea-level, was constructed by the Austrian government in 1820—25. The bold and skilful construction of the road and the grandeur of the scenery render this one of the most remarkable routes in Europe. The vast glaciers and snow-fields of the Ortler and Monte Cristallo present a striking contrast to the vine-clad slopes of the Val Tellina, and the luxuriant southern vegetation of the banks of the Lake of Como. Pedestrians are strongly recommended not to avail themselves of any of the short cuts (by which a saving of 3—4 M. is effected), as all the finest views are from the road itself. Since the evacuation of Lombardy by the Austrians, the road on the Tyrolese side has been sadly neglected, but repairs are contemplated during the present year.

The road ascends on the l. bank of the *Inn*, passing the *Martinswand* (3778 ft.), a precipice where the Emp. Maximilian I. nearly lost his life in 1493, whilst engaged in chamois-hunting. At the base of the cliff lies

8 M. *Zirl* (2082 ft.) (*Löwe). On the r. rises the ruined castle of *Fragenstein*. Near

9¹/₄ M. *Telfs* (Post) the road crosses the Inn and passes the considerable (l.) Cistercian monastery of *Stams*, founded in 1271 by the mother of Conradin, the last of the Imperial family of Hohenstaufen. Beyond

8 M. *Silz* (Steinbock), with a handsome modern church, rises the wooded *Petersberg* on the l., crowned with the ruined castle of that name. Beyond *Haimingen* the road crosses the Inn to *Magerbach* (*Inn by the bridge) and skirts the base of the *Tschürgant* (7745 ft.). A remarkable view is obtained here of the masses of debris with which the *Ache*, descending from the *Oetzthal*, covers the entire valley.

11½ M. **Imst** *(*Post)*, a well-built market-town at the base of the *Laggersberg* and the *Platteinkogl*. The road again descends and approaches the Inn at the base of the Laggersberg. The small village of *Mils* possesses a pretty modern church. Beyond *Starkenbach* the imposing ruins of the *Kronburg* rise on a lofty eminence on the opp. bank of the Inn. Near *Zams* (2722 ft.), before the bridge is reached, a field-road diverges r. to a beautiful waterfall (10 min.), not visible from the high-road. The bridge over the Inn, frequently the scene of fierce struggles, was destroyed in 1703 by the Tyrolese, and those of the French who had already crossed were thus captured.

14 M. **Landeck** (2651 ft.) *(*Schwarzer Adler; Post; Goldener Adler)*, a considerable village on both banks of the Inn, is commanded by the ancient castle of the same name, now tenanted by poor families. A road leads hence over the *Arlberg* to Feldkirch in the valley of the Rhine, and to the railway from Rorschach to Coire.

The Inn here forces its way through a narrow ravine and forms several rapids. To the r. a waterfall of the *Urgbach*. The *Pontlatzer Bridge*, 6 M. from Landeck, by which the road crosses to the l. bank, has frequently proved a most disastrous spot to the armies of Bavaria.

On the r., on a precipitous rock above Prutz, stand the ruins of the castle of *Laudegg*. Near it, on the height, is the village of *Ladis*, 1 hr. from *Prutz*, with sulphur-baths; ½ hr. higher up is *Obladis*, a charmingly situated sanitary establishment. *Prutz* (Rose), where the road returns to the r. bank of the Inn, lies in a swampy plain at the entrance of the *Kaunserthal*.

9¼ M. **Ried** (2881 ft.) *(*Post; Adler)* is a thriving village. The castle of *Siegsmundsried* is the seat of the local authorities; on the S. side a Capuchin monastery. At *Tösens* the Inn is again crossed.

9¼ M. *Pfunds* (*Traube) consists of two groups of houses, separated by the river. Above Pfunds the new road again crosses the Inn and gradually ascends on the r. bank, hewn at places in the perpendicular rock, and supported by solid masonry. The route is here remarkable for the picturesque views it affords of the narrow valley of the Inn, as well as for the grand construction of the road itself. The finest point is at **Hoch-Finstermünz**, about 4½ M. from Pfunds, a small group of houses on the road, one of which is an *Inn. Far below is the old *Finstermünz* (3294 ft.), with a tower and a bridge over the Inn. These, with the defile through which the river issues from the Engadine, and the mountains in the background, form a very striking picture.

9½ M. **Nauders** (4437 ft.) *(Post; Mondschein)*; the old castle of *Naudersberg* contains the district courts of judicature.

The road now ascends to the *Reschen-Scheideck*, its culminating point (4898 ft.), the watershed between the Black Sea and the Adriatic. Near the village of *Reschen* (4574 ft.) (*Stern), by the muddy lake of that name, a strikingly magnificent *view is disclosed. The entire background is formed by the snow and ice fields of the Ortler chain. The *Etsch*, Ital. *Adige*, rises near Reschen, flows through the lake, and also through the *Mittersee* and *Heidersee*, which the road passes farther on.

9 M. *St. Valentin auf der Heide* (4626 ft.) (*Post), formerly the hospice of the bleak and rocky *Malser Heide*. The beauty of the view increases as the road approaches the *Vintschgau* (Val Venosta). The Ortler continues to fo m the imposing background. As the road descends, the villages of *Mals*, *Glurns*, and *Tartsch*, when viewed from the height, almost appear to form a single town. To the r., before Mals is reached, is seen the village of *Burgeis*, with its red spire, and the castle of *Fürstenburg*, now occupied by a number of poor families. Farther on, the Benedictine Abbey of *Marienberg* lies on the mountain to the r.

7 M. **Mals** (3355 ft.) *(Post; Hirsch; Gans)* is a market town of Roman origin. Beyond it the ancient tower of the *Fröhlichsburg* is passed. In the distance to the r., not far from the commencement of the Stelvio route, on the opposite bank of the Etsch, rises the handsome half-ruined castle of *Lichtenberg*. L. of the road, near *Schluderns*, is the *Churburg*, a château of Count Trapp, containing a valuable collection of ancient armour. At *Spondinig* the road crosses the broad, marshy valley of the Etsch and the river itself by a long bridge, the frontier between the Upper and Lower Vintschgau.

9¼ M. **Prad** (3271 ft.) *(Post)*, or *Bivio di Prad*, is an insignificant village at the foot of the Stelvio route, which now enters a narrow valley, traversed by the *Trafoi-Bach*. On the height to the r. lies the village of *Stilfs*, Ital. *Stelvio*, whence this route derives its appellation, although it does not pass through Stelvio itself. The houses are perched on the rocks like swallows' nests.

Pedestrians may avoid the dusty and monotonous high road from Mals viâ Spondinig to Prad by proceeding from Mals across the valley to *Glurns*, a small town with an ancient church, and thence, skirting the mountain by the castle of *Lichtenberg* and *Agums*, to Prad, a walk of 2½ hrs.

At *Gomagoi* (Inn), the Austrian custom-house, where large 'Defensive Barracks' were erected in 1860, the wild *Suldenthal*, 9 M. in length, opens on the E.

9 M. **Trafoi** (5544 ft.) *(*Post)* consists of some half dozen houses. It derives its name *(tres fontes)* from the **Three Holy Springs*, situated low down in the valley at the foot of the Ortler, and well deserving a visit ($3/4$ hr.).

The vast *Mondatsch* or *Madatsch Glacier*, descending from the Ortler, extends many hundred feet into the valley. The *Madatsch-Spitz* is a black, rocky peak protruding from the ice. Lower down, the two *Trafoi Glaciers* descend from the Ortler. In the background to the N. rises the broad snow pyramid of the *Weisskugel*, the second highest peak of the Oetzthal ice-mountains.

7 M. **Franzenshöhe** (7356 ft.), formerly a post-station, destroyed by Italian irregular troops in 1848, and subsequently partially restored, now affords shelter for sheep. The road ascends, skirting the talk-slate precipices by numerous windings, and passes under dilapidated wooden galleries. Vegetation gradually disappears, and scanty moss alone is seen clinging to the rocks. The road here is seldom entirely free from snow except in warm seasons. Icicles frequently hang from the roofs of the galleries as late as July.

The summit of the **Stelvio Pass** (9239 ft.), Germ. *Stilfser Joch*, 8 M. from the Franzenshöhe, is the boundary between Austria and Italy. A workmen's house stands at the top.

A footpath ascends by the house to the l. in 20 min. to a rocky summit which commands an almost unlimited * panorama. The view of the **Ortler** (12,851 ft.), the loftiest mountain in Germany, is particularly striking. Its snowy dome appears quite near, and is surrounded by numerous snow and ice-peaks: S.E. the lofty *Königswand* (or *Monte Zebrù*, 12,706 ft.), farther S.E. the *Monte Cevedale*. Nearer are vast masses of ice *(Monte Cristallo)* and the ravines of the Stelvio route; S. in the distance the three snow-clad peaks of the *Corno dei Tre Signori*; to the N.W. the Engadine range; to the N.E. the snowy *Weisskugel* and the Oetzthal Mts. The barren red *Monte Pressura* in the foreground (1 hr. ascent; view more extensive) intercepts the view of the Münsterthal.

Immediately to the l. of the road rise the huge icy masses of *Monte Cristallo*. Occasional glimpses are obtained of the Münsterthal.

$9^1/_2$ M. **S. Maria** (Inn), the Italian custom-house, is situated in a bleak mountain basin, almost destitute of vegetation, surrounded by barren mountain ridges, and about 900 ft. below the summit of the pass ($1/2$ hr. walk). By carriage hence to Bormio (p. 55) in less than 2 hrs. (in the reverse direction a good walker will accomplish the journey more expeditiously than a carriage).

The road next reaches the *Cantoniera al Piano del Brauglio* in a green valley, with the *'Abitazione del R. Cappellano'* and a chapel; then the *Casino dei rotteri di Spondalonga*, a house occupied by road-menders.

The road descends by innumerable windings *('giravolte')*, which the pedestrian can generally avoid, skirts the rocky mountain slope and passes a number of waterfalls.

A succession of galleries, partly of wood and partly hewn in the rocks, protect the road against avalanches and waterfalls and convey it through the defile termed '*Il Diroccamento*'. The *Cantoniera Spondalonga* (6906 ft.) was destroyed by the Garibaldians in 1859 and has since been a ruin. Adjacent to it are two picturesque waterfalls of the *Brauglio*, which is precipitated from a cleft in the rock above. Then the *Cantoniera di Piatta Martina*, a refuge for travellers.

A number of waterfalls are next passed. Farther on, the *Brauglio* is precipitated from a rock on the r., a waterfall commonly termed the *Source of the Adda*. A magnificent view is now soon disclosed, comprising the valley from Bormio to Ceppina, S.W. the *Monte Colombano* (9931 ft.), W. the *Val Pedenos*, S.E. the snow-clad *Gavia* (11,759 ft.) and the ice-pyramid of the *Piz Tresero* (11,877 ft.). To the r. lies the old bath-establishment on the verge of a deep, gloomy ravine.

Beyond the *Galleria dei Bagni*, the last tunnel, a fine view is obtained near the bridge. To the r. of the road, perched upon the face of the rocks, the *Bagni Vecchi*, or *Old Baths*, now come into view. Far below flows the *Adda*. The *New Baths, or *Bagni Nuovi* (4190 ft.) (R. 2, B. 1, A. $^1/_2$ fr.), situated on a terrace commanding a fine survey of the valley of Bormio and the surrounding mountains, are much frequented in July and August, but are closed about the end of September. The mineral water (containing salt and sulphur, 117°) is conducted hither by pipes from the springs at the old bath, 1 M. higher up. The windings of the road terminate at

$11^1/_2$ M. **Bormio** (3927 ft.) *(Posta)*, a poor and insignificant place notwithstanding its seven towers. Ancient pictures in the pilgrimage-church of *S. Cristoforo*.

About 3 hrs. from Bormio, on the Frodolfo in the *Val Furva*, is situated **S. Caterina** (6076 ft.), a comfortable bath-establishment, generally crowded in summer. The water, which is strongly impregnated with carbonic acid gas, is largely exported. — The ***Monte Confinale** (11,369 ft.) is frequently ascended from St. Caterina (in $3^1/_2$ hrs., not fatiguing). It affords an admirable survey of the Ortler-chain; W. the Bernina-group, S.W. the Mte. della Disgrazia, S. the Adamello, etc.

Another excellent point of view is ***Piz Umbrail** (9954 ft.). The Stelvio-road is followed as far as the 4th Cantoniera (Inn), 9 M. from Bormio; then a tolerable footpath ascends N.W., across meadows, where numerous Alpine plants are found, to the top, whence a splendid view of the Mts. of Tyrol and Bernina. Carriages to the Cantoniera may be hired at Bormio. Guide unnecessary.

The road now intersects the valley in a straight direction, crossing the muddy *Frodolfo*, which below the bridge unites with the Adda, and then turns to the S. This broad and green portion of the valley *(Piano di Bormio)*, extending as far as the village of *Ceppina* and enclosed by lofty mountains, presents a somewhat barren aspect. Below Ceppina is the hamlet of *S. Antonio* with brickworks; then *Morignone* in a green dale, the church of which stands on the hill above.

The defile of *La Serra*, 1 M. in length, here separates the '*Paese Freddo*', or district of Bormio, from the *Val Tellina*, which till 1797 belonged to the Grisons, then to Austria, and has since 1859 been Italian. The broad valley is watered by the *Adda*, the inundations of which often cause considerable damage. The vineyards on the slopes yield excellent red wine. The climate is considered unhealthy, and cretinism is not unfrequent. — The *Ponte del Diavolo* was destroyed by the Austrians in 1859. Near the issue of the defile are the ruins of a house; farther on, to the r., fragments of a former fortification. The valley now expands, and the vegetation of the south gradually develops itself.

12 M. **Bolladore** *(*Posta)*. On the mountain slope to the W. rises the picturesque church of the village. Then *Grosotto*, a village of some importance.

To the N. rises the precipitous *Piz Masuccio* (9249 ft.), a landslip from which in 1807 blockaded the narrow bed of the Adda and converted the populous and fertile valley, as far as *Tovo*, into a vast lake. At *Lovera*, 3 M. from Tirano, the depth of the water (18 ft.), with an inscription recording the disaster, may be seen on one of the houses. The devastation caused by subsequent inundations is still observable. The road now descends from the district of *Sernio*, passing vine-clad hills, to

11 1/2 M. **Tirano** (1522 ft.) *(Due Torri)*, a small town containing old palaces of the Visconti, Pallavicini, and Salis families. Here, too, inundations of the Adda have frequently proved very destructive.

About 3/4 M. farther, on the r. bank of the Adda, lies **Madonna di Tirano** (*Molinari*, near the church). The Church, a resort of pilgrims, contains fine wood-carving near the organ. (The road which here diverges to the r. leads to *Poschiavo*, and over the *Bernina* to the Upper Engadine; see *Baedeker's Switzerland*. The '*Confine Svizzero*' is 3/4 M. N.W. of Madonna di Tirano.)

The road next crosses the *Poschiavino*, a stream descending from the Bernina glaciers. *Tresenda* is the point where the new road over the Monte Aprica diverges (R. 31). About halfway up the N. slope of the valley rises the ancient watch-tower of *Teglio*, whence the valley *(Val Teglino)* derives its name. Near Sondrio the churches of *Pendolasco* and *Montagna* are seen on the hill to the r.

18 M. **Sondrio** (1141 ft.) *(Corona* or *Posta; Maddalena)*, capital of the Valtellina, is situated on the *Malero*, an impetuous mountain-torrent which has frequently endangered the town, but is now conducted through a broad artificial channel. The former

Nunnery, an extensive edifice outside the town, is now a prison; the castle of the former governors is employed as barracks.

Farther to the W. rises the church of *Sassella*, built on a rocky eminence and supported by galleries. Vines, mulberries, and pomegranates flourish luxuriantly in the valley, whilst in the background the snowy peaks of the *Monte della Disgrazia* (12,057 ft.), one of the Bernina range, tower above the landscape.

16¼ M. **Morbegno** *(*Regina d'Inghilterra* or *Posta)* is noted for its production of silk. The lower part of the Valtellina is rendered unhealthy by the inundations of the Adda. Before reaching 9¼ M. **Colico** (p. 49) the Splügen route is joined (R. 5).

8. From Innsbruck to Verona by the Brenner.

Railway from *Innsbruck* to *Bozen* in 5½—6½ hrs., fares 6 fl. 12, 4 fl. 59, 3 fl. 6 kr.; from *Bozen* to *Verona* in 5½—6¼ hrs., fares 8 fl. 82, 6 fl. 62, 4 fl. 41 kr.; i. e. exclusive of 'agio' (difference between value of paper and silver money) and stamp dues. There are two stations at Verona (comp. p. 163), a fact which should be borne in mind in sending off luggage. Views on the *right* as far as the summit of the Brenner.

The *Brenner*, the lowest pass over the principal chain of the Alps, is traversed by the oldest of the Alpine routes, employed as early as the Roman period and rendered practicable for carriages in 1772. The railway, opened on Aug. 17th, 1857, is one of the grandest modern structures of the kind, and affords the most direct communication between Germany and Italy. It ascends for 21 M. with an incline of 1:40 to the culminating point (4604 ft.). The descent to Brixen (1923 ft.), a distance of 30 M., is less rapid. The scenery of the Brenner Railway is inferior to that of the Semmering, its tunnels and viaducts are less imposing. The expense of the undertaking has also been considerably less.

Soon after leaving Innsbruck the train passes the Abbey of *Wiltau* (r.) and penetrates the hill of *Isel* by means of a tunnel 700 yds. in length. It then ascends on the r. bank of the *Sill*, by a passage hewn in the rocks; far below roars the impetuous river. Near stat. *Patsch* the *Rutzbach*, which descends from the picturesque *Stubaythal* to the Sill, is precipitated from a narrow gorge on the r. Thus far there are seven tunnels.

The valley contracts, and the scenery becomes wilder. Four more tunnels are passed through, the longest of which is 920 yds. The Sill is crossed twice.

Stat. **Matrey** (3472 ft.) *(*Krone)*, with the château of *Trautson*, the property of Prince Auersperg, is charmingly situated.

Stat. **Steinach** *(Post; Steinbock)* has been entirely re-erected since a conflagration in 1853. The line passes the village of *Stafflach* and ascends far above the level of the Sill. Three tunnels, then stat. *Gries*. Beyond it, to the S., rises the ruined Castle of *Lueg*, formerly a robbers' stronghold. The train ascends in long curves, high above the valley, passes the small green *Brennersee* (well stocked with trout), and reaches

Stat. **Brenner** (4604 ft.), with the former *Post-House*, the watershed between the Black Sea and the Adriatic. View obstructed by wood. The *Sill*, which rises in the vicinity, falls into the Inn; the *Eisack*, on the farther side of the pass, descends to the Adige. The line now follows the course of the Eisack and descends gradually (2 tunnels) to stat. *Schelleberg*, where it enters the *Pflersch-Thal* (far below, to the l., is the continuation of the railway; fine view). About $1/2$ hr. later it re-enters the Eisackthal by the Aster Tunnel, and reaches the low-lying stat. *Gossensas*. This is one of the most interesting portions of the line.

The train, which runs high above the Eisack, passes at places through wild rocky scenery, and reaches

Stat. **Sterzing** (3280 ft.) *(*Post; Krone; *Rose)*, a prosperous place, deriving much of its wealth from the mines formerly worked here. It is situated in the broad *Sterzinger Moos*, or *Upper Wippthal*. The old building, and arcades of the small town are very picturesque.

From Sterzing to Franzensfeste the valley of the Eisack is wild and romantic, the mountains lofty and extremely precipitous. High above are the castles of *Sprechenstein* on the l. and *Reifenstein* on the r.

Stat. *Freienfeld*. L. rise the ruins of the castle of *Welfenstein*, where several Roman remains have been found. Stat. *Grasstein*. The railway now enters a narrow defile in which the *post-inn of *Mittewald* is situated. The lower extremity of the defile (extensive view towards Brixen), termed the *Brixener Klause*, near *Unterau* (2429 ft.), was strongly fortified in 1833—38. These works (**Franzensfeste**), which are very conspicuous when viewed from the S., command the Brenner route to Italy, whilst the route to Carinthia, which here diverges E. through the Pusterthal, will be guarded by a new fortress, now about to be constructed. The station is at a considerable distance from the fortress.

The group of houses with the new church, to the l. in the valley below, is the monastery of *Neustift*, founded in 1142. The vegetation now assumes a more southern character. Vineyards and plantations of chestnuts become more frequent.

Stat. **Brixen** (1923 ft.), Ital. *Bressanone* (**Elephant*, adjoining the post-office; **Sonne*, unpretending; *Goldenes Kreuz*, all in the town, $3/4$ M. from the stat.), contains a number of churches with altar-pieces by Tyrolese masters. At the S.E. extremity of the town is the *Episcopal Palace* with an extensive garden.

Beyond Brixen, near *Sarns* on the l. bank of the Eisack, rises the castle of *Paltaus*.

Stat. **Klausen** *(Gans; Rössel)*, consisting of a single narrow street, is situated in a defile, as its name imports. The Benedictine monastery of *Seben*, crowning the cliffs on the r., commands a most striking view. The *Loretto Chapel*, adjoining the

Capuchin Monastery (where visitors apply for admission), contains the most valuable collection of ecclesiastical treasures in the Tyrol.

Below Klausen the valley contracts. The line skirts the precipitous porphyry cliffs. Above, on the heights, extends a broad and fertile tract, sprinkled with numerous villages, of which the traveller in the gorge perceives no trace.

Stat. *Waidbruck*. Near *Kollmann* (Kreuz) the *Grödenerbach* descends from a rocky ravine to the Eisack. Above it rises the *Trostburg* with its numerous towers and pinnacles, the property of Count Wolkenstein. This is the most striking point in this picturesque valley of the Eisack.

Stat. **Atzwang** (1478 ft.) *(*Post)*. Four short tunnels, then stat. *Blumau*. The valley again contracts. Beyond the defile an extensive plantation of chestnuts on the slope of the mountain is passed. The line now enters the wide basin of Bozen, a district of the most luxuriant fertility, resembling a vast v'neyard.

Bozen (928 ft.), Ital. *Bolzano (Kaiserkrone; Mondschein; Erzherzog Heinrich; *Badl*, outside the town, on the high-road to Meran; *Schwarzer Adler; Rail. Restaurant)*, with 9000 inhab., the most important commercial town in the Tyrol, is delightfully situated at the confluence of the Eisack and the *Talfer*, which descends from the *Sarnthal* on the N. The E. background is formed by the strikingly picturesque dolomite mountains of the Fassathal. Most of the houses have openings in the roofs, covered by projecting eaves, to admit light and air. Many of the streets are traversed by channels of fresh water, which in summer contribute in some degree to mitigate the oppressive heat.

The Gothic **Parish Church* is of the 14th and 15th cent. The W. Portal, with two lions of red marble, is an imitation of the Lombard style. Beaut'ful tower of perforated work, completed in 1519. On the E. side a gateway, bearing the inscription '*Resurrecturis*', leads to the **Cemetery*, which is surrounded by arcades. A chapel adjoining the sacristy in the *Franciscan Monastery* contains a finely carved old German altar. — The **Calvarienberg* (25 min. walk; ascent across the railway embankment) commands a fine view of the town and environs.

Beyond Bozen the train crosses the *Eisack*, which lower down falls into the *Etsch* (or *Adige*). The latter becomes navigable at stat. *Branzoll* (Ital. *Bronzollo*). Beyond stat. *Auer* (Ital. *Ora*), where the road through the Fleimserthal commences, the train crosses the river. Next stat. **Neumarkt**, Ital. *Egna (Krone; Engel)*, with a population in which the German element still preponderates, lies on the l. bank of the Adige and consists of a single street only.

To the r. on the slope of the mountain lie the villages of *Tramin*, *Kurtatsch*, and *Margreid*. Stat. *Salurn* is the last place where German is spoken. The village itself lies on the l. bank of the river, commanded by a dilapidated castle. The bottom of the valley is here flat and marshy.

The *Rocchetta Pass* on the r. leads to the *Val di Non*. *Mezzo Tedesco* and *Mezzo Lombardo* (or *Deutsch* and *Wälsch-Metz*), situated on different sides of the pass separated by the *Noce*, are both Italian.

S. Michele Lombardo, or *Wälsch-Michael* (Adler), with a handsome old Augustine monastery, founded 1143, but now suppressed, is the station for the Val di Non. The line now crosses to the l. bank of the Adige. Next stat. *Lavis* on the *Avisio*, which here descends from the *Val Cembra*. This impetuous torrent with its different ramifications is crossed before its junction with the Adige by a bridge 1000 yds. in length.

Trento (730 ft.), or *Trent*, Lat. *Tridentum* (*Europa, the dining-room contains portraits of princes who once lodged here, e. g. Count Artois, subsequently Charles X. of France, Eugene Beauharnais, viceroy of Italy, etc.; *Hôtel de la Ville, both near the stat., R. and L. 80, B. 50, A. 25 kr.; Corona. — 2nd cl. Al Rebecchino next to the Hôtel de la Ville; Aquila Bianco; Castello. Café near the Europa), with 14,000 inhab., formerly the wealthiest and most important town in the Tyrol, founded according to tradition by the Etruscans and mentioned by Strabo, Pliny and Ptolemy, possesses numerous towers, palaces of marble, dilapidated castles and broad streets, and is surrounded by imposing groups of rocks. Above the town rises the considerable castle of *Buon Consiglio*, once an archiepiscopal residence, now a barrack.

The *Cathedral, founded 1048, commenced in its present form in 1212, and completed in the 15th cent., is a structure in the Romanesque style, surmounted by two domes. At the N. portal, as at Bozen, is a pair of lions (p. 59). In the S. transept are several old monuments, half-faded frescoes, and by the wall the porphyry tombstone of the Venetian general Sanseverino, whom the inhabitants of Trent defeated and killed at Calliano (see below) in 1487. In the Piazza of the cathedral are the courts of judicature and the guard-house.

S. Maria Maggiore (with an admirable organ), where the celebrated Council of Trent held its sessions in 1545—63, contains a picture on the N. wall of the choir (covered by a curtain) with portraits of the members of the council: 7 cardinals, 3 patriarchs, 33 archbishops, and 235 bishops. Adjacent to the S. side of the choir is a column dedicated to the Virgin, erected in 1855 on the 300th anniversary of the festival celebrated in commemoration of the Council.

The rocky eminence of *Verruca*, or *Dos Trento*, situated on the r. bank of the Adige, was fortified in 1857, and is not accessible to strangers without special permission. The best point of view in the environs is the terrace of the *Capuchin Church*, on the opposite side of the valley.

From Trent to Venice by the Val Sugana, 115 M. Diligence 3 times daily between Trent and Borgo (1 fl. 40 kr.); twice daily from Borgo by Primolano to Bassano and Treviso; thence to Venice by railway in 1 hr. Arrival at Venice see p. 184.

This direct route (although not the most expeditious) to Venice traverses the beautiful and romantic *Venetian Mountains*. The road, which ascends soon after Trent is quitted, is hewn in the rocks as far as Pergine. Near

9 M. *Pergine*, an extensive prospect is enjoyed; beyond it, on a commanding, rocky height, rises the handsome castle of that name. To the r. lies the picturesque lake of *Caldonazzo*, which is drained by the *Brenta* (on the mountains S.W. lies *Calceranica*, whence a fine view is obtained). Then the smaller lake of *Levico*, in which *Monte Scanupia* (7133 ft.) is reflected. The *Val Sugana* commences here. The principal town in the valley is

18½ M. **Borgo** (*Croce*), where silk is extensively produced. Below the town rises the beautiful château of *Ivano*.

Near *Grigno* the valley of *Tesino* opens on the N., watered by the *Grigno*. Its inhabitants frequently emigrate as dealers in engravings. The proprietors of several of the best shops of this description in Europe are natives of this valley. Near

16 M. *Primolano*, the road traverses a magnificent, rocky ravine and crosses the Venetian frontier. In a rocky cavity beyond the village are situated the ruins of the castle of *Covelo*, a mediæval stronghold, to which access could only be obtained by means of a windlass. *Valstagna* is inhabited chiefly by straw-hat makers. (About 12 M. S.W. is situated *Asiago*, with 5000 inhab., capital of the **Sette Comuni**, or seven parishes where an unintelligible German patois is spoken in the midst of an Italian population. Till 1797 they formed an independent republic under the protection of Venice. The dialect is, however, rapidly giving way to Italian.)

From the height of *Rubio*, about 10 M. from *Primolano*, the road commands a charming and picturesque view of the river districts of the Astico and the Piave and of the Vicentine and Euganean Mts. as far as Venice. The ravine of the *Brenta* now expands, a broad plain with extensive olive-plantations comes into view, and the road reaches

18 M. **Bassano** (*S. Antonio*, near the chief piazza; *Luna*, in the suburbs), a picturesquely situated town (15,000 inhab.), surrounded by lofty and venerable ivy-clad walls. One of the six gates was erected by Palladio. In the centre of the town rises the once fortified tower of the tyrant Ezzelino, which commands a fine view and contains a library and armoury. Bassano possesses no fewer than 35 churches, the chief of which is the *Cathedral*, containing some fine pictures, many of them by Giacomo da Ponte, surnamed Bassano, this town having been his birthplace. His best work, a Nativity, is in the *Oratorio S. Giuseppe*. The *Villa Rezzonica*, 1½ M. from the town, contains several valuable works of art, e. g. Canova's Death of Socrates; delightful views hence, extending to the Euganean hills and the mountains of the Sette Comuni (application for admission must be made the day previous to the intended visit).

On Sept. 8th, 1796, Napoleon defeated the Austrians under Wurmser near Bassano, four days after the battle of Roveredo. A number of skirmishes also took place here between the French and Austrians in 1801, 1805, and 1813. In 1809 Napoleon constituted the district of Bassano a Duchy, with which he invested Maret, his secretary of state.

(**Possagno**, Canova's birthplace, is beautifully situated at the base of the mountains, 12 M. N.E. of Bassano. The road thither is rugged and hilly. The church, in the form of a circular temple, resembling the Pantheon at Rome, was designed by Canova and contains his tomb. The altarpiece also was painted by him. The bridge which here spans the river by a single arch, 117 ft. in length, was erected in accordance with a bequest by Canova to his native town. The *Palazzo*, as his house is termed, contains models and casts of his works.)

14 M. *Castelfranco*, an ancient town surrounded by walls and towers,

was the birthplace of the painter Giorgione. The principal church contains a *Madonna by him; in the Sacristy a fresco by Paolo Veronese representing Justice.

16 M. **Treviso**, and railway thence to Venice, see R. 39.

From Trent to Verona by Riva and the Lago di Garda. To Riva 25 M., omnibus once daily (9 a. m.) for 2 fl.; one-horse carr. 8, two-horse 14 fl. Steamer from Riva to Peschiera in 4½ hrs., see p. 151. Railway from Peschiera to Verona in 1 hr., see p. 151.

This route is far preferable to the direct railway-route, on account of the charming scenery of the Lago di Garda. The traveller from Bozen, whose time is limited, may shorten the route by proceeding by railway as far as stat. Mori (10 M. from Riva), instead of quitting the train at Trent. This approach to the lake is also very attractive. — Omnibus daily between Mori and Riva (coupé 1 fl.); office in Riva at the Café Andreis under the arcades.

The route through the *Val Sarca*, especially the portion between Trent and the bridge over the Sarca, presents a succession of charming and occasionally strikingly imposing landscapes. At Trent the road crosses the Adige, traverses the suburb *Piè di Castello* and ascends. Fine retrospect from the height (1½ M.). A wild and rocky defile *(Buche di Vela)* is now entered, terminating in a species of (1½ M.) fortified vault, beyond which the road emerges suddenly on a smiling and fertile district. Farther on (1½ M.) the view of *Terlago* and its lake at the base of *Monte Gazza* (6300 ft.) is beautiful and imposing. 1½ M. *Vigolo*. 3 M. **Vezzano** *(Corona)*, the principal place between Trent and Arco. At (1½ M.) *Padernione* the road turns to the r. and passes the *Lake of Toblino* and the picturesque castle of that name. Below *Le Sarchè* the Sarca emerges from a gorge, and the road to Giudicaria diverges (see below). 3 M. Bridge over the Sarca, scene of a skirmish between Italians and Austrians in 1848. 1½ M. *Pietra Murata*. Near (4½ M.) *Drò* is the ruined *Castello di Drena* on an eminence to the l.

The road now enters a more fertile district. 3 M. **Arco**, with church of somewhat oriental aspect. The vegetation now becomes most luxuriant (olives, pomegranates, figs, grapes). The peaches and other fruit of Arco are in high repute. N., on a precipitous height, rises the castle of Arco, with well-kept gardens. The road which turns to the r. from the S. Gate of Arco leads to (3¾ M.) **Riva** (p. 153).

The line continues to traverse the broad and fertile valley of the Adige, the former marshes of which have been almost entirely drained. To the S.W. of Trent, on the r. bank of the Adige, is the village of *Sardagna*, with a considerable waterfall. Next stat. *Matarello*. On a height near stat. *Calliano* rises the extensive castle of *Beseno*, the property of Count Trapp. Rocky debris in the vicinity indicate the scene of a former landslip.

Roveredo *(Cavalotte; Corona)*, a town with 8000 inhab., is noted for its thriving silk-culture (upwards of 120,000 lbs. are annually produced in the district between Trent and Verona). At the '*Filande*', 60 in number, the silk is wound from the cocoons; the '*Filatorie*' are the spinning-establishments. Southern fruits and excellent red wine are also produced in the neighbourhood. The most remarkable building is the old *Castello* in the Piazza del Podestà.

The lower part of the valley of the Adige, as far as the Italian frontier, is termed *Val Lagarina*. On the r. bank lies *Isera*, with vineyards, numerous villas, and a waterfall. On the l. bank, E. of the railway, near *Lizzana*, is a castle, which about the year 1302 was tenanted by Dante who had been banished from Florence as an adherent of the Ghibellines.

The line follows the l. bank of the Adige. Next stat. *Mori*; the village itself lies in a ravine on the opposite bank, on the road leading to Riva (p. 153); and is noted for its excellent asparagus.

Omnibus from stat. Mori to *Riva* on the Lago di Garda in 2 hrs. (fare 80—90 kr.), twice daily in connection with the trains from Bozen (comp. p. 62).

Near *S. Marco* on the l. bank are the traces *(Slavini)* of a vast landslip, which is said to have overwhelmed a town here in 833, and is described by Dante *(Inferno XII, 4—9)*. At *Serravalle*, the ancient fort which guarded the defile, the valley contracts.

Stat. *Alà* (Posta), a place of some importance, with 3800 inhab., boasts of once celebrated velvet-manufactories. Stat. *Avio* is the last in the Austrian dominions. The village, with a well preserved castle of Count Castelbarco, lies on the r. bank.

Peri is the first Italian station. The ridge of *Monte Baldo* (7090 ft., p. 154), on the W., separates the valley of the Adige from the Lago di Garda. Stat. *Ceraino*. The line now enters the celebrated *Chiusa di Verona*, a rocky defile penetrating the limestone mountains and affording space for the river, road, and railway only. This important military point was defended against the Milanese in 1155 by the German army commanded by Otho of Wittelsbach, in the reign of Frederick Barbarossa. (On an eminence on the r. bank is situated *Rivoli*, stormed several times by the French in 1796 and 1797 under Masséna, who derived his ducal title from this village.)

Next stat. *Domegliarà*. On the opposite bank of the Adige a range of hills extends into the plain as far as *Custozza*, far below Verona, whence the Piedmontese were driven by the Austrians in 1848. On the same ground the battle of June 20th, 1866, took place, in which the Italians were defeated by the Austrians under Archduke Albert, and compelled to retreat across the Mincio. At some distance to the W., on the farther side of the Mincio, which emerges from the Lago di Garda, *Solferino* is situated, where the memorable battle of June 24th, 1859, was fought.

Stat. *Pescantina*, then *Parona*. The line crosses the Adige, and at *S. Lucia* (p. 151) reaches the Verona and Milan line. A short distance farther is the railway-station (outside the Porta Nuova) on the S. side of

Verona, see R. 33.

9. From Vienna to Trieste. Semmering Railway.

Austrian S. Railway. Expr. in 14^1/$_2$ hrs., ordinary trains in 22—23 hrs.; fares 28 fl. 26, 21 fl. 20, 14 fl. 13 kr. (express ^{1}/$_5$ th more). Fifty lbs. of luggage free, provided it is at the station at least ^{1}/$_2$ hr. before the departure of the train; otherwise the whole must be paid for. Best views generally on the left. For farther particulars see *Bœdeker's S. Germany*.

The station of the S. Railway is between the Belvedere and the Favorite 'Lines', or boundaries of the city. The train, soon after starting, affords a good survey of Vienna, the environs, and the surrounding ranges of mountains. On the mountains to the r. near stat. *Brunn* are several ruined castles, of which *Liechtenstein*, one of the most important, was destroyed by the Turks. Near stat. *Mödling* (Hirsch) the *Brühl*, a picturesque rocky valley is disclosed to view; branch-line hence E. to *Laxenburg*. Near Baden several picturesque ruins rise on the r. The view to the l. over the broad plain, sprinkled with villages, is bounded by the *Leytha Mts*.

Baden *(Stadt Wien; *Schwarzer Adler)*, a considerable town with a number of handsome villas, the Rom. *Thermae Pannonicae*, is celebrated for its mineral springs. The 'Ursprung', or principal spring (72—100° Fahr.), rises at the base of the *Calvarienberg*, the summit of which commands an extensive prospect.

Vöslau *(*Schweizerhof)* yields one of the best Austrian red wines. Near *Leobersdorf* the barren *Schneeberg* (6882 ft.) rises on the r.

Neustadt, or *Wienerisch-Neustadt (Hirsch; Ungar. Krone*, both in the town; *Stadler*, near the station), has been entirely rebuilt since a conflagration in 1834 (popul. 14,500). On the E. side is the former ducal *Castle* of the Babenberg family, converted in 1752 into a military academy. Branch-line in 2 hrs. S.E. to *Oedenburg*, which lies 7 M. to the W. of the saline *Neusiedler See*.

On the r. beyond Neustadt the *Schneeberg* rises on the r., the *Leytha* range on the l. R., in the distance, the well-preserved castle of *Sebenstein*, the property of Prince Liechtenstein. Near stat. *Ternitz* the *Schneeberg* is again visible on the r. Stat. *Pötschach*, a manufacturing place. On the height to the l. near Gloggnitz rises the castle of *Wartenstein*. The *Gloggnitzer Schloss* on the hill, with its numerous windows, was a Benedictine Abbey till 1803.

At stat. **Gloggnitz** (1415 ft.) *(*Rail. Restaurant)* the ***Semmering Railway** commences (best seats on the l.). The locomotive reduces its speed. Fine retrospect of Gloggnitz. In the valley of the green *Schwarzau* is the imperial paper-factory of *Schleglmühl*. L. the three-peaked *Semmering*, W. in the background the *Raxalp*. The line describes a wide circuit round the N. slope of the valley and crosses the *Valley of Reichenau* by a large viaduct (300 yds. long). Incline 1 : 40. Two small tunnels, then stat. *Eichberg*, 575 ft. above Gloggnitz. Extensive prospect over the plain.

The *Gotschakegel* is now skirted and two more tunnels are traversed. Stat. *Klamm;* the half-ruined castle of Prince Liechtenstein, on a rocky pinnacle, was once the key of Styria. Far below runs the old Semmering road; the green dale visible beyond the next tunnel is the *Untere Atlitzgraben*. The *Weinzettelwand* is next skirted by a long gallery; then a tunnel, and two bridges which carry the line to the S. slope of the *Obere Atlitzgraben*. After traversing three more tunnels the train reaches

Stat. **Semmering** (2970 ft.), the culminating point of the line. At the highest point of the high road (3289 ft.) is the *Erzherzog Johann Inn*, 1 M. from the stat. In order to avoid the remaining portion (300 ft.) of the ascent the line now penetrates the highest part of the Semmering, the boundary between Austria and Styria, by means of a tunnel nearly 1 M. in length, beyond which several peaceful dales are passed. Next stat. **Mürzzuschlag** *(*Bräuhaus; Elephant; Rail. Restaurant)*, 2235 ft. above the sea-level. The line now follows the *Mürz*, the picturesque, pine-clad valley of which contains numerous forges. To the r. in the valley, beyond *Krieglach*, is the new château, and on the height the old castle of *Mitterdorf*. Then *Kindberg* and *Kapfenberg* with the castles of the same names. Near stat. *Bruck* rises the ancient castle of *Landskron*.

Bruck *(*Eisenbahn-Gasthof; Adler; Mitterbräu)* is a small town at the confluence of the Mürz and the *Mur*. The line now enters the narrow valley of the Mur. Stat. *Pernegg*, with château. The forges of *Frohnleiten* on the r. bank and the castle of *Pfannberg* on the l. belong to Prince Lobkowitz. *Schloss Rabenstein* on the r. bank is the property of Prince Liechtenstein. The line next passes the *Badelwand* and skirts the river by means of a rocky gallery of 35 arches, above which the high road is situated. Stat. *Peggau* possesses silver and lead mines.

The train crosses the Mur, passes stat. *Klein-Stübing*, and enters the fertile basin in which Gratz is situated. On an eminence to the W. rises the picturesque Gothic pilgrimage-church of *Strassengel* (1443 ft.). To the r. rises the castle of *Gösting*, the property of Count Attems, a favourite resort of the Gratzers. Farther on is the castle of *Eggenberg*, 3 M. from Gratz.

Gratz (1170 ft.) (On the r. bank of the Mur: *Elephant, R. 1 fl.; Gold. Ross; *Florian; Drei Raben. — On the l. bank: *Erzherz. Johann; Stadt Triest; Gold. Krone; Ungar. Krone), the capital of Styria (63,700 inhab.), picturesquely situated on both banks of the Mur, which is here crossed by four bridges, is one of the most agreeable towns in Austria. The **Schlossberg*, which rises about 400 ft. above the river, commands one of the finest views in Germany, embracing the course of the Mur and the populous valley, enclosed by picturesque mountains: N. the Schöckel (4711 ft.), N.W. the Upper Styrian Mts., S.W. the Schwanberg Alps, S. the Bachergebirge. The Gothic *Cathedral* dates from 1446. The *Landhaus*, or *Council Hall*, an extensive and imposing pile, was erected in 1569. The **Johanneum*, a spacious edifice with gardens, was founded by Archduke John in 1811 as an institution for the promotion of agriculture and practical science in Styria. It contains specimens of the staple commodities of this district, and a well arranged natural history museum.

As the train proceeds, indications of the richer vegetation of the south become more apparent. On the mountains to the r. rises the castle of *Premstätten;* on the l. beyond stat. *Karlsdorf* the castle of *Weisseneck*. The mountains on the r. separate Styria from Carinthia.

Near *Wildon* the *Kainach* is crossed. R., near *Leibnitz* is the archiepiscopal castle of *Seckau;* farther on, the castles of (l.) *Lubeck*, and (r.) *Ehrenhausen*. *Spielfeld*, the next castle which comes in view, once belonged to the Duchess de Berry, whose sumptuous château of *Brunnsee* is $4^1/_2$ M. distant. Diligence and omnibus in 4 hrs. from stat. *Spielfeld* to the Baths of *Gleichenberg*, which were known as early as the Roman period.

The train quits the Mur and enters the mountainous tract which separates the Mur from the Drau. Near *Pössnitz* a viaduct 700 yds. in length (64 arches) and a tunnel of equal length are traversed.

Marburg *(Stadt Wien; Stadt Meran*, the nearest to the station) (popul. 8000), is the second town in Styria. To the S.W. extends the long range of the *Bacher-Gebirge*, clothed with vineyards and forest. Branch-line from Marburg to Klagenfurt and Villach.

A pleasing glimpse is obtained from the train as it crosses the *Drau*. Stations *Kranichsfeld* and *Pragerhof* (whence a line leads to *Pest*, skirting the long Plattensee). Beyond stat. *Pöltschach* the scenery improves. The *Baths of Rohitsch*, which attract many visitors, lie 12 M. to the S.E., near the Croatian frontier.

The German language is now replaced by a Sclavonic or Wend dialect. The line winds through a scantily populated district. The valleys are generally narrow and picturesque, the mountains richly wooded. Several unimportant places are passed, and at length an extensive view of a populous and undulating plain, bounded by the Carinthian Alps, is suddenly disclosed.

Cilli (796 ft.) *(Krone; Rail. Restaurant)*, an ancient town, founded by the Emp. Claudius *(Claudia Celleia)*. Roman reliefs and memorial stones are still found imbedded in the walls. On a wooded mountain in the vicinity rise the ruins of the castle of *Obercilli;* on the slope to the N.E. stands the Lazarist monastery of *St. Joseph* with its two towers.

The train crosses the green *Sann* several times, and then enters the narrow and wooded valley of that stream. This is the most interesting part of the line. Many of the highest peaks in the vicinity are picturesquely crowned with white churches and chapels. *Markt Tüffer*, with ruined castle, possesses mineral baths of some note (102° Fahr.); so also *Bad Tüffer* (known to the Romans) and *Teplitz* (= warm bath in Sclavonic). The two last, with attractive grounds and promenades, are much visited, especially from Trieste.

Steinbrücken is a flourishing village on the *Save* or *Sau*, which here unites with the Sann. Branch-line hence S.E. to *Agram*. The train now proceeds for 1 hr. in the narrow valley of the Save, enclosed by lofty limestone cliffs and often affording but little space for the river and railway. Productive coal mines near stat. *Hrastnig*; Stations *Triffail*, *Sagor*, the first place in Carniola, and *Sava*.

The valley now expands. The white château of *Bonowicz* and the distillery below belong to a merchant of Vienna. At *Littai* the Save is crossed. Scenery still very picturesque. At the influx of the *Laibach* into the Save, the line quits the latter and enters the valley of the former river. The lofty mountain-range now visible is that of the *Julian* or *Carnian Alps*; in clear weather the *Terglou* (10,258 ft.) is seen towards the N.W. Stat. *Salloch*; then

Laibach (1020 ft.) *(*Stadt Wien; Elephant)*, Sclav. *Ljubljanu*, on the *Laibach*, the capital of Carniola, with 21,000 inhab., situated in an extensive plain enclosed by mountains of various elevations. An old *Castle*, now used as a prison, rises above the town, commanding a magnificent prospect. The *Cathedral*, an edifice in the Italian style, is decorated with stucco and numerous frescoes of the 18th cent.

The line now traverses the marshy *Laibacher Moos* by means of an embankment, $1^1/_3$ M. in length, and crosses the Laibach, which here becomes navigable, although only 3 M. below the point where it issues from the rocks near Oberlaibach.

Near stat. *Franzdorf* the line is carried past *Oberlaibach* and enters a more mountainous district by means of a viaduct 600 yds. long, 128 ft. high in the centre, and supported by a double series of arches (25 in number). Stat. *Loitsch* (1595 ft.) (Post or Stadt Triest).

Quicksilver Mines of Idria, 15 M. N.W. of Loitsch; carriage thither in 4 hrs., 6—8 fl. for the excursion; inspection of the mines 3—4 hrs.; drive back 4 hrs. The entrance to the mines is approached by 787 steps hewn in the limestone-rock, in the ancient town of **Idria** (1584 ft.) *(Schwarzer Adler)*, which lies in a sequestered valley. Drops of the pure metal are everywhere visible adhering to the ore. The latter is brought to the surface in tuns from a depth of 2661 ft., conveyed to the stamping-mills, and thence by means of canals to the washing houses, where the superfluous earthy particles are removed. It is then melted in furnaces, the fumes from which are conducted to the cooling chambers, where the metal is deposited in showers of minute globules. Annual yield 125 tons, part of which is converted into cinnabar on the spot.

Next stat. *Rarek*. The water of the *Zirknitzer See*, $3^1/_2$ M. S.E., enclosed by lofty mountains, disappears in the clefts of the rock and emerges in the Laibach Valley lower down as the *Bistriza* and *Boruniza*. Then stat. **Adelsberg** (1818 ft.) *(*Krone; Eisenbahn)*, Sclav. *Postojna*. The celebrated **Stalactite Caverns*, known in the middle ages and accidentally re-discovered in 1816, are $3/_4$ M. W. of Adelsberg; about $2^1/_2$—3 hrs. are occupied in exploring them. For a detailed description see *Baedeker's S. Germany*.

The train now traverses a dreary, inhospitable plain, strewn with blocks of limestone, termed the **Karst** (Ital. *Carso*, Sclav. *Gabrek*), which commences before Adelsberg is reached and extends from Fiume (p. 71) to Görz (p. 215). The surface is intersected by numerous gorges and occasionally covered with thickets of underwood. Curious funnel-shaped cavities in the rocks are observed here. The N.E. wind *(Bora)*, which often rises to a hurricane in this district, has been known to overturn loaded waggons.

At stat. *Prestanek* the train crosses the *Poik*. Beyond stat. *St. Peter* it passes through six tunnels. Next stations *Lesetsche* and *Divazze*. Beyond stat. *Sessāna* (1672 ft.) the high road is crossed, and the train descends to stat. *Prosecco* and stat. *Nabresina*, where the line to Venice by Udine diverges (carriages generally changed here). As the train descends in long curves to Trieste a magnificent *view of the blue Adriatic, Trieste, and the Istrian coast is obtained (best seats on the r.). *Grignano*, the last station, is in a straight direction not above $1^1/_2$ M. below Prosecco. On the *Punta Grignana*, which here projects into the sea, is situated the handsome château of *Miramar*, formerly the residence of the ill-fated Emp. Maximilian of Mexico. The train then passes through a long tunnel and reaches the station of

Trieste. Hotels. Hôtel de la Ville (Pl. a), R. $1^1|_2$ fl., L. 40, B. 70, A. 40 kr.; *Grand Hôtel (Pl. b); *Victoria (Pl. c); Hôtel de France (Pl. d); Albergo Daniel (Pl. e). — *Cafés:* Hôtel de Ville; Specchi, Piazza Grande; several near the post-office and many others. — *Restaurants:* Toni, Zum Tiroler, both in the old town; Solder's Garden, below the castle, fine prospect, concerts frequently; Monte Verde and others with gardens.

Fiacres to or from the station, one-horse 50 kr., two-horse 1 fl., at night 20 kr. more; drive in the town, $1/_4$ hr. 30 or 45 kr., $1/_2$ hr. 50 or 80, $3/_4$ hr. 75 kr. or 1 fl. 10 kr., 1 hr. 1 fl. or 1 fl. 80 kr., each additional $1/_4$ hr. 20 or 30 kr.; luggage 15 kr. — *Omnibus* to all the hotels 20, at night 30 kr.

Steamboats of the 'Austrian Lloyd' to Venice (R. 39) three times weekly, to Istria once (to Pola twice) weekly; to Greece, Constantinople, and the Levant once weekly; to Alexandria four times monthly.

Baths. *Warm* at Oestereicher's, near the Artillery Arsenal, and at the Hôtel de la Ville. *Cold* at the Maria bath-estab., opp. the Hôtel de la Ville; Angeli, in the harbour; Boscaglia, between the

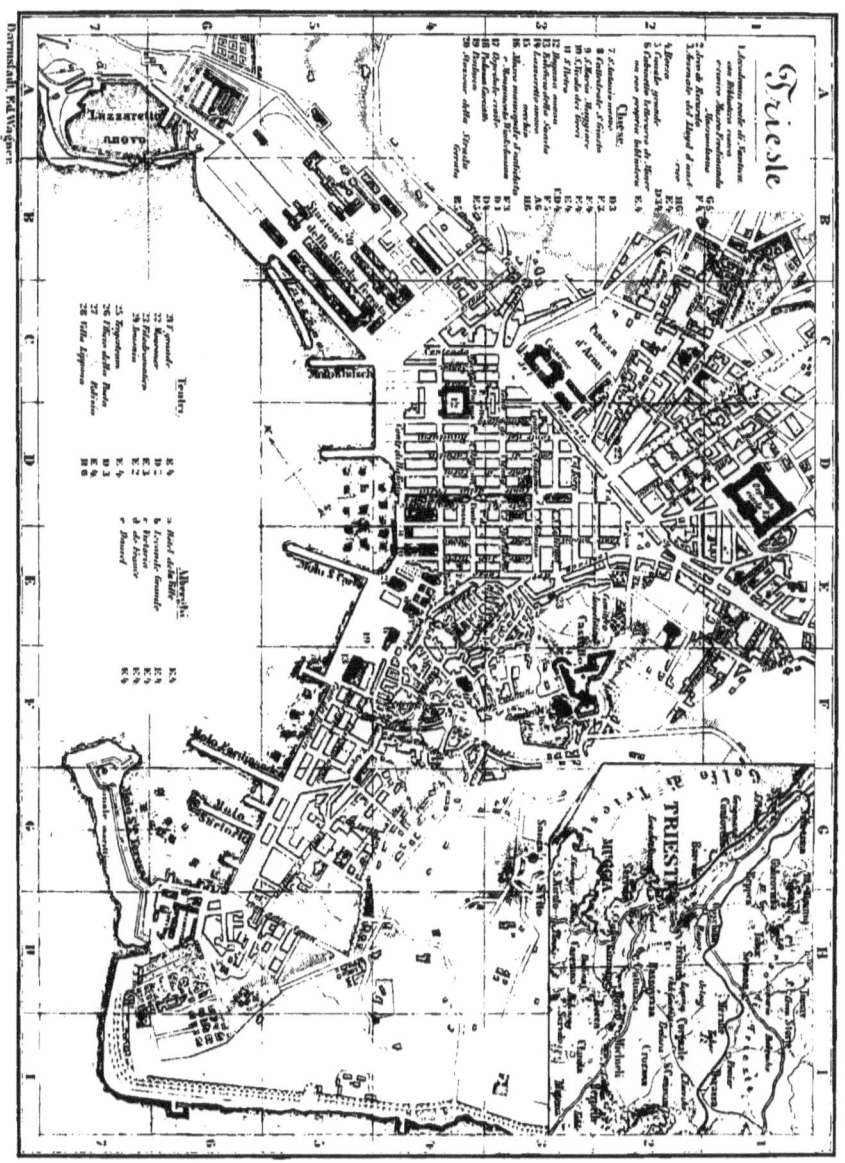

Molo del Sale and the Molo Klutsch; Military Swimming Bath, l. below the lighthouse. Ferry to the baths 4, back 2 soldi. — *Boats* 1—1½ fl. per hour.

Theatres. Teatro Grande (Pl. 21), opp. the Tergesteo; Teatro Mauroner (Pl. 22), Corsia Stadion; Teatro Filodrammatico (Pl. 23); Armonia (Pl. 24).

English Church Service performed by a resident chaplain.

Trieste (more fully described in *Baedeker's S. Germany*), the *Tergeste* of the Romans, capital of Illyria, situated at the N.E. extremity of the Adriatic, is the most important sea-port of Austria (popul. 64,095). It was constituted a free harbour by Emp. Charles VI. in 1719, and may be termed the Hamburg of S. Germany. Every European nation has a consul here. The population is most heterogeneous, but the Italian element predominates.

The *Harbour* is the focus of animation. On the N. is the new *Lazzaretto*, erected in 1769, one of the most extensive in Europe. A lofty *Lighthouse* rises on the S.W. Molo. The old Lazzaretto is now used as an arsenal.

The well-built *New Town*, adjoining the harbour, is intersected by a *Canal* (Pl. 5), by means of which vessels are enabled to discharge their cargoes close to the magazines of the merchants. At the extremity of the Canal is the modern church of *S. Antonio* (Pl. 7) in the Greek style.

Near the Hôtel de la Ville is the *Greek Church (Pl. 10) (divine service at 6 a. m. and 5 p. m.), sumptuously fitted up. To the l. of the Hôtel de la Ville is the *Palazzo Carciotti*, with a large green dome. In the vicinity is the *Tergesteo (Pl. 25), an extensive pile of buildings, the exterior of which is occupied by shops, and the interior by a glass gallery in the form of a cross, where the *Exchange* (12—2 o'clock) is situated. The principal part of the edifice is occupied by the offices and *Reading Room of the '*Austrian Lloyd*', a steamboat-company established in 1833. Strangers are seldom denied access. The *Old Exchange* in the vicinity is disused. In front of it a fountain and a *Statue of Leopold I.* erected in 1660.

The *Corso*, the principal street of Trieste, connecting the *Piazza Grande* with the *Piazza of the Exchange*, separates the new town from the old. The latter, nestling round the hill on which the castle rises, consists of narrow and steep streets, not accessible to carriages. To the l. on the route to the cathedral and the castle is situated the *Jesuits' Church* (*S. Maria Maggiore*, Pl. 9), containing a large modern fresco by *Sante*. Nearly opposite is the *Piazzetta di Riccardo*, named, it is said, after Richard Cœur de Lion, who was imprisoned here after his return from Palestine. The *Arco di Riccardo* (Pl. 2) is believed by some to be a Roman triumphal arch, by others to have appertained to an aqueduct.

The *Cattedrale S. Giusto* (Pl. 8) originally consisted of a basilica, a baptistery, and a small Byzantine church, dating from the 5th and 6th cent., which in the 14th cent. were united so as to form a whole. The tower contains Roman columns; Six Rom. tombstones (busts in relief) are immured in the portal, and several Rom. inscriptions will be observed. The altar-niches of the interior contain two ancient mosaics, representing Christ and Mary. The S. aisle contains the tombstone of Don Carlos, pretender to the Spanish crown.

A former burial-ground adjoining the church is now used as a repository of *Roman Antiquities* (Pl. 16) of no great value (key kept by the sacristan of the cathedral). Winckelmann, the eminent German antiquarian, who was robbed and murdered by an Italian at the Locanda Grande in 1768, is interred here. A monument was erected to his memory in 1832.

Fouché, once the powerful minister of police of Napoleon I., died at Trieste in 1820 and was interred on the terrace in front of the church. Fine view of the town and sea hence; still more extensive from the height on which the *Castle* stands.

A long avenue, commanding a succession of beautiful views, ascends gradually from the *Campo Marzo*, on the E. side of the town, to *Servŏla*, $2^1/_2$ M. distant. Another attractive walk is by the *Acquedotto*, through a picturesque valley to the *Boschetto*, a very favourite resort; thence by a shady path to the 'Jäger', a good point of view.

Pleasant excursion to the château of *Miramar*, formerly the property of the Emp. Maximilian of Mexico (d. 1867). It is easily reached from the railway-stat. Grignano (p. 68), or by carriage (2—3 fl.). The situation and views are charming.

Excursions by boat to *S. Bartŏlo*, to *Muggia*; also to the extensive *Wharves of the Lloyd Co.* ($1^1/_2$ hr.), opposite to Servola (adm. daily, except Sundays, festivals, and the hours 11—1 o'cl.; attendant $^1/_2$—1 fl.).

From Trieste to Pola and Fiume steamboat twice weekly; in 10 hrs. to Pola (reaching Fiume on the following morning, but once weekly only); fares 5 fl. 40, 3 fl. 65, 1 fl. 75 kr. — Those who proceed as far as Fiume may return thence by diligence to Trieste in 11 hrs. ($6^1|_2$ fl.).

The steamer skirts the undulating, olive-clad coast of Istria. In a distant bay S.E. lies *Capo d'Istria* with an extensive house of correction. On an eminence rises the church of *Pirano*; the town itself, with 9000 inhab., is picturesquely situated in a bay; the pinnacles and towers of the former fortress peep from amidst olive-plantations. The lighthouse of *Salvore* is next passed, then *Umăgo*, the castle of *Daila*, *Cittanova*, *Parenzo* (with remarkable cathedral), a basilica of 961), and *Orsēra*. In the distance to the E. rises *Monte Maggiore* (4400 ft.). The vessel now stops at *Rovigno* (Sismondi), a prosperous town with 14,000 inhab.; staple commodities wine, oil, and sardines. To the r. near *Fasăna* rise the *Brionian Islands*, separated by a narrow strait from the mainland. The grand amphitheatre of Pola now comes in sight. The excellent harbour, the principal station of the Austrian fleet, but of no commercial importance, is defended by two towers.

Pola (*Hôtel de la Ville*), an insignificant place with 1200 inhab., is of very ancient origin, having been probably founded by Thracians. It was afterwards the *Pietas Julia*, a war-harbour of the Romans, from which period its magnificent and highly interesting antiquities date. These may be visited in the following order (guide unnecessary):

The **Temple of Augustus and Roma* (B. C. 19), 27 ft. in height and 53 ft. in width, with a colonnade of six Corinthian columns 23 ft. in height, and with admirably executed decorations on the frieze, is almost in perfect preservation. The collection of antiquities in the interior is insignificant.

In the vicinity stood a temple of *Diana*, or more probably of *Roma*, of which the posterior wall only is preserved. This fragment was employed about the year 1300 in the construction of the *Palazzo Pubblico*, which is incorporated with it with considerable skill.

The traveller now proceeds across the market-place towards the S. and at the end of a long street reaches the *Porta Aurata*, an elegant isolated arch in the Corinthian style, 23 ft. in height, erected by the Sergian family. At some distance to the r. stood the ancient *Theatre*, the site of which only is now recognisable by a semicircular depression in the hill. The remnants were employed in 1630 in the construction of the fort.

Excavations which are still prosecuted have brought to light the ancient *Porta Erculea* and the *Porta Gemina*. The latter formed the entrance to the Roman capitol, the site of which is now occupied by the *Castle*. On the E. side of the latter is a *Franciscan Monastery*, erected in the 13th cent., now a military magazine. It possesses fine cloisters, and an elegant Romanesque portal on the W. side. The laurel-tree in the court is said to be a scion of that which yielded its foliage to grace Cæsar's triumphal entry into the capitol!

Beyond the latter the *Arena is reached. It was erected about the period of the Antonines (A. D. 150) and could accommodate 15,000 spectators. Height 80 ft., diameter 354 ft. The lower stories consist of two series of arches (72 in number) 19 ft. in height, one above the other; the upper story is a wall with square openings for windows. The exterior is in admirable preservation, but the interior presents a scene of desolation; the arrangements for the *Naumachia* in the centre can alone now be traced. Four gates, with projecting buttresses of which the object is unknown, form the entrances.

The steamboat (once weekly) generally quits Pola late in the evening and arrives at Fiume early on the following morning. The broad *Quarnero Bay* is traversed. To the l. rises *Monte Maggiore* (4688 ft.); r. in the distance the Croatian Mts. of which the *Capella* range is the most prominent.

Fiume, Illyr. *Reka (Rè d'Ungheria)*, the capital of the Hungarian coast-district, with 15,319 inhab., contains little to interest the traveller. On the height, $1/2$ hr. walk from the inn, is the castle of *Tersato*, the property of the Austrian Marshal Nugent. A small temple here contains a good collection of ancient reliefs, busts, statues, etc. In the vicinity a much frequented *Pilgrimage-Church*, with an image of the Madonna of Loreto. *View of the Bay of Quarnero with its islands, Fiume, and the adjoining coast.

NORTHERN ITALY.

10. Turin, Ital. *Torino.*

Arrival. There are 3 rail. stations at Turin: 1. The *Stazione Centrale*, or *Porta Nuova* (Pl. G, 7, 8), a handsome edifice with waiting-rooms adorned with frescoes, the terminus of all the lines; 2. *Stazione Porta Susa* (Pl. C, 5, 6), 11—20 min. by train from the central station, first stopping-place of all the trains of the Novara-Milan line (conveniently situated for many travellers; omnibuses and carriages meet every train); 3. *Stazione Succursale*, on the l. bank of the Dora, stopping-place of the slow trains of the Novara line.

Hotels. *Europa (Pl. a), Piazza Castello 19, spacious apartments, R. from $2^1/_2$, L. $^3/_4$, B. $1^1/_2$, D. 4, A. 1 fr.; *Hôtel Trombetta (Pl. c, formerly *Feder*), Via S. Francesco di Paola 8, near the corner of the Via di Po, R. $2^1/_2$, D. $3^1/_2$, A. 1 fr.; Bonne Femme or Grand Hôtel d'Angleterre (Pl. f), Via Barbaroux 1. — Second class, with restaurants: Caccia Reale (Pl. g), Via della Caccia 2; Concordia (Pl. h), Via di Po 20; Liguria, Via Nuova 31; Tre Corone, Via S. Tommaso; Bologna, Piazza d'Armi; *Dogana Vecchia, Via Corte d'Appello 4, near the Palazzo di Città (Pl. 27), D. 3 fr.; Albergo del Moro, Piazza Carlo Emanuele; Albergo di Roma, Via Nuova, etc. — Table d'hôte generally at 5 o'clock, also D. à la carte, or at a fixed charge ($3^1/_2$ to 4 fr.). The *Grissini*, long and thin rolls, so termed from a physician of that name, are said to be particularly wholesome. Best wines: *Barbera*, *Barolo*, *Nebiolo*, *Grignolino*.

Restaurants. Cambio, Piazza Carignano 2, good wines; Paris (Pl. k), Via di Po 21, good cuisine, D. 4 fr.; Biffo, Piazza Vitt. Eman. 7; S. Carlo (Pl. n); Concordia (Pl. h), Via di Po 20; Meridiana (Pl. m); Due Indie, Via Guasco 4. — The Restaurant in the Nuovo Giardino Pubblico at the *Valentino* (p. 79) is much frequented in the evening. Good wines in the Trattoria d'Oriente, Via Lagrange, and in the Coccagna, Via Dora Grossa.

Cafés: *de Paris (Pl. k); S. Carlo, Piazza S. Carlo 2; Nazionale, Via di Po 20; Madera, Via Lagrange 10; Brunetti, Via Lagrange; Atene, Piazza Carlo Alberto; Borsa, Via Nuova 25; Roma, corner of the Via di Po and Via Carlo Alberto; Bava Giuseppe, Via di Po 24. Ices everywhere, *sorbetti* and *pezzi duri* (hard ices). A favourite morning beverage is a mixture of coffee, milk, and chocolate, '*un bicchierino*' 20 c. — *Confectioner:* Bass, Piazza Castello, S. side. — *Beer:* bottle 20 c., generally bad. *Vienna Beer:* Città di Graz, in the Corso near the stat.; Rè di Prussia, Via Nuova 22 (30 c.); Birraria di Vienna, Via Lagrange 6 (20 c.).

Fiacres, or *Cittadine*, stand in the Piazza Castello, Via Nuova and Piazza S. Carlo; per drive (*corsa*) 75 c., at night (12—6 a. m.) 1 fr. 20 c.; per hr. (*ora*) 1 fr., each following $^1/_2$ hr. 75 c., at night 1 fr. 50 c. and 1 fr. Larger articles of luggage 20 c. each; two-horse carr. per drive 2, per hr. $2^1/_2$ fr. — Omnibuses run frequently from the Piazza Castello to each of the four gates, fare 10 c.

Railway E. to Alessandria (Genoa, Bologna) see RR. 12, 13; S. to Saluzzo, Brà, and Cuneo (Nice) in $2^1/_2$ hrs. (R. 17); S.W. to Pinerolo (p. 80) in 1 hr.; W. to Susa (Mont Cenis, p. 33) in $1^3/_4$ hr.; N.E. to Ivrea (p. 81); Biella and Novara (Arona, Milan), see R. 18.

Diligence (from Cuneo) to Nice: Office *Ballesio*, Strada Cavour (coupé 25, intérieur 23 fr.).

Post Office (*posta lettere*), Via d'Angennes 10. **Telegraph Office**, Via d'Angennes 8.

Bookseller, Loescher, Via Carlo Alberto 5, with circulating library of English, French, German, and other books.

Parade with military music in front of the W. Portal of the Palazzo Madama and at the Royal Palace daily at 12 and 5 o'clock. Military music on Sunday 12—2, in summer in the Giardino Reale, in winter in the Piazza Castello.

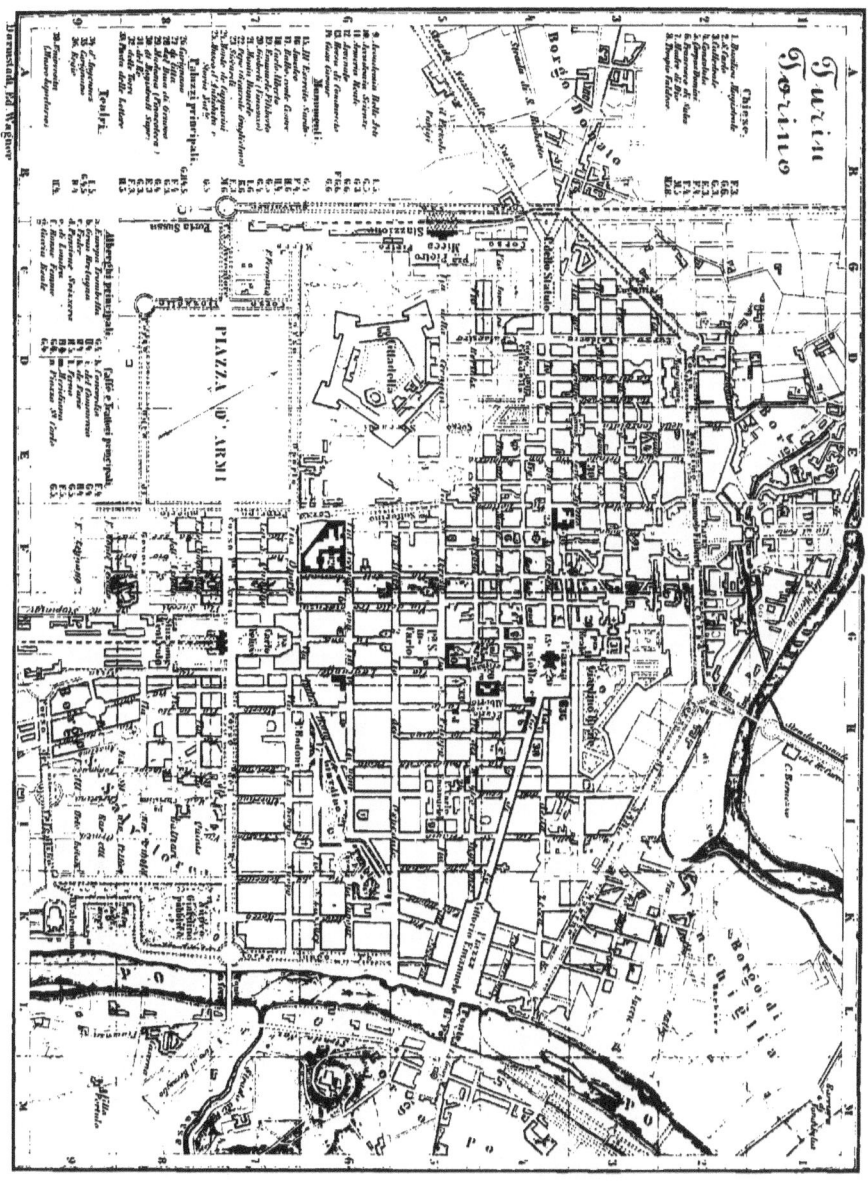

Baths, Via del Po 51 (1 fr. 25 c.) and Via della Consolata. *Swimming Bath* (scuola di nuoto) above the old bridge over the Po (p. 79), 60 c.

Commissionaires, or *ciceroni*, loiter in great numbers about the Piazza Castello and Carignano and often annoy strangers by their importunity (5 fr. per day).

Theatres. Teatro Regio (P. 36), in the Piazza Castello, with seats for 2500, generally open during the Carnival only; Carignano (Pl. 35), in the Piazza of that name, open during the greater part of the year; D'Augennes (Pl. 34), comedies in the Piedmontese dialect; Nazionale, for operas, Via Borgo Nuovo; Rossini, Via di Po 24; Scribe, Via Zecca 29, French; Gerbino, corner of Via Ripari and Via del Soccorso, Italian comedies; Vittorio Emanuele, Via Ippodromo 11, a circus; Balbo, Via Andrea Doria near the Giardino pubblico; Alfieri, Piazza Solferino, day-theatre etc.

Consuls. *British*, Via di S. Filippo 20. *American*, Via de' Fiori 19.

English Church Service performed in a chapel at the back of the Tempio Valdese (Pl. 8).

Principal Attractions: Armoury (p. 74), Picture Gallery (p. 76) and Museum of Antiquities, monuments in the cathedral (p. 78), Campo Santo (p. 80), view from the Capuchin monastery (p. 79).

Turin (820 ft.), the Roman *Augusta Taurinorum*, founded by the Taurini, a Ligurian tribe, destroyed by Hannibal B. C. 218 and subsequently re-erected, was the capital of the County of Piedmont in the middle ages, and in 1418 became subject to the Dukes of Savoy, who frequently resided here. From 1859 to 1865 it was the capital of Italy and residence of the king. Population (in 1813 only 66,000) 180,520 (1500 Protest., 2000 Jews). The University has a staff of 65 professors and is attended by 2000 students. Turin is situated on the *Po*, which rises on Monte Viso, about 45 M. to the S.W., and is augmented by the waters of the *Dora Riparia* (p. 33) below the city. The extensive plain of the Po is bounded on the W. by the *Graian* and *Cottian Alps*, and on the E. by a range of hills rising on the r. bank, opposite the city (Mt. of the Capuchins and Superga, p. 80). The town has lost much of its importance by the removal of the court. The French language is more universally employed here than in any other Italian town.

On Sept. 7th, 1706, a celebrated battle was fought under the walls of Turin between the Imperial army of Germany with its allies under Prince Eugene, and the French, in which the latter were signally defeated (comp. p. 80). In consequence of this victory the House of Savoy regained possession of the duchy, and by the Peace of Utrecht (1713) obtained the royal dignity which it still possesses.

The architecture of the city, its spacious squares, and regular streets (formerly termed *contrada*, now generally *via*) indicate its comparatively modern origin, most of the older buildings having been destroyed during the siege of 1706. The fortifications were demolished by the French in 1801, when they were in possession of the city and environs. The citadel, another old structure, was levelled in 1857 to make way for the railway.

The most animated streets are the *Via Nuova*, *Via di Dora Grossa*, and especially the broad and handsome ***Via di Po**, leading from the *Piazza Castello* to the bridge over the Po, and skirted on both sides by arcades *(portici)*. The best shops are in the Piazza Castello; those in the direction of the Po, towards the Piazza Vittorio Emanuele, are inferior.

The **Palazzo Madama** (Pl. 29), the ancient castle, a lofty and cumbrous pile in the centre of the Piazza Castello, is the sole mediæval structure of which Turin boasts. It owes its present appellation to the mother of King Victor Amadeus II., who as Dowager Duchess *('Madama Reale')* occupied the building, and embellished it in 1718 by the addition of a magnificent double flight of steps and the façade with marble columns on the W. side. The original towers on the E. side are still standing. Until 1865 the Palazzo Madama was the seat of the Italian senate and contained the *Royal Picture Gallery*, recently transferred to the Palazzo dell' Accademia delle Scienze (p. 75). — In front of the Palace stands a *Monument to the Sardinian Army*, erected by the Milanese in 1859. It was executed by *Vinc. Vela*, and represents a warrior in white marble defending a banner with his sword; the relief represents Victor Emmanuel on horseback at the head of his troops.

On the N. side of the Piazza Castello is situated the **Palazzo Reale**, or *Royal Palace* (Pl. 31), erected about the middle of the 17th cent., a plain structure of brick, sumptuously fitted up in the interior. The palace-yard is separated from the Piazza by a gate, the pillars of which are decorated with two groups in bronze of Castor and Pollux, designed by *Abbondio Sangiorgio* in 1842. To the l. in the hall of the palace, to which the public are admitted, in a niche near the staircase, is the '*Cavallo di marmo*', an equestrian statue of Duke Victor Amadeus I. (d. 1675); the statue is of bronze, the horse in marble; beneath the latter are two slaves. The royal apartments are generally accessible in the absence of the king. The private library contains a very copious collection of historical and genealogical works, and a valuable cabinet of drawings. Visitors apply to the custodian in the palace itself. The *Palace Garden (Giardino Reale)*, entered from the arcade, N. E. of the Palazzo Madama, is open Sund. and Thursd. $10^1/_2$—4 o'clock (a military band frequently plays here; comp. p. 72). Adjacent to the Giardino Reale is the *Zoological Garden*, containing a fine collection of foreign animals (cards of admission are issued by the administration of forests at the palace). — Commissionaires may be dispensed with for the palace and armoury.

The long S. E. wing of the edifice contains the ***Armoury** (*Armĕria Reale*, Pl. 11), entered from the arcade, opposite of the Palazzo Madama to the N.E. It is open to the public on Sundays, 12—3 o'clock, and daily at the same hours by tickets (obtained between 11 and 12 o'clock at the office of the secretary of the library, under the Armoury). The collection is very choice and in admirable order (custodian 1 fr.).

In the centre of the 1st Saloon is a handsome modern *Marble Group by *Finelli*, representing St. Michael with raised sword keeping down Satan in fetters, presented in 1844 by '*M. Cristina di Borbone vedova del Re Carlo Felice*'. This room contains chiefly models of modern weapons; also busts of celebrated Piedmontese and Savoyards. Here, too, is preserved the valuable gift presented to Victor Emanuel by the ladies of Bologna in 1860, consisting of a saddle and caparison wrought in purple and silver; a sword presented by Rome in 1859, a crown by Turin in 1860, and a sword in 1865, on the occasion of the Dante Festival; also flags from the wars of 1848—49, the costume of the notorious brigand *Monaco*, etc. The extensive Hall, adjoining the saloon, contains cavalry-accoutrements; the first sword to the r. above (No. 949) in cabinet *K*. is by *Benvenuto Cellini*. The finest suits of armour are those of the Brescian family *Martinengo*. A saddle of Emp. Charles V. in red velvet. By the door a gigantic suit worn by an equerry of Francis I. of France at the battle of Pavia. Over the door a bust of King Charles Albert (d. 1849); also two of his swords and two Austrian flags captured in 1848 at the battle of Somma Campagna. A cabinet here contains a rare and valuable collection of 32 halberds, the sword worn by Napoleon at the battle of Marengo, and the armour used by Prince Eugene at the siege of Turin. (A small adjacent room is occupied by a very extensive Collection of Coins, trinkets, mosaics, carved ivory, etc.) On the r., as the large saloon is re-entered, are two French eagles of the Italian Imperial guards, with names of battles on the back. Under glass a *shield by *Benvenuto Cellini*, embossed and inlaid with gold, representing scenes from the wars of Marius against Jugurtha. A number of ancient helmets are also preserved here. The sword of the Imperial General Johann v. Werth (d. 1652) bears a curious German inscription in verse.

In the *Piazza Carignano* near the Piazza Castello, to the S., rises the ponderous **Palazzo Carignano** (Pl. 26), which till 1865 was the seat of the Italian Chamber of Deputies and of the Council of State, now destined for the municipal authorities, and furnished with a new façade at the back, in the Piazza Carlo Alberto. — In the Piazza Carignano, in front of the palace, stands the finely-executed marble statue of the philosopher and patriot *Gioberti*, by *Albertoni*, erected in 1859. — In the Piazza Carlo Alberto (E. side of the Palazzo Carignano) is the bronze monument of *King Charles Albert* (Pl. 18), designed by *Marochetti* and cast in London. The pedestal, rising on four steps of Scottish granite, consists of two sections; at the corners below are four colossal statues of Sardinian soldiers; above them are four allegorical female figures, representing Martyrdom, Freedom, Civic Equality, and Statute Law. The fine equestrian statue of the king, with raised sword, appears somewhat diminutive, owing to the height of the pedestal and the dimensions of the figures at the corners.

Near the Palazzo Carignano, Via dell' Accademia 4, is the **Palazzo dell' Accademia delle Scienze** (Pl. 10), containing a picture-gallery and museums of natural history and antiquities. To the r. on the ground-floor are the Egyptian, Roman, and Greek sculptures; on the 1st floor the natural history collection, and on the 2nd floor smaller Egyptian antiquities and the picture gallery. The latter is open to the public daily 9—4 o'clock (but closed on Sund., Tuesd. and Thursd. 1—3). The other collections are accessible Sund, Tuesd., and Thursday 1—3. Access to all may be obtained daily, 10—4 o'clock, by payment of a fee.

The **Natural History Museum** contains fossil impressions of fish; a cabinet with fossil teeth and bones of an antediluvian '*Tetralophodon Arvernensis*', found during the construction of the railway; opposite to it a gigantic '*Glyptodon clavipes*' from the La Plata district; beetles, butterflies, bats, etc. — The *Mineralogical Collection* is considered very valuable.

The ***Museum of Antiquities** (*museo di antichità ed egizio*) consists of two sections. A vaulted hall to the r. on the ground-floor contains the large Egyptian sphynxes, idols, monuments, sarcophagi, mosaic pavements and reliefs; over the sitting figure of Sesostris is an inscription in honour of the celebrated Parisian antiquarian Champollion. None of the ancient statues are of very great value. Then a collection of statuettes, reliefs, bronzes, vases, and mediæval curiosities; a *statuette of Minerva in bronze, found in the Versa, should be carefully inspected. The other section of the museum is on the 2nd floor (visitors ring a bell on the r.), comprising the smaller antiquities: mummies, papyrus writings, scarabees, statuettes, trinkets, vases, etc. In the centre of the second room is the formerly celebrated *Tabula Isiaca*, found under Pope Paul III. (d. 1549) in the Villa Caffarelli at Rome, a tablet of black porphyry with hieroglyphics and figures partially inlaid with silver. Attempts to decipher the characters have elicited the most profound and erudite explanations and conjectures from savants during nearly three centuries, but it has been recently proved that the tablet was manufactured at Rome under Hadrian. It is therefore nothing more than a comparatively modern and worthless imitation of Egyptian workmanship. The celebrated papyrus with the annals of Manetho, discovered by Champollion, is also preserved here. A number of Roman and mediæval antiquities here are at present in disorder.

The **Picture Gallery**, or *Pinacoteca*, consists of 15 rooms containing 506 paintings, many of them very valuable (catalogue 1 fr.). 1st Room: Princes of the House of Savoy and battle-pieces. Beginning on the r.: 4. *Van Schuppen*, Prince Eugene on horseback; 17. *Hugtenburg*, Battle of Turin (1706); 18. Battle of Oudenarde (1708), by the same; 28. *Horace Vernet*, Charles Albert at a review; 30. *Van Dyck*, Prince Giacinto. — The 2nd, 3rd and 4th Rooms contain works of the school of Vercelli and Monferrato, of no great value. In the 2nd R.: 50. *Sodoma* (*Giov. Ant. Bazzi*, 1477 —1549), Holy Family; 54. *Gaudenzio Ferrari*, Descent from the Cross; 55. *Sodoma*, Madonna and saints. — 5th Room: 93. *Fra Angelico*, Madonna; 98. *Botticelli*, Tobias led by angels; 101. *Fr. Francia*, Entombment; 112. *Beccafumi*, Holy Family; 127, 128. *Bronzino*, Portraits of Cosmo I. and his consort Eleonora; 129. Pope Paul III., an old copy from Titian. — 6th Room: *157. *Paolo Veronese*, The Queen of Sheba before Solomon; 161. *Caravaggio*, Musician. — 7th Room: 166. *Badalocchio*, St. Jerome with the skull; 167. *Bassano*, Smithy; 174. *Ribera*, St. Jerome; 182. Finding of Moses, a copy from P. Veronese. — 8th Room: porcelain-paintings by *Constantin* of Geneva, copied from celebrated originals. — 9th Room: fruit and flower-pieces. Then a corridor with copies. — 10th Room: *234. *Paolo Veronese*, Mary Magdalene washing the Saviour's feet; 236. *Guido Reni*, Group of Cupids; 237, 238. *Poussin*, Waterfall, Cascades of Tivoli; 239. *Guercino*, S. Francesca; 242. Ecce Homo, by the same; 251. *Strozzi*, Homer. — 11th Room: 257. *Sassoferrato*, Madonna della rosa; 258. Madonna, by the same; 260, 264, 271, 274. *Albani*, The four Elements; 276. *Carlo Dolci*, Madonna; 295. *Maratta*, Madonna; 299, 300. *Angelica Kauffmann*, Sibyls; 303. *Nogari*, Smokers. — 12th Room: Netherlands and German school; *338. *Van Dyck*, Children of Charles I. of England; 351. Princess Isabella of Spain, by the same. — 13th Room, comprising the greatest treasures of the collection: 355. *Mantegna*, Madonna and saints; *358. *Hans Memling*, History of the Passion; *363. *Van Dyck*, Prince Thomas of Savoy; 366. *Wouverman*, Cavalry attacking a bridge; *373. *Raphael*, Madonna della Tenda (a very fine picture, although its genuineness has been questioned); 376. *Sodoma*, Lucretia killing herself; 384. *Van Dyck*, Holy Family; 386. *Honthorst* (*Gherardo delle Notti*), Samson overcome by the Philistines;

392. *Velasquez*, Philip IV. of Spain; 393. *Rubens*, Holy Family. — 14th Room: 410. *Floris*, Adoration of the Magi; 428. *Teniers the Y.*, Card-Players; 430. *Rembrandt*, Portrait; 450. *Rembrandt* (?), a Rabbi; 458. *Schalken*, Old woman. — 15th Room: 478, 483. *Claude Lorrain*, Landscapes.

The **Accademia Albertina delle Belle Arti** (Pl. 9), Via dell' Accademia 10, contains a small collection of pictures; among them a Madonna ascribed to Raphael, a cartoon by Leon. da Vinci, and 24 cartoons by Gaudenzio Ferrari.

The **Museo Lapidario** in the court of the University (Pl. 38) contains Roman inscriptions, antiquities, etc. Statues of Prof. *Riberi* (d. 1851) and Dr. *Luigi Gallo* (d. 1867) have been erected here. The corridor of the first floor is adorned with busts of celebrated professors.

The extensive **Arsenal** (Pl. 12) is not accessible without special permission from the office of the minister of the exterior. It comprises gun-foundries, laboratories, artillery-workshops, an armoury, library, and collection of maps.

The **Monuments** of Turin are very numerous (pp. 74, 75). In the spacious Piazza S. Carlo rises the **Equestrian Statue of Emanuel Philibert* (Pl. 19), Duke of Savoy (d. 1580), surnamed '*Tête de Fer*'. The statue is in bronze, designed by *Marochetti* and placed on a pedestal of granite. On the W. side is represented the Battle of St. Quentin, gained by the duke under Philip II. of Spain against the French; E. the Peace of Cateau Cambrésis (1558), by which the duchy was restored to the House of Savoy. The duke as '*pacem redditurus*' is in the act of sheathing his sword. — The *Piazza del Palazzo di Città* is adorned with a monument (Pl. 16) of *Amadeus VI.* (d. 1383), Count of Savoy, surnamed the '*conte verde*', the conqueror of the Turks and restorer of the imperial throne of Greece. This bronze group, designed by *Palagi*, was erected in 1853 as a '*monumento di gloria nazionale e domestica*', in commemoration of the marriage of the present king in 1843. The marble statues in front of the portico of the Town Hall, r. *Prince Eugene* (d. 1736), l. *Prince Ferdinand* (d. 1855), Duke of Genoa and brother of the king, were erected in 1858; that of *King Charles Albert* (d. 1849) in the hall, was erected in 1859; that of the present king in 1860. Opposite to these statues are several *Memorial Tablets*. — In the Piazza Savoia rises the '*Monumento Siccardi*' (Pl. 23), an obelisk 74 ft. in height, erected in 1854 to commemorate the abolition of ecclesiastical jurisdiction and the establishment of the constitution. It derives its appellation from the minister of justice *Siccardi*, at whose instance it was erected with the consent of the king and the Chambers. The names of all the towns and provinces which voted for the suppression of the spiritual courts are inscribed on the column. — Count *Camillo Cavour* (d. 1861) was born (1810) in the house at the corner of the Via Cavour and the Via Lagrange, where a memorial tablet records the fact. A statue of Cavour in the Exchange (Via Alfieri 9) was inaugurated in 1862. — In front of the old Citadel in the Via della Cernaja is a monument in bronze, erected by King Charles Albert in 1834, in memory of *Pietro Micca*, the brave '*soldato minatore*', who at the sacrifice of his own life saved the citadel of Turin, Aug. 30th, 1706, by springing a mine when the French grenadiers had already penetrated to the very gates. — Opposite rises the statue of Count *Alex. Lamarmora* (d. 1855 in the Crimea). — Between the Piazza Carlo Felice and Via Lagrange is the statue of the mathematician Count *Lagrange* (d. 1813 at Paris). — Monument of Manin see p. 79.

Most of the churches of Turin are uninteresting. The **Cathedral** (Pl. 3), erected in the Renaissance style in 1498, possesses a handsome marble façade. Over the W. Portal in the interior is a copy of the Last Supper of Leonardo da Vinci (p. 117); over the second altar on the r. are 18 small pictures, blackened with age, erroneously attributed to Alb. Dürer. The ceiling-paintings and high altar-piece are of no great artistic merit. The seats of the royal family are on the l. of the high altar. Behind the high altar is situated the **Cappella del SS. Sudario* (open during the morning mass till 9 o'cl.), erected in the 17th cent. by the Theatine monk *Guarini*, a lofty circular chapel of dark brown, almost black marble, with which the monuments strikingly contrast, separated from the choir by a glazed partition and connected with the cathedral by a lofty staircase. This is the burial-chapel of the Dukes of Savoy, adorned with statues in white marble erected by King Charles Albert in 1842 to the most illustrious members of his family. They are adorned with symbolical figures and furnished with inscriptions: (r.) *Emanuel Philibert* (d. 1580), 'restitutor imperii', by Marchesi; Prince *Thomas* (d. 1656), by Gaggini; *Charles Emanuel II.* (d. 1675), by Fraccaroli; *Amadeus VIII.* (d. 1451), by Cacciatori. The chapel also contains the marble monument of the late Queen of Sardinia (d. 1855), by Revelli: '*Conjugi dulcissimae Mariae Adelaidi posuit Victorius Emanuel 1856*'. The chapel is lighted by a cupola above in a peculiar manner, by which the effect is enhanced. In a species of urn over the altar is preserved the *SS. Sudario*, the linen cloth in which the body of the Saviour is said to have been enveloped. The door in the centre leads to the upper corridors of the royal palace, which serve as a public thoroughfare.

Corpus Domini (Pl. 5), near the Piazza del Palazzo di Città (p. 77), was erected in 1647. In 1753 the church was restored by Count Alfieri, then 'decurione' of the city, and lavishly decorated with marble, gilding, and paintings. Rousseau, when an exile from Geneva at the age of 16, was here admitted within the pale of the Rom. Catholic Church, in 1728, but in 1754 again professed himself a convert to Calvinism at Geneva.

S. Massimo, Via S. Lazzaro, by the Giardino Pubblico, is in the style of a Roman temple, surmounted by a dome. The façade is adorned with statues of the 4 Evangelists. Some good modern frescoes in the interior, and several statues by Albertoni.

La Consolata (Pl. 4), containing a highly revered Madonna, has been formed by the union of three churches; present structure of the 17th cent. The chapel to the l. beneath the dome contains the kneeling statues of Maria Theresa, Queen of Charles Albert, and Maria Adelaide, Queen of Victor Emanuel (both of whom died in 1855), erected in 1861.

The handsome **Protestant Church** *(Tempio Valdese,* Pl. 8), the first erected in Turin in consequence of the introduction of religious toleration in 1848, is situated not far from the railway-station, in the street leading thence to the elegant suspension-bridge across the Po *(Stradale del Rè).*

In the Via Montebello rises the new *Synagogue*, a building of several stories, resembling a tower, the basement of which is surrounded by a colonnade.

On the N.E. side of the city the *Dora Riparia* (p. 73) is crossed by a handsome *Bridge* of a single arch of 160 ft. span. The *Po* flows on the S.E. side. A **Bridge** of 5 arches, constructed of granite in 1810, crosses the Po opposite the Piazza Vittorio Emanuele, at the extremity of the long Via di Po. *(Swimming Bath* above the bridge, p. 73.)

To the W. of this bridge, somewhat inland, is situated the **Giardino Pubblico,** now a play-ground for children. It contains a monument to *Daniele Manin* (d. 1857), the dictator of Venice, representing the Republic of Venice with a palm-branch in her right hand and with her left resting on the medallion of Manin. Beneath the medallion are the words, '*Unificazione, indipendenza d'Italia*'. There are also monuments here to the minister and historian *Cesare Balbo*, the Piedmontese General *Bava*, and the Neapolitan General *Pepe*.

A favourite promenade in the evening is the **Nuovo Giardino Pubblico,** above the iron bridge on the l. bank of the Po (Restaurant see p. 72), which comprises also the *Botanical Garden* and extends to the royal château *Il Valentino*, a clumsy building of the 17th cent., now occupied by the *Polytechnic School* ('scuola superiore d'applicazione degli Ingegneri').

Beyond the stone bridge, on the r. bank of the Po, a number of steps ascend to the spacious dome-church of **Gran Madre di Dio** (Pl. 7), erected in 1818 in imitation of the Pantheon at Rome, to commemorate the return of King Victor Emmanuel I. in 1814. The groups sculptured in stone on the flight of steps are emblematical of Faith and Charity. The lofty columns of the portico are monoliths of granite.

On the wooded hill to the r. rises the **Capuchin Monastery,** 1/4 hr. walk from the bridge, approached by broad paths on the S. and N. sides. The latter is to be preferred, because shady and not paved. The terrace in front of the church (morning best time for a visit) commands a fine *survey of the river, city, plain, and the chain of the Alps in the background, from which (r.) the snowy summit of Monte Rosa rises prominently, then the Aiguille de Sassière and Mont Iséran; farther W. is the valley in which Susa (p. 33) is situated, S. Michele della Chiusa (p. 33), rising conspicuously on a lofty peak, above it Mont Cenis, farther S.W. Monte Viso. This hill of the Capuchins has always been a point of great importance in the military history of Turin and was fortified until 1802. A *Hospital* was added to the monastery buildings by King Charles Albert in 1840.

The *Cemetery (Cimitério, or Campo Santo, open 10—5), 1½ M. N.E. of Turin (fiacre 1 fr.), on the road to Chivasso (see p. 110), is superior in extent and arrangement to most of the Italian burial-grounds, but contains few monuments worthy of note. The wall enclosing it is skirted by a continuous arcade, divided by a long arcade in the centre. A separate space on the N. side is reserved for the interment of non-Romanists.

The *Superga (2555 ft.), the royal burial-church, a handsome structure with a colonnade in front and surmounted by a dome, conspicuously situated on a hill E. of Turin, is well worthy of a visit (2 hrs. walk) and commands a splendid view. Prince Eugene is said to have reconnoitred the hostile camp from this height before the commencement of the battle of Turin (1706), and, observing symptoms of irresolution in their movements, to have observed to the Duke of Savoy: '*Il me semble, que ces gens là sont à demi battus*'. The latter on this occasion vowed to erect a church here in honour of the Virgin, in case of the successful issue of the battle. The structure was commenced in 1717 and completed in 1731. The kings of the House of Savoy are interred here, the last of whom was Ch. Albert in 1849.

The adjacent edifice is an *Ecclesiastical Seminary*. A thanksgiving festival is celebrated here annually on Sept. 8th, to commemorate the liberation of Turin from the French yoke. The pleasantest route to the Superga is to descend by boat (*barchetta*) on the Po (also an omnibus every 1|2 hr.) to the *Madonna del Pilone*, where donkeys (*somarelli*, 1½ fr.) may be engaged for the ascent of the hill.

Pleasant Excursion from Turin to the *Valleys of the Waldenses* (*Vallées Vaudoises*), extending along the French frontier, about 30 M. to the S.W. The well-known and interesting Prot. communities (about 25,000 souls) who have occupied these valleys for 600 years, have steadily adhered to the faith for which they were formerly so cruelly persecuted. Their language is French. Railway from Turin to **Pignerol** (Ital. *Pinerolo*) in 1½ hr.; fares 3 fr. 55, 2 fr. 55, 1 fr. 70 c.; omnibus thence in 1 hr. to **La Tour**, Ital. *Torre Luserna* (*L'Ours; Lion d'Or*), the chief of these communities, which possesses excellent educational establishments. — From Pignerol a road ascends the valley of the *Ancone* by *Perosa* and *Fenestrelle*, a strongly fortified place, to the French fortress of *Briançon* in the lofty valley of the *Durance*. At *Cesanne* this road unites with that from Susa (p. 33).

11. From Turin to Aosta.

Railway to Ivrea in 2 hrs. (3 trains daily); fares 6 fr. 85, 5 fr. 80, 3 fr. 45 c. — Diligence thence to Aosta in 9 hrs.

From Turin to *Chivasso* see p. 110. Between the depressions of the lower mountains the snowy summits of Mont Blanc are visible in the background; to the r. of them the pointed peak of the Great St. Bernard; the highest peak farther E. is Monte Rosa.

At *Chivasso* carriages are changed. Next stations *Montanāro*, *Calūso*, and *Strambīno*, villages of some importance. To the l. Mont Blanc is visible; facing the traveller is Monte Rosa. To the l. of the latter a glimpse of the Matterhorn is obtained for a short time, but it is soon concealed by the nearer mountains.

Ivrea (766 ft.) *(Europa)*, a town with 9600 inhab., is picturesquely situated on the *Dora Baltea* (French *Doire)*, on the slope of a hill crowned by an extensive and well-preserved ancient *Castle*, with three lofty towers of brick, now a prison. Adjacent is the modern *Cathedral*, the interior of which was restored in 1855. An ancient sarcophagus adorns the adjoining Piazza. Ivrea is an episcopal see and capital of the province of that name. Strabo relates that at *Eporedia*, the present Ivrea, 36,000 Salassi, inhabitants of the valleys of Aosta (p. 83), were captured by the Romans and sold as slaves.

Ivrea may be termed one of the S. gateways to the Alps. The luxuriantly fertile valley, where mulberries, grapes, and other fruits are abundantly produced, is here $1^1/_2$ M. in breadth. The road now follows the course of the *Dora Baltea* as far as Aosta. On a height to the r. stands the well-preserved, pinnacled castle of *Montaldo* (a waterfall in the neighbourhood); several other ruins crown the hills farther on. The vines which clothe the slopes are here carefully cultivated. The road passes the villages of *Settimo-Vittone* and *Carema*. At

12 M. **Pont St. Martin** *(Rosa Rossa)* the road crosses the *Lysbach*, which descends from Monte Rosa. The bold and slender bridge which crosses the brook higher up is a Roman structure. This and the ruined castle here are most picturesque adjuncts to the scenery. Several forges are situated on the banks of the Dora.

Beyond *Donnaz* the road ascends rapidly through a profound defile. On the l. flows the river, on the r. rises a precipitous rock. The pass is suddenly terminated by the picturesque ***Fort Bard** (1019 ft.), which stands on a huge mass of rock in a most commanding position. The fort is of very ancient origin. In 1052 it was taken by Duke Amadeus of Savoy after a long and determined siege. In May, 1800, three weeks before the battle of Marengo, an Austrian garrison of 400 men here kept the entire French army in check for a week after their passage of the St. Bernard. The French, however, succeeded in conveying a small field-piece to the summit of *Monte Albaredo*, which overtops the fort, whence they partially disabled the battery commanding the entrance to the town.

The new road, hewn in the solid rock, no longer leads by the village of *Bard*, but follows the course of the Dora, below the fort. On the l. the *Val di Camporciero*, or *Champorcher*, opens.

7½ M. **Verrex** (1279 ft.) *(Ecu de France*, or *Poste;* *Couronne)* is situated at the entrance of the (r.) *Val de Challant*.

The valleys of Aosta and Susa (p. 33) were alternately occupied by the Franks and the Lombards, and belonged for a considerable period to the Franconian Empire, in consequence of which the French language still predominates in these Italian districts. Bard is the point of the transition from Italian to French, while at Verrex the latter is spoken almost exclusively.

Above Verrex the valley expands. The ruined castle of *St. Germain*, loftily situated, soon comes in view. The road ascends through the long and steep *Defile of Montjovet*. The rock-hewn passage is supposed to have been originally constructed by the Romans. The *Doire* forms a succession of waterfalls in its rugged channel far below. The small village of *Montjovet*, on the roofs of which the traveller looks down from the road, appears to cling precariously to the rocks. The castle of St. Germain is again visible from several different points of view.

As soon as the region of the valley in which Aosta is situated is entered, a grand and picturesque landscape, enhanced by the richest vegetation, is disclosed to view. The *Pont des Salassins* (comp. pp. 81, 83), a bridge crossing a profound ravine, commands a magnificent view. On the l. rises the castle of *Usselle*.

Near **St. Vincent** *(Lion d'Or; Ecu de France)* a mineral spring rises, and a bath-establishment has been erected here. Hotels better than at (1½ M. farther)

9 M. **Châtillon** (1736 ft.) *(Palais Royal; Lion d'Or; Trois Rois)*, capital of this district, possessing a number of forges and handsome residences. To the N. opens the *Val Tournanche*, through which a bridle-path leads to the *Matterjoch* (10,998 ft.) and *Zermatt*, and thence to *Vispach* (p. 36) in the Rhone Valley (see *Bædeker's Switzerland)*.

The road is shaded by walnut and chestnut-trees and trellised vines. The wine of *Chambave*, about 3 M. from Châtillon, is considered one of the best in Piedmont. A slight eminence here commands an imposing retrospect; to the E. rise several of the snowy summits of Monte Rosa, r. Castor and Pollux *(Les Jumeaux)*, l. the peak of the Matterhorn and the Matterjoch (see above). The entire background is formed by the Mont Blanc chain.

To the l., at the entrance of the valley, stands the picturesque castle of *Fenis*. The poor village of *Nus*, with fragments of an old castle, lies midway between Châtillon and Aosta.

A footpath leads from *Villefranche* to the castle of *Quart*, situated on the hill above (now used as an hospital) and descends on the other side. Beautiful view from the summit.

15 M. **Aosta** (1962 ft) (*Hôtel du Montblanc, at the upper end of the town, on the road to Courmayeur, R. 2, D. 3½, A. 1 fr.; *Jean Tairraz*, the landlord, is well acquainted with the environs; Couronne in the market place, R. 2, B. 1½ fr.), the *Augusta Praetoria Salassorum* of the Romans, now the capital (7760 inhab.) of the Italian province of that name, lies at the confluence of the *Buttier* and the *Doire*, or *Dora Baltea*. The valley was anciently inhabited by the Salassi, a Celtic race, who commanded the passage of both the Great and Little St. Bernard, the two most important routes from Italy to Gaul. They frequently harassed the Romans in various ways, and on one occasion plundered the coffers of Cæsar himself. After protracted struggles this tribe was finally extirpated by Augustus, who founded Aosta to protect the high roads, named it after himself, and garrisoned it with 3000 soldiers of the Prætorian cohorts. The antiquities still extant testify to its ancient importance. The *Town Walls* are flanked with strong towers. The double *S. Gate* resembles the Porta Nigra of Treves in miniature; near it is the fine *Arch* of a bridge, half-buried. The magnificent *Triumphal Arch* is constructed of huge blocks and adorned with 10 Corinthian half-columns. There are also ruins of a basilica etc.

The modern *Cathedral* possesses a singular Portal, with frescoes; above it the Last Supper in terra cotta, gaudily painted. Near the church of *St. Ours* are cloisters with handsome early Romanesque columns. Modern *Town Hall* in the spacious market-place (the *Piazza Carlo Alberto*).

From Aosta over the *Great St. Bernard* to *Martigny* (p. 35), and from Aosta to *Courmayeur* and round Mont Blanc to *Chamouny*, see *Baedeker's Switzerland*. One-horse carr. to St. Remy (where the carriage-road to the Great St. Bernard at present terminates) 15, to Courmayeur 20, to Châtillon (p. 82) 12 fr. Diligence to Courmayeur and Pré St. Didier.

12. From Turin to Piacenza by Alessandria.

Railway in 4½—6½ hrs.; fares 20 fr. 75, 14 fr. 55, 10 fr. 40 c.

From Turin to *Alessandria* see R. 13. Beyond Alessandria the train traverses the *Battle-field of Marengo* (p. 146). The village of that name is close to (N.W.) the first stat. *Spinetta*. Next stat. *S. Giuliano*. The train then crosses the *Scrivia* and reaches **Tortona** *(Croce Bianca)*, the ancient *Dertona*, a small town with a *Cathedral* erected by Philip II. in 1584, and containing a remarkably fine ancient sarcophagus.

Branch Railway to Novi (p. 146), by stat. *Pozzuolo*, in 35—45 min. (2 fr. 10, 1 fr. 50, 1 fr. 5 c.); only two trains daily, three on Sundays.

A fertile tract is traversed, and near stat. *Ponte* the impetuous *Curone* is crossed. **Voghera** *(Italia; Albergo del Popolo)*, a town with 10,173 inhab. on the l. bank of the *Staffora* (perhaps the ancient *Iria*), was once fortified by Giov. Galeazzo Visconti. The old church of *S. Lorenzo*, founded in the 11th cent., was remodelled in 1600. This town was frequently mentioned in the war of 1859.

On the high road from Voghera to the next station *Casteggio*, to the S. of the railway, is situated *Montebello*, where the well known battle of June 9th, 1800 (five days before the battle of Marengo), took place, and whence Marshal Lannes obtained his ducal title. Here, too, on May 20th, 1859, the first sanguinary encounter took place between the Austrians and the united French and Sardinian armies. *Casteggio*, a village on the *Coppa*, is believed to be identical with the *Clastidium* so frequently mentioned in the annals of the wars of the Romans against the Gauls. Hence by Pavia (and the Certosa) to Milan see R. 27.

The train skirts the base of the N. spurs of the *Apennines*, on which several unimportant places are situated, and at stat. *Arena-Po* enters the plain of the Po, in which it proceeds, at some distance from the river, till it reaches Piacenza. Stat. *Castel S. Giovanni* is situated in the former Duchy of Parma. *S. Niccolò*, the last station before Piacenza, lies in the plain of the *Trebia*, memorable for the victory gained by Hannibal, B. C. 218, over the Romans, whom he had already defeated near Somma (p. 141) a short time previously.

Piacenza, French *Plaisance* (*S. Marco, R. 1½, D. 3 fr.; Italia; "Croce Bianca; Caffè Battaglia in the Piazza; Caffè Grande in the Str. di S. Raimondo, S. of the Piazza), situated near the S. bank of the Po, which is here crossed by a bridge of boats (iron bridge in course of construction), is a large and dreary town with 39,318 inhab. It was founded by the Romans, B. C. 219, as *Colonia Placentia*, at the same time with Cremona. In the middle ages the town was frequently the subject of fierce party-struggles between the Scotti, Torriani and Visconti. In 1488 it was plundered by Francesco Sforza, a blow from which it never entirely recovered. In 1545 it finally came into the possession of the Farnese family and was united to Parma. In the *Piazza de' Cavalli* is situated the **Palazzo del Comune*, erected in 1281, in a combined Gothic and Romanesque style, with handsome colonnade. In front of it stand the equestrian *Statues of the Dukes Alessandro* and *Ranuccio Farnese*, erected 1620—24 and executed by Francesco Mocchi, a pupil of Giovanni da Bologna. Alessandro attained to great distinction in the wars in the Netherlands as governor under Philip II. He took Antwerp in 1585, besieged Paris in 1591, and died at Arras in 1592. He was succeeded by his tyrannical son Ranuccio (d. 1622).

S. Francesco, situated in the Piazza, with Gothic interior, was erected in 1278. The principal street to the E. leads to the *Cathedral, dating from 1132, a Romanesque-Lombard edifice adorned with admirable frescoes by Guercino (prophets and sibyls) and Lodovico Caracci, and pictures by Procaccini and E.

Sirani. The ancient crypt is borne by 100 columns. In the vicinity is *S. Antonino*, formerly the cathedral, dating from 903, 1104, and 1561, with a fine old vestibule termed 'Il Paradiso'.

S. Maria della Campagna (at the W. extremity of the town), erected by Bramante, but disfigured by renovations, contains some finely executed frescoes by Pordenone.

**S. Sisto*, at the N. end of the town, is the richest church in Piacenza, for which, about 1518, Raphael painted his master-piece, the Sistine Madonna (Madonna with St. Sixtus and St. Barbara, now at Dresden). It was sold in 1753 to King Augustus III. of Poland for 20,000 ducats and replaced by a copy by Nogari. The church contains pictures by Camillo Procaccini, Palma Giovine, etc.; also the monument of Margaret of Austria, daughter of Charles V. and wife of Ottavio Farnese, Duke of Parma, father of Alessandro Farnese.

To the N. of the town is the *Palazzo Farnese*, erected in a magnificent style by Vignola (1507 to 1573), during the reign of Margaret, one of his first great works. It was never completed and is now a barrack. On the S.W. side of the town is the *Citadel*, erected in 1547, and strongly fortified by the Austrians in 1848.

About 24 M. to the S. W. in the valley of the Trebbia, is situated the small town of **Bobbio**, celebrated for the *Library* of the monastery founded here by St. Columbanus in 712, which on the dissolution of the abbey was dispersed to Rome, Paris, Turin, etc. This library contained the palimpsests from which the erudite *Angelo Mai* (born at Bergamo in 1782, librarian of the Vatican in 1819, cardinal in 1833, d. at Albano near Rome in 1854) brought to light so many valuable ancient works, among others 'Cicero de Republica' in 1822.

The remains of the ancient town of ***Velleia**, which is believed to have been buried by a landslip under the Emp. Probus (about 278), is also 24 M. distant from Piacenza. A great number of antiquities excavated here in 1760—75 are now preserved in the museum at Parma. An amphitheatre, temple, forum, etc. have also been discovered. The route to Velleia is by *S. Polo; S. Giorgio*, on the *Nure*, with a villa of the Scotti erected by Vignola; *Rezzano*, and *Badagnano* (where the carriage-road terminates).

13. From Turin to Genoa.

Railway in 4¹/₄—5³/₄ hrs. (Alessandria is about half-way); fares 18 fr. 30, 12 fr. 80, 9 fr. 15 c.

The line at first proceeds S., at some distance from the l. bank of the *Po*, which here skirts the base of the extreme spurs of the *Apennines* rising on its r. bank. Near stat. *Moncalieri*, where the line turns to the E., the river is crossed by a bridge of 7 arches, each with a span of 50 ft. On an eminence above Moncalieri, which is picturesquely situated on a range of hills, rises the handsome royal château, where Victor Emmanuel I. died in 1823. A final retrospect is now obtained of the hills of Turin; to the l. the conspicuous snowy summits of the Alps (p. 80). At stat. *Trufarello* the line to *Cuneo* (p. 108) diverges to the r. (S.). Next stations *Cambiano*, *Pessione*, *Villanuova*, *Villafranca*, *Baldichieri*, and *S. Damiano*. The line penetrates farther into the heart of the mountains (numerous cuttings), crosses the *Borbone*, and reaches the valley of the *Tanaro*, the l. bank of which it follows as far as Alessandria.

Asti *(Leone d'Oro*, R. 2½, B. 1½ fr.; *Albergo Reale)*, a town (20,239 inhab.) with numerous towers, the birthplace of the tragic dramatist *Alfieri* (d. 1803), l es to the l. of the line. Its wine and its horticulture enjoy a high reputation. The Gothic *Cathedral*, erected in 1348, contains a Nativity by a master of the Cologne School. The Piazza is adorned with a *Statue of Alfieri*, by Vini, inaugurated in 1862. To the r. and l., at some distance from the town, rise the vine-clad hills which yield the excellent wine of Asti.

The next stations are *Annone*, *Cerro*, *Felizzano*, and *Solero*. The country is flat and fertile; the Tanaro flows on the r. Before Alessandria is reached, the line to Arona (R. 25) diverges to the N. The train now crosses the Tanaro by a bridge of 15 arches, winds past the fortifications, and reaches **Alessandria**, see p. 145.

From Alessandria to **Genoa**, see p. 146.

14. Genoa, Ital. *Genŏva*, French *Gênes*.

Hotels, almost all of unattractive exterior. *Hôtel Feder (Pl. a), formerly the Palace of the Admiralty, new proprietor, entrance Rue Bogino 9, R. 3 fr. and upwards, L. 1, B. 1½, D. 4, A. 1 fr. — Hôtel d'Italie (Pl. b), R. from 2½, L. 1, D. 4, A. 1, omn. 1¼ fr.; Quattro Nazioni (Pl. d), Palazzo Serra; Hôtel de la Ville (Pl. c), R. 2½, L. 1, D. 4½, A. 1, omnibus 1½ fr.; Hôtel Royal (Pl. e); *Croce di Malta (Pl. f), R. 2, L. ¾, A. ¾, D. 4, omnibus 1 fr.; Grande Bretagne; °di Genova (Pl. h), near the Teatro Carlo Felice; *Hôtel de France (Pl. g), opposite the Hôtel Feder, recommended; Pension Suisse, R. 2, D. 3, A. 1½ fr.; Albergo della Vittoria, Piazza dell' Annunziata 16, R. 2½, L. ¾, A. ¾ fr.; Hôtel de l'Europe, Via Teodoro, R. 1—1½ fr. and Hotel Smith, near the exchange, Via Ponte Reale, are unpretending, but well spoken of. Hôtel National, near the station (Pl. C, 2). — Those who make a prolonged stay at any of the hotels should come to a preliminary understanding as to the charges.

Restaurants etc. *Concordia, Via Nuova, opp. the Palazzo Rosso (Pl. 16), dinner 4—5 fr., good ices 60 c., music frequently in the evening. *Café d'Italie at Acqua Sola (p. 93), in summer only, D. 4 fr.; Caffè dell'Acquasola, corner of Via and Salita Acquasola. Café de France, Via Carlo Felice, D. 2½ fr.; Rossini, opp. the post-office; Caffè Elvetico, Via Giulia; Caffè del Centro, Via Nuova 8; Caffè dell'Omnibus, Via Lomellina, etc.; Rossini, opp. the post-office. *Trattoria della Confidenza, Via Carlo Felice 9, D. 3—4 fr.; Trattoria dell' Unione, Piazza Campetto 9; Tratt. Nazionale, Via S. Luca 9. — *Birraria Müller*, Via Caffaro.

Consulates. English, Salita di S. Caterina; American, Salita de' Cappuccini, at Acquasola; Prussian, Palazzo Spinola, Via Orefici.

Steamboats: to *Leghorn* (R. 48) daily in 9 hrs., fares 32½, 20½ fr.; to *Spezia* (R. 49) daily exc. Sund. in 5—6 hrs.; to *Leghorn*, *Civitavecchia*, *Naples* and *Messina*, twice weekly; to *Marseilles* (p. 22), several times weekly in 18—20 hrs., fares 76, 58, 37 fr.; to *Nice* (p. 100) daily at 10 p. m. in 9—10 hrs., fares 27½, 17½ fr.; to *Sardinia* by Leghorn 3 times weekly;

of which the usurper died, and, with the aid of the French, the Genoese supremacy over Corsica was re-established. In 1746 new disasters were caused by the occupation of the city for some time by the Imperial army

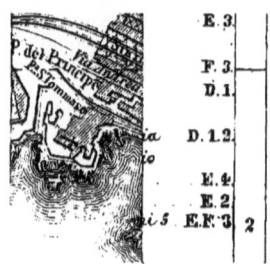

weekly in 18—20 hrs., fares 76, 58, 37 fr.; to *Nice* (p. 100) daily at 10 p. m. in 9—10 hrs., fares 27½, 17½ fr.; to *Sardinia* by Leghorn 3 times weekly;

to *Tunis* once weekly. Embarcation in each case 1 fr. for each pers., incl. luggage.

Small boat with one rower per hr. 2 fr. (2—4 pers.).

Baths, Via delle Grazie 11, Piazza Sarzano 51, Via delle Fontane 12, 80 c. *Sea-bathing* estab. at the Punta della Cava (Pl. H, 8), to which omnibuses (20 c) run during the summer, and at Pegli (p. 94), accommodation very poor. Swimmers are recommended to bathe from a boat.

Post Office, Piazza delle Fontane Morose, open 8 a. m. to 8 p. m.

Telegraph Office in the Palazzo Ducale (Pl. 13).

Carriages for the whole day, one-horse 10, two-horse 15 fr., half a day 5 or 10 fr.; per hr., one-horse $1^1\!/_2$ fr., each following $^1\!/_2$ hr. 75 c.; per drive 80 c., at night $1^1\!/_4$ fr.

Omnibuses traverse the city in every direction, fare 20 c. From the Piazzo Carlo Felice to the railway 20 c. — Smaller vehicles run to places in the environs, but are often crowded.

Diligences. *Messageries Impériales* to Nice and Spezia, from the Piazza Brignole, opp. the Palazzo Brignole (comp. p. 94).

Commissionaires 5 fr. per day.

Money. The Genoese *Soldo* = 4 Centesimi only (1 fr. = 25 Genoese soldi, 1 lira Genovese = 80 c., used only by the humbler classes). The usual soldo of 5 c. is called *Palanca* at Genoa, as well as in Tuscany.

English Church Service in an apartment in the Via Assarotti. *Presbyterian* at the Waldensian church in the same street.

Principal Attractions: Ascent of the Madonna di Carignano (p. 88); walk on the terrace of the harbour (p. 89) and through the line of streets mentioned p. 88; visit to the Palazzo Pallavicini (p. 91), Brignole (p. 91) and Doria (p. 92); drive to the Villa Pallavicini (p. 93).

The city of **Genoa** (127,986 inh.), justly termed '*la superba*', owing to its beautiful situation and its numerous palaces of marble, rises from the sea on the slope of the mountain, like a grand amphitheatre. Genoa was celebrated as a harbour at a very remote age, and as early as the Roman period was the great mart for the products of the coast-districts of the Mediterranean. The city in its present dimensions, however, dates from the middle ages. At the commencement of the 10th cent. a republic, presided over by doges, was constituted here. The citizens participated in the crusades, and acquired valuable possessions in the distant East. Their great rivals were the Pisans and Venetians, with whom they waged fierce and interminable wars (pp. 266, 188).

The **Internal History** of Genoa consists of a succession of violent, and frequently sanguinary party-struggles, originated chiefly by the *Doria* and *Spinola* families (Guelphs) and those of the *Grimaldi* and *Fieschi* (Ghibellines) to which the Doges, the presidents of the republic belonged. *Andrea Doria* (p. 92) at length restored peace by the establishment of a new constitution. The unsuccessful conspiracy of Fieschi in 1547 is the last instance of an attempt to make the supreme power dependent on unbridled personal ambition. The power of Genoa was, however, already on the wane. The Turks conquered its Oriental possessions one by one, and the city was subjected to severe humiliations by its powerful Italian rivals, as well as by the French (who took Genoa in 1684). In 1736 the ambition of *Theodore de Neuhof*, a Westphalian nobleman, occasioned great disquietude to the republic. He was created king by the inhabitants of Corsica, who had been subjects of Genoa, but now threw off their yoke. The Genoese pronounced the newly elected king a traitor against the 'majesty of the people' ('*Qual seduttore del popolo, reo di lesa maestà*'), in consequence of which the usurper fled, and, with the aid of the French, the Genoese supremacy over Corsica was re-established. In 1746 new disasters were caused by the occupation of the city for some time by the Imperial army of Germany. After the battle of Marengo (1800) Genoa was taken possession of by the French. In 1805 it was formally annexed to the Empire of France, and in 1815 to the Kingdom of Sardinia. — An old Tuscan saying, the first part of which is not untrue, is very characteristic of the former rivalry between them and the Genoese, whom it pronounces to possess: 'mare senza pesce, montagne senza alberi, uomini senza fede, e donne senza vergogna'.

The city possesses a double line of **Fortifications**. The first of these, about 7 M. in length, encloses the city itself, the other consists of a broad rampart, 20 M. in length, which extends along the hills at some distance from Genoa and at the most elevated points is furnished with small fortified towers and intrenchments, completed in 1632, and recently strengthened.

Genoa is the most important commercial town and seaport in Italy. The average number of sailing-vessels from foreign ports which enter the harbour is 1700 annually, of steamboats 800. In the coast trade 5000 sailing vessels and 1400 steamers touch here annually. The annual imports are valued at 300 million fr., the exports at 120 million. Of the imports about one-third is from England, and a large proportion of the remainder from France and North America. The traffic of Genoa has been doubled within the last twelve or fourteen years.

The former opulence of the city is still evidenced by the numerous and magnificent palaces of bygone ages. All the streets are paved with slabs of marble, but many of them are so narrow, steep, and tortuous as to be inaccessible to carriages.

The great artery of the traffic of Genoa is a line of broad streets, which, like the Boulevards at Paris, encircle the city, commencing at the Railway Station, passing the *Monument of Columbus* (p. 92), continued by the *Via Balbi*, passing *S. Annunziata* (p. 91); then by the *Via Nuovissima*, *Via Nuova*, *Piazza delle Fontane Morose* (or *della Posta*), *Via* and *Piazza Carlo Felice*, *Piazza Nuova*, and thence by the *Cattedrale S. Lorenzo* (*Strada Carlo Alberto)* to the *Harbour*. The principal churches and palaces are situated in this line of streets. Many of them were erected by *Galeazzo Alessi* (a pupil of Michael Angelo, born at Perugia 1500, d. 1572), whose example was generally followed in the construction of subsequent palaces. Between these loftily situated streets and piazzas a complete labyrinth of narrow streets and lanes descend to the harbour, those adjacent to which are the most ancient.

The unparalleled beauty of the situation and the interesting reminiscences of its ancient magnificence render a visit to Genoa very attractive. The stranger is recommended to proceed first to the church of ***S. Maria di Carignano** (Pl. 13), situated on one of the highest points at the S.E. extremity of the city. This structure, in the form of a Greek cross, with a lofty dome, designed by the above-mentioned Galeazzo Alessi, is an imitation of the original design of St. Peter's at Rome, and is remarkable for the harmonious symmetry of the interior. The great attraction is the *view from the highest gallery of the dome (ascended by commodious and well lighted staircases, 249 steps in all), extending over the city, harbour and fortifications, and W. and E. over the well populated coasts (W. the *Riviēra di Ponente*, R. 15; E. the *Riviēra di Levante*, R. 49), bounded on the E. by the picturesque promontory of *S. Martino d'Albaro*, and stretching to the S. over the vast blue expanse of the Mediterranean. In clear weather even the island of Corsica is said to be visible in the extreme distance (sacristan 25 c., his attendance for the ascent is unnecessary). The *Ponte Carignano*, a bridge 90 ft. in height, by means of which the street crosses a lower quarter of the city, was formerly regarded as a marvel of architectural skill.

The *Harbour *(Porto)* forms a semicircular bay, about $2^1/_2$ M. in diameter, into which two substantial *Piers* of considerable length project. That on the E. is the *Molo Vecchio*, with the small, old lighthouse; on the W. the *Molo Nuovo*, adjoining which is the new lighthouse, or *Lanterna*, the dazzling reflectors of which are 520 ft. above the sea-level. The summit commands a fine view; the arrangements of the interior may also be inspected (fee $^1/_2$ fr.). On the N. E. side is the *Royal War Harbour (Darsena Reale)* with the *Arsenal (Arsenale di Marina)*, accessible by special permission only. It was here that Gian Luigi de' Fieschi was accidentally drowned in 1547, when he with the other conspirators against Andrea Doria had taken possession of the harbour. The *Dogana* is established in the building of the *Banco di S. Giorgio*, an institution founded in 1346, but suppressed during the French Revolution. The large hall contains two series of Statues of Genoese celebrities, some of them of the 15th cent.

On the E. side is the **Free Harbour** *(Porto Franco)*, where numerous vessels lie at anchor. The quay is connected by rails with the railway station. A lofty wall with arcades separates the harbour from the houses (most of them six stories in height) of the long Via Carlo Alberto and the Piazza di Scaricamento, in which almost all the hotels are situated. These arcades are the favourite haunt of the red-capped denizens of the harbour, the sailors and boatmen, the porters, valets-de-place, etc. The best point for surveying the scene which here presents itself is the *Gran Terrazzo Marmoreo* (ascended at the N. extremity), the marble platform of these arcades, $^1/_3$ M. in length and 20 paces in width. This terrace affords a most agreeable *walk in the early morning, but later in the day it is exposed to the sun. The stranger, as he approaches the arcades, is immediately assailed by the boatmen with offers of their services (p. 87). The finest view of the city from the harbour is about $^3/_4$ M. from the coast. — A cannon fired in summer at 9 p. m. is a signal for all the sailors to repair to their vessels.

Genoa possesses 82 Churches, of which a few only need be mentioned:

*S. Lorenzo (Pl. 9), the cathedral, erected in 1100 on the site of an older structure, was frequently altered in the 15th and 16th cent., so that it now exhibits three distinct styles of architecture (Romanesque, Lombard-Gothic, Renaissance). The façade, constructed of alternate layers of black and white marble, is embellished by recumbent lions, of which the lower, on the r. and l. of the flight of steps, are modern. Over the principal portal are old reliefs of Christ and the emblems of the four Evangelists; beneath them the martyrdom of St. Lawrence.

The Interior, with its circular vaulting and octagonal dome, is supported by 16 Corinthian columns and 4 pillars, above which there is a second series of columns. The 2nd Chapel on the l. (di S. Giovanni Battista) contains six marble statues by *Matteo Civitali*, and a John the Baptist and Madonna and Child by *Sansovino*. In the vaulting of the choir, the martyrdom of St. Lawrence by *Tavarino*, executed at the beginning of the 17th cent.; choir-stalls in 'tarsia' (inlaid work) by *Fr. Zabello*. In the Sacristy is preserved the vessel (*Vaso Catine*) from which Christ and his disciples are said to have partaken of the paschal lamb, captured at Cesarea by the Genoese during the Crusades.

A short distance hence, adjoining the *Piazza di Scaricamento*, is the **Exchange** (*Borsa*, Pl. 7), erected in the 16th cent., with a statue of *Cavour* by Vinc. Vela.

In the *Piazza Nuova*, somewhat higher, is situated **S. Ambrogio** (Pl. 12), a Jesuit church with dome, sumptuously decorated with marble, mosaics, gilding, and ceiling-paintings. The high altar-piece (Circumcision) is by *Rubens;* the chapel of the Virgin (3rd on the r.) contains an Assumption by *Guido Reni*.

Adjoining the latter is the handsome **Palazzo Ducale** (Pl. 22), now the *Town Hall*, constructed entirely of white marble. In the niches above are placed allegorical warlike figures, and eight statues of the Doges, who formerly resided here. The palace has been entirely modernized since a conflagration in 1777. The *Telegraph Office* is now in this edifice.

Farther N. in the street, to the l. of the Piazza Carlo Felice, is situated **S. Matteo** (Pl. 14), a small church erected by the Dorias in 1278, containing numerous mementoes of that illustrious house. The façade is completely covered with inscriptions dedicated to members of the family, and great numbers of their epitaphs, and a few mutilated statues, are preserved by being built into the walls of the interesting cloisters. The palace in the corner opposite, the lower story covered with black and yellow marble, bears the inscription: '*Senat. Cons. Andreae de Oria, patriae liberatori munus publicum*'; i. e. the edifice was a gift to Andrea Doria from the senate.

In the spacious *Piazza Carlo Felice* the extensive **Teatro Carlo Felice** (Pl. 36), erected in 1827, is situated. Adjacent to it is the *Accademia delle Belle Arti* (Pl. 1), containing a small collection of pictures (1st floor) and a library. The latter, which comprises numerous modern works, is accessible daily.

In the vicinity, *Via Carlo Felice 12*, is the ***Palazzo Pallavicini** (Pl. 26), several rooms in which contain good pictures (fee 1 fr.): *Lucas of Leyden*, The Virgin, a picture with wings, and an Entombment; *A. Dürer*, Repose during the flight to Egypt; *Schidone*, Madonna; *Van Dyck*, James I. of England and his family; *Guercino*, Mucius Scævola; *Lucas of Leyden*, Descent from the Cross; *An. Caracci*, Magdalene (on copper); *Van Dyck*, Portrait. — Permission is also obtained here (r. on the ground floor, 3rd door), on presenting a visiting-card (personally or through a valet-de-place), to visit the Villa Pallavicini (p. 93); the number of the party must be stated.

Not far distant hence, *Via Nuova 18*, is the ***Palazzo Brignole** (called *Palazzo Rosso* from its red façade, Pl. 25), sumptuously fitted up, containing the most extensive gallery in Genoa (fee 1 fr.):

1. Sala della Gioventù: *Rubens*, Satyr. — 2. Sala Grande, the ceiling adorned with coats of arms. — 3. Sala della Primavera: **Van Dyck*, three portraits, the Prince of Orange, Antonio Brignole on horseback, and a Marchesa Brignole; other portraits by *Gaetani*, *Tintoretto*, *Moretto*, *Titian*, *P. Bordone*, *Francia*, *Giov. Bellini*; Bearing of the Cross, *Van Dyck*. — 4. Sala d'Estate: *Lanfranco*, Bearing of the Cross; *Paolo Veronese*, Sketch for the Adoration of the Shepherds; *Lucas of Leyden*, Portrait, and St. Jerome. — 5. Sala d'Autunno: Portraits by *Bassano* and *Tintoretto*; *Bonifazio*, Adoration of the Magi; *Guido Reni*, Christ with the globe, *Madonna; *Guercino*, Madonna with John the Baptist, SS. John and Bartholomew; *A. del Sarto*, Madonna. — Sala dell'Inverno: Portraits by *P. Bordone* and *Rubens*; *Leonardo da Vinci (Luini?)*, John the Baptist; *Van Dyck*, the tribute-money. — 7. Sala della Vita Umana: *Van Dyck*, two fine family portraits; *P. Veronese*, portrait. — 8. Sala delle Arti Liberali: nothing of importance.

Opposite is the **Palazzo del Municipio**, or *Town Hall* (Pl. 23), erected by the Dorias, with the chief guard-house of the municipal guard, containing a few pictures, reminiscenses of Columbus, a large ancient bronze-tablet of the year B. C. 187, recording the decision pronounced by Roman commissaries in a dispute between Genoa and a neighbouring fort, etc.

In a small Piazza at the extremity of the *Via Nuova* and *Via Nuovissima* stands the Capuchin church of ***SS. Annunziata** (Pl. 10), erected in 1487, possessing a portal with marble columns, but with an unfinished and unsightly brick façade. In the interior this is the most sumptuous church in Genoa. The nave and aisles are supported by twelve columns of white marble inlaid with red. The vaulting and dome are richly decorated with gilding and painting.

In the broad and handsome *Via Balbi*, which leads hence to the station, next to the Annunziata on the r. (No. 1), is situated the **Palazzo Marcello Durazzo** or *della Scala* (Pl. 20), with handsome façade, erected by *Bart. Banchi* in the 17th cent.; the imposing court and marble steps were added during the last century by *Tagliafico*. The interior contains several good family portraits by *Van Dyck* (those of two children the best), vases by *Benvenuto Cellini*, etc.

Opposite to the latter (No. 4) is the **Palazzo Balbi** (Pl. 19), erected at the commencement of the 17th cent., possessing a handsome court with columns. The upper story contains a picture-gallery (fee 1 fr.):

1st Room: *Van Dyck*, Equestrian figure; *Bernardino Strozzi*, Joseph interpreting the dream. — 2nd R.: *Van Dyck*, Madonna; *Michael Angelo* (?), Christ on the Mt. of Olives; *Titian*, Madonna with SS. Catharine and Dominicus. — 3rd R.: *Van Dyck*, Two family-portraits (the head of the equestrian figure is said to be a portrait of Philip II., painted by Velasquez, in order to save the picture from destruction, over that of Balbi, who had meanwhile been banished). — 4th R.: *Caravaggio*, Conversion of St. Paul. — 5th R.: *Bassano*, Fair. — 6th R., a long gallery containing numerous small pictures: *Titian*, Portrait of himself; *Spagnoletto*, Philosopher and Mathematician; *Memling*, Crucifixion; *Breughel*, Temptation of St. Antony.

Farther on, to the r., is the *University* (Pl. 54), with handsome staircase (the university itself was founded in 1812), established in a palace also erected by the Balbi family. It contains a library, natural history museum, a small botanical garden and a few bronzes by Giovanni da Bologna. On the l. is the **Royal Palace** (*Palazzo Reale*, Pl. 21), erected by the Durazzo family (accessible daily in absence of the royal family). The interior is richly fitted up, but the antiquities and pictures are of no great value, the finest objects in the collection having been removed to Turin.

In an open space, farther on, rises the **Statue of Columbus** (Pl. 47), who was born at *Cogoleto* (p. 95) in 1447. The monument, erected in 1862, stands on a pedestal adorned with ships' prows. At the feet of the statue, which rests on an anchor, kneels the figure of America. The monument, which consists entirely of white marble, is surrounded by allegorical figures in a sitting posture, representing Religion, Geography, Force, and Wisdom. Between these are reliefs of scenes from the history of Columbus, with the inscription of dedication. Opposite to the monument is situated the *Palace of Columbus*, with the inscription: '*Cristoforo Colombo Genovese scopre l'America*'. — A niche on a house (the 5th to the N. from the commencement of the street of the harbour, p. 89) contains a small statue of Columbus, with the inscription: '*Dissi, volli, credi, ecco un secondo sorger nuovo dall' onde ignote mondo*'.

To the W. of the railway-station is situated the ***Palazzo del Principe Doria** (Pl. 24) (p. 87), remodelled by *Andrea Doria* (well known from Schiller's '*Fiesco*'), the '*padre della patria*' (d. 1560, at the age of 95), as the long Latin inscription in front of the edifice records.

Ariosto says of this illustrious prince in his poems: '*Questo è quel Doria, che fa dai pirati sicuro il vostro mar per tutti i lati*'. The palace was presented to him in 1522, and the restoration conducted by Montorsoli. It was decorated with frescoes by Pierino del Vaga, a pupil of Raphael, and renovated in 1845. Visitors are conducted through the great entrance-hall, a corridor hung with portraits of the Doria family, and a saloon with a large ceiling-painting representing Jupiter overthrowing the giants. The latter also contains a portrait of the aged prince (who was admiral of the fleets of the Pope, of Emp. Charles V., and of Francis of France, as well as of that of Genoa) with his favourite cat. The elder branch of the Doria family, to whom the palace now belongs, generally resides at Rome.

The garden of the palace, extending towards the harbour, contains remarkably fine orange-trees. At the extremity, towards the sea, rises an extensive Loggia with arcades. The gardens on the hill opposite, with a statue of Hercules ('Il Gigante') in a niche, also appertain to the estate. They command a fine survey of the harbour.

Palazzo Spinŏla, Via Nuova 54 (Pl. 34), formerly *Grimaldi*, containing some good pictures, and another *Palazzo Spinola* (Giov. Battista), in the Piazza Fontane Morose (Pl. 35), as well as several other of the palaces of the Genoese nobility, which are remarkable either for their architecture or their collections, may also be visited by those who have leisure.

The most favourite promenade is the small park *(Giardino Pubblico)* of *Acqua Sola (Pl. 41), adorned with a fountain, situated on an eminence at the N.E. extremity of the city (approached most conveniently from the Piazza delle Fontane Morose by the street ascending opposite the post-office). The *Caffè dell' Italia* (p. 86), with a pleasant garden, and well fitted up, is a popular resort here. During the military concerts on Sunday afternoons the grounds are crowded. Pleasing views to the E. and S., especially over the open sea. Adjoining the N. side of the promenades of Acqua Sola is the *Villa Negro* (Pl. 46), the property of the city, and open to the public, with well-kept garden. Winding promenades ascend hence to a bastion at the back of the villa, about 150 ft. above Acqua Sola, commanding a fine survey of the city, the harbour, and environs.

The most delightful excursion in the environs is to the *Villa Pallavicini (admission see p. 91), at *Pegli*, 7½ M. W. of Genoa, a station on the Genoa and Nice Railway (p. 95; in 35 min., fares 1 fr. 10, 88, and 55 c.). The station is immediately opposite to the entrance of the villa. One of the gardeners (fee 2 fr. for 1 pers., more for a party) of the Marchese conducts visitors through the grounds and the park, the inspection of which occupies about 2 hrs. They extend to a considerable height on the slopes rising from the coast and display the richest luxuriance of southern vegetation. Cedars, magnolias, magnificent oleanders, azalias, camellias, etc. here flourish in the open air. Several points of view afford the most charming prospects of Genoa, the sea, coast, and mountains. The highest of these points is occupied by a building in the mediæval style with a tower, whence an extensive and magnificent panorama is enjoyed. The other attractions are the Mausoleum, the remains of an ancient Roman burial-place, a stalactite grotto (with a subterranean piece of water, over which visitors are conveyed by a boat; fee $^1/_2$ fr.), beneath the bridge a striking glimpse of the lighthouse of Genoa and the sea; kiosks in the Pompeian, Turkish, and Chinese style, obelisk, fountains, etc. may also be inspected. The gardens also contain a few examples of the coffee, vanilla, cinnamon, pepper, sugarcane, camphor, and other plants, which will interest the visitor.

Pegli (*Grand Hôtel de la Méditerranée*, well spoken of; *Hôtel Gargini*, both facing the sea. *Hôtel Michel*, opp. the station, dear), a small ship-building town, with 4000 inhab., is much resorted to as a sea-bathing place, especially by Italians.

15. From Genoa to Nice by the Riviera di Ponente.

95 M. Steamboat (French Co. *Fraissinet*, office in the Piazzi Banchi) in 8—10 hrs., on Mond. and Frid. at 8 p. m.; fares 27$^1/_2$ or 17$^1/_2$ fr. Also (Italian Co. *Peirano d'Annovaro*) on Mond., Wed. and Frid. at 9 p. m., returning from Nice on Tuesd., Thursd., and Sat. at 9 a. m.; fares, incl. dinner, 32$^1/_2$ or 22$^1/_2$ fr. — Since the opening of the railways between Genoa and Savona, and between Mentone and Nice, the Land Journey by the celebrated *Route de la Corniche* along the charming *Riviera di Ponente* is far preferable to the steamboat voyage. Railway to Savona in 2$^1/_2$ hrs.; fares 4 fr. 85, 3 fr. 40, 2 fr. 45 c. The line between Savona and Mentone is partially finished, but will probably not be opened for several years. After a delay of 1$^1/_2$ hr. passengers are conveyed hence to Mentone by the diligences of the French Messageries Impériales (afternoon and evening only; office at Genoa in the Piazza Brignole, nearly opp. the palace of that name, where through-tickets to Nice can be obtained: 1st cl. by rail. and coupé of diligence 45, 1st cl. and intérieur or banquette 38 fr.; office at Savona in the Albergo Svizzero). The diligence journey from Savona to Mentone occupies 15 hrs. Travellers who pay one-half more for their tickets may break their journey wherever they please, and resume it on the following day. — Carriages require two days for the journey from Savona to Mentone. Charge for two-horse carr. 100—120 fr. ('cabriolet', or front seat with hood, must be expressly included in the bargain); one-horse carr. 80 fr. (sufficient for 2 pers. with moderate luggage). The first demands of the voituriers are generally exorbitant. Travellers by carr. are recommended to spend the night at Oneglia (p. 96). The midday train should be taken from Genoa to Savona, in order that all the necessary arrangements may be made on the day previous to starting for Mentone. — Railway from Mentone to Nice in 1$^1/_4$ hr., fares 2 fr. 80, 2 fr. 10, 1 fr. 55 c.

With regard to the rail. and dilig. communication in the reverse direction, comp. p. 102.

This journey is extremely attractive. The road affords the most delightful succession of charming and varied landscapes, traversing bold and lofty promontories, wooded hills, and richly cultivated plains near the coast. At some places the road passes precipitous and frowning cliffs, the bases of which are lashed by the surf of the Mediterranean, whilst the summits are crowned with the venerable ruins of towers, erected in bygone ages for protection against pirates. At other places extensive plantations of olives, with their grotesque and gnarled stems, bright green pine-forests, and most luxuriant growths of figs, vines, citrons, oranges, oleanders, myrtles, and aloes meet the view. Numerous palms too occasionally diversify the landscape (at S. Remo and Bordighera). Many of the towns are picturesquely situated on gently sloping heights (Porto Maurizio, S. Remo, Bordighera, Ventimiglia); others, commanded by ancient strongholds and castles, are perched like nests among the rocks (Roccabruna, Eza). Small churches and chapels, peering from the somber foliage of cypresses, and gigantic grey pinnacles of rock, rising proudly above the smiling plains, frequently enhance the charms of this exquisite scenery. Finally, the vast expanse of the sea itself, with its ever varying hues, constitutes one of the principal attractions. At one time it is observed bathed in a flood of sunshine, at another its beautiful blue colour arrests the eye; immediately beneath the spectator, roaring breakers are frequently visible, whilst farther off the snowy crests of the waves are gradually lost to view in the purple distance. — The inns are generally good, but dear.

The railway skirts the coast, and runs parallel with the high road. Of the numerous promontories penetrated by tunnels that of Voltri, the first after starting, is the most extensive. Stations *S. Pier d'Arena*, *Cornigliano*, *Sestri a Ponente*, and *Pegli* (see p. 94). Stat. *Pra*, to the l. on the coast. Stat. *Voltri*, a town with 11,000 inhab. at the mouth of the *Ceruso*, carries on a considerable traffic in 'confitures.'

Beyond Voltri a long tunnel. Stat. *Arenzano*, surrounded by villas in the midst of cypresses, oleanders, and aloes; beautiful retrospect of the coast as far as Genoa. Three tunnels are next passed through. *Cogoleto* is said to have been the birthplace of Columbus (p. 92). A poor tavern here bears the inscription:

> *Hospes, siste gradum. Fuit hic lux prima Columbo;*
> *Orbe viro majori heu nimis arcta domus!*
> *Unus erat mundus. 'Duo sunt', ait ille. Fuere.*

Stat. *Varazze*, or *Voragine*, a town on the coast with 8000 inhab., is an important ship-building place. On both sides of it the coast is rocky. Huge masses of rock, cuttings, and tunnels are successively passed.

Next stations *Celle*, *Albissola* at the mouth of the *Sansobbia*, and *Savona*, where the line at present terminates (comp. p. 94).

Savona (**Albergo Svizzero*, dilig. office, R. 2, D. 4, B. 1½, A. 1 fr., omnibus ¾ fr.; *Italia*, both in the Piazza of the theatre), the most important town on the route, with 19,000 inhab., was the capital of the Montenotte department under Napoleon I. The harbour, which is commanded by a fort, always presents a busy scene. The cathedral contains several good pictures; so also the former church of the Dominicans, especially an Adoration of the Magi by *Dürer*. The handsome theatre, erected in 1853, near which the diligence halts, is dedicated to the poet *Chiabrera*, who was a native of this place. Savona was the birthplace of the popes Sixtus IV. and Julius II. (della Rovere). Pius VII. was detained as a prisoner here for some time.

The High Road at first leads between houses, and then approaches the sea. At the promontory of *Bergeggi* it is hewn in the rock, and defended by fortifications. Churches surrounded with cypresses, olive-plantations, and ruined castles on the promontories, above which are pine-forests, constitute the principal features of the scenery. *Spotorno*, a village. Then *Noli*, a small town, shaded by dense plantations of olives, and overlooked by the ruins of a castle. Beyond the town the road gradually ascends (*retrospect) the promontory of Noli, the extremity of which is penetrated by a tunnel *(Galleria di Noli)*. A second castle-crowned promontory rises on the l., while the road leads inland over a height. Farther on is the village of *Varigotti* on the slope to the r., almost entirely concealed by olives. Then a second tunnel.

14$^3/_4$ M. (from Savona) **Finale** *(Grand Hôtel de Venise)* is a small seaport possessing a fort, and a cathedral with double columns of white marble, dome, and rich gilding. The road becomes wilder, and passes through a third tunnel. *Borgio*, with its two towers, remains on the r. Then *Pietra*, with 1160 inhab. On the r. of the road near Loano are two suppressed monasteries. *Monte Carmelo*, the higher of the two, was erected by the Doria family in 1609.

Loano (*Albergo d'Europa) possesses a twelve-sided church with a dome, also erected by the Doria's. Beyond the village of *Ceriale* the mountains recede from the coast, and the road leads inland across vine and olive-clad fields and orchards to *Albenga*, an ancient town, the Roman *Albigaunum*. Considerable remnants of a Roman bridge are seen by the road side, $^1/_4$ M. before the town is reached. Several lofty towers here belong to ancient residences of noble families. The cathedral possesses an elegant tower and façade. All the buildings are constructed of brick. The road again approaches the sea, opposite to the rocky *Isola Gallinara* (surmounted by a tower), ascends for some distance, and then descends to

Alassio (Hôtel de la Belle Italie), a small seaport with 4000 inhab., which carriages do not usually enter. Then *Lagueglia;* charming retrospective view, beyond which the road ascends to a considerable height, and passes the frowning and barren *Capo della Croce*, with a lighthouse, and the *Capo delle Mele*.

Cervo and *Diano Marino*, picturesquely situated on the slopes, are next reached. *Diano Castello* lies farther inland. Extensive olive-plantations are here traversed. Magnificent retrospect as the road ascends the next promontory. Then a descent to

38 M. **Oneglia** (*Hôtel Victoria*, charges according to agreement), a small seaport with 6440 inhab., most beautifully situated. Beyond it the broad, stony channel of a mountain-torrent is crossed by a suspension-bridge. *Porto Maurizio* (Hôtel de France), through which the road next leads, is a naval station and harbour of some importance, very picturesquely situated on an eminence on the coast, surrounded by dense groves of olives. Invalids sometimes spend the winter here.

The low and massive towers which rise on the r. and l. of the road near the shore, beyond the next village of *S. Lorenzo*, and have been partially converted into dwelling-houses, were erected for protection against Saracen marauders in the 9th and 10th cent. Some of them have lately been removed to make way for the railway. The next places are *S. Stefano, Riva*, and *Taggia-Bressano*. The road then leads round the *Capo Verde* to

22 M. **S. Remo** (*Hôtel Victoria, *H. d'Angleterre, Pension Anglaise, 8—9 fr. per diem, all three on the Savona road; H. Grande Bretagne, *H. Royal, R. 2½, B. 1½, D. 4, A. ½, pens. 7—10 fr., both in the principal street in the lower part of the town; *Gr. Hôtel de Londres, on the road to Nice. — Café Garibaldi; Café Victoria. — *English Church Service; Dr. Rose*, Engl. physician), a town with 10,000 inhab., with a small harbour commanded by a fort. The older part of the town consists of a curious labyrinth of lanes, flights of steps, archways, and decaying walls, rising on the slope of the hill, and surrounded by gardens in terraces. On a cypress-clad height to the E. rises a white church, surmounted by a dome, whence a fine view is obtained. On the r., outside the W. gate of the town, a public garden, planted with cypresses, palm and orangetrees, etc., has recently been laid out. S. Remo, which possesses the same advantages of climate as Mentone, is also frequently resorted to as a winter-residence.

A family here named Bresca is said to have obtained from Pope Pius V. in 1588 the privilege of sending a vessel annually to Rome laden with palms, for the decoration of the churches there on Palm Sunday. This was a reward for a service rendered by an ancestor of the family. When the pope was superintending the erection by Domenico Fontana of the great obelisk of the Circus of Nero in the Piazza of St. Peter at Rome, an operation accomplished by means of 40 windlasses worked by 800 men and 140 horses, a sudden and most critical stoppage took place. The sailor *Bresca*, notwithstanding the severe penalties with which persons breaking the silence were threatened, shouted: ',Water on the ropes!' His suggestion was acted upon, and the work successfully completed in consequence.

The road passes several plantations of palms, then skirts the *Capo Nero* at a considerable height above the sea.

Bordighera (*Hôtel d'Angleterre, expensive), situated on a hill abutting on the sea, consists of the upper and the lower town. The road leads through the latter only. The former however commands a magnificent *view of the bay (from the terrace of a small café near the issue towards Ventimiglia). Around the town are seen numerous groves of palms *(phœnix dactylifera)*, the dates of which however have no commercial value. Aloe-plants are here employed as hedges for the fields. Near Ventimiglia a chalybeate bath is passed *(Hôtel des Sources d'Isola Buona)*, beyond which the broad and stony bed of the *Roja* is crossed by a bridge of eleven arches.

Ventimiglia (Hôtel de l'Europe), a place of some importance, is very picturesquely situated on a hill, and is now the Italian frontier-fortress. Beyond it the road again ascends. The highest part is defended by fortifications and gates. In descending, the traveller obtains an extensive view of the French coast. The road next passes through several small villages, and is shaded by picturesque and venerable groups of olive-trees (several good retrospective views). On a hill to the r. are the ruins of a Rom. fort. Then *Mortola*, with its church, picturesquely situated on a promontory. A ravine is now skirted, and the road finally ascends a height whence Mentone is visible. Immediately beyond it is the Ital. 'dogana' or custom-house. *Grimaldi* lies on a height to the r. Charming country-houses with orange and lemon gardens are passed. Luxuriant southern vegetation. The French frontier is at the *Pont St. Louis* which crosses the rocky gorge.

22 M. **Mentone**, French *Menton*.

Hotels and Pensions. In the *E. Bay*, towards the Italian frontier: *Grande Bretagne, pension 9 fr. and upwards; *Grand Hôtel de la Paix, expensive, pension 12—15 fr.; *Hôtel des Anglais, well fitted up; *Iles Britanniques, Grand Hôtel, these three with garden. All these houses are beautifully situated on the coast. — Farther back: *Hôtel et Pension d'Italie; near the Pont St. Louis (see above); Pension de l'Univers, with view of Mentone. — *In the town:* Angleterre; *Hôtel du Midi; *Hôtel Victoria, newly fitted up, all looking inland. — In the *W. Bay:* *Hôtel de la Méditerranée, expensive; *Londres; *Turin, pleasant rooms facing the sea, R. 3, L. 1/2. A. 1, B. 1½, D. 4 fr.; *Louvre, and Beau Séjour, farther from the sea, sheltered from the wind. Near the stat.: Hôtel Splendide, a magnificent estab., and Hôtel du Parc, both new. — 3/4 M. from the town: Hôtel du Pavillon and Prince de Galles. — *Pensions:* *Villa Germania of Dr. Genzmer; *Pension Hemmelmann; Pension des Etrangers et du Wurtemberg; Mme. Martel; *Pension Camous; Pension Suédoise, and many others, pension generally 9—15 fr. per day, according to situation and requirements.

In both bays there is also a great number of charmingly situated and occasionally very handsomely furnished villas, a list of which may be obtained of the *Agence des Propriétaires*, Quai Bonaparte. The rents vary from 1000 to 7000 fr. and upwards for the season. Private apartments for the season, from 400 fr. upwards, are also to he had, where the visitor may have his own 'menage', and live at considerable less expense than at a pension. Invalids should enquire whether it is desirable in their respective cases to be near, or at some distance from the sea.

The Cercle Philharmonique contains a reading-room, and balls and concerts are frequently given; subscription 60 fr. for the season, ladies 48 fr.; per month 15 fr., ladies 12 fr.

Restaurants etc. Hôtel de Paris; Hôtel du Parc (see above); Café de la Victoire; Café de Paris; Restaurant du Cercle; London Tavern; beer in all.

Physicians. *Drs. Bennet, Marriott,* and *Siordet,* English; *Drs. Bottini* and *Farina,* Italian; *Drs. Stiege, Genzmer* and *Dührsen,* German. — Chemists: *Albertotti, Gras,* who make up Engl. and Germ. prescriptions.

Poste aux Lettres, near the Hôtel Victoria. — *Telegraph Office:* Avenue Victor Emanuel 19.

Bankers: *Palmaro; Bioves and Co.* — **Booksellers:** *Papy; Giordan.* — **Photographers:** *Noack, Anfossi,* both in the Avenue Victor Emanuel.

Omnibuses run frequently through the town during the Season (30 c.). Diligence by Turbia to Nice once daily, coupé 4 fr., intérieur and banquette 3 fr.

Carriages. Drive in the town, one-horse carr. 1 fr., two-horse 1½ fr.; for half a day one-horse 8—10, per day 12—15 fr., two-h. 25 fr. — *Donkeys* 5 fr. per day, 2½ fr. for half a day, and gratuity.

English Church Service during the season.

Mentone, a small town with 5600 inhab., formerly belonging to the principality of Monaco, then under the Sardinian supremacy, finally became French by the events of 1860. It is charmingly situated on the Bay of Mentone, which is divided into the *Baie de l'Est* and the *Baie de l'Ouest* by a rocky promontory. It is protected by a vast wall of rock from the N. winds, and is considered to be one of the most favourable spots for a winter-residence on the Riviera di Ponente (mean temperature about 5° Fahr. higher than at Nice, a cold wind however generally prevails towards noon). The vegetation is luxuriant. The numerous orange and lemon groves are interspersed with gnarled carob-trees (ceratoria siliqua), figs, olives, etc. The *Promenade du Midi* and the *Jardin Public* are the favourite afternoon resorts of visitors. The ruined castle on the above mentioned rocky promontory, which has been converted into a burial-ground, affords a fine view. Another picturesque point is the monastery of *S. Annunziata*, to which a rough path ascends (in ½ hr.) from the Turin road (to the l. immediately beyond the railway). A pleasant and sheltered walk to *Capo Martino*, which bounds the Bay of Mentone on the W.

Pleasant excursion (comp. map, p. 104) from Mentone by (4 M.) *Castellaro* to the summit of the **Berceau** (3—4 hrs.). Magnificent prospect embracing the mountains of the coast, the blue expanse of the Mediterranean, and Corsica in the distance. — To *S. Agnese* in 3—3½ hrs., returning to Mentone by *Gorbio* and *Roccabruna* (5—6 hrs.). — To *Camporosso* situated 3½ M., and *Dolce Acqua* 7 M. inland from Ventimiglia (p. 97).

The High Road from Mentone to Nice, 18¾ M. (by diligence or carr.), the so-called '*Route de la Corniche*', traverses the most beautiful part of the Riviera, and is far preferable to the railway (see below). It ascends through the most luxuriant vegetation, and commands a charming retrospect of Mentone and the coast as far as Bordighera. Then a view of *Monaco* (see below), to which a road descends to the l. beyond the highest point of the road. To the r. of the road higher up *Roccabruna* is visible. Then **Turbia** with its huge Roman tower, the remains of the *Tropaea Augusti* (whence the name 'Turbia'), erected to commemorate the subjugation of the Ligurian tribes (A. D. 13). Here another very beautiful view is enjoyed. E. the wild mountains and the entire coast from Ventimiglia to Bordighera; W. (view in this direction from a point a few steps above the tower) the Mediterranean, the French coast near Antibes, the island of St. Marguerite, the Montagnes de l'Estérel, and other distant coast hills. The road attains its culminating point in a bleak mountain-district ¾ M. beyond Turbia. On the l. is *Eza* (p. 100), a group of grey and venerable houses with a white campanile, perched on an isolated rock rising abruptly from the valley. Farther on, the wooded promontory of St. Hospice (p. 106), *Beaulieu* (p. 106), *Villafranca* (p. 105), beyond which a view is obtained of the beautiful valley of *Nice* (p. 100), with its villas, monasteries, villages, and green hills.

The Railway (fares etc. see p. 94) from Mentone to Nice skirts the coast the whole way, and affords very inferior views to the magnificent and lofty carriage-road. It crosses the *Borigli*, penetrates *Capo Martino* by means of a tunnel, and stops at stat. *Cabbe-Roquebrune*. The village (Ital. *Roccabruna*) lies on the hill to the r., in the midst of orange and lemon groves, and overtopped by a ruined castle. Next stat. *Monte Carlo* (for the Casino, p. 100); then

Monaco (*Hôtel de Paris*, a large estab., near the Casino; *H. et Pens. Suisse*, *H. du Louvre*, both smaller; *Angleterre*, *H. des Bains*, both near the stat.; all these near the sea; *Prince Albert*, in the town above. — Carr. from stat. to town 1½/₂, per hr. 3 fr.), picturesquely situated on a bold and prominent rock, capital (1500 inhab.) of the diminutive principality of that name, to which Mentone and Roccabruna also belonged down to 1848. This little independent state was mediatized by France in 1860, and the once powerful princes, who were anciently renowned for their naval exploits, have retained but little of their former privileges. The palace (accessible daily, 2—5 p. m.) contains a suite of sumptuously furnished apartments. Pleasant promenades extend round the extremity of the rock. Monaco is visited on account of the mildness of its climate in winter, and as a sea-bathing place in summer, but the chief attraction to many is the 'tapis vert'. The *Casino*, which contains the rooms dedicated to play, is situated on a promontory to the E. of the town, surrounded by beautiful grounds (café, music in the afternoon), and commanding a fine view.

Beyond Monaco the train passes through 3 long and several shorter tunnels. Stat. *Eza*; the village, situated on an isolated rock on the r., high above the line, was once a stronghold of Saracen freebooters, who levied contributions on the surrounding district. Then *Beaulieu* (p. 106), and *Villafranca* (p. 105). The train now enters the valley of the *Paglione* by means of a tunnel nearly 1 M. in length, crosses the stream, passes through another tunnel, and reaches the station of **Nice** on the r. bank of the river.

16. Nice (Ital. *Nizza*) and its Environs.

Comp. Map p. *104.*

Hotels. On the Quais Masséna and St. Jean Baptiste (r. bank of the Paillon): *Hôtel Chauvain, *Hôtel de la Paix, *Grand Hôtel, all of the 1st class; *Hôtel de France, R. 3, L. 1, B. 1½|₂, D. 5, A. 1 fr. — At the Jardin Public: *Grande Bretagne, Angleterre. — In the Promenade des Anglais: *Hôtel des Anglais, Hôtel du Luxembourg, *Hôtel de la Méditerranée, de Rome, all 1st cl. — In the Avenue du Prince Impérial: *Iles Britanniques, des Empereurs, Ganter's Hôtel et Pension, Maison Dorée, Deux Mondes. — W. of these, in the streets Boulevard de Longchamp, Rue Masséna, Grimaldi, St. Etienne, Delphine: Hôtel du Paradis, du Louvre, Royal, Julien, Chamonix, all new. Same direction, farther to the W.: Hôtel de l'Europe, Hôtel Helvétique, the latter less expensive, both Rue de France. East of the Aven. du Prince Impérial, in the Rue Gioffredo, du Temple etc.: Hôtel et Pension du Colorado, Windsor, des Colonies, the two latter recommended for moderate requirements. — In the Boulevard Carabacel, in a sheltered position: *Hôtel de Nice, a large estab.; Europe et Amérique, Hôtel de Paris, Périno; near them Hôtel Victoria, Prince de Galles, Hôtel et Pension Carabacel. — On the l. bank of the Paillon: Hôtel de Gênes et de Turin, de la Ville, Lyon et Paris, *Hôtel des Etrangers, Rue du Pont Neuf, well spoken of, D. 3, R. 3, B. 1½|₂ fr.; Hôtel

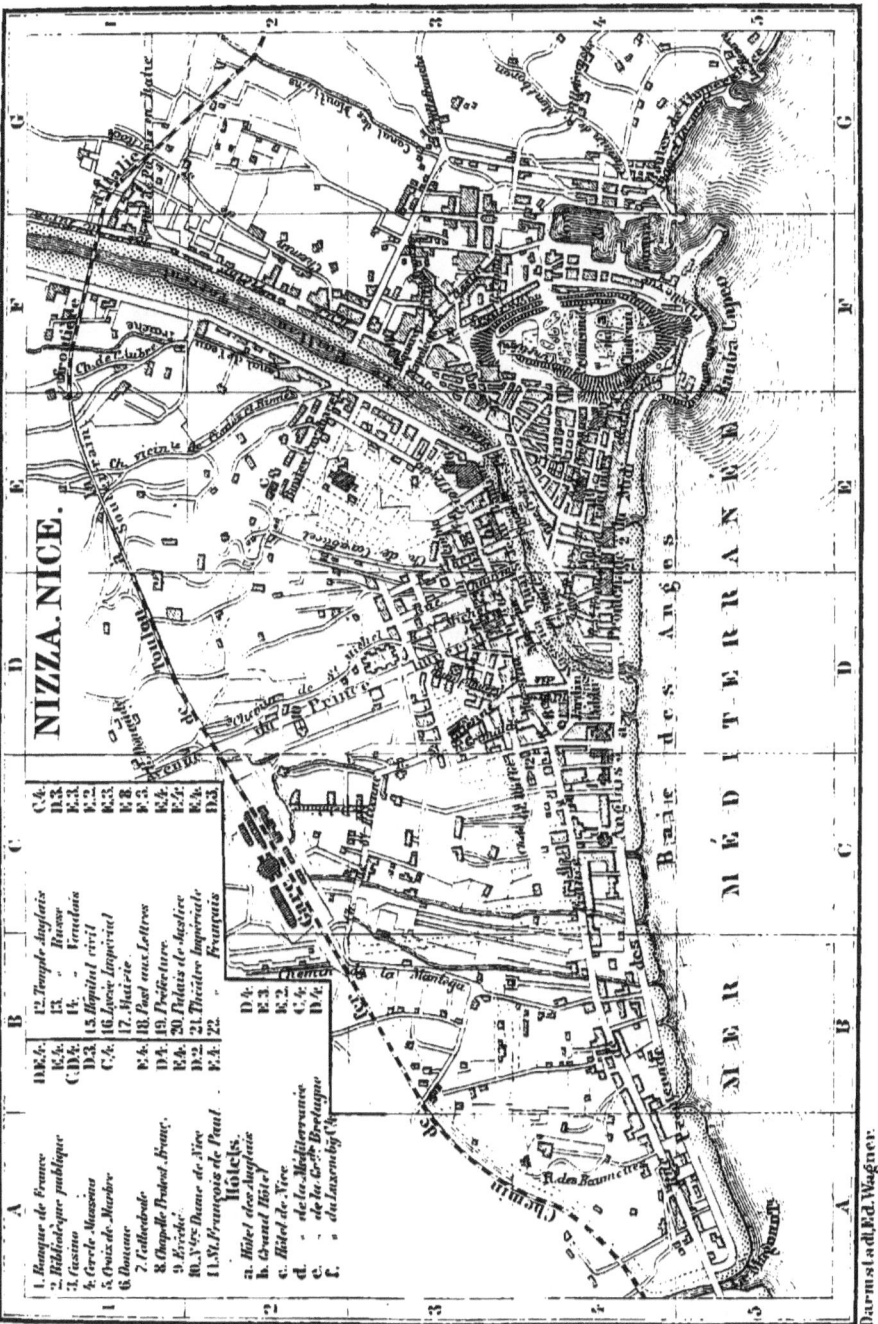

de l'Univers, Place St. Dominique, R. and L. 3, A. 1/2, D. 3 1/2, omnibus 1 fr. — In the Rue des Ponchettes, at the W. base of the Castle Hill: *Hôtel et Pension Suisse, on the coast, R. 2 1/2, L. and A. 1, B. 1 1/4, D. 3 1/2, pension 6 1/2–10 fr., recommended; *Hôtel des Princes, farther back. — Opposite the station: *Hôtel du Midi, new, R. 2, D. 3 fr., L. 40 c.; Hôtel de Paris.

Pensions. Besides the above mentioned hotels: In the Promenade des Anglais, Pension Rivoir, Lombard, Anglaise. In the streets W. of the Avenue du Prince Impérial: *Milliet, at some distance from the sea, well fitted up; *Internationale, with garden; Pension Royale, Raissan, Longchamp. Towards the E.: Pension d'Allemagne, Russe. In the Quartier Carabacel: Pension des Etrangers, de Genève, de Venise. — At *Cimiès* (p. 104): Pension Garin, Pension Victor. The usual charges at most of these establishments are 7—10 fr. per day.

Restaurants. *Restaurant Français *(Augier)*, at the 1st floor of the Café de la Victoire, Place Masséna; Maison Dorée and Deux Mondes, see above; Restaurant Américain, Avenue du Prince Impérial; Restaurant du Jockey Club, Boulevard de Longchamp; Restaurant Polonais and Scala, Rue Grimaldi; Frères Provençaux and *Léonard, Rue St. François de Paule; Restaur. de la Réserve, Boulevard de l'Impératrice, E. of the harbour; Rest. du Midi, de Paris, both near the stat.

Cafés. *Café Impérial (with restaur.) and *Café Américain, both in the Promenade du Cours; Café de la Victoire, Place Masséna; Grand Café, Quai St. Jean Baptiste; Maison Dorée and Deux Mondes (see above). — Lyons and Strasbourg beer in all. — Best *ices* at Rumpelmeier's, Place Etienne. — *Preserved Fruits:* Brondet, Rue François de Paule; Escoffier, Place Masséna; Musso, Rue Pont Neuf.

Fiacres are stationed in the Place Charles Albert, Place Masséna, Boulevard du Pont Vieux etc. — One-horse: per drive 75 c. (1 fr. 25 c. at night); for 1 hr. 2 fr. 10 c. (2 fr. 60 c. at night), each additional 1/2 hr. 80 c. (1 fr. 30 c. at night). Carriages with two seats only at somewhat lower rates. Two-horse: per drive 1 fr. (at night 1 1/2 fr.); for 1 hr. 2 fr. 60 c. (at night 3 fr. 10 c.), each additional 1/2 hr. 1 fr. 40 c. (at night 1 fr. 35 c.). From the stat. to the town: 1–2 pers. one-horse 1 fr. 25 (at night 1 fr. 75), 3–4 pers. 1 fr. 50 and 2 fr.; two-horse carr. 2 pers. 2 and 2 1/2, 4 pers. 2 1/4 and 2 3/4 fr.; trunk 25 c., drive from one hotel to another 25 c. — To *Villafranca* and back, one-horse carr. with 2 seats 4, with 4 seats 5, two-horse 6 fr.; charges for a prolonged stay according to tariff. No fees.

Omnibuses cross the town in several directions (25 c.); from the stat. to the town 30 c.; trunk 25, hat-box 10 c.; to Villafranca and Beaulieu every 2 hrs., starting from the Pont vieux, l. bank of the Paillon.

Horses may be hired of Nigio, Ruelle St. Michel, Mouton, Rue Pastorelli etc.; 6–10 fr. for a ride of 3–4 hrs. In winter a horse may be hired by the month for 250–350 fr., in summer for less.

Vetturini. Plana, 8 Rue de la Terrasse; Clessy; Loupias, etc. To Savona (p. 95) in 2–2 1/2 days with 4 horses 200–250, with 2 horses 100–150 fr., less in summer. A written contract should be made.

Donkeys 3–4 fr. per day and 1 fr. for the attendant; half-day 1 1/2–2 fr.

Booksellers. Librairie Étrangère of *Barbéry*, with circulating library, Jardin Public; Visconti's reading-room, well supplied with newspapers, Rue du Cours, with garden.

Post Office, Place Napoléon, 7 a. m. to 6, in summer to 7 p. m.; Sund. 7–12, 4–6 only. — *Telegraph Office*, Promenade du Cours.

Physicians. Drs. Travis, Gurney, Crothers, Crossby, Blest, Zürcher, Lippert, Proell, Rehberg etc.; Dr. Jansen, homœopathist. — *Dentist:* Weber, 8 Rue Carabacel. — *Chemist:* Daniel, 3 Quai Masséna.

Bankers. Florès, Prussian and Dutch consul, Boulevard du Midi 3; Avigdor aîné et fils, Quai St. Jean Baptiste.

Baths. *Warm Baths:* Bains Polithermes, Rue du Cours; Turn, Rue du Temple, both well fitted up. — *Turkish Baths:* Hammam, Place

Grimaldi (4 fr.); another in the Rue Chauvain 2. — *Sea-baths* opposite the Promenade des Anglais, 40 c. to 1 fr.

Shops. The best are on the Quai St. Jean Baptiste and the Quai Masséna. — *Photographer:* Blanc, Prom. des Anglais.

Casino (*Cercle International*), a new building on the Promenade des Anglais, embellished with the armorial bearings of different states, containing a reading-room, restaurant, concert and ball room, etc. Subscription for 1 pers. 15 fr. per week, 30 fr. per month, 100 fr. for the entire season, for each additional member of the same family one-half more.

Theatres. Théâtre Impérial, Rue St. François de Paule, Ital. opera; Théâtre Français, Rue du Temple, opéras, comedies, etc.

Military Music several times weekly, in the Jardin Public, 2—4 o'clock.

Railway from Nice to Toulon and Marseilles see R. 1; to Mentone see pp. 99, 100.

Steamboats (different companies: *Fraissinet*, Place Bellevue 6, on the quay; *Peirano, Danovaro & Co.*, office in the Corso, to the r. of the flight of steps ascending to the terrace; *Valery Frères et Fils*, Quai Lunel 14: to Genoa (p. 86) several times weekly in 9—10 hrs., $32^1/_2$, $22^1/_2$ or 12 fr., cabin on the deck $42^1/_2$ fr.; to *Spezia* $50^1/_2$, $34^1/_2$, 15 fr.; to *Leghorn* $58^1/_2$, $40^1/_2$, 20 fr.; to *Civitavecchia* $87^1/_2$, $57^1/_2$, 30 fr.; to *Naples* $132^1/_2$, $92^1/_2$, 40 fr. — To Marseilles (p. 22) twice weekly in 12 hrs., 30, 12, 8 fr. — To Corsica (R. 54) in 12 hrs., 30, 20, 15 fr.

Messageries Impériales (office in the Place Charles Albert) to *Genoa* twice daily in 19 hrs. (comp. p. 94): from Nice to Mentone, and from Savona to Genoa by railway. Coupé 45, intérieur or banquette 38 fr., both incl. 1st cl. by rail.; by paying 67 fr. for coupé, or 48 for intérieur, the traveller is entitled to break his journey at Oneglia (p. 96), and have a seat reserved for him on the following day. — Diligence (office in the Boulevard du Pont Neuf) to *Mentone* (by Turbia) daily at 3 p.m. in $3^1/_2$ hrs., fares 4 and 3 fr.

House Agents. Samaritani, Lattès, Dalgoutte, Tiffen, to whom a percentage is paid by the proprietors. Visitors may therefore make a more advantageous bargain without their intervention. Houses and apartments to let are indicated by tickets. A single visitor may procure apartments for the winter in the town for 300—700 fr.

The hirer is recommended not to take possession until the contract (upon stamped paper) has been signed by both parties. This document should if possible contain stipulations with regard to every detail, e.g. damage done to furniture and linen, compensation for breakages, etc. This will be found the best preventive against the disputes which frequently arise on the termination of the contract.

English Church in the Rue de France, service also at Carabacel. *Scotch Church*, Rue Masséna 5.

Climate. The bay of Nice is sheltered from the N., N.E., and N.W. winds by the lower terraces of the Alpes Maritimes (culminating in *Mont Chauve*, Ital. *Monte Calvo*, 2672 ft.), a natural barrier to which it owes its European reputation for mildness of climate. The mean winter temperature is 10—15° Fahr. higher than that of Paris, summer temperature 5—10° lower. Frost is rare. The *Mistral*, or N.W. wind, the scourge of Provence, is seldom felt, being intercepted by the Montagnes du Var and de l'Estérel. The E. wind, however, which generally prevails in the spring, is trying to delicate persons. Sunset is a critical period. As the sun disappears, a sensation similar to that of a damp mantle being placed on the shoulders is experienced. This moisture, however, lasts 1—2 hrs. only. — Those who contemplate a brief visit only should avoid the rainy season, which usually commences about the beginning of October and lasts 5—6 weeks.

Nice, the capital (50,000 inhab.) of the French Département des Alpes Maritimes, was founded by the Phocian inhabitants of Marseilles in the 5th cent. B. C., and named *Nikaea*. Till 1388 it belonged to the County of Provence, afterwards to the Dukes of Savoy; in 1792 it was occupied by the French, in 1814 restored to Sardinia, and in 1860 finally annexed to France together with Savoy. The meeting of Charles V. and Francis I. which took place here through the intervention of Pope Paul III. in 1538 resulted in a temporary armistice only, as the emperor and the king had conceived such a profound mutual aversion for each other that nothing would induce them to meet in person. Nice was the birthplace of the French general Masséna (born in 1758) and of Giuseppe Garibaldi (b. July 4th, 1807). Halévy, the composer of opera music, died here in 1862. The dialect of the natives is a mixture of Provençal and Italian.

In winter Nice is the rendezvous of numerous invalids and persons in robust health from all parts of Europe, especially from England, Russia, and Germany, who assemble here to escape from the rigours of a northern winter. The annual number of visitors is still on the increase, and living becomes dearer in the same proportion. In summer the town is deserted.

Nice is beautifully situated on the broad *Baie des Anges*, which opens towards the S., at the mouth of the *Paglione*, or *Paillon* (a small stream, frequently dried up). The broad and stony bed of the river, with handsome quays on each bank, divides the town into two halves. On the l. bank is the *Old Town*, with its narrow, dirty lanes, which however have been superseded by better streets near the shore (Boulevard du Midi, and Promenade du Cours). On the r. bank is the *Strangers' Quarter*, which already surpasses the old town in extent, and is intended to occupy the entire space bounded on the W. by the brook *Magnan*, and on the N. by the railway (the Quartier de la Croix de Marbre stretches along the coast to the W., the Quartier Carabacel to the N.E. along the bank of the Paillon).

Nice contains no churches or other buildings worthy of notice. A *Marble Cross* in the Rue de France, commemorating the above-mentioned meeting of Charles V. and Francis I., has given its name (Croix de Marbre) to this entire quarter of the town. The *Square*, a broad space formed by covering in the Paillon between the Pont Vieux and Pont Neuf, is embellished by a *Statue of Masséna* (see above) in bronze, erected in 1867; in front Clio is represented on the pedestal writing his name on the page of history; at the sides are reliefs. The *Town Library* (40,000 vols., accessible daily 10—3, on Sundays 10—12 o'clock) in the Rue St. François de Paule 2, contains a few Rom. antiquities (milestones etc.), and a nat. hist. Cabinet.

The **Jardin Public** (military music, see p. 102) at the embouchure of the Paillon, and the ***Promenade des Anglais** adjoining it on the W., which was laid out by English residents in 1822—24, and greatly extended in 1862, are the principal rendezvous of visitors. These grounds stretch along the coast for 1½ M. as far as the brook *Magnan*, and are bordered with handsome hotels and villas (at the beginning of the promenades is the Casino, mentioned p. 102). On the l. bank of the Paillon, which is crossed here by the Pont Napoleon, they are continued by the *Boulevard du Midi* (p. 103).

To the E. of the town rises the **Castle Hill,** 300 ft. in height (ascent from the E. side, 20 min.), crowned by the ruins of a castle destroyed by the Duke of Berwick under Louis XIV. in 1706, now converted into beautiful grounds, where palms, oranges, cypresses, and aloes flourish luxuriantly. The platform on the summit, erected in honour of the emperor, commands an admirable view in every direction: S. the Mediterranean; W. the French coast, the promontory of Antibes, the two Iles de Lérins, the mouth of the Var (which till 1860 formed the boundary between France and Sardinia), beneath the spectator Nice itself; N. the valley of the Paglione, the monasteries of Cimella, or Cimiès, and St. Pons, in the distance the castle of St. André, Mont Chauve, the Aspremont, and the Alps; E. the harbour, the mountains and Fort Montalban, and the promontory of Montboron which separates the roadsteads of Villafranca (p. 105) and Nice. The S. slope of the castle-hill, which descends precipitously towards the sea, is termed the *Rauba-Capeu* ('hat-robber', owing to the prevalence of sudden gusts). — The *Cemeteries*, with the exception of the English, are on the N. side of the castle-hill.

At the base of the castle-hill on the E. lies the small **Harbour,** termed *Limpia* from an excellent spring *(limpida)* which rises near the E. pier. It is accessible to small vessels only; those of large tonnage cast anchor in the bay of Villafranca (p. 106). The Place Bellevue adjoining the harbour is embellished with a *Statue of King Charles Felix* in marble, erected in 1830. On the farther side of the harbour is the *Boulevard de l'Impératrice* (Restaur. de la Réserve, p. 101).

The Environs of Nice afford a variety of beautiful excursions, and abound in attractive villas and luxuriant vegetation (olives, oranges, figs, etc.).

The Franciscan monastery of **Cimiès,** Ital. *Cimella*, is situated 3 M. to the N. of Nice. The best, although not the shortest route to it is by the new road ascending to the E. from the Boulevard Carabacel (Pl. E, 2), which on the top of the hill intersects the site of a Rom. *Amphitheatre* (210 ft. long, 175 ft. wide). About $1/4$ M. to the r. from the cross-road immediately beyond the amphitheatre the traveller reaches the monastery (two pictures by Bréa in the chapel), re-erected in 1543 after its destruction by the Turks. It stands on the site of the Rom. town *Cemenelium*, to which the above-mentioned amphitheatre and a quadrangular structure, commonly termed a '*Temple of Apollo*', appertained. Traces of baths etc. have also been discovered.

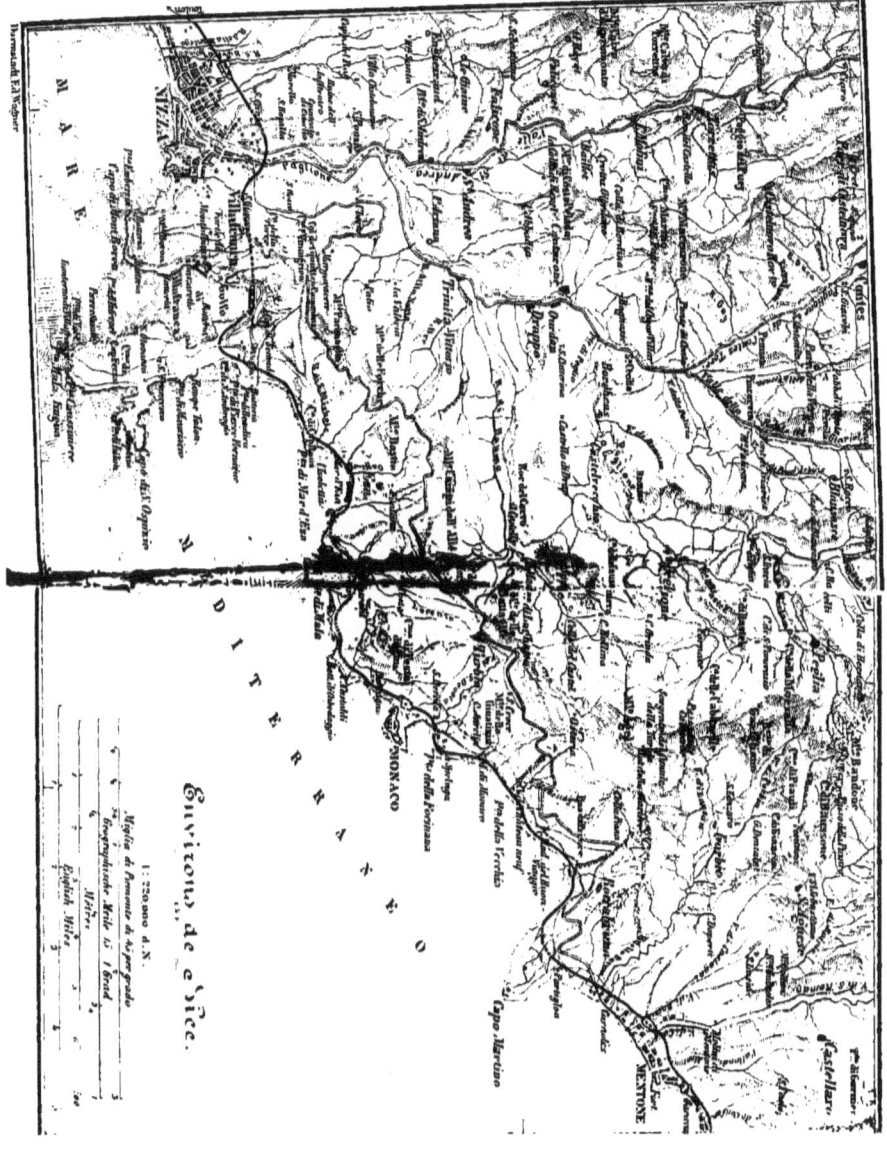

The *Villa Clary* (accessible), below Cimiès, on the road to St. André (see below), possesses the finest orange and lemon-trees at Nice and a number of rare plants.

A good carr.-road ascends on the r. bank of the Paglione to the (40 min.) monastery of **St. Pons**, founded in 775 on the spot where St. Pontius, a Roman senator, suffered martyrdom in 261. It was destroyed by the Saracens in 890, and the present edifice erected in 999. Here in 1388 the treaty was concluded by which the County of Nice was annexed to the Duchy of Savoy. The château of **St. André** (Restaurant, closed in summer) which is reached in $1/2$ hr. more, erected in the 17th cent., is now unoccupied. It stands on an eminence, at the base of which ($1/4$ hr. walk) is the grotto *les Cluses de St. André*, or rather a natural bridge over a brook, crossed by the road. An avenue of cypresses leads from the château to the grotto (15 min.).

The traveller may extend his excursion still farther in this direction. Beyond the château of St. André the road enters a dreary and desolate rocky gorge, almost entirely destitute of vegetation, lying between *Mont Chauve* (or *Monte Calvo*, p. 102) and *Mont Maccaron*. Beyond it, cultivated land is again reached. The road next reaches the antiquated village of **Torretta** (7 M. from Nice, carr. 10 fr.), with the picturesque ruin of that name *(Fr. La Tourette)*. The tower of the castle commands a very singular survey of the sterile mountain scene, especially of Mont Chauve, the Aspremont, and the deserted village of Château Neuf (see below), high on a barren ridge of rock; to the S. Montalban and the sea.

About $1^1/2$ M. farther is the dilapidated village of **Château Neuf**, founded on the ruins of former fortifications and probably employed in the 15th and 16th cent. by the inhabitants of Nice as a place of refuge from Turkish invaders. It has recently been abandoned by most of its inhabitants on account of the want of water. This is another fine point of view.

To the E. of the harbour La Limpia rises the **Montboron**, a promontory 890 ft. in height, which separates Nice from Villafranca. The summit, reached by a bridle-path in $1^1/2$ hr., commands an extensive prospect. The mountains of Corsica are visible towards the S. in clear weather.

The Road to Villafranca (2 M.; for its commencement in Nice see Pl. G, 4), recently constructed by the French government, leads round the promontory of Montboron and passes a number of villas, the most conspicuous of which is the *Villa Smith*, a red building in the oriental style. Immediately beyond the extremity of the cape a view is obtained of the small seaport of ***Villafranca**, Fr. *Villefranche* (carr. from Nice see p. 101, rowing-boat 10 fr.), very beautifully situated on the *Bay of Villafranca*, which is enclosed by olive-clad heights (to the l. on the height rises Fort Montalban). Villafranca, which was founded in 1295 by Charles II. of Anjou, as king of Sicily, is now a French naval station, where several large vessels are generally lying at anchor. In returning to Nice the traveller should take the old road (1½ M.), which crosses the promontory and affords a fine view on the descent. Rail. stat. at Villafranca (see p. 100) close to the sea.

If the road which ascends the hill to the l. above Villafranca be followed for 1½ M. farther, a road to the r. crossing the railway by a stone bridge will lead the traveller (¾ M. farther) to **Beaulieu** (rail. stat. to the l. of the bridge, see p. 100), an insignificant village situated in the midst of rich plantations of olives, figs, carob-trees, lemons, and oranges. Many of the olive-trees are remarkably large, one of them measuring 22 ft. in circumference. Beaulieu lies in a wide bay, bounded on the S. by the long peninsula of **St. Hospice.** At the foot of the latter lies the village of *S. Giovanni*, or *St. Jean* (dear inn), 1¾ M. from Beaulieu, a favourite resort of excursionists from Nice. Tunny fishing is successfully carried on here in the months of February, March, and April. At the extremity of the peninsula are the ruins of an old Saracen castle, destroyed in 1706 under Louis XIV. (see p. 104), and the ruined chapel of St. Hospice. Instead of proceeding to St. Jean by the above route, the traveller may be ferried across the bay to the creek of *Pasbles* (60 c.), and thence cross the peninsula on foot to St. Jean.

To the W. of Nice pleasant walks are afforded by the valley of the **Magnan** (p. 103), in which a road ascends to (2 M.) the church of *La Madeleine.* The beautiful, sheltered banks of the **Var,** which falls into the Baie des Anges (p. 103) 4¾ M. to the W. of Nice, are also worthy of a visit.

Route de la Corniche by Turbia to Mentone see p. 98.
Monaco see p. 99.

17. From Nice to Turin by the Col di Tenda.

Messageries to Cuneo in 22—23 hrs. (delay is sometimes occasioned in winter by the snow on the Col di Tenda, which is crossed in sledges); Railway from Cuneo to Turin in 2½ hrs.; fares 9 fr. 60, 6 fr. 70, 4 fr. 80 c. Through-tickets for the entire journey from Nice to Turin may be procured for 32 fr., entitling the holder to a seat in the 2nd cl. of the railway.

This is a very attractive route, especially for those coming from Turin. The views during the descent from the Col di Tenda to the Mediterranean are strikingly beautiful.

The road crossing the Col di Tenda (5883 ft.) was constructed by Charles Emmanuel in 1591 and improved by Victor Amadeus III. in 1780 (as two inscriptions on the road record). It is inferior to the majority of the skilfully constructed modern Alpine roads, being in many places only 12 ft. in width, and generally unprotected by a parapet or railing. The descent is therefore somewhat unpleasant, especially at the sharp turnings on the N. E side of the mountain. During 3—4 months of the year the road is traversed by sledges only. A violent wind often prevails at] the summit of the pass, especially in the afternoon, and sometimes seriously retards the progress of the mules which are used for the journey (generally six in number, harnessed by twos). — About half way up is the opening of a tunnel, commenced by the Duchess Anne of Savoy in order to avoid the highest part of the pass. The works were stopped at the time of the French occupation in 1792 and have never been resumed. The tunnel, if completed, would be upwards of $2^1/_4$ M. in length.

The road leads from Nice on the bank of the Paglione, through the villages of *La Trinità-Vittoria*, *Drappo;* beyond the latter it crosses and quits the river.

$13^3/_4$ M. **Scarena**, Fr. *Escarène*. The road hence to Sospello traverses a sterile and unattractive district. The barren rocks which enclose the bleak valley are curiously stratified at some places. The road ascends to the *Col di Braus* (3243 ft.). To the S., on a lofty rock to the r., is seen the castle of Châtillon, or Castiglione, near Mentone. At the foot of the pass on the E. lies

$16^1/_2$ M. **Sospello**, French *Sospel* (1173 ft.) *(Hôtel Carenco)*, situated in the valley of the *Bevera* (affluent of the Roja, see below), in the midst of olive-plantations and surrounded by lofty mountains. (New road from Sospello to Mentone in course of construction.) The road now ascends to the *Col di Brouis* (2071 ft.). Near the summit of the pass a final view is obtained of the Mediterranean. District unattractive, mountains bleak and barren. Then a descent to

15 M. *Giandola* (1249 ft.) (Hôtel des Etrangers; Poste), grandly situated at the base of lofty slate-rocks. *Breglio*, a town with 2500 inhab. and the ruined castle of *Trivella*, lies lower down on the r.

The road now ascends the narrow valley of the *Roja*, which falls into the sea near Ventimiglia (p. 97). *Saorgio*, rising in terraces on a lofty rock on the r., with the ruins of a castle in the Oriental style, destroyed by the French in 1792, commands the road. On the opposite side is a monastery of considerable extent. The valley contracts, so as barely to leave room for the river and the road between the perpendicular rocks. Several small villages are situated at the points where the valley expands. Beyond *Fontana* the road crosses the Italian frontier. The southern character of the vegetation now disappears. Then *Borgo S. Dalmazzo*, with 3800 inhab., where an old abbey is fitted up as a hydropathic establishment, resorted to in summer by some of the winter residents of Nice.

$13^3/_4$ M. *Tenda* (Hôtel Royal; Hôtel Impérial) lies at the S. base of the Col di Tenda. A few fragments of the castle of the unfortunate *Beatrice di Tenda* (comp. p. 147) are picturesquely situated on a rock here.

The road traverses a dreary valley by the side of the Roja and ascends by 50 zigzags on the barren mountain, passing several refuges, to the summit of the **Col di Tenda**, or *di Cornio* (5883 ft.) where the Alpes Maritimes (W.) terminate and the Apennines (E.) begin. The view embraces the chain of the Alps from Mont Iséran to Monte Rosa; the plains of Piedmont are concealed by intervening mountains. Monte Viso is not visible from the pass itself, but is seen from a point a short distance beyond it, near the 4th Refuge. The descent is very steep. The road follows the course of the *Vermanagna* to

22 M. *Limone* (3282 ft.) (Hôtel de la Poste), an Italian excise-station, and then becomes more level. The valley of the Vermanagna, which is now traversed, is at some places enclosed by wooded heights, at others by precipitous limestone cliffs. To the l. rises the magnificent pyramid of the *Monte Viso* (12,582 ft.).

9½ M. *Robillante*.

11 M. **Cuneo**, or *Coni* (1497 ft.) *(Hôtel de la Poste; Hôtel de Londres)*, a town with 23,000 inhab., at the confluence of the *Stura* and the *Gesso*, was once strongly fortified. After the battle of Marengo (p. 146) the works were dismantled in accordance with a decree of the three consuls (at the same time as the citadels of Milan and Tortona and the fortifications of Ceva and Turin) and converted into pleasure-grounds. In the principal street are arcades with shops on either side. The *Franciscan Church*, like most churches of this order beyond the Alps, is in the Gothic style (12th cent.), which was regarded by the Italians as the architecture most expressive of the simplicity and austerity inculcated by the Franciscans. — Cuneo is a great depôt for wares on their route from Nice to N. Italy and Switzerland. A considerable fair is held here in autumn. — Pleasant walk to the *Madonna degli Angeli*, at the confluence of the Gesso and the Stura.

About 7 M. S. E. of Cuneo, in the Val Pésio, is the romantically situated **Certosa di Val Pésio**, now employed as a hydropathic establishment, also frequented as quarters for the summer by those in search of retirement. — In the Val di Gesso, about 10 M. S. W. of Cuneo, are the Baths of Valdieri, the waters of which somewhat resemble those of Aix-les-Bains in Savoy (p. 30).

The Railway to Turin intersects the fertile plain, bounded on the W. by the Alpes Maritimes and, farther distant, the Cottian Alps, and on the E. by the Apennines. *Centallo*, the first station, with 4900 inhab., possesses remnants of mediæval walls and towers. Next stat. *La Maddalena;* then **Fossano**, an episcopal residence, on the l. bank of the *Stura*, beautifully situated on an eminence, with ramparts and a mediæval castle.

Savigliano *(Corona)* is a pleasant town on the *Macra*, enclosed by old fortifications. The principal church contains pictures by

Mulinari (1621—93), a native of Savigliano, surnamed *Caraccino*, as an imitator of Caracci.

Branch Line W. to Saluzzo (in 1/2 hr.; fares 1 fr. 80, 1 fr. 25, 90 c.), capital of the province (formerly of a marquisate) of that name, with 15,814 inhab. The higher part of the town, with its precipitous streets, affords a fine prospect over the Piedmontese plain. Saluzzo was the birthplace of *Silvio Pellico* (p. 196), to whom a monument was erected here in 1863.

Next stat. *Cavaller Maggiore*, formerly fortified.

Branch Line to Alessandria in 5 hrs.; fares 10 fr. 80, 7 fr. 55, 5 fr. 40 c. Stat. *Madonna-Pilone;* then **Brà**, a prosperous town with 12,946 inhab. (staple commodities cattle, corn, and wine). The church of *Sta. Chiara* was erected in 1742 by Vettone in the richest style of that period. Next stations *S. Vittoria*, where the line reaches the *Tanaro; Monticelli, Musolto;* the Tanaro is crossed, and **Alba**, with 9336 inhab., reached. The cathedral of *S. Lorenzo* dates from the 15th cent. Stations *Nejve, Castagnole, Costigliole, S. Stefano-Belbo*, on the river of that name, the valley of which the train traverses for a considerable distance; *Canelli, Calamandrana*, and *Nizza di Monferrato*, whence a good road leads to Acqui (p. 146). Stat. *Incisa*, a considerable distance from the railway, is situated on the Belbo. Then *Castelnuovo, Bruno, Bergamasco, Origlio, Cantalupo* and **Alessandria**, see p. 145.

Near the next stat. *Racconigi* is a royal château, once a favourite residence of Charles Albert (d. 1849), who caused it to be restored and embellished, and furnished with pleasant grounds. Stat. **Carmagnola**, a town with 12,894 inhab., was the birthplace (1390) of the celebrated military commander *Francesco Bussone*, son of a swine-herd, and usually termed *Count of Carmagnola*, who reconquered a considerable part of Lombardy and the possessions of Giangaleazzo for Duke Filippo Maria Visconti. He afterwards became an object of suspicion to the duke and fled to Venice, where he was elected generalissimo of the army, with which he conquered Brescia and Bergamo and won the battle of Macalo (1427). His fidelity being again suspected, he was recalled to Venice by the Council of Ten and received with great pomp. On the departure of the army, however, he was thrown into prison, put to the torture, and on May 5th, 1432, beheaded between the two columns in the Piazzetta (p. 196). Bussone's brief and chequered career is the subject of a tragedy by Manzoni. — (Railway from Carmagnola S. to Savona, p. 95, to join the Genoa and Nice line, in course of construction.)

Stat. *Villastellone*.

A road leads hence W., crossing the Po, to the town of **Carignano** (7800 inhab.), on the high road from Turin to Nice, 4 1/2 M. distant. Several of the churches are interesting. *S. Giovanni Battista* was erected by Count Alfieri. *Sta. Maria delle Grazie* contains the monument of Bianca Palæologus, daughter of William IV., Marquis of Montferrat, and wife of Duke Charles I., at whose court the 'Chevalier Bayard' was educated. Carignano, under the title of a principality, was an appanage of Thomas Francis (d. 1656), fourth son of Charles Emmanuel I., and ancestor of the present royal family. Prince Eugene, uncle of the king, is entitled 'Prince of Carignano.'

At stat. *Trufarello* the line unites with that from Turin to Alessandria. Journey hence to

Turin see p. 85.

18. From Turin to Milan by Novara.

Railway in $3^3/_4$—$5^1/_2$ hrs.; fares 16 fr. 95, 11 fr. 95, 8 fr. 55 c. — The seats on the left afford occasional glimpses of the Alps. — Fiacres and omnibuses see pp. 72, 112.

The *Dora Riparia* is crossed, then, beyond the stat. of *Succursale di Torino* and *Settimo*, the *Stura*, farther on the *Malon* and *Orco*, all of them tributaries of the *Po*, the l. bank of which is skirted by the line. Stat. *Brandizzo*.

Chivasso *(Moro)* lies near the influx of the Orco into the Po. Branch-line hence to *Ivrea*, see p. 80. Beyond stat. *Torrazza di Verolan* the *Dora Baltea* (p. 80), a torrent descending from Mont Blanc, is crossed. Several unimportant stations, beyond which the line turns to the N.E.

Stat. *Santhià* possesses a church, restored in 1862 with great taste, and containing a picture by Gaud. Ferrari in 10 sections.

Branch Line N. to Biella in 1 hr., by *Saluzzola* and *Candelo*. **Biella** *(Albergo della Testa Grigia; Italia)*, an industrial town and seat of a bishop, possesses streets with arcades and a fine cathedral in a spacious Piazza, where the episcopal palace and seminary are also situated. The palaces of the old town, rising picturesquely on the hill, are now tenanted by the humbler classes. Celebrated pilgrimage-church of the *Madonna d'Oropa*, 8 M. farther up the valley (omnibus thither). On the way to it two admirably situated hydropathic establishments are passed.

The line skirts the ancient high road. Stat. *S. Germano*; then **Vercelli** *(Tre Re; Leone d'Oro; Posta)*, an episcopal residence with 19,352 inhab. The church of *S. Cristoforo* contains pictures by G. Ferrari and B. Luini. *S. Caterina* also contains a work of Ferrari. The library of the cathedral contains a number of rare and ancient MSS.

Branch Line S. to Valenza (p. 145) in $1^1/_4$—$1^1/_2$ hr., fares 4 fr. 65, 3 fr. 25, 2 fr. 35 c. Stat. *Asigliano, Pertengo, Balzola*; near **Casale** the Po is crossed; next stat. *Borgo S. Martino, Giarole, Valenza*.

The train crosses the *Sesia* (p. 144), which descends from Monte Rosa. To the l. rise the Alps, among which the magnificent Monte Rosa group is especially conspicuous. Stations *Borgo Vercelli, Ponzana*, and

Novara *(*Rail. Restaurant; Tre Re)*, a fortress and episcopal residence (14,395 inhab.), commanded by the stately tower of the church of S. Gaudenzio, which was erected by Pellegrini about 1560 and contains several good pictures by Gaudenzio Ferrari. The tower, ascended by 300 steps, commands a very extensive prospect, especially picturesque towards the Alps. The *Cathedral*, a Romanesque structure with nave and double aisles, connected with the Baptistery by an atrium or entrance-court, is a picturesque pile. The market-place is surrounded by colonnades. The whole town, with its Italian architecture and numerous shops, is attractive and interesting. In the Corso Cavour, at the entrance to the town from the station, stands a *Monument of Cavour*, by Dini, erected in 1863; near the Porta Mortara another to *Charles*

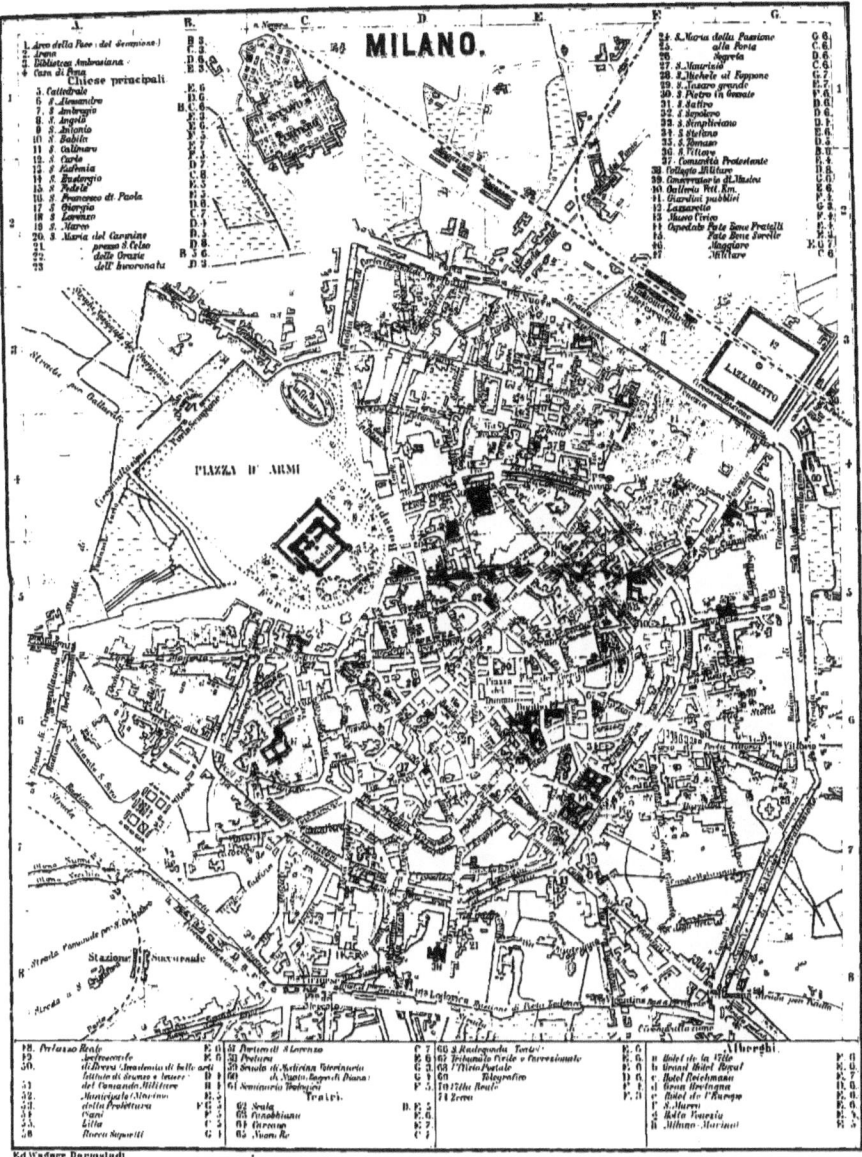

Albert. Novara was the scene of a victory gained by the Austrians under Hess over the Piedmontese in 1849, in consequence of which Charles Albert abdicated.

The celebrated philosopher *Petrus Lombardus* (d. 1164 as Bishop of Paris), surnamed the 'Magister Sententiarum' and a pupil of Abælard, was born near Novara about 1120.

Branch Line to Gozzano from Novara in $1^1/_4$ hr.; fares 4 fr., 2 fr. 80 c., 2 fr. — Stations *Caltignaga*, *Momo*, *Borgomanĕro* (a thriving town with 7800 inhab.), *Gozzano* (near it *Bolzano*, an episcopal château with a church and seminary); diligence hence to Orta and Omegna (see p. 143).

At Novara the Turin and Milan line is crossed by that from Arona to Genoa (R. 25). Stat. *Trecate*. Near stat. *S. Martino* the line crosses the Ticino by a broad and handsome stone bridge of 11 arches, which the Austrians partially destroyed before the battle of Magenta, but not sufficiently to prevent the passage of the French. Traces of the inundation of the autumn of 1868 are still visible near the bridge.

Farther on, the *Naviglio Grande* (p. 113), a canal connecting Milan with the Ticino and the Lago Maggiore, is crossed. On the r. before stat. *Magenta* is reached is a monument erected to Napoleon III. in 1862, to commemorate the victory gained by the French and Sardinians over the Austrians on June 4th, 1859, in consequence of which the latter were compelled to evacuate the whole of Lombardy. The French General Mac Mahon, who distinguished himself here, was shortly afterwards created marshal and Duke of Magenta. A number of hillocks with crosses in a low-lying field opposite the station mark the graves of those who fell in the struggle. A monument to commemorate the battle was inaugurated in 1862. On an eminence in the burial-ground a small chapel has been erected.

Next stations *Vittuone* and *Rhò* (p. 142). The line intersects numerous fields of rice, which are kept under water during two months in the year, and soon reaches **Milan** (see below).

19. Milan, Ital. *Milano*, Lat. *Mediolanum*.

Arrival. The railway-station, an imposing structure, is decorated with handsome frescoes. The arrangements are also admirable. Omnibuses from most of the hotels are in waiting; charge generally 1 fr. each passenger. Fiacre from the station to any part of the town 1 fr., at night 1 fr. 25 c., each article of luggage 25 c. Omnibus to the cathedral 25 c. Porterage to the town for luggage under 100 lbs. 50 c. according to tariff.

Hotels. *Hôtel de la Ville (Pl. a), Corso Vittorio Emanuele, opposite the church of S. Carlo, R. 3, A. 1, B. $1^1/_2$, D. $4^1/_2$ fr.; on the ground-floor the large *Café Europa*; *Hôtel Cavour, in the Piazza Cavour, near the station, new and quiet, R. from 2 fr., D. 5 fr.; *Grand Hôtel Royal (Pl. b), R. $2^1/_2$, L. 1, D. 4, B. $1^1/_2$, A. 1 fr.; Hôtel Reichmann (Pl. c), Corso di Porta Romana, R. $2^1/_2$, B. 1, D. $3^1/_2$, A. 1 fr., L. 75 c.; *Gran Bretagna (Pl. d), similar charges; *Hôtel de Milan, Corsia del Giardino 22, new, R. $2^1/_2$, A. 1 fr., L. 75 c.; *Hôtel de l'Europe, Corso Vittorio Emanuele 9; *Roma, Corso Vittorio Emanuele 7, R. 2 fr., A. 75, L. 75 c., with restaurant, no table d'hôte; Francia, Corso Vitt. Emanuele.

112 *Route 19.* MILAN. *Theatres.*

— Albergo Manin, Via Manin 15; S. Marco; *Bella Venezia, Piazza S. Fedele; *Ancora; *Pozzo, Via Asole 8, near the Ambrosiana, R. 1¹|₂ —3, B. 1¹|₂, D. 2³|₄, L. ¹|₂, A. ³|₄ fr.; Trois Suisses; Pension Suisse, commercial. — Albergo Firenze, Via Principe Umberto near the station; Borsa, Via Rebecchino 16; Aquila, Via S. Margarita, moderate; Leone; Passerella; Bissone; Rebecchino; Agnello, Corso Vitt. Emanuele 4, all in the Italian style, with restaurants.

Restaurants *(Trattorie*, comp. Introd. V). *Cova, with garden, near the Scala, concerts on Sund. and Thursd.; *Borsa, near the Scala, expensive; Accademia, near the latter; Biffi, Gnocchi, in the Galleria Vittorio Emanuele (see below); *Rebecchino, near the Piazza del Duomo; Rinascimento, with garden, by the Porta Venezia; Milano, Via del Giardino. Isola Botta, outside the town, by the Triumphal Arch (p. 119), a favourite resort on holidays. Dinner-hours 3—7 p. m.

Cafés (comp. Introd. V). Café in the *Giardino Pubblico* (p. 120); Europa; *Merlo (best ices), Corso Vitt. Emanuele; *Biffi, *Gnocchi, both in the Galleria Vittorio Emanuele; Cova (see above); Martini near the Scala; delle Colonne, Corso Venezia 1; Capello, Via Capello 14 etc. A déjeûner à la fourchette may be procured at most of the cafés; also Vienna (35 c.) and Chiavenna beer (30 c.). Ices *(sorbetto)* after 4 p. m. and *granita* (half-frozen) at an earlier hour are one of the chief specialties of the cafés. — *Beer* at the Birraria Nazionale, opposite the cathedral, and the Birraria della Scala, adjoining the Scala.

Baths, Corso Vittorio Emanuele 26. *Swimming-bath* outside the Porta Venezia.

Fiacres (*'Broughams'*). Drive *(corsa)* of less than ¹|₂ hr. between 6 a. m. and 1 a. m. 75 c., between 1 and 6 a. m. 1 fr. 25 c., each article of luggage 25 c. From the stat. to the town or vice-versâ 1, at night 1¹|₄ fr.

Omnibuses from the Piazza del Duomo to the different gates 10 c., to the railway-station 25 c.; the most frequented are the '*Porta Ticinese*' and the '*Porta Garibaldi*' lines.

Railway to Camerlata (Como, R. 20), Novara (Genoa, Turin, Arona, R. 18), Venice (R. 27), Pavia, and Piacenza (Bologna, Ancona, R. 40).

Diligence *(Impresa Merzario*, Via di S. Dalmazio 2, near the Scala) daily: to *Coire* by the *Splügen* once in 25 hrs. (RR. 20, 21, 5), by the *Bernardino* in 26¹|₂ hrs. (RR. 23, 4, 6); to *Lucerne* by the *St. Gotthard* once in 27¹|₂ hrs. (RR. 20, 22, 4); to *Sion* by the *Simplon* once in 29 hrs. (RR. 25, 19, 3).

Post Office (Pl. 53), near the cathedral, at the back of the Palazzo Reale, Via Rastrelli 4919, open from 8 a. m. to 9 p. m. — **Telegraph Office** by the *Borsa*, Piazza dei Mercanti (Pl. 8).

Theatres (comp. Introd. VI). *Teatro della Scala* (Pl. 63); *alla Canobbiana* (Pl. 64), only during the Carnival, both with ballet; *S. Radegonda* (Pl. 66), operas, a theatre of the second class; *Carcăno* (Pl. 65), generally operas. Performances at the *Scala theatre during the autumn and Carnival only; arrangements of the interior worthy of inspection (1 fr.).

Shops. *Photographs, books, maps:* Artaria e Figlio, Via S. Margherita. — *Silks:* Manfredi, Zanardi, et Cie., Via Rastrelli, near the post-office. — *Haberdashers:* Martinelli e Landi, Corso Vittorio Emanuele 28.

English Church Service, Vicolo San Giovanni della Conca 12.

Principal Attractions: Cathedral, ascend tower; Galleria Vittorio Emanuele; Brera (picture-gallery); Arco della Pace; S. Maria delle Grazie and Leonardo da Vinci's Last Supper; S. Ambrogio, the oldest, and S. Alessandro, the most sumptuous of the churches; Piazza de' Mercanti; between 6 and 7 p. m. walk in Corso Vittorio Emanuele or outside the Porta Venezia.

Milan, surnamed '*la grande*', entirely reconstructed after its total destruction in 1162 by the Emp. Fred. Barbarossa, is the capital of Lombardy and one of the wealthiest manufacturing towns (silk being one of the staple commodities) in Italy. The population, exclusive of the garrison and the suburbs, is 212,240;

the circumference of the city is upwards of 9 M. It is situated on the insignificant river *Olona*, which however is connected by means of the *Naviglio Grande* (p. 111) with the Ticino and Lago Maggiore, by the *Naviglio di Pavia* (p. 147) with the Ticino and the Po, and by the *Naviglio della Martesana* with the Adda (p. 121), Lake of Como, and Po.

The favourable situation of Milan in the centre of Lombardy has always secured for it a high degree of prosperity. Under the Romans it was one of the largest cities in Italy, but its repeated destruction has almost entirely annihilated all the monuments of that period. Its heroic struggles against the German emperors are well known. With the exception of S. Ambrogio and a few other churches, the city was totally destroyed in 1162 by the emperor Frederick Barbarossa, but in 1167 rebuilt by the allied cities of Cremona, Brescia, Bergamo, and Mantua. It was subsequently governed by the Visconti (1312—1447), then by the Sforza family (1447—1535). Milan with the rest of Lombardy afterwards fell into the hands of the Spaniards, and in 1714 became Austrian. In 1796 it became the capital of the 'Cisalpine Republic', then (till 1815) that of the kingdom of Italy. The bloody insurrection of May 17th, 1848, compelled the Austrians to evacuate the city, and after they regained possession of it frequent manifestations of popular feeling were exhibited. No town in Italy has improved since the events of 1859 in such a marked degree as Milan.

The old part of the town, a portion of which consists of narrow and irregular streets, is enclosed by canals, beyond which suburbs (borghi), named after the different gates, have sprung up. Of the latter, eleven in number, the principal are the Porta Venezia at the extremity of the handsome new Corso Venezia, the prolongation of which, the Corso Vittorio Emanuele, the principal street of Milan, leads to the cathedral; the Porta Sempione (p. 119) and between these the Porta Garibaldi, erected 1828, so named and furnished with an appropriate inscription in 1859.

The most celebrated of the 80 Churches of Milan is the ****Cathedral** (*Cattedrale*, Pl. 5) (travellers are cautioned against engaging a valet-de-place to accompany them, as they will on entering be consigned into the hands of another member of the fraternity, and thus have to pay both), dedicated to '*Mariae Nascenti*', as the inscription on the façade announces, and as the gilded statue on the tower (erected under Napoleon I.) over the dome also indicates. It is regarded by the Milanese as the eighth wonder of the world, and is, next to St. Peter's at Rome and the cathedral at Seville, the largest church in Europe. The interior is 477 ft. in length, 186 ft. in breadth; nave 158 ft. in height, 35 ft. in breadth. The dome is 214 ft. in height, the tower 360 ft. above the pavement. The roof is adorned with 98 Gothic turrets, and the exterior with no fewer than 4500 statues in marble. The structure was commenced by Enrico Gamodia (Heinrich Arler of Gmünd) in 1386, one year after the cathedral of Prague had been completed by Peter Arler of Gmünd. The principal parts of it were finished at the close of the 15th cent.

In 1805 Napoleon caused the works to be recommenced, and at the present day additions and repairs are constantly in progress.

After the cathedral of Seville, it is the largest existing example of (Italian) Gothic architecture. It consists of nave with double aisles, and transept with aisles. It is supported by 52 pillars, each 15 ft. in diameter, the summits of which are adorned with canopied niches with statues instead of capitals. The pavement consists entirely of mosaic in marble of different colours. The vaulting is skilfully painted in imitation of open-work in stone.

By the principal inner portal are two huge monolith columns of granite from the quarries of Baveno (see p. 139). The band of brass in the pavement close to the entrance indicates the line of the meridian. By the W. wall of the S. (r.) transept is the *Monument which Pope Pius IV., uncle of S. Carlo Borromeo, caused to be executed by *Leone Leoni* in 1564, to the memory of his brothers Giacomo and Gabriele Medici. The colossal statue in the middle represents the first of these brothers. (Tickets for the roof are obtained here.) The staircase leading to the dome is on the S. side of the S. transept. The altar of the Offering of Mary (E. wall of S. transept) is adorned with fine Reliefs by *Ag. Buzzi*; adjacent is the Statue of St. Bartholomew by *Marco Agrate*, anatomically remarkable, as the saint is represented flayed.

The door of the S. Sacristy (r. in the choir) is remarkable for its richly sculptured decorations in the Gothic style (the treasury here may be inspected, fee 1 fr.; among other valuables it contains silver statues, life-size, of S. Ambrogio and S. Carlo Borromeo, and the ring and staff of the latter). A short distance farther is the marble *Monument of Cardinal Marino Carraccioli* (d. 1538), by whom Emp. Charles V. was crowned at Aix-la-Chapelle in 1520. The stained glass in the three vast choir windows, comprising 350 representations of scriptural subjects, were executed by *Alois* and *Giov. Bertini* of Guastalla during the present century; most of them are copies from old pictures. Before the N. Sacristy is reached the visitor passes the *Statue of Pius IV.* in a sitting posture, by *Angelo Siciliano*. The door of this sacristy is also adorned with fine sculptures in marble.

By the E. wall of the N. transept is an altar with the Crucifixion in high relief, by *Ant. Prestinari*. In the centre of the N. transept, in front of the altar, is a valuable *Bronze Candelabrum*, decorated with jewels, presented by Giov. Batt. Trivulzio in 1562.

At the corner of the N. transept and aisle is an Altar-piece, painted in 1500 by *Fed. Baroccio*, representing S. Ambrogio releasing Emp. Theodosius from ecclesiastical penalties. Upon the adjoining altar of St. Joseph the Nuptials of Mary, by *F. Zuccheri*. The following chapel contains the old wooden *Crucifix* which S. Carlo Borromeo, barefooted, bore in 1576 when engaged in his missions of mercy during the plague. Beneath the 5th (from the entrance) window of the N. aisle is a Monument, with relief of the Virgin in the centre, by *Marchesi*; r. and l. the two SS. John by *Monti*. Not far from the N. side door is the *Font*, consisting of a sarcophagus of porphyry beneath a canopy. It was originally the sarcophagus of S. Dionysius, but was appropriated to its present use by S. Carlo Borromeo. The canopy is by *Pellegrini*.

In front of the choir, beneath the dome, is the subterranean *Cappella S. Carlo Borromeo*, sumptuously decorated with gold and precious stones (accessible in summer 5—10, in winter 7—10 a. m.; at other times 1 fr.; for showing the relics of the saint 5 fr.).

No one should omit to undertake the ascent of the *Roof and Tower of the Cathedral. The staircase ascends from the corner of the r. transept; ticket 20 c.; map of town and environs $1^1/_2$ fr., which will prove more useful than the services of a commissionaire (1/2 fr.). The visitor is recommended to ascend at once to the highest gallery of the tower (by 194 steps in the interior and 300 on the exterior of the edifice) and after having surveyed the prospect to descend and examine the details of the architecture of this vast marble structure. A watchman at the summit possesses a good telescope, by means of which the statues, especially the four by Canova, should be inspected. The cathedral is opened at 5 a. m. The earlier the ascent of the tower is undertaken, the greater the probability of a fine view of the Alps.

View. To the extreme l., S. W., Monte Viso, then Mont Cenis (p. 32); farther distant, between these two, the Superga (p. 80) near Turin; Mont Blanc, Great St. Bernard; Monte Rosa, the most conspicuous of all; l. of the latter the prominent Matterhorn; then the Cima di Jazi, Strahlhorn, and Mischabel; N.W. the Monte Leone by the Simplon (p. 37); the Bernese Alps; N. the summits of the St. Gotthard (p. 42) and Splügen (p. 48), and E. in the distance the peak of the Ortler (p. 54). S. the Certosa of Pavia (p. 147) is visible, farther E. the towers and domes of Pavia itself, in the background the Apennines.

To the S., opposite the cathedral, is situated the *Palazzo Reale* (Pl. 45); on the N. side is the dog and bird market.

The *Piazza del Duomo* forms the central point of the traffic of Milan. It was formerly confined between narrow lanes, but has recently been greatly extended by their removal. Farther improvements are contemplated, with a view to impart a more uniform appearance to the Piazza and render it a more worthy adjunct of the cathedral. The principal work which has been undertaken and completed since the emancipation of Milan from the Austrian yoke is the *Galleria Vittorio Emanuele* (Pl. 40), connecting the Piazza del Duomo with the Scala. This is the most extensive and attractive of all the European structures of the description. It was commenced in March, 1865, by the architect *Mengoni*, and inaugurated in Sept., 1867. The expense of the construction amounted to 8 mill fr. (320,000 *l.*). Length 320 yds., breadth 16 yds., height 94 ft. The form is that of a Latin cross, with an octagon in the centre, over which rises a cupola 180 ft. in height. The decorations are well-executed and bear testimony to the good taste of the Milanese. It is adorned with 24 statues of celebrated Italians: at the entrance from the Piazza del Duomo, Arnold of Brescia and G. B. Vico; in the octagon r. Cavour, Emanuel Philibert, Vittore Pisano, Gian Galeazzo Visconti; Romagnosi, Pier Capponi, Macchiavelli, Marco Polo; Raphael, Galileo, Dante, Michael Angelo; Volta, Lanzone, Giov. da Procida, Beccaria; at the r. lateral issue Beno de' Gozzadini and Columbus, at the l. lateral issue Ferruccio and Monti; at the entrance from the Scala, Savonarola and Ugo Foscolo. The frescoes of the upper part of the octagon represent the four quarters of the globe; on the entrance-arches are Science, Industry, Art, and Agriculture.

8*

The gallery, which contains attractive shops, is lighted in the evening by 2000 gas-jets.

In the Piazza della Scala, where the theatre of that name is situated, it is intended to erect a monument to Leonardo da Vinci, the pedestal of which will be adorned with statues of his four pupils Salaino, Beltraffio, Marco da Oggionno, and Cesare da Sesto. Leonardo (1452—1519) of Florence was the founder of the Lombard school of painting and the most illustrious master of whom the Milanese can boast.

*S. Ambrogio (Pl. 7), situated in the distant W. quarter of the city, founded by St. Ambrose in the 4th cent. on the ruins of a temple of Bacchus, dates in its present form from the 12th cent. The style is Romanesque, but the effect is greatly marred by the pointed vaulting. In front of the church is a fine oblong forecourt or quadriporticus of the 9th cent., surrounded by arcades containing ancient tombstones, inscriptions, and half-obliterated frescoes. The gates of this church are said to be those which St. Ambrose closed against the Emp. Theodosius after the cruel massacre of Thessalonica; a portrait of the saint is on the l. side of the principal entrance. The Lombard kings and German emperors formerly caused themselves to be crowned here with the iron crown, which since the time of Frederick Barbarossa has been preserved at Monza (p. 121).

The interior is at present undergoing restoration. The 2nd chapel on the r. is decorated with frescoes by *Gaudenzio Ferrari*, representing the Bearing of the Cross, the Mourning of the Virgin, and the Descent from the Cross The 4th chapel on the r., the Cappella delle Dame, contains a kneeling *statue of St. Marcellina, by *Pacetti*. In the 7th chapel a Madonna with St. John and Jerome, by *Luini*. Beneath the pulpit is an early Christian sarcophagus of the 6th cent., said to be that of Stilicho. The canopy over the high altar is borne by four columns of porphyry; in front of it is the tombstone of Emp. Lewis II. (d. 875). The choir contains an ancient episcopal throne. The high altar is furnished with a cover *(paliotto)* in enamel of the 9th cent., a master piece of its time, executed by Wolsinius (5 fr. are exacted for showing it). By the high altar is an *Ecce Homo, painted al fresco by *Luini*, and preserved under glass. In the Tribuna *mosaics of the 9th cent., earlier than those at St. Mark's in Venice: Christ in the centre, at the sides the history of Ambrose. — At the entrance to the crypt Christ among the scribes, a fresco by *Borgognone*. The crypt contains the tombs of SS. Ambrose, Protasius, and Gervasius.

S. Alessandro (Pl. 6), the most sumptuously decorated church in Milan, was erected in 1602. The high altar is richly adorned with precious stones, but destitute of works of art.

S. Carlo Borromeo (Pl. 12), in the Corso Vittorio Emanuele, is a rotunda in the style of the Pantheon at Rome, 150 ft. in height, consecrated 1747. It contains two groups in marble by *Marchesi*, and modern stained glass by *Jose Bertini* (the finest r. of the entrance: S. Carlo Borromeo among those sick of the plague).

The church of *S. Lorenzo (Pl. 18) is the most ancient structure in Milan; the interior is supposed to have appertained to the Thermae, or to a temple erected by the Emp. Maximian. Although frequently altered at subsequent periods, it is still an object of great interest to architects. It is an octagon surmounted by a dome. On the four principal sides are semi-circular apses in two stories, each supported by four columns. The whole is characterized by simple dignity. — R. of the church is the *Chapel of St. Aquilinus*, containing very ancient mosaics and the sarcophagus of the founder, the Gothic king Ataulph (d. 416). — The extensive *Colonnade of 16 Corinthian columns in the same street also appertained originally to the same ancient structure.

*S. Maria delle Grazie (Pl. 22), near the W. gate *(Porta Magenta)*, an abbey-church of the 15th cent., was partially erected by *Bramante* (choir, transept, and dome). The 4th chapel on the r. contains frescoes by *Gaudenzio Ferrari* (Crucifixion, Christ crowned with thorns, Christ scourged), and an altar-piece (Descent from the Cross) by *Caravaggio*. In the 6th chapel frescoes by *Fiamingo*. R. by the organ a Madonna by *Luini*. In the sacristy two frescoes by *Luini*. St. John, altar-piece by *Oggionno*.

In the S.E. angle of the small piazza to the N. of this church is the entrance to the refectory of the former convent of *Sta. Maria delle Grazie* (now used as a cavalry-barrack), containing the celebrated **Last Supper of *Leonardo da Vinci* (the 'custode del cenacolo' is generally in the refectory). The picture is unfortunately in bad preservation, chiefly from having been painted on the wall in oils. A fresco by *Donato Montorfano* (Crucifixion) of 1495, opposite the Last Supper, is in a much better condition.

S. Maria di S. Celso (Pl. 21), near the *Porta Lodovica*, also erected by *Bramante*, contains a Baptism of Christ (behind the high altar) by *Gaudenzio Ferrari*, a Madonna adoring the Child, surrounded by John the Baptist, St. Rochus and the founders of the picture, by *Borgognone* (1st chapel l.) etc. Adjacent to this church is *S. Celso*, a Romanesque structure, but partially removed in 1826.

S. Maurizio (Pl. 27), or *Monastero Maggiore*, a small church in the Corso di Magenta, contains *frescoes by Luini in the nave and choir (the best are the two adjoining the high altar).

The picture-gallery in the opposite *Palace of the Duca Litta* was dispersed on the death of the proprietor in 1866.

Of the palaces of Milan, the following deserve special mention: *Palazzo Marino* (Pl. 52), now Municipio, a colossal structure adjoining the Scala; *Palazzo Ciani* (Pl. 54, Corso Venezia 59 —61), an edifice in terra cotta, completed in 1861, adorned with heads of Victor Emmanuel, Garibaldi, Napoleon, etc.; *Palazzo Saporiti* (Pl. 56), with façade adorned with columns and statues.

The *Brera (Pl. 50) or *Palazzo delle Scienze ed Arti*, accessible daily in summer 9—4, in winter 9—3, on Sundays 12—4 o'clock, formerly a *Jesuits' College*, contains the *Picture Gallery* and *Library of the Academy* (170,000 vols., about 1000 MSS.), and a collection of *Casts* from the antique. The court contains statues in marble of the political economist Count *Pietro Verri*, the architect Marchese *Luigi Cagnola* (d. 1833), *Tommaso Grossi*, the mathematicians *Gabrio Piola* and *Fra Bonaventura Cavalieri* (d. 1647), and of *Carlo Ottavio Castiglione;* in the centre of the court a bronze statue of Napoleon I., as a Roman emperor, with a long staff in his left hand and in the right a statue of Victory, by *Canova*, considered one of his finest works. By the staircase, to the l., the statue of the celebrated jurist *Beccaria* (d. 1794), who in his treatise '*dei delitti e delle pene*' was the first to call in question the justice of capital punishment; to the r., that of the satirist *Gius. Parini* (d. 1799), professor of rhetoric at the college of the Brera. On the wall of a back-staircase to the library is the Marriage of Cana, a fresco by *Calisto Piazza da Lodi*.

The ***Picture Gallery** *(Pinacoteca)* in 13 rooms, contains upwards of 400 oil paintings, and admirable frescoes which have been carefully detached from old monastery-walls. Each picture is furnished with the name of the painter.

1st and 2nd Ante-Chambers: Frescoes by *Luini*, *Ferrari*, *Bramantino*, and *Marco da Oggionno*. *Luini:* 20. and 31. Angels; 33. Nativity; 34. Interment of St. Catharine; *36. Madonna with St. Antony and St. Barbara; 50. *Gaudenzio Ferrari*, Adoration of the Magi. — Oil-paintings. 1st Saloon: 6. *Titian*, St. Jerome; 10. *Van Dyck*, Madonna and St. Antony of Padua; 18. *Domenichino*, Madonna with saints and angels; 26. *Paris Bordone*, Baptism of Christ; 36. *Dan. Crespi*, Bearing of the Cross; 47. *Tintoretto*, Pietà. — 2nd S. (l.): 45. *Garofalo*, Mourning for the dead Saviour; 56. *Moretto*, Madonna among clouds with three saints; *58. *Timoteo Vite da Urbino*, Annunciation; 60. *Palma Vecchio*, Adoration of the Magi; 61. *Paolo Veronese*, Marriage of Cana; 71. *P. Veronese*, St. Cornelius, the pope and other saints. — 3rd S.: *90. *Gentile Bellini*, Preaching of St. Mark; 105. *Mantegna*, Saints; 112. *Paolo Veronese*, Christ with the Pharisces; 117. *Martino da Udine*, St. Ursula and her virgin followers; 118. *Garofalo*, Crucifixion. — 4th S.: 142. *Franc. Francia*, Annunciation; 144. *Vittore Carpaccio*, St. Stephen and scribes; 188. *Giov. Bellini*, Pietas. — 5th S.: nothing of importance. — 6th S.: **230. *Raphael's* far-famed Sposalizio (Marriage of the Virgin), an early work of the master, and strongly resembling the Sposalizio of Perugino, now at Caen; 251. *Rembrandt*, Portrait; 184. *Cesare da Sesto*, Madonna; 247. *Luini*, Madonna; 416. Drawing of the head of Christ for Leonardo da Vinci's Last Supper (p. 117), preserved under glass; 254. *Velasquez*, Sleeping monk; *214. *Guercino*, Abraham and Hagar. — 8th. S.: 237. *Guido Reni*, Peter and Paul; 226. *Mantegna*, Body of Christ, drawing under glass. — 9th S.: *136. *Van Dyck*, Female portrait; *279. *Sassoferrato*, Madonna and Child; 257. *Bonifazio*, Moses and Pharaoh's daughter; *Lotto*, three admirable portraits. — 10th S.: 280. *Luca Giordano*, Madonna and Saints; 429. *Guido Reni*, Madonna (a copy); 290. *Federigo Baroccio*, Martyrdom of St. Vitus; 294. *Pietro da Cortona*, Madonna with saints; 332. *Salvator Rosa*, Landscape and hermits. — 11th S.: 342. *Marco da Oggionno*, St. Michael and Lucifer; 343. *Gaudenzio Ferrari*, Martyrdom of St. Catharine; 354. *Crespi*, Presentation in the Temple; 355. *Enea Salmeggia*, surnamed *Talpino*, Madonna with saints; 370. *Borgognone*, Assumption. — 12th and follg. S.: Modern pictures and casts.

The ground-floor contains the recently opened Museo Archeologico (10—3 daily, 50 c.; Sundays 12—4 gratis), containing a collection of ancient and mediæval sculptures and inscriptions. In the centre the *monument of Barnaba Visconti (dethroned in 1385 by his nephew Gian Galeazzo), the sarcophagus adorned with reliefs, in front the 4 Evangelists, at the back the Coronation of Mary, at the sides Crucifixion and Entombment; above is the equestrian statue of the prince, with traces of gilding. Recumbent statue of Gaston de Foix (d. 1512, see p. 256), by *Agostino Busti*, surnamed *Il Bambaja*. Marble door attributed to *Michelozzo*. — An annual exhibition of art also takes place here, generally in September.

The celebrated **Biblioteca Ambrosiana** (Pl. 3), open 10—3 o'clock (fee to the library-attendant 1 fr., to the custodian of the pictures 1 fr.; picture-gallery, or *Pinacoteca*, open to the public on Wednesdays 10—2½, entrance from the reading-room), contains 60,000 vols. and 15,000 MSS. and palimpsests, or *codices rescripti*, some of them very valuable. The library was founded in 1609 by the archbishop Cardinal Fed. Borromeo, to whom a statue was erected in front of the building in 1865.

Codice Atlantico, i. e. original drawings and MSS. of *Leonardo da Vinci*; Virgil with marginal notes by *Petrarch*; a number of miniatures; letters of S. Carlo Borromeo, Tasso, Galileo, Liguori, etc. Then, Christ crowned with thorns, al fresco, *Bernardino Luini*; Cupid in marble, *R. Schadow*; several reliefs and bust of Byron by *Thorwaldsen*; mosaics, coins, old woodcuts, and drawings by celebrated masters. On the walls above about 60 oil-paintings: *Guido Reni*, Christ on the Cross; *Titian*, Adoration of the Magi; old copy of Leonardo da Vinci's Last Supper; Spinning girl, marble statue by *Schadow*; Eve, *Barocci*; *Raphael's* cartoon for his School of Athens, and the cartoon for the battle of Constantine, a fragment; Beatrice d'Este, by *Leonardo da Vinci*, also drawings by him; three studies for *Michael Angelo's* Last Judgment; cartoon for a Sposalizio (see p. 118) by *Gaudenzio Ferrari; Luca d'Olanda (Lucas of Leyden)*, Adoration of the Magi; *Raph. Mengs*, Portrait of Pope Clement XIII.; models of obelisks and Trajan's Column at Rome. In the court Rom. inscriptions. — Fine stained glass by *Jose Bertini* (p. 116).

The **Ospedale Maggiore** (Pl. 46), a vast and remarkably fine brick structure, commenced 1457, contains no fewer than 9 courts. The principal court is extensive and surrounded by arcades. The entire edifice is covered externally with terra cotta, in a style frequently observed in other Milanese buildings.

The **Castle** (Pl. C, 4, 5), once a residence of the Visconti and Sforza, the fortifications of which have recently been strengthened, is now a barrack. By the spacious exercising-ground, or *Piazza d'Armi*, behind the castle, is the **Arena** (Pl. 2) (fee ½ fr.), a species of circus for races etc. founded by Napoleon I. The grass-seats are capable of accommodating 30,000 persons.

Opposite the castle, on the N.W. side of the Piazza d'Armi, is the ***Arco della Pace** (Pl. 1), or *Arco di Sempione*, a triumphal arch in the Roman style, commenced in 1804 by Napoleon as a termination to the Simplon route, completed by the Emp. Francis in 1830, the destination and decoration having been altered (ascended by means of 107 steps). The former inscriptions in honour of Emp. Francis have been superseded by others commemorating the emancipation of Italy in 1859. This lofty gateway, with three passages, consisting entirely of blocks of white marble, was erected by *L. Cagnola* (p. 118), and is adorned with numerous reliefs and statues.

On the platform is the goddess of Peace in a chariot with 6 horses, at the four corners Victoriæ on horseback. Side towards the town: by the inscription, on the r. and l., the river-gods of the Po and Ticino. L. beneath the cornice, the entrance of Emp. Francis into Milan in 1825, above it the battle of Kulm, below it the surrender of Dresden. R. the foundation of the Lombard and Venetian kingdom, above it the passage of the Rhine, below it the taking of Lyons, all by *Pompeo Marchesi*. Beneath the great arch the foundation of the 'Holy Alliance' in two reliefs. On the W. side the battle of Arcis-sur-Aube, E. the victory of Lyons, by *Marchesi*. Side towards the country: river-gods of the Tagliamento and Adige, by *Marchesi*. Beneath the cornice on the l. the Congress of Vienna, institution of the order of the Iron Crown, taking of Paris; r. Peace of Paris, entry of the Allies into Paris, entry of General Neipperg into Milan in 1814.

The **Giardino Pubblico** (Pl. 41) is a favourite promenade, near the *Porta Venezia*, especially frequented on Sunday afternoons. The *Corso*, or promenade of the fashionable world, is 6—7 p. m. in the Corso Vittorio Emanuele and outside the Porta Venezia.

These grounds have been enlarged by the addition of the *New Giardino Pubblico*, by the Porta Nuova, in commemoration of the liberation of Italy from the Austrian yoke, and now extend from the Porta Venezia to the Porta Nuova. They consist of fine avenues, artificial sheets of water, and even a small deerpark. On a small island is a marble statue to *Carlo Porta*, 'poeta Milanese'. In front of the entrance to the new garden rises the *Statue of Cavour* in bronze, on a lofty pedestal of granite, in front Clio entering his name on her tablets, at the back the date 1865. Several other statues also adorn the gardens.

By these grounds rises the **Museo Civico** (Pl. 43) (admission on Tuesd., Wed., and Sat. 11—3 o'clock, 50 c.; on Thursd. gratis), containing natural history collections: on the 1st floor palæontology and ethnography (also a phrenological collection of skulls), on the 2nd floor zoology. At the entrance are busts of former directors.

20. From Milan to Como. The Brianza.

Comp. Map, p. 124.

Railway from Milan to Camerlata in 1½ hr.; fares 5 fr. 45, 4 fr., 2 fr. 85 c.; omnibus thence in 20 (in the reverse direction 35) min. *to Como* and the steamboats, 50 c. Through-tickets to Como, Tremezzina, Cadenabbia, Bellaggio, Menaggio, and Colico may be purchased at the railway-station at Milan. Tickets for luggage must be given up at Camerlata; otherwise it will remain there till claimed.

The railway traverses the fertile plain, luxuriantly clothed with vineyards, mulberry-plantations, and fields of maize, and intersected by innumerable canals and cuttings for purposes of irrigation. First stat. *Sesto*.

Monza (*Palazzo Reale; *Angelo*; *Falcone*; **Albergo del Castello*) is a town with 15,587 inhab. Leaving the station and following the Corso d'Italia to the r., the traveller reaches the *Cathedral*, the principal attraction here. It was erected in the 14th cent. on the site of a church founded in 595 by the Lombard queen Theodolinda. It consists of nave and transept, and two aisles with chapels.

Interior. In the N. aisle the sarcophagus of Queen Theodolinda; in the E. transept reliefs of the 13th cent., supposed to represent the coronation of Emp. Otho III., or that of Henry III. — In a casket forming the centre of a richly decorated cross over the altar, r. of the choir, is preserved the celebrated Iron Crown, with which 34 Lombard kings were crowned. The last coronations for which this venerable relic was employed were those of the Emp. Charles V., of Napoleon in 1805, and of Emp. Ferdinand I. in 1838. It consists of a broad hoop of gold adorned with precious stones, round the interior of which is a thin strip of iron, said to have been made from a nail of the true Cross brought by the empress Helena from Palestine. In 1859 it was carried off by the Austrians, but after the peace of 1866 was restored to its former repository. — The Treasury contains several objects of historical interest: a hen with 7 chickens in gold, representing Lombardy and its 7 provinces, executed by order of Queen Theodolinda; the queen's crown, fan, and comb; two silver loaves, presented by Napoleon I. after his coronation; the cross which was placed on the breast of the Lombard kings at the moment of their coronation; goblet of Berengarius; diptychs (ivory tablets with reliefs) etc.; then, in a cabinet outside the treasury, the mummy of one of the Visconti, who died in 1413. The treasury is shown for a fee of 1 fr. for 1—2 pers.; it also contains a model of the iron crown.

The *Broletto*, or town-hall, of the 13th cent., with round arched windows and tower, is believed to be part of a palace of the Emp. Frederick I. and the Lombard kings. The royal *Summer Palace* near Monza is a large building with an extensive and beautiful park, traversed by the Lambro. The church of the *Madonna di Tirano* contains frescoes by Luini, Gaudenzio Ferrari, and Cesare da Sesto.

From Monza to Lecco omnibus twice daily. 14 M. *Carsaniga*. The beautiful hills of the Brianza to the l. (see below) are studded with country-residences of the wealthy Milanese. A bridge constructed in the 14th cent. (see p. 130) crosses the Adda where it emerges from the Lake of Lecco. 14 M. *Lecco*, see p. 130.

The hilly tract which comes in view farther on, r. of the railway, is the fertile Brianza (see below), with its numerous country-residences. The train passes through several tunnels and reaches stat. *Desio*, then **Seregno**, a town with 5000 inhab.

The Route to Bellaggio through the Brianza, strongly recommended to pedestrians, especially to those who have seen the Lake of Como from the steamboat only, is conveniently made from Seregno. The traveller should, however, drive as far as *Canzo* (p. 122), a distance of 16¼ M., and proceed thence on foot. At the station of Seregno carriages are generally in waiting to convey passengers to Canzo, fare 5—7 fr., but exorbitant demands are frequently made. An omnibus (3 fr.) runs in the morning daily, except Sundays, from Canzo to Seregno, returning in the evening; the traveller therefore who avails himself of this conveyance must pass the night at Canzo, in which case he will be enabled to start on his walk early on the following morning. A carriage-road leads from Canzo to Bellaggio, but the country is very hilly, and walking is pleasanter and hardly less expeditious than driving.

The road from Seregno to Canzo intersects the W. side of the **Brianza**, an undulating, grassy, partially wooded, and extremely fertile tract, 12 M. in length, 6 M. in breadth, extending between the *Lambro* and the *Adda*, and stretching N.E. to the vicinity of Lecco (p. 130). At **Inverigo**, about one-third of the way, rises the *Rotunda, a handsome and conspicuous country-residence with small park and admirably kept garden, the property of the Marchese Cagnola, situated on an eminence in the midst of vines, mulberry and other fruit-trees, and commanding an extensive prospect.

Where this road crosses that from Lecco to Como, near *Erba* (p. 128), several small lakes are situated, W. the *Lago d'Alserio*, E. the *Lago di Pusiano*. The road now enters a more mountainous district, and the scenery becomes more attractive. *Caslino*, possessing considerable silk-factories (*filatorie*), rises picturesquely on the slope of the hill. The road follows the course of the small river *Lambro*.

Canzo (*Croce di Malta*, the first house on the l. An agreeable liqueur, called *Vespetro*, is manufactured at Canzo), almost contiguous to *Asso*, 1¼ M. beyond. At the entrance of Asso is a very extensive silk-manufactory (*Casa Versa*).

The road now gradually ascends for a considerable distance in the picturesque valley of the *Lambro*, the Vall' Assina, the slopes of which are well wooded; it passes through several villages, (2¼ M.) *Lasnigo*, (2¼ M.) *Barni* and *Magreglio*, where the ascent becomes more rapid; first view of both arms of the Lake of Como from the eminence near the (1¼ M.) *Chapel*.

Delightful *survey of the entire W. arm to Lecco and far beyond, from the rear of the first church of (1¼ M.) **Civenna**, with its graceful tower. The road now runs for 2¼ M. along the shady ridge of the mountain which extends into the lake at Bellaggio; beyond the chapel the following striking views are obtained: the W. arm of the lake (of Como), the Tremezzina with the Villa Carlotta and Cadenabbia (p. 126), the E. arm (Lake of Lecco), a large portion of the road of the E. shore, the entire lake from the promontory of Bellaggio to Domaso (p. 130), and the rising ground with the Serbelloni park (p. 127).

The road winds downwards for about 3 M., passing the *Villa Giulia* (p. 128) on the r., and ½ M. before Bellaggio is reached, the church-yard of the place, containing the monument of the painter *Carlo Bellosio*, several of whose pictures are to be seen at Bellaggio. From Civenna to the hotels at *Bellaggio* on the lake (p. 126) 2 hrs. walk.

A longer route which will reward the pedestrian is by the **Monte S. Primo** (5200 ft.). Ascent from Canzo with guide in 4—5 hrs., descent to Bellaggio 2½ hrs. Magnificent panorama from the summit, comprising the Brianza as far as Milan, the Lago Maggiore, Lago di Varese, the Lake of Como to the N. as far as the Alps from Monte Rosa to the Splügen.

Farther on, beyond stat. *Seregno*, the long, indented *Monte Resegone* rises on the r. Stat. *Camnago*, then a small tunnel, and stat. *Cucciago*. Above **Camerlata** (*Café della Stazione ed Albergo;* a good *trattoria*, opposite the post-office, near the station) rises the lofty old tower of the *Castello Baradello*, once frequently occupied by Frederick Barbarossa. The harbour of Como is 1½ M. from the station at Camerlata; omnibus thither in 20 min. (50 c.).

Diligence from Camerlata to *Varese* (p. 131) on the arrival of the trains from Milan; on the arrival of the first train also to *Laveno* (p. 138) on the Lago Maggiore, in 5 hrs. From the Corona (see below) omnibus (2 fr. 10 c.) to *Capolago* (p. 132) in connection with the steamboat to Lugano. In the morning and evening Swiss diligence (from the stat. at Camerlata) to *Lugano* (p. 133) in 3½ hrs., *Bellinzona* (p. 44) in 7½ hrs., *Lucerne* (over the St. Gotthard, R. 4) in 25½ hrs., *Coire* (over the Bernardino, R. 6) in 24½ hrs. (in the morning only); see p. 112.

Como (705 ft.) (*Angelo; *Italia, R. from 1½, L. ½, B. 1, D. 3, A. ½ fr.; both on the harbour, with cafés and restaurants; in the vicinity a bath-establishment; *Trattoria di Frasconi Confalonieri, a restaurant in the Italian style, near the harbour, at the W. end of the gallery. Corona, outside the Porta Milanese), with 20,614 inhab., birthplace of the younger Pliny and of the experimental philosopher Volta (d. 1826; his statue by P. Marchesi is on the W. side of the town near the harbour), is situated at the S. extremity of the S.W. arm of the Lake of Como, enclosed by an amphitheatre of mountains.

The *Cathedral, commenced 1396, completed 1521, constructed entirely of marble, is one of the best in N. Italy. Over the portal reliefs (adoration of the Magi) and statuettes (Mary with S. Abbondio, St. Protus, etc.). At the sides of the principal entrance are statues of the elder and the younger Pliny, erected 1498.

The gaudy vaulting, restored in 1838 at an expense of 600,000 fr., mars the effect of the interior, the proportions of which are imposing and resemble those of the Certosa near Pavia (p. 147). The windows of the portal contain fine modern stained glass, representing the history of S. Abbondio. To the r. on entering is the monument of Cardinal *Tolomeo Gallio*, a benefactor of the town, erected in 1861. Farther on, over the altar of S. Abbondio on the r. the Adoration of the Magi, by *Bern. Luini*, and the Flight into Egypt, by *Gaud. Ferrari*. Over the altar of St. Jerome a Madonna by *B. Luini*. In the N. transept the Altare del Crocefisso of 1498, with a fine statue of St. Sebastian. In the choir the Apostles, by *Pompeo Marchesi*. The sacristy contains pictures by *Guido Reni*, *Paolo Veronese*, etc. In the l. aisle the altar of the Mater Dolorosa with an Entombment by *Tommaso Rodari* (1498). At the altar di S. Giuseppe: *G. Ferrari*, Nuptials of the Virgin, in style resembling Raphael; *B. Luini*, Nativity; St. Joseph, a statue by *P. Marchesi*, and a basrelief below, the last work of this master; at the entrance the busts of Pope Innocent XI. (Odescalchi) and Carlo Ravelli, bishop of Como.

Adjoining the church is the *Town Hall (Broletto)*, completed in 1215, constructed of alternate courses of different-coloured stones. Behind the cathedral is the handsome *Theatre*, erected 1813. The old church of *S. Fedele*, of the 10th cent., is in a remote part of the town. Extensive silk and weaving factories.

On the promenade outside the town is the church *Del Crocefisso*, richly decorated with marble and gold, of the 17th cent.; beyond it, to the l., on the slope of the mountain about 1 M. from the town, is the fine old *Basilica S. Abbondio* of the 11th cent.; iron foundries in the vicinity.

Walk on the E. Bank of the Lake. Two roads lead from Como along the slopes on the E. bank of the lake. The lower of these passes several hamlets and villas. The upper (after 2 M.) affords a view of magnificent snow-mountains towards the W., and leads by *Vico*, *Sopra-Villa*, and *Cazzanore*, leaving the Villa Pliniana (p. 125) far below, to *Riva di Palanzo* (osteria on the lake), whence the traveller may cross to the steamboat-stat. *Carate* on the opposite bank.

From Como to Lecco by Erba, diligence daily in 3 hrs. (steamer see p. 124). Como is quitted by the Porta Milanese. The road gradually ascends the hills to the E. The view of the Lake of Como is concealed by the beautifully wooded *Monte S. Maurizio;* to the S. a survey is obtained of the district towards Milan and the Brianza (see p. 121). The church of *Camnago*, a village situated N. of the road, contains the tomb of Volta (see above). Farther on, S. of the road is the sharp ridge of *Montorfano* near a small lake. Near *Cassano* is a curious leaning campanile. Beyond *Albesio* a view is disclosed of the plain of Erba *(Pian d'Erba)* and the lakes of Alserio, Pusiano, and Annone, above which the *Corni di Canzo* (4503 ft.) and the *Resegone di Lecco* (6151 ft.) rise on the E.

Near (10½ M.) **Erba** (1017 ft.) *(Inn)*, a small town in a luxuriantly fertile district, are several handsome villas; the *Villa Amalia* on the W.

side commands a charming view of the Brianza. Near *Incino*, with its lofty Lombard campanile, once stood the *Forum Licini* of the Romans, mentioned by Pliny together with Como and Bergamo.

Before the road crosses the *Lambro*, which is here conducted by an artificial channel to the Lago di Pusiano, the road to stat. Seregno (p. 121) diverges to the r., that to Bellaggio to the l. (see p. 121). *Penzano* on the N. bank of the *Lago di Pusiano* is next reached, then *Pusiano* itself. Beautiful glimpse N. of the *Vall' Assina* (p. 122) and of the Corni di Canzo, S. of the Brianza. Near *Civate* is the double *Lago d'Annone* (E. rises the Resegone di Lecco), connected by the *Ritorto* which the road follows, with the Lake of Lecco. The latter is reached at *Malgrate*, on the W. bank, with numerous silk-factories. Opposite to it lies Lecco (p. 130).

21. Lake of Como.

Plan of Excursion. The most beautiful point on the Lake of Como is Bellaggio (p. 126), which is admirably situated for a stay of several days and for short excursions. — Those who wish to visit the Lakes of Como and Lugano (p. 132) and Lago Maggiore (p. 137) without loss of time should pursue the following route, starting from Milan: train at 10. 50 a. m. in 2 hrs. to Como (Cathedral); proceed by steamboat $1^1/4$ p. m. in $1^1/2$ hr. to Cadenabbia or Bellaggio, spending the night there. In the evening and next morning visit Villa Carlotta, Serbelloni, and Melzi; by steamboat in $1/4$ hr. or by rowing-boat, to Menaggio; thence by omnibus at 11 a. m. (fare $2^1/2$ fr.) in 2 hrs. to Porlezza, in time for the steamboat which starts for Lugano at 1. 15 p. m. (Sund. and Tuesd. excepted), arriving in 1 hr. (2 fr. or 1 fr.), early enough to leave time for the ascent of Monte S. Salvadore. From Lugano Diligence to Luino at 9 a. m. in $2^3/4$ hrs., steamboat from Luino in $1^1/2$ hr. to the Borromean Islands, thence in 1 hr. to Arona. The above information is obtained from the time-tables of last summer.

Steamboat 3 times daily from Como to Colico in $3^1/2$ hrs.; to Lecco (railway to Bergamo) 3 times weekly at $5^1/2$ a. m., returning at $1^3/4$ p. m. Fares from Como to Colico 4 fr. or 2 fr. 10 c., from Como to Cadenabbia or Bellaggio 2 fr. 55 or 1 fr. 40 c. Stations: *Torno*, *Moltrasio*, *Carate*, *Laglio*, *Torriyia*, *Nesso*, *Argegno*, *Campo*, *Lenno*, *Tremezzina*, *Cadenabbia* (pier), *Bellaggio* (pier), *Varenna*, *Menaggio* (pier), *Bellano*, *Rezzonico*, *Dervio*, *Cremia*, *Dongo*, *Gravedona*, *Domaso*, *Colico*; tickets (gratis) for the ferry-boats attached to the steamboat tickets (the boatmen however expect a trifling gratuity). Between Cadenabbia, or Menaggio, and Bellaggio, the steamboat is the cheapest mode of conveyance, especially for single travellers. Those who embark at intermediate stations between Como and Colico must provide themselves with a ticket at the pier; otherwise they are liable to be charged for the whole distance from Como or Colico.

Rowing-boats (*barca*). First hour $1^1/2$ fr. for each rower, each additional hour 1 fr. each rower. From Bellaggio to Cadenabbia and back (or viceversâ) 3, with 2 rowers 4 fr.; Bellaggio-Menaggio and back 4 fr.; Bellaggio-Varenna and back 4 fr.; Bellaggio, Villa Melzi, Villa Carlotta, and back 4 fr. — One rower suffices, unless the traveller is pressed for time; a second may be dismissed with the words 'basta uno!' When travellers are not numerous, the boatmen readily reduce their demands. Those who wish to ascertain beforehand what they will have to pay, should put the following question: *Quanto volete per una corsa d'un ora (di due ore)? Siamo due (tre, quattro) persone. E troppo, vi daro un franco (due franchi* etc.). On paying the fare, it is usual to give an additional '*buonamano*' of $1/2$ fr. or 1 fr. according to the length of the excursion.

The **Lake of Como** (699 ft.; greatest depth 1929 ft.), Ital. *Lago di Como* or *Il Lario*, the *Lacus Larius* of the Romans, extolled by Virgil *(Georg. II. 159)*, is in the estimation of many the most beautiful of the lakes of N. Italy. Its length from

Como to its most N. extremity is 30 M., from the Punta di Bellaggio (p. 128) to Lecco 12²/₃ M.; greatest width between Menaggio and Varenna 2¹/₂ M.

Numerous bright villas of the Milanese aristocracy, surrounded by luxuriant gardens and vineyards, are scattered along the banks of the lake. In the forests above, the brilliant green of the chestnut and walnut contrasts strongly with the greyish tints of the olive, which to the unaccustomed eye bears a strong resemblance to the willow. The mountains rise to a height of 7400 ft. The scenery of the lake, as seen from the deck of the steamboat, though on a far grander scale, faintly resembles the Rhine, the banks on both sides being perfectly distinguished by the traveller. At Bellaggio (p. 128) the lake divides into two branches, termed respectively the Lakes of Como and Lecco. The Adda enters at the upper extremity and makes its egress near Lecco. The W. arm, or Lake of Como, has no outlet. — The population of the banks of the lake is of an industrious character, and principally occupied in the production and manufacture of silk. — The *Lacus Larius* derives a classic interest from its connection with the two Plinies, natives of Como, the elder of whom prosecuted his philosophical researches in the surrounding district. — The lake abounds in fish; trout of 20 lbs. weight are not unfrequently captured. The 'Agoni' are a small, but palatable variety.

The prospect from the quay at Como is limited, but as soon as the steamer has passed the first promontory on the E. the entire beauty of the lake is disclosed to the view.

Lake of Como.

Western Bank.

Villa Raimondi, formerly *Odescalchi*, the most extensive on the lake, is situated at *Borgo Vico*, the N.W. suburb of Como. *Villa d'Este* (now an hotel), for a considerable period the residence of Queen Caroline (d. 1821), the unfortunate consort of George IV.; *Villa Pizzo*, formerly belonging to the Archduke Rainer (d. 1853).

Villa Passalacqua, with its numerous windows, resembles a manufactory.

Near *Moltrasio* is a picturesque waterfall. *Carate*; in the background rises the *Monte Bisbino* (4382 ft.). — *Villa Colobiano*, a green and red structure. The lofty pyramid, with the inscription 'Joseph Frank' and a medallion, was erected by a professor of Pavia of that name (d. 1851), grandson of the celebrated phy-

Eastern Bank.

Villa Trubetzkoi, a cottage in an angle near the rock, belongs to a Russian prince of that name; *Villa Napoli*, a castellated edifice; *Villa Taglioni*, with a Swiss cottage, formerly the property of the famous danseuse, now belonging to her son-in-law Prince Trubetzkoi; *Villa Pasta* was the residence of the celebrated singer (d. 1865); *Villa Taverna*, formerly *Faroni*.

Torno is surrounded by villas.

Villa Pliniana at the end of the bay, at the entrance of a narrow gorge, a gloomy square edifice, erected in 1570 by Count Anguissola, one of the four conspirators who assassinated Duke Farnese at Piacenza, now the property of the princess Belgio-

Western Bank.

sician Peter Frank of Vienna. The professor left the sum of 25,000 fr. for this purpose, from which it may be inferred that he did not do much to merit the remembrance of posterity. — *Laglio*, with *Villa Gaggi*, now *Antongina*.

Villa Galbiati, completed 1855, is gaily painted on the exterior; then *Torrigia* and *Brienno* with numerous laurels.

Argegno, at the mouth of the *Intelvi Valley*.

Sala, with the small island of *S. Giovanni*, or *Comacina*, frequently mentioned in the annals of mediæval warfare, once fortified and now occupied by a small church.

Campo lies in a bay formed by the promontory of *Lavedo*, which here projects far into the lake. On its extremity glitters the *Villa Balbianello*, with its colonnade, the property of Count Arcomati.

Tremezzo (Albergo Bazzoni) is almost contiguous to Cadenabbia; between them the Villa Carlotta is situated. This district, termed the *Tremezzina*, is not inaptly called the garden of Lombardy.

Cadenabbia (*cà de navia*, 'ship-houses') (*Bellevue, R. 2, D. 4, pension 7 fr.; Ville de Milan, formerly Majolica, pension 5—8 fr.; *Belle Ile, moderate), halfway between Como and Colico. In

Eastern Bank.

joso, whose name figured so conspicuously in the disturbances of 1848. It derives its name of *Pliniana* from a neighbouring spring which daily changes its level, a peculiarity mentioned by Pliny. Extracts from his works *(Epist. IV. 30, Hist. Nat. II. 206)* are inscribed on the walls of the court.

Quarsano and *Careno*.

Nesso, at the foot of the *Piano del Tivano* (3742 ft.), *Nesso Sopra*, and *Nesso Sotto*; near the latter in a rocky gorge is a waterfall of considerable height, frequently dry in summer.

Lezzeno; here the lake is very deep.

Bellaggio (708 ft.) (*Grande Bretagne, *Genazzini, both beautifully situated on the lake; R. 2½, D. 3½ fr., pension 7 fr.; Hôtel Suisse, Hôtel Florence, Ital. style, both also on the lake. Boats see p. 124), at the W. base

| Western Bank. | Eastern Bank. |

Western Bank.

a garden sloping down to the lake, in the midst of lemon and citron trees, stands the celebrated *Villa Carlotta, or *Sommariva*, from the Count of that name whose property it formerly was. In 1843 it came into the possession of Princess Albert of Prussia, from whose daughter *Charlotte* (d. 1855) it derives its present appellation. The widower of the latter, Duke George of Saxe-Meiningen, is the present proprietor. Visitors ring at the entrance to the garden and ascend the broad flight of steps, where they are received by the intendant (1 fr., more for a party).

Interior. The Marble Hall contains a frieze decorated with celebrated reliefs by Thorwaldsen, representing the Triumph of Alexander (for which a sum of nearly 15,000 *l.* was once paid by Count Sommariva); also several statues by Canova (Cupid and Psyche, Magdalene, Palamedes, Venus, and Paris); bust of Count Sommariva; Mars and Venus, by *Acquisti*; Cupid giving water to pigeons, by *Bienaimé*, etc. — The Billiard Room contains casts, and a small frieze in marble on the chimney-piece said to be an early work of Thorwaldsen. — In the Garden Saloon several modern pictures, and a marble relief of Napoleon as consul, by *Lazzarini*.

The *Garden* (attendant 1/2 fr.), although less richly stocked than those of Melzi and Serbelloni, may also be visited; pleasant view towards Bellaggio.

Behind the 'Milan' hotel rises a rock, *Il Sasso S. Martino*, on which stands a small church, *Madonna di S. Martino*, commanding a beautiful view; ascent 1½ hr., path in some places destroyed by torrents. — The *Monte Crocione*, a more lofty mountain to the W., commands

Eastern Bank.

of the promontory which separates the two arms of the lake, perhaps the most delightful point on any of the lakes of Upper Italy. To the l., close to the steamboat-pier, is situated the *Villa Frizzoni*, the property of a wealthy silk-merchant of that name from the Engadine. — A short distance S. of the village is the *Villa Melzi, erected by *Albertolli* for Count *Melzi d'Erile*, who was vice-president of the Italian Republic under Napoleon in 1802, and afterwards Duke of Lodi. It now belongs to his grandson the Duca di Melzi, and is hardly less attractive than the Villa Carlotta (intendant 1 fr., more for a party).

Vestibule. Copies of ancient busts in marble by *Canova*; the mother of Napoleon, by *Canova*; bust of the present proprietor, portrait-busts, etc.; David, by *Fraccaroli*; Spring, by *Pandiani*, etc. — The walls of the other apartments are embellished with appropriate frescoes. Thus in the dining-room, genii bringing game, fruit, vegetables, etc.; in the same room a Venus by *Pompeo Marchesi*, and a bust of Michael Angelo. In the other rooms a portrait of Napoleon I. as the president of the Italian Republic, by *Appiani*; a Bacchante and a bust of Michael Angelo by *Canova*.

The *Garden (attendant 1/2 fr.) exhibits all the luxuriance and fragrance of Southern vegetation (magnificent magnolias, camellias, cedars, Chinese pines, gigantic aloes, etc.). — The *Chapel* in the garden contains monuments in marble to the two former proprietors, and to the mother of the present duke, by *Nessi*. In another part of the garden Dante and Beatrice, by *Comolli*.

Higher up stands the *Villa Serbelloni; the building itself has more the character of an old farm-house than a ducal residence, but the **view from the

Western Bank.
a striking view of the Monte Rosa chain, the Bernese Alps and Mont Blanc, the lakes and the plain of Lombardy (a fatiguing ascent of 6—7 hrs.; guide 5 fr.; in order to avoid the heat the traveller should start at 2 or 3 a. m.).

Eastern Bank.
park, which extends to the extremity of the wooded promontory, is magnificent. It extends over the lake in both directions, and embraces the Lake of Lecco (see p. 130); this is generally considered the finest view on the lake. Charming glimpses of Varenna, Villa Balbianello, Carlotta, etc. (fee $1/2$ fr. to each attendant, for a party more). At the entrance of the park and at the hotels, small objects tastefully manufactured in olive-wood are sold as souvenirs. A short distance S. of this, in the direction of the *Lake of Lecco*, is the **Villa Giulia** (beautiful flowers), the property of King Leopold of Belgium. Adjacent to the latter is the *Villa Paldi*. — Excursion to *Monte S. Primo* see p. 122.

Here, at the *Punta di Bellaggio*, the two arms of the lake, the *Lago di Como* and the *Lago di Lecco*, unite to form the Lake of Como, properly so called.

Lake of Como.

Western Bank.
Menaggio *(Vittoria,* new; *Corona)* possesses an extensive silk-spinning establishment, to which visitors are readily admitted. On the lake, S. of the village, the handsome *Villa Mylius*. A road leads hence to Porlezza on the Lake of Lugano (9 M.; omnibus daily at 11 a. m., see p. 136). On an eminence ($1/2$ hr.), near the church of *Loveno* (*Inn), stands the **Villa Vigoni** (*view), formerly the property of Herr Mylius, of Frankfurt, a liberal patron of the fine arts (d. 1845), and the benefactor of the entire neighbourhood, as the monuments to

Eastern Bank.
Varenna *(*Albergo Reale)* is charmingly situated. In the vicinity, especially towards the N., are some remarkable galleries in the rock on the Stelvio route (p. 49). Most of the marble quarried in the neighbourhood is cut and polished in the town.

About $3/4$ M. to the S. of Varenna is the cascade of the *Fiume Latte* ('milk brook', from its colour), which is precipitated in several leaps from a height of 900 ft., and contains an imposing volume of water in the spring.

The *Torre di Vezio* situated still higher commands a noble prospect.

Western Bank.

his memory testify. The villa contains some admirable works in marble (Eve, Jesus in the temple, the Finding of Moses, Ruth) by modern Italian sculptors, reliefs by *Thorwaldsen* (Nemesis, in the temple, erected by Herr Mylius to his son's memory) and *Marchesi*; in the garden-saloon a *group by *Argenti*, the proprietress with her children.

The steamer next passes a wild, yellowish-brown cliff, *Il Sasso Rancio* ('the orange-rock'), which is traversed by a dangerous footpath. This route was undertaken in 1799 by the Russians under General Bellegarde, on which occasion many lives were lost.

S. Abbondio is the next village. *Rezzonico (Raetionicum)*, with the picturesque ruins of a fortress of the 13th cent.

Cremia with handsome church; then *Pianello*.

On rocks rising precipitously above *Musso* are situated the ruins of the *Castle of Musso*, the count of which after the battle of Pavia (1525) established an independent principality, embracing the entire Lake of Como. Then *Dongo*, with a monastery. Above it, on the height to the r., lies *Garzeno*, whence a somewhat neglected path crosses the *Passo Jorio* to Bellinzona.

Gravedona (Hôtel del Sasso), the most populous village on the lake, is picturesquely situated at the entrance of a gorge. The handsome villa with four towers at the upper

Eastern Bank.

Gittana is the station for the hydropathic establishment of *Regoledo* (pension 6 fr., 'per le operationi idropatiche' 2 fr.); donkey from Gittana to Regoledo 1 fr., horse or chaise-à-porteurs 2 fr.

Bellano lies at the base of *Monte Grigna* (7136 ft.), at the mouth of the *Pioverna*, the valley of which extends to the neighbourhood of Lecco, and contains flourishing iron-works.

Dervio, at the mouth of the *Varrone*, is situated at the base of the abrupt *Monte Legnone* (8559 ft.) and its spur *Monte Legnoncino* (4947 ft.). *Corenno* and *Dorio* are the following villages.

Western Bank.
extremity was built by the Milanese Cardinal Gallio. The church, dating from the 13th cent., contains two Christian inscriptions of the 5th cent.

Domaso, charmingly situated, possesses several handsome villas, especially *Villa Calderara* and *Villa Lasquez*.

Eastern Bank.
Colico (*Albergo Piazza Garibaldi*, on the lake; *Isola Bella*; both in the Italian style), comp. p. 49. The *Monte Legnone*, mentioned above, may be ascended hence without difficulty in 7—8 hrs.

From Colico to Chiavenna Swiss diligence (also an omnibus, 2½ fr.) twice daily in 3 hrs.; thence daily (twice in summer) over the Splügen to Coire (R. 5) in 13½ hrs.

From Colico to Sondrio in the Val Tellina diligence twice daily in 5 hrs., also an omnibus (comp. pp. 49, 57).

Lake of Lecco.

From Bellaggio to Lecco and back steamboat 3 times weekly, see p. 124.

The S. E. arm of the Lake of Como is worthy of a visit, although inferior in attraction to the other parts. Lecco is charmingly situated. The E. bank of the lake is so precipitous that it was formerly traversed by a path for goat-herds only, but in 1832 a road was constructed on it with the aid of embankments, tunnels, and galleries. Three of the latter near *Olcio* are together 1000 yds. in length. It affords admirable views of the lake.

After the steamer has steered round the *Punta di Bellaggio*, the Villa Giulia (p. 128) is left on the r.; adjoining it is *Visgnola*; farther on, *Limonta*; on the opposite (l.) bank *Lierna* and *Sornico*, r. *Onno*, l. *Olcio*, then *Mandello* on an flat tongue of land. Opposite the latter is the market-town of *Parè*, separated from Malgrate by the promontory of S. Dionigio. *Malgrate* itself lies at the entrance of the Val Madrera, through which the road by Erba to Como leads (p. 124). The lake here gradually contracts to form the *Adda*, by which river it is drained. A stone bridge of ten arches, *Il Ponte Grande*, leads to Lecco, on the opposite bank; it was constructed in 1335 by Azzone Visconti, and furnished with fortified towers at the extremities. Fine view of the town from the bridge.

Lecco (*Albergo d'Italia; Croce di Malta; Leone d'Oro*) is an industrial town with 8000 inhab., possessing silk, cotton, and iron manufactories, situated at the S. extremity of the E. arm of the Lake of Como, and admirably described in Manzoni's '*Promessi Sposi*.' Pleasant walks to the height of *Castello* and the pilgrimage-church on the *Monte Baro* (view of the Brianza).

A short distance below Lecco the Adda again expands into the *Lago di Garlate*, and further down, into the small *Lago di Olgirate*. A navigable canal connects *Trezzo* with Milan. — From Lecco to Milan railway by Bergamo in 3 hrs., see p. 150.

22. From the Lake of Como to the Lake of Lugano and the Lago Maggiore.

1. From Como to Laveno direct.

30 M. The road traverses a beautiful district of Lombardy, commanding views of several lakes, of Monte Rosa and the Simplon chain, and of other high mountains. One-horse carr. from Como to Laveno 20, two horse 30 fr.; a drive of about 6 hrs. Diligences and omnibus see p. 122.

The road ascends through the long S. suburb of S. Bartolommeo, skirts the base of an eminence surmounted by the ruins of the *Castello Baradello* (p. 122), and leads to *Camerlata* (p. 122), station of the railway for Milan. It then turns E. to *Rebbio*, *Lucino* and *Lurate Abbate*, traversing a luxuriantly fertile district containing numerous villas of the Milanese aristocracy. At *Olgiate* the road attains its culminating point (777 ft. above the Lake of Como), whence a view of the Alps is obtained; through the deep opening to the N., which indicates the situation of the Lake of Lugano, the chapel on the Monte S. Salvadore (p. 134) near Lugano is visible. The road next passes the villages of *Solbiate* and *Binago*, descends rapidly by *Malnate*, and crosses the *Lanza*, near its influx into the *Olona*, which after a farther course of 30 M. washes the walls of Milan.

Varese (*Angelo;* **Stella;* **Corona; Leon d'Oro*, starting point of the diligences), a wealthy town halfway between Como and Laveno, is often visited in summer by the wealthy Milanese, who possess villas in the environs. *S. Vittore*, the principal church, contains a St. George by *Crespi* and a Magdalene by *Morazzone*. A diligence runs daily from Varese to *Marchirolo*, *Ponte Tresa* (p. 135), and *Porto (Morcote*, p. 136), fare 1½ fr.; also to *Luino* (p. 136), 1½ fr.

Railway from Varese to Milan (37½ M.) in 2¼ hrs.; fares 7 fr. 30, 5 fr. 35, 3 fr. 80 c. — Stations *Gazzada*, *Albizzate*, **Gallarate**; from the latter to Milan see p. 141.

The road to Laveno leads by *Masnago* (1 hr. to the N. is the **Madonna del Monte*, p. 136) and *Cosciago*, and ascends to *Luinate*, whence a beautiful view S.W. is obtained of the *Lake of Varese* and the small adjacent *Lake of Biandrone*, also of the farther distant lakes of *Monate* and *Comabbio*. The next village is *Barrasso*, then *Comerio* (745 ft. above the lake), with a number of pleasant villas, whence the road, passing near the N.W. extremity of the Lago di Varese, gradually descends to *Gavirate;* in the vicinity of the latter are quarries of the 'marmo majolica', a species of marble used for decorative purposes. For a short distance the road commands a view of Monte Rosa. *Cocquio* and *Gemonio* are situated r. of the road. Farther on, the *Boesio*, which flows through the *Val Cuvio*, is crossed, and, beyond *Cittiglio*, its r. bank skirted. The road then leads past the S. base of the *Sasso del Ferro* to

Laveno (p. 138), where the steamboats do not always touch, comp. p. 137. Small boat to the Borromean Islands and Pallanza with 3 rowers 10—12 fr.; to Isola Bella 1½ hr., thence to Isola Madre in 20 min., to Pallanza in 20 min. more.

2. From Como to Luino by Lugano.

To Lugano 10 M., to Luino 12 M. more. Swiss diligence from Camerlata to Lugano twice daily in 3½ hrs., from Lugano to Luino once daily in 2¾ hrs. — Omnibus from Como to Capolago see p. 122. Steamer from Capolago to Lugano see p. 133. On re-entering the Italian dominions (at Fornasette, p. 135) from the Canton of Ticino the formalities of the custom-house must be undergone.

The road leads through *Borgo Vico*, the W. suburb of Como, and ascends the *Monte Olimpino*, commanding charming retrospects of the lake, Como, the Villa Raimondi (p. 125) etc., above which the Corni di Canzo rise on the l. and the rocky eminence crowned with the Castello Baradello on the r. *Ponte Chiasso* is the Italian frontier custom-house for travellers from Switzerland. *Chiasso* (784 ft.) (Angelo, or Posta) is the first Swiss village; then (1½ M.) *Balerno* and (1½ M.).

Mendrisio (1199 ft.) *(Angelo)*, a small town with 2200 inhab., in a rich and productive district, with large wine-cellars and handsome hospital.

***Monte Generoso** (5561 ft.) *(Monte Gionnero* or *Monte Calvaggione)*, the Rigi of Italian Switzerland, should be ascended by those whose time permits, especially as the paths have recently been improved and an inn has been erected on the mountain. The latter is reached in 2½ hrs. from Mendrisio, the summit in 1½ hr. more. Guides (unnecessary) and horses at Mendrisio. The **Hôtel du Généroso*, situated on an open plateau, and containing a post and telegraph office, the property of *Dr. Pasta* of Mendrisio, at whose expense the new paths have been formed, is a comfortable house and well adapted for a prolonged stay. — A good bridle-path from Mendrisio, passing the wine-cellars of the village of *Salorino*, ascends by zigzags (pedestrians may go through Salorino and follow the telegraph-wires) to a shaded dale, at the upper extremity of which (1¼ hr., halfway to the hotel) there is a spring in the rock, and a hut where refreshments may be obtained. The path then leads through a beautiful grove of chestnuts, and farther on through a beech-wood to the (1¼ hr.) hotel, ¼ hr. from which, on the other side of the hill, is the chalet of *Cassina* with a fine breed of cattle. From the hotel to the summit an ascent of 1½ hr., crossing pastures, and passing the different summits of the Monte Generoso. On the top a hut to afford shelter, and about 100 paces from it a scanty spring. The *view embraces the lakes of Lugano, Como, Varese, and the Lago Maggiore, the populous district of Lombardy, and to the N. the entire Alpine chain. Excellent grapes and figs thrive luxuriantly at the base of the mountain, which is clothed higher up with chestnuts, beeches, and finally pines. A variety of the rarest plants also grow here. — Monte Generoso may also be ascended from *Rovio*; laborious ascent, 4—5 hrs.

At **Capolago** (*Inn* on the lake) the road reaches the ***Lake of Lugano**, or *Lago Ceresio* (930 ft.), the scenery of which is little inferior to that of its more celebrated neighbours Como and Maggiore. In the vicinity of Lugano the banks are picturesquely studded with villas and chapels, and planted with the vine, fig, olive, and walnut. The W. side of the S. arm also presents several delightful points of view. On the N. bank, *Gandria* with its terraced gardens (on lofty arcades) and vineyards is charmingly situated at the base of *Monte Brè*. Beyond this point the lake assumes a wilder character. The rocks are so abrupt in some places that scarcely sufficient space is left for the footpath at their base. At the N. extremity of this bay *Porlezza* (p. 136), a harbour and seat of the Italian custom-house, is situated. Small boat to Lugano 10—12 fr.

Beyond Capolago the road, commanding a succession of beautiful views, leads on the E. bank of the lake by *Melano* and *Maroggio* to *Bissone*, where it crosses the lake by means of an unsightly stone dyke, or dam, $1/2$ M. in length, 24 ft. in width, completed in 1846 at a cost of 700,000 fr. Each extremity of this structure is provided with an arch. The road then passes *Melide*, on a promontory opposite Bissone, and skirts the lake, passing the E. base of *Monte S. Salvadore* (p. 134). The white dolomite, of which the mountains chiefly consist here, changes near Melide to dark porphyry, and as *S. Martino* is approached, there is a gradual transition to shell-limestone. Lugano does not come in view until the road turns round the N. base of Monte S. Salvadore, where the striking beauty of the situation at once becomes apparent.

Lugano. Hotels. *Hôtel du Parc, in the former monastery of *S. Maria degli Angioli*, on the S. side of the town, R. 2—3, L. $3/4$, B. $1^1/2$, D. excl. W. at 5 o'clock 4, A. 1 fr.; pension in summer 6—9 fr., in winter $5^1/2$—6 fr. — Grand Hôtel Suisse and Hôtel de la Couronne, tolerable, but without view. — Post and telegraph office in the Gov. Buildings (p. 134).

Diligence to *Luino* (p. 138) once daily in $2^1/2$ hrs., coupé 3 fr. 60', intérieur 2 fr. 90 c.; steamboat-tickets for Lago Maggiore are also issued at the office (two-horse carr. 20, one-horse 12 fr., incl. fee); to *Lucerne* by the St. Gotthard twice daily; to *Coire* by the Bernardino once daily; to *Camerlata* twice daily.

Steamboat to *Capolago* 1 fr. or 60 c.; to *Porlezza* 2 or 1 fr.

Boats to Porlezza (p. 136) with one rower 7 fr., two 12 fr., three $16^1/2$ fr.; to Capolago 6, 10, or 12 fr., incl. fee.

English Church Service at the Hôtel du Parc during the season.

Lugano (932 ft.), the principal town of the canton of *Ticino*, with 5600 inhab. (28 Prot.), is charmingly situated on the lake of the same name and enjoys a southern climate (the aloe blooms here in the open air), without the oppressive heat of the Italian towns. It is a most agreeable place for a lengthened sojourn; the environs display all the charms of Italian mountain scenery; numerous white villas and country-seats are scattered along the verge of the lake; the lower hills are covered with vineyards and gardens, contrasting beautifully with the dark foliage of the chestnuts and walnuts in the background. To the S., immediately above the town, rises *Monte S. Salvadore*, wooded to its summit (p. 134); among the mountains towards the N. the double peak of *Monte Camoghè* (p. 44) is conspicuous.

The interior of the town with its arcades, workshops in the

open air, and granite-paved streets also presents a thoroughly Italian appearance. On market-day (Tuesday) the Italian costume is to be seen here in every variety.

The monasteries here were formerly very numerous, but were suppressed between 1848 and 1853, with the exception of two. The most important was *S. Maria degli Angioli*, now the *Hôtel du Parc*. The adjacent church contains three *Frescoes* by Luini, the *Crucifixion, one of his finest works, the Last Supper (on the l. wall) in three sections, formerly preserved at the Lyceum, and a Madonna (1st chap. on the r.).

S. Lorenzo, the principal church, on an eminence (fine view from the terrace), said to have been designed by Bramante, has a tastefully adorned marble façade. The white marble reliefs represent the busts of the four Evangelists, Solomon and David.

Adjoining the Theatre are the handsome *Government Buildings*, with the inscription: *In legibus libertas; quid leges sine moribus et fides sine operibus?*

In a small temple at the *Villa Tanzina*, 1/4 M. S. of the Hôtel du Parc, is a bust of Washington: '*magnum saeculorum decus*'. The proprietor of the villa, in which apartments are let, is an Italian who acquired a fortune in America. — The garden of the neighbouring *Villa Vasalli* contains some fine cypresses. — Superb view from the tower in the garden of the *Villa Enderlin*, to which access is permitted by the proprietor.

The beautiful *Park of M. *Ciani* (d. 1867) extends along the N. bay of the lake; strangers are readily admitted (gardener 1 fr.). The proprietor, a native of Milan, has erected a marble *Monument* in the park to the memory of his parents, the work of the sculptor *Vela*.

Opposite the Hôtel du Parc, on the new and spacious quay, is a *Fountain*, with a *Statue of William Tell*, 8 ft. in height, in white sandstone, designed by *Vinc. Vela*, and erected at the cost of M. Ciani.

In front of the church of *S. Pietro* near *Pambio*, 1 1/2 M. S.W., stands a *Statue* (also by Vinc. Vela) of *Captain Carloni* who was killed in 1848 near Somma Campagna, fighting as a volunteer '*per la libertà e l'indipendenza d'Italia*'. — 1 M. to the W. of Pambio, in the churchyard of *S. Abbondio*, near the (5 min. W.) church of that name, is a white marble *Monument of the Torriani family, also by Vela, an admirably executed work.

Delightful excursion to ***Monte S. Salvadore** (2982 ft.), ascent 2 hrs., descent 1 1/2 hr., guide (4 fr.) superfluous, as the path cannot be mistaken; horse 9 fr., mule 8 fr., incl. fee. 10 min from the Hôtel du Parc, between a detached house and the wall of a garden, a good paved path diverges to the r. from the road to Como; 2 min. farther, where the path divides, not to the r., but straight on to the houses; between these the road ascends, past the handsome and conspicuous (25 min.) *Villa Marchino*, to (5 min.) the village of Pazzallo, from which Monte Rosa is visible through a mountain-gorge. Here the path diverges to the l. from the broad road, through the gateway of the fourth house, and ascends to the l. by a stony but easy ascent in 1½ hr. to the Chapel on the summit (to which pilgrimages are made). Near the chapel is a small house with a spring, which however is frequently closed; in this case no refreshment of any kind can be obtained. The *view embraces all the arms of the Lake of Lugano, the mountains and their wooded slopes, especially those above Lugano, sprinkled with numerous villas. To the E. above Porlezza is Monte Legnone (p. 129), to the l. of which, in the extreme distance, are the snowpeaks of the Bernina; N. above Lugano the double peak of Monte Camoghè (p. 44), l. of this the distant mountains of St. Gotthard; W. the chain of Monte Rosa, with the Matterhorn and other Alps of the Valais to the r. This view is seen to the greatest advantage in the morning, when Monte Rosa gleams in the sunshine. In descending, the route through *Carona* (1966 ft.) and *Melide* (somewhat longer) may be chosen.

The ascent (2½ hrs.) of *Monte Brè, N.E. of Lugano, is another easy excursion, scarcely less interesting than the former. A road runs inland towards several mills at the foot of the mountain. Thence a broad and well-constructed path winds upwards to the r. to the small village of Desago, passing a few groups of houses. Another route to Desago from the town runs along the lake to the foot of the mountain, and then ascends from hamlet to hamlet, through gardens etc. Above Desago the path divides; both routes are broad, and well-constructed, leading round the mountain to the village of Brè on its farther side (Inn, bread and wine only). The route to the r., above the lake, is of surpassing beauty, that to the l. also commands a fine inland view. Near the church of Brè a narrow forest-path ascends to the summit of the mountain. This path also divides; the branch to the r. traverses the highest ridge of the hill, that to the l. leads to a spur of the mountain in the direction of Lugano. The summit may be attained by either. The view of the several arms of the Lake of Lugano, especially in the direction of Porlezza, and the surrounding mountains, is remarkably fine. Lugano itself is not visible from the summit, but from the above-mentioned spur a good view of it may be obtained. All these paths are easily traced. From Lugano to Brè about 1½ hr.; from Brè to the summit by the longest way about 1 hr.

Monte Caprino, opposite Lugano, on the E. bank of the lake, is much frequented on holidays by the townspeople, who possess wine-cellars *(cantine)* in the numerous cool grottoes by which the side of the mountain is honey-combed. These receptacles are guarded by numerous huts, which from a distance present the appearance of a village. Good wine of icy coolness may here be obtained ('Asti' is particularly recommended). These cellars should be visited on account of their truly Italian characteristics.

Beyond Lugano the road gradually winds upwards to the W., turns S. past the small *Lake of Muzzano*, crosses the *Agno*, and leads through the village of that name (967 ft.), and a short distance farther reaches the W. arm of the Lake of Lugano. Near *Magliaso*, with an ancient castle of the Beroldingen family, the lake is quitted, but another of its bays is touched near *Ponte Tresa* (so called from a bridge across the Tresa, here connecting the Swiss and Lombard banks). This bay is so completely enclosed by mountains, that it appears to form a distinct lake; it is connected with the Lake of Lugano by a narrow channel only. The *Tresa*, which here emerges from the lake, falls into the Lago Maggiore ¾ M. S.W. of Luino. The road follows its course as far as the Italian frontier at *Fornasette*, where luggage is examined. The road then descends and soon affords a view of the Lago Maggiore.

Luino, see p. 138.

3. From Cadenabbia (p. 126) or Menaggio (p. 128) by Porlezza and Lugano to Laveno (or Luino, comp. No. 2).

Omnibus and steamer see p. 124. One-horse carr. from Menaggio to Porlezza in 2 hrs., 6 fr.; boat thence to Lugano in 3 hrs., 7—12 fr., from Lugano to Porto in 3 hrs., 5—6 fr.; or the traveller may prefer to proceed direct by boat from Porlezza to Porto, a Lombard harbour at the S.W. bay of the Lake of Lugano; one horse carr. from Porto to Laveno in 4 hrs., 12—15 fr.

The journey from Cadenabbia or Menaggio to Porlezza (9 M.) is strongly recommended to the notice of the pedestrian, as the road leads through a succession of imposing and attractive mountain-scenes. The Villa Vigoni (p. 128) lies r. of the road, to the N. The retrospect from the height near *Croce*, 2 M. from Menaggio, is lovely. To the W. *Monte Crocione* on the l. and *Monte Galbiga* (5593 ft.) in front rise abruptly. The road then descends to the small *Lago del Piano* and the village of *Tavordo*. **Porlezza** (*Inn* on the lake) (p. 133) is nearly 2 M. farther. Attempts at extortion are frequently made here by the fraternity who prey upon travellers.

The scenery of the E. arm of the Lake of Lugano is of a severe character. Soon after Porlezza is quitted, the Monte S. Salvadore (p. 134) becomes conspicuous to the S.W. The lake becomes more attractive as Lugano is approached. *Gandria*, *Lugano* (where travellers to Luino descend), stone bridge near *Melide* see p. 133. *Morcote* lies on a tongue of land which forms the S. base of Monte S. Salvadore.

Porto (see above) is the seat of the Italian custom-house. The road, which at first ascends rapidly, commands picturesque retrospects. Beyond *Induno* (*Inn), 6 M. from Porto, the road to Varese is quitted and that r. to *S. Ambrogio* followed.

The village lies 3 M. N. of Varese (p. 131) and 1½ M. S. E. of the base of the ***Madonna del Monte**, a celebrated resort of pilgrims. Fourteen chapels or stations of various forms, adorned with frescoes and groups in stucco, have been erected along the broad path, by which the monastery and church on the mountain (2841 ft.) are attained in 1 hr. The view hence is not less celebrated than the peculiar sanctity of the spot. The small lakes of Comabbio, Biandrone, and Monate, that of Varese, two arms of the Lago Maggiore, a portion of the Lake of Como, and the expansive and fruitful plain as far as Milan are visible. A far more comprehensive view, including the glacier-world also, is obtained (best by morning-light) from the *Tre Croci* (3966 ft.), 1 hr. N. W. of the Madonna. Several cabarets adjoin the monastery. Donkeys and guides (unnecessary) are to be found at the foot of the mountain.

The road then leads from S. Ambrogio to *Masnago*, where it joins that leading from Varese to Laveno, see p. 131.

23. Lago Maggiore. Borromean Islands. From Arona to Milan.

Steamboats ply on the lake 3 times daily during the summer: from Magadino to Arona in $5^1/_2$ hrs., from Luino to Isola Bella in $2^1/_4$ hrs., from Isola Bella to Arona in $1^1/_4$ hr.; fares from Magadino to Arona 4 fr. 80 or 2 fr. 65 c., from Luino to Isola Bella 1 fr. 85 or 1 fr. 15 c., from Isola Bella to Arona 1 fr. 70 or 95 c., *landing and embarking included*. The 1st class only is protected from the sun by an awning. The steamboats are the best and cheapest conveyance to Isola Bella, especially for a single traveller (from Pallanza 60, from Stresa 40 c.); and, as they touch at the island 4—5 times daily, frequent opportunities are afforded for the excursion. Stations on the **E. Bank** (those are printed in *Italics*, with which the steamers do not communicate regularly; those in wider print have piers; for particulars see the '*Horaire pour la Navigation à vapeur du Lac Majeur*', which may be obtained at all the principal inns on the banks): Magadino, *Locarno*, *Ascona*, Brissago, Canobbio, *Maccagno*, Luino, *Cannero*, *Oggebbio*, *Ghiffa*, *Porto Val Travaglia*, *Laveno* (comp. p. 138), Intra, Pallanza, *Suna*, *Feriolo*, Isola Bella, Stresa, Belgirate, Lesa, Meina, *Angera*, Arona. — On board the boats from Sesto Calende and Arona to Magadino, agents of the innkeepers at Magadino offer to provide passengers with carriages for the passage of the St. Gotthard (see p. 38, private posting).

Boats. Travellers coming from the Simplon usually take a boat at Baveno (p. 139) to visit the Borromean Islands. The charge for an excursion not exceeding 2 hrs. is fixed for each rower at $2^1/_2$ fr.; for 1—3 pers. 2 rowers, for 4—6 pers. 3, more than 6 pers. 4 rowers, so that the half-hour's passage to Isola Bella is somewhat expensive. Half-way between Stresa and Baveno, opposite the island, there is a ferry-station where 1—2 fr. is exacted for a passage of scarcely 10 min.; the boatmen demand 5 fr. The passage from Stresa for 1—2 pers. costs 2 fr., for 3 or more with 2 rowers 4 fr., according to tariff. For the return from the island to the mainland, to Baveno, Stresa, etc., the boatmen demand 5 fr., but they reduce their terms as the time for the departure of the steamboat approaches (see above). From Isola Bella to Isola Madre and back, incl. stay, 3 fr. with two rowers.

Diligence from Arona twice daily in 6 hrs. to Domo d'Ossola (p. 37), in correspondence with the diligence over the Simplon (R. 3). — From Luino Swiss diligence daily in $2^3/_4$ hrs. to Lugano, see p. 132. — From Magadino (in $1^3/_4$ hr.) and Locarno (in $2^1/_4$ hrs.) Swiss diligence twice daily to Bellinzona (see p. 44), thence in summer twice daily over the Bernardino to Coire in 17 hrs. (RR. 6, 5).

Lago Maggiore (645 ft., greatest depth 2838 ft.), the *Lacus Verbanus* of the Romans, is 45 M. in length and averages 3 M. in width; greatest depth 2666 ft. The canton of Ticino possesses only the N. bank for a distance of 9 M.; this portion of the lake is also called the *Lake of Locarno*. The W. bank beyond the brook *Valmara*, and the E. bank from *Zenna* belong to Italy. Its principal tributaries are on the N. the *Ticino (Tessin)*, on the W. the *Tosa*, on the E. the *Tresa*, flowing from the Lake of Lugano. The river which emerges from the S. extremity of the lake retains the name of *Ticino*. The N. banks are bounded by lofty mountains, for the most part wooded, whilst the E. shore towards the lower extremity slopes gradually away to the level of the plains of Lombardy. The W. bank affords a succession of charming landscapes. The water is of a green colour in its N. arm, and deep blue towards the S.

The Steamboat leaves *Magadino*, the most N. harbour (p. 51), and steers first N.W. to

Locarno (651 ft.) (*Corona, on the lake; *Albergo Svizzero, R. 1½ fr., higher up in the town, clean), with 2982 inhab., one of the three capitals of the Canton Ticino, alternately with Bellinzona (p. 44) and Lugano (p. 133) the seat of the government, situated on the W. bank of Lago Maggiore, at the mouth of the *Maggia*. Politically Locarno is Swiss, but the character of the scenery and of the population is thoroughly Italian. The *Collegiate Church* contains a few good pictures. The handsome *Government Buildings* are situated in a large piazza and the public garden. The pilgrimage church of **Madonna del Sasso* (1159 ft.), on a wooded eminence above the town, commands a remarkably fine view.

On the principal market-day (every alternate Thursday) a variety of the most picturesque costumes from the Canton of Ticino, Lombardy, and Piedmont may be observed. Great national festival on Sept. 8th, the Nativity of the Virgin.

The boat now follows the W. bank, passes *Ascona* with its castle and seminary, *Ronco*, and *Brissago* (*Albergo Antico), a delightful spot, with picturesque white houses conspicuous from a great distance, and an avenue of cypresses leading to the church. The slopes above the village are covered with fig-trees, olives and pomegranates; even the myrtle flourishes in the open air. Then *S. Agata* and **Canobbio** *(Serpente)*. The latter, one of the oldest and most prosperous villages on the lake, is situated on a promontory at the entrance of the *Val Canobbino*, and enclosed by richly-wooded mountains. A short distance inland is situated the new hydropathic estab. of *La Salute*, the property of Dr. Fossati-Barbò (pension 8 fr., omnibus at the pier).

The boat now steers for the E. bank, touches at *Maccagno*, and stops at **Luino** *(*Hôtel du Simplon; Posta*, at the pier), with the château of *Grivelli* surrounded by pines, the station for Lugano (p. 133). On the W. bank rise two grotesque-looking castles *(Castelli di Cannero)*, half in ruins, the property of Count Borromeo. In the 15th cent. they harboured the five brothers Mazzarda, notorious brigands, the terror of the district. **Cannero** is beautifully situated in the midst of vineyards and olive-groves, which extend far up the slopes of the mountain. The W. bank is clothed with the richest vegetation, and studded with innumerable white houses and a succession of picturesque villages.

The next small villages of *Oggebbio* and *Ghiffa* on the W. bank, and *Porto Valtravaglia*, on the E., as well as the more important **Laveno** *(*Posta; Moro; Stella)*, are only occasionally touched at by the steamers. The latter, beautifully situated in a bay at the mouth of the *Tresa*, was formerly a strongly fortified war-harbour of the Austrians (omnibus to Varese and Como see

p. 122). Charming survey of the lake and mountains from *Fort Garibaldi*, 1½ M. from Laveno. Behind Laveno rises *Il Sasso del Ferro* (3491 ft.), the most beautiful mountain on the entire lake, commanding a magnificent view of the lake, the plain as far as Milan and the Monte Rosa chain. The five peaked summit of Monte Rosa is in this neighbourhood also visible from the lake.

At the boat approaches Intra, a rotunda with a statue, belonging to the *Villa Prina*, becomes visible. The valley, which here opens to the W., suddenly discloses a strikingly picturesque view of the N. neighbours of Monte Rosa: the Cima di Jazi, Strahlhorn, and the Mischabel with its three peaks. They are lost to view as the steamboat turns the point between Intra and Pallanza, but soon re-appear and remain visible until Isola Bella is reached. From the island itself they are hidden by the mountains of the valley of the Tosa.

Intra *(Vitello d'Oro)*, a flourishing town with a number of manufactories, most of them founded by Swiss, is situated on an alluvial soil, between the mouths of two mountain-streams, the *S. Giovanni* and *S. Bernardino*. Omnibus daily between Intra, Pallanza, Gravellona, Omegna, and Orta, comp. R. 24.

On the promontory of *S. Remigio*, which here projects into the lake, stands a church on the site of an ancient Roman temple of Venus. This is the widest part of the lake. The little **Isola S. Giovanni**, one of the Borromean group, with its chapel, house, and gardens, is the property of Count Borromeo.

Pallanza *(Hôtel de Pallanza*, new; *Posta, at the wharf; *Italia)*, the seat of the authorities of the province, is a thriving little town (4000 inhab.), most delightfully situated opposite the Borromean Islands. — Boat with two rowers to the islands and back 4 fr., an excursion of 3 hrs.; to Baveno 3 fr.; Diligence to Domo d'Ossola in 5 hrs., on the arrival of the boat from Magadino. Omnibus to Orta, see above.

The lake here forms an expansive bay, 4½ M. long and 2¼ M. wide, extending in a N.W. direction, at the N. extremity of which is the influx of the impetuous *Tosa*. On its N. E. bank lies *Suna*, on the opposite bank *Feriolo* (Leone d'Oro), where the Simplon route (p. 38) quits the lake; a few of the steamboats only touch at these two places. Farther on is **Baveno** *(Beaurivage; Bellevue)*, a village with 1300 inhab., where travellers from the Simplon usually halt in order to visit the

***Borromean Islands**. The steamboats touch at the most S. of these, the *Isola Bella*, which with the *Isola Madre* is the property of the Borromeo family. Between these lies the *Isola dei Pescatori*, or *Superiore*, the property of the fishermen by whom it is occupied; to the N. is the *Isola S. Giovanni* mentioned above. Count *Vitalio Borromeo* (d. 1690) erected a château on ***Isola Bella**, and converted the barren rock into beautiful gardens, rising on 10 terraces 100 ft. above the lake, and containing the most luxuriant products of the south: lemon-trees, cedars, magnolias, cypresses, orange-trees, laurels, magnificent oleanders, etc. The evening light is most favourable for the charming prospect which is here enjoyed. Grottoes of shells, fountains (dry), mosaics, statues, etc. meet the eye in profusion, but in questionable taste.

The *Château*, the size of which is quite disproportionate to the extent of the island, is richly decorated, and contains a *Collection of Pictures* more numerous than valuable. The N. wing is in ruins. The view through the arches of the long galleries under the château is very striking. A domestic hurries visitors through the apartments (fee 50 c. to 1 fr. for each pers.), and consigns them to a gardener, who shows the garden with equal dispatch for a similar fee. Adjacent to the château is the *Hôtel du Dauphin*, or *Delfino* (R. 2, L. 1/2, B. 1, D. at 4 o'cl. 4, A. 3/4 fr., Pension 7—8 fr.). The steamboats do not always touch at Isola Bella; comp. the '*Horaire*', mentioned p. 137. Excursion of 2 hrs. by boat to the other islands with one rower 2 1/2, with two 5 fr.

The **Isola Madre** on its S. side resembles the Isola Bella, and is laid out in 7 terraces with lemon and orange-trellises; on the upper terrace, a dilapidated 'Palazzo'. On the N. side, it is laid out with walks in the English style, which render it a pleasanter resort than the Isola Bella. On the rocks on the S. side are many beautiful aloes, some of which are generally in flower (fee 1 fr.). — The **Isola dei Pescatori** is entirely occupied by a small fishing-village, the single open space being just sufficient for drying the nets.

The scenery of the Borromean Islands rivals that of the Lake of Como in grandeur, and perhaps surpasses it in softness of character. Monte Rosa is not visible; the snow-mountains to the N. W. are the glaciers and peaks of the Simplon; of the nearer mountains the most conspicuous are the white granite-rocks near Baveno (p. 38). The traveller coming from the N. cannot fail to be struck with the loveliness of these banks, studded with innumerable habitations, and clothed with southern vegetation (chestnuts, mulberries, vines, figs, olives), the extensive lake with its deep blue waters, and the beautiful girdle of snowy mountains, combining the stern grandeur of the High Alps and the charms of a southern clime. Rousseau at one time intended to make the Borromean Islands the scene of his 'Nouvelle Héloïse', but considered them too artificial for his romance, in which human nature is pourtrayed with such a masterly hand.

The steamboat now steers S. to

Stresa [*Hôtel des Iles Borromées (diligence office), R. 2—3, B. 1 1/2, A. 3/4, D. 3 1/2 fr., Pension in summer 7 1/2—9 1/2 fr., in winter 5—6 fr., 1/4 M. to the N., recommended for a prolonged stay, boat 1 1/2 for the first, 1 fr. for each subsequent hr. — Hôtel de Milan, R. 1 1/2—2, D. 3, A. 1/2, Pension 6—7 fr., well spoken of; Hôtel du Simplon, both new; Albergo Reale, Ital. inn. *One-horse carr.* to Domo d'Ossola 15—20 fr., *two-horse* 30—35 fr.; to Arona with one horse 6 fr.; carriages for the Simplon route to Sion may also be procured]. The handsome *Rosminian Monastery* halfway up the mountain is now a college. At the N.

extremity of the village is the *Palazzo Bolongaro*. Beautiful cypresses in the *Churchyard*. — Ascent of Monte Motterone see p. 142.

As the boat pursues its course along the W. bank, the construction of the high-road, in many places supported by piers of masonry, attracts attention owing to the difficulties which had to be overcome. The banks gradually become flatter, and Monte Rosa makes its appearance in the W. The boat touches at *Belgirate* (Grand Hôtel du Port-Franc), *Lesa*, and *Meina* on the W., and at *Angera* on the E. bank (at which the steamers touch once only), and finally stops at the Arōna station. The handsome château above Angera belongs to Count Borromeo.

Arona (*Italia, or Posta, diligence office; *Albergo Reale, both near the steamboat quay; *Café* adjoining the Albergo Reale; *Café du Lac* by the quay); an ancient town on the W. bank, with 3153 inhab., extends upwards on the slope of the hill. In the principal church of *S. Maria*, the chapel of the Borromean family, r. of the high altar, contains an *Altar-piece, the Holy Family, by *Gaudenzio Vinci*, a master rarely met with; it is surrounded by 5 other smaller pictures, the upper representing God the Father, at the sides eight saints and the donatrix.

On a height overlooking the entire district, $1/2$ hr. N. of the station and pier, is a colossal **Statue of S. Carlo*, 70 ft. in height, resting on a pedestal 42 ft. high, erected 1697 in honour of the celebrated Cardinal, Count Carlo Borromeo, Archbishop of Milan, born here in 1538, died 1584, canonized 1610.

The head, hands, and feet of the statue are of bronze, the robe of wrought copper. Notwithstanding its enormous dimensions, the statue is not devoid of artistic merit. The various parts are held together by iron clamps, and by stout masonry in the interior. By means of ladders, kept in readiness in the neighbourhood (fee), the lower part of the robe can be attained on the W. side, whence the interior may be entered. The venturesome climber may now ascend by means of iron bars to the head of the statue, which will accommodate 3 persons. A window is introduced at the back of the statue. The suffocating heat and the number of bats which infest the interior render the ascent far from an enjoyable undertaking.

The adjacent church contains a few relics of S. Carlo. The extensive building in the vicinity is an *Ecclesiastical Seminary*. Railway from Arona by Novara to Genoa and Turin see R. 18.

From Arona to Milan.

42 M. — Railway in $2^1/_4$–$2^1/_2$ hrs.; fares 8 fr. 5, 5 fr. 85, 4 fr. 15 c.

The line follows the S. bank of the lake, crosses the *Ticino (Tessin)*, the boundary between Piedmont and Lombardy (till 1859 the boundary between Sardinia and Austria), and reaches *Sesto-Calende* (Posta) at the S. E. extremity of the Lago Maggiore, at the efflux of the Ticino. Stat. *Vergiate*, then *Somma*, where P. Corn. Scipio was defeated by Hannibal, B. C. 218. The district continues arid and sandy as far as stat. **Gallarate** (the junction of the Varese line, p. 131), a town with 5200 inhab.

at the S. E. base of a range of hills which form the limit of the vast and fruitful plain, planted with maize, mulberries, and vines, extending hence to Milan.

Next stat. *Busto Arsizio*, the church of which, designed by Bramante, contains frescoes by Gaudenzio Ferrari. Then stat. *Legnano*, where in 1175 Frederick Barbarossa was defeated by the Milanese. Stat. *Parabiago*. Stat. *Rhò* (p. 111) possesses a church (Madonna dei Miracoli) by Pellegrini, which however remained unfinished till near the middle of the present century. Last stat. *Musocco*.

Milan see R. 19. Omnibuses and fiacres see p. 112.

24. From Stresa to Varallo.
Monte Motterone. Lake of Orta. Val di Sesia.

Three days suffice for a visit to this district, which, though seldom visited, is one of the most beautiful of the S. Alps. Travellers from the Simplon (R. 3) should, after visiting the Borromean Islands, commence this excursion at Stresa (p. 140) and terminate it at Arona; or Gravellona (p. 38) may be taken as the starting-point, and Stresa the termination, in which case the portion between Orta and Varallo must be traversed twice. From Stresa or Isola Bella to Orta 7, from Orta to Varallo 5 hrs. walking; from Varallo to Arona or Novara about 6 hrs. drive. — A guide (to the summit of the pass 4, to Orta 8 fr. and gratuity) should be taken as far as the culminating point of the pass, or to the chalets, especially if the traveller propose to ascend to the summit of the mountain (strongly recommended in fine weather, 2 hrs. additional). A supply of provisions is also necessary for the excursion, as little except milk can be procured. At Orta, mules at high charges.

The *Monte Motterone*, a long mountain-ridge, separates Lago Maggiore from the Lake of Orta. The footpath which traverses it from Stresa to Orta commences opposite Isola Bella, at the landing-place of the boats, and ascends rapidly by the r. bank of the brook as far as the (½ hr.) village, beyond which it pursues a N. direction through the chestnut-wood on the slope of the mountain (½ hr.), commanding a beautiful view of the Lago Maggiore. On (½ hr.) emerging from the wood, the path ascends to the W., traversing heath and pasture; in ½ hr. it passes three rocks, crosses the brook, and (¾ hr.) reaches a small group of houses (*'Ristorante all' Alpe Volpe'*), 10 min. below the culminating point of the pass. The summit of the mountain may be attained hence in 1 hr.

The extensive prospect commanded by the summit of ***Monte Motterone** (4811 ft.) or *Margozzolo*, which might be termed the Rigi of the S. Alps, embraces the entire amphitheatre of mountains from Monte Rosa to the Ortler in the Tyrol. To the r. of Monte Rosa appear the snow-mountains of Monte Moro, Pizzo di Bottarello, Simplon, Monte Leone, Gries, and St. Gotthard; farther E. the conical Stella above Chiavenna, and the long, imposing ice-range of the Bernina, which separates the Val Bregaglia (p. 49) from the Valtellina (p. 56). At the spectator's feet lie six different lakes, the Lake of Orta, Lago Maggiore, Lago di Monate, Lago di Comabbio, Lago di Biandrone, and Lago di Varese; farther to the r. stretch the extensive plains of Lombardy and Piedmont, in the centre of which rises the lofty cathedral of Milan. The Ticino and the Sesia meander like silver threads through the plains, and by a singular optical delusion frequently appear to traverse a lofty table-land. The simultaneous view of the Isola Madre in Lago Maggiore and the Isola S. Giulio in the Lake of Orta has a remarkably picturesque effect. The mountain itself consists of a number of barren summits, studded with occasional chalets, shaded by trees. At its base it is encircled by chestnut-trees, and the foliage and luxuriant vegetation of the landscape far and wide impart a peculiar charm to the picture.

At the chalets, 25 min. from the summit of the pass, milk may be procured; (¼ hr.) the solitary church of *Madonna di Lucciago*, (¾ hr.) *Chegino*, (¼ hr.) *Armeno*, (40 min.) *Masino* are successively passed, and (½ hr.) the high-road is reached (¾ M. from Orta) near the pension *Ronchetti Posta*. A short distance beyond the latter a path diverges from the road to the r., ascending in 10 min. to the *Sacro Monte* (see below), which may now in passing be most conveniently visited.

Orta (1214 ft.) (**Leone d'Oro; *Ronchetti* or *Hôtel S. Giulio*, both on the quay; one-horse carr. to Gravellona 8 fr.), a small town with narrow streets, paved with marble slabs, is most picturesquely situated on a promontory extending into the lake, at the base of a precipitous cliff. At the S. entrance of the town is the handsome villa of the Marquis Natta of Novara.

Omnibus and Diligence from Orta daily to *Omegna* (Posta), at the N. extremity of the Lago di Orta, and by *Gravellona* (p. 38) to *Pallanza* (p. 139); also from Orta by *Buccione*, a village at the S. end of the Lago di Orta, commanded by the old *Castello di Buccione*, to *Gozzano*, the terminus of the Novara-Gozzano railway.

Above Orta rises the **Sacro Monte** (ascent between the two hotels), a beautifully wooded eminence, laid out as a park, on which 20 chapels were erected in the 16th cent. in honour of S. Francis of Assisi, each containing a scene from the life of the saint. The life-size figures are composed of terra cotta, highly coloured, with a background al fresco; as a whole, though destitute of artistic worth, the representations are animated and effective. The best groups are in the 13th, 16th, and 20th chapels, the latter representing the canonization of the saint and the assembly of cardinals. The °*Tower* on the summit of the hill commands an admirable panorama; the snowy peak of Monte Rosa rises to the W. above the lower intervening mountains. The '*Eremita del Monte*' expects a fee of 1 fr., for showing the above-mentioned three chapels.

In the **Lake of Orta** (1½ M. in width, 9 M. in length), opposite to Orta, rises the rocky island of **S. Giulio,** covered with trees and groups of houses. The Church, founded by St. Julius, who came from Greece in 379 to convert the inhabitants of this district to Christianity, has been frequently restored; it contains several good reliefs, some ancient frescoes, and in the sacristy a Madonna by *Gaudenzio Ferrari*.

On the W. bank of the lake, opposite the island, the white houses of the village of **Pella** peep from the midst of vineyards and groves of chestnut and walnut-trees. Passage from Orta to Pella 2 fr. with 2 rowers.

A path towards the S. winds upwards from Pella, through a grove of chestnut and fruit trees, in 20 min. to the *Madonna del Sasso*, the picturesque church of the village of *Boletto*. An open space by the church, on the verge of a precipice several hundred feet above the lake, commands a fine prospect.

At Pella mules may be procured for the journey over the Colma to Varallo (5 hrs., guide unnecessary). A steep path ascends the hill to the W., traversing luxuriant gardens (vines, figs, pumpkins, and fruit-trees); in 12 min. the ascent to the r. must be avoided. In 1 hr. from Pella, *Arola* is reached, at a small chapel beyond which the ascent to the r. must again be avoided; the path pursues a straight direction and soon descends. The *Pellino*, a mountain-torrent, descending from the Colma, forms (5 min.) a picturesque waterfall. Beautiful retrospective views of the lake. The path now ascends through a shady wood, between disintegrated blocks of granite which crumble beneath the touch, to the **Col di Colma** (2½ hrs. from Pella), a ridge connecting *Monte Pizzigone* with *Monte Ginistrella*. The prospect of the Alps is beautiful, embracing Monte Rosa, the lakes of Orta and Varese, and the plain of Lombardy. The entire route is attractive. In descending on the W. side (to the r.) the traveller overlooks the fruitful *Val Sesia*, with its numerous villages. The path, again traversing groves of chestnut and walnut-trees, carpeted with turf and wild-flowers, now leads through the *Val Duggia* to (1 hr.) *Civiasco* and (1 hr.)

Varallo (1299 ft.) (**Italia; *Posta; Falcone Nero*), the principal village (3200 inhab.) in the valley of the *Sesia*, which is frequently dry in summer. The old town and the Sacro Monte, when seen through the arches of the bridge, have an extremely picturesque aspect.

The **Sacro Monte**, the object of numerous pilgrimages, rises in the immediate vicinity of the town. It is attained in ¼ hr. by a path shaded by beautiful trees, but the enjoyment is somewhat marred by the importunities of numerous beggars. The summit, surmounted by a chapel and crucifix, commands a magnificent view. Besides the church there are in all 46 Chapels or Oratories on the summit and slopes of the Sacro Monte, many of them buried among the trees, containing representations of scenes from the life of the Saviour, in terra cotta, with life-size figures arranged in groups. Each chapel is devoted to a different subject; the 1st, for example, the Fall, the 2nd the Annunciation, and so on to the 46th, which contains the Entombment of the Virgin. Some of the frescoes by *Pelegrino Tibaldi* and *Gaudenzio Ferrari* are well worthy of inspection. This '*Nuova Gerusalemme nel Sacro Monte di Varallo*' was founded by Bernardino Caloto, a Milanese nobleman, with the sanction of Pope Innocent VIII. As a resort of pilgrims, it did not come into vogue until after the visits of Cardinal Borromeo (p. 141) in 1578 and 1584, from which period most of the chapels date.

Varallo is admirably adapted as head-quarters for excursions to the neighbouring valleys, being easily accessible, and in beauty and grandeur of scenery surpassed by no other Alpine district (comp. *Baedeker's Switzerland*).

A carriage-road (omnibus twice daily) descends the picturesque valley of the Sesia to (6 M.) *Borgo-Sesia*, (7½ M.) *Romagnano* (Post); then quitting the Val Sesia, by *Sizzano*, *Fara*, *Briona* to *Novara* (p. 110).

25. From Arona to Genoa.

Railway in 5—6 hrs.; fares 19 fr. 65, 13 fr. 10, 9 fr. 85 c.; no luggage free except small articles carried in the hand. Good railway refreshment-rooms at Novara and Alessandria. Those who have quitted Arona late in the day will prefer spending the night at Alessandria to performing the interesting journey through the Apennines in the dark.

The railway at first commands picturesque views (to the l.) of the S. extremity of *Lago Maggiore* (p. 141) and the mountains of the *Brianza* (p. 121). Numerous cuttings and embankments. A flat, agricultural district extending as far as Alessandria is soon reached. The Ticino flows at some distance to the l.

The first stations are *Borgo-Ticino*, *Varallo-Pombia*, and *Oleggio* (to the r. a fine glimpse of the Monte Rosa chain). Then stat. *Bellinzago*, and **Novara** (p. 110), where the Arona and Genoa line is crossed by that from Milan to Turin (R. 18); to *Turin* in 3 hrs., fares 10 fr. 45, 7 fr. 85, 5 fr. 25 c.

Next stations *Vespolate*, *Borgo Lavezzaro*, *Mortara*, the last of which was taken by storm by the Austrians two days before the battle of Novara (p. 111). To the r. and l. are numerous fields of rice, which are laid under water during two months in the year.

Branch Line from Mortara (in 20 min.; fares 1 fr. 45, 1 fr. 5, 75 c.) N.E. to **Vigevano** *(Albergo Reale)*, a town of considerable importance in the silk-trade, with 15,000 inhab., situated near the r. bank of the Ticino. Spacious market-place surrounded by arcades. A direct line from Vigevano to Milan is in course of construction.

Next stations *Valle*, *Sartirana*, *Torre-Beretti* (railway to Pavia see p. 149).

To the l. the long chain of the *Apennines* forms a blue line in the distance. Rice-fields are seen in every direction. The line crosses the *Po* by means of a bridge of 21 arches, and traverses sandy hills planted with vines. Beyond stat. **Valenza** (branch-line to Pavia, see p. 149, to Vercelli p. 110) the train passes through a tunnel $1^1/_3$ M. in length. Then stat. *Val Madonna*; several picturesquely situated small towns lie on the chain of hills to the r. The *Tanaro* is then crossed, and some fortifications passed.

Alessandria *(Hôtel de l'Univers*, R. $1^1/_2$, B. 1 fr.; *Europa*; *Victoria*; *Aquila*; **Railway Restaurant)*, a town with 54,000 inhab., situated on the *Tanaro*, in a marshy district, an important stronghold of the Italian kingdom, was founded in 1167 by the Lombard towns in alliance against the Emp. Frederick Barbarossa and named after Pope Alexander III. It is surnamed *della paglia*, i. e. of straw, perhaps because the first houses were built of clay and straw. The town contains nothing to detain the traveller.

Carriages are usually changed here. Railway W. to Turin, see R. 13; E to Piacenza, Parma, Modena, Bologna (Faenza, Ancona), RR. 12, 40; to Cavaller-Maggiore p. 109.

Branch Line to Acqui from Alessandria, in a S. direction, in 1 hr. 10 min.; fares 3 fr. 75, 2 fr. 65, 1 fr. 90 c. — Acqui, the *Aquae Statielae* of the Romans, an episcopal town on the *Bormida* with 8600 inhab., is well known for its mineral waters, which resemble those of Aix-la-Chapelle in their constituent parts and effects. The *Cathedral*, with its double aisles, dates from the 12th cent. Near Acqui the Austrians and Piedmontese were defeated by the French in 1794. Good wine is produced in the vicinity. This line will be prolonged to *Cairo* and *Savona* (p. 95), where it will unite with the coast-line from Genoa to Nice.

The line crosses the *Bormida*, which a short distance below Alessandria falls into the Tanaro. About $1^1/_4$ M. E. of the bridge, in the plain between the Bormida and the *Scrivia*, is situated the small village of *Marengo*, near which, on June 14th, 1800, the battle which influenced the destinies of the whole of Europe was fought. The French were commanded by Napoleon, the Austrians by Melas. The battle lasted 12 hrs., and the French lost Desaix, one of their best generals.

The district which the railway now intersects is at first flat; in the distance rise the Apennines. Next stat. *Frugarōlo*. Stat. **Novi** [Branch-line to Pavia and Milan see R. 26, to Piacenza see R. 12], situated on the hills to the r., commanded by a lofty square tower, is known as the scene of the victory gained by the Austrians and Russians under Suwarow over the French on Aug. 15th, 1799. At stat. *Serravalle* the train enters the mountainous district; then *Arquata*, with a ruined castle on the height. Between this point and Genoa there are eleven tunnels. The train winds its way through profound rocky ravines *(la bocchetta)*, traversing lofty embankments and several times crossing the mountain-brook *(Scrivia)*. The scenery is imposing and beautiful. Stat. *Isola del Cantone;* on the height to the r. the ruins of an old castle. Stat. *Busalla*, the culminating point of the line, 1192 ft. above the sea-level, is the watershed between the Adriatic and the Mediterranean.

The last tunnel, the *Galleria dei Giovi*, is upwards of 2 M. in length, the transit occupying 7 min. Then several short cuttings. The landscape becomes more smiling; the hills, planted with the vine and corn, gradually become more thickly sprinkled with the villas of the Genoese.

To the r., on the loftiest summit of the mountain near stat. *Pontedecimo*, rises the white church of the *Madonna della Guardia*. Next stat. *Bolzaneto* and *Rivarolo*. The railway now crosses the *Polcevēra*, the stony channel of which is occasionally covered by an impetuous torrent. On the summits of the heights to the l. are towers appertaining to the former fortifications of Genoa. The last stat. *S. Pier d'Arēna* is a suburb of Genoa. On the r. are the lighthouse and citadel, beneath which the train enters the town by a tunnel. R., before the station is entered, stands the *Palazzo del Principe Doria*.

Genoa, see p. 86.

26. From Milan to Genoa by Pavia.
Certosa di Pavia.

Railway from Milan to Genoa in $4^3/_4$—$5^1/_2$ hrs.; fares 17 fr. 25, 12 fr. 25, 8 fr. 75 c. An early train should be selected in order that nothing of the remarkable scenery of the Apennines be lost. Those who desire to visit both the Certosa and Pavia from Milan are recommended to take a return-ticket to Pavia, inspect the town (in about 3 hrs.), and then drive (one-horse carriage 4—5 fr.) to the Certosa, a pleasant journey of 50 min., skirting a canal. A visit to the Certosa occupies $1^1/_2$—2 hrs.; thence to stat. Certosa a walk of $^1/_4$ hr. (small café at the station).

The train to Pavia at first follows the Piacenza line, then diverges to the S.W. before stat. *Rogoredo* is reached. The high road, which in a straight direction follows the *Naviglio di Pavia* (p. 113), a broad canal, lies on the r. Below Pavia, near the union of this canal with the *Ticino*, there are some remarkable locks. The district is flat; underwood and rice-fields are traversed alternately. Stations *Locate* and *Villamaggiore*.

On the high road, to the W. of the railway, is situated *Binasco*, a small town with an ancient castle, in which, on Sept. 13th, 1418, the jealous and tyrannical Duke Fil. Maria Visconti caused his noble and innocent consort Beatrice di Tenda (p. 107) to be executed.

If the traveller prefer to visit the Certosa on the way to Pavia, the train is quitted at stat. *Guinzano* or *della Certosa*, whence the path planted with willows is followed, and the long garden-wall of the monastery skirted towards the r. (walk of $^1/_4$ hr.). The *Sagrestano* should be enquired for at the entrance. A French lay-brother generally officiates as guide (fee for 1 pers. 1 fr.). The monastery at present numbers 31 inmates.

The celebrated *Certosa, or Carthusian monastery, founded in 1396 by Gian Galeazzo Visconti, suppressed under Emperor Joseph II., was restored to its original destination in 1844 and placed at the disposal of the Carthusians. The **Façade, commenced in 1473 by Ambrogio Borgognone, an example of the richest Renaissance style, is entirely covered with marble of different colours and most tastefully decorated; below are medallions of the Roman emperors, above them scenes from sacred history, the foundation of the monastery, and a number of statuettes of apostles and saints. This is unquestionably the finest work of this decorative description in N. Italy, though it is far inferior to the façades of the cathedrals of Orvieto and Siena. The nave, commenced in 1396 by *Marco di Compione*, in the Gothic style, with aisles and 14 chapels, is surmounted by a dome. The *Interior* (nave, transept, and side-chapels only accessible to ladies) is sumptuously and tastefully fitted up. Beautiful pavement of modern mosaic. The chapels and altars are adorned with valuable columns and precious stones; the frescoes and paintings by Borgognone, Procaccini, Crespi, Guercino, Bianchi and others are of no great value; fine Madonna and Child by *Luini*, al fresco. The magnificent **Monument of Gian Galeazzo Visconti* in the S. transept, in white marble, was designed by Galeazzo Pellegrini in 1490, but not completed till 1562. The N. transept contains the monument of Duke *Ludovico Sforza* and his consort *Beatrice d'Este* (d. 1497). The *Choir possesses a fine altar with carving of the 16th cent. The stalls are adorned with figures of apostles and saints, designed by Borgognone. Beautiful wood-carving in the old sacristy, N. of the choir. In the new sacristy is an altar-piece, representing the *Assumption, by Andrea Solari, the upper part of the picture by Bernardino Campi of Cremona. The front portion of the * *Cloisters* is finely decorated in terra cotta. Around the extensive posterior cloisters are situated the 24 different dwellings occupied by the monks, each consisting of three rooms and a small garden. — The battle of Pavia, at which Francis I. of France was taken prisoner by Emperor Charles V., took place in 1525 near the Certosa.

Pavia (*Croce Bianca; Lombardia; Pozzo*, near the bridge over the Ticino; *Tre Re*, starting-point of the diligences, R. $1^1/_2$, L. $^1/_2$ fr.; *Café* at the corner of the Corso Vittorio Emanuele and the Corso Cavour), with 25,000 inhab., situated near the confluence of the Ticino and the Po, the *Ticinum* of the ancients, subsequently *Papĭa*, was also known as the *Città di Cento Torri* on account of its hundred towers, many of which still exist. In the middle ages it was the faithful ally of the German emperors until it was subjugated by the Milanese; it is still partly surrounded by the walls and fortifications of that period. At the N. end of the town is situated the *Castle*, erected by the Visconti in 1460 – 69, now employed as a barrack. The *Corso Vittorio Emanuele*, intersecting the town in a straight direction from N. to S., from the Porta di Milano to the Porta Ticinese, leads to the covered *Bridge (a pleasant promenade with picturesque view) over the *Ticino*, which is here navigated by barges and steamboats. A chapel stands on the bridge, halfway across.

N. of the Corso, near the bridge over the Ticino, is situated the *Piazza del Duomo* with the *Cathedral* (Pl. 4), an extensive rotunda with four arms, designed by Bramante, but never completed. In the interior, on the r., is the sumptuous **Arca di S. Agostino*, adorned with 290 figures (of saints and allegorical personages), commenced, it is supposed, in 1362 by Bonino da Campiglione, by whom the figures on the tombs of the Scaliger family at Verona (p. 165) were executed. The lance of Roland is also preserved here. Then, r. of the entrance, a large model of the church, in wood, executed according to the original design. — *S. Michele* (Pl. 7), a Romanesque structure erroneously attributed to the Lombard kings, belongs to the latter

A		B		C		D	
1 Bagni pubblici	A. 5.	13. San Primo	C. 5.	26. Pio Ritiro di S. Croce		B. 3.
2 Casa d'Industria	C. 4.	14. San Giacomo e Filippo	C. 5.	27. " " " S. Margherita		C 5. 6.
3 Castello	C. 3.	15. Canepa nova	C. 4.	28. Seminario Vescovile		C. 5.
Chiese:		16. Collegio Borromeo	C. 5. 6.	29. Teatro		B. 3.
4. Cattedrale	B. 4.	17. " " Caccia	B. 3.	30. Ufficio della Posta		B. 4.
5. San Teodoro	A. 3.	18. " " Ghislieri	C. 4.	31. Università		B. 4.
6. S. Maria del Carmine	B. 4.	19. Ginnasio	C. 4.			
7. San Michele	B. 5.	20. Orto botanico	D. 4.			
8. San Francesco	C. 4.	21. Ospitale Civico	B. 4.	Alberghi:		
9. Santa Maria in Betlemme	A. 6.	22. " " Militare	A. 4.	a. Croce bianca		
10. San Gervaso	A. 3.	23. Palazzo Civico o Broletto	B. 4.	b. Lombardia		
11. Gesù	B. 4.	24. " " Vescovile	B. 4.	c. Pozzo		
12. San Marino	B. 5.	25. Pio luogo degli Esposti	C. 4.	d. Tre Re		

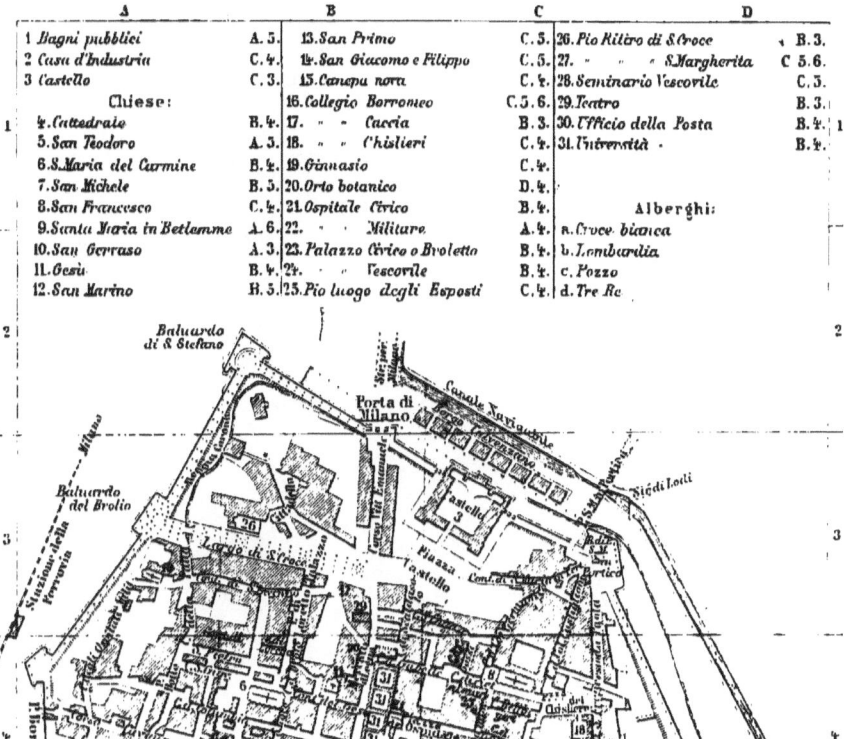

part of the 11th cent., but has been recently restored. The façade is adorned with numerous reliefs of great antiquity. The nave and aisles are supported by four pillars, from which rise double round arches. The very short choir terminates in an apse. Over the centre of the transept rises a dome. The crypt is beneath the choir. — *S. Maria del Carmine* (Pl. 6), an extensive and venerable edifice of 1325, is architecturally interesting. In the Piazza del Carmine, opposite the church, is a handsome court of the 15th cent. — The *University* (Pl. 31), the oldest in Europe, said to have been founded by Charlemagne, situated in the Contrada Malaspina, is externally a much more considerable structure than that of Padua (p. 178); the different courts of the interior are surrounded by handsome arcades and embellished with numerous memorial-tablets, busts, and monuments of celebrated professors and students of this university. In the first court is a marble statue of the mathematician *Antonio Bordoni* (d. 1864). — At the entrance to the court of the *Casa Malaspina*, near Porta Castello, at the N.E. extremity of the town, are the busts of *Boëthius* and *Petrarch*. The former, when confined here by Emperor Theodosius, composed his work on the 'Consolation of Philosophy'; the latter once resided here with his daughter and son-in-law. His grandson, who died at the Casa Malaspina, was interred in the neighbouring church of S. Zeno. A short poem of Petrarch in allusion to this event, in six Latin distiches, is one of the many inscriptions on the wall opposite the entrance.

Railway from Pavia to Valenza in 2 hrs.; fares 5 fr. 75, 4 fr. 5, 2 fr. 90 c. The line crosses the Ticino and intersects the *Lomellina*, or broad plain of the Po, in a S.W. direction. After a number of unimportant stations are passed, the line reaches *Torre-Beretti*, then *Valenza* (p. 145).

Beyond Pavia the line crosses the Ticino, and a short distance farther the Po and one of its small affluents. Stations *Cava*, *Bressana*, *Calcababbio*, and

Voghera; this and the journey to Tortona see p. 84. Novi and the journey to

Genoa see p. 146.

27. From Milan to Verona.

Railway in 5½—7 hrs.; fares 18 fr. 56, 13 fr. 53, 10 fr. 61 c. Finest views to the left.

The train starts from the station outside the Porta Tosa. First stat. *Limito* and *Melzo*. Near stat. *Cassano*, a considerable village with handsome houses, the blue *Adda*, which issues from the Lake of Como near Lecco (p. 130), is crossed. At *Treviglio* the line turns to the N. (Branch-line to *Cremona*, see R. 32.)

Bergāmo (1250 ft.) (*Italia, R. from 2 fr., L. ½, A. ½ fr.; *Venezia, moderate; *Caffè Centrale), capital of the district, or 'Delegation', consisting of two distinct quarters, the new town *(Borgo*

S. Leonardo) and the old town *(Città)*, is an important commercial place with 35,197 inhab., celebrated for its great Fair, the *Fiera di S. Alessandro*, held annually from the middle of August to the middle of September. The *New Town*, containing the *Fiera*, or site of the fair, the corsia, and the new town-hall *(municipalità)*, is situated on level ground. The *Old town* on the hill, connected with the lower town by means of the Strada Vittorio Emanuele, and consisting principally of very steep streets, is the seat of the government-offices and courts of judicature. The *Promenade* affords a fine view of the richly cultivated plain and the beautiful amphitheatre formed by the surrounding mountains, especially those to the N.E. The *Castle*, rising on the hill to the N.W. above the old town, commands a more imposing and extensive prospect. In the market-place, now the *Piazza Garibaldi*, is situated the *Palazzo Nuovo*, seat of the municipal authorities, erected in the Renaissance style by Scamozzi, but still in an unfinished condition. Opposite to it is the library in the Gothic *Palazzo Vecchio*, or *Broletto*, the ground-floor of which consists of a hall supported by pillars and columns. Here stands the *Monument of Torquato Tasso*, whose father *Bernardo* was born at Bergamo in 1493; near it a handsome fountain. At the back of the Broletto is situated *S. Maria Maggiore*, erected 1173 in the Romanesque style (entrance on the S. side), with ancient portals, supported by lions, on the N. and S. sides. Adjoining the former is the rich Renaissance façade of the chapel of the Colleoni. The interior contains some ancient pictures, fine *carved work on the choir-stalls, admirable inlaid wood (intarsia) by the Bergamasque Giov. Franc. Capo Ferrato, the handsome monument of the celebrated composer *Donizetti* of Bergamo (d. 1848), by *Vinc. Vela*, and opposite to it that of his teacher *Simone Mayr* (d. 1845). The *Cappella Colleoni*, in the early Renaissance style, contains the monument of the founder Bart. Colleoni (d. 1475), with reliefs representing the Bearing of the Cross, Crucifixion, and Descent from the Cross; above them is the gilded equestrian statue of Colleoni. Adjacent is the much smaller, but beautifully executed monument of his daughter Medea. — *S. Grata*, adjacent to a nunnery, contains fine paintings and reliefs. On the slope of the hill, in the street leading to the lower town, is situated the *Accademia Carrara*, a school of art containing models and pictures; in the small cabinet Pius VII., by Canova.

From Bergamo to Lecco railway in $1^1/_4$ hr.; fares 4 fr., 2 fr. 90, 2 fr. 5 c.; from Lecco to *Varenna* and *Colico* see p. 130.

The line now describes a wide curve towards the S.E., and at stat. *Seriate* crosses the *Serio*. Stations *Gorlago* and *Grumello* (hence to the Lago d'Iseo see p. 159). At stat. *Palazzolo* the *Oglio* (p. 159), descending from the Lago d'Iseo, is crossed. Then stat. *Coccaglio*, with the monastery of *Mont' Orfano* on a height, stat. *Ospedaletto*, and stat. *Brescia* (see R. 30), commanded by its castle.

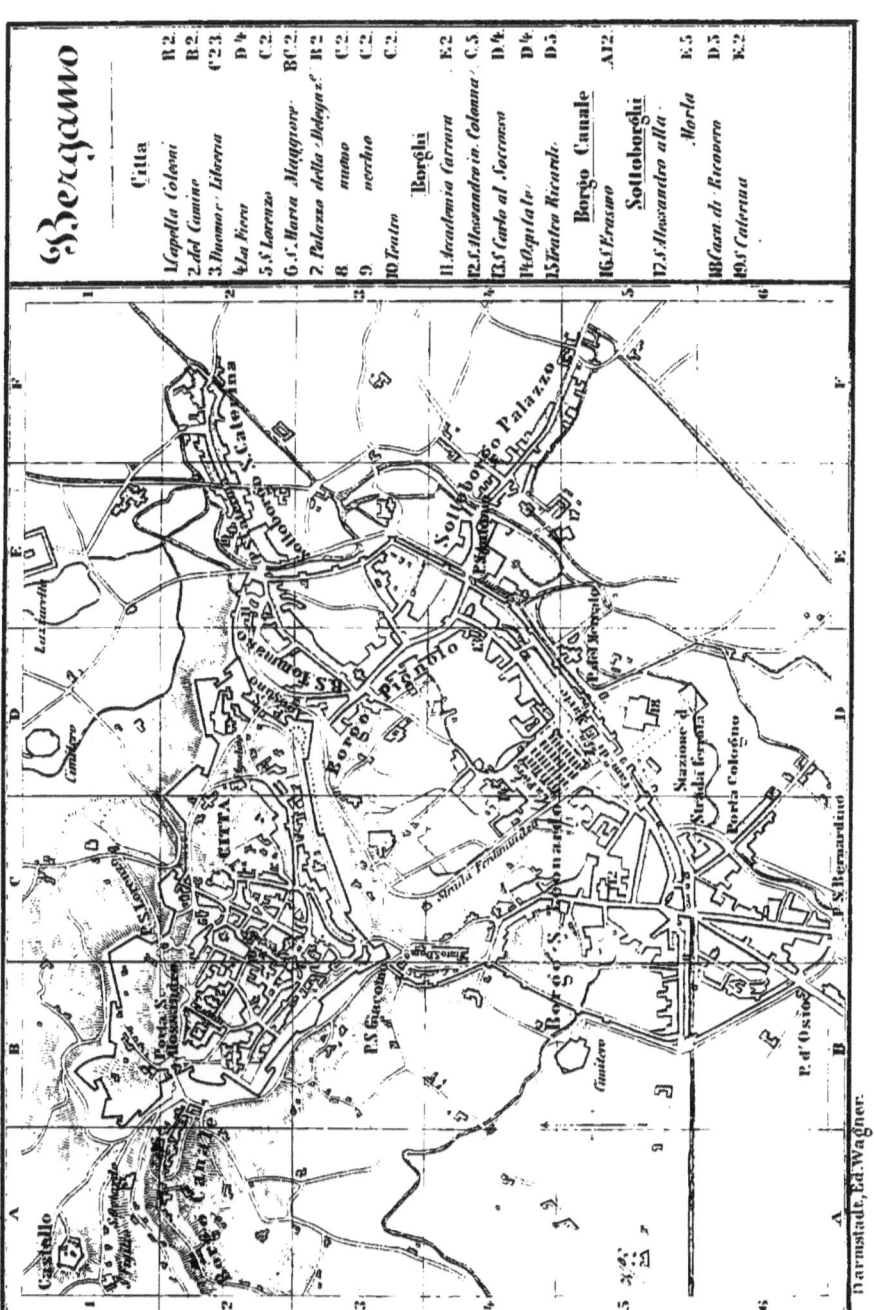

The slopes near Brescia are sprinkled with numerous villas. The red colour of the mountains is due to the presence of abundant iron-ore (comp. p. 155). The line speedily quits the hilly district. Stat. *Rezzato*. Near stat. *Ponte S. Marco* the *Chiese* is crossed. Beyond stat. *Lonato* is a short tunnel and a long cutting.

A long viaduct now carries the line to **Desenzano** (p. 152), a harbour at the S.W. extremity of the *Lago di Garda* (see below). The railway affords an admirable survey of the lake and the peninsula of *Sermione* (p. 152), connected with the land by a narrow isthmus. The venerable castle with its pinnacles and tower is especially conspicuous.

Next stat. *Pozzolengo*. In this district, extending from the banks of the lake to a point considerably beyond *Guidizzolo* (on the road from Brescia to Mantua), the obstinate and sanguinary battle of Solferino was fought on June 24th, 1859, between the united French and Italian armies and that of Austria. The defeat of the latter shortly afterwards led to the Peace of Villafranca (p. 169). The total extent of the line of battle amounted to upwards of 15 M. The village of *Solferino* (Inn, good red wine; guides) lies on the heights to the S., about 5 M. from the railway; carriage thither and back, from stat. Desenzano 15 fr.

The train next reaches (in 20 min. from Desenzano) **Peschiera** (*Railway Restaurant;* the station is $3/4$ M. from the town; in the latter: *Tre Corone*, dear), a fortified town situated at the S.E. extremity of the Lago di Garda, at the efflux of the *Mincio* from the lake. In 1848 Peschiera was taken by the Piedmontese after a gallant defence by the Austrian General Rath. The villages of *Volta* and *Goito*, situated at some distance to the S., were also the scene of battles during the same year.

Beyond Peschiera the train crosses the Mincio. Stat. *Castelnuovo;* the village is picturesquely situated on the l. Beyond a chain of hills, penetrated by means of several cuttings, the train reaches stat. *Somma Campagna*, then *S. Lucia*, and finally

Verona, see p. 163.

28. The Lago di Garda.

Steamboat on the W. Bank between Desenzano and Riva twice weekly in $4^1/2$ hrs.; fares 4 fr. 35, 2 fr. 40 c.; stations *Salo*, *Maderno*, *Gargnano*, *Tignale*, *Tremosine*, *Limone*, *Riva*. — On the E. Bank between Riva and Peschiera, also twice weekly, in $4^1/2$ hrs.; fares 4 fr. 50, 2 fr. 50 c.; stations *Malcesine*, *Assenza*, *Castelletto*, *Torri*, *Garda*, *Bardolino*, *Lazise*, *Peschiera*. — Restaurant on board the steamers.

The **Lago di Garda**, the *Lacus Benacus* of the Romans, the largest of the N. Italian lakes, is 37 M. in length, and $2^1/2$—14 M. in width. Area 189 sq. M., depth in many places upwards of 1000 ft. The greater part of it belongs to the kingdom of Italy, the N. extremity only with Riva being Austrian.

The lake is rarely perfectly calm, and in stormy weather is almost as violently agitated as the sea itself, a circumstance recorded by Virgil (Georg. II. 160). The bluish green water, like that of all the Alpine lakes, is remarkably clear. The *carpione*, or salmon-trout, which attains a weight of 25 lbs., the *trutta*, or trout, 1—1½ lb., the *sardenne*, etc. are excellent fish, and form one of the chief articles of commerce here.

The banks, although inferior in attraction to those of the Lake of Como, present a great variety of beautiful landscapes, enhanced by the imposing expanse of the water. Those of the S. half are flat and well cultivated, but they begin to assume a bolder appearance between Capo S. Vigilio and a point to the N. of Salò, where the lake contracts. The vegetation is luxuriant, especially on the more sheltered W. bank. Even the sensitive lemon arrives at maturity here (but nowhere else in N. Italy, except on the Riviera di Ponente, see p. 94), but the trees require to be carefully covered in winter. This is accomplished with the aid of numerous white pillars of brick, 8—20 ft. in height, erected at regular intervals, and united by means of transverse beams at the top. The fruit is more bitter and aromatic than that of Sicily, suffers less from carriage, and keeps longer. Price in the most productive seasons 3—4 fr. per hundred, frequently however as high as 10 fr. (as in 1869).

Desenzano (**Mayer's Hôtel*, with fine view of the lake; *Vittoria*; *Aquila*), a thriving little town with 4000 inhab., at the S.W. angle of the lake, is a station on the railway from Milan to Verona (R. 27). Omnibus from the steamboat to the train 50 c., luggage 25 c.

To the E., not quite halfway to Peschiera (p. 154) the narrow promontory of *Sermione* ('*Sirmio, peninsularum insularumque ocellus*'), 3 M. in length, projects into the lake, which here attains its greatest width. The poet Catullus once resided and composed his poems in a villa on this peninsula. The ruins still exist, consisting of two vaults, remains of a bath, etc. A castle was also erected here by the Scala family, who for upwards of a century (1262—1389) were princes of Verona.

The Steamboat runs near the bank, but does not touch at the small villages of *Moniga* and *Manerba*. Opposite to the promontory of *S. Vigilio* (p. 154) it next passes the small *Isola di S. Biagio* and the beautiful, crescent-shaped island of *Lecchio*, or *Isola dei Frati*, the property of the Marchese Scotti of Bergamo. The latter was fortified by the Italians in 1859, but the works have since been removed. The steamer now steers to the W. and enters the bay of **Salò** (*Gambĕro*, Ital. style, but comfortable), a delightfully situated town with 3400 inhab., surrounded with terraces of fragrant lemon-groves. The *Monte S. Bar-*

tolommeo, at the foot of which the town lies, affords a charming view, especially by evening light. (Diligence to Brescia see below.) *Gardone* is the next village; then *Maderno*, on a promontory extending far into the lake, beyond which rises the *Monte Pizzocolo*. Farther on are *Toscolano*, *Cocina*, and *Bogliaco*. At the latter a large country-residence of Count Bettuno. Most of the lemon-gardens belong to members of the Italian nobless. Then **Gargnano** (**Albergo del Cervo*), an important looking village (4000 inhab.) in the midst of lemon and olive plantations, and one of the most attractive points on the lake (diligence hence twice daily to Brescia by Salò, Gavardo, and Rezzata).

The mountains now become higher. *Muslone*, *Piovere*, *Tignale*, and *Oldese* are four small villages almost adjacent. Then *Tremosine*, on the hill, scarcely visible from the lake, to which a steep path ascends on the precipitous and rocky bank. In a bay farther on are seen the white houses of *Limone*, also surrounded by lemon and olive plantations. The Austrian frontier is passed a short distance beyond *La Nova*. A view is soon obtained of the **Fall of the Ponal*, which presents a more imposing appearance seen from the steamboat than from the bank (see below). Finally

Riva (*Albergo Traffellini al Sole d'Oro, R. 80, L. and A. 50 Austr. kr.; *Giardino; Albergo del Popolo, also a good restaurant; Café Andreis, under the arcades near the quay; *Baths* in the lake at Traffellini's 30 kr.; public baths to the W. of the town), charmingly situated at the N. extremity of the lake, and bounded by precipitous mountains on the E. and W. The *Church of the Minorites*, at the entrance to the town from Arco, erected in the 16th cent. and decorated with stucco and gilding, is an admirable example of its style. It contains altar-pieces by Guido Reni, Palma Vecchio, etc. The *Parish Church* in the town contains modern pictures and frescoes. The watchtower of *La Rocca* on the lake, fortified anew since 1850, and the old *Castello*, high on the mountain to the W., greatly enhance the picturesqueness of the place. The situation of Riva is sheltered and healthy, the heat of summer being tempered by the proximity of the lake, and is also frequently resorted to as a winter residence. Private apartments easily procured on moderate terms. Luggage is examined on arriving at, and on departing from Riva by Austr. and Ital. officials respectively.

Excursions: **Fall of the Ponal** (2 hrs.). The high road is followed to the entrance of the Ledro Valley. Here by a path l., across a bridge, an ascent, and finally a descent to the cascade. (Boat thither 2 fl.) The new *Road from Riva to Brescia through the Ledro Valley is very interesting and commands magnificent views.

Monte Brione, with a fort, between *Riva* and *Torbole*, $1/2$ hr. N.E., commands a fine view. — Pleasant excursions N.E. to the *Castello of Arco*; N. to the falls of the *Varrone* and castle of *Tenno*, ascending to the *Villa Fiorio*, returning by *Pranzo*.

Monte Baldo (7195 ft.), a ridge 45 M. long, separating the lake from the Adige, is best ascended from *Nago*, 8 M. E. of Riva. The highest point on the N. is the *Altissimo di Nago* (6624 ft.), reached in 4¹/₂ hrs. with guide; extensive panorama, embracing a large portion of N. Italy and the snowy Ortler.

Giudicaria. The road thither ascends the Ledro Valley (fall of the Ponal see above) to (6 M.) *Molina*, past the *Lago di Ledro* through (1¹/₂ M.) *Mezzo Lago*, (1¹/₂ M.) *Pieve*, (³/₄ M.) *Bezzecca*, (³/₄ M.) *Enguiso*, (³/₄ M.) *Leuzumo*, and across the *Monte Tratta* to (3 hrs.) *Campi* and back (3 M.) to Riva. — Or in a N. direction by *Tenno*, *Balino*, *Fiave*, and *Campo* to *Stenico*, where there is a fine waterfall; then to the r., by the road which leads through a picturesque rocky ravine, by the Baths of *Cumano* to *Le Sarchè*. Thence either down the valley of the *Sarca* to *Arco* and Riva, or by *Vezzano* to *Trent* (comp. p. 62).

From Riva to Mori (rail. station, p. 63), 10 M., omnibus twice daily in 3 hrs. by *Torbole*, a harbour on the N.E. bank of the lake, and *Nago*, which affords a magnificent retrospect. The road ascends a wild and rocky height, passes the picturesque lake of *Loppio* and reaches *Mori* (p. 63).

Ten min. after the steamboat has quitted Riva the above mentioned fall of the Ponal comes in view. *Torbole* (see above) is left on the l. The steamer now steers S. to **Malcesine** (2000 inhab.), a good harbour on the E. bank, with an old castle of Charlemagne, which was subsequently a robbers' stronghold. Gœthe, while sketching this ruin, narrowly escaped being arrested as a spy by the Venetian government. The castle has since been restored. Beyond it is the rock of *Isoletto*, then *Cassone*, and a short distance farther the small island of *Tremelone*. The next places of importance are *Castello*, *S. Giovanni*, *Castelletto*, *Montagna*, and somewhat inland *Torri*. The banks gradually become flatter. The promontory of *San Vigilio*, sheltered from the N. wind by the Monte Baldo, extends far into the lake, and is the most beautiful point of view on the E. bank. The surrounding hills are planted with vines, olives, and fig-trees. The village of **Garda** (1100 inhab.), beautifully situated in a bay at the influx of the *Tesino* which descends from the Monte Baldo, gives its name to the lake. The château belongs to Count Albertini of Verona. To the S. in the distance is the peninsula of *Sermione* (p. 152). The next places are *Bardolino* (2000 inhab.) with a harbour, *Cisano*, and *Lazise* (2600 inhab.), another harbour.

Peschiera *(Restaur.* near the quay) (see p. 151) at the efflux of the *Mincio* from the lake, is a station on the railway between Milan and Verona. Stat. 1¹/₄ M. from the lake, omnibus 75 c.

29. From Pavia to Brescia by Cremona.

Railway in 5 hrs.; fares 13 fr. 90, 9 fr. 80 c., 7 fr. None of the stations are worthy of note except Cremona, but this line is important as affording the most direct communication between Genoa and Verona (or the Brenner Railway).

The line intersects the fertile plain watered by the Po and the Olōna. Stations *Motta San Damiano*, *Belgiojoso* with hand-

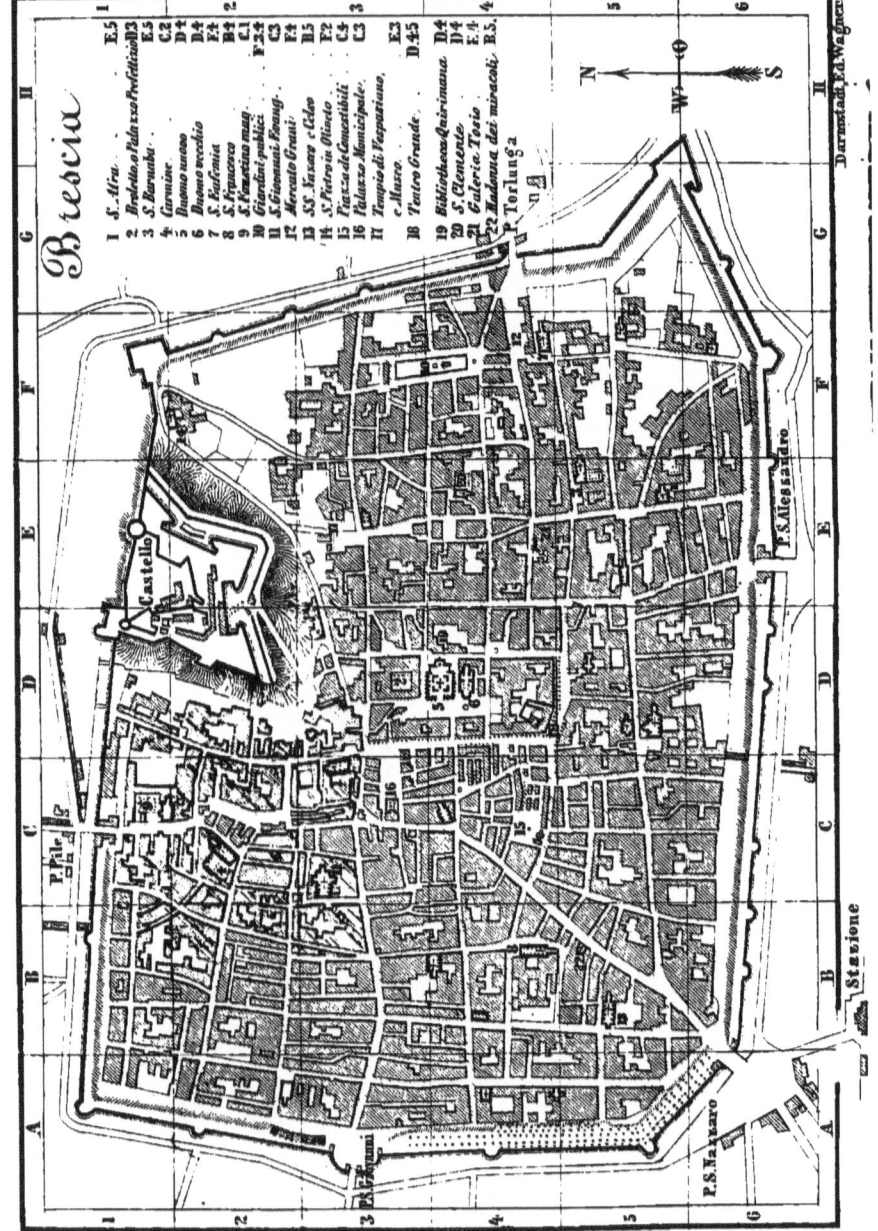

some château; near *Corteolona* the Olona is crossed. Then *Miradolo*, *Chignolo* on a small tributary of the Po, *Ospedaletto* and *Casalpusterlengo*, where the line from Piacenza to Milan (R. 40) is crossed. Stat. *Codogno;* near the fortified *Pizzighettone* the Adda, here navigable, is crossed. The district is here considered unhealthy. Stations *Acquanegra* and *Cava Tigozzi*.

Cremona (p. 162) is a terminus stat. whence the train backs out.

From Cremona to Brescia the line proceeds due N., following the direction of the high road, through a flat district. Stations *Olmeneta*, *Robecco-Pontevico*, beyond which the *Oglio*, a considerable affluent of the Po, is crossed. *Verolanuova*, *Manerbio*, then across the *Mella*, to *Bagnolo* and *S. Zeno Golzano*.

Brescia see below.

30. Brescia.

Hotels. Albergo Reale, R. 2½, D. 3, A. 1 fr.; Albergo Fenice in the Piazza del Duomo; Italia, well spoken of; Torre di Londra; *Gambero and *Scudo di Francia, moderate; Capello.

Cafés. Several adjacent to the theatre and in the Piazza del Duomo. — *Restaurant*: Wührer, near S. Clemente (Pl. 20).

Fiacres *(Cittadine)* 85 c. per drive, 1¼ fr. per hour.

Diligences twice daily to Edolo, 5 fr. 80 c. (comp. p. 159). From Brescia to Iseo 1 fr. 70 c., from Edolo to Pisogne 3 fr. — Railway by Cremona to Pavia see R. 29.

Brescia (482 ft.) vied with Milan at the commencement of the 16th cent. as one of the wealthiest cities of Lombardy, but in 1512 was sacked and burned by the French under Gaston de Foix, after an obstinate defence. Five years later Brescia was restored to the dominions of Venice, to which it belonged till 1797, but it has never recovered its ancient importance. On April 1st, 1849, the town was bombarded and taken by the Austrians under Haynau.

The town, with 40,500 inhab. and numerous iron-works, is delightfully situated at the base of the Alps. Previous to the events of 1848 the town and its environs constituted a vast manufactory of weapons *('Brescia armata')*, which furnished a large proportion of the arms used by the Austrian army. At the present day its energies are devoted to the service of Italy.

The **Duomo Nuovo** (Pl. 5), or episcopal cathedral, commenced in 1604, the dome not finally completed till 1825, is one of the best churches of that period.

Interior. By the first pillar on the r. is the large *monument of Bishop Nava (d. 1831), with groups in marble and a relief by Monti of Ravenna; by the first pillar on the l. the monument of Bishop Ferrari. The second altar on the r. is adorned with modern statues in marble of Faith by *Selvaroni*, and Hope, by *Emanueli*, and a modern painting, Christ healing the sick, by *Gregoletti*. Then (3rd altar on the r.) a sarcophagus with reliefs, date about 1500, containing '*Corpora D. D. Apollonii et Philastri*', transferred hither in 1674 from the crypt of the old cathedral. High altarpiece an Assumption by *Zoboli*, designed by *Conca*. In the dome the 4 Evangelists in marble.

The *Duomo Vecchio*, commonly termed **La Rotonda** (Pl. 6), situated on the low ground to the S. of the Duomo Nuovo, is shown by the sacristan (½ fr.) of the new cathedral (whose dwelling is at the back of the choir of the latter). This massive structure is circular, as its name implies, and surmounted by a dome. The pillars are painted so as to resemble columns. Substructure very ancient, supposed to date from the 9th cent. The dome and cupola date from the 12th cent., the addition at the back is of a later period. At the second altar on the r. is the monument of Bishop Lambertino (d. 1349) with reliefs. Altarpiece an Assumption by *Moretto*. Beneath the circular part of the edifice is the crypt, or *Basilica di S. Filastrio*, supported by 42 columns.

The **Broletto** (Pl. 2), adjoining the cathedral on the N., is a massive and extensive building of the 12th cent., subsequent additions to which have almost entirely obliterated its original form. It was anciently the seat of the municipal authorities, and is now occupied by courts of judicature. A portion of it serves as a prison. The campanile on the S. side, termed *La Torre del Popolo*, appertains to the original edifice.

Opp. the E. side of the Duomo Nuovo is the entrance to the ***Biblioteca Quiriniana** (or *Biblioteca Comunale*, Pl. 19; fee ½ fr.), comprising 40,000 vols., bequeathed to the town in 1750 by Cardinal *Quirini*. Several curiosities are preserved in a separate cabinet (adm. daily except Wedn. 11—3, in winter 10—3, Sund. 2—5 o'cl.; vacation from Dec. 24th to Jan. 1st and from Oct. 1st to Nov. 2nd, on high festivals, and during the carnival).

A Book of the Gospels of the 9th cent. with gold letters on purple vellum; a Koran in 12 vols., adorned with miniatures and gilding; a *cross 4 ft. in height *(Croce Magna)*, of gold, decorated with cameos and jewels and portraits of the Empress Galla Placidia and her sons Honorius and Valentinian III., resembling modern miniatures, the whole a most valuable specimen of the workmanship of the 4th cent.; a small cross adorned with gold and pearls and a fragment of the 'True Cross', said to have been worn by St. Helena. The *Lipsanoteca*, carved in ivory, a cross composed of the sides of an ancient relic-casket, with representations from Scripture, of the 4th or 5th cent. The *Dittico Quiriniano*, carved in ivory, presented by Pope Paul II., and other diptychs (ivory tablets with reliefs). Several calendars carved on a staff. Two caskets containing letters which passed between Napoleon and Canova. — In a separate room old Books of the Gospels with miniatures; a MS. of *Dante* on parchment, with miniatures; a *Petrarch* of 1470 with various illustrations ('*Petrarca figurato*') and written annotations; a *Dante* with notes, printed at Brescia in 1487; the *Codice Eusebiano*, a concordance of the 11th cent. with miniatures; Madonna painted on lapis lazuli by *Titian*.

The ***Museo Patrio** (Pl. 17), accessible gratis 11—3 o'cl. daily, on Sund., holidays, and during the vacations, Sept. and Oct., on payment of a fee; visitors knock at the door), is established in the three (restored) cellæ of a Corinthian temple of Hercules, excavated in 1822, erected by Vespasian, according to inscriptions of A. D. 72. The lofty substructures, the steps, the bases and portions of the shafts of the columns, in white marble, are still well preserved.

The principal Cella contains inscriptions and mosaic pavements. In the hall on the r. are mediæval and other curiosities, ornaments, the monument of Count Pitigliano, weapons, medals (those of the Napoleonic period very numerous). In the hall on the l. ancient sculptures, the most valuable of which is a fine statue of **Victory**, excavated in 1826, a bronze figure about 6 ft. in height, with a silver wreath of laurel round the head, in the left hand a shield on which she is about to write, beneath the l. foot a helmet; this is one of the rarest existing specimens of the ancient Greek plastic art. Also a number of coins and medals, ornaments, busts in gilded bronze, etc.

The *Galleria Tosi (or *Museo Civico*, Pl. 21), Contrada Tosi, Quartiere VIII., No. 596 (accessible daily 11—3 o'clock, on Sundays and festivals and during the vacations, Sept. and Oct., on payment of a fee), bequeathed with the palace to the town by Count Tosi, contains a number of ancient and modern pictures, drawings, engravings, modern sculptures, etc. in a series of small apartments.

In a room on the ground-floor the Laocoon, a group in marble by *Ferrari*; bust of Galileo by *Monti*; copies of Canova's colossal busts of himself and Napoleon, by *Gandolfi*; *Moretto*, Virgin and Saints, from the church of St. Afra. — In the ante-chamber on the first floor a bust of Count Tosi by *Monti*. — 1st Room : *Andrea del Sarto* (?), Holy Family; *Fra Bartolommeo*, Holy Family; *Caravaggio*, Lute player. — 2nd R.: *Moretto*, Tullia d'Arragona; *Francesco Francia*, Madonna; *Lor. Lotto*, Nativity; *Moretto*, Herodias, The disciples at Emmaus. — 3rd R.: *Albano*, Venus and the Graces; *Clouet*, Henry III. of France; *Giorgione*, Nativity (formerly in the old cathedral); *Cesare da Sesto*, Youthful Christ (?); *Ann. Caracci*, St. Francis; *Raphael*, Christ crowned with thorns, a small and exquisite work (covered). — Cabinets with interesting drawings and engravings (by *A. Dürer* etc.). — 4th R.: *Migliara*, La Certosa near Pavia; *Borsato*, Winter at Venice; *Vernet*, Night; *Domenico Presenti*, Church of St. Celso at Milan, in water-colours; *Basiletti*, Ischia; *Canella*, Dyeing-works; *Granet*, Choir with monks. — In the adjacent cabinet a bust of Eleonora d'Este, by *Canova*; in the passage a boy treading out grapes, by *Bartolini*. — Corridor with drawings. — In the chapel a statue of the youthful Saviour, by *Marchesi*. — 5th R.: *Baruzzi*, Silvia, statue in marble. — 6th R.: *Canella*, Night, and other pictures by the same master; *Azeglio*, Episode from Ariosto. — 7th R.: *Basiletti*, *Renica*, *Riccardi*, *Bisi*, Ital. landscapes. — 8th R.: *Day and *Night, reliefs by *Thorwaldsen*. — 9th R.: Marble statues: *Franceschetti*, Flora; *Gandolfi*, Genius of Music; *Thorwaldsen, Ganymede; *Pampaloni*, Boy praying; *Gherardo of Obstal*, Sacrifice of Isaac. — 10th—13th Rooms: Modern pictures: *Hayez*, Jacob and Esau; *Appiani*, Madonna; *Palagi*, Newton; *Belzuoli*, Copy of Raphael's School of Athens; *Podesti*, Tasso at the court of Ferrara; *Diotti*, Death of Ugolino; *Schiavoni*, Raphael and the Fornarina; *Hayez*, Departure of the Greeks, etc.

S. Clemente (Pl. 20), near the Tosi Gallery to the S., is a small church containing the tomb of the painter *Alessandro Bonvicini*, surnamed *Moretto* (d. 1564), a monument recently erected to him, and five of his works: r. 2nd altar, SS. Cecilia, Barbara, and Lucia; l. 1st altar, St. Ursula; 2nd altar, St. Jerome; 3rd altar, Abraham and Melchisedech; *high altar-piece, St. Clement and other saints. Moretto is a highly esteemed master; one of his pictures, representing Fathers of the church, was purchased in 1857 by the Städel Institute at Frankfurt for 35,000 fl. (2980 *l.*).

*S. Afra** (Pl. 1) was erected in 1580 on the site of a temple of Saturn. 1st altar on the r., Nativity of Mary, by *Bagnadore;* 2nd altar, Baptism of S. Afra, by *Bassano;* 3rd altar, Assumption by *Passerotti;* 4th altar, Virgin, S. Latinus, S. Carlo, and many other saints, a confused crowd of figures, all of the same size, by *Procaccini*. High altar-piece, Ascension, in which the blue of the sky is somewhat too predominant, by *Tintoretto*. Over the N. door, *Christ and the adulteress, by *Titian*, one of the great artist's finest works (generally covered). Over the N. altars: Christ in the house of Simon the Pharisee, by *Alessandro Maganza;* *Martyrdom of St. Afra, by *P. Veronese;* Brescian martyrs, by *Palma Giovine*.

S. Nazaro e Celso (Pl. 13), near the gate leading to the railway-station, erected in 1780, contains several good pictures. *High altar-piece by *Titian*, in five sections, the Resurrection being the principal subject, on the r. St. Sebastian and St. Rochus, l. St. Nazarus and St. Celsus with the portrait of the founder of the picture, above these the Annunciation. Over the 1st altar on the l. the *Coronation of the Virgin by *Moretto;* over the 2nd altar on the l. Nativity, with S. Nazaro and S. Celso, also by *Moretto*.

Madonna dei Miracoli (Pl. 22), not far from S. Nazaro, is a small church with four domes and richly decorated façade in the early Renaissance style, erected towards the close of the 15th cent.; over the 1st altar on the r. a *Madonna and Child, with St. Nicholas, by *Moretto*.

The ***Palazzo Comunale** (Pl. 16), usually termed **La Loggia**, situated in the handsome Piazza Vecchia, is the town-hall of Brescia, erected by *Formentone* in 1508 on the ruins of a temple of Vulcan, and completed in the latter half of the 16th cent. by *Jacopo Sansovino* and *Palladio*. The exterior of this imposing structure is somewhat overladen with ornament. In the angles of the arches of the lower part is a series of busts of Roman emperors as medallions.

On the opposite side of the Piazza, above an arcade, rises the **Torre dell' Orologio,** or clock-tower, with a large dial marking the hours according to the Italian computation (1 to 24). The bell is struck by two iron figures as in the clock at Venice (p. 195). — To the l. of this edifice rises a *Monument*, erected by the king in 1864, in honour of the natives of Brescia who fell during the gallant defence of their town against the Austrians in the insurrection of 1849, or were subsequently shot by order of Haynau.

The ***Campo Santo,** ½ M. beyond the Porta S. Giovanni, is one of the finest in N. Italy. It is approached by a triple avenue of cypresses diverging to the l. from the high road (see below). The long halls, with niches resembling the columbaria of the ancients, were erected in 1815. Beyond the chapel in the centre new halls have been constructed. In the intervening space rises a rotunda terminating in a column, at the back of which is a mortuary chapel. — Fine view from the gate of the *Castello*.

31. From Brescia to Tirano in the Valtellina.
Lago d'Iseo. Monte Aprica.

Distance about 78$\frac{1}{2}$ M. From Brescia post-omnibus daily at an early hour from the Albergo Reale, halting at *Pisogne* (1 hr.) and at *Breno* (1 hr.) and arriving at *Edolo* in the evening, fare 7 fr. Diligence from Edolo to *Tirano* (4 fr.) 3 times weekly; one-horse carr. about 10 fr. This direct route is recommended to the notice of travellers who are already acquainted with the Lake of Como and desire to reach the upper Val Tellina and the Stelvio or Bernina from Brescia. The scenery from Iseo onwards is beautiful the whole way.

The omnibus quits Brescia by the Porta S. Giovanni (to the l. is the avenue of cypresses leading to the *Campo Santo*, see above), and after a drive of $\frac{1}{2}$ hr. diverges to the r. from the Milan road. The country is flat. *Camignone* is first reached; then, near *Provaglio*, the mountainous region is attained.

11$\frac{1}{2}$ M. **Iseo** *(*Leone)*, situated on the lake of that name, is a busy place of some importance. Steamboat twice daily from *Sarnico* (Leone d'Oro) at the S. extremity of the lake by Iseo to Lovere (p. 160) and back, in correspondence with the diligences between Grumello (p. 150) and Sarnico, Brescia and Iseo, and Lovere and Edolo; drive from Sarnico to Lovere 2$\frac{1}{4}$ hrs.

The ***Lago d'Iseo** (*Lacus Sebinus*, 620 ft. above the sea-level, greatest depth 979 ft.), about 15 M. in length from the S. to the N. extremity, in the centre 900 ft. deep, and averaging 1$\frac{1}{2}$ M. in breadth, somewhat resembles an *S* in form. The *Oglio* enters the lake between Pisogne and Lovere and emerges from it near Sarnico. The scenery vies in beauty with that of the Lago di Garda, the soil is admirably cultivated, and the vegetation of a luxuriant, southern character. The *Mezz-Isola*, an island 1$\frac{1}{2}$ M. in length, consisting of a lofty ridge descending precipitously on the E. side (at the S.E. base of which lies *Peschiera d'Iseo*, and at the N.W. base *Siviano*, two fishing-villages), rises picturesquely and boldly in the middle of the lake. Opposite Peschiera lies the islet of *S. Paolo*.

The new *road, skirting the rocks of the E. bank, commencing at *Sale Marazzino* and terminating at *Pisogne*, a distance of 6 M., is little inferior in the boldness of its structure to that on the banks of the Lake of Como (p. 130). Immediately to the l. lies the lake, whilst on the r. the rocks rise precipitously, in some places overhanging the road, which is carried through a number of galleries and supported by solid masonry. From Iseo it winds through a succession of vineyards, which occupy the valley and its slopes, and reaches the bank of the lake at *Sulzano*, opposite to the island mentioned above. On the mountain, far above, is seen the white church of *S. Rocco;* then, farther on, the ruins of the monastery of *S. Loretto* on a rock in the lake. *Sale Marazzino* (Albergo della Posta), consisting of a long row of houses, is the largest village on the road. Then *Marone*, at the W. base of *Monte Guglielmo* (6019'; ascent 4 hrs., beautiful view), and

11½ **Pisogne** *(Albergo Grisoni)*, at the N. E. extremity of the lake. Towards the close of this portion of the route the scenery is strikingly beautiful, especially where the lake terminates in a rounded bay, and where **Lovere** *(S. Antonio*, or *Posta; Leone d'Oro;* *Canone *d'Oro)*, with its busy harbour, which formerly afforded the sole outlet to the industry of the Val Camonica, lies picturesquely on the N. bank. The long and handsome *Palazzo Tadini*, a conspicuous point in the distance, contains a collection of antiquities, pictures, and specimens of natural history, and in the family chapel a monument by Canova. Omnibuses between Lovere and Edolo, and Lovere and Bergamo (p. 150).

The road now quits the lake and traverses a fertile, alluvial tract. To the l. flows the *Oglio*, a considerable river, which is crossed at *Darfo*. The road now skirts the W. side of the valley, which presents the usual characteristics of the valleys of the S. Alps, being richly productive of maize, grapes, mulberries, etc., and enclosed by lofty, wooded mountains. The dark rocks (verrucano) here contrast peculiarly with the light (triassic) formations.

At *Cividate* the Oglio is crossed by two bridges. On the height a very picturesque deserted monastery. Near Breno a broad hill, planted in numerous terraces with vines and mulberries, and surmounted by a ruined castle, rises from the valley.

14 M. **Breno** *(Pellegrino; Albergo d'Italia*, of very small pretension) is the capital of the *Val Camonica*, which is 36 M. in length, extends from Lovere and Pisogne to the *Monte Tonale* (p. 161), and produces a considerable quantity of silk and iron. The construction of the lake-road (p. 159) at a cost of 200,000 fr., defrayed by this district alone, bears ample testimony to the prosperity of the inhabitants.

The road now crosses a mountain-torrent descending from *Monte Pizzo*, the indented ridge of which peeps from an opening on the r. A massive mountain of basalt here extends towards the road; near the summit columnar basalt is occasionally visible. Beyond *Capo di Ponte* (1373 ft.) the character of the scenery gradually changes. The valley contracts, maize and mulberries become rarer, whilst numerous chestnut-trees flourish on the slopes and in the valley itself. The road ascends slightly.

16½ M. **Edolo** (2285 ft.) *(Due Mori; Leone)*, a mountain-village possessing iron-works, lies in a basin on the *Oglio*, which here descends from the rocks and forms a waterfall. (Diligence to Tirano see p. 159; one-horse carriage to Tirano in 6 hrs., 10 fr.; to Lovere in 9 hrs., 15 fr. Distance from Edolo to Tirano 25 M.)

The new Tonale Route, here diverging N. E. to the **Monte Tonale** (6403 ft.) is one of the most important military routes from the Tyrol to N. Italy, formerly intended by the Austrian government to supersede the much loftier Stelvio Route (p. 51). the maintenance of which was attended with far greater expense. The road leads on the E. side of the Monte Tonale, which forms the boundary between Lombardy and the Tyrol, through the *Val di Sole (Sulzberg)* and *Val di Non (Nonsberg)*, which descend to *S. Michele Lombardo* (or *Wälsch-Michael*), a station on the railway from Bozen to Verona (p. 60), in the valley of the Adige.

The new road, which crosses numerous bridges and consists almost exclusively of solid masonry, gradually ascends beyond Edolo on the N. slope of the mountain. At *Cortĕno*, a village with a large church and handsome parsonage, the new road is joined by the old, which leads on the r. (S.) bank of the *Corteno*. Beyond it is a picturesque rocky gorge. High up on the r. lies the village of *Galleno*. Near the poor village of *S. Pietro* the highest point of the **Passo d'Aprica** (3991 ft.) is reached. The boundary-stone between the *Val Camonica* and the *Val Tellina* stands on the old road to the l.. about half-way between Edolo and Tirano. The inn *Alla Croce d'Oro* is ¾ M. farther. *Aprica*, 1½ M. W. of S. Pietro, is another village consisting of rude huts only.

A view of the Val Tellina, with Sondrio in the background, is now soon disclosed. The broad, gravelly channel of the *Adda* (p. 56) and the devastation frequently caused by the stream are well surveyed hence. Several snowy peaks of the spurs of the *Bernina* come in view to the N.; lower down, above Tresenda, rises the square watch-tower of *Teglio* (p. 56). On the road is situated the **Belvedere* (Inn), 1½ M. from Aprica. Fine view of the valley of the Adda.

The admirably constructed road now descends through plantations of chestnuts, in a long curve, to *La Motta;* it finally reaches the bottom of the valley of the Adda by means of two tunnels, and crosses the river near *Tresenda* (p. 56). In tolerably dry seasons when no inundation of the Adda need be apprehended, pedestrians are recommended to quit the high road, a few paces from the point where it turns to the W., by a footpath to the r., at first somewhat steep. which near the village of *Staziona* crosses a brook, passes through an opening in the wall, and reaches *Madonna di Tirano* (p. 56) in 1½ hr. A saving of 4½ M. is thus effected. From Tresenda to Tirano about 6 M. *Tirano* (1413 ft.) see p. 56. Those whose destination is Sondrio need not proceed first to Tirano, but carriages are seldom to be obtained at Tresenda.

32. From Milan to Cremona.

Railway in 3¹/₄ hrs.; fares 11 fr. 90, 8 fr. 65, 6 fr. 15 c.

From Milan to *Treviglio* see p. 149. The train here diverges to the S.E. First stat. *Caravaggio*, birth-place of the painter Michael Angelo Amerighi da Caravaggio, with the pilgrimage-church of the *Madonna di Caravaggio*. Next stat. *Casaletto-Vaprio*; then *Crema*, an industrial town (9000 inhab.) with an ancient castle and an episcopal residence.

Next stations *Castellone*, *Soresina*, *Casalbuttano*, *Olmenetta*. The station at Cremona is outside the Porta Milanese.

Cremona *(Sole d'Oro; Italia; Cappello;* carriages per drive ¹/₂, per ¹/₂ hr. 1 fr.), situated in a fertile plain on the l. bank of the Po, with 31,000 inhab., possesses streets and piazzas on an extensive scale, bearing testimony to its ancient importance. The original town was wrested by the Romans from the Gallic Cenomani and colonized by them at various periods, the first of which was at the commencement of the Punic wars (B. C. 218). It suffered seriously during the civil wars and was several times reduced to ruins, but was restored by the Emp. Vespasian. The Goths and Lombards, especially King Agilulf, as well as the subsequent conflicts between Guelphs and Ghibellines, occasioned great damage to the town. Cremona espoused the cause of Frederick Barbarossa against Milan and Crema, and afterwards came into the possession of the Visconti and of Francesco Sforza, since which period it has appertained to Milan. On Feb. 1st, 1702, *Prince Eugene* here surprised the French marshal *Villeroi* and took him prisoner. In 1799 also the Austrians here defeated the French.

The manufacturers of the far-famed violins and violas of Cremona were *Amati* (1590—1620), the two *Guarneri* (1552—80 and 1717—40) and *Stradivari* (1670—1728).

In the principal *Piazza* rises the Torrazzo, a tower 372 ft. in height, said to be the loftiest in Italy, founded 754, completed 1284, connected with the cathedral by a series of loggie. The summit commands an extensive prospect. Here, too, is situated the *Palazzo *Pubblico* (Pl. 12), containing a richly decorated chimney-piece, by G. C. Pedone, 1512. — The *Cathedral (Pl. 3), a German-Lombard structure of 1107, possesses a rich façade decorated with columns. In the interior are frescoes from the life of Mary, by *Boccaccino* and *Meloni*, and pictures by *Pordenone* and others. In the vicinity are the octagonal *Battisterio* (Pl. 1) of 1167, and the *Campo Santo* (Pl. 2), with ancient mosaics (entrance r. of the cathedral, No. 10). *S. Agostino e Giacomo in Braida* (Pl. 6) of the 14th cent., contains paintings by *Pietro Perugino* and *Galeazzo Campi*. *S. Sigismondo*, 1¹/₂ M. from the town, on the road to Mantua (E.), possesses pictures

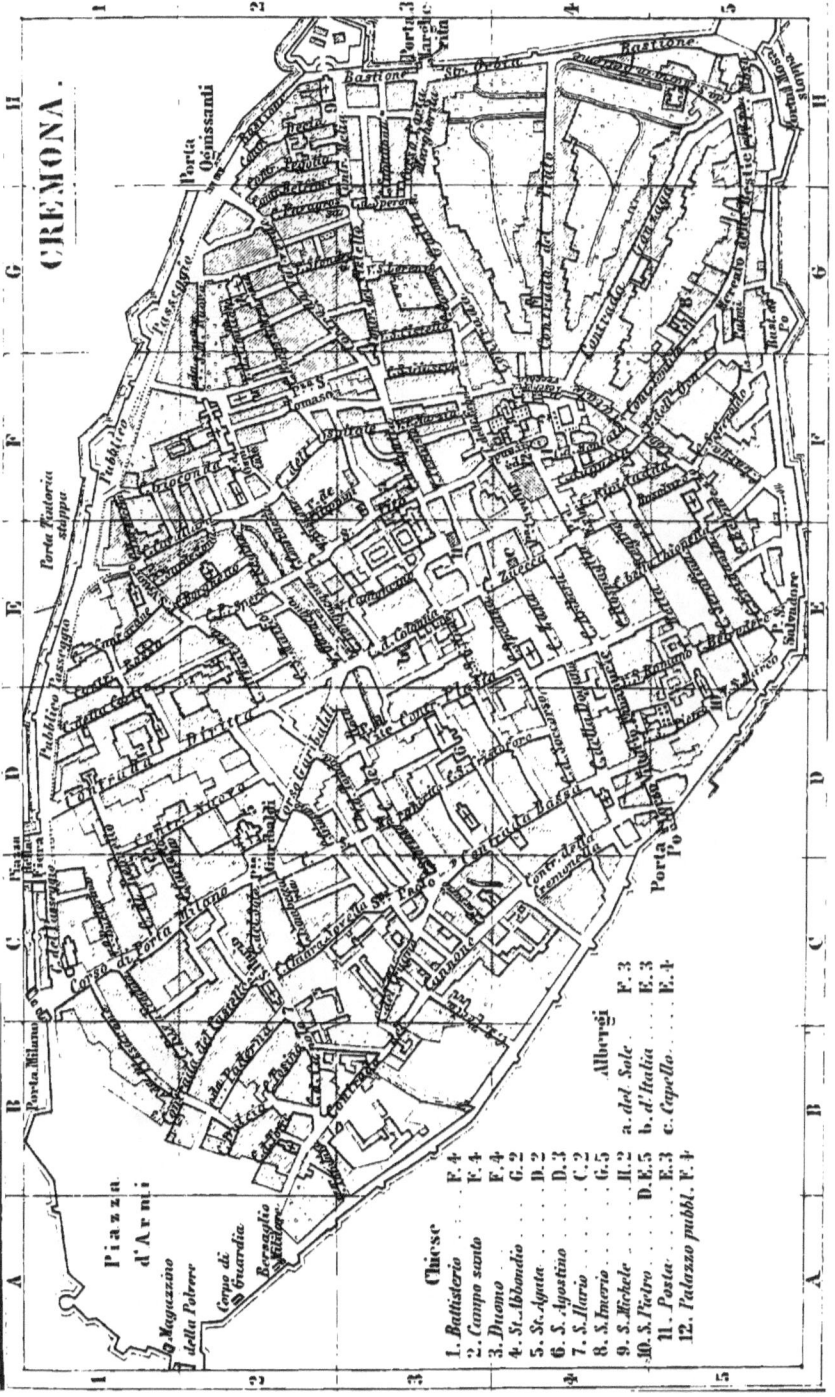

by *Campi* and *Boccaccino*. — Cremona also boasts of a number of handsome Pa la ces, e. g. that of *San Secondo*, with sculptures by Sacchi. — Pict u re Ga lle ri cs of the Marchese *Pallavicini*, Conte *Schizzi*, *C. Pedretti*, *Ala di Ponzone*, etc. — Near the village of *Le Torri* is situated the beautiful *Villa Sommi*.

In the château of Soncino on the *Oglio*, 20 M. N. W. of Cremona, *Ezzelino da Romano*, once the powerful representative at Padua and Verona of the Emperor Frederick II., renowned for his bravery, as well as for his relentless cruelty, died on Sept. 27th, 1259, eleven days after he had been wounded at the battle of Cassano (p. 149). Even whilst in prison he displayed his indomitable and haughty spirit, spurned from his presence the monks who proffered the consolations of religion, refused to take food and medicine, and tore the bandages from his wounds. The talented painter *C. F. Lessing* derived from this history the subject of one of his finest works (in the Städel Gallery at Frankfurt on the Main).

From Cremona to Brescia and to Pavia see p. 154.

From Cremona to Mantua see p. 172. — From Cremona to Parma diligence (from the Albergo d'Italia) daily in 7 hrs. by *Casal Maggiore;* the traveller will, however, find it more convenient to drive to the (15 M.) railway-station *Firenzuola* (p. 217). — The road from Cremona to Piacenza intersects the plain on the r. (S.) bank of the *Po*, after having crossed the river with its numerous islands 1½ M. beyond the former town. Stations *Monticelli*, *S. Nazzaro;* then *Caorso*, where the river formed by the *Chiavenna* and *Riglio* is crossed. At *Roncaglia* the *Nure* is crossed, after which the road proceeds W. to *Piacenza* (see p. 84).

33. Verona.

Hotels. Due Torri (Pl. 46), R. 3, L. 1, B. 1½, D. 4, A. 1 fr.; *Torre di Londra (Pl. 47), similar charges; Gran Czara di Moscovia (Pl. 48); Hôtel Rainer il gran Parigi, in the Corso, R. from 1½, L. ½. D. 2½, A. ½ fr.; *S. Lorenzo, with restaurant, on the Adige, in the third narrow street W. of the Porta Borsari; Colomba d'Oro, R. 1½ fr., well spoken of; Aquila Nera, near the church of St. Eufemia and the Piazza d'Erbe. Albergo della Posta, near the post-office; Palma d'Oro, Via Perar, near the Teatro Ristori.

Restaurants. *Del Teatro Filarmonico on the S. side of the Piazza Brà. Beyond the gateway, immediately to the r. by the moat, is the *Birraria al Giardino S. Luca (with baths). Aquila Nera see above. Crespi, near the Ponte delle Navi (p. 168).

Cafés. Europa and *Vittorio Emanuele in the Piazza Brà, where a military band plays every evening. *Caffè Dante, in the Piazza de' Signori.

Bookseller. Münster, in the Via Nuova, the principal business street, leading from the Brà to the Piazza delle Erbe.

Fiacres. Drive of ¼ hr. 60 c., ½ hr. 1 fr., 1 hr. 1½ fr., each subsequent hr. 1 fr. 25 c.; in the evening 40 c. per hr. more. From the station to the town and vice-versâ 65 c.; luggage 20 c. for each person. These fares are for 1—2 pers.; for each additional pers. ⅓rd more. Omnibus from the stat. to the town 30 c.

Railway Stations. Verona possesses two stations (to which the traveller's attention is directed in case of mistakes about luggage etc.), one outside the *Porta Vescovo*, 1½ M. E. of the Piazza Brà, the other outside the *Porta Nuova*, ¾ M. to the S. — Railway to *Bozen* and *Innsbruck*, see R. 8; the trains start from the station beyond the Porta Vescovo, but halt at the station outside the Porta Nuova; to *Mantua* (R. 34) from the Porta Nuova. (The Austrian, as well as the Italian paper-currency should be avoided by those crossing the frontier in either direction.)

Principal Attractions (all of which may be seen in one day): Arena and Piazza Brà, then across the Adige to the Palazzo Pompei (on the way thither is S. Fermo Maggiore, p. 167), back by the Via Leoni to the Piazza de' Signori, with the tombs of the Scaligers; S. Anastasia, the Cathedral, and across the Ponte di Ferro to S. Giorgio; drive along the Corso, from the Porta Borsari to the Porta Stuppa and S. Zeno, then back to the Giardino Giusti.

Verona (157 ft.), the *Bern* of early German lore, with 60,000 inhab. and a garrison of 6000, situated at the base of the Alps, on the rapid *Adige*, which is crossed by 5 bridges, is the most important fortress, and next to Venice the most considerable town in Venetia.

The *Amphitheatre (Pl. 24; entrance from the W. side by the arcade marked 'V') bounds on one side the principal square of Verona, the *Piazza Brà (Praedium)*. This celebrated arena, probably erected under Diocletian (A. D. 284), is 106 ft. in height, 546 ft. long, 436 ft. wide (the arena itself 239 ft. long, 141 ft. broad), circumference 492 yds. Around the amphitheatre rise 45 tiers of steps, 18 inches in height, 26 inches in width, of grey marble (modern), on which it is calculated that 27,000 spectators could be accommodated. A small portion only of the external wall, blackened by age, is still standing. The arcades (72 in all) are let by the town at high rents to dealers in wares of every description.

On the S. side of the Brà are the old and new *Guard Houses*, on the N. several large cafés, on the W. the *Old Town Hall*, now a barrack. The W. corner is occupied by the *Teatro Filarmonico* (Pl. 41), with the *Museo Lapidario* (Pl. 29), a valuable collection of Roman and Greek inscriptions, basreliefs, Roman statues, etc.

N. E. of the Brà, in the Corso, is the *Porta de' Borsári*, a triumphal arch (or, according to others simply a gateway of the old town-wall), occupying the entire breadth of the street, consisting of two entrance-archways surmounted by two galleries, with façade towards the exterior of the town, erected under the Emperor Gallienus, A. D. 265.

The Corso leads in a straight direction to the once busy scenes of mediæval life. On the r. the traveller first reaches the **Piazza delle Erbe**, the fruit and vegetable market, formerly the forum of the Republic. At the upper end of it rises a *Marble Column*, which till 1797 bore the lion of St. Mark to indicate the supremacy of the Republic of Venice. The *Fountain* is adorned with a statue of 'Verona', part of which is ancient. The *Tribuna*, with its canopy supported by four columns, in the centre of the Piazza, anciently served as a court of judicature. Many of the surrounding houses are adorned with frescoes in the old Veronese style, recently restored, such as the *Casa Mazzanti* near the column, and the *Casa dei Mercanti* of the 14th cent., adorned with a statue of the Madonna. Opposite to it is the *Tower of the Municipio*, upwards of 300 ft. in height. A short street to the l. of the latter leads to the small

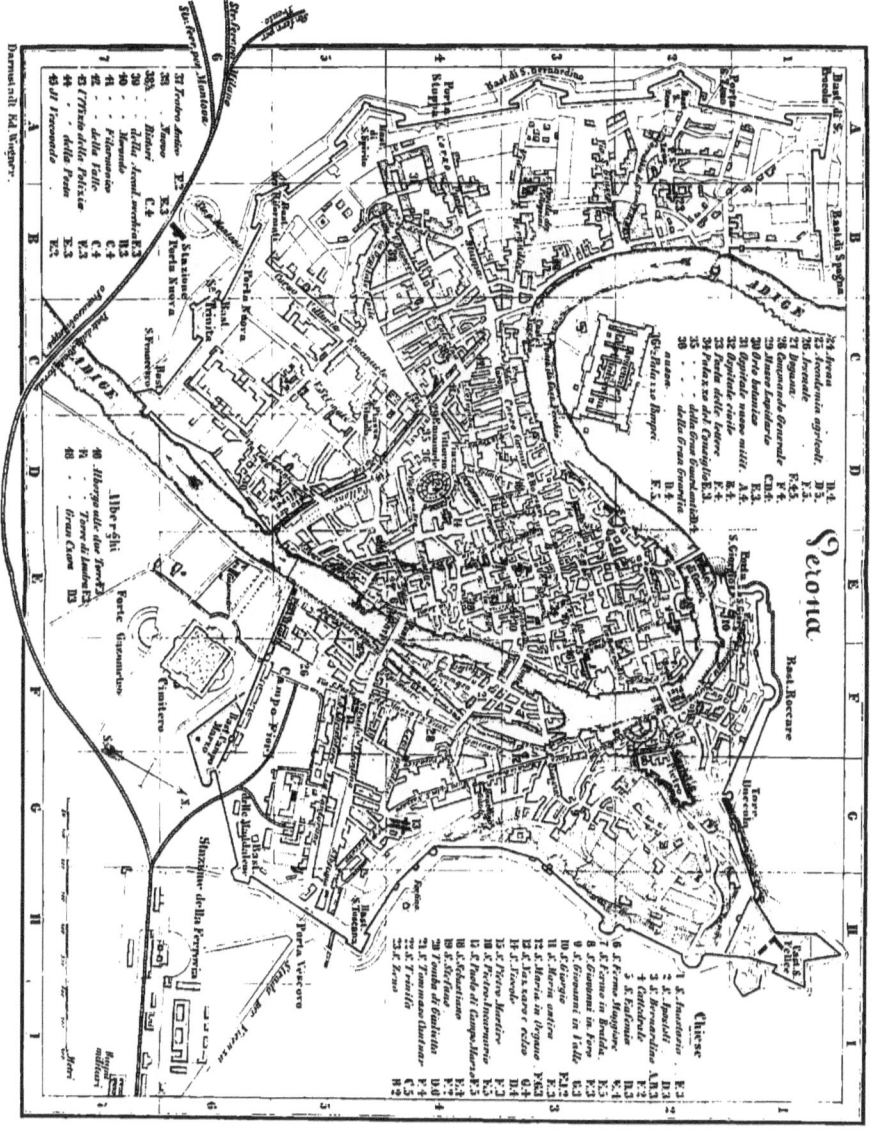

***Piazza dei Signori,** a square surrounded by imposing edifices. Immediately to the r., by the tower already mentioned, is the *Municipio*, or *Town hall*, with a remarkably picturesque court. In the angle diagonally opposite is situated the *Old Town Hall*, or **Palazzo del Consiglio** (Pl. 34), usually termed *La Loggia*, erected at the beginning of the 16th cent. by Fra G.ocondo da Verona. This edifice is adorned with statues of celebrated natives of the town, among whom are Cornelius Nepos and Catullus. ('Mantua Virgilio gaudet Verona Catullo'. *Ovid.* — 'Tantum magna suo debet Verona Catullo, quantum parva suo Mantua Virgilio'. *Martial.*) In the middle of the piazza rises a marble *Statue of Dante*, who, as recorded by the inscriptions on the monument and on the palace adjoining the Loggia at a right angle, found an asylum here with the Scaligers after his banishment from Florence.

The passage on the r. side of the Loggia leads direct to the modernized Romanesque church of *S. Maria Antica* (Pl. 11), and the imposing Gothic ***Tombs of the Scaligers,** who for upwards of a century (1262—1389) held the chief power in the republic of Verona. The ladder which forms their crest also recurs frequently on the railings. The largest of these monuments, that at the corner of the street, was executed by *Bonino du Campione* for *Can Signorio* (d. 1375) during his life-time. It consists of a sarcophagus resting on a pedestal supported by columns of moderate height, over which rises a canopy crowned w.th an equestrian statue of the prince. On the square columns in the middle are 6 Christian heroes, in niches higher up are the Christian virtues. On the other side next to the Piazza dei Signori, is the monument of *Mastino III.* (d. 1351), another sarcophagus with canopy and equestrian statue. Between these two principal monuments are four large *Sarcophagi*, the three first dating from 1311. The last is that of *Can Grande II.*, who in 1359 was assassinated in the public streets by his brother Can Signorio. Over the church-door the sarcophagus and equestrian statue of *Can Grande (Francesco della Scala*, d. 1329); adjoining it, also on the church wall, that of *Giovanni della Scala* (d. 1350); finally that of *Mastino I.* (d. 1277) (fee to custodian 30 c.).

In the vicinity is ***S. Anastasia** (Pl. 1), a fine Gothic church of the beginning of the 14th cent., with façade of brick partially covered with marble. The interior, supported by 12 circular columns, is remarkable for the boldness and symmetry of its proportions, but the vaulting is painted with questionable taste. It contains several good tombstones.

On the two first pillars, as supporters of the basin for consecrated water, are two beggars in white and grey marble, that on the l. executed by *Gabriel Cagliari*, father of Paul Veronese, that on the r. by *Aless. Rossi* in 1591. The chapel of the Pellegrini, on the r. by the high altar, is adorned with reliefs of the 14th cent., representing the history of Christ from the Nativity to the Resurrection, and contains two monuments of the Pellegrini in red marble.

To the l. of the church, over a gateway adjoining the small church of *S. Pietro Martire* (Pl. 15), is the dingy marble sarcophagus of Count Castelbarco, beyond it another similar monument, and two still more ancient in front of the pediment of the church.

The **Cathedral** (Pl. 4) is an imposing Gothic structure of the 14th cent., with choir and Romanesque façade of the 12th cent. Behind the columns of the handsome portal are the two paladins of Charlemagne, Roland and Oliver, in half-relief. The front columns rest on griffins. In the interior, over the 1st altar on the l., is an *Assumption by *Titian*. Elegantly wrought roodloft of marble, designed by *Sanmicheli*. The handsome cloisters are supported by arches on double columns of red marble in two stories, one above the other (entrance l. of the façade).

Between the Cathedral and the Vescovado is *S. Giovanni in Fonte*, the ancient Baptistery, a basilica of the 12th cent.

On the l. bank of the Adige is situated **S. Giorgio** (Pl. 10; entrance by a side-door on the N. when the front-door is closed), completed in 1604, surmounted by a dome, and containing some admirable pictures. On the W. wall, over the door, Baptism of Christ, by *Tintoretto;* 1st altar l., St. Ursula and her companions, the Saviour above, painted in 1545 by *Franc. Carotto;* 4th altar l., *Madonna with two saints, God the Father above, three angels with musical instruments below, by *Girolamo dai Libri*. R. in the choir the Miracle of the Five Thousand, by *Paolo Farinati;* l. Shower of manna, by *Fel. Brusasorzi*, both pained in 1603. *High altar-piece, Martyrdom of St. George, by *P. Veronese* (generally covered).

On the r. about the middle of the Corso, on the way to S. Zenone (see below) is the *Castello Vecchio* (Pl. C, 3), the ancient palace of the Scaligers, now an arsenal, connected with the opposite bank of the Adige by a bridge *(Ponte di Castello)* constructed in the 14th cent. The continuation of the Corso leads to the *Porta Stuppa* (or *Palio)*, once admired and described by Gœthe, the finest of the gates of Verona, erected by *Michele Sanmicheli* (1484—1549), the most famous builder of fortifications of his time. — To the N. of this point, by the monastery of S. Bernardino, is the *Cappella dei Pellegrini* (Pl. 3), a very interesting sample of early Renaissance, also by Sanmicheli. It is surmounted by a dome and is unadorned with painting and gilding.

***S. Zenone** (Pl. 23) is a Romanesque basilica of most noble proportions. The nave in its present form dates from the 12th, the choir from the 13th cent.

The Portal is embellished with marble reliefs of 1178, the subjects of which are derived from Scripture, from the creation of woman and the

Fall to the Betrayal by Judas and the Crucifixion. The hunting-scene to the r. in one of the lower sections is known as the 'Chase of Theodoric', an allusion to his having embraced the heretical Arian doctrines. Then representations from the life of St. Zeno, and of the months, beginning with March. The doors, consisting of a number of small brazen plates with reliefs (of which the oldest are very rudely executed), are said to have been presented by Dukes of Cleve (on the Rhine). The two columns of the Portal rest on lions (comp. p. 59). To the r. by the church is a round altar supposed to be of Roman origin.

In the Interior, l. of the entrance, is a large ancient vase of porphyry, 27 ft. in circumference. In the r. Aisle Christ and the 12 Apostles, a series of statues in marble, some of them painted, supposed to be coeval with the reliefs on the portal. The faded remnants of old frescoes probably date from the 13th cent. From both aisles steps descend to the spacious and lofty Crypt with the tomb of St. Zeno, the 40 columns of which have interesting capitals. (The entrance descending from the nave has recently been discovered, and is to be restored.) To the r. in the Choir, above the crypt, is the very ancient painted marble figure of St. Zeno, Bishop of Verona, holding his episcopal staff and (as patron-saint of fishermen) a fishing-rod with a silver fish. Behind the high altar is a *picture (covered) by *Mantegna*, in excellent preservation, consisting of 3 compartments, a Madonna and angels, with groups of saints on the r. and l.

A door in the N. aisle leads to the admirably preserved *Cloisters, supported by a series of elegant double columns of great antiquity, having been restored (according to an old inscription) as early as 1123. Immediately to the r. two tombstones are recognised as pertaining to the Scaliger family by the ladder represented on them. — On the S. side of the church is a small disused Cemetery whence a general view of the church with its campanile of 1045 (restored 1120) is best obtained. At the entrance of a disused Mausoleum, with a sarcophagus and two columns (descent by 12 steps), a stone bears an inscription: 'The sepulchre of Pepin, King of Italy, the Son of the Emperor Charlemagne'. Adjacent is a very large Roman sarcophagus.

Within a closed garden (visitors ring at the gate facing them, 2—3 soldi) in the Vicolo Franceschine, a side-street of the Via Cappuccini, is situated the former Franciscan Monastery (Pl. 20), where a partially restored chapel contains a rude sarcophagus in red Verona marble, called without the slightest authority the 'Tomb of Juliet' (fee 25 c.). Shakespeare's play of 'Romeo and Juliet' is founded on events which actually occurred at Verona. 'Escalus, Prince of Verona' was Bartolommeo della Scala (d. 1303), one of the ruling princes of the Scaliger family (comp. p. 165). The lofty and narrow house of Juliet's parents (Pl. E, 4) in the street of S. Sebastiano (formerly Capelletti), now a tavern, still bears the hat (over the entrance to the court) which was the distinctive emblem in the armorial bearings of the family.

Pursuing a N. direction hence, the traveller reaches **S. Fermo Maggiore** (Pl. 6), dat ng from the commencement of the 14th cent. The architecture of the exterior should be inspected. The façade is of brick, with enrichments in marble. The interior is modernized; beautiful ceiling in walnut-wood, and also remains of old frescoes. L. of the entrance is a Resurrection carved in wood. The Cappella del Sagramento on the l. contains an altarpiece by *Carotto*, painted in 1528; above are the Virgin and St. Anna, beneath are John the Baptist, St. Sebastian, and other saints.

The *Ponte delle Navi* in the vicinity was erected to replace a bridge destroyed by an inundation in 1757. Immediately to the r. beyond it, at the beginning of the promenade, is situated the **Palazzo Pompei** (Pl. 36 1/2), an architecturally interesting edifice, erected by *Sanmicheli*, presented by the family to the town, and now containing the *Museo Civico* (fee 1 fr.).

On the G r o u n d Fl o o r are several rooms containing casts, antiquities, and fossils from the Monte Bolca; in the 4th is a *drawing by *Andrea Mantegna*. — The P i n a c o t e c a, or picture-gallery on the first floor, contains principally works of the Veronese school. 1st R o o m: nothing worthy of note. — 2nd R. (to the r. of the first). Without numbers: *Paolo Morando* (d. 1522), Two saints; *Giac. Bellini*, The Crucified, all three 'a tempera'; 25. *Girolamo Santa Croce*, Madonna and child with saints. — 3rd R. Old paintings on wood: 52. *Vittore Pisano*, Madonna in the garden; 68. *Cimabue*, History of the creation and of the Old Testament, in thirty sections, on a gold ground. — 4th R. (to the l. of the first): 74¹. *Paolo Veronese*, Descent from the Cross; 74². *P. Veronese*, Portrait. — 5th R.: 90. *P. Veronese*, St. Cecilia and saints, a fresco transferred to canvas; 94. *Girolamo dai Libri*, Holy Family; 97. *Jacopo Ligozzi*, Surrender of Verona to the Republic of Venice in 1405. — 6 t h R.: 99—109: *Paolo Morando*, Scenes from the Passion. — 7 t h R.: nothing interesting. — 8 t h R.: a corridor with engravings, some of them by *Agostino Caracci, Rembrandt*, and *Dürer*. — 9 t h, 10th, 11th R.: nothing of importance. — 12th R. (to the l. of the eleventh): 185. *Palma Vecchio*, Dominican monk. — An adjacent room without a number contains two large pictures of scenes from the history of Verona: 220. *P. Farinati*, Battle of the Veronese against Fred. Barbarossa at Vigasi in 1164; 224. *F. Brusasorci*, Victory of the Veronese over the inhabitants of the banks of the Lago di Garda in 849. — 14th, 15th, 16th R.: nothing important.

A few minutes S. of the Palazzo Pompei the traveller reaches the *Porta S. Vittoria*, which leads to the uninteresting **Campo Santo**, enclosed by a Doric colonnade, connecting the lofty church with two temples. The summit of the pediment is adorned with a marble group of Faith, Hope, and Charity, by *Spazzi*.

A fine *view of Verona and its environs, as well as the Alps and distant Apennines, is obtained from the somewhat neglected **Giardino Giusti** on the l. bank of the Adige (access daily; visitors ring at a gate on the r.; fee 20 c.), celebrated for its numerous (upwards of 200) cypresses, some of which are 400—500 years old, and said to exceed 120 ft. in height. The campanili of *S. Lucia* (1 1/2 M.) and *S. Massimo* are conspicuous objects in the landscape. *Somma Campagna* (p. 151) and *Custozza* (p. 169) lie 10—12 M. to the S.W.

The view is still finer from the **Castello S. Pietro** (ascent by the *Ponte della Pietra*; permission obtained at the office of the commandant at the entrance), the ancient castle of 'Dietrich of Bern', the hero of German lore. It was entirely remodelled by Galeazzo Visconti in 1393, destroyed by the French in 1801, and refortified by the Austrians in 1849. At its base, immediately below the bridge, are the remains of an ancient semicircular Roman *Theatre* (Pl. 37), excavated in the court of a private house.

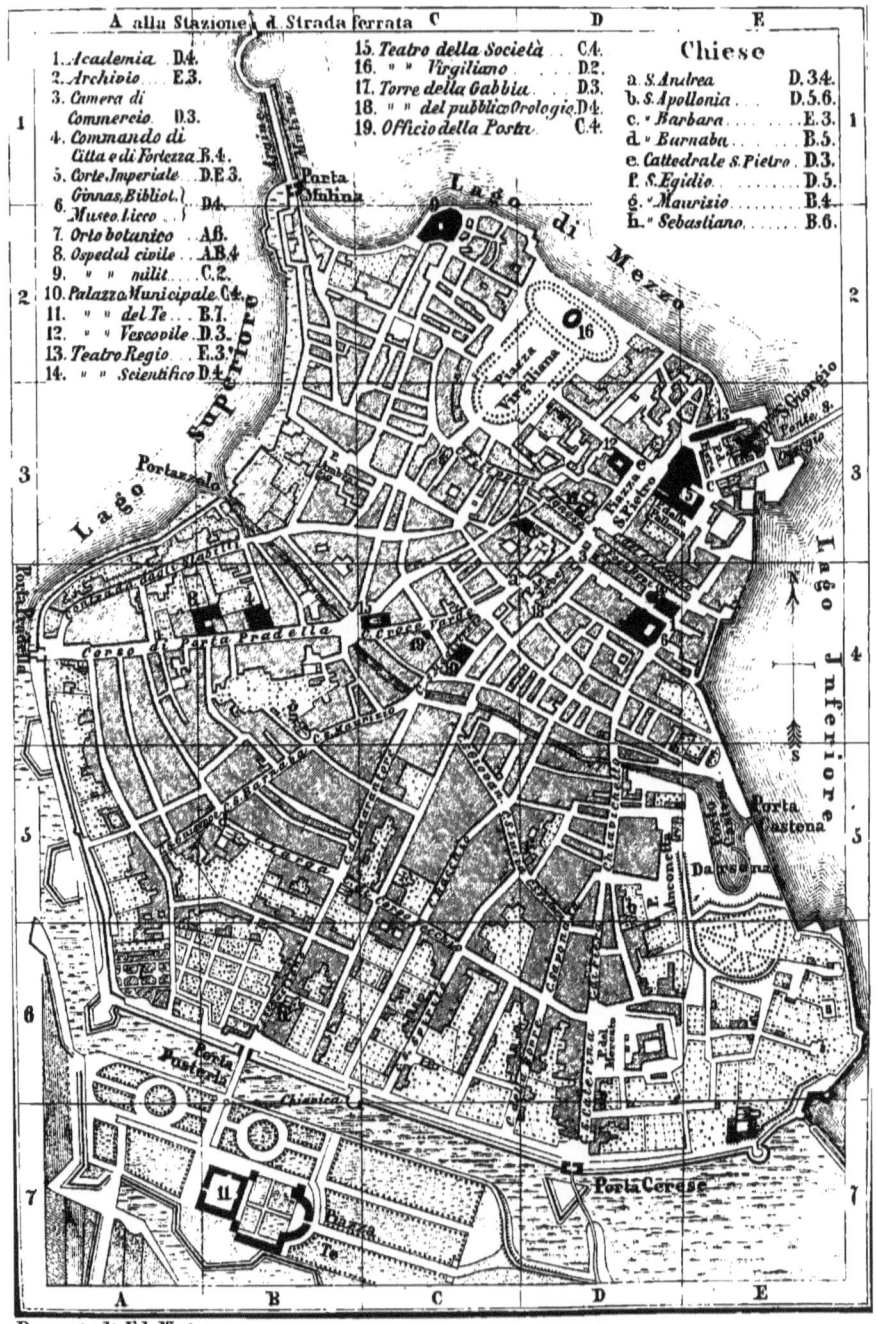

34. From Verona to Mantua.

From Mantua to Modena, Reggio, Parma, Cremona or Brescia.
22¹/₂ M. Railway in 1¹/₄ hr.; fares 4 fr. 40, 3 fr. 20, 2 fr. 80 c.

Soon after quitting the station outside the Porta Nuova (p. 163) the train quits the Milan line (R. 27) and leads to the S., across a richly cultivated and productive plain. Fields of rice are occasionally seen, especially near Mantua. Stat. *Dossobuono*, then *Villafranca;* here was signed the celebrated treaty between the French and Austrian Emperors, July 11th, 1859, which terminated the Italian war and was confirmed by the Peace of Zürich. About 5 M. to the N.W. lies *Custozza*, where the Italians were defeated by the Austrians in 1848 and 1866. Next stations *Mozzecane*, *Roverbella*, and *Mantua*.

The railway-station is about 2¹/₂ M. distant from the town. Omnibuses to the hotels in 30—40 min. (1 fr.); they start from the hotels for the station 1¹/₂ hr. before the departure of the train. Fiacre 2, there and back 3 fr. Midway between the station and the town rises the *Citadel of Mantua*, where Andreas Hofer, the Tyrolese patriot, was shot by order of Napoleon on Feb. 20th, 1810. He was originally interred in the garden of the curé, but his remains were conveyed to the Tyrol in 1823. A monument marks the spot where the execution took place. The road next crosses the *Argine Mulino* (i. e. mill-dam), a long covered bridge constructed in 1257, with 12 mills named after the 12 Apostles. It separates the Lago Superiore (W.) from the Lago di Mezzo (E.), two lakes formed by the *Mincio* (which descends from the Lake of Garda, p. 151), and unites the citadel with the town. The *Palazzo Cavriani*, the garden-wall of which is adorned with the busts of celebrated natives of Mantua, is next passed.

Mantua, Ital. *Mantŏva* ("Aquila d'Oro or Leone; "Croce Verde or Fenice, R. 2, L. ¹/₂, A. ³/₄ fr., both in the centre of the town, in the Contrada Croce Verde. — *Carriages* per drive 60 c., 1st hr. 1 fr. 50 c., each following ¹/₂ hr. 50 c., to the station see above. — *Diligences* see above), a very ancient town founded by the Etruscans, with 30,000 inhab. (3000 Jews), is a strongly fortified place, bounded on the N.W. by the *Lago Superiore*, on the N.E. by the *Lago di Mezzo*, on the E. by the *Lago Inferiore*, and on the S. and S.W. by marshy land, which in case of a siege is capable of being laid under water. The aspect of the town is unattractive and dull, although it contains a number of spacious palaces. The traffic of the place is chiefly confined to the arcades of the *Contrada Croce Verde* and the *Piazza d'Erbe*, near S. Andrea. In the *Piazza S. Pietro*, the N.E. corner of Mantua, are situated the cathedral and the *Corte Imperiale* (pl. 5), the ducal palace of the Gonzagas, part of which is now employed as a barrack. The latter contains apartments with magnificent ceilings and mosaic pavements, Flemish tapestry (9 designs by *Raphael*), etc.; in the chamber of the archives are frescoes by *Andrea Mantegna* (d. 1506) and *Giulio Romano* (or *Pippi*, d. 1546), whose school of painting was established at Mantua; in the upper story a room with the signs of the constellations; in the Uffizio della Scalcheria scenes from the chase of Diana, by *G. Romano;* also, in the principal saloon, Night, Day, and Olympus; in a distant room of the old wing of the palace, History of the Trojan war. Opposite to the palace is Giulio Romano's house. His tomb was in the church of *S. Barnaba* (Pl. d), but has disappeared since the remodelling of the edifice. — A long bridge leads N.E. between the Lago di Mezzo and the Lago Inferiore to *Borgo S. Giorgio*, a kind of suburb also appertaining to the fortifications.

*S. *Andrea* (Pl. a), the finest church of Mantua, is a structure in the Italian style of very imposing proportions. It was erected in 1492 from designs by the Florentine Leo Battista Alberti, but the dome was not added till 1782. The façade, with a spacious portico, is of white marble; the square tower, built of red brick, is surmounted by an elegant octagonal superstructure with Gothic spire, affording a good survey of the town and its peculiar situation.

The Interior, consisting of nave without aisles, covered by massive barrel vaulting, the panels of which are partly painted. 1. Large Chapel r. St. Antony admonishing the tyrant Ezzelino, painted in 1844 by Count Arrivabene. At the sides are frescoes representing Hell, Purgatory, and Paradise according to Dante. — 3rd Chap., the *Cappella S. Longino*, contains a sarcophagus with the inscription: *Longini ejus, qui latus Christi percussit, ossa.* The frescoes, designed by *Giulio Romano*, represent the Crucifixion, beneath is Longinus, on the opposite side the finding of the sacred blood. The saint is said to have brought hither some drops of the blood of Christ, which were preserved in an altar (destroyed by Hungarian soldiers in 1848) in the *Crypt*, beneath the high altar. The S. Transept contains the monument of Bishop Andreasi (d. 1549), by a pupil of Michael Angelo. The swan is the distinctive emblem in the armorial bearings of Mantua. — Choir. Martyrdom of St. Andrew, al fresco by *Anselmi*, a pupil of Paolo Veronese. In the corner to the l. by the high altar is the marble figure of Duke Guglielmo Gonzaga, founder of the church, in a kneeling posture. — N. Transept. Monument of Pietro Strozzi, with caryatides, designed by *Giulio Romano*. — Another monument with the recumbent figure of a Count Andreasi, was also designed by *G. Romano*. — The 1st Chapel l. of the W. portal contains the tomb of the painter Andrea Mantegna (d. 1506), with his *bust in bronze. The frescoes which cover the walls and the dome, and exhibit a rare harmony of colouring, are of the 18th cent., most of them by *Campi*.

The *Cathedral of S. Pietro* (Pl. e), a basilica with double aisles, transept surmounted by a dome, rows of chapels with domes on each side, and a very unsuitable façade, was almost entirely constructed by *Giulio Romano*. The colossal unfinished tower is of much earlier origin.

In the vicinity to the W. is a very extensive space, planted with trees and bounded by the Lago di Mezzo on the N., termed the *Piazza Virgiliana*, adorned with a bust of Virgil, who was born in the neighbouring village of *Pietōle* (see below). The *Teatro Virgiliano* (Pl. 16) is employed for open-air performances on summer evenings. Beyond the theatre, from the parapet towards the Lago di Mezzo, a superb view of the Tyrolese Alps is enjoyed in favourable weather.

The *Accademia Virgiliana di Scienze e Belle Arti* (Pl. 1) contains a few frescoes and sculptures, a collection of casts, etc. of little value. Behind it is the *Liceo* (Pl. 6) with a library (one of the rooms of which contains the Trinity, by *Rubens*) and museum. Several admirable antiquities are preserved in the latter; by the entrance busts of Euripides and another Greek poet (erroneously called Virgil's bust); statue of Apollo in the archaic style; torso of Venus; bust of Juno, designated as Ino Leucothea; numerous busts of emperors, inscriptions, sarcophagus-reliefs, etc.

Immediately without the *Porta Pusterla*, the S.W. gate, is situated the *Palazzo del Tè (Pl. 11) (contracted from Tajetto), erected by *Giulio Romano*, and containing in apartments of comparatively small dimensions some of that master's largest frescoes. In the vaulted saloon the Fall of the giants, then the History of Psyche, that of Phaëton, the Zodiac, the Triumph. Fine friezes in plaster and mosaic pavements.

Pietole, supposed to be the *Andes* of the Romans and the birthplace of Virgil, lies about 3 M. S.E. of Mantua, near the efflux of the Mincio from the Lago Inferiore.

The high road from Mantua to Modena (diligence daily in 7½ hrs., 6 fr.) passes the *Palazzo del Tè* (see above) and traverses the forests of *Serraglio* and *Bagnolo*. At *Porto S. Benedetto* the *Po* is crossed by a ferry; farther on, *S. Benedetto*, *Moglia*, and **Novi** (2400 inhab.), not to be confounded with the place of that name on the railway between Alessandria and Genoa (p. 146).

[10]½ M. E. of Novi is situated **Mirandola**, formerly the capital of a duchy which belonged to the Pico family, a town with broad streets and picturesque, antiquated buildings. It was originally subject to the jurisdiction of the abbey of *Nonantola* (p. 225) and after many vicissitudes came into the possession of the Counts of Pico, who retained their supremacy for upwards of three centuries. *Alexander I.* was the first of the family who bore the title of Duke of Mirandola and Concordia. *Francesco Maria*, the last duke, sold his dominions to Modena in 1710. The *Old Palace* of the dukes, the *Cathedral*, and the church of *Gesù* should be visited.]

The road, skirting several canals, next leads to **Carpi**, with 5000 inhab., an episcopal see, possessing a *Cathedral* attributed to Bramante (?), an old tastle, a modern palace, and spacious streets. — *Correggio* (p. 218) is situaced 7 M. to the S.W. Before the road reaches **Modena** (p. 222) it passes the *Citadel* of that town.

From Mantua to Reggio (37½ M.) diligence daily in 7½ hrs. Near *Borgoforte* the road crosses the Po and reaches **Guastalla** (*Posta*), a small town on the r. bank of the *Po*, which in the 16th cent. gave its name to a principality of the *Gonzagas*, Dukes of Mantua. They became extinct in 1746, and their territory fell to Parma. In the market-place is the bronze *Statue of Ferdinand I. Gonzaga* (d. 1557 at Brussels), by *Leone Leoni*. From Guastalla to Reggio 10 M. *Reggio* see p. 217.

From Mantua to Parma (30 M.) diligence daily in 6½ hrs.; fare 7, coupé 8 fr. — A short distance beyond the town the road diverges to the l.

from that which leads to Cremona (see below), and passes *Montanara* and *Campitello*. It then crosses the broad channel of the *Oglio*, and leads by *Sabbionetta* to **Casalmaggiore** (Croce Verde), whence an omnibus runs to Verona. A ferry here crosses to the r. bank of the Po. Then **Colorno** on the *Parma*, with an extensive, but now neglected ducal château, with pleasure-grounds and hothouses. From this point to Parma 9½ M. — *Parma* see p. 219.

From Mantua to Cremona (43½ M.) diligence daily in 10 hrs. (railway projected). The road passes *Curtatone*; then, near the influx of the Mincio into the Lago Superiore, the church of *S. Maria delle Grazie*, founded in 1399, a celebrated place of pious resort, remarkable principally for a number of life-size figures in wax, presented by various devotees. The next places are *Castellucchio*, *Marcaria*, *Bozzolo* (4000 inhab.), where the old road to Parma diverges to the r.; *Piadena*, whence another road leads to Parma; *Cicognolo*, and 10 M. farther *Cremona* (p. 162).

From Mantua to Brescia (39 M.) diligence daily in 9 hrs., passing through *Goito*, *Guidizzolo* (both scenes of engagements during the war of 1848), *Castiglione* (for the capture of which in 1796 Marshal Augereau was afterwards created Duc de Castiglione by Napoleon), *Montechiaro*, *Brescia* (see p. 155).

35. From Verona to Venice. Vicenza.

Railway in 3¼—4 hrs. (distance 72 M.); fares 13 fr. 95, 10 fr. 15, 7 fr. 25 c. Best views generally to the l. — Arrival at Venice see p. 184. Venice being a free port, travellers entering it are exempt from the payment of imposts, but those quitting it are subjected to the formalities of the *dogana*.

Railway-stations at Verona see p. 163. Soon after quitting the station outside the Porta Nuova the train crosses the *Adige* below the town. On the r. and l. are a number of detached forts, which render Verona the strongest fortress of N. Italy. The line skirts the S. spurs of the Alps and intersects the great Venetian plain. Vineyards, mulberry plantations, and fields o. Indian corn intersected by cuttings for their irrigation are passed in unbroken succession.

Near *S. Michēle* on the l. stands the pinnacled castle of *Montario*, formerly the property of the Scaliger family (p. 165). Stat. *S. Martino*. Stat. *Caldiēro* possesses mineral springs which attract many visitors and were known to the Romans. On the hill to the l. the slender campanile of *S. Vittōre*. *Villanuova* and the castle of *Soave*, once belonging to the Scaligers, on the height to the l. present a good picture of a mediæval fortified town.

Next stat. *S. Bonifacio*. *Arcŏle*, 3½ M. to the S., was the scene of the battle of 15th—17th Nov., 1796, between the Austrians and the French under Bonaparte, Masséna, Augereau, and Lannes. Stat. *Lonigo*; the village lies 4½ M. S.E., at the W. base of the *Monti Berici*, a chain of volcanic, wooded hills, between which and the spurs of the Alps the line now runs to Vicenza. Stat. *Montebello* is not to be confounded with the place (p. 84) of that name in Piedmont. Beautiful view towards the mountains; the stately château belongs to Count Arrighi. L. on the height the castles of the *Montecchi*, then stat. *Tavernelle*.

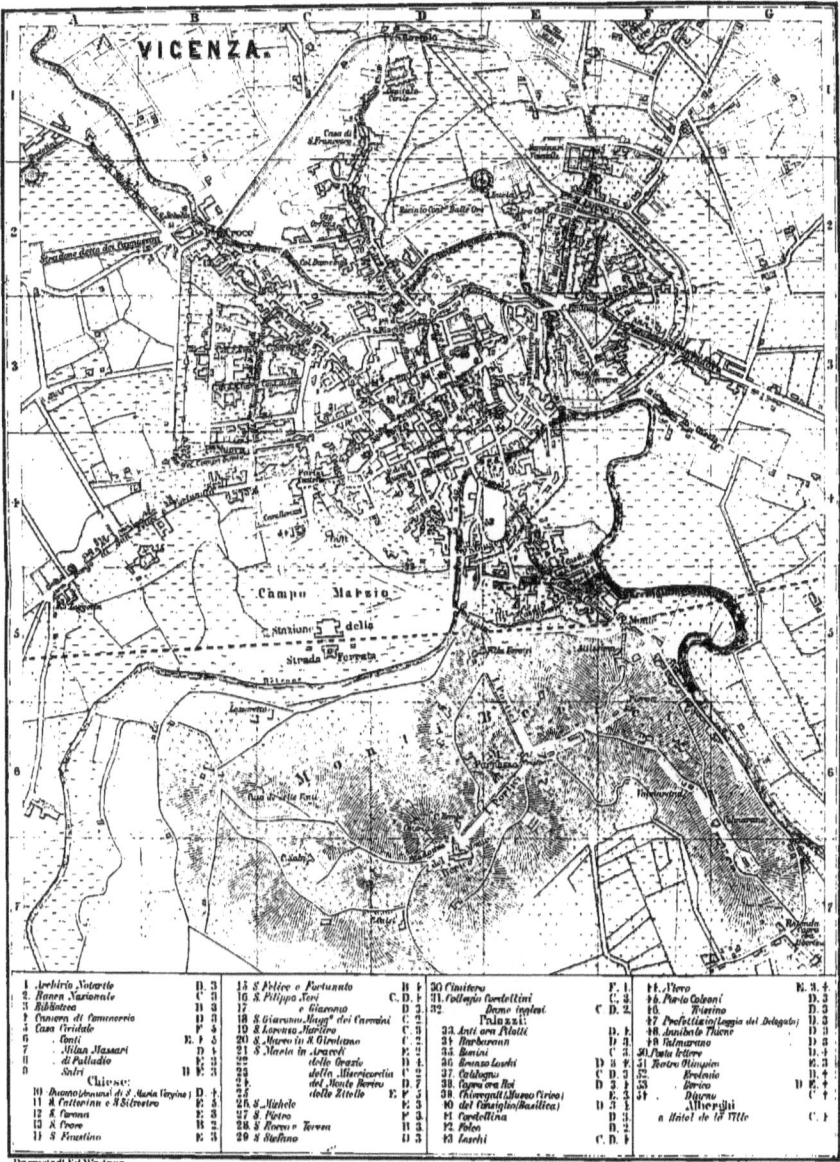

Vicenza (*Hôtel de la Ville, at the railway-gate, R. from 2 fr., D. 3, A. and L. 1 fr.; Stella d'Oro, in the Corso; Due Mori e Gran Parigi, good cuisine; Albergo e Trattoria ai tre Garofani, both in the Contrada delle due Ruote; Caffè Principe Umberto and Nazionale, in the Corso; Garibaldi, Piazza de' Signori; *Railway Restaurant), the *Vicetia* of the ancients, with 33,000 inhab., situated on the *Bacchiglione*, is celebrated as the birthplace of Palladio (1518—80), who erected his finest secular structures here (churches at Venice see p. 201). His successors *Scamozzi*, *Longhena*, and others adhered uniformly to his style, so that the town presents a remarkably handsome and harmonious appearance.

The town is entered by the W. gate (near the entrance the *Palazzo Gusano*, now Hôtel de la Ville), and the long *Corso Principe Umberto*. On the l. the new church of *S. Filippo Neri* (Pl. 16).

A short street leads r. from the Corso to the handsome *Piazza de' Signori*, with two columns of the Venetian period. Here rises the *Palazzo del Consiglio*, or *Basilica* (Pl. 40), a double series of grand and elegant open arcades, the lower with Doric, the upper with Ionic columns, surrounding the Palazzo della Ragione (town-hall). These arcades, commenced in 1549, are one of Palladio's earliest works. The lofty and slender red tower is of later date. Opposite the Basilica is the *Loggia del Delegato* or *Palazzo Prefettizio* (Pl. 47), also by Palladio (1571) In the Piazza, near the Basilica, stands a good *Statue of Palladio* in marble, by *Gajassi*, erected in 1859.

On the l. at the E. extremity of the Corso is the small *Casa di Palladio* (Pl. 8); then r., in the Piazza Vittorio Emanuele, the *Museo Civico* (Pl. 39), a handsome modern edifice, connected with the *Palazzo Chieregati* (see above), and containing several collections (access daily 9—5, $^1/_2$ fr.).

On the Ground Floor Roman antiquities from an ancient theatre. The Upper Floor contains the ***Pinacoteca**. 1st Room: 14. *Montagna*, Adoration of the Child; 213. *Bassano*, same subject; 6. *Montagna*, Madonna with SS. Clara and Catharine. Colossal bust of Garibaldi by *Barrera*. The shoes worn by the Doge during his nuptial procession (p. 199) etc. — 2nd R.: 1. 36. *Montagna*, Madonna enthroned with four saints; 32. *Bernardino da Murano*, same subject. — 3rd R.: 58. *Parmegiano*, Dead Saviour and saints; 56. *Titian*, Magdalene; 54. *Paolo da Venezia*, Death of Mary, painted in 1333; 53. *Correggio*, St. Catharine of Siena; 50. *Mozzetto*, Madonna; 35. *Gior. Bellini*, Madonna; 31. *P. Veronese*, Madonna; *10. *Cima da Conegliano*, Madonna with John the Baptist and St. Jerome, painted in 1489. — The next rooms contain nothing of importance. A separate room is devoted to drawings and various reminiscences of Palladio. — The *Nat. History Collection* comprises some very fine fossils; e. g. a fish, a palm, a crocodile found in a bed of coal in 1865, etc.

In the vicinity is the *Teatro Olimpico* (Pl. 51; fee $^1/_2$ fr.), designed by Palladio, but not completed till 1584, after his death. It was inaugurated by the performance of the 'Œdipus Tyrannus' of Sophocles. Palladio is said to have adhered to the directions given by Vitruvius with regard to the construction of ancient theatres, but the result differs materially from what would have been anticipated. The perspective of the scena is very remarkable; it is closed by a façade adorned with statues, through three doors in which a glimpse of the distant prospect is obtained. The orchestra is in front of the scena.

Besides the above mentioned, the following structures of Palladio may be noticed: *Palazzo Barbarano* (Pl. 34), *Tiene* (Pl. 48), *Valmarano* (Pl. 49), *Porto Coleoni* (Pl. 45), and the *Rotonda* (see below).

The *Cathedral* (Pl. 10) the aisles of which have been converted into chapels, is a broad and low structure containing nothing remarkable. The church of *S. Corona* (Pl. 12), a brick edifice with plain Lombard façade, contains a Baptism of Christ by G. Bellini, and an Adoration of the Magi by P. Veronese.

The pilgrimage-church of the *Madonna del Monte* (Pl. 24), situated on *Monte Berico*, outside the *Porta Lupia*, is approached by an arcade 2000 ft. in length, supported by 180 pillars. This passage was sharply contested in 1848 by the Piedmontese, who had fortified the hill with its villas, and the Austrians. A portion of the fortification is still left. *View pleasing, inn tolerable.

On the hill of S. Sebastiano, at the N.E. base of Monte Berico (not visible from the road thither), $1^1/_2$ M. from the town, is situated the celebrated *Villa Rotonda Palladiana* (Pl. G, 7) of the Marchesi Capra, with an Ionic colonnade surmounted by a pediment on each of the four sides. In the centre is a circular hall with a dome.

The *Baths of Recoaro* (Inn), about 25 M. (by carr. in 4 hrs.) N.W. of Vicenza are picturesquely situated and much frequented, especially in July and August. The mineral water contains iron.

Pojana is the only station between Vicenza and Padua. Country flat; S. in the distance rise the Monti Euganei (p. 179).

Padua see p. 175. To the l. as the train proceeds the Tyrolese Alps are perceived in the distance. Near stat. *Ponte di Brenta* the line crosses the *Brenta*; at stat. *Dolo* a lofty, slender campanile; at stat. *Marano* an arm of the Brenta is crossed. From stat. *Mestre* the line by Treviso and Udine to Trieste (R. 39) diverges to the N. — Venice, with its dark blue line of towers and churches rising from the sea, now gradually comes into view. The various islands with their groups of houses appear to float in the water. The line passes *Fort Malghera* and two large barracks on the l. and reaches the colossal *Bridge, one of the greatest existing structures of the kind (supported by 222 arches, length $2^1/_3$ M., breadth 28 ft.), by means of which the train crosses the *Lagune* (p. 190) in 8 min. and reaches the station at the N.W. extremity of **Venice** (R. 38).

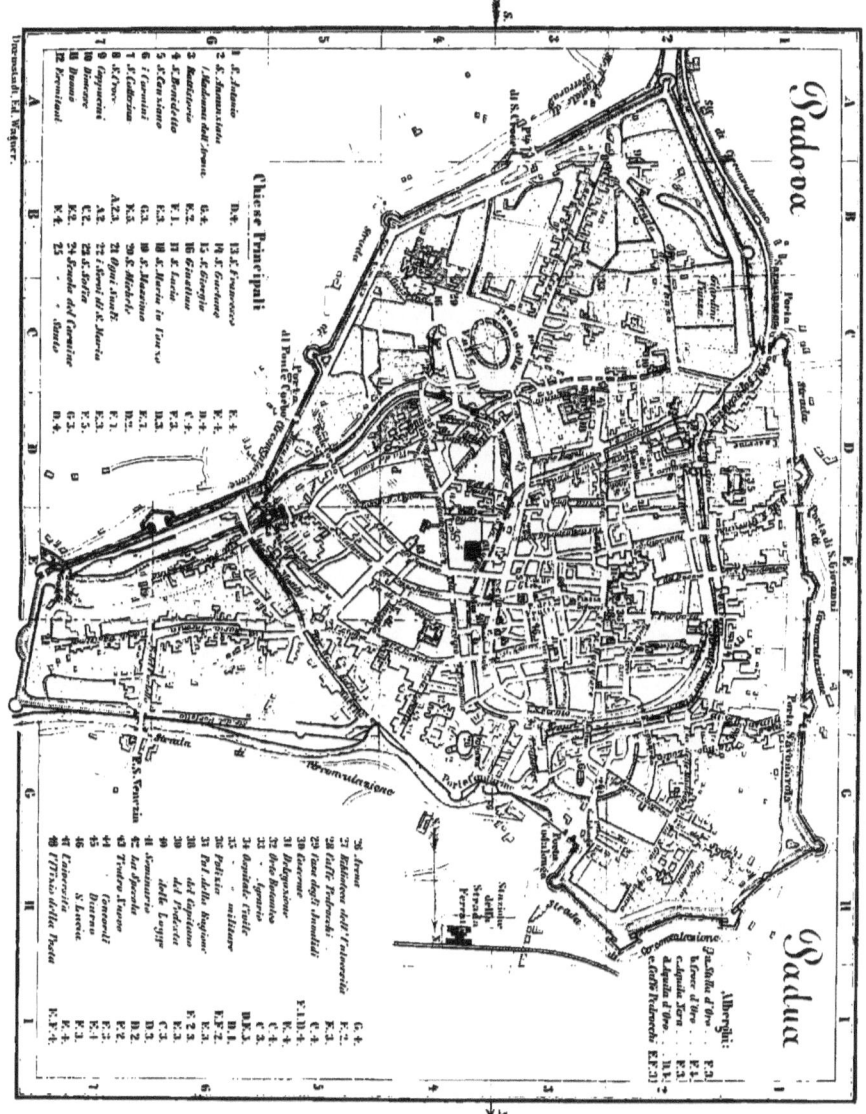

36. Padua, Ital. *Padŏva,* Lat. *Patavum.*

Hotels. Stella d'Oro, in the Piazza Garibaldi, R. 2¹/₂, D. 4, A. ³/₄, L. ¹/₂ fr.; *Aquila d'Oro, near S. Antonio, R. 2, L. ¹/₂, D. 4, A. ³/₄, Omnibus ³/₄ fr.; Croce d'Oro, in the Piazza Cavour; Aquila Nera, in the same Piazza, opposite Café Pedrocchi; Albergo al Paradiso, adjacent to the Stella d'Oro.

Cafés. *Pedrocchi (Pl. 28), opposite the University, an imposing edifice with halls and columns of marble; *Vittoria, in the Piazza Unità d'Italia. — Birraria di Franc. Stoppato, Via Eremitani; also on the ground-floor of the Albergo del Paradiso (see above). Ristoratore at the back of the Café Pedrocchi.

Fiacres, or '*Broughams*', to or from the station 1 fr., luggage 40 c., ¹/₂ hr. 1¹/₂ fr., 1 hr. 2 fr., drive in the town 50 c., at night 25 c. more. *Omnibuses* from the hotels meet each train.

Padua is a town of very great antiquity, tracing its origin traditionally to Antenor, brother-in-law of Priam. In 1405 it placed itself under the protection of the republic of Venice, to which it adhered until that state ceased to exist. From the middle ages down to the present time Padua has derived great celebrity from its *University*, which was founded by Emp. Frederick II. in 1238. The town, a quiet place with 51,000 inhab., occupies an extensive area. Narrow streets and arcades are interspersed with a number of spacious gardens.

***St. Antonio** (Pl. 1), the Basilica of St. Antony of Padua (d. 1231), commonly known as '*Il Santo*', is supposed to have been designed by Nicola Pisano in 1237, but was not commenced till 1259. The principal part of the church was completed in 1307, the remaining portions not before 1475; the whole was restored in 1749 after a conflagration. This vast structure with its seven domes is more extensive across the transepts than S. Marco at Venice. Over the portal of the façade, which is 110 ft. in width, stands a statue of the saint; in the lunette Madonna with SS. Bernardino and Antonio, a fresco by *Mantegna*. The church is 280 ft. in length, 138 ft. in width across the transepts, and 116 ft. high in the centre. The nave and aisles are supported by 12 pillars; the semicircular choir possesses 8 clustered columns and a series of 8 chapels.

At the entrance, in the nave r. and l. two handsome 'benitiers', with statuettes of St. John the Baptist and of Christ, dating from the commencement of the 16th cent.

R. Aisle. On the 1st pillar on the r. a *Madonna in Trono with SS. Peter, Paul, Bernard, and Antony, an altar-piece by *Antonio Boselli* of Bergamo. — *1st Chapel:* Altar with reliefs in bronze by *Donatello*, representing the miracles of St. Antony; r. the sarcophagus of General *Gattamelata* (p. 176) and his son. — By the second pillar beyond this is the tasteless monument of Professor *Ottavio Ferrari* (d. 1684).

R. Transept. **Cappella S. Felice*, with frescoes from the history of Christ and St. James, by *Jac. d'Avanzo* (d. 1370), restored in 1773, also architecturally interesting. — At the back of the choir is the circular *Cappella del Santuario* with statues of Faith, Love, Penitence, and Humility, by *Filippo Parodi*; the rich treasure of the church is preserved here. — On the N. side of the choir is the *Cappella del B. Luca Belludi,* a pupil of

S. Antony, with frescoes by *Giov.* and *Ant. Padovano*, badly restored in 1786; the walls are covered with a large number of votive paintings.

L. Transept. **Cappella del Santo;* the façade has four columns and two elegant corner pillars adorned with reliefs; between the five arches are the Evangelists; above is the inscription: *Divo Antonio confessori sacrum Rp. Pa. po.* The walls are embellished with nine *reliefs of the 16th cent. by the *Lombardi, Sansovino,* etc., representing the miracles of St. Antony. The bones of the saint repose beneath the altar which is also adorned with many votive tablets. Two magnificent candelabra (groups in marble beneath, the upper parts of silver).

L. Aisle. Imposing *Monument of the Venetian Admiral *Caterino Cornelio* (d. 1674). with two figures as supporters, two prisoners in fetters, and the life-size statue of the admiral by *Giusto le Curt*; *Monument of *Antonio de' Roicelli* (d. 1466), of admirable workmanship; by the last pillar (1st from the W. portal) the monument of Count *Sicco;* opposite to it is the last altar, that of St. Stanislaus, with a vault which once belonged to the kingdom of Poland; adjacent to it is a relief by *Luigi Ferrari* to the memory of the Princess *Jablonowska* (d. 1846).

In the Choir are 12 reliefs in bronze, representing scenes from the Old Testament, most of them executed by *Vellano*, the teacher of Donatello, at the end of the 15th cent. The features of the full-length figure of St. Antony are said to be a faithful portrait. The reliefs on the altar are by *Donatello.* Adjacent to the altar is a bronze *Candelabrum, 11 ft. in height, by *Andrea Riccio*, adorned with a variety of Christian and heathen representations. The Crucifix in bronze, with the Virgin and the tutelary saints of Padua, is by *Donatello.*

Nave. On the 2nd pillar on the l. the *Monument of *Alessandro Contarini* (d. 1553), General of the republic of Venice, with six slaves as supporters. On the opposite pillar (2nd on the l.) is the simple and chaste Monument of *Cardinal Bembo* (d. 1547); on the 4th pillar on the l. the Monument of the Venetian Admiral *Hieronymus Michiel* (d. 1557).

The Cloisters, which are entered from the S. aisle, contain a number of ancient tombstones.

The *Scuola del Santo*, adjoining the church, the assembly-hall of the brotherhood of St. Antony, is adorned with frescoes by *Titian* and his pupils (Nos. 1, 11, and 12 are by Titian himself, being among his earlier works, 1500—1520; the finest (No. 11) represents *St. Antony rescuing a woman who is on the point of being killed by her jealous husband. The written catalogue may be consulted). The adjacent old chapel of *S. Giorgio* contains mural paintings of 1384, by *Jacŏpo d'Avanzo.*

In front of the church is the equestrian Statue of *Erasmo da Narni*, surnamed *Gattamelāta*, commander of the army of the Republic of Venice in 1438—41, cast in bronze by *Donatello*, the first great specimen of bronze-casting of the modern period of Italian art (15th cent.).

Eremitani (Pl. 12), an Augustine church of the middle of the 13th cent., judiciously restored a few years ago, with painted vaulting of wood, is a very long structure, and destitute of aisles, columns, and pillars.

The church contains two old monuments of Princes of Carrara, the ancient lords of Padua. The walls of the Choir are covered with indifferent frescoes by *Guariento* (15th cent.), representing scenes from the history of the Augustine Order, subsequently restored. — The celebrated frescoes of *Mantegna* in the chapel of *S. Jacopo e Cristoforo*, adjacent to the church on the r., are in a very damaged condition: l. the history of St. James, r. that of St. Christopher (of the latter the lower part only is by Mantegna; the small lance-bearer, whose head alone now remains recognisable, on the l. is the painter himself. The upper scenes are by *Anuino*, a pupil of Mantegna). The terra cotta altar, Madonna and Saints by *Giovanni da Pisa*, a pupil of Donatello; behind it, Assumption of the Virgin, by *Pizzolo*. The chapel to the r. of the high altar contains a Coronation of Mary of the school of Giotto. — The Sacristy (entrance l. of the choir) contains an altar-piece by *Guido Reni* (covered), representing John the Baptist; on the wall to the l. is a relief by *Canova*, a mourning figure in a sitting posture with a pelican (emblem of parental affection), in memory of a *Prince of Orange* (d. 1799), who was a general in the Austrian service.

In a large garden adjoining the Piazza in front of the church (if closed, visitors ring at the large wooden gate), is situated the *Madonna dell' Arena (Annunziata, Pl. 2), a small Romanesque burial-chapel, erected in 1303. The walls are completely covered with a series of **Frescoes*, most of them in good preservation, by *Giotto*, painted in 1304. Those on the N. side represent the history of the Saviour in 18 sections, from the Nativity to the Descent of the Holy Ghost; on the S. (window-side) are 16 representations, also from the New Testament. In the choir is represented the Life of the Virgin (in inferior preservation); on the W. wall is a single painting, grandly conceived, representing the Last Judgment, supposed to have been composed from suggestions by Dante, who was then on a visit to his friend Giotto (custodian 1/2 fr.). Morning light is the most favourable. (Photographs from the originals may be purchased of Naya at Venice, 1 1/2 fr. each.)

The **Cathedral** (Pl. 11), dating from the latter half of the 16th cent., with a façade totally destitute of ornament, is unattractive. The *Baptistery* (Pl. 3), which adjoins it on the N., is a brick structure of the 12th cent., adorned with ancient and nearly obliterated frescoes.

The **Palazzo della Ragione** (Pl. 37), now the *Municipio*, situated between the Piazza d'Erbe and the Piazza di Frutti, a '*Juris Basilica*' as the inscription records, was erected in the 11th cent. and remodelled in 1420. It is celebrated for its great *Hall*, with vaulted wooden ceiling, said to be one of the largest in the world, 272 ft. in length, 92 ft. in breadth, 80 ft. in height (custodian 1/2 fr.). It contains a wooden model of a large horse by Donatello, which has given rise to a variety of conjectures, but was probably employed by the artist for his equestrian statue of Gattamelata (see above). It closely resembles the third horse to the r. on St. Mark's at Venice (p. 192), which was probably the original model. Beneath the external gallery are Roman antiquities, most of them inscriptions. Behind the horse is the tombstone of T. Livius Halys, a freedman of the family of the historian Livy, who is believed to have been born at Abano (p. 179). The Palazzo della Rag one also contains a *Pinacoteca, or *Picture Gallery* (entrance to the l. in the street leading to the university, ascent by a stair opposite the gate), recently founded and enriched with a number of valuable works from dissolved monasteries; it contains few works of great value, but is well worthy of a visit. Catalogues are provided for visitors.

1st Saloon: 58. *Titian*, Christ, Mary, and Apostles; 40. *Guido Reni*, Portrait; 30. *Guercino*, St. John. — 2nd S.: 56. *Palma Vecchio*, Jacob's blessing; *114. *Mantegna*, Warrior, with his back to the spectator; 15, 16. *Titian*, Portraits; 20. *Giovanni Bellini*, Portrait. — 3rd S.: 21. *Palma Vecchio*, Madonna, with portraits of the donors; 34. *Mantegna*, Resurrection; 38. *Luigi Vivarini*, Portrait of a pope; 45. *Marco Basaiti*, Madonna and Child with saints. — 4th S.: *Campagnola*, Beheading of John the Baptist, a large fresco transferred to canvas. — 5th S.: *70. *Girolamo Romanino* (beginning of 16th cent.), Madonna with SS. Benedict and Justina on the l., and SS. Protasius and Scholastica on the r.; 71. *G. Romanino*, Last Supper; 81. *Romanino*, Madonna with SS. Benedict and Scholastica. — A stair descends from this saloon to the 6th S. (on the lower floor): 24. *Girolamo del Santo*, Entombment, a fresco. — 7th S.: 23. *Garofalo*, Holy Family; 43. *Bassano*, Noah entering the ark; 60. *Velasquez*, Portrait; 6. *Maratta*, Portrait of Donatello. — 8th S.: 30. *Agapiti* (1497), Enthroned Madonna with saints. — 9th S.: Casts, bronzes, etc. — 11th S.: Majolicas, coins, reliefs. — The Biblioteca Municipale (10,000 vols.), which is also established here, contains little to interest the stranger.

The *Palazzo del Podestà*, in the Piazza d'Erbe, and the *Palazzo del Capitaneo*, with a central tower, in the Piazza de' Signori (now the Piazza dell' Unità d'Ital'a), also merit inspection.

The **Loggia del Consiglio**, or *Gran Guardia*, in the Piazza dell' Unità d'Italia, W. of the Palazzo della Ragione, is a very elegant example of the early Renaissance style. It possesses a deep vestibule with an open arcade above a broad and lofty flight of steps.

The **University** (Pl. 47), opposite the Café Pedrocchi (p. 175), is established in a building termed '*Il Bò*', from a former tavern in the vicinity with the sign of the ox. Beneath the handsome colonnades in the court, erected in 1552 by *Jac. Sansovino*, are numerous inscriptions and coats of arms of distinguished '*cives academici*'.

Padua has also dedicated a number of monuments to the '*auditores Patavini*', or students of the university who distinguished themselves in after-life. A double series of statues, a few only of which possess artistic merit (e. g. those of *Poleni* and *Capello* by Canova), adorn the *****Piazza Vittorio Emanuele**, formerly termed *Prato della Valle* from its original condition as a grassy dale (now a promenade, $1/4$ hr. walk from the university). In the inner row to the l. No. 63. *Savonarola*, 74. *Steph. Buthori*, 75. *John Sobieski*; in the external row *Tasso*, *Ariosto*, *Petrarch*, *Galileo*. This spacious Piazza presents a busy scene at the time of the fair *(fiēra)*, which commences on the festival of St. Antony (June 13th).

Opposite to the Prato N.W., in front of the Gothic halls of the *Palazzo della Loggia* (Pl. 40), a modern structure of brick and stone, are the two marble *Statues of Dante* and *Giotto*, by

Vincenzo Vela, erected in 1865. To the E. of the Prato is situated the church of

*S. Giustina (Pl. 16), an edifice of strikingly noble and imposing proportions, especially in the interior, completed in 1549 by *Andrea Riccio* or *Briosco*. It possesses a nave with two aisles, four domes and an unadorned façade of brick, approached by a handsome flight of 12 steps, of the entire breadth of the structure. The church is paved with black, yellow, and red marble. In the l. transept is the sarcophagus of St. Luke, in the r. transept that of St. Matthew. Over the high altar, which contains the tomb of St. Justina, is the *Martyrdom of St. Justina, by *Paolo Veronese*. Magnificently carved *Choir-stalls by Tavolino (1550), in 50 different sections, each representing a subject from the New Testament above, and one from the Old below. In the chapel on the r. of the choir is represented the Virgin with the body of Christ, at the sides John and Mary Magdalene, a large group in marble by *Parodi*. The old choir, the sole remnant of the original church, also possesses fine carved stalls. — To the N. in the vicinity is the **Botanical Garden** (Pl. 32), the oldest in Europe, containing a number of fine examples of trees peculiar to the south.

Commissionaires here generally urge the stranger to visit the *Castello Pacerotti*, a miniature imitation of a feudal castle, erected about 1830, containing old armour, an imitation of the dungeons at Venice, implements of torture, etc., but not worthy of a visit.

37. From Padua to Bologna by Ferrara.

97½ M. Railway in 3—5 hrs.; fares 14 fr. 50, 11 fr. 10, 7 fr. 95 c.

The line skirts the navigable *Canale di Battaglia*. To the r. rise the *Monti Euganei*, an isolated volcanic chain of hills (12 M. in length, extending from N. to S.; 6 M. in breadth, from E. to W.), containing extensive quarries of trachyte, and affording interesting excursions from Padua. Their culminating point is *Monte Venda* (1890 ft.), with the ruins of a monastery.

Stat. *Abano;* the small town itself, the birth-place of the historian Livy, lies at some distance to the r. of the line. In the vicinity is *Bagni* (i. e. 'Baths', a well-appointed establishment), the *Aquae Patavinae*, or *Fons Aponi* of the Romans, on the E. slope of the Monti Euganei, with warm springs and mud-baths.

Stat. *Montegrotta*. To the r., beyond a long tunnel, is seen the old and well-preserved castle of *Cattājo*, the property of the Duke of Modena, adorned with numerous frescoes by Celotti. It was erected by the now extinct Venetian family Obïzzo, who, according to a notice on a family-portrait, claim to have invented the howitzer. The castle contains very extensive collections of antiquities, mediæval curiosities, weapons, guns, artillery-models, and (in the chapel) old Italian pictures.

Stat. *Battaglia* possesses warm baths of considerable repute. The principal spring adjoins the château of the Countess Wimpffen, the proprietress of the watering-place. About 3 M. S.W. of Battaglia, on the slopes of the Monti Euganei, is situated *Arquà*, a small town celebrated as Petrarch's favourite retreat, where he died (in 1374). His house and tombs one are shown. The latter is adjacent to the church; the bust was erected in 1667.

Stat. *Monselice*, a town at the base of the Monti Euganei, with a ruined castle, was formerly a fortress.

Stat. *Este*. The town, the *Ateste* of Tacitus, lies $3^1/_2$ M. to the N., on the road which here diverges to Mantua. It possesses the old ancestral residence of the House of Este, a fine p azza, and the church of S. Martino with a leaning tower.

The line now quits the canal, and near stat. *Stanghella* crosses the *Gorzone Canal*. The district is fertile, but flat and marshy. Near *Boara* a small new fort is passed and the *Adige* crossed.

Stat. **Rovigo** *(Cappa d'Oro; Corona Ferrea)*, on the *Naviglio Adigetto*, is an episcopal residence and the capital of a 'Delegation'. Here, too, there is a leaning tower.

Adria, $16^1/_2$ M. to the E., on the *Bianco Canal*, occupies the site of the very ancient Etruscan town of the same name, whence the Adriatic derives its appellation. The sea, which has gradually receded, owing to alluvial deposits and other causes, is now 17 M. distant.

Stat. *Arquà*. The line crosses the *Bianco Canal* near the *Bosaro*, and near

Stat. *Polesella* reaches the *Po*, here the boundary between Venetia and the Romagna. The l. bank of the Po is now followed. Stat. *Paviole;* then *S. Maria Maddalena*. The river is then crossed, and the train reaches stations *Pontelagoscuro*, and

Ferrara (Europa, opposite the post-office; Stella d'Oro, opposite the castle, R. 2, L. $^1/_2$, B. $^1/_2$ fr.; Tre Corone, R. $1^1/_2$, A. $^1/_2$ fr., tolerable; Ristoratore di Pasqua Crovetto, Piazza del Commercio, opp. the palace; Caffè del Commercio, in the same piazza), situated near the ancient *Forum Alieni*, $3^1/_2$ M. S. of the Po, in the midst of a fruitful, but unhealthy plain. It is the capital of a Delegation, with 27,688 inhab., and possesses broad, deserted streets, decaying palaces, and other imposing reminiscences of its golden period. It once numbered 100,000 inhab., enjoyed great commercial prosperity, and was the seat of the renowned court of the illustrious House of Este, to which several great patrons of literature and art in the middle ages belonged. Ariosto and Tasso were among the most brilliant stars of this court.

The family of Este was of Tuscan extraction. *Azzo I.* became Count or Margrave of Este under Emp. Henry III. His eldest son *Welf* (founder of the younger branch of the *Guelphs*) was invested with the Duchy of Bavaria, which had belonged to his grandfather, the last male repre entative of the elder branch of the Guelphs, and his son *Henry the Proud* became the founder of the families of Brunswick and Hanover. *Giulio*, the second son of Welf, was the ancestor of the dukes of Ferrara and Modena. *Obizzo III.*, who added Modena and Reggio to his dominions (d. 1352), considera-

bly extended the power of his house, which from an early period was a liberal patron of art and science. In 1452 *Borso* received the title of Duke of Modena and Reggio from Emp. Frederick III., and that of Duke of Ferrara from Pope Paul II. He died in 1471. His brother *Hercules I.* (1471–1505), and the son of the latter, *Alphonso I.* (1505–34), husband of the infamous Lucrezia Borgia, were powerful and influential princes. Cardinal *Hippolytus d'Este*, Archbishop of Milan, brother of Alphonso, was the friend and patron of *Ariosto*. *Hercules II.* (1534–58), son of Alphonso, was the husband of *Renata*, daughter of Louis XII. of France, patroness of the Reformers Calvin and Marot, to whom she accorded an asylum. Having declared herself in favour of the reformed doctrines, she was separated from her husband and children. Her son *Alphonso II.* (1558–97) raised the glory of Ferrara to its culminating point, but with him the family became extinct, his three marriages being childless. He was the patron of the poets *Tasso* and *Guarini* (author of the 'Pastor Fido', born at Ferrara in 1537, died at Venice in 1612). Goethe in his 'Torquato Tasso' has drawn a faithful picture of the court of Ferrara about the year 1575, although a somewhat ideal colouring has been imparted to some of the characters. His description of the attachment of Tasso to *Eleonora* (1537–81), the youngest unmarried sister of the duke, is however not without foundation. *Anna* (1531–1607), one of the sisters, was married to the Duc de Guise, and afterwards to the Duc de Nemours; *Lucrezia* (1534–98), the other sister, was the wife of the Duke of Urbino. Alphonso II. was succeeded by *Cesare d'Este*, descendant of a natural son of Alphonso I., but only as duke of Modena and Reggio, Ferrara and Comacchio having been claimed by Pope Clement VIII. as vacant fiefs. In the history of art and science the renown of the House of Este is immortal.

'Whoe'er in Italy is known to fame
This lordly House as frequent guest can claim.'

Several celebrated painters who lived at Ferrara must also be mentioned: *Cosimo Tura*, a pupil of Mantegna; *Lorenzo Costa*, who subsequently became a follower of Francesco Francia at Bologna; then, at the commencement of the 16th cent., *Dosso Dossi* and *Benvenuto Tisio*, surnamed *Garofalo* (1481–1559), an adherent of Raphael. *Titian* also occasionally resided at Ferrara, where he painted his 'Cristo della Moneta', now at Dresden.

The *Palace* (Pl. 17), an ancient and picturesque edifice with four towers, is situated in the centre of the town. It is now the seat of the local authorities, the telegraph-office, etc. The custodian shows several dungeons, and among them one at the base of the 'lion tower', where on May 21st, 1425, the Marquis Nicholas III. caused his faithless wife Parisina Malatesta and his natural son Hugo, her paramour, to be beheaded. Lord Byron in his poem of 'Parisina' substitutes the name of Azzo for Nicholas as being more metrical. The *Sala del Consiglio* (or *Sala de' Giganti*) in the building of the prefecture, contains frescoes by Dosso Dossi, representing wrestling-matches of the ancient palæstra. The *Sala dell' Aurora*, with frescoes by the same master, is accessible only by special permission of the prefect.

The *Piazza Grande (Ariostea)* is adorned with a *Statue of Ariosto* on a lofty Corinthian column with pedestal.

The *Cathedral* (*S. Paolo*, Pl. 1), of 1135, possesses an imposing façade with three series of round arches, one above the other. The projecting portal, adorned with sculptures and four lions, was added at a subsequent period. The tower rises above the choir. The spacious interior is adorned with paintings of no great value by *Garofalo*, *Cosimo Tura*, *Dosso Dossi*, and *Guercino* (St. Lawrence). At the S. corner of the cathedral rises a handsome *Campanile* of four massive stories, erected under *Ercole II.* (p. 181).

S. Francesco (Pl. 7), dating from the end of the 15th cent., is entirely covered with domes. The interior, consisting of nave and aisles with chapels on each side, is adorned with frescoes and other paintings by *Garofalo*, *Ortolano*, etc. and monuments of the House of Este, also that of *Giambattista Pigna*, secretary of Alphonso II. and rival of Tasso. A famous echo here (at the commencement of the nave) is said to answer 16 times when awakened with due energy.

S. Benedetto (Pl. 3), dating from the same period, consists of nave and aisles supported by pillars, with a series of chapels on each side. The circular vaulting is interrupted by the domes. The monument of Ariosto was removed hence to the library (p. 183) in 1801. The former monastery is now a hospital. It is adorned with frescoes by *Scarsellino* and *Dosso Dossi;* that of the ante-chamber of the refectory bears a representation of Paradise, with saints and angels, among which Ariosto caused himself to be painted.

S. Domenico (Pl. 6) is adorned with statues on the façade by *Ferreri*, and with paintings in the interior by *Garofalo* and *Carlo Bonone*. The celebrated *Celio Calcagnini* of Ferrara (1479—1541), who to some extent anticipated Copernicus in his discoveries respecting the solar system, the contemporary and friend of Ariosto, bequeathed his library to the adjacent monastery. His bust is placed over the entrance, and beneath it is inscribed his humiliating avowal, that the principal lesson he had derived from his long and indefatigable studies was to despise knowledge and everything human.

S. Maria del Vado (Pl. 11), one of the oldest churches of Ferrara, consists of a nave divided into three parts with flat ceiling resting on 10 columns, and surmounted by a dome supported by pillars. It contains admirable paintings by *Carlo Bonone* (Marriage of Cana, Coronation of Mary, etc.), *Dosso Dossi*, and *Palma Vecchio*.

S. Paolo (Pl. 13) is adorned with paintings by *Bonone* and *Scarsellino*, and contains the monument of *Antonio Montecatino*, the friend and minister of Alphonso II.

The *ature *Palazzo de' Diamanti* (Pl. 30), a handsome square structure, erected in 1492 and remodelled in 1567, contains the *Ateneo Civico* and the *Civic Picture Gallery* (open daily 9—3 o'clock), most of the pictures in which have been obtained from suppressed churches. *Garofalo* and *Dosso Dossi* are particularly well represented.

1st Room: 87. *Tintoretto*, Madonna del Rosario, with SS. Dominicus,

Maurice, and George. — 2nd Room: 74. *Panetti* (d. 1531, master of Garofalo), Annunciation; 18. *Boccaccino* (d. 1515), Death of the Virgin; 23. *Costa* (1480—1530), Adoration of the Child with 4 smaller pictures. — 3rd Room: 45. *Garofalo*, Large fresco, symbolical of the victory of Christianity over Judaism. — 4th Room: *72. *Palma Vecchio*, Jesus and the Pharisees; 28. *Cremonese*, St. Mark; *48. *Garofalo*, Madonna del Riposo; 47. *Garofalo*, St. Peter the Martyr; 26. *Carpi* (d. 1567), St. Antony of Padua, causing an infant to speak and bear testimony to the honour of its mother; *46. *Garofalo*, Adoration of the Magi. — 5th Room: 34. *Dosso Dossi*, St. John the Evangelist in the island of Patmos; 49. *Garofalo*, Madonna del Pilastro; 50. *Garofalo*, Adoration of the Magi (the artist has painted a 'garofalo' or carnation by way of signature); 73. *Panetti*, Mary's meeting with Elisabeth; 51. *Garofalo*, Christ on the Mt. of Olives. — 6th Room: 60. *Guercino*, Beheading of St. Maurelius; 53. *Garofalo*, Slaughter of the Innocents; 56. *Garofalo*, Finding of the Cross; *55. *Garofalo*, Raising of Lazarus. — 7th Room: 89. *Timoteo della Vite*, Assumption. — 8th Room: 33. *Dosso Dossi*, Madonna surrounded by saints, a very large picture in several divisions.

The *Studio Pubblico* or *Università* (Pl. 22), a school of medicine, mathematics and jurisprudence, contains a valuable collection of coins and Greek and Latin inscriptions, and a *Library* of 100,000 vols. and 1100 MSS. Among the latter are several cantos of the 'Orlando Furioso' in *Ariosto's* handwriting, with numerous corrections, and a copy of *Tasso's* 'Gerusalemme Liberata', likewise with corrections; also letters written by Tasso in prison; *Guarini's* MS. of the 'Pastor Fido'; a number of ancient illuminated choir-books. Among the printed books are 52 old editions of *Ariosto*. His monument, formerly in S. Benedetto, has also been preserved here since 1801.

The simple *House of Ariosto* (Pl. 25), which he erected for himself and occupied during the latter part of his life, Via dell' Ariosto No. 67, has been the property of the town since 1811. It bears the inscription, composed by the poet himself:

'Parva, sed apta mihi, sed nulli obnoxia, sed non
Sordida, parta meo sed tamen aere domus.'

A few reminiscences of Ariosto are shown in the interior.

Whilst the poet was studying law, which however he soon exchanged for poetry, he resided in the *Casa degli Ariosti*, near the church of S. Maria di Bocche. He quitted this house on his father's death. *Guarini's House* still belongs to his descendants.

The *Hospital of St. Anna* (entrance in the Stradella Giovecca, next door to the Europa, Pl. 29) is interesting as the place where *Tasso* was kept in confinement for seven years (from 1579) by order of Alphonso II. It is generally supposed the poet incurred the displeasure of his patron by his passion for the Princess Leonora, the sister of Alphonso. The dungeon in which he is supposed to have been incarcerated is shown. The names of Byron and other poets are written on the walls.

In the church of *S. Giorgio*, outside the Porta Romana, Pope Eugene IV. opened the council convened with a view to effect a union of the Greek and Roman churches, in the presence of the Greek Emp. John Palæologus in 1438. This locality being considered unhealthy, the seat of the Council was afterwards transferred to Florence.

From Ferrara to Bologna by railway in 1—1½ hr. The train proceeds S. and crosses the *Cavo Tassone Canal*, which communicates with the *Pò di Primaro*, and traverses flat, well cultivated land (rice-fields). Stations *Poggio Renatico*, *Galliera*, *S. Pietro in Casale*, and *San Giorgio*.

From S. Giorgio an excursion may be made to (5 M.) **Cento**, a small town on the *Reno*, birthplace of the great painter *Guercino* (d. at Bologna 1666). Several of the churches, especially those of **S. Biagio* and the *Madonna del Rosario*, contain admirable works by *Guercino*, who was greatly attached to his native town. His house, where he received many illustrious visitors, is still shown. In the centre of the town is his statue by *Galetti*. — Near Cento is situated *Pieve di Cento*, a small town with the pilgrimage-church of *S. Maria Assunta;* the high altar-piece is an *Assumption by *Guido*.

Next stations *Castel Maggiore* and *Corticella*. As Bologna is approached the rich fertility of the soil continues to increase.

Bologna see R. 43.

38. Venice (Venezia).

Arrival. The railway-station is confined and noisy. The porters with badges convey the luggage to an omnibus-boat (p. 186) or to a private gondola, according to the wish of the traveller, to whom an official presents a number for a gondola and a printed tariff of fares from the station to any part of the city (as far as S. Marco 1 fr., to more distant points 1 fr. 25 c., each box 15 c.; with two rowers double these charges). A second generally proffers his services, but may be dismissed with the words 'basta uno!' The 'omnibus' is a very slow craft, often crowded and affording no view. — Gondola tariff for those who arrive by sea see p. 185.

Hotels (comp. Introd. V). Grand Hôtel Royal (Danieli, Pl. a), in the former *Palazzo Bernardi*, Riva degli Schiavoni, E. of the Palace of the Doges, R. from 3, L. 1, B. 2, D. 4, A. 1 fr.; *Europa (Pl. b), in the former *Palazzo Giustiniani*, on the Grand Canal, opposite the Dogana di Mare and near the Piazza of St. Mark, similar charges. *Hôtel Barbesi (Pl. c), in the *Palazzo Zucchelli*, on the Grand Canal, opposite the church della Salute; *Vittoria (Pl. g), R. 2½ fr. and upwards, D. 4, L. and A. 1, B. 1½ fr., situation not favourable. — *S. Marco (Pl. e), in the Piazza of St. Mark, in the old Procuratie, similar charges; *Hôtel Bellevue (Pl. d), N. side of the Piazza of St. Mark, R. 3 fr. and upwards, B. 1½, A. 1 fr.; Hôtel New York, in the former *Palazzo Ferro* (p. 209), new, well spoken of; *Luna (Pl. f), to the W. of and opposite to the former Imperial Garden, close to the Piazza of St. Mark, similar charges; *Città di Monaco (*Munich Hotel*) (Pl. l), on the Grand Canal, near the Piazza of St. Mark, R. 2½ fr., L. 75, A. 60 c.; Città di Roma, S. Moisè, Piscina, new; Hôtel Pension Suisse, on the Grand Canal, opposite S. Maria della Salute; *Italia (Pl. h), newly fitted up; *Hôtel Bauer (Pl. m), S. Moisé, Calle lunga, with Restaurant; Pension Anglaise in the former *Palazzo Giustinian Vescovi*, Grand Canal, recommended; Vapore (Pl. i), S. Gallo (Pl. k), with good restaurant; Leon bianco, Calle de' Fabbri, N. of the Piazza of St. Mark; Sandwirth, Riva degli Schiavoni, moderate. — Hôtel Garni au Beau-Rivage, 'dependance' of Hôtel Danieli (see above), Riva degli Schiavoni; Scharfnagels Hôtel Garni by the Campanile, well spoken of, R. and L. 2½ fr. per day, 50 fr. per month. — Strangers are cautioned against sleeping with open windows on account of the gnats. Mosquito-curtains afford the best protection against these pertinacious intruders. Pastilles ('*fidibus contro le zanzare*'), sold by the chemists,

are generally effectual in dispersing them. *Drinking-water* is bad at Venice; a new conduit is projected.

Private Apartments, to which the attention is attracted by notices on the shutters or in the windows, are easily obtained. The rents of those on the *Grand Canal* and the *Riva degli Schiavoni* are the highest. The *Fondamenta della Zattere* is a quiet and agreeable situation (e. g. in the Calle del Ridotto, R. 1—2 fr. per day, 30—50 fr. per month). It is usual to pay for one month in advance, before which the tenant is recommended to see that every necessary arrangement is made, *'tutto compreso'*.

Restaurants (*Trattorie*, comp. Introd. V). On the first floor of the *Café Quadri; *Gallo (good Italian cuisine); *Hôtel Bauer (see above); to the r. in the same street, farther on, Città di Firenze, good wine, Calle del Ridotto, opp. the Europa; *Leon Bianco (p. 184). These are among the best establishments of their kind; most of the others are deficient in cleanliness and comfort. — The wines of *Cyprus* and *Samos* are the best at Venice. — Beer at *Bauer* and *Grünwald* (Hôtel Bauer, p. 184); at the *Città di Genova* (see above), and at most of the cafés.

Cafés (comp. Introd. V). In the *Piazza of St. Mark*, S. side: *Florian; Café Svizzero. N. side: Degli Specchi; *Quadri (recommended for breakfast). After sunset hundreds of chairs and small tables are placed in front of these cafés for the accommodation of customers. Strangers must here submit, with the best grace they can, to the importunities of flower-girls, hawkers, musicians, etc. The cafés on the *Riva degli Schiavoni* are also much frequented, although less fashionable: Briciacco (good ices), Alle Nazioni, etc.

Boats take the place of fiacres at Venice. The light, old Venetian Gondola, with a low black canopy or cabin (*felze*) and black leather seat, accommodates 2—3 pers. They are painted black in conformity with a law passed in the 15th cent. The Barca, a modern institution, is a larger craft, open at the sides, covered with coloured material, and accommodating 6 or more pers. The heavy indented iron prow (*ferro*), resembling a halberd, is partly designed to counterbalance the weight of the rower, and partly as a measure of the height of the bridges, which cannot be passed unless the ferro, the highest part of the craft, clears them. The rower himself is hailed as '*Poppe*', from the *poppa* on which he stands.

Charges. Gondola with one rower (*barcajuola*), according to the most recent tariff, a copy of which the gondolier is bound to exhibit if desired, for the first hour, or for each trip 1 fr., for each additional hour 75 c.; for the whole day (of 10 hrs.) 5 fr. To or from the station see p. 184. Luggage 15 c. From the steamers to the Piazzetta (two rowers required) 50 c., to the Rialto Bridge 2 fr., beyond it 2½ fr. From the Piazzetta to the Giardini Pubblici 50 c. After sunset one-half more. For short distances more favourable terms may frequently be made. For a second rower double the ordinary fare is charged. One, however, suffices for the gondola, and even for the barca if not heavily laden, unless greater speed than usual is desired. Officious loiterers who assist passengers to disembark expect a gratuity of a few centimes.

It is usual for the passenger, after having selected a gondola or barca, to mention his destination and the fare to the gondolier; e. g. '*alla stazione un franco, S. Giovanni e Paolo mezzo franco*' etc. Should the proper fare be declined, application is made to another. If the gondola be hired by the hour, the passenger shows his watch and remarks: '*all' hora*'. The highest demands are generally made at the Piazzetta and Riva and in the vicinity. It need hardly be observed that the intervention of a commissionaire or waiter in the hiring of a boat causes the fare to be considerably raised. A second rower, who is generally desirous of being engaged, may be dismissed with the words '*basta uno*'. According to the official regulations gondoliers guilty of extortion or want of respect are liable to severe punishment.

Generally speaking the gondoliers are respectable and trustworthy, and it is usual to give them a trifling gratuity in excess of the fare (for a whole day 50 c. to 1 fr.). — The shouts of the gondoliers on turning a corner are peculiar, e. g. *già è* (boat ahead!), *premè* (pass to the *r.*!), *stall* (pass to l.!), etc.

Omnibus Boats (Pl. 20) ply, on the arrival of every train, from the station to the *Riva del Carbon* (near Ponte Rialto) and the *Piazzetta*. Fare 25 c., gratuity 5 c., each heavier article of luggage 15 c.; the porter belonging to the boat, who conveys luggage to the hotel, also expects a fee. On quitting the railway station, the traveller who purposes employing one of these conveyances names his hotel or other destination and is conducted by the railway-officials to the proper boat (comp. p. 184). Omnibuses to the station (in 20 min.) start from the *Molo*, E. of the Piazzetta, ³/₄ hr. before the departure of each train (their station is by the first bridge, the *Ponte della Paglia*, nearly under the *Bridge of Sighs*). Omnibus to the Lido 25 c.

Ferries (*Traghetti*) across the Grand Canal (5 c., after dusk 8 c.), 15 in number, see Plan.

Guides (*Huber*, *Schneider*, *Fuchs*, *Joseph Scholl*, *Ferrari*, *Fassetta*, *Carabba*, *Nicola* etc.) are to be met with before 9 a. m. or about 8 p. m. in the Piazza of St. Mark. Each hotel generally has its own guide. Parties of strangers are frequently formed by the guides, who undertake to conduct them to all the principal sights of Venice at a charge of 3—4 fr. each pers., which includes gondola-fares, gratuities, etc., but, as the number is usually unlimited, this wholesale system cannot be recommended, the members of the party being entirely deprived of their independence. The traveller, alone, or accompanied by a few friends, will find it far preferable to have a guide at his own disposal. In this case the fee including all expenses, is 20 fr. (i. e. 5 fr. for the guide and about 15 fr. for gondolas, fees, etc.).

It must, however, be observed that the following pages, coupled with a slight acquaintance with the Italian language, will enable the stranger entirely to dispense with the services of a guide. The principal objects of interest should be visited in a definite order, such as that suggested below, and the most direct routes ascertained from the Plan, in order that the proper orders may be given to the gondolier at each stage of the route.

Plan of Visit. A stay of 3—4 days may suffice when time is limited, in which case the following plan is recommended, but may be modified at discretion.

Afternoon or Evening of arrival. In order to gratify their first curiosity, and obtain a general idea of the peculiarities of Venice, strangers are recommended to undertake a preliminary '*Voyage of Discovery*' from the Piazzetta along the *Grand Canal* (see p. 208) to its extremity (near the railway-station is the church *Degli Scalzi*, see p. 207, which should now be visited on account of its remoteness from the other points of attraction); then beneath the iron bridge (p. 212) to the *Canal di Mestre*, l. of which is the Jews' quarter (the *Ghetto*, inhabited by the lowest classes); back hence by the Grand Canal to the *Ponte Rialto*, where the gondola should be quitted. Then on foot (the best mode of forming acquaintance with the customs and character of the people) through the *Merceria* (pp. 187, 195) to the Piazza of St. Mark. The whole expedition will occupy 2—2¹/₂ hrs.

1st Day. ***S. Marco* (p. 192); **Palace of the Doges* (p. 195); * *S. Giorgio Maggiore* (p. 203) (ascend campanile); *Redentore (p. 206); * *S. Sebastiano* (temporarily closed, see p. 207).

2nd Day. *Pal. Emo Treves* (p. 209); *S. Maria della Salute* (p. 206); ***Accademia delle Belle Arti* (p. 199); **S. Stefano* (p. 208); * *Frari* (p. 202); **Scuola di S. Rocco* (p. 207).

3rd Day. *S. Salvadore* (closed, see p. 207); **Pal. Vendramin* (p. 211); *Museo Correr (p. 211); **Madonna dell' Orto* (p. 205); *Gesuiti* (p. 203); *S. Maria de' Miracoli* (p. 205).

4th Day. **S. Zaccaria* (p. 208); *S. Maria Formosa* (p. 205); * *S. Giovanni e Paolo* (p. 203); *S. Francesco della Vigna* (p. 201); *Arsenal* (open till 3 p. m.); *Giardini Pubblici* (view, p. 212).

Finally ascend *Campanile* of S. Marco, p. 194.

Those who make a longer stay may visit the *Lido* (p. 212), and make excursions to the N. to *Murano*, *Burano*, and *Torcello* (p. 213, 5 hrs. there and back); to the S. to *S. Lazzaro* (p. 205), *Malamocco*, and *Chioggia* (p. 213). — Every leisure hour should be devoted to S. Marco and its environs.

Access is obtained to the —

Churches usually from 6 a. m. till 12 or 1 o'clock, after which application must be made to the sacristan (*nonzolo*, fee 30—50 c.), for whom one of the officious loungers in the neighbourhood may be sent (5 c.).

**Academy (p. 199) 9—4 daily, on Sundays and festivals 10—4 o'clock.

*Arsenal (p. 198) 9—3 daily.

***Palace of the Doges* (p. 195) 9—4 daily, on Sundays and festivals 10—4.

*Museo Correr (p. 211) Mond., Wed., Sat. 10—4.

Permanent Exhibition of Art (p. 210) in the Pal. Mocenigo open daily, adm. 25 c.

Seminario Patriarcale (p. 209) daily.

The *Private Palaces* (*Vendramin, *Emo-Treves*, *Fini-Wimpfen*, *Pesaro*) are usually accessible from 9 or 10 a. m. till 3 or 4 p. m. — When the proprietors are residing in them, application should be made on the day previous to the visit, but is often dispensed with (fee to attendant 1 fr., to porter 25—50 c.).

Baths of various descriptions, also for swimming (*galleggiante*), are situated between the Riva degli Schiavoni and the Isola *S. Giorgio*, but are used during the three summer-months only (bath 1 fr.). Ferry from the Piazzetta to the baths 10 c.; the word '*bagno*' is a sufficient direction to the gondolier. Swimmers (1 fr.) ask at the establishment for a ticket for the '*vasca*' (basin); a separate bath (1½ fr.) is a '*camerino*'; common bath for ladies (*sirene*) 1 fr. 40 c.; separate bath for ladies 3 fr. No gratuities are expected. The proper period for bathing is when the tide commences to rise; at low tide the water is shallow and muddy. — The baths on the Lido (p. 212) are more agreeable. In summer a steamboat plies every hour between the Riva degli Schiavoni and the Lido in 12 min., returning after a halt of ½ hr. From the landing-place to the baths a walk of ¼ hr. Bath 1 fr., less to subscribers. — *Warm Baths* at most of the hotels, and at *Chitarin's*, near S. Maria della Salute, 1½—2 fr.

Consulates. *British*, S. Maria del Giglio, Calle Gritti o del Campanile 2489; *American*, S. Maria del Rosario, Fondamenta Venier 709; *French*, S. Stefano, Calle Giustiniano 2891; *Prussian*, S. Benedetto, Calle Ramo Contarini Pal. Cavalli 3978; also others for all the principal European states.

Post Office (*Uffizio della Posta*, comp. Introd.) (Pl. 39) in the Palazzo Grimani, on the Grand Canal, by the Campo S. Luca, not far from the Ponte Rialto. Letter-boxes in the Piazza of St. Mark, at the Utfizio del Lloyd, etc. — Telegraph Office behind the W. side of the Piazza of St. Mark, above the guard house.

Booksellers. Münster, Piazza of S. Mark, S.W. corner; Giusto Ebhard, S. Luca, Calle de' Fuseri 4355, next to the Vittoria; both with circulating libraries. — *Photographers*: Naya, Riva degli Schiavoni 4206; Ponti, Riva degli Schiavoni 4178; both of whom have shops in the Piazza of St. Mark.

Steamboat Office (*Uffizio del Lloyd Austriaco*) in the Piazzetta, below the Zecca (Pl. 54). To *Trieste* three times weekly; to *Chioggia* daily at 5 or 6 p. m. (fares 2 or 1½ fr.), on Sundays 8 a. m. (return-tickets 3½ fr.).

Theatres (comp. Introd. VI). Della Fenice (Pl. 100) is the largest in Venice, capable of accommodating 3000 spectators; internal arrangements worthy of inspection; performances during the Carnival only, sometimes also in June and July. The following are employed throughout the whole year: Apollo (Pl. 101), Rossini (Gallo) (Pl. 102), and Camploy (S. Samuele) (Pl. 104). Malibran (Pl. 53), open-air theatre.

Shops (comp. Introd. VI). The best are in the *Piazza of St. Mark*, in the *Merceria*, a narrow line of streets leading from the Piazza of St. Mark to the Ponte Rialto, and in the *Frezzaria*, entered from the Piazza of St. Mark, opposite to the church. The Venetian pearls and jewellery enjoy a high reputation; ornaments in mosaic, glass and shells are also well executed here. The most extensive manufactory of mosaic is that of *Salviati*, on the Canal Grande, in the Campo S. Vito, not far from S. Maria della Salute. At most of the shops two-thirds or even one-half of the price first demanded are often taken.

English Church Service, Palazzo Contarini degli Scrigni, Grand Canal, near the iron bridge. — *Scotch Presbyterian Church* on the Grand Canal, not far from S. Maria della Salute.

History. The modern Venetia was inhabited during the Roman period by the *Veneti*, whose principal towns were Patavium, Altinum, Aquileia etc. These were successively destroyed, after the fall of the W. Roman Empire, by the hordes of barbarian invaders by whom Italy was now overrun, and their inhabitants took refuge on the islands of the Lagune, founded a new state there, and at an early period carried on a considerable commerce with the Levant. The necessity of a constitutional government was soon felt, and in 697 *Pauluccio Anafesto* was elected the first doge. In 819 the doge *Angelo Participaco* transferred the seat of government from Malamocco to Rialto, which he connected with the adjacent islands by means of bridges, thus laying the foundation of the modern city of Venice.

During the following centuries, notwithstanding continual internal dissensions, the might of Venice steadily increased. The foundation of its subsequent greatness, however, was principally laid at the period of the Crusades (1097—1271), which the shrewd policy of Venice contrived to turn to its own aggrandizement. In 1177, under the Doge *Sebastiano Ziani*, the celebrated meeting of Emp. Frederick I. with Pope Alexander III. (p. 197) took place at Venice. *Enrico Dandolo* (1192—1205), one of the most powerful of the doges, conquered Constantinople in 1204 with the aid of French crusaders. In consequence of this the Byzantine Empire was divided, and Venice obtained possession of the coast-districts of the Adriatic and Egyptian seas and numerous islands, among which was Candia. Under the successors of Enrico Dandolo the republic underwent severe contests with Genoa, which occasioned the loss of the Venetian conquests in the East, but at length terminated with the total defeat of Genoa in 1252, under *Andrea Dandolo*. His successor *Marino Falieri* contemplated the overthrow of the aristocratic form of government, but his scheme was discovered, and he was beheaded on April 17th, 1355 (p. 196). During the reign of *Andrea Contarini* (1367—82) Padua, Verona, Genoa, Hungary, and Naples formed an alliance against Venice. In 1379 the Genoese took possession of Chioggia, but were surrounded in the Lagune and compelled to surrender, June 24th, 1380. In 1381 the peace was concluded by which Venice lost all its possessions on the mainland.

The republic, however, soon recovered from these reverses. In 1386 *Antonio Venier* (1382—1400) took possession of the island of Corfu, then of Durazzo, Argos, etc. Under *Michele Steno* (1400—14) the Venetian general *Malatesta* conquered Vicenza, Belluno, Feltre, Verona, and Padua (1405); in 1408 the republic gained possession of Lepanto and Patras, in 1409 of Guastalla, Casalmaggiore, and Brescello. In 1421 *Tommaso Mocenigo* waged war successfully against Hungary. In 1416 the Venetian fleet under *Loredan* had already conquered the Turkish at Gallipoli, and in 1421 subjugated all the towns of the Dalmatian coast, so that Venice was now in possession of the entire coast district from the estuary of the Po as far as the island of Corfu.

Mocenigo's successor was *Francesco Foscari* (1423—57). In 1426 Brescia fell into the hands of the Venetian general *Carmagnola*, but in 1431 his successful career was terminated by a suspicion of treason, and in 1432 he was executed by order of the Council of Ten. In 1449 the Venetians gained possession of Crema, but were unable to prevent the elevation of Sforza to the dignity of Duke of Milan (1450).

In 1457 Foscari, now enervated by old age and domestic misfortunes, was deposed by the Council of Ten in consequence of the intrigues of his enemies. Under *Cristoforo Moro* (1462—71) the Morea was conquered by the Turks. In 1480, in consequence of the renunciation of Catharine Cornaro, wife of king James of Cyprus, this island came into the possession of Venice, and in 1483 the republican dominions were farther augmented by the island of Zante.

The close of the 15th cent. may be designated as the culminating point of the glory of Venice. It was now the grand focus of the entire commerce of Europe, numbered 200,000 inhab., and was universally respected and admired. Its annual exports were valued at 10 millions ducats, 4 millions of which were estimated as clear profit. It possessed 300 sea-going vessels with 8000 sailors, and 3000 smaller craft with 17,000, as well as a fleet of 45 galleys manned by 11,000 men, who maintained the supremacy of the republic over the Mediterranean. With the commencement of the 16th cent. the power of Venice began to decline. Its commerce was gradually superseded to a great extent by that of the Portuguese, in consequence of the discovery of the new sea-routes to India. The League of Cambray, formed by the Pope, the Emperor, and the kings of France and Arragon against Venice in 1508, and the victory of the French at Agnadello in 1509 occasioned serious losses to the republic. The wars between Emp. Charles V. and Francis I. of France (1521—30) were also very prejudicial to Venice, and its power was still more thoroughly undermined by the extension of the Osman empire in Europe and Asia. In 1540 Nauplia, the islands of Chios, Paros, and others were lost, and in 1571 Cyprus, notwithstanding its brave defence by *Bragadino*. In the naval battle of Lepanto (Oct. 1st, 1571) the Venetian fleet greatly distinguished itself. In 1659 the island of Candia was conquered by the Turks. In 1684 the Venetians under *Francesco Morosini* and *Königsmark* were victorious in the Morea and conquered Coron, Patras, Corinth, etc.; in 1696 and 1698 they again defeated the Turkish fleets, and by the Peace of Carlowitz in 1709 they retained possession of the Morea; but in 1715 the Turks reconquered the peninsula, and in 1718 were confirmed in their possession by the Peace of Passarowitz.

From this period Venice ceases to occupy a prominent position in the history of Europe. It retained its N. Italian possessions only, observed a strict neutrality in all the contests of its neighbours, and continued to decline in power. On the outbreak of of the French Revolution Venice at first strenuously opposed the new principles, on the victorious advance of the French it endeavoured to preserve its neutrality, and repeatedly rejected Buonaparte's proposals of alliance. Irritated by this opposition, the French broke off their negotiations and took possession of the city on May 16th, 1797. By the Peace of Campo Formio (1797) Venetia was adjudged to Austria, by that of Pressburg (1805) to the kingdom of Italy. In 1814 Venice was again declared Austrian, and remained so until 1848, when a revolution broke out, and the citizens endeavoured to re-establish their ancient republican form of government, under the presidency of *Manin*. Their renewed independence, however, proved most disastrous and short-lived. The city was torn by internal dissension, and at the same time besieged by the Austrians. After a siege of 15 months it was compelled to capitulate to *Radetzky*, in August, 1849, a victory which cost the Austrians upwards of 20,000 soldiers. The war of 1859 did not affect the supremacy of Austria over Venetia, the re-union of which with Italy was finally effected by the events of 1866.

In the History of Art Venice occupies a prominent position. The Venetian School of painting, which was especially celebrated for the brilliancy of its colouring, boasts of many illustrious names. The most conspicuous painters of the 15th cent. were *Antonio Bartolommeo* and *Luigi Vivarini* of Murano, *Vittore Carpaccio*, *Gentile* and *Giovanni Bellini*. The Madonnas of the latter are remarkable for their grace and tenderness. Among his numerous pupils, *Giambattista Cima* of Conegliano and *Giorgio Barbarelli* of Castelfranco ('*Il Giorgione*', 1478—1511) were the most distinguished. The next well-known names are *Jacopo Palma il Vecchio* of Bergamo, *Paris Bordone*, and *Pordenone*, but the most celebrated of all is that of *Titian* or *Tiziano Vecellio* (1477—1576), whose marvellous power of lifelike delineation and richness of colouring are unparalleled. His greatest contemporaries were the talented masters *Jacopo Robusti*, surnamed '*Tintoretto*' (1512—94), *Paolo Cagliari*, surnamed '*Veronese*' (1528—88) from his native town, and *Jacopo da Ponte* of Bassano; then *Bonifazio*, *Alessandro Bonvicini*, surnamed '*Il Moretto*', and *Giov. Batt. Morone*. In the 17th cent. *Palma Giovine* and *Padovanino* attained a well-merited reputation, but the art was now decidedly on the decline. The only subsequent names worthy of mention are *Rosalba Carriera* (d. 1757), paintress of miniatures, *Antonio Canale*, surnamed '*Canaletto*' (d. 1768), and *Tiepoletto* (d. 1769), the mannerist.

Venice is adorned with several structures in the Byzantine and Gothic styles, but its architecture did not attain to a high degree of perfection until the period of the Renaissance. To this epoch belong the great masters *Pietro* and *Tullio Lombardo*, and the brothers of the latter, who were also architects, *Michele Sanmicheli*, *Jac. Sansovino*, *Antonio da Ponte*, *Palladio*, *Scamozzi*, and *Longhena*. — Of late years the reputation of Venice as a cradle of art has commenced to revive in a very marked degree.

Venice, the population of which had after its dissolution as an independent state (1797) dwindled from 200,000 to 60,000, gradually regained its former importance under the Austrian regime, owing in a great measure to its advantages as a *Free Harbour*. Its prosperity, however, again sustained severe injury from the revolution of 1848 and the war of 1859, and it now remains to be proved whether the Italian government will adopt measures calculated to neutralize the physical and moral degeneracy which have resulted from these vicissitudes. The city at present contains 106,000 inhab., of whom more than one-fourth are in receipt of relief as paupers. The 15,000 houses and palaces of Venice are situated on three large and 114 small islands, formed by 147 canals, connected by 378 bridges (most of them of stone), and altogether about 7 M. in circumference. The city is surrounded by the *Lagune*, a shallow bay about 25 M. in length and 9 M. in width, protected from the open sea by long sandhills *(lidi)*, which are converted into a still more efficient bulwark by means of dams *(murazzi)* of solid masonry, averaging 30 ft. in height and 40—50 ft. in width. Towards the Lagune the Murazzi are perpendicular, whilst towards the sea they descend in four terraces. The Murazzi on the Lido from *Palestrina* to *Chioggia* date from the last period of the republic. The *Diga of Malamocco*, a pier which extends for a distance of $1^1/_4$ M. into the open sea, was constructed by the Austrian government after 1825, in order to prevent the harbour of Malamocco from becoming filled up with mud.

The Lagune are connected with the open sea by means of four entrances, of which those of the *Lido* and *Malamocco* alone are available for vessels of heavy tonnage. The steamers usually enter by the *Porto di Lido* (p. 216), but in stormy weather occasionally employ that of Malamocco.

The Lagoons are termed either '*lagune vive*', or '*lagune morte*', about one half of them belonging to each class. In the former the tide rises and falls about 2 ft.; the latter, shallower, and situated nearer the mainland, are unaffected by the tide. Venice is situated in the '*laguna viva*'.

At high water innumerable stakes, protruding from the water in groups of the most varied form, mark the situation and shape of the low sand-islands which surround the city on every side, forming a complicated network of navigable channels, most of them accessible to small boats only.

Most of the houses rise immediately from the canals *(rii)*, or are separated from them by narrow streets only, here termed (as in Spain) *calli* (sing. *il calle*) and paved with broad slabs of stone, or occasionally with brick or asphalt. These lanes form a labyrinth from which the stranger will sometimes find it difficult to extricate himself. For expeditions of any length walking cannot be recommended, and in such cases the Venetians themselves generally employ a gondola or barca.

The ***Piazza of St. Mark,** usually termed '*La Piazza*' (the other small open spaces are termed *campi*), is 575 ft. in length, on the W. side 185 ft., and on the E. 268 ft. in breadth. On three sides it is enclosed by imposing structures, which appear to form one vast marble palace, blackened by age and the action of the elements; on the E. it is bounded by the Church of St. Mark and the *Piazzetta* (p. 195), a small piazza, the S. side of which adjoins the Lagune. These palaces were once the residence of the 'procurators', the highest officials of the republic, whence their appellation of **Procuratie:** N. the *Procuratie Vecchie*, erected at the close of the 15th cent.; S. the *Procuratie Nuove*, commenced by Scamozzi in 1584, now a royal palace; the modern edifice on the W., termed the *Atrio* or *Nuova Fabbrica*, was erected under Napoleon in 1810 on the site of the former church of S. Geminiano. The ground-floors of these structures consist of arcades, in which the cafés and shops mentioned at pp. 185, 187 are established. — The Piazza of St. Mark is the grand focus of the public life of Venice. Here on summer evenings, after sunset, all who desire to enjoy the fresh air congregate, and the prince, as well as the humbler classes, may be seen enjoying their sorbetto in front of the cafés. The scene is most animated towards 9 p. m., especially on the evenings when the military band plays in the Piazza (Sundays, and usually on Tuesdays and Thursdays also, 8—10 o'clock). On these occasions the Piazza presents a busy scene until after midnight; on other evenings the crowd generally disperses about 10 o'clock. In winter the band plays on the same days 2—4 p. m., and the Piazza is then the promenade of the fashionable world. At an early hour in the morning a few visitors to the cafés may be seen indulging in coffee, but these are rarely natives of Venice. The Venetians themselves are seldom visible at a very early hour, and the Piazza is comparatively deserted except at the hours already mentioned. The Piazza with its adjuncts (the Procuratie, St. Mark's, the Palace of the Doges, Piazzetta, and Lagune) presents a strikingly imposing aspect by moonlight.

Numerous pigeons flock daily to the Piazza at 2 p. m. to be fed at the expense of the city. According to tradition, Admiral Dandolo, whilst besieging Candia at the commencement of the 13th cent., received important intelligence by means of carrier-pigeons from the island, the conquest of which was greatly facilitated in consequence. He then despatched the birds to Venice with the news of his success, and since that period their descendants have been carefully tended and highly revered by the citizens. They nestle in the nooks and crannies of the surrounding buildings and are generally seen in great numbers in the evening, perched on the façade of St. Mark's.

The three lofty *Flagstaffs (Pili)*, or masts of cedar in front of the church, rising from pedestals resembling candelabra, executed in 1505, once bore the banners of the kingdoms of Cyprus, Candia and the Morea, to commemorate their subjugation by the republic. On Sundays and festivals the Italian colours are now hoisted here.

**S. Marco (Pl. 17), the Basilica of St. Mark, the tutelary saint of Venice, was erected in 976—1071 in the Romanesque-Byzantine style which is peculiar to Venice, and decorated with lavish and almost oriental magnificence during subsequent centuries. The façade received some additions in the Gothic style in the 14th cent. The form of the edifice is that of a Greek cross (with equal arms), covered by a dome in the centre and one at the extremity of each arm. Externally and internally the church is adorned with five hundred columns of marble, the capitals of which present an exuberant variety of styles. The mosaics, the oldest dating from the 10th cent., cover an area of 40,000 sq. ft., whilst the interior is also profusely decorated with gilding, bronze, and oriental marble. The aggregate effect may be termed picturesque, or even fantastic, rather than impressive. Since 1807 St. Mark's has been the cathedral of Venice, a dignity formerly enjoyed by S. Pietro di Castello (p. 206).

Over the principal portal are Four Horses in gilded bronze, 5 ft. in height, which were long supposed to be the work of a Greek master (*Lysippus*); they are now, however, believed to date from the period of the Roman Empire, probably from the time of Nero. They are finely excecuted and are especially valuable as the sole specimen of an ancient quadriga which has come down to posterity uninjured by the ravages of time. They probably once adorned the triumphal arch of Nero, then that of Trajan. Constantine caused them to be conveyed to Constantinople, whence the Doge Dandolo brought them to Venice in 1204. In 1797 they were carried by Napoleon I. to Paris, where they afterwards occupied the summit of the triumphal arch in the Place Carrousel. In 1815 they were brought back to Venice by the Emp. Francis and restored to their former position.

Façade. *Mosaics in the arches, best surveyed from the steps of the flagstaffs. Below, over the principal entrance, the Last Jugdment, executed in 1836, r. the embarcation of the body of St. Mark at Alexandria, its disembarcation at Venice, both executed 1660; l. the veneration of the saint, of 1728, and the church of St. Mark into which the relics are conveyed, of the 13th cent. — Above are the four horses in front of the great arched window, l. and r. are four mosaics of the 17th cent., Descent from the Cross, Christ in Hell, Resurrection, Ascension.

Entrance Hall (*Atrio*), the entire breadth of the church: the vaulting consists entirely of mosaic, of which the *older* portion (12th cent.) represents Old Testament subjects, beginning on the r. with the Creation; the *modern* part, scenes from the New Testament; over the entrance to the church is St. Mark, executed in 1545 from a design by Titian. The *Capitals of the Columns* are said once to have belonged to the Temple at Jerusalem. The three red slabs commemorate the reconciliation between the Emp. Fred. Barbarossa and Pope Alexander III., which was here effected on July 23rd, 1177, through the mediation of the Doge Seb. Ziani. According to an old tradition the emperor kneeling before the pope said: '*non tibi sed Petro*', to which the pope replied '*et mihi et Petro*'. In the corner to the l. is the tomb of *Daniele Manin*, president of the republic in 1848, erected in 1868., the only interment which has taken place in the church for upwards of three centuries.

Interior, 86 yds. in length, 70 yds. in width. Over the *Entrance-door* Christ, Mary, and St. Mark, of the 11th cent., one of the oldest mosaics in the church. The smooth, slippery marble pavement is very uneven at places from having settled. By the screen, r. and l. of the approach to the high altar, are two *Pulpits* in coloured marble. The mosaic (of 1542) above in the N. aisle (l.) represents the genealogy of Mary. On the *Screen* are 14 statues in marble (of 1393), representing St. Mark, Mary, and the 12 Apostles, with a bronze Crucifix. On the *Arches* on each side of the *Choir* are 6 reliefs in bronze, by Sansovino (d. 1570), representing events from the life of St. Mark. On the parapet of the *Stalls* the 4 Evangelists in bronze, by Sansovino, and 4 Fathers of the church, by Cagliari (1614).

The *High Altar (Altare Maggiore)* stands beneath a canopy of verde antico, borne by four columns of marble (with reliefs of the 11th cent.). The *Pala d'Oro*, enamelled work with jewels, wrought on plates of gold and silver, executed at Constantinople in 1105, constitutes the altar-piece, which is uncovered on high festivals only. (It was originally intended to embellish the *front* of the altar.) Beneath the high altar repose the relics of St. Mark, as the marble slab at the back records. — Behind the high altar is a second altar with four spiral columns of alabaster, of which the two white ones are semi-transparent, said to have once belonged to the Temple of Solomon.

The *Sacristy (Sagrestia)*, to the l., possesses some fine mosaics on the vaulting; cabinets with inlaid work of 1523; by the door leading from the high altar, reliefs in bronze by Sansovino (1556). Entrance to the Crypt see p. 194.

R. of the high altar: *Cappella di S. Clemente*, with altar relief of the 16th cent., representing SS. Nicholas, James, and Andrew and the Doge Andr. Gritti. In front of the *Cappella del Sagramento*, in the r. transept, are two rich candelabra in bronze; on the other side a corresponding pair.

In the r. aisle, near the W. portal, is the *Battisterio*, in the centre of which is a large bronze font of 1545; above is John the Baptist. Also the monument of the Doge And. Dandolo (d. 1354). The stone over the altar is from Mt. Tabor. L. of the altar the head of John the Baptist, of the 15th cent.; beneath it is the stone on which he is said to have been beheaded. — From the Baptistery the stranger enters the *Cappella Zen, containing the handsome monument of Cardinal Giambattista Zeno (d. 1501), wrought entirely in bronze; on the sarcophagus is the figure of the cardinal, over life-size; beneath are the six Virtues. The *altar and canopy are also cast in bronze, with the exception of the frieze and the bases of the columns. Over the altar are groups in bronze, of the Madonna, St. Peter, and John the Baptist; on the altar itself a relief of the Resurrection. To the r. and l. two lions in coloured marble.

In the r. transept is the entrance to the *Treasury (Tesoro di S. Marco*, open on Mondays and Fridays $12^1/_2$—2 o'clock, not on festivals), containing candelabra by *Benvenuto Cellini*; cover of the books of the Gospels from the church of St. Sophia at Constantinople, decorated with gold and jewels; a crystal vase with the 'Blood of the Saviour', a silver column with a fragment of the 'True Cross', a cup of agate with a portion of the 'skull of St. John', the sword of the Doge Morosini, cuneiform writings from Persepolis, an episcopal throne of the 7th cent., said to be that of St. Mark, and a number of other curiosities.

The Crypt, freed from water and restored in 1868, also deserves a visit; open 12—2 o'clock, entrance by the first door to the r. in the Sacristy (p. 194).

A walk (in the company of the sacristan, $1/2$ fr.) round the *Gallery* within and without the church is recommended, as a better general view of the building may thus be obtained, and the mosaics more minutely inspected. The ascent is from a door to the r. in the principal portal, which the sacristan opens.

On the *S. Side* of the church are two short square *Columns, inscribed with Coptic characters, brought hither from Ptolemais in 1256, from the church of St. Saba which was destroyed by the Venetians. From the *Pietra del Bando*, a block of porphyry at the S.W. corner, the decrees of the republic were anciently promulgated. Two curious *Reliefs* in porphyry are immured by the entrance to the Palace of the Doges, representing two pairs of knightly and armed figures embracing each other. They are said also to have been brought from Ptolemais and have given rise to a great variety of conjectures, according to the most recent of which they represent four emperors of Byzantium of the 11th cent., and once adorned the pedestal of an equestrian statue.

Opposite St. Mark's, to the S. W., rises the isolated square ***Campanile** of St. Mark (Pl. 4), 304 ft. in height, which is always accessible to the public (doorkeeper 10 c. on entering). The ascent by a winding inclined plane, and finally by a few steps, is easy and well-lighted. The watchman at the summit is provided with a telescope and opens the door to the second gallery for a trifling gratuity. The *view comprises the city, the Lagune (comp. p. 190), the Alps, and a portion of the Adriatic; W. the Monti Euganei near Padua (p. 179), rising from the Lagune; E. in clear weather the Istrian Mts. (p. 70), rising above the Adriatic, a magnificent spectacle towards sunset. The ascent of the campanile is recommended to the stranger, both for a preliminary survey, and as an appropriate termination to his visit to Venice. The *Bronze Doors of the *Loggetta*, or vestibule, on the E. side (16th cent.) of the campanile, cast in 1750, merit inspection. This chamber once served as a waiting-room for the procurators, whose office it was, during the sessions of the great Council, to command the guards. It is now employed for public auctions and 'tombola' (lottery) drawings. The bronze statues of Peace, Apollo, Mercury, and Pallas, and the reliefs on the coping are by *Sansovino*.

The **Clock Tower** *(La Torre dell' Orologio)*, with the Italian dial (1—24, at present twice 1—12), on the opposite side, a the E. extremity of the old Procuratie, rises over a gateway, resembling a triumphal arch, restored in 1859. On the platform are two Vulcans in bronze, who strike the hours on a bell. The custodian of the clock, who lives in the building, shows and explains the mechanism (fee $^1/_2$ fr.). The entrance is beneath the archway. The *Merceria* (p. 187), the principal commercial street of Venice, here quits the Piazza of St. Mark and leads to the *Ponte Rialto* (p. 210).

On the W. side of the **Piazzetta** is the *Library *(Libreria Vecchia, or Antica Libreria di S. Marco)*, commenced by Sansovino in 1536, a magnificent structure of the 16th cent. and one of the finest secular edifices in Italy. In the direction of the Lagune are two *Granite Columns*, one of which bears the *Winged Lion of St. Mark*, the emblem of the tutelary saint of Venice; the other is surmounted by *St. Theodore* on a crocodile, the patron of the ancient republic. This is the headquarters of the gondoliers. On the Lagune, between the Library and the former Imperial Garden, is situated the *Zecca* or *Mint*, from which the well known Venetian coin, the Zecchino or sequin derives its name.

The ****Palace of the Doges** *(Palazzo Ducale*, Pl. 60), the W. side of which, 245 ft. in length, faces the Piazzetta, and the S. side, 234 ft. in length, looks towards the Molo, was founded in 800, subsequently destroyed five times, and as often re-erected in a style of greater magnificence. The present sumptuous structure, in the Venetian-Gothic style, dates from the 14th cent. On the W. towards the Piazzetta, and on the S. towards the Molo the palace is flanked by two colonnades of 107 columns (36 below, 71 above), one above the other, with pointed vaulting. The mouldings of the upper colonnade, termed '*La Loggia*',· are remarkable for their richness. From between the two columns of red marble (9th and 10th from the principal portal) in the Loggia, the Republic anciently caused its sentences of death to be published. The capitals of the short columns below are richly decorated with foliage, figures of men and animals, etc. On the corner-pillar by the portal is a group representing the Judgment of Solomon, the '*justizia alla vedova*', as the long inscription terms it. (Porphyry-reliefs on the corners to the l., see p. 204.) The fine Portal adjoining St. Mark's, constructed of marble of different colours, and recently restored. is termed the *Porta della Carta*, from the placards formerly exhibited here to announce the decrees of the republic. *Justice* is represented in the pediment.

The *Court, begun at the close of the 15th cent. when the Venetian Renaissance had attained its zenith, but only partially completed, possesses an admirable finished façade on the E. wing. In the centre of the court two *Cistern-fronts* in bronze. To the

r. on the façade of the *Clock Tower* is a statue of the Venetian general Duke Francis Maria I. of Urbino (d. 1625). One of the highest windows to the l. is that of the former prison of the poet Count Silvio Pellico, who was subsequently incarcerated from 1822 to 1830 in the Spielberg at Brünn (in Moravia).

The *Scala dei Giganti*, the flight of steps by which the palace is entered, derives its appellation from the colossal statues of Mars and Neptune above, executed by *Sansovino* in 1554. On the highest landing of these steps the doges were once wont to be crowned. Opposite the latter are two statues, Adam and Eve, by *Antonio Rizzo* (1462). The site of the Scala dei Giganti was formerly occupied by another flight of steps, on which the ill-fated Doge *Marino Falieri*, when in his eightieth year, was beheaded as a traitor, April 17th, 1355.

Around the upper colonnade are placed the busts of a number of Venetian scholars, artists and doges. The first staircase is the *Scala d'Oro*, constructed by Sansovino, once only accessible to those whose names were entered as Nobili in the Golden Book. Guides (unnecessary except for the prisons, which scarcely merit inspection) are here in readiness to conduct visitors through the palace of the doges. Fee 1 fr. for a single visitor, $1^1/_2$—2 fr. for a party (to each of the three custodians of the different apartments 20—30 c., for a party $^3/_4$ fr.). The visitor then ascends the next broad staircase closed by a gate, leading in a straight direction to the principal saloons designated as No. I., and to the r. to the Archæological Museum, No. II.; one story higher is No. III., with the inscription 'Storia Naturale'. Guide unnecessary; information if required is obtained from the custodians (fee prohibited).

I. A door (generally open; if not, visitors ring) leads straight on to the rooms of the Library, the first of which is the *Sala del Maggior Consiglio. In this large saloon (154 ft. long, 75 ft. broad, 45 ft. high) the Nobili, whose names were entered in the 'Golden Book', and who constituted the highest authority in the Republic, formerly held their sessions. In 1848—49 the deputies under the Dictator Manin also assembled here. On the frieze are the portraits of 76 doges, commencing with Angelo Participaco (d. 827); on the walls 21 large pictures by *Bassano*, *Paolo Veronese*, *Tintoretto*, etc., painted to commemorate the achievements of the Republic, especially against Fred. Barbarossa. On the E. wall *Jac. Tintoretto's* Paradise, said to be the largest oil-painting in the world, containing a perplexing multitude of figures. — The series of *Historical Pictures* commences on the S. wall: 1. Doge Enrico Dandolo and French Crusaders swear an oath of alliance at St. Mark's in 1201, for the purpose of liberating the Holy Land, by *Giov. Le Clerc;* 2. Surrender of Zara to the Crusaders in 1202, by *Dom. Tintoretto* (placed over the door to a balcony, which affords a fine view of the Lagune and the islands of S. Giorgio and Giudecca); 4. Alexius, son of the dethroned Greek Emp. Isaac Angelos, requesting the aid of the Venetians in behalf of his father in 1202, by *Andrea Vicentino;* 7. Count Baldwin of Flanders elected Greek Emp. in the church of St. Sophia, 1204, by *Andr. Vicentino;* 8. Coronation of Baldwin by the Doge Enrico Dandolo, 1204, by *Aliense*. (Above this, a black tablet on the frieze among the portraits of the Doges bears the inscription: *Hic est locus Marini Falethri decapitati pro criminibus;* see above.) *9. Return of the Doge Andr. Contarini from the victory over the Genoese fleet near Chioggia, 1378, by *Paolo Veronese*; 10. Pope Alexander III. presenting gifts to the Doge Ziani in recognition of his defence of the papal throne against Fred. Barbarossa, e. g. a ring, the symbol with which the Doge annually 'wedded the Adriatic', 1177, by *Giulio dal Moro*; 11. (over the door) Conclusion of peace between the Pope, Doge, and Emp. Fred. Barbarossa, by *Girolamo Gambarato*; *12. Fred. Barbarossa kneeling before the Pope (p. 189), by *Federigo Zuccaro*; 13. Pope Alexander granting permission to Otho, son of the Emperor, to repair to his father in order to negotiate a peace, by *Palma Giovine*; 14. (over the door) The Doge presenting the son of the Emperor to the Pope, by *Andr. Vicentino*; 15. Battle of Salvore (Pirano, p. 70), defeat of the Imperial fleet, and capture of Otho, 1177, by *Dom. Tintoretto*; 16. (over the window) Departure of the Doge with the papal benediction, by *Paolo Fiammengo*; 17. The Pope presenting a sword to the Doge, by *Franc. Bassano*; 18. The ambassadors of the Pope and the Doge presenting to Fred. Barbarossa at Pavia a petition for a cessation of hostilities, by *Jac. Tintoretto*; 19. (over the window) Presentation of the consecrated candle, by *Leandro Bassano*; 20. Parting audience of the ambassadors of the Pope and the Doge on their departure for Parma, 21. Meeting of Pope Alexander III. and the Doge Seb. Ziani at the monastery della Carità, both by *pupils of P. Veronese*. The ceiling-paintings are by *P. Veronese*, *Bassano*, *Tintoretto*, and *Palma Giovine*; the large central painting, representing the Glory of Venice, is by *P. Veronese*.

In the Passage a bust of the Emp. Francis. The Sala dello Scrutinio, or voting hall, is decorated similarly to the preceding saloons. On the frieze are the portraits of 39 doges down to Lodovico Manin (1797). On the wall of the entrance: Last Judgment, by *Palma Giovine*. On the *left wall*: 1. Victory of the Venetians over King Roger of Sicily in 1148; 2. Subjugation of Tyre under Domenico Michieli in 1125; 3. (over the door to the balcony, which affords a good survey of Sansovino's library) Victory of Dom. Michieli over the Turks at Jaffa in 1123; 4. Victory in the lagoons over Pepin, son of Charlemagne in 811; 5. Siege of Venice by Pepin in 809. — *Opp. the entrance:* Monument to the Doge Francesco Morosini 'Peloponnesiacus', who in 1684—90 conquered the Morea and Athens (p. 189). — On the *right wall:* 6. Lazaro Mocenigo conquers the Turks near the Dardanelles in 1657; 7. (over the window towards the court): Destruction of Margaritino in 1571; 8. Battle of Lepanto, in the same year; 9. (over the second window) Conquest of Cattaro in Dalmatia during the war against Genoa in 1378; 10. Re-capture of Zara in 1346. — On the *ceiling* several other scenes from the history of the Republic.

The celebrated *Library of St. Mark*, containing many rare MSS., and the valuable and extensive *Collection of Coins*, is only accessible by special permission.

II. The Archæological Museum, occupying the apartments in which the doges resided till the close of the 16th cent., contains ancient sculptures in marble. 1st Saloon: colossal Minerva; 4. candelabrum-pedestals (Nos. 68. and 70. the finest); two colossal *Muses (from the amphitheatre at Pola). — 2nd S.: 102. Copy of the Cupid, bending his bow, of Praxiteles, in Parian marble; 112. Odysseus in a posture of attack; 113, 187. Two heads of Pan; 138. Leda; *148. Ganymede carried off by the eagle, restored. The chimney-piece dates from the close of the 15th cent. — 3rd S.: old maps; in a cabinet the celebrated *Map of the World by the Camaldulensian monk Fra Mauro, 1457—59; six tablets of carved wood by Hadgi Mehemet of Tunis (1559), representing the globe. — 4th S.: 195. Fragment of a sarcophagus; 196. another with the destruction of the children of Niobe; 231. Fragment of a Greek frieze, battle of the Greeks and Trojans around the ships; 239. Four-sided base of a candelabrum. — 5th S.: 250. Colossal head of a satyr; 299. Colossal female head.

III. *Upper Story:* Sala della Bussola, once the ante-chamber of the three Inquisitors of the Republic; by the entrance is an opening in the wall, formerly decorated by a lion's head in marble, into the mouth of which (*bocca di leone*) documents containing secret information were formerly thrown. This apartment contains two pictures by *Aliense:* r. Taking of Brescia, 1426, and l. Taking of Bergamo, 1427. — Sala del Consiglio dei Dieci: Pope Alexander III. and the Doge Ziani, the conqueror of Emp. Fred. Barbarossa, by *Bassano*; Peace of Bologna, concluded in 1529 between Pope Clement VII. and Emp. Charles V., by *Marco Vecellio*; on the ceiling near the entrance, portraits of an old man and a handsome woman, by *Paolo Veronese*. The visitor now retraces his steps through the Sala della Bussola and enters the Stanza dei tre Capi del Consiglio, with ceiling-paintings (an angel driving away the vices) by *Paolo Veronese*; chimney-piece by *Sansovino*; caryatides by *Pietro da Salò*. — A passage leads hence to the Atrio Quadrato, with ceiling-painting by *Tintoretto*, representing the Doge Priuli receiving the sword of justice. — Sala delle quattro Porte: doors designed by *Palladio*, 1575; r. Verona reconquered by the Venetians, 1439, by *Giov. Contarini*; the Doge Ant. Grimani kneeling before Religion, by *Titian*; l. the Arrival of Henry III. of France at Venice, by *Andrea Vicentino*; the Doge Cicogna receiving the Persian ambassadors in 1585, by *Carletto Cagliari*. — Sala del Senato (door on the r.): over the throne, Descent from the Cross by *Tintoretto*; on the wall, the Doge Franc. Venier before Venice, the Doge Cicogna in presence of the Saviour, Venetia on the Lion against Europa on the Bull (an allusion to the League of Cambray, see p. 189), all three by *Palma Giovine*; the Doge Pietro Loredano imploring the aid of the Virgin for Venice, by *Tintoretto*; ceiling-painting, Venice the queen of the ocean, by *Tintoretto*. — Beyond this room (to the r. of the throne) is the Ante-Chamber to the chapel of the doges, containing the cartoons of the mosaics on the W. portal of S. Mark. — In the Chapel over the altar a Madonna by *Sansovino*. — Sala del Collegio: r. the Nuptials of St. Catharine (beneath, the Doge Franc. Dona), Virgin in glory (with the Doge Niccolò da Ponte), Adoration of the Saviour (with the Doge Aloise Mocenigo), all three by *Tintoretto*; over the throne a memorial picture of the *Battle of Lepanto, Christ in glory (beneath, the Doge Venier, Venetians, St. Mark, St. Justina, etc.), both by *Paolo Veronese*; opposite, the Prayer of the Doge Andrea Gritti to the Virgin, by *Tintoretto*. Ceiling-paintings, Neptune and Mars, Faith, Venetia on the globe with Justice and Peace, all by *Paolo Veronese*. — Anticollegio: *Rape of Europa, by *Paolo Veronese*; Jacob's return to Canaan, by *Bassano*; Forge of Vulcan, Mercury with the Graces, opposite to it Minerva driving back Mars, and Ariadne and Bacchus, all four by *Tintoretto*. — Ceiling-painting, Venetia enthroned, by *Paolo Veronese*.

On the E. side the Palace of the Doges is connected with the *Carceri* or *Prigioni*, constructed 1512—97 by Giov. da Ponte, by means of the lofty **Bridge of Sighs** *(Ponte dei Sospiri)*. The *Piombi*, or prisons beneath the leaden roof of the Palace, were destroyed in 1797; the *Pozzi*, or half-ruined dungeons on the farther side of the narrow canal on the E. side of the Palace, have been disused since the commencement of the 17th cent. These once dreaded prisons, where so many victims of a bigoted and tyrannical age have languished, contain absolutely nothing to interest the traveller beyond the mere historical associations. A good survey of the Bridge of Sighs (application may be made to a custodian) is obtained from the *Ponte della Paglia* (Pl. F, 4), which connects the Molo with the adjacent

Riva degli Schiavoni, a quay paved with unpolished slabs of marble, and presenting a busy scene. Numerous sailors of all nations, from the vessels which lie in the vicinity, are seen lounging here or congregated at the cafés. From the Riva a view is obtained of the *Giardini Pubblici* (p. 212), situated on the prolongation of the bank at the S.E. extremity of Venice.

The ***Arsenal** (Pl. 3; adm. 9—3 o'cl. on presenting a visiting-card) at the time of the Republic employed 16,000 workmen, now 2000 only. The decline of Venice is nowhere so apparent as here. At the outer entrance are the four antique lions, brought here in 1687 as trophies from the Piræus; the large one on the l., the body of which is covered with inscriptions no longer legible, is conjectured once to have stood on the battle-field of Marathon.

Interior. On the external wall of the magazine is a monument of Count Schulenburg, a general of the Republic (d. 1747). The collection of weapons, a great part of which the Austrians carried off in 1866, contains the remains of the Bucentoro, a vessel destroyed by the French, from which the Doge was wont annually on Ascension Day to throw the ring (p. 197) into the Adriatic, which he thus symbolically wedded. Here, too, is a marble monument to Admiral Angelo Emo (d. 1792) by *Canova*; opposite to it the suit of armour of Henry IV. of France, presented to the Republic; several trophies of historical interest, banners from the battle of Lepanto, armour of former doges, revolvers and breech-loaders of a primitive description of the 16th cent., a finely executed culverin of steel, adorned with reliefs, instruments of torture, iron helmet of Attila, king of the Huns, model of an ancient Venetian vessel, model of the piles on which Venice is to a great extent built, bust of Napoleon of 1805. — The extensive wharves and workshops are now comparatively deserted. The state-bark employed by Victor Emanuel in 1866 is also shown (additional fee).

The ****Accademia delle Belle Arti** (Pl. 1) in the suppressed *Scuola della Carità*, the assembly-hall of this brotherhood, on the Grand Canal, opposite the S. extremity of the iron bridge (p. 209) and 1/2 M. from the Piazza of St. Mark, may easily be reached on foot. (On the way thither are situated *S. Maria Zobenigo*, p. 206, and *S. Stefano*, p. 208.) The entrance is in the cloisters, to the l., then an ascent to the first floor. Admission on week-days 9—3, on festivals 11—2 o'clock (visitors ring). Trifling fee to the custodian at the door. Permission to copy is granted, if written application, coupled with a recommendation from the stranger's consul, be made. Full-size copies not generally allowed. The gallery contains almost exclusively pictures by Venetian masters: Titian, Paolo Veronese, Tintoretto, the elder and the younger Palma, Pordenone, Giorgione, Bassano, etc.

Beyond the Corridor, which contains numerous architectural drawings, the 5th and 6th saloons (p. 200) are passed on the l., and the room without number, mentioned at p. 200, on the r., and in a straight direction the visitor enters the

Sala I. (ancient pictures): 1. *Bart. Vivarini*, Mary and four saints, painted in 1464; 5. *Lorenzo Veneziano* and *Franc. Bissolo*, Altar-piece in sections, in the centre the Annunciation, above it God the Father; 11. *Vincenzo Catena*, St. Augustine; 18. *Aloiso Vivarini*, St. Antony; 21. *Bartolommeo Vivarini*, S. Clara; *23. *Giovanni d'Alemagna* and *Antonio da Murano*, Madonna enthroned, with four Fathers of the church, painted in 1496.

Sala II. (*dell' Assunta*), the ceiling richly gilded, in the lunettes portraits of painters of the Venetian school, painted 1849—55, the light unfavourable. Opposite to the staircase: ***24. *Titian*, Assumption (Assunta, whence the name of the saloon). Farther on, to the r.: 25. *Tintoretto*, The Fall of man; *31. *Marco Basaiti*, Call of the sons of Zebedee (James and John); 33. *Titian*, Entombment, his last picture, with which he was still engaged at the time of his death, in his 99th year, completed by *Palma Giov.*; 35. *Titian*, Assumption, his first picture; 38. *Giov. Bellini*, Virgin and Child with six saints; 40. *Palma Giov.*, The three horsemen of the Apocalypse; *45. *Tintoretto*, St. Mark releasing a condemned slave; 47. *Padovanino*, Marriage of Cana; 50. *Bonifazio*, The adulteress before Christ; 51. *Tintoretto*, Portrait of the Doge Luigi Mocenigo; 55. *Paolo Veronese*, Virgin in glory, beneath is St. Dominicus, distributing crowns of roses to the pope, emperor and king, doges, cardinals, etc.; 54. *Bonifazio*, Solomon's judgment; 59. *Palma Vecchio*, Assumption; 60. *Rocco Marconi*, Christ, Peter and John; 62. *Paolo Veronese*, Scourging of St. Christina.

    Sala III. (adjoining the Assunta on the r.): Marble bust of *Giov. Bellini*; *Titian*, St. Nicholas; *P. Veronese*, Martyrdom of St. Sebastian (both the property of the Church of St. Sebastian, p. 207).

    Sala IV. (to the l., reached by a staircase), academic assembly-hall, with numerous old drawings, among them those of *Leonardo da Vinci* particularly interesting; several reliefs, and an urn containing the r. hand of Canova (this saloon is open on Tuesd. and Sat. only, 12—3 o'clock).

    Sala V. (containing the *Pinacoteca Contarini*, presented in 1843 by Count Contarini): 1. 84. *Palma Vecchio*, Christ and the widow of Nain; *94. *Giov. Bellini*, Madonna, painted 1487; 107. *Sassoferrato*, St. Cecilia; 110. *Andrea Cordele Agi*, Madonna with St. Catharine and St. John; 124. *Vinc. Catena*, Madonna with John the Baptist and St. Jerome; 125. *Cima da Conegliano*, Madonna with John the Baptist and St. Peter; 132. *Boccaccino da Cremona*, Madonna and saints; 151. *Jacques Callot*, Market at Impruneta near Florence, a large picture with numerous figures and groups; 164. *Callot*, Pont Neuf at Paris (?).

    Sala VI. (*Cabinetto Contarini*), containing 66 small pictures. The most interesting, as affording samples of the Venetian costumes and habits of the past century, are Nos. 229, 230, 231, 241, 242, 243, all by *Pietro Longhi*.

    Opposite to the 5th saloon is a room without a number, where the pictures of S. Salvadore (p. 207) and S. Sebastiano (p. 207) are kept during the restoration of these churches: *Giov. Bellini*, Christ and the disciples at Emmaus; *P. Veronese*, St. Mark, St. Luke, Queen Esther, Esther and Ahasuerus, Triumph of Mordecai, etc.

    Sala VII. contains a number of sculptures, among which are groups of Ethiopian slaves in ebony, bearing Japanese vases, executed about the middle of last century.

    Sala VIII.: 266—268. Portraits attributed to *Holbein*; 283. *Mantegna*, St. George.

    Sala IX. (long corridor): 277. *Lucas Cranach* (?), Lot and his daughters; *280. and *281. *Hondekoeter*, Hen and chickens, Victorious cock; 295. *Tintoretto*, Portrait of Antonio Capello; 301. *Titian*, Portrait of his own mother; 306. *Tinelli*, Portrait; 313. *Bellini*, Madonna; 315. *Corn. Engelbrechtsen*, Crucifixion; 318. *Greg. Schiavone*, Madonna; 319. *Titian*, Portrait of Jacopo Soranzo; 326. *Bonifazio*, Madonna and saints; 337. *Bissolo*, Madonna and saints; 338. *Mierevelt*, Portrait of a general; 349. *Antonello da Messina*, Mater Dolorosa; 350. *Titian*, Portrait of Priamo da Lezze; 352. *Tommaso da Modena*, St. Catharine.

    Sala X.: 361. *Montagna*, Madonna and saints; *366. *Titian*, John the Baptist in the wilderness; 367. *Bassano*, Holy Family; 372. *G. Bellini*, Madonna and sleeping Child.

    Sala XI. contains old Italian pictures of little value.

    Sala XII.: 404. *Andrea Busati*, St. Mark enthroned, St. Andrew, and St. Francis; most of the other pictures are unimportant.

    Sala XIII. (*Pinacoteca Renier*, presented by Countess Renier in 1850) · 424. *Giov. Bellini*, Madonna with St. Paul and St. George; 429. *Cima*, Entombment; 432. School of *L. da Vinci*, Jesus and the scribes; *436. *Giov. Bellini*, SS. Mary, Magdalen, and Catherine.

    Sala XIV.: 456. *Cima*, Christ with SS. Thomas and Magnus; 460. *Bassano*, Portrait of a doge; 465. *Titian*, Portrait of Antonio Capello (see above, Sala IX.).

    *Sala XV.: *Canova's* original model of the group of Hercules and Lychas; 473. *Pietro da Cortona*, Daniel in the lions' den; *487. *Titian*, Presentation of Mary in the Temple; 486. *Pordenone*, Mary and saints; 490. *Pordenone*, Four saints; 489. *P. Veronese*, Annunciation; *492. *Paris Bor-*

done, The fisherman presenting to the doge the ring received from St. Mark; 495. *Rocco Marconi*, Descent from the Cross; *500. *Bonifazio*, Banquet of Dives; 505. *Bonifazio*, Saviour and saints; 516. *Bonifazio*, Christ and the Apostles; 519. *Paolo Veronese*, Madonna and saints; 524. *Bonifazio*, Slaughter of the Innocents.

*Sala XVI. contains very large pictures only: 529. *Gentile Bellini*, Miraculous finding of a fragment of the 'True Cross' which had fallen into the canal; 533, 537, 539, 542, 544, 546, 549, 552, 554, 560. *Vittore Carpaccio*, History of St. Ursula, painted in 1475—95; 534. *Marco Basaiti*, Jesus on the Mt. of Olives; 547. *Paolo Veronese*, Jesus in the house of Levi; *555. *Gentile Bellini*, Procession in the Piazza of St. Mark, painted in 1491 (interesting as showing the aspect of the piazza at that date, differing materially from its present form); 559. *Carpaccio*, Martyrdom of the 10,000 Christians on Mt. Ararat, painted in 1515.

Sala XVII.: 572. *Bonifazio*, Adoration of the Magi; 582. *Cima*, Madonna and saints; 593. *Palma Vecchio*, Peter and saints.

Sala XVIII. contains modern pictures of professors and pupils of the Academy.

Sala XIX. contains pictures from 1700, most of them mediocre: 644. *Canaletto*, Architectural piece; 656. and 661. *Carriero*, Portraits in chalks.

Sala XX. Modern pictures.

By the 4th Saloon to the l. (p. 200) a staircase leads back to the Sala dell' Assunta.

The unfinished fragment of a three-storied open hall by *Palladio*, behind the Academy, merits the inspection of architects.

Churches. Venice possesses 90, of which the following are the most remarkable. They are usually open from 6 to 1 o'clock (comp. p. 187). The description of the interior commences in each case on the r. side.

Santi Apostoli (Pl. 5), erected in 1672, contains the *Cappella Cornaro*, which appertained to the former church, and possesses rich decorations of the 16th cent. and two monuments of the Corner family. In the *Cappella Maggiore*: r. Last Supper, by *Cesare da Conegliano*; l. Fall of Manna, by *Paolo Veronese*.

S. Crisostomo (Pl. 14), near the Ponte Rialto, to the N., erected 1483, is in the Renaissance style; 1st altar r., Three saints, by *Bellini*; principal altar, St. Chrysostom and saints, by *Seb. del Piombo*; base of the altar, *Entombment, a high relief by an unknown master. Altar to the l., Coronation of the Virgin, and the 12 Apostles, reliefs by *Tullio Lombardo*.

S. Francesco della Vigna (Pl. 9), interior constructed in 1534 by *Sansovino*, façade by *Andr. Palladio* 1568—72.

R. of the entrance: Font with St. John the Baptist and St. Francis, statuettes in bronze by *Vittoria*. In the 1st chapel on the r., Last Supper, by *Franc. Santacroce*; 3rd chapel fitted up with coloured marble, property of the Contarini family; 4th chapel, Resurrection, by *Paolo Veronese*. In the r. transept, Enthroned Madonna, by *Fra Antonio da Negroponte*. L. of the high altar the *Cappella Giustiniani*, the altar entirely covered with reliefs in marble, Last Judgment beneath, above (as altar-piece) St. Jerome and four saints, over them Madonna and angels, at the sides of the chapel 12 prophets and the 4 Evangelists, higher the history of Jesus in 18 sections, below on the altar the history of St. Jerome in 3 sections, the whole an admirably executed work of the 15th cent. — In the chapel of the N. transept a Madonna and four saints, by *Bellini*. Over the pulpit, God the Father and Christ, by *Girolamo Santacroce*. In the 5th chapel to the l. (at the principal door), a Madonna and four saints, by *Paolo Veronese;* 3rd chapel, fitted up with white marble, containing busts of the Patriarch and the Doge Sagredo, erected in 1743; over the altar the statue of S. Gherardo.

****Frari** (*S. Maria Gloriosa dei Frari*, Church of the Franciscans, Pl. 10), a cruciform church with aisles, in the pointed style, supported by 12 circular pillars, one of the largest and most beautiful structures in Venice, was erected by *Nicola Pisano* in the middle of the 13th cent. It contains numerous monuments, sculptures and pictures, and like S. Giovanni e Paolo (p. 203) is the last resting-place of many eminent men.

R. Aisle. Adjoining the 1st altar the *Monument of Titian (d. 1576), erected by Emp. Ferd. I., completed by *Luigi* and *Pietro Zandomeneghi* in 1852, a vast architectural group; beneath are two figures with tablets bearing inscriptions. In the centre, above the dedication 'Tiziano Ferdinandus I. 1852', between four columns Titian sitting by an angel and uncovering the statue of Sais; on the columns are figures of Sculpture, Architecture, Painting, and Xylography. On the wall are reliefs of the three most celebrated pictures of Titian, the Assumption (p. 199), Martyrdom of St. Peter (p. 204), and Martyrdom of St. Lawrence (p. 208); above, l. and r. of the vaulting, Entombment and Annunciation, his last and first pictures; above these the lion of St. Mark. — By the 2nd altar the monument of a Prince of Modena (d. 1660), with a statue; 3rd altar, St. Jerome, a statue by *Alessandro Vittoria*, said to possess the features and figure of Titian when in his 98th year; 4th altar, Martyrdom of St. Catharine by *Palma Giovine*.

R. Transept. *Monument of Jacopo Marcello, a sarcophagus borne by male figures; altar-piece in four sections by *Bart. Vivarini*. Over the door of the sacristy the Mausoleum of Benedetto Pesaro (d. 1503). — In the Sacristy, opposite the door, a shrine with reliefs in marble of the 17th cent.; *altar-piece, a Madonna and saints, by *Bellini;* on the wall to the l., Madonna and saints, attributed to *Titian*. — In the church, l. of the entrance to the sacristy, the monument with equestrian statue of Paolo Savelli (d. 1405).

Choir Chapels. *2nd Chapel on the r.:* on the r. the monument of Duccio degli Alberti, l. that of an unknown warrior, both of the 14th cent. — *Choir:* r. mausoleum of the Doge Franc. Foscari (d. 1457), l. that of the Doge Niccolò Tron (d. 1473), both by *Ant. Rizzo.* — *Chapels l. of the Choir:* 1st, altar-piece, Madonna and saints, by *Bern. Licinio;* 2nd, monument of Melch. Trevisano (d. 1500), the altar in coloured and gilded carved wood, in the centre John the Baptist in wood, by *Donatello;* 3rd, altar-piece, St. Ambrose and saints, by *Vivarini* and *Marco Basaiti*, r. St. Ambrose on horseback expelling the Arians, by *Giov. Contarini.*

L. Transept. Altar-piece in 3 sections, St. Mark with saints, by *Bart. Vivarini;* monument of Generosa and Maffeo Zen, 15th cent.

L. Aisle. *Baptistery:* altar-piece in marble, St. Peter, Mary and 8 saints, of the 15th cent.; over the font a statue of John the Baptist, by *Sansovino*. Farther on: Tomb. of Jac. Pesaro (d. 1547); *altar-piece, Madonna with saints and members of the Pesaro family, by *Titian*, who has introduced a portrait of himself as Joseph; *mausoleum of the Doge Giov. Pesaro (d. 1659), a rich and handsome architectural monument occupying the entire wall, with fantastic figures (in bad taste) of negroes as bearers. *Mausoleum of Canova (d. 1822), '*principis sculptorum aetatis suae*', erected in 1827 from the master's own design for Titian's monument ('*ex conlatione Europae universae*'), executed by *Fabris*. — By the W. portal the sarcophagus of Pietro Bernardo (d. 1538).

In the Nave a high parapet of marble, covered with two series of reliefs, separates the seats of the monks from the rest of the church. Gracefully carved stalls, by *Marco da Vicenza* in 1468, half Gothic in style.

The adjacent monastery contains the *Archives*, one of the most magnificent collections of this description in the world. In the 298 saloons and chambers about 14 million documents are preserved, the earliest dating from 883.

Gesuiti (Pl. 11), erected 1715—30 in the baroque style, entirely clothed in the interior with marble inlaid with verde antico, is most sumptuously decorated like all the churches of this order. At the high altar are 10 spiral columns of verde antico, in the centre a globe, with God the Father and the Son. The marble mosaic pavement in front of the altar resembles a carpet. The chapel to the r. of the high altar contains the monument and statue of Orazio Farnese (d. 1654); in the chapel on the l. is the monument of the Doge Pasquale Cicogna (d. 1595); l. Assumption, an altar-piece by *Tintoretto*. In the 1st chapel on the l. of the principal door the *Martyrdom of St. Lawrence, an altar-piece by *Titian*, unfortunately darkened by age.

***S. Giorgio Maggiore** (Pl. 12), a cruciform church with dome, and apses terminating the transepts, commenced by *Palladio* in 1560, is situated on a fortified island opposite the Piazzetta, and belongs to the adjoining Benedictine monastery.

Over the door in the interior a portrait of Pope Pius VII., in commemoration of an ordination of Cardinals held by him here in 1800. To the r. the monument of Lorenzo Venier (d. 1667). Over the 1st altar, Nativity, by *Bassano*; 2nd, Crucifix in wood, by *Michelozzo Michelozzi*; 3rd altar, Martyrdom of several saints; 4th altar, Coronation of the Virgin, the two last by *Tintoretto*. — C h o i r : r. Last supper, l. rain of Manna, both by *Tintoretto*; over the high altar a *group in bronze by *Girolamo Campagna*, representing God the Father on a gilded globe borne by the 4 Evangelists, beside them two angels; two candelabra in bronze dating from the 17th cent.; the 48 *choir-stalls, admirably carved in wood in the 17th cent. by *Alberto de Brule* of Flanders, represent scenes from the life of St. Benedict. — In the *Corridor*, r. of the choir the mausoleum of the Doge Domenico Michiel (d. 1127), erected in 1637; in a chapel behind it, Descent from the cross by *Tintoretto*. — To the l., farther on in the church, Resurrection and Martyrdom of St. Stephen, both by *Tintoretto*; Virgin and Child, a group over life-size by *Girolamo Campagna*; last altar, Martyrdom of St. Lucia, by *Bassano*; monument of the Doge Marc Antonio Memmo (d. 1616).

A staircase in 32 spiral windings, well lighted and of easy ascent, leads to the summit of the *Campanile*, which commands the finest *View in Venice of the city, the Lagune, the distant Alps, etc.

***S. Giovanni e Paolo**, popularly known as '*S. Zanipòlo*', (Pl. 15), commenced 1240, completed 1430, is a very spacious and magnificent Gothic edifice, supported by ten circular columns, and surmounted by a dome. This church, next to St. Mark's the most imposing at Venice, was formerly the burial-church of the doges, whose funeral-service was always performed here, and may be termed the Westminster Abbey of Venice.

R. A i s l e . *Mausoleum of the victorious Doge Pietro Mocenigo (d. 1476), with 15 statues; the sarcophagus is '*ex hostium manubiis*' (from the spoils of his enemies). A pyramid to the memory of the painter Melch. Lanza (d. 1674); monument of Marc Antonio Bragadino (d. 1571), who long defended Famagosta in Cyprus against the Turks, and after its surrender was barbarously flayed alive, as the picture above indicates; altar-piece in 9 sections by *Bellini*, or *Carpaccio*; monument of the Senator Alb. Michiel (d. 1589). In the chapel: altar-piece, Descent from the Cross, by *Pietro Liberi*. Over the doors the °Mausoleum of Bertucci, Silvestro, and Elisabetta Valier with their statues, a rich architectural monument in marble of the 18th cent., embellished with numerous small statues and reliefs. In the chapel below the monument, l. St. Hyacinth crossing a river dry-shod, by *L. Bassano*. The following chapel contains six reliefs in bronze and wood, scenes from the life of St. Dominicus, 1720.

R. Transept. At the corner, St. Augustine, an oil-painting by *Vivarini*; tomb of General Niccolò Orsini (d. 1509) with equestrian statue; beneath it an oil-painting, St. Mark aiding in the manning of the fleet, by *Giambatt. del Moro*; St. Antony, an altar-piece by *Lorenzo Lotto*; stained glass designed by *Vivarini* (1473); altar-piece, Christ, SS. Andrew and Peter, by *Rocco Marconi*. — The chapels on the r. and l. of the choir, recently restored, contain nothing worthy of note.

Choir. Tombs of the Doges (r.) Michele Morosini (d. 1382) and °Leonardo Loredano (d. 1521), (l.) °Andrea Vendramin (d. 1478) (by *Alessandro Leopardo*, one of the most sumptuous and beautiful monuments in Venice), and °Marco Corner (d. 1368), the latter Gothic.

L. Transept. Above, by the entrance to the chapel of the Rosary, a °group in marble by *Antonio Dentone*, of the 15th cent., representing St. Helena presenting General Vittore Capello with the marshal's baton; over the door the monument of the Doge Antonio Venier (d. 1400). — The adjacent (on the l.) *Cappella del Rosario*, founded in 1571 to commemorate the victory of Lepanto, was destroyed by fire in Aug., 1867. Of its former valuable contents nothing remains except the blackened and mutilated remnants of the admirable reliefs in marble, representing scenes from the life of the Saviour and that of the Virgin, executed by different masters from 1600 to 1732. At the time of the conflagration the celebrated picture by *Titian* representing St. Petrus Martyr attacked and murdered in a wood, and a Madonna by *Bellini* had unfortunately been deposited in the chapel during the execution of repairs in the church, and also became a prey to the flames. — Farther on in the church, Monument of the wife and daughter of the Doge Antonio Venier, 1411; monument, with equestrian statue, of Leon. da Prato (d. 1511).

L. Aisle. Over the door of the *Sacristy* busts of Titian and the two Palmas, by *Jac. Alberetti*, 17th cent. — °Mausoleum of the Doge Pasquale Malipiero (d. 1462); Monument of the senator Bonzio (d. 1501), beneath it statues of SS. Thomas and Peter the martyrs; in the niches, r. the painted recumbent effigy of the Doge Michele Steno (d. 1413), l. that of Aloysius Trevisan (d. 1528); monument, with equestrian statue, of General Pompeo Giustiniani; °monument of the Doge Tommaso Mocenigo (d. 1423); monument of the Doge Niccolò Marcello (d. 1474). — 2nd altar, l. of the principal entrance: Ancient copy of Titian's martyrdom of St. Peter (see above), presented by King Victor Emanuel to replace the destroyed picture; monument, with equestrian statue, of Orazio Baglioni (d. 1617); over the last altar a statue of St. Jerome by *Aless. Vittoria*; adjoining it, the monument of the Marquis de Chasteler (d. 1825), born at Mons in Belgium, who distinguished himself in the Tyrolese war (1809). Mausoleum of the Doge Giov. Mocenigo (d. 1485). Over the *Principal Entrance* the mausoleum of the Doge Aloiso I. Mocenigo, his wife, and the Doge Giov. Bembo (d. 1618).

Adjoining S. Giovanni e Paolo is the magnificent *Façade (of 1485) of the *Scuola di S. Marco* (now a hospital), with singular reliefs in perspective, two lions, and the achievements of St. Mark. To the S., on a lofty and elegant pedestal of marble, rises the equestrian *Statue of Bart. Colleoni* (d. 1475), general of the republic, modelled by *Andr. Verocchio*, cast in bronze by *Aless. Leopardo*.

S. Giuliano *('San Zulians')* (Pl. 16) was erected by *Sansovino* in 1553 and consecrated in 1580. The chapel adjacent to the high altar contains a marble relief of the Sleeping Saviour, by *Girolamo Campagna*.

S. Lazzaro, the Armenian Mechitarist monastery on the island of that name, 2 M. S.E. of Venice, possesses a valuable Oriental library and an extensive printing-office.

****S. Marco**, see p. 192.

S. Maria Formosa (Pl. 18) was erected in 1492. Over the 1st altar, *S. Barbara and four saints, with a Pietà above, by *Palma Vecchio*; 2nd, Mary, Anna, and St. Joachim, by *Bart. Vivarini*. In the r. transept, Last Supper, by *L. Bassano*; in the choir modern frescoes, painted by *Paoletti* in 1844, representing Abraham's Sacrifice, Christ driving out the money-changers etc. — The court of the neighbouring *Palazzo Grimani* (Pl. 30; reached by crossing the Ponte Ruga Giuffa, to the E. at the back of the church, and following the first side street to the l.) contains an ancient colossal statue of *Marcus Agrippa*, supposed to have once adorned the Pantheon at Rome; opposite to it, a statue of *Augustus*, partially modern.

S. Maria dei Miracoli (Pl. 20), a small, early Renaissance structure, erected 1480, is entirely covered on the façade and in the interior with valuable marble. The quadrangular choir with dome, 12 steps higher than the nave, is peculiar (beneath it is the sacristy). On the r. and l. are ambos, or lecterns, where the epistles and gospels are read, the usual arrangement in the ancient Christian churches. The *decorations are by *Pietro Lombardo*. The coffered barrel-vaulting is sumptuously painted and gilded. The church was restored in 1869.

S. Maria dell' Orto (Pl. 21), in a remote situation on the N.E. side of the city, possesses a *Façade in the most elegant late Gothic style, commenced 1473, and recently restored. It contains numerous pictures by *Tintoretto*, and the tomb of that master.

R. 1st altar: *"Cima da Conegliano*, St. John the Baptist with SS. Peter, Mark, Jerome, and Paul. Between the 3rd and 4th altars: Monument of Hieronymus Caraccio (d. 1657) in the baroque style. Above the entrance of the sacristy, Virgin and Child, high-relief by *Giovanni de Sanctis*. — In the Sacristy: 28 portraits of Venetian Saints, and a Descent from the Cross, School *of Giorgione*. — Chapel to the r. of the choir: *Girolamo di S. Croce*, SS. Augustine and Bonaventura. In the choir r. the Last Judgment, l. Adoration of the golden calf, large works by *Tintoretto*. Over the high altar an Annunciation, by *Palma Giovine*, with surrounding pictures by *Tintoretto*. — Chapel to the l. of the choir, on the wall r. *"Palma Vecchio*, St. Stephen and four Saints; altar-piece a copy from Bordone. — In the l. aisle the Capp. Contarini, containing busts of six members of the celebrated family of that name; among them that of the Cardinal (d. 1542), by *Alessandro Vittoria*; altar-piece by *Tintoretto*, Miracles of St. Agnes; l. *Palma Giovine*, Crucifixion. 1st chapel l. of the entrance: altar-piece by *Bellini*, Madonna (restored); l. *Lor. Lotto*, Lamentation over the body of Christ.

***S. Maria della Salute** (Pl. 22), a spacious and handsome church, surmounted by a dome, at the E. extremity of the Canal Grande, adjacent to the Dogana di Mare (p. 209), was erected 1631-32 by *Longhena*, a successor of Palladio.

The three chapels on the r., contain Madonnas by *Luca Giordano;* in the last chapel on the l., Descent of the Holy Ghost, by *Titian.* The columns by which the vaulting of the choir is supported are from a Roman temple at Pola (p. 71). On the high altar a large candelabrum in bronze, of admirable workmanship; the Virgin banishing the demons of the plague, a group in marble by *Le Curt.* On the ceiling eight medallions with portraits of the evangelists and the fathers of the church by *Titian. Outer Sacristy:* *Pietà, a relief of the 15th cent. by *Dentone* (?); *St. Mark and 4 saints, by *Titian*; St. Sebastian, by *Marco Basaiti.* — *Sacristy:* by the entrance-door, St. Roch and other saints, by *Girolamo da Treviso;* r. Madonna, *Sassoferrato;* l. Marriage of Cana, *Tintoretto;* Ceiling-paintings by *Titian.*

S. Maria Zobenigo (Pl. 23), on the way from the Piazza of St. Mark to the Academy (p. 199), was erected in 1680 by the Barbaro family *('barbaro monumento del decadimento dell' arte').* The niches of the façade contain statues of members of the family. At the base of the lower row of columns are plans of Zara, Candia, Padua, Rome, Corfu, and Spalato, hewn in the stone; on the bases of the columns are representations of naval battles. This curious façade is the only part of the church worthy of note.

S. Pantaleone (Pl. 26), S.W. of, and not far from the Frari (p. 202), was erected in 1668—75. The chapel l. of the high altar contains (r.) a *Coronation of the Virgin by *Giovanni* and *Antonio da Murano,* painted in 1444; also an *Entombment in high relief, of the same date.

S. Pietro di Castello (Pl. 27), a church with a dome, on the island on the E. side of Venice, commenced by *Smeraldi* in 1596, is said to have been designed by *Palladio* in 1557. Till 1807 it was the cathedral of the Patriarch of Venice, whose adjoining palace was converted by Napoleon into a barrack; on the same occasion St. Mark's became the cathedral.

The interior of the church offers little to interest the visitor. In the chapel of the l. transept are two reliefs in marble, executed by *Mich. Ongaro* in the 17th cent.; they represent the consecration by Pope Paul V. of the Patriarch Vendramin as cardinal, and an allegory of death. To the r. beyond the second altar is a marble throne from Antioch, alleged to be that of St. Peter.

The handsome and lofty adjacent *Campanile* dates from 1474.

***Redentore** (Pl. 28), on the Giudecca, erected in 1576 by *Andr. Palladio,* a spacious church with portal borne by columns, is a fine and interesting structure especially in the interior.

On the r., 1st Chapel: Nativity, by *Francesco Bassano;* 2nd, Baptism, *Carletto Cagliari;* 3rd, Scourging, *Tintoretto;* 3rd Chapel on the l., Descent from the Cross, *Palma Giov.;* 2nd, Resurrection, *F. Bassano;* 1st, Ascension, *Tintoretto.* In front of the high altar, Christ bearing the Cross, behind it a Descent from the Cross, a relief in marble. The Sacristy contains the three finest *Madonnas (covered by curtains) of *Giovanni Bellini;* the best is that with the sleeping Child.

The church belongs to the neighbouring Franciscan monastery.

S. Rocco (Pl. 29), in the rear of the Frari (p. 202), erected at various periods between 1490 and 1725, is adorned with rich marble sculpturing of the 15th cent. The chapel r. of the high altar contains a picture (covered) by *Titian*, representing Christ dragged to the Cross. The adjacent *Scuola di S. Rocco (Pl. 45), containing the council-halls of the brotherhood, commenced in 1517, possesses a most magnificent façade, and handsome staircase and hall; bronze gates in front of the altar, by *Joseph Filiberti* of Florence, 1756; a number of pictures by *Tintoretto*, among them his chef-d'œuvre, a *Crucifixion, of 1565; also an Annunciation and Ecce Homo by *Titian*. The church is accessible daily 9 – 4 o'clock (custodian 1/2 fr.).

S. Salvadore (Pl. 30), on the way from the Piazza of St. Mark to the Rialto Bridge (p. 210), completed in 1534 (façade 1663), surmounted by three flat domes which rest on circular vaulting, is one of the finest churches in Venice in this style. At present the church is undergoing restoration and not accessible (some of the pictures are i the Academy, p. 199).
R. Aisle. Between the 1st and 2nd altars the monument of Proc. Andrea Dolfin (d. 1602) and his wife; between the 2nd and 3rd, that of the Doge Franc. Venier (d. 1556), an architectural °monument by *Sansovino*; over the 3rd altar (also by *Sansovino*) an Annunciation by *Titian*. — Transept: r. the monument of Catharine Cornaro (d. 1510), Queen of Cyprus, who abdicated in 1489 in favour of Venice. — Choir. °Transfiguration, high altar-piece by *Titian*; behind it an altar-piece chased in silver, with 27 scriptural representations, executed about 1290. — In the Chapel on the l., Christ at Emmaus, by *Giov. Bellini*. — L. Aisle. Monument of three cardinals of the Cornaro family. — Over the altar l. of the organ, statue of St. Jerome, by *T. Lombardo*. Monument of the brothers Girolamo (d. 1567) and Lorenzo Priuli (d. 1559), with gilded recumbent figures of the doges, a lofty architectural monument.

Gli Scalzi (Pl. 31), the sumptuous church of the order of barefooted monks, immediately to the E. of the railway-station, erected 1649—89, affords an excellent sample of the decorative style of the 17th cent. It was greatly damaged by the bombardment of 1849, but was restored in 1860. Behind the high altar a Madonna by *Bellini*. (The church is closed at noon.)

S. Sebastiano (Pl. 33), in the S.W. quarter of the city, near the Canal della Giudecca, contains a number of works by *Paolo Veronese*, and his tomb. It was erected in 1506—18 and is now undergoing restoration, but will shortly by re-opened. Several of the pictures are temporarily removed to the Academy (p. 200).
S. Side. 1st altar, St. Nicholas, painted by *Titian* in his 86th year; 2nd, Madonna, a small picture by *Paolo*; 3rd, °Madonna with John, a group in marble by *Tommaso da Lugano*; 4th, Christ on the Cross, and the Maries, by *Paolo*; °monument of Bishop Livio Podocataro (d. 1555), by *Sansovino*. — Choir. Altar-piece, Madonna in glory and four saints, on the wall to the r. °Martyrdom of St. Sebastian, l. °Martyrdom of SS. Mark and Marcellinus, all three by *Paolo*. — Organ, on the external wing the Purification of Mary, on the inner the Pool of Bethesda, both by *Paolo*; to the l. the bust, and near it the tomb of the master (d. 1588), bearing the inscription: '*Paulo Caliaro Veronensi pictori, naturae aemulo, artis miraculo,*

superstite fatis, fama victuro.' — Sacristy. Ceiling-paintings by *Paolo*, Coronation of the Virgin, in the corners the 4 Evangelists. Farther on in the church the *Bust of the Procurator Marcantonio Grimani (d. 1565), by *Vittorio*; 2nd altar, Baptism of Christ, by *Paolo*; ceiling-paintings also by *Paolo*, aided by his brother *Benedetto Cagliari*.

S. Simeone Piccolo (Pl. 34), opposite the railway-station, W. of the iron bridge, erected 1718—38, with portal resting on columns, is surmounted by a dome in imitation of the Pantheon at Rome. The interior possesses nothing remarkable.

***S. Stefăno** (Pl. 35), on the way from the Piazza of St. Mark to the Academy (p. 199), is a Gothic church of the 14th cent., with an elegant façade in brick, and a peculiar vaulting of wood (restored).

Entrance-wall, above the principal door, equestrian statue of Dom. Contareni, middle of 17th cent.; adjacent the *tomb of the physician Jacopo Suri ano (d. 1551). On the Pavement of the nave is the large tombstone of the Doge Francesco Morosini 'Peloponnesiaci' (d. 1694), the cap and baton of office in bronze. — Adjacent to the Sacristy in the r. aisle a Madonna with saints, a relief in bronze of the 16th cent.; in the sacristy admirably executed small marble statues of John the Baptist and St. Antony by *Pietro Lombardo*; Madonna and Saints by *Palma Vecchio*. — Choir. On the lateral walls statues of the 12 Apostles and four saints, and reliefs of the 4 Evangelists and two Fathers of the church. In front of the high altar two candelabra in gilded bronze, 1577; behind it several choir-stalls carved and inlaid. — 3rd altar, l. statues of St. Jerome and St. Paul by *Pietro Lombardo*. Stained glass windows of no great value.

***S. Zaccaria** (Pl. 36), near the Riva degli Schiavoni, erected 1457—1515, in the round-arch style, supported by six Corinthian columns, possesses a handsome façade. The recess of the high altar is in the Gothic style. Over the entrance the statue of St. Zacharias by *Aless. Vittoria*.

The walls of the Nave are covered with large pictures, all of them, except those over the altars, representing memorable events in the history of the church. R. of the entrance, over the basin for holy water, a statuette of John the Baptist by *Al. Vittoria*. The third arcade leads to the Coro delle Monache (choir of the nuns): *Enthroned Madonna and saints, on the wall to the r., by *Palma Vecchio* (?); over the door, Nativity of John the Baptist, by *Tintoretto*. In the Cappella di S. Tarasio (2nd on the r.) two gilded *altars in carved wood, of 1443—44, with old Italian pictures by the *Vivarini* of Murano. Here, too, is the entrance to the *Crypt*, belonging to the original structure, which was burned down in 1105. — Altar of the choir, Circumcision, by *Giovanni Bellini*. In the l. aisle, the tombstone of *Alessandro Vittoria* (d. 1605), with a bust by the master himself, '*qui vivens vivos duxit e marmore vultus*'. 2nd altar (l.), *Madonna enthroned and four saints, by *Giov. Bellini*. This picture was taken to Paris by the French in 1797, but restored in 1815.

The ****Grand Canal** *('Canalazzo')*, the main artery of the traffic of Venice, nearly 2 M. in length, and 100—200 ft. in width, intersects the city from N.W. to S.E., dividing it into two unequal parts, and resembling an inverted *S* in shape. The Canal Grande occupies the same position at Venice as the Corso at Rome, the Toledo at Naples, or the Boulevards at Paris. Thousands of gondolas and barcas are here seen gliding in every direction. Handsome houses and magnificent palaces rise on its banks. The Grand Canal is the street of the Nobili, the ancient aristocracy of Venice. Little commercial traffic is here carried on, the channel being too shallow for sea-going vessels. A trip on the canal is most instructive and entertaining; it will bear frequent repetition and will afford the traveller the best opportunity for carefully inspecting and studying the architecture of the principal palaces. The gondolier points out the most important edifices. The posts *(pali)* were formerly the distinguishing marks of the palaces of the nobles, and are still so to some extent, being painted with the heraldic colours of their proprietors. The following, commencing from the Piazzetta, are the most striking:

Left.

Dogana di Mare (Pl. 37), the principal custom-house, erected 1682 by Benoni; the vane surmounting the large gilded ball on the summit of the tower is a gilded Fortuna.

Seminario Patriarcale (Pl. 99), containing a collection of statues, architectural fragments, etc., most of them from secularized churches and monasteries of Venice, a collection of coins, a library, and the small Gallery Manfredini (open daily).

S. *Maria della Salute*, see p. 206.

Pal. Dario-Angarani (Pl. 59), in the style of the Lombardi (15th cent.).

Pal. Venier, a grand building, but unfinished.

Pal. Da Mula, pointed style of the 15th cent.

Pal. Zichy-Esterhazy (Pl. 95).

Pal. Manzoni-Angarani (Pl. 78), of the period of the Lombardi (15th cent), formerly an edifice of great magnificence, and the sole palace which stood in a feudal relation to the republic, now in a dilapidated condition (at present undergoing restoration).

Right.

Palazzo Giustiniani, now the Hôtel Europa (Pl. b), in the pointed style of the 15th cent.

Pal. Emo-Treves (Pl. 61); in one of the apartments is a group of Hector and Ajax, over life-size, Canova's last work (fee 1 fr.).

Pal. Tiepolo-Zucchelli (Pl. 91), now Hôtel Barbesi.

Pal. Contarini, 15th cent.

**Pal. Contarini-Fasan*, restored in 1867,

Pal. Ferro (Pl. 47), now Hôtel New York, both handsome structures in the pointed style of the 14th cent.

Pal. Fini (Pl. 62), the property of the Countess Wimpffen, containing a small collection of modern pictures, works of art and curiosities (adm. daily 10—4 o'clock, fee 1 fr.).

**Pal. Corner della Cà Grande* (Pl. 54), erected by Jac. Sansovino in 1532, with spacious internal court, now the seat of the government authorities.

**Pal. Cavalli* (Pl. 50), the property of the Duke of Bordeaux, in the pointed style of the 15th cent.

Campo della Carità. — I r o n B r i d g e, constructed in 1854. — *Campo S. Vitale* (bridge-toll 2 c.).

Left.

Accademia delle Belle Arti, see p. 199.

Palazzi Contarini degli Scrigni (Pl. 51), one of the 16th, the other of the 15th cent., erected by Scamozzi (the picture-gallery formerly here has been presented to the Academy, see p. 200).

**Pal. Rezzonico* (Pl. 88), a spacious structure of the 17th and 18th cent., erected by Longhena and Massari.

Right.

Pal. Giustinian-Lolin (Pl. 69), of the 17th cent., the property of the Duchess of Parma.

Pal. Grassi (Pl. 72), of the 18th cent., belongs to Baron Sina.

Left.

Two *Pal. Giustiniani* (Pl. 68).

**Pal. Foscări* (Pl. 66), in the pointed style of the 15th cent., a handsome structure, now the property of the city, situated at the point where the Canal turns to the E.

Pal. Balbi (Pl. 42), a Renaissance structure, erected by Aless. Vittoria, a pupil of Sansovino. This portion of the Canal, and especially the two palaces, are a favourite subject with artists.

Pal. Grimani, Renaissance style.

Pal. Persico (Pl. 83).

Pal. Pisani (Pl. 85), in the pointed style of the 14th cent. The celebrated picture of Darius and Alexander, by Paolo Veronese, formerly here, is now in England.

Pal. Barbarigo della Terrazza (Pl. 43) was once celebrated for its picture-gallery, which in 1850 became the property of the Emp. of Russia.

Pal. Grimani, in the Renaissance style.

Pal. Bernardo (Pl. 46), in the pointed style.

**Pal. Tiepŏlo-Stürmer* (Pl. 90), in the Renaissance style.

Right.

Pal. Moro-Lin (Pl. 82), 17th cent., erected by Mazzoni.

Pal. Contarini delle Figure (Pl. 53), in the early Renaissance style, 1504—64, with shields and trophies suspended from the walls.

Pal. Mocenigo (Pl. 81), three contiguous palaces, that in the centre occupied by Lord Byron in 1815; that on the N. (Pl. 30) contains the Exhibition of Art mentioned p. 187 (with Titian's picture, The Saviour's Blessing).

**Pal. Corner-Spinelli* (Pl. 56), in the early Renaissance style, erected by Lombardi, the property of the danseuse Taglioni.

**Pal. Cavalli*, in the pointed style of the 15th cent., now occupied by the Consulate of Prussia.

**Pal. Grimani* (Pl. 70), a Renaissance edifice, chef d'œuvre of Michele Sanmicheli, dating from the middle of the 16th cent., now the post-office.

**Pal. Farsetti* (Pl. 65, originally *Dandolo*), in the Romanesque style of the 12th cent., with an admixture of Byzantine and Moorish features, is now the seat of the municipal authorities *(municipio)*.

**Pal. Loredan* (Pl. 74), coeval with the last, was once the residence of king Peter Lusignan of Cyprus, husband of Catharine Cornaro (comp. Pal. Corner, p. 211), whose armorial bearings are seen on different parts of the edifice; it is now also occupied by the Municipio (see above).

Pal. Dandolo (Pl. 58), once the unpretending residence of the celebrated Doge Enrico Dandolo (a small café on the ground floor).

**Pal. Bembo* (Pl. 45), in the pointed style of the 14th cent.

Pal. Manin (Pl. 77), with façade by Jac. Sansovino, 16th cent., was the property of the last Doge Lod. Manin, who on the approach of the French in May, 1797, resigned his office; it is now the *Banca Nazionale*.

"**Ponte di Rialto** (i. e. 'di rivo alto'), constructed in 1588—91 by Antonio da Ponte (or perhaps by Andrea Boldù), 158 ft. long, 46 ft. wide, consists of a single marble arch of 74 ft. span and 32 ft. in height, resting on 12,000 piles. It is situated midway between the Dogana di Mare and the railway-station, and till 1854 (p. 209) was the sole connecting link between the E. and W. quarters of Venice. On the r. bank, near the bridge, is the *Fish Market*, abundantly supplied on Fridays. On the l. is the *Fruit* and *Vegetable Market*, where excellent fruit may generally be purchased in the morning. At the back of the market-place is a short column of Egyptian granite, to which a flight of steps ascends. The kneeling figure which serves as a supporter is termed *Il Gobbo di Rialto*. From this column the laws of the Republic were promulgated.

Left.

Pal. de' Camerlinghi (Pl. 49), in the early Renaissance style of 1525, once the residence of the republican chamberlains or officers of finance, now the seat of a court of judicature, was erected by Bergamasco.

Pal. Corner della Regina (Pl. 55) was erected by Rossi in 1724, on the site of the house in which Catharine Cornaro, Queen of Cyprus, was born; it is now a monte di pietà or pawn-house.

Pal. Pesăro (Pl. 84), a Renaissance edifice of the 17th cent. by Longhena (accessible daily 9—4 o'clock, attendant 1 fr., porter 20 c.), contains a series of sumptuous apartments adorned with pictures of no great value.

Church of *S. Eustachio* ('*S. Stae*').

Pal. Tron, 16th cent.

Pal. Battagia, erected by Longhena.

**Fondaco de' Turchi* (Pl. 64), Romanesque style of the 10th cent., once (after 1621) a Turkish depôt, is undergoing restoration.

Civico Museo Correr (Pl. 57), accessible Mond., Wednesd., and Sat. 10—4 o'clock, comprising pictures and drawings by old masters, bronzes, carved wood and ivory, coins, etc.; also a large bird's eye view of Venice, carved in wood by Dürer (?) in 1500; mementoes of Canova, modern statues (Hagar, by Lucardi), zoolog. collection. The following pictures deserve mention: 27. *Mantegna*, Transfiguration; 14. *Gent. Bel-*

Right.

**Fondaco de' Tedeschi* (Pl. 63), an early Renaissance structure (1506), erected by Fra Giocondo da Verona (p. 165), was once a depôt of the wares of German merchants. It was originally decorated externally with paintings by Titian and his pupils, of which few vestiges now remain. The building is now employed as a custom-house (*Dogana*).

Pal. Mangilli-Valmarana (Pl. 76) built by Vicentini.

Corte del Remer, 13th cent.

Pal. Michieli dalle Colonne, 17th cent.

Pal. Sagredo, pointed style of the 14th cent.

**Cà(sa) d'Oro* (Pl. 48), the most elegant of the palaces in the pointed style of the 14th cent.

Pal. Grimani della Vida (Pl. 71), 16th cent., was erected by Sanmicheli.

Pal. Erizzo, in the pointed style of the 15th cent.

**Pal. Vendramin Calergi* (Pl. 94), early Renaissance style, erected in 1841 by Pietro Lombardo, one of the finest palaces on the Canal Grande, and well worthy of a visit, is the property of the Duchess of Berry. The motto on the exterior is '*non nobis*'. The interior, magnificently fitted up, contains some fine old (Palma Giovine, Tintoretto, Bordone) and modern pictures (generally accessible daily, porter 25 c., attendant 1 fr., more for a party).

Left.
lini, Franc. Foscari; 16. *Giov. Bellini*, Mocenigo; 44. *Leonardo da Vinci*, Caesar Borgia; 127—139. *Piet. Longhi*, Pictures characteristic of Venice; 175. *L. Cranach*, Resurrection; several Dutch masters; 144. *Aless. Longhi*, Goldoni; 81. *P. Veronese*, Sketch of the Marriage of Cana (in the Louvre). — The u p p e r floor contains an insignificant z o o l o g. collection.

Right.

Pal. Labia (Pl. 73), 17th cent., at the union of the Cannaregio with the Canal Grande.

Near it, immediately beyond the bridge *(Ponte di Cannaregio)* is (l.) the *Pal. Manfrin* (Pl. 75), containing a picture-gallery, the greatest treasures of which were sold in 1856. It still comprises 300 works, some of them valuable (Descent from the Cross by *Titian;* Lucrezia by *Guido Reni;* Noah entering the Ark, a large cartoon by *Raphael*, etc.), all for sale (admission daily 10—3, $^1|_2$ fr.).

Gli Scalzi (church of the barefooted monks) see p. 207.

New Iron Bridge, completed 1858 (bridge-toll 2 c.).

S. Simeone Piccolo, see p. 208.

Stazione della Strada Ferrata (Rail. Station), omnibus - boats etc. see p. 184).

To the l., near the point where the Canal turns to the N.W., is situated the well-kept **Giardino Papadopŏli** (Pl. 40). On the N. side of the railway-station is the **Botanical Garden**, *Orto Botanico* (Pl. C, 2), the cacti of which are said to be the largest in Europe.

At the S.E. extremity of Venice *(Punta della Motta)* are the **Giardini Pubblici** (Pl. I, 5), laid out by Napoleon in 1807, the space having been obtained by the demolition of several monasteries. They are $^1/_4$ M. in length and 120 yds. in width, and are planted with six rows of acacias and sycamores. At the S. extremity is a small shrubbery, with a poor café. The grounds, which are generally almost deserted, afford fine views of the town and Lagune. On Sundays and Mondays they are a favourite promenade, especially frequented by women of the humbler classes (gondola thither from the Piazzetta 50 c.). They are approached by the *Via Eugenia*, constructed in 1810 by Eugene Beauharnais, viceroy of Italy, by bridging over a canal.

Campo di Marte (Pl. B, 4), the military exercising-ground, an island on the W. side of Venice, surrounded with avenues, also affords a pleasant walk, especially towards sunset.

A visit to the **Lido** ($^1/_2$ hr. from the Piazzetta; steamer and baths in summer, see p. 187) is one of the best excursions for enabling the stranger to form an accurate idea of the situation and topography of Venice. A second rower is recommended for this trip, as, in the case of the wind rising, one is insufficient.

Murano is situated on an island about $1^1|_2$ M. N. of Venice. The route to it passes the C e m e t e r y I s l a n d *(Cimiterio)*, with the church of *S. Michele*. — The *C a t h e d r a l *(S. Donato)*, a vaulted church supported by columns, with transept resting on pillars, vies with St. Mark's itself in the splendour of its interior, its columns of Greek marble, mosaics, etc. An inscription on a marble slab inserted in the mosaic pavement of the church bears the date 1111. Over the side-door on the r. a Madonna with saints, by *Lazzaro Sebastiani*. — S. Pietro e Paŏlo is a simple and spacious basilica of 1509. Near the door of the sacristy, to the l., is an Assumption by *Marco Basaiti*, in bad preservation, and a Madonna with saints and angels, by *Giov. Bellini* (between the 2nd and 3rd altars on the r.). — Murano (4000 inhab.) possesses an extensive manufactory of glass beads, mosaics in glass, objects in crystal, etc. The Museo (adm. 40 c.) contains a good collection of these articles.

Torcello, about 7½ M. N. E. of Venice, also situated on an island, the ancient *Altinum* (traces of which may still be observed beneath the surface of the water), and belonging to the town of *Burano*, on a neighbouring island (6000 inhab.), is a poor place, consisting of a few small houses only. The two well-preserved churches are the sole attraction. The *Cathedral (*S. Maria*), erected in the 7th cent., restored in 1008, is a basilica in the early Christian style, supported by columns resembling those of Murano. The principal object of interest is the ancient arrangement of the semicircular seats of the priests on the tribuna, rising in steps and commanded by the lofty episcopal throne in the centre. On the W. wall of the interior is a large *Mosaic of the 12th cent., representing the Sacrifice of Christ, the Resurrection, Last Judgment, etc., recently restored. An octagonal Baptistery adjoins the cathedral. — **S. Fosca*, dating in its present form from the 12th cent., is externally octagonal (interior intended to be surmounted by a dome, but at present covered with a flat roof). On five sides it is enclosed by a beautiful arcade, supported by columns (16 in number, and 4 cornerpillars), a structure worthy of the notice of architects.

Chioggia, 30 M. to the S., an ancient town (26,700 inhab.) at the end of the lagoons, was founded about the same period as Venice, by which it was soon conquered. During the war with Genoa it was taken by the Genoese (1378), but recovered by the Venetians the following year (comp. p. 188). The inhabitants have always differed materially in language and customs from the other inhabitants of the lagoon-districts. None of the churches are worthy of note. The *Murazzi* (p. 190) may most conveniently be inspected in the course of an excursion to Chioggia (by steamer of the Austr. Lloyd in 2 hrs., p. 187; also pleasure-trips occasionally).

39. From Venice to Trieste.

a. *By Land, viâ Udine*.

Railway in 10 hrs.; fares 25 fr. 80, 19 fr. 35, 12 fr. 90 c. — Austrian custom-house formalities at Cormons. Railway-station at Venice see pp. 174, 184.

Bridge across the *Lagune*, and *Fort Malghera* see p. 174. At *Mestre* the line diverges N. from that to Padua. Stations *Mogliano*, *Preganziolo;* then

Treviso *(Posta; Aquila; Quattro Corone)*, capital of an episcopal diocese, with 22,000 inhab. The handsome, but unfinished old cathedral of *S. Pietro* contains pictures by Bellini and Paris Bordone, and a celebrated work of Fra Marco Pensabene, commonly attributed to Seb. del Piombo. The *Town Hall* and *Theatre* are fine edifices. The *Monte di Pietà* (pawn-office) contains a good Giorgione, representing the Entombment, supposed by some to be the last work of this master, finished by Titian. The *Villa Manfrini* possesses extensive gardens. The French Marshal Mortier was styled Duke of Treviso. (Route to Trent through the Val Sugana see R. 8.)

Stat. *Lancenigo*. Beyond stat. *Spressiano* the line crosses the *Piave* and approaches the mountains. Stat. *Piave*.

Conegliano *(*Posta)*, birthplace of the celebrated painter Cima (d. 1517), surnamed *da Conegliano*, is commanded by an extensive and conspicuous castle on an eminence. The French Marshal Moncey bore the title of Duke of Conegliano.

From Conegliano to Belluno to the N., viâ *Ceneda*, *S. Croce*, and *Capo di Ponte*, diligence once daily in 6 hrs.

Belluno (1365 ft.) *(Due Torri*, R. and L. 1 fr. 60, A. 50 c.), capital of a province, with 14,600 inhab., situated on a hill between the *Ardo* and the *Piave*, which here unite, presents all the features of a Venetian town. Of its 14 churches the *Cathedral*, erected by Palladio, is the finest. It contains several good altar-pieces and an ancient sarcophagus. The massive campanile, 216 ft. in height, commands a beautiful prospect. An old sarcophagus of some artistic merit adorns the small Piazza in front of the church of S. Stefano. The triumphal arch outside the gate, completed in 1815 and dedicated to the Emp. Francis, was probably originally intended, like that at Milan, as a monument in honour of Napoleon.

Stat. *Pianzano*. Stat. *Sacile*, a town on the *Livenza*, surrounded by walls and fosses, exhibits traces of its ancient importance. The palace of the Podestà (chief magistrate) is a handsome building. An engagement between the French and Austrians took place here in 1809. Stat. *Pordenone*, probably the *Portus Naonis* of the Romans, was the birthplace of the painter of that name. The principal church contains a St. Christopher by him.

Beyond stat. *Casarsa*, the train crosses the broad channel of the *Tagliamento* by an iron bridge $1/2$ M. in length. The stony deposits of the stream have raised its bed so considerably that the next stat. *Codroipo* (Imperatore), situated between the Tagliamento and the *Corno*, lies 28 ft. below the level of the bottom of the former river.

Campo Formio, a small village to the r. of the railway, is memorable as the place where the treaty, by which the Republic of Venice was dissolved, was concluded between France and Austria, Oct. 17th, 1797. An insignificant house where the plenipotentiaries met is still shown. The next important station is

Udine *(Europa; Stella; Croce di Malta)*, an ancient town with 25,000 inhab., formerly the capital of the Austrian province of Friaul, and a place of great importance, surrounded by walls of considerable antiquity. In the centre is the old town, with walls and fosses. Above it rises the castle, on an eminence, which according to tradition was artificially thrown up by Attila, in order that he might thence survey the conflagration of Aquileia (p. 215).

Udine may in some respects be termed a miniature Venice, as it presents several points of resemblance to the metropolis to which it was so long subject. It possesses a town-hall similar to the palace of the doges, two columns like those of the Piazzetta of Venice, and a campanile with two figures which strike the hours. The *Cathedral*, a Romanesque structure, contains a few interesting pictures, and some fine sculpturing in wood and stone. In the episcopal palace a ceiling-painting by Giovanni da Udine may be inspected. The *Castle*, now a prison, commands an extensive survey of the surrounding plain. The *Campo Santo* of Udine is very remarkable and merits a visit.

Cividale, the ancient *Forum Julii*, interesting on account of its numerous Roman antiquities, lies 9 M. to the E. of Udine.

The train now proceeds in a S.E. direction. Stations *Buttrio*, *S. Giovanni Manzano* (Italian frontier, custom-house formalities for travellers from Trieste), *Cormons* (Austrian custom-house), and **Gorizia**, Germ. *Görz (Tre Corone; Trieste)*, charmingly situated on the *Isonzo* in a hilly district (13,300 inhab.). Cathedral worthy of notice. In the upper part of the town is the dilapidated castle of the former counts of the place, partly used as a prison. The preserved fruit of Gorizia is highly esteemed; the best may be purchased of Redaelli.

Charles X. of France (d. 1836) is interred in the chapel of the monastery of *Castagnovizza*, on a height above the town. In the vicinity rises the *Monte Santo*, with a pilgrimage-church, commanding a fine view.

To the E. of stat. *Monfalcone* (Leone d'Oro), the train reaches the *Adriatic*.

Aquileia, 18 M. to the W., once one of the most important provincial towns of ancient Rome, at that period strongly fortified, was the principal bulwark of Italy on the N. E. frontier. The population in the time of Augustus, who frequently visited the town, is computed to have been 100,000 souls. It was at that epoch the great centre of the traffic between Italy and the N. and E. of Europe, and supplied the inhabitants of Illyria and Pannonia with grain, oil, and wine, in return for slaves and cattle. The incursions of the Romans into these districts were always undertaken from this point. In 452 Attila, exasperated by the obstinate resistance he encountered here, caused the city to be plundered and destroyed. The sole trace of its ancient glory is the *Cathedral*, erected in 1019—42, once the metropolitan church of the patriarchs of Aquileia. The place is now a poor village with 500 inhab., but interesting on account of the valuable antiquities frequently found in the neighbourhood. The collections in the Battisterio by the cathedral, of Count Cassis, M. Zandonati, etc. may be visited. In 1862 an extensive Castellum Aquæ was discovered between *Monastero* and *Aquileia*. One of the principal curiosities is a fine mosaic, with the Rape of Europa.

At *S. Giovanni* the *Timavo* (the *Timavus* of the Romans, Virg. Æn. I. 244—246), which under the name of *Recca* (or Rjeka, i. e. river) is lost in the grottoes of the Carso, near St. Canzian, re-appears after a subterranean course of 23 M. and falls into the Adriatic 1½ M. lower down. Farther on is *Duino*, with an ancient castle of Prince Hohenlohe.

At *Nabrēsina* (Daniel, near the stat.) the line unites with the Vienna and Trieste Rail.; hence to Trieste see p. 68.

Trieste, and excursions to Pola and Fiume see R. 9.

b. *Sea Voyage to Trieste*.

Steamboat three times weekly, corresponding with the express train to Vienna, usually starting at midnight, and reaching Trieste on the following morning; fares 9 or 6½ fl.; return-tickets, available for a fortnight, 13 or 10 fl. — Gondolas etc., see p. 185.

The steamer starts from the Canal S. Marco, opposite the Piazzetta, passes the *Giardini Pubblici* (p. 212), the small island of *S. Elena*, and the fortified island of *S. Andrea del Lido*, which commands the entrance to the harbour of the *Lido* (p. 190). The navigable channel is indicated by stakes. Beautiful retrospect of Venice on moonlight nights. As Trieste is approached a view is obtained of the distant, snow-clad *Julian Alps*, the lighthouse of *Salvore*, *Pirano*, S.E. the coast of Istria and *Capo d'Istria* in a bay, and finally of the charmingly-situated Trieste itself.

40. From Milan to Bologna.

Railway in 5¾—7 hrs.; fares 24 fr. 70, 19 fr. 15, 14 fr. 15 c.

At stat. *Rogoredo* the line to Pavia diverges to the r. (S.). Stat. *Melegnano*, formerly *Murignano*, is a memorable place in the annals of mediæval and modern warfare. Here on Sept. 15th, 1515, Francis I. of France, in his campaign against Milan, defeated the Swiss allies of the city, 15,000 of whom fell in the action. In the environs, and especially in the town itself, a sanguinary conflict took place between the French and the Austrians, June 7th, 1859, in consequence of which the latter were compelled to retreat. The rear-guard of the army, then on its retreat from Magenta (p. 111), was commanded by Benedek. The French troops were commanded by Marshal Baraguay d'Hilliers.

Stat. *Tavazzano*. Innumerable cuttings for the purposes of irrigation and drainage here intersect the plain.

Lodi *(Sole; Europa; Tre Rè)*, 4½ M. E. of which lies *Lodi Vecchio*, the ancient Roman colony of *Laus Pompeia*, is a town with 18,150 inhab., one of the bitterest enemies of Milan in the middle ages. It is celebrated as the scene of Napoleon's storming of the bridge over the Adda, May 10th, 1796. Excellent Parmesan cheese (p. 219) is manufactured in the neighbourhood. The *Cathedral* contains an ancient relief of the Last Supper. The church of **Incoronata*, erected by Bramante in 1476, is a fine sample of the Renaissance style.

Next stations *Secugnago*, *Casalpusterlengo*, *Codogno*.

From Casalpusterlengo and Codogno branch-line to Pavia see p. 155, to Cremona p. 155; comp. R. 29.

The following stations are *S. Stefano* and **Piacenza** (p. 84), where carriages are frequently changed.

The line now follows the direction of the *Via Æmilia*, a Roman road constructed by, and named after the consul M. Æmilius Lepidus, B. C. 187. This great route led hence to Parma, Reggio, Modena, Bologna, Forli, and Rimini (Ariminum) on the Adriatic, from which the other consul C. Flaminius Nepos simultaneously constructed the *Via Flaminia* through Umbria and Etruria to Rome. Many traces of these roads are still observed, especially as most of the modern routes in Italy follow the direction of those constructed by the Romans.

The train passes *S. Lazaro*, an ecclesiastical seminary greatly enriched by the eminent Cardinal Alberoni in the 18th cent. He was born at Firenzuola in 1664 (d. 1752). The church contains his tomb and pictures by *Perugino, Zucchero*, etc.

Near stat. *Ponte Nure* the *Nure* is crossed. The train passes *Fontana Fredda*, where Theodoric the Great and the Lombard kings once possessed a country-residence. The *Arda* is now crossed, and stat. *Firenzuola* reached, a small but thriving place, whence a visit may be paid (rough road viâ *Castel Arquato*) to the ruins of *Velleia* (p. 85).

Stat. *Alseno;* then **Borgo San Donino** *(Croce Bianca; Angelo)*, a small town, the ancient *Fidentia Julia*. It received its appellation in 387 from St. Dominicus, who had suffered martyrdom about a century earlier, under Maximian, and to whom the ancient *Cathedral*, a Lombard structure, embellished with rude sculptures, is dedicated. Next stat. *Castel Guelfo*, with the *Torre d' Orlando*, a ruined castle erected by the Ghibelline Orlando Pallavicino about 1407, for protection against the Guelph Ottone Terzi of Parma. The line crosses the river *Taro* by a bridge of 20 arches, constructed 1816—21 (under Marie Louise, ex-Empress of the French, Duchess of Parma), whence a charming view is obtained of the chain of the Apennines. The peasant-women here wear quaint and picturesque costumes.

Parma, see p. 219.

S. Ilario is the only station between Parma and Reggio; before it is reached the train crosses the *Enza*, formerly the boundary between the duchies of Parma and Modena.

Montecchio, 5 M. to the S., was the birthplace of Attendolo Sforza, father of Francesco Sforza, from whom the dukes of Milan of the second dynasty were descended.

The train crosses the *Crostolo*, and reaches

Reggio *(Posta*, in the principal street; **Caffè Avanzi)*, the ancient *Rhegium Lepidi*, a town with broad, well-constructed streets with arcades (popul. 21,174). The house in which the poet *Lodovico Ariosto* (d. 1533) was born in 1474, near the Palazzo del Comune, is still shown. In the Piazza is situated the **Cathedral*, erected in the 15th cent.; at the principal entrance are colossal statues of Adam and Eve by Clementi of Reggio, a pupil of Michael Angelo. The church contains other statues and sculptures by the same master, e. g. the monuments of Horatius Malegutius and of Ugo Rangoni, Bishop of Reggio (in the chapel r. of the choir). In the 1st chapel on the l. is the tomb with bust of Clementi, 1588. At the entrance to the Municipio is a marble bust of General Cialdini, who was born here. — The church of the **Madonna della Chiara*, erected in 1597, from Balbi's design, in the form of a Greek cross surmounted by a dome, is adorned with frescoes by Luca Ferrari (1605—54) of Reggio, a pupil of Guido Reni, by Tiarini of Bologna of the school of Caracci, and by Spada, etc. — *S. Prospero*, at the back of the cathedral, was erected in the 16th cent. on the site of an ancient Lombard structure, to which the six marble lions of the façade originally appertained; in the interior are frescoes (badly preserved) by Campi and Procaccini, and pictures by Tiarini. — The *Madonna della Concezione* is a handsome modern church adjoining the theatre. — Reggio also possesses a *Library* and a *Museum*, containing the natural history collection of the celebrated *Spallanzani*, born at Reggio in 1729 (d. 1799).

Diligence from Reggio in 8 hrs. to *Mantua*, corresponding with the trains.

Scandiano, 7 M. S. E. of Reggio, was the birthplace of the poet *Matteo Maria Bojardo* (1434—94), author of 'Orlando Innamorato'. Princes and men of letters (Petrarch among others) were frequent visitors at the château of the Bojardi, afterwards that of the Bentivogli.

Correggio, 9 M. N. E. of Reggio, formerly the capital of a principality belonging to the Duchy of Modena, was the birthplace (in 1494) of the celebrated painter *Antonio Allegri da Correggio*. Old copies of his two earliest works are preserved here.

Canossa, a village 11½ M. S. W. of Reggio, is commanded by the ruins of a castle of Countess Mathilde of Tuscany, situated on a rocky eminence. Here during three days, Jan 25th—28th, 1077, the Emp. Henry IV. performed penance in presence of Pope Gregory VII. It is reached from Reggio by the road leading to *Sassalba*, *Fivizzano*, *Sarzana*, and *Spezia* on the Mediterranean.

A short distance beyond Reggio the railway passes *S. Maurizio*, where Ariosto frequently resided at the house of the Maleguzzi. *Rubiera*, with a castle of the Bojardi (see above), is the only station between Reggio and Modena. The *Secchia* is then crossed.

Modena see R. 42.

The line continues to follow the direction of the Via Æmilia (p. 216). Near *S. Ambrogio* the *Panaro*, formerly the boundary between the Duchy of Modena and the States of the Church, is crossed. Stat. *Castel Franco*, a small town, is believed to have been the place *(Forum Gallorum)* where Antony was defeated by Octavian and Hirtius, B. C. 43. In the vicinity is the *Forte Urbano*, erected by Pope Urban VIII., now in a dilapidated condition.

Near stat. *Samoggia* and stat. *Lavino* the rivers of these names are crossed; then the narrow *Reno*, the ancient *Rhenus* or *Amnis Bononiensis*. Between *La Crocetta* and *Trebbo*, 1½ M. l. of the railway, a small island is situated in the river, supposed to be that on which the triumvirate, or alliance between Octavian, Antony, and Lepidus, regulating their administration of the Empire, was concluded about the close of Oct., B. C. 43, after the termination of the war of Mutina.

Farther on, an attractive district is traversed, and a view is obtained of the *Monte della Guardia* (p. 234) and the pilgrimage-

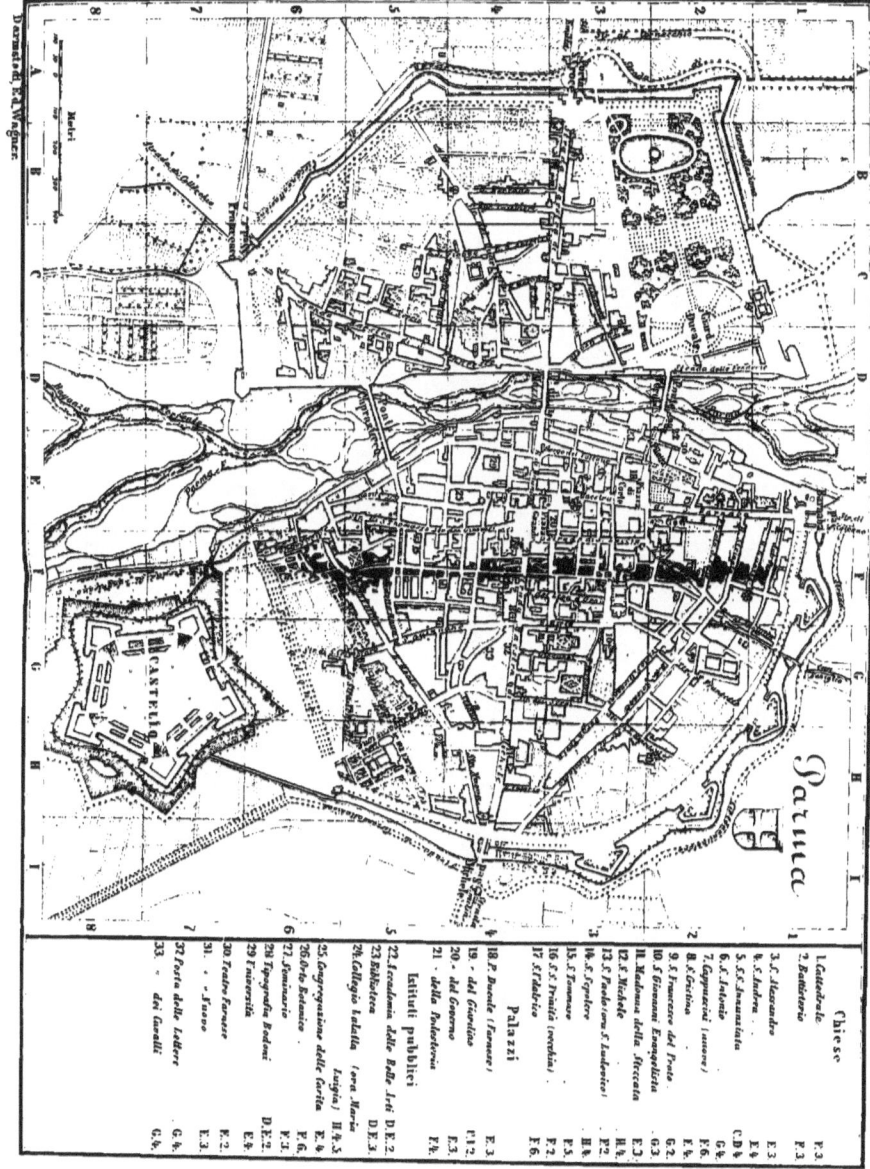

church of the Madonna di S. Luca. To the r. rises the tower of the Certosa (p. 233) with the Campo Santo. The approach to Bologna is remarkably picturesque.

Bologna see R. 43.

41. Parma.

Hotels. *Albergo della Posta, in the principal street, adjacent to the post office, R. 1½, L. ½, A. ½, Omnibus ¾ fr.; Concordia; Italia (Pension Suisse), Via S. Lucia, near the Piazza Grande, with restaurant; Pavone; Croce Bianca.

Restaurants. *Italia (see above), entrance from the side street; Café Cavour, Via S. Lucia.

Fiacres to or from the station 1 fr., two-horse 1 fr. 60 c.; at night 1½ or 2 fr.; omnibus 40 or 50 c., trunk 20 c.

Parmesan Cheese (*Parmeggiano*), here termed *Grana*, is strictly speaking a misnomer, as it is manufactured in Lombardy, in the district between the Ticino, Po, and Adda, and not in the neighbourhood of Parma. The most esteemed quality is produced at *Gorgonzola*, between Milan and Bergamo, about 2¼ M. N. of rail. stat. Melzo (p. 149).

Parma, situated on the river *Parma*, a town of entirely modern aspect, but of very ancient origin, was founded by the Etruscans, conquered by the Romans, and in B. C. 183 constituted a Roman colony at the same time with Mutina (Modena). It was subsequently extended by Augustus, and termed *Colonia Julia Augusta Parma*. In the middle ages it was the seat of the Guelphs, in 1245 besieged by Emp. Frederick II., and was afterwards the scene of a succession of fierce struggles between the rival Visconti, Scaligers (p. 165), Terzi, etc. In 1545 it became the seat of princes of the house of Farnese, who were Dukes of Parma and Modena, and in 1731 it was annexed to the dominions of Spain. In 1815 it became the capital of the Duchy of Parma under Marie Louise, ex-Empress of the French (d. 1848); its political independence was finally terminated by the well-known events of 1859—60.

Parma, capital of an episcopal diocese, with 47,067 inhab., possesses a university, numerous spacious, neglected looking edifices, and broad streets. The ancient *Via Æmilia* (p. 216) intersects the town, from the *Porta S. Michele* to the *Porta S. Croce*, crossing the *Piazza Grande with the *Palazzo del Comune*, or *del Governo* (Pl. 20), whence two streets to the r. lead to the *Piazza del Duomo*. The

***Cathedral** (Pl. 1), an admirable example of the Lombard-Romanesque style, begun 1117, but not completed till the 13th cent., is a cruciform structure surmounted by a dome, with somewhat raised choir above a crypt, and a broad façade with a triple columnar gallery. The three portals are embellished with two huge lions and four of smaller size, executed in 1281 by *Bono da Bisone*, and sculptures by *Bianchino*, 1493.

The Interior, consisting of nave and aisles, rests on 14 articulated pillars, above which runs a fine triforium. The 5th Chapel on the l. is adorned with ancient frescoes of Giotto's school. In the l. Transept (ascend steps) a Madonna in Gloria, as altar-piece, of the school of Raphael. The octagonal **Dome** is adorned with an *Assumption by *Correggio* (p. 218), to whom Parma is chiefly indebted for its importance in the history of art; this was one of the last (1522—30) great works of the master, but has unfortunately been almost entirely obliterated owing to the dampness of the church. The figures and groups of angels are especially admired. Noon is the most favourable hour for inspecting the painting. Persons not liable to dizziness may ascend to the dome itself, but the advantange thus gained is questionable. (Copies in the picture-gallery, see p. 221.) To the r. above the tribune are portraits of Correggio and his family. In the Choir, David and St. Cecilia, by *Camillo Procaccini*. The Crypt, a spacious cruciform structure with 38 columns, contains monuments of the Canon Montini, the jurist Prati, Bernardo degli Uberti etc. — In the 3rd chapel from the altar a Descent from the Cross, a relief by *Benedetto Antelami*, 1178. The Cap. S. Agata, the first beyond the side-entrance, contains a monument (1713) to the memory of *Petrarch*, who was archdeacon of the cathedral of Parma.

The *Baptistery (Pl. 2), constructed of white marble darkened by age, consisting of six stories with colonnades, was designed by *Benedetto Antelami*, and erected 1196—1270. It is externally octagonal, with four round-arched portals. Around almost the entire structure runs a series of medallions, representing various animals of symbolical import. The portals are adorned with scriptural subjects (e. g. that on the W. with the Last Judgment). All these sculptures are by *Antelami* and *Filippo Mazzuoli*. The flat roof is surmounted by eight turrets.

The Interior (closed; key in the house opposite the S. entrance) is sixteen-sided, with three stories, and graceful columns on the walls. The sculptures have only been partially completed. The old frescoes in the dome, of the school of Giotto (14th cent.), represent the history of John the Baptist, with a number of saints below. The entire population of Parma since the year 1216 is said to have been baptized here. The font dates from 1294.

In the rear of the cathedral is situated the church of

*S. Giovanni Evangelista (Pl. 10), appertaining to an ancient Benedictine monastery, now restored. This elegant cruciform structure, surmounted by a dome, with aisles and two series of chapels, was erected in 1510 by *Bernardino de' Zaccagni*.

Interior. In the two first chapels on the l., frescoes by *Parmeggianino* (SS. Lucia and Apollonia, two deacons, S. Giorgio and S. Agata); in the 2nd chapel on the r., Nativity, by *Fr. Francia*, 1518. The sombre **Dome** is adorned with *frescoes by *Correggio*, representing Christ in glory, surrounded by apostles and angels, painted in 1520—24 (the best time to inspect them is at noon or 4 p. m.; copies in the picture-gallery, see p. 221). The half-dome of the Choir contains a Coronation of Mary, after Correggio, by *Mazzuoli* (the original of the principal group is in the Library, p. 222; copies by Ann. and Ag. Caracci in the picture-gallery, see p. 221). In the archway of the door of the sacristy (l. transept) *S. Giovanni by *Correggio*. Among the guests who have been entertained in the monastery were King Charles Emmanuel, when a fugitive in 1798, Pope Pius VI. as a prisoner of the French in 1799, and Pope Pius VII. in 1805.

*Madonna della Steccata (Pl. 11), an imitation of St. Peter's, designed by *Francesco Zaccagna* in 1521, s tuated in the street leading from the principal piazza to the (formerly) ducal palace, is regarded as the finest church in Parma. It contains frescoes by *Anselmi* and *Parmeggianino*, monuments of Sforzino Sforza,

Bertrand Rossi, Ottavio Farnese, and in the crypt the tomb of Alessandro Farnese. The *monument of Count Neipperg, second husband of the empress Marie Louise of France, a group in white marble by *Bartolini* (1829), formerly in S. Paolo, has been transferred hither.

In the *Piazza di Corte* is situated the *Palazzo Ducale (Pl. 18), which contains reminiscences of Marie Louise, and a collection of French pictures by *David, Gérard, Le Gros*, etc.

To the N.E. of the Palazzo Ducale, which is passed on the r., is the *Palazzo Farnese, containing a very valuable collection of antiquities and pictures, as well as a considerable library (visitors cross the court and ascend a broad flight of steps to the l.), accessible daily 9—4, and on festivals 10—2 o'clock.

On the first floor is the Museo di Antichità, containing Rom. antiquities, most of them from Velleia (p. 85). The two first rooms contain inscriptions from Velleia and Parma, and a mosaic representing a gladiator. — 3rd R.: Bronzes; statuette of the drunken Hercules with dedication inscribed on it; head of Hadrian in gilded bronze; candelabra; the *Tabula Alimentaria* of Trajan, containing directions with regard to the maintenance of poor children. — 4th R.: Several Egyptian antiquities, statuettes in bronze, two heads of Jupiter. — 5th R.: Bust of Marie Louise by *Canova*; four statues with drapery, from Velleia, admirably executed. Finally a collection of coins, with well-preserved specimens in gold, and trinkets of the later period of the Empire. — Strangers may also obtain access to two rooms containing architectural fragments from the Roman theatre at Parma, and curiosities dating from the most ancient 'flint-period' in Italy, similar to those found in the barrows of England and the lake-dwellings of Switzerland.

The *Picture Gallery is on the second floor. The 1st Room contains nothing worthy of note. — 2nd R.: l. the celebrated *Madonna della Scala (formerly in the church della Scala) by *Correggio*, al fresco, unfortunately seriously damaged. — Next two rooms unimportant. — 5th R.: Christ in glory, with the Madonna, SS. John, Paul, and Catharine, attributed to *Raphael*; *Murillo*, Job; *Van der Helst*, Portrait. — 6th R.: Descent from the Cross, and Martyrdom of Placidus and Flavia, by *Correggio*; *Fr. Francia*, Madonna; *Cima da Conegliano*, two Madonnas; Portrait of Erasmus, attributed to *Holbein*; Head by *Leon. da Vinci*. — The adjoining room contains water-colour *copies of the works of Correggio, by the talented engraver *Toschi* (d. 1854). — 7th R.: *Correggio*, Madonna di S. Girolamo. — 8th R.: *Toschi*, Drawings after Correggio. — 9th R.: *Correggio*, Madonna della Scodella, considered the chef d'oeuvre of this great master. — 10th R.: Portraits. — 11th R.: Landscapes. — 12th R.: Works by modern artists; two colossal statues of Hercules and Bacchus in basalt, found in the imperial palaces at Rome. — 13th R.: Over the entrance, on the r. and l., and also at the farther extremity of the room, *copies of Correggio's Coronation of Mary (in S. Giovanni, p. 220) by *Annibale* and *Agostino Caracci*. Then to the r., farther on: *Fr. Francia*, Descent from the Cross, and Enthroned Madonna; *Lod. Caracci*, Entombment of Mary; *Titian*, Christ bearing the Cross; *Giov. Bellini*, Christ as a boy with the Scriptures; l. *Annib. Caracci*, Descent from the Cross. Statue of Marie Louise in a sitting posture, in marble, by *Canova*. The door to the l. at the upper extremity of the room leads to the former studio of the engraver *Toschi*, which contains admirable engravings from Correggio, Raphael, etc.

The door opposite to the picture-gallery in the same story leads to the *Library (Pl. 23), containing 80,000 vols. and 4000 MSS.; several of the latter are of Oriental origin, amongst them the Koran which the Emp. Leopold I. found in 1683 in the tent of the grand vizier Cara Mustapha after the raising of the siege of the Vienna; the 'livre d'heures' (prayer-book) of Henry II.; a Dante written by Petrarch in 1370; the original fresco of *Correggio's* Coronation of Mary from S. Giovanni (p. 220); a room with frescoes by *Franc. Scaramuzza*, now the director of the academy, representations from the 'Divine Comedy', completed in 1857.

Here too is the decaying **Teatro Farnese** (keys kept by the custodian of the picture-gallery, fee 30 c.), erected in 1618—28 by Duke Ranuccio Farnese. The former ducal *Tipografia* (Pl. 28), founded by *Bodoni* in 1766, is celebrated for its admirable printing.

The custodians of the picture-gallery also keep the keys (fee 50 c.) of the

*Convento di S. Paolo (Pl. 13), formerly a Benedictine nunnery, now an educational establishment, an insignificant structure, but remarkable for the charming *Frescoes by *Correggio* in the *Camera di S. Paolo*, one of the apartments, which was thus decorated by order of the abbess Giovanna da Piacenza in 1519 (the best preserved works of the master): over the chimney piece Diana, on the ceiling Cupids and emblems of the chase, on the frieze the Graces, Fortuna, Adonis, etc. The most favourable light is in sunny weather, 10—12 a. m. The adjacent room was adorned with paintings by *Al. Alardi* (d. 1528).

Quitting the museum and crossing the small river *Parma* by the *Ponte Verde*, the stranger soon reaches the (formerly) *Ducal Garden*, at the N. extremity of which is situated the ***Palazzo del Giardino** (Pl. 19), erected by Ottavio Farnese, and adorned with numerous frescoes. One of the apartments contains the Rape of Europa, the Triumph of Venus, the Marriage of Peleus and Thetis, etc., by *Agostino Caracci*.

The garden adjoins the *Stradone*, a promenade encircling the town, and laid out on the site of the former fortifications.

From Parma to Mantua diligence twice daily, see p. 171.

42. Modena.

Hotels. Albergo Reale (Pl. a), R. 2, L. 1|2, D. 3—4, A. 3|4 fr.; Albergo S. Marco (Pl. b); Mondatora (Pl. c); Leopardo (Pl. d). — Caffè Nazionale; Corso Vittorio Em. — *Arena Goldoni*, an open-air theatre near the Porto Bologna (1 or 1|2 fr.). — *Zanichelli*, bookseller, Corso di Via Emilia.

Modĕna, with 55,000 inhab., formerly the capital of the duchy of that name, and now of the province of Emilia, is situated in a fertile plain between the *Secchia* and the *Panaro*. It possesses broad streets, spacious arcades, a university, academy of art, etc. It was the *Mutina* of the ancients, in the dominions of the Gallic Boii; it became a Roman colony B. C. 183, situated on the high road from Rome to Mediolanum (Milan), and therefore a place of importance.

After the murder of Cæsar, Brutus was besieged here during 4 months, Dec. 44 to April 43 B. C., by Antony (*Bellum Mutinense*); but the latter was defeated by Octavian with the consuls Pansa and Hirtius, and compelled to raise the siege. — In the middle ages Modena belonged to the estates of the Countess Mathilde, but eventually obtained its independence and became the scene of violent conflicts between the Guelphs and Ghibellines.

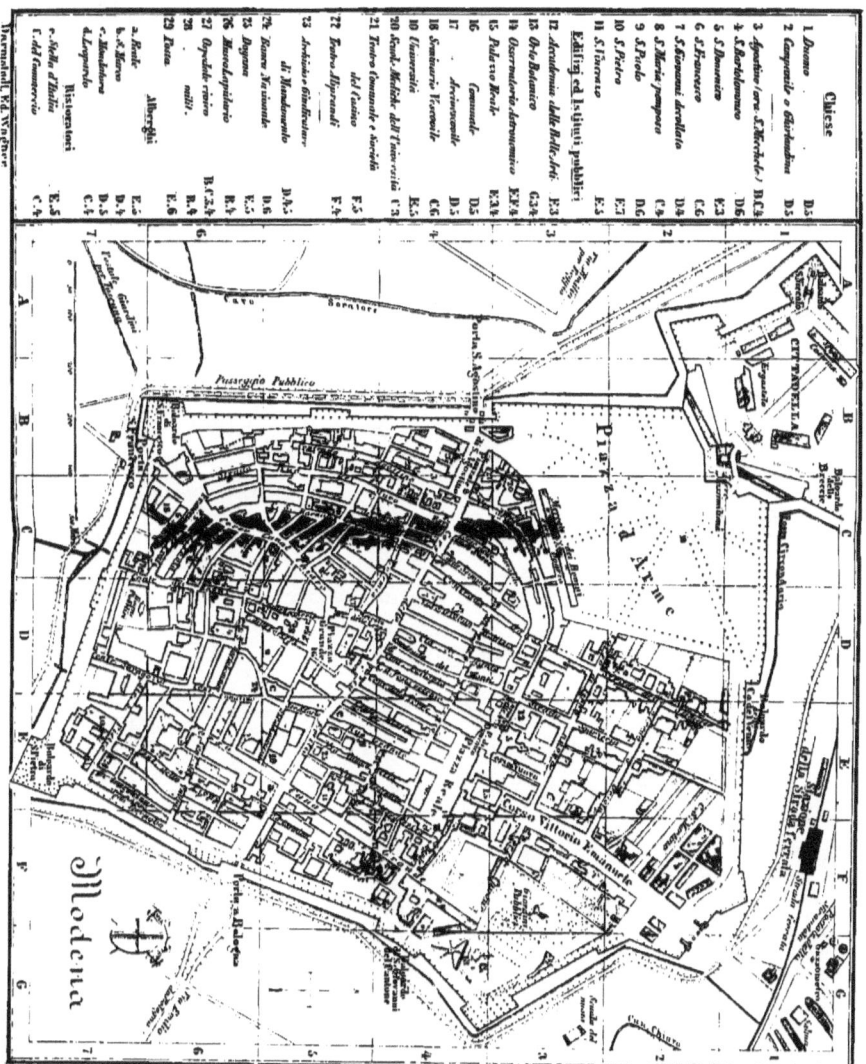

In 1288 *Obizzo d'Este* gained possession of the supreme power, which his descendants continued to enjoy. In 1452 *Borso* was created *Duke of Modena* by Emp. Frederick III., and in 1470 obtained the title of Duke of Ferrara from Pope Paul II. The House of Este now soon attained the zenith of its glory. *Hercules I.* (1471–1505) and his son Cardinal *Hippolytus d'Este* (1479–1520) were the patrons of Ariosto, and *Alphonso II.* (1558–97) the patron of Tasso (comp. p. 181). On the death of Alphonso II., without issue, the states of Modena and Reggio (but not that of Ferrara) fell to his kinsman *Cesare d'Este* (1598), husband of Virginia de' Medici, daughter of Grandduke Cosmo I. of Florence. *Hercules III.* (d. 1803), who by the Peace of Luneville lost Modena in 1801, was the last of the family of Este. Through his daughter Beatrice, who married Archduke Ferdinand, the duchy came into the possession of the younger branch of the House of Austria. Francis V., the last duke, quitted his dominions in consequence of the events of 1859 and went over to the Austrians.

The *Cathedral (Pl. 1), begun in the Romanesque style in 1099, consecrated in 1184, has a superstructure of later date. The façade is relieved by a large wheel-window and a single gallery of columns which is continued round the entire building. The portals are adorned with the often recurring marble lions. The rude sculptures of the façade, representing the history of the first men and the death of King Arthur, are by *Nicolaus* and *Guilelmus* (about 1099); on the S. side, to the r. near the choir, is the history of St. Geminianus, a relief by *Agostino da Firenze*, 1422.

The Interior is low and heavy, but of imposing proportions. The nave and aisles are supported by alternate pillars and columns, over which runs a triforium; below are round arches and galleries supported by columns; above, the arches are pointed. Pulpit by *Tommaso di Campione*, 1322; behind it, to the l., a very ancient font, adapted for the purpose from the capital of a column. Choir-stalls by *Cristoforo Lendenari*, 1465; r. in the choir sculptures of the 16th cent., representing the history of the Passion. In the 2nd chapel l., an altar of terra cotta; 3 rd chapel l., a Coronation of Mary with saints on a gold ground, by *Serafinus de Serafinis*, the oldest extant picture of the school of Modena; 4th chapel l., St. Sebastian with John the Baptist and other saints, by *Dosso Dossi*. By the l. entrance to the choir are several fine monuments of the Rangoni family, especially that (designed by *Giulio Romano*) of Claudio, Count of Castelvetro (d. 1537), husband of Lucrezia, daughter of the celebrated and erudite Pico of Mirandola (p. 171); also that of Hercules III. of Este (d. at Treviso in 1803). The crypt, supported by 30 slender columns, with four lions at the entrance, contains the tomb of St. Geminianus; over the altar on the r. a Madonna and four saints by *Mazzoni*.

The *Campanile, or *La Ghirlandina* (Pl. 2), erected 1224—1319, 315 ft. in height, is one of the four finest in N. Italy. It leans slightly towards the rear of the cathedral, which is itself somewhat out of the perpendicular.

In the campanile an old *Secchia*, or pitcher, is preserved, which the Modenese *(Geminiani)* captured from the Bolognese *(Petronii)* at the battle of Rapolino, Nov. 15th, 1325. *Alessandro Tassoni* of Modena (1565–1635) has humorously described this incident in his comic epic poem 'La Secchia Rapita' (1616). A monument to his memory was erected in 1860 in the principal street, behind the cathedral.

S. Pietro (Pl. 10) is a spacious church with double aisles, façade of brick, and barrel-vaulting. Over the 3rd altar on the r. an Assumption by *Dosso Dossi*; in the chapel r. of the choir, Mourning for the dead Christ, in terra cotta, by *Antonio Begarelli* of Modena (d. 1555). The six statues in the nave are by the same master. The Madonna and Child with saints, a group in the r. transept, was commenced by Begarelli and completed by his nephew Lodovico.

S. Francesco (Pl. 6) contains a *Descent from the Cross (in the chapel l. of the choir) by *Begarelli*, an imposing composition in terra cotta, with 13 life-size figures.

S. Agostino, now *S. Michêle* (Pl. 3), contains the tombs of the celebrated savants *Carolus Sigonius* (1524—85) and *Lod. Ant. Muratori* (1672—1750) of Modena. The latter was especially eminent as an historian of Italy; a monument to him has been erected in the Piazza Muratori, in the Corso della Via Emilia.

Opposite to S. Agostino is the church of *S. Maria Pomposa* (Pl. 8); 1st altar r., Pietà by *Begarelli*.

The **Museo Lapidario**, in a court to the l. of S. Agostino, contains several ancient inscriptions and mediæval sarcophagi.

The *Palazzo Ducale (Pl. 15), a magnificent edifice, commenced under Francis I. in 1634 by the Roman *Bartolommeo Avanzini*, contains a Picture Gallery (open daily 9—3; entrance at the back of the palace, 2nd floor).

2nd Room: *Gherardo da Harlem*, Crucifixion; *Bianchi Ferrari* (master of Correggio), Annunciation; *Filippo Lippi*, Madonna; *Mantegna*, Crucifixion. — 3rd R.: *Correggio*, Angels; then 9 frescoes from the Æneid by *Niccolò da Modena* (1512—71), transferred to canvas. — 4th R.: *Titian*, Portrait of a woman; *Palma Vecchio*, Madonna with saints; *Bonifazio*, Adoration of the Magi; *Cima da Conegliano*, Descent from the Cross. — 5th R.: *Guido Reni*, Christ on the Cross. This and the 8th R. contain a number of drawings, unfortunately in disorder. — 6th R.: *Garofalo*, Madonna and saints; *Dosso Dossi*, Adoration of the Child, and other pictures. — 8th R.: Landscapes by *Claude Lorrain* and *Canaletto* (among the drawings the Judgment of Paris and the Flight of Helen are worthy of note). — 9th R.: *Andrea del Sarto*, Madonna. — 10th R.: Pictures by *Malatesta*, director of the gallery. (An adjoining room, usually closed, containing the portrait of a Benedictine by *Murillo*, a Madonna by *Sassoferrato*, and a small St. John by *Bern. Luini*, leads to another apartment with a collection of mediæval curiosities). — 11th R.: Large pictures by *Dosso Dossi*, *Procaccini*, etc.; four landscapes by *Salvator Rosa*.

On the first floor of the palace is the **Library** *(Biblioteca Estense)*, with 90,000 vols. and 3000 MSS. (closed Aug. 1st to Oct. 1st), transferred by Duke Cesare d'Este from Ferrara to Modena in 1598, when Pope Clement VIII. claimed the Duchy of Ferrara as a vacant fief. The three eminent scholars *Zaccaria*, *Tiraboschi*, and *Muratori* (see above) were once librarians here. Some of the MSS. are very valuable, e. g. a collection of Provençal poems by Ferrari (1254), Dante with miniatures of the 14th cent. The same building also contains the Cabinet of Coins and the *Archives.

The well-kept *Gardens* of the palace (closed in rainy weather only), as well as the ramparts of the town, afford pleasant promenades.

From Modena to Mantua, diligence twice daily, see p. 171.

BOLOGNA. *43. Route.* 225

Nonantŏla, a small town 5¹/₂ M. N.E. of Modena, possesses an Abbey founded in the 18th cent., frequently mentioned in the wars between Bologna and Modena, and once noted for its wealth and its magnificent Library (the latter has been described by *Tiraboschi*). The *Church* and the *Seminary* with lofty tower are the most remarkable edifices.

Vignŏla, 12¹/₂ M. S.E. of Modena, on the *Panaro*, is situated on an eminence and commands the landscape far and wide. The celebrated *Muratori* and the architect *Giacomo Barozzi da Vignola* were born here.

Duke Francis III. of Modena constructed (about 1779) a bold and interesting, but now much neglected road hence to Pistoja, a distance of 46 M., leading by *Formigine*, *Serra*, *Paullo*, *Pieve a Pelago*, and *Fiumalbo*, at the base of the lofty *Monte Cimone*, where charming views of the Apennines are obtained. — To the W. of this road, about 10¹/₂ M. S.W. of Modena, is situated **Sassuola**, a small town on the *Secchia*, with a ducal *Villa and beautiful park. The neighbouring mountain *Zibio* is remarkable for its naphtha springs and occasional volcanic eruptions.

43. Bologna.

Hotels. *Hôtel Brun (*Pension Suisse*, Pl. a), in the Palazzo Malvasia, Strada Ugobassi, R. 3, D. 4, A. 1 fr., from the Loggia good survey of the town; Albergo Bologna (formerly *Tre Mori*), S. Marco (Pl. b), Pellegrino (Pl. c), all in the Strada Ugobassi, R. 2 fr. and upwards; Commercio, Italia, both in the Via di Petra Fitta. — Pace, Aquila, in the Calca Vinazzi, a side street of Ugobassi; Europa, Str. Ugobassi; Tre Re, R. 1¹/₂, L. ¹/₂, A. ¹/₂ fr., Omnibus 60 c.; Quattro Pellegrini, Bella Venezia, these three in the Mercato di Mezzo; Cannon d'Oro, corner of Via Porta Nova and Via Gombruti, R. 1¹/₄—2 fr.

Restaurants. *Ristorante Felsineo, Mercato di Mezzo near the Piazza Vitt. Em., on the 1st floor; *Caffè del Corso, Strada S. Stefano; also in most of the hotels. (The '*Mortadella*', or Bologna sausage, and the '*Cervellato*', a variety used in winter, are much esteemed by the natives.)

Cafés. The most frequented, in the arcades near the Palazzo Pubblico, and in the streets S. of S. Petronio, are somewhat sombre and uninviting. La Barchetta; Majani (confectioner); *delle Scienze, Via Miola; del Commercio, opposite Hôtel Brun; Caffè de' Negozianti; *del Corso (see above); Caffè de' Servi, Via Maggiore. — *Beer:* *Birraria e Caffeteria della Ditta Neviani in the side passage of the Piazza, E. of S. Petronio; *Birraria e Ristoratore Milano, Via Miola, adjacent to the Caffè delle Scienze; Nuovo Caffè del Pavaglione in the Piazza, W. of S. Petronio; Mayr's Fabbrica di Birra, Via Pratello; Brewery at the S.W. side of the Piazza d'Armi, etc.

Railway Station outside the *Porta Galliera*, N.W. of the Montagnola (p. 233). Railway to Ancona see R. 44; to Ferrara (and Ponte Lagoscuro) see R. 37; to Ravenna (by Castel Bolognese) see R. 46; to Florence (by Pistoja) see R. 47; to Piacenza see R. 40.

Post Office (Pl. 80), in the street S.W. of Hôtel Brun, adjoining the church of S. Francesco. — *Telegraph Office* in the Palazzo Comunale, 1st floor.

Fiacres. Per hr. 1¹/₂, each additional ¹/₂ hr. ³/₄ fr.; per drive ³/₄ fr.; to or from the station, with or without luggage, 1 fr. To S. Michele, for the first hr. 2¹/₂, each additional ¹/₂ hr. ³/₄ fr. After 10 p. m., in winter past 9 p. m., 50 c. more.

Baths. Bagni di S. Lucia, Strada Castiglione; alla Carità, Strada Ugobassi; delle Moline, Via delle Moline, near the Montagnola. Vapour-baths, corner of Via Repubblicana and Vicolo della Maddalena.

Theatres. Teatro del Comune (Pl. 72), the largest, erected by Bibiena in 1756 on the site of the Palazzo Bentivoglio. Contavalli (Pl. 73), established in 1814 in the former church of the Carmelites; del Corso (Pl. 74); Teatro Brunetti, in a side-street of the Strada Castiglione; Arena del Sole, Via de' Malcoltenti, near the Montagnola, open-air

BÆDEKER. Italy I. 2nd Edit. 15

theatre. *Marionette Theatre* in the evening in the Piazza Vittorio Emanuele.

Shops. The best are in the arcades near the Palazzo Pubblico.

The situation of Bologna is considered healthy, although the summer is frequently very hot and the winter keen. The character of the natives is generally described as spirited and restless. Art and science have attained a high degree of development here. The town is sometimes termed '*Bologna la grassa*', owing to its reputation for wealth and good-living. The neighbourhood produces tolerable wines and excellent fruit. The grapes are delicious; the yellow *Uva Paradisa* is a variety capable of being kept for a considerable time. — The once favourite lap-dogs of Bologna are now almost entirely extinct. Soap, maccaroni, and liqueurs are among the most esteemed commodities of the place. — The *Giuoco di Pallone*, or ball-game, is regarded at Bologna not only as an exercise, but also as an interesting spectacle; a large saloon (Pl. 76) in the Promenade Montagnola (p. 233) is fitted up for the purpose.

Principal Attractions: Piazza Vitt. Em. with Pal. Pubblico and del Podestà, *S. Petronio, *S. Domenico, S. Stefano, S. Giacomo Maggiore, S. Cecilia, *Accademia delle Belle Arti, the Leaning Towers, Loggia de' Mercanti, *Campo Santo, and, if possible, the *Madonna di S. Luca for the sake of the view. If time remains, the Arciginnasio Antico, the University, the Palaces Bacciocchi, Bevilacqua, etc. may be visited.

Bologna, one of the most ancient and important towns in Italy, the capital of the *Romagna*, or *Æmilia* as it was anciently termed, is situated in a fertile plain at the base of the Apennines, between the *Reno*, the *Aposa*, and the *Savena*. Popul. 89,850. It possesses 130 churches, 20 monasteries, and a venerable and celebrated university, whence the inscription on old coins '*Bononia docet*'.

The town was founded by the Etruscans and named *Felsina*, but was afterwards conquered by the Gallic Boii, and by them termed *Bononia*. In the Punic War it espoused the cause of Hannibal, after which, B. C. 190, it was converted into a Roman colony, at the same time as Cremona and Placentia, by the consul C. Lælius, and as such was a place of a great importance. During the period of the Empire it was even occasionally the residence of the monarchs themselves. It subsequently belonged to the Greek Exarchate, then to the Lombards and Franks. Charlemagne constituted Bologna a free town (whence its motto '*Libertas*'), and its commerce and prosperity rapidly increased. In 1119 the *University*, one of the oldest in the world, was founded, and as a *School of Jurisprudence*, where Irnerius and other celebrated jurists taught, soon attained an European reputation, and was visited by many thousand students annually. In 1262 the number is said to have nearly attained to 10,000; at the present day there are 400 only. Irnerius introduced the study of the Roman Law, whilst his successors the *Glossators* devoted their energies to its interpretation. The study of medicine and philosophy was introduced at a later period, and a theological faculty established by Pope Innocent VI. The anatomy of the human frame was first taught here in the 14th cent., and here galvanism was discovered by *Jos. Galvani* in 1789. It is a remarkable fact that the university of Bologna has numbered members of the fair sex among its professors. Thus in the 14th cent. *Novella d'Andrea*, a lady of great personal attractions, who is said to have been concealed by a curtain during her lectures; at a subsequent period *Laura Bassi* (mathematics and physical science), Mme. *Manzolina* (anatomy), and more recently (1794—1817) *Clotilda Tambroni* (Greek).

Bologna acted a very prominent part in the contests of the Guelphs and Ghibellines, espoused the cause of the former, and allied itself with the Pope against Emp. Frederick II. In a sanguinary encounter at Fossalta, in May, 1249, King *Enzio*, son of the Emperor, was captured by the Bolognese, and kept in confinement by them for the rest of his life (22 years). He was the founder of the family of the Bentivogli, afterwards so powerful, who after protracted feuds entered into an alliance with the papal throne. During several centuries the town was the scene of the party-struggles of the Bentivogli, Visconti, and other families, until in 1512 *Pope Julius II.* incorporated it with the States of the Church.

In 1515 the interview of Pope Leo X. with Francis I. of France took place at Bologna, and in 1529, 1530, and 1532 those of Clement VII. with Emp. Charles V. Here, too, in 1547 the Council of Trent assembled. In 1796 Bologna was annexed to the 'Cisalpine Republic' by Napoleon, in 1815 it again became subject to the States of the Church; in 1831 and 1849 revolutions broke out, and in 1859 the town finally united itself to the kingdom of Italy.

In the History of Art Bologna occupies a meritorious, but not independent position, more especially in the provinces of sculpture and architecture. *Francesco Francia* (1518) was the first painter of note here; then pupils of Raphael, such as *Bagnacavallo* and *Innocenzo da Imola*, and the adherents of the schools of Leonardo da Vinci and Correggio. During the latter half of the 16th cent. the School of the Caracci, of which eclecticism is the principal characteristic, was established at Bologna. Its founders were *Lodovico Caracci* and his cousins and pupils *Agostino* and *Annibale*. Their most illustrious pupils were *Guido Reni, Albano, Domenichino* (or *Domenico Zampieri), Tiarini*, and *Barbieri. Guercino* is also considered to belong to this school.

The antiquated aspect of the town, its picturesque mediæval architecture, lofty arcades, numerous old palaces, and venerable churches surmounted by quaint-looking towers, all bear testimony to the peculiar character of the place. The dialect spoken by the lower classes is almost wholly unintelligible to strangers.

The *Piazza Vittorio Emanuele (Pl. F, 4) (formerly *Piazza Maggiore*, or *del Gigante*), in the centre of the town, the mediæval 'forum' of Bologna, is one of the most interesting in Italy. It is adorned with a **Fountain** by *Laureti;* the bronze statue of Neptune was executed by *Giov. da Bologna* (born 1524 at Douay in Flanders) in 1564. It is said to weigh 10 tons, and to have cost 70,000 ducats.

In this Piazza is situated the **Palazzo Pubblico**, or *del Governo* (Pl. 45), commenced in 1290, adorned with a Madonna on the façade by *Niccolò dell' Arca*, and a bronze statue of Pope Gregory XIII. (Buoncompagni of Bologna) by *Menganti*, transformed in 1796 into a statue of St. Petronius. The grand staircase in the interior was designed by *Bramante;* the chapel with the 'Madonna del terremoto' is of 1505. The galleries and halls are decorated with frescoes; statue of Hercules in the hall of that name, by *Alfonso Lombardi;* in the Sala Farnese a statue of Paul III., etc.

Opposite to the latter is the **Palazzo del Podestà** (Pl. 44), of 1201, with façade of 1485, where King Enzio (p. 226) was kept a prisoner by the Bolognese, but derived great solace from his attachment to the beautiful Lucia Vendagoli, from whom the Bentivoglio family (p. 276) is descended. The great hall is termed after him *Sala del Rè Enzio*. The conclave for the election of Pope John XXIII. was held here in 1410. The palace contains the *Civic Archives*, with a number of ancient documents.

15*

The adjoining **Portico de' Banchi,** erected by *Vignola* is used for shops etc. Opposite to it is

*S. Petronio (Pl. 1), the largest church in the town, commenced in the Tuscan-Gothic style in 1390 from a design by *Antonio Vincenzi*, but never completed. It possesses an imposing transept and an octagonal dome rising above the crossing between four towers. The construction was abandoned in 1659, when the nave and aisles as far as the transept only were completed, being now terminated by an apse of the breadth of the nave. Length 383 ft., breadth with the chapels 156 ft. (originally projected length 798 ft.). The nave is of vast and noble dimensions, the aisles are flanked with series of chapels. The church is supported by 12 pillars with pointed vaulting, beneath which are small circular windows. The sculptures of the bare façade, representing saints, date from 1393; those of the principal entrance are by *Jacopo della Quercia*, 1425; side-doors, 1525.

Over the principal entrance of the church once stood during three years a bronze statue by *Michael Angelo*, of Pope Julius II. with the keys and a sword in his left hand. In 1511 it was destroyed by the populace and sold as old metal to the Duke of Ferrara, who employed it in casting a piece of ordnance ('Giuliano').

The Interior is adorned with numerous sculptures and pictures, many of them of great value. The handsome marble screens by which most of the chapels are enclosed, dating from the 14th, 15th, and 16th cent., should be observed. In the 1st Chapel on the r. the Madonna della Pace by *Hans Ferrabech*, and an altar-piece (God the Father with angels) by *Giacomo Francia*; in the 2nd Chapel (r.) curious old frescoes of the year 1407. Between the 3rd and 4th chapels the tombstone of Archb. Oppizzoni (d. 1855). 4th Chapel: Old stained glass by *Jacob of Ulm*. 8th Chapel: Canopy by *Vinc. Franceschini;* inlaid stalls by Fra Raffaele da Brescia. 9th Chapel (di S. Antonio): Statue of the saint, an early work of *Sansovino*, and Miracles wrought by him, in grisaille, by *Girolamo da Treviso;* fine stained glass from designs by *Pellegrino Tibaldi*. Opposite to the 11th Chapel: Assumption of Mary, a high-relief by *Nicolo Tribolo*. The sacristy contains pictures of no great value. The Reverenda Fabbrica (workshop) on the l. (W.) side of the choir contains 40 sketches of the unfinished façade, by *Palladio, Giulio Romano, Vignola* etc., an interesting collection; also a model of the church in wood. The Cappella Bacciocchi (7th from the entrance on the l.) contains the monument of princess Elisa Bacciocchi (d. 1820), grand-duchess of Tuscany and sister of Napoleon, and of her husband Felix; opposite to it, that of two of her children, both admirable groups in marble by the two *Franzoni*. Over the altar a Madonna by *Lorenzo Costa*. The 4th Chapel (on the l.), the oldest in the church, consecrated in 1392, contains ancient frescoes: Adoration of the Magi, with Paradise and Hell beneath, recalling Dante's poem; altar with sculptures in marble, and stained glass by *Jacob of Ulm*, also worthy of note. Between this and the 3rd chapel are two clocks manufactured by Fornasini in 1756, one of which gives the solar, the other the mean time. On the pavement of the l. aisle is the meridian-line drawn by the celebrated astronomer *Gian. Domenico Cassini* in 1653.

To the S. E. of S. Petronio is situated the **Arciginnasio Antico** (Pl. 4, entrance under the Portici del Pavaglione), erected as a university in 1562, and since its transference to the Palazzo Cellesi (p. 230) employed as a *Biblioteca Comunale* (open daily 10—4, exc. Sund.; several valuable MSS.). The Loggie of the court contain numerous monuments, adorned with armorial bearings, to the memory of professors of the university (Muratori, Peggi, Malpighi, Mariani, etc.). The museum of antiquities here is of little value.

***S. Domenico**, formerly *S. Bartolommeo* (Pl. 10), was rededicated to St. Dominic, who was born in Castile in 1170, and died here in 1221. The church, which is in the circular style, dates from the 12th cent., but was completely remodelled during the 18th.

Interior. 3rd Chapel on the r., on the lower part of the altar a Madonna by *Franc. Francia*, under glass; 5th Chapel on the r., old Italian Madonna; 6th Chapel on the r., that of S. Domenico, containing the tomb of the saint, a sarcophagus ('arca') of white marble dating from 1267, with reliefs from the life of the saint, by pupils of *Giovanni Pisano;* reliefs of the front probably by the master himself, those of the base by *F. Lombardi.* The kneeling *angel on the l. and St. Petronius are by *Michael Angelo.* Additions were made to the work in 1469 and 1532. In the half-dome over the 'arca' a transfiguration of the saint, by *Guido Reni*. In the Choir magnificent inlaid stalls by *Fra Damiano da Bergamo*, 1528—51, among the finest of the kind in Italy. Between the 1st and 2nd chapels on the l. of the choir is the monument of 'Hencius Rex', or king Enzio (p. 227), frequently restored; in the 2nd chapel that of Taddeo Pepoli, of 1337; opposite to it a portrait of St. Thomas Aquinas (d. 1274). In the l. aisle is the Cappella del Rosario with handsome frescoes by *Guido Reni* and *Lod. Caracci*, containing monuments of Guido Reni (d. 1642) and of the talented paintress *Elisabeth Sirani* (died of poison at the age of 25, in 1655). In the vestibule of the side-entrance is the monument of the jurist Alessandro Tartagni, by *Francesco di Simone* (1477).

In the Piazza di S. Domenico, besides two columns with statues of the saint and the Madonna, are two curious old *Monuments* of the 13th cent., the more important of which, standing alone, was erected in honour of *Rolandino Passeggieri*, who distinguished himself in the contests between the town and the Emp. Fred. Barbarossa (restored in 1868).

***S. Stefano** (Pl. 36), a pile consisting of seven different churches, containing ancient columns and mural paintings, bears an inscription on the exterior, recording that it was founded on the site of a temple of Isis, probably in the 15th cent. The churches are not all on the same level, the last having been constructed as a crypt below the first, and have been differently arranged and fitted up according to the period of their erection. The round church with the tomb of St. Petronius is the oldest and most important at Bologna. An open court, termed the *Atrio di Pilato* forms the centre of the pile; it contains a Coronation of Mary, fresco by *Bagnacavallo*, and a Christ on the cross, with St. Jerome and other Saints, by *Fr. Francia*. The neighbouring monastery, now suppressed, possesses fine cloisters of the 11th cent.

S. Giacomo Maggiore (Pl. 13), founded 1267, consisting of a nave with barrel-vaulting of 1497, is adorned with several excellent pictures.

On the altar, immediately to the r. of the entrance, is the 'Vergine della Cintura', attributed to *Franc. Francia* (covered with a view of the town of Bologna, over which angels hover); 7th Chapel on the r. Marriage of St. Catharine, by *Innocenzo da Imola;* 9th Chapel, St. Rochus with an angel, by *Lod. Caracci;* 11th Chapel, erected by *Pellegr. Tibaldi*, and decorated by him with frescoes. In the Choir large paintings of the Resurrection etc. by *Tommaso Lauretti*. In the 3rd of the choir-chapels a gilded altar with numerous saints, 1. on the wall a large painted crucifix by *Simone de' Crocefissi* (1319?); 5th Chapel, sculptures in marble by *Gius. Mazza*; 6th °Cap. de' Bentivogli contains a Madonna, the best work of *Fr. Francia*, and frescoes by *Lorenzo Costa*; opposite to it the monument of *Antonio Bentivoglio* (d. 1435) by *Jacopo della Quercia*. The 9th Chapel in the left aisle contains a Presentation in the Temple, by *Agost. Caracci*.

The sacristan of S. Giacomo is also the custodian of the adjacent oratory of *S. Cecilia (Pl. 6), erected in 1481 by Giovanni Bentivoglio, and adorned with superb paintings. The frescoes by *Fr. Francia* and his pupils represent the legend of St. Valerian and St. Cecilia (Nos. 1. and 10. by *Fr. Francia*, 2. and 9. by *Costa*, 3. and 8. by *Giacomo Francia*, 4. by *Chiodarolo*, 5., 6., and 7. by *Aspertini*.

Among the other churches may be mentioned:

S. Giovanni in Monte (Pl. 15), one of the oldest churches in Bologna, founded by St. Petronius in 433, was re-erected in the Gothic style in 1221, restored 1824. It is adorned with paintings by *Lor. Costa* (Coronation of Mary in the choir) and *Guercino* (3rd chapel r.). The 7th chapel on the l. contained Raphael's St. Cecilia (now in the museum, p. 231) till 1796. The 6th chapel on the l. contains an admirable bronze statue of Christ over the altar.

S. Martino Maggiore (Pl. 26), a church of the Carmelites in the Gothic style, dates from 1313. The 1st chapel on the l. contains an Enthroned Madonna with angels, by *Fr. Francia*; over the 5th altar on the l. an Assumption by *Lorenzo Costa*; 5th altar r., Madonna and two saints, by *Amico Aspertini*.

S. Pietro, the cathedral (Pl. 2), begun in 1605, with circular vaulting, and destitute of aisles, has a series of spacious chapels on each side, over which is a triforium. In the chapter-room St. Peter with the Madonna; above the choir an Annunciation, the last work of *Lod. Caracci*. — Adjoining it on the N. is the *Palazzo Arcivescovile* (Pl. 42), with a handsome court constructed by Tibaldi in 1577. — In the vicinity, to the N.W. of S. Pietro, is the small church of the *Madonna di Galliera* (Pl. 20), possessing an interesting, but dilapidated façade of 1470.

S. Vitale ed Agricola (Pl. 38) was consecrated by St. Petronius in 428. The large chapel on the l. contains an altar-piece by *Fr. Francia*; the frescoes on the r. side are by *Giac. Francia*, those on the l. by *Bagnacavallo*.

If the traveller who has come from S. Cecilia continue to follow the Strada Luigi Zamboni (formerly Str. S. Donato), he will soon reach (on the r.) the **University,** established since 1803 in the former *Palazzo Cellesi* (Pl. 47), with a superb court, erected by Triachini, after that of Salerno the oldest in Italy, founded 1119, now possessing a staff of 58 professors (400 stud.) and a considerable number of scientific institutions (clinical hospital, anatomical theatre, natural history collections, botanical garden, and observatory). The *Museum of Antiquities* contains inscriptions, sculptures etc. The extensive *Library* of 100,000 vols. is accessible daily, except Sundays, 9—3 o'clock. The oldest of the MSS. is that of Lactantius; also letters from Voltaire to Fred. the Great, miniatures, etc. The celebrated linguist *Giuseppe Mezzofanti* (born at Bologna 1776, cardinal under Pope Gregory XVI. in 1837, died at Naples 1849), professor of Oriental languages at the university, was once librarian here. At the age of 35 he is said to have spoken 18 languages fluently, and at the period of his death no fewer than 42. — The *Archives* comprise a number of ancient documents on papyrus, the Codex Diplomaticus Bononiensis in 44 vols. etc. — The *Tower* commands a good survey of the town.

Crossing the Via Zamboni the traveller next reaches the **Accademia delle Belle Arti* (Pl. 39), established in the former College of the Jesuits. It contains on the ground-floor collections of casts etc., and on the first floor a collection of weapons *(Oploteca)*, the latter comprising arms captured from the Turks, Venetians, etc.; also a superb **Picture Gallery*, or *Pinacoteca*, consisting chiefly of works of the Bolognese School (accessible daily, 9—3 o'clock). Visitors ring. Catalogue (1½ fr.) unnecessary; fees prohibited.

1st Room (opposite the entrance): 82. *Fr. Francia*, Scene from the life of Christ; also pictures by *Guercino*, the two *Sirani*, the *Caracci, Massari*, and *Lavinia Fontana*. — 2nd R.: r. 37. *Ann. Caracci*, Madonna with saints; 2. *Albano*, Baptism of Christ; *42. *Lod. Caracci*, Madonna with SS. Dominicus, Francis, Clara, and Mary Magdalene, being portraits of members of the Bargellini family, at whose cost the picture was painted; *206. *Domenichino*, Martyrdom of St. Agnes; *36. *Ann. Caracci*, Madonna with SS. Lewis, Alexis, John the Baptist, Francis, Clara and Catharine; 35. *Ag. Caracci*, Assumption; 47. *Lod. Caracci*, Conversion of Paul; 183. *Tiarini*, Nuptials of St. Catharine; 34. *Ag. Caracci*, Communion of St. Jerome; 46. *Lod. Caracci*, Preaching of John the Baptist. — 3rd R.: r. 198. *Giorgio Vasari*, Banquet of Gregory the Great, who here bears the features of Clement VII.; 80. *Fr. Francia*, Madonna with SS. Augustine, Sebastian, and John the Baptist; 210. Youthful John, after *Raphael*; 26. *Bugiardino*, Nuptials of St. Catharine; **152. *Raphael's* St. Cecilia listening to the heavenly music in an ecstatic trance, surrounded by SS. Paul, John, Augustine, and Mary Magdalene. This exquisite picture (which should be viewed from some distance), the gem of the collection, was painted for the chapel of the Bentivogli in S. Giovanni in Monte (p. 230). It was at Paris, 1796—1815. A duplicate figure of the saint alone was purchased some years ago by the King of Bavaria. 133. *Bagnacavallo*, Holy Family; 81. *Fr. Francia*, Madonna and saints adoring the Child; *78. *Fr. Francia*, Madonna with SS. Augustine, Sebastian, John the Baptist, etc., painted in 1490; 197. *Perugino*, Madonna in glory with Saints; 79. *Fr. Francia*, Madonna with John the Baptist and St. Augustine; 90. *Innocenzo da Imola*, Holy Family; 89. *Inn. da Imola*, The Archangel Michael conquering the dragon, with SS. Peter and Augustine. — 4th R.: *137. *Guido Reni*, Samson victorious over the Philistines; 12. *Guercino*, William of Aquitaine receiving the robe of the Order of St. Felix; *136. *Guido Reni*, Crucifixion ('Cristo dei Cappuccini', the high altar of whose church it formerly adorned), one of his finest works; 208. *Domenichino*, Martyrdom of St. Peter; *134. *Guido Reni*, Madonna della Pietà, below are St. Petronius, Carlo Borromeo, Dominicus, Francis, and

Proculus; the picture was painted in 1616 for the Town Council, who rewarded the painter with a valuable gold chain and medal, in addition to his remuneration; *135. *Guido Reni*, Slaughter of the Innocents; 138. *G. Reni*, Madonna del Rosario, painted on silk in 1630 (as a procession-flag). — In the Corridor: r. *Cima da Conegliano* Madonna; l. 275. *Raph. Mengs*, Portrait of Clement XIII. — 5th R.: Altar-pieces of the 14th and 15th cent. by *Vitale*, *Simone da Bologna*, *Jacopo Avanzi*, *Antonio* and *Bartolommeo Vivarini* of Murano (about 1450); in the centre, 360. *Niccolò Alunno da Foligno*, Madonna adoring the Child, on the back, Annunciation, presented by Pope Pius IX. in 1856; 102. Wings of an altar-piece (now in the Brera at Milan, p. 118) by *Giotto*, from the church degli Angioli, with SS. Peter, Paul, and the angels Michael and Gabriel. — 6th R.: above the door, 292. *Innocenzo da Imola*, Virgin and Child with saints; several pictures of *Guido Reni*, the *Caracci*, etc. A number of pictures from suppressed monasteries, by Francia and others, are still in disorder.

At the E. extremity of the Mercato di Mezzo, almost in the centre of the town, are the **Leaning Towers**, the most singular structures in Bologna. The **Torre Asinelli** (Pl. 78), erected in 1109 by *Gherardo degli Asinelli*, is 272 ft. in height and 3 ft. 4 in. out of the perpendicular. A rough staircase of 447 steps leads to the summit, which commands a fine view towards Verona, the Monti Euganei (p. 179), and the Alps. The **Torre Garisenda** (Pl. 79), erected in 1110 by *Filippo* and *Ottone Garisendi*, is 138 ft. high only, but is 8 ft. out of the perpendicular towards the S., and 3 ft. towards the E. Since the last measurement (1772), it is said to have settled still farther. Dante (Inferno XXXI, 136) compares the giant Antæus, who bends towards him, to this tower, 'when a cloud passes over it'. Their obliquity has been occasioned by the settling of the foundations (comp. p. 268), in consequence of which the Garisenda was never completed. — In this piazza is situated **S. Bartolommeo di Porta Ravegnana** (Pl. 3), erected in 1653, a church in the baroque style surmounted by a dome, containing pictures by *Lod. Caracci*, *Albani*, *Guido Reni*, *Tiarini*, etc. — The *Palazzo della Mercanzia, or *Loggia de' Mercanti* (Chamber of Commerce, Pl. 43), farther S., at the corner of the streets S. Stefano and Castiglione, is a beautiful Gothic structure, said to have been erected in 1294, restored by the Bentivogli in 1493. It contains the armorial bearings of all the jurists who taught law here from 1441 to 1800.

Of the **Palaces** the following are the most interesting:

Pal. Bacciocchi, formerly *Ranuzzi* (Pl. 52), possesses a façade by *Andrea Palladio* and a colonnade by *Bibiena*. It was once the residence of Napoleon's sister Elise Bacciocchi, and still contains a number of portraits and statues of members of the Buonaparte family.

Pal. Bargellini, now *Davia*, Strada Maggiore, with the studio of Prof. Baruzzi, one of Canova's most eminent pupils.

Pal. Bentivoglio (Pl. 53), erected in the 16th cent. on the site of the ancient mansion of this powerful family, which was destroyed under Pope Julius II., was frequently a residence of princes.

Pal. Bevilacqua Vincenzi (Pl. 54), attributed to *Bramantino*, possesses a magnificent court. The Council of Trent (p. 60) held its sessions for a short period here in 1547.

Pal. Fava (Pl. 57) is decorated with beautiful *frescoes by the *Caracci* from the history of Jason and Æneas.

Pal. Pepoli (Pl. 64), date 1344, is the castellated seat of this once influential family.

Pal. Tanari (Pl. 67) and *Pal. Zambeccari di S. Paŏlo* (Pl. 69) possess paintings by *Domenichino*, *Innocenzo da Imola*, the *Caracci, Carlo Dolce, Guercino*, etc.

Pal. Zampieri (Pl. 70), with the inscription '*Galleria Zampieri*', is always accessible ($1/_2$ fr.). It is adorned with admirable frescoes from the history of Hercules by the *Caracci* and *Guercino*. The old and celebrated picture-gallery it once contained has been sold. The collection made by the present proprietor, comprising several good works of the Bolognese school, is also for sale.

The adjoining *House of Rossini* (Pl. 71), in the Via Maggiore, was erected by the great composer in 1825, and furnished with inscriptions from Cicero and Virgil. The houses of *Guercino* and *Guido Reni*, the latter with frescoes by the master himself, are also pointed out.

The **Collegio di Spagna** (Pl. 40), in the Strada Saragozza, founded in 1364 by Cardinal Albornoz, contains frescoes (damaged) by the *Caracci* and *Bagnacavallo*. The Coronation of Emp. Charles V. at S. Petronio (p. 228) by the latter is very interesting on account of the portraits of the principal characters, who were contemporaries of the artist.

Within the wall, on the N. side of the town, near the *Porta Galliera* leading to the station, rises **La Montagnōla**, a slight eminence, converted during the first French occupation into a promenade, and still a favourite popular resort. Fine view of the town, with the villas on the spurs of the Apennines in the foreground. Here is situated the *Giuoco di Pallone* (Pl. 76, p. 226). The Austrians were attacked here by the Bolognese in 1848 and compelled to evacuate the town. On the S. is the *Piazza d'Armi*.

The *Strada Saragozza* leads to the gate of that name at the S.W. extremity of the town. Outside this gate, $3/_4$ M. S. of the town, rises ***S. Michele in Bosco**, once an Olivetan monastery (suppressed 1797), now a royal château. The church contains remnants of frescoes by *Bagnacavallo* and others. The court of the buildings is adorned with finely executed *frescoes by the *Caracci* and their pupils, from the history of St. Benedict and St. Cecilia, but unfortunately much injured.

Outside the *Porta S. Isaia*, at the W. extremity of the town is situated the ***Certosa** (formerly a Carthusian monastery), erected in 1335, and consecrated in 1801 as a *Campo Santo*.

The route to it is the principal road from the gate; after 1/3 M. a cross indicates the way to the cemetery, which is reached about 3/4 M. farther (custodian 1/2 fr.). This burial-ground is one of the most interesting in Italy. The church contains a few paintings by *Sirani* and others; in the cloisters a number of old tombstones; in the arcades modern monuments, most of them in marble. In the centre are the ordinary graves. Among the many illustrious names on the former are those of the erudite *Gaspar Garatoni* (d. 1817) and the talented *Clotilda Tambroni* (d. 1817) (p. 226). Noble families of the town also possess vaults here. Thus the monument of *Letizia Murat Pepoli* (d. 1859), with a statue of her father King Murat ('propugnatore dell' italica indipendenza'), executed by Vinc. Vela in 1865. A rotunda here contains the busts of celebrated professors, *Mezzofanti, Galvani, Costa, Schiassi, Mattei* (teacher of Rossini) etc.

On the *Monte della Guardia*, a fortified eminence outside the Porta Saragozza (2 1/2 M.), lies the sumptuous pilgrimage-church of the ***Madonna di S. Luca**, erected by *Dotti* in 1731, so called from an ancient picture of the Virgin pretended to have been painted by St. Luke, brought from Constantinople in 1160. A passage leads to a colonnade of 635 arches (constructed 1676—1739), about 1 M. in length, extending along the height. Remarkably fine view from the summit, extending from the Apennines to the Adriatic. The finest points are beneath the portal of the church and by the new intrenchments.

44. From Bologna to Ancona.

Railway in 5 1/4—8 hrs.; fares 22 fr. 45, 18 fr., 13 fr. 50 c. — Beautiful views of the sea between Rimini and Cattolica, then beyond Pesaro. A seat on the *left* should therefore be selected.

From the railway-station on the N. side of the city the line runs parallel with the high-road in the direction of the ancient Via Æmilia, and as far as Forli traverses fertile plains in nearly a straight direction; in the distance to the r. the spurs of the Apennines. Stat. *Mirandola* and *Quaderna*. Stat. *Castel S. Pietro*, on the *Silaro*, with a castle erected by the Bolognese in the 13th cent.

Imola *(S. Marco)*, on the *Santerno*, is an ancient town with 26,000 inhab. and seat of a bishop (since 422), the Roman *Forum Cornelii*, incorporated with the States of the Church in 1509, birthplace of St. Petrus Chrysologus, archbishop of Ravenna (d. 449); his tomb is in the cathedral of *S. Cassiano*, where the remains of the saint of that name also repose.

The line crosses the Santerno and soon reaches stat. **Castel Bolognese** (poor Restaur.), an ancient stronghold of the Bolognese, constructed in 1380. Branch-line hence to *Ravenna* see p. 248. Then across the river *Senio*, ancient *Sinnus*, to

Faenza *(Corona; Posta)*, a town with 36,000 inhab. on the *Lamone* (ancient *Anemo*). the *Faventia* of the Boii, the scene of Sulla's victory over Carbo. In the middle ages it was the witness of numerous feuds, a circumstance alluded to by Dante, Inferno XXVII, 49:

'*Le città di Lamone e di Santerno
Conduce il lioncel dal nido bianco.*'

A small lion on a white ground belonged to the armorial bearings of Mainardo Pagani, prince of Imola and Faenza at the period alluded to. Faenza was afterwards (in 1376) taken and plundered by *Sir John Hawkswood*, the commander of the troops of Pope Gregory XI., and in 1509 annexed by Pope Julius II. to the States of the church.

The town is celebrated for its pottery (whence the term '*faïence*'), and contains considerable silk and weaving manufactories.

The cathedral of *S. Costanzo* contains a *Holy Family by *Innocenzo da Imola*, and bas-reliefs by *Benedetto da Majano*.

The *Capuchin Monastery*, outside the town, possesses a good picture by *Guido Reni*, a *Madonna and St. John.

In *S. Maglorio* a *Madonna, attributed to *Giorgione*, more probably by *Girolamo da Treviso*. By the latter a fine fresco (1533), Madonna with saints, in the *Commenda* (in the Borgo), where there is also a *Collection of Pictures* by native masters, such as Bertucci etc.

The *Palazzo Comunale* was in the 15th cent. the scene of the murder of Galeotto Manfredi by his jealous wife Francesca Bentivoglio; the grated window in the centre, where the deed was perpetrated, is still shown.

In 1782 the *Canale Zanelli* was constructed from Faenza to the *Po di Primaro* near *S. Alberto*, in order to connect the town with the Adriatic.

A good road leads from Faenza to *Ravenna* (diligence 3 times weekly), and another by Marradi and Borgo S. Lorenzo to *Florence* (corriere daily; diligence 3 times weekly in 12 hrs.; office, Corso 68).

The line intersects the plain in a straight direction, the *Lamone* is crossed, then the *Montone*, which falls into the Adriatic not far from Ravenna.

Forlì *(Posta)*, the ancient *Forum Livii*, founded by M. Livius Salinator after the defeat of Hasdrubal, is a well-built-town with 36,000 inhab., seat of the cardinal-legate till 1848. The nuptials of Athaulf, king of the Visigoths, with Galla Placidia, sister of the Emp. Honorius were solemnized here in 410. Forlì was long an independent state, in which the Guelphs retained their ascendancy till 1315. The Ordelaffi then usurped the supreme power, and in 1504 the town was finally annexed to the States of the Church by Julius II.

The **Cathedral of S. Croce* contains a chapel of the Madonna del Fuoco; in the dome of the latter *frescoes by *Carlo Cignani* (1686—1706): Assumption of the Virgin. The painter is buried in the chapel. A Ciborium from a design by Michael Angelo, a casket of relics of the 14th cent., and the sculptures of the principal door of the 15th cent. are worthy of notice.

S. Girolamo contains a Madonna with angels by *Guido Reni*, in the 1st chapel to the r. *frescoes by *Melozzo* and *Palmezzano*.

S. Mercuriale possesses a *painting by *Innocenzo da Imola*, sculptures of 1536, and several good pictures by *Marco Palmezzano*, an artist of this town. Lofty campanile.

On a house adjoining that of the druggist *Morandi*, are remains of fine frescoes by *Melozzo da Forli* (about 1470). The *Pinacoteca* (in the *Ginnasio Comunale*, Piazza di S. Pellegrino) contains good pictures by *Marco Palmezzano*, *Cignani*, *Fra Angelico*, *Lorenzo di Credi*, etc.

The *Piazza* with the *Palazzo Comunale* and other edifices deserves a visit.

The *Citadel*, constructed in 1361, now serves as a prison. In the 15th cent. it was occupied by Girolamo Riario, nephew of Pope Sixtus IV., who married Catharina Sforza, the natural daughter of Gian Galeazzo. This prince was implicated in the conspiracy of the Pazzi, in consequence of which he was assassinated by his own officers in his palace at Forli. Notwithstanding this, his widow Catharine Sforza took possession of the citadel and defended it bravely. In 1499 she again heroically resisted the attacks of the united forces of the French and the Pope under Cesare Borgia, till her stronghold was reduced to the utmost extremities and captured, and she was carried off as a prisoner to the Castle of St. Angelo. — The poet Cornelius Gallus, the historian Flavio Biondo, and the anatomist Morgagni were natives of Forli.

A road leads from Forli on the l. bank of the Ronco to *Ravenna* (about 15 M.); another through the Apennines by *Rocca S. Casciano* and *S. Benedetto* to *Florence*, diligence 3 times weekly, corriere daily at noon.

The line to Rimini crosses the *Ronco* and passes stat. *Forlimpopoli*, the ancient *Forum Popilii;* to the r. on the hill, *Bertinoro* with its productive vineyards; then by *Polenta* and across the *Savio (Sapis)* to the town of

Cesena *(*Posta*, or *Leone Bianco)*, with 7777 inhab., surrounded by beautiful meadows and hills, and embellished with handsome palaces, one of the most ancient episcopal sees in Italy, where St. Philemon is said to have held the office as early as the year 92. In ancient history Cæsena is frequently mentioned as a town of the Cisalpine Gauls. During the middle ages it was at first an independent state, then became subject to the Ghibelline family of Montefeltro, and shortly afterwards to the Malatesta, who were partizans of the Guelphs. This rapid change of rulers is alluded to by Dante, Inf. XXVII, 52:

*'Cosi com' ella sie' tra il piano e il monte,
Tra tirannia si vive e stato franco.'*

On Feb. 1st, 1377, the town was cruelly sacked by Cardinal Robert of Geneva, and subsequently by Cesare Borgia, after which it was incorporated with the states of the Church.

In the *Piazza* is the handsome *Palazzo Pubblico with a statue of Pius VI., who was born at Cesena in 1717. In the interior a *Madonna with saints, by *Francesco Francia*. The *Capuchin Church* possesses a fine picture by *Guercino*.

The chief attraction is the *Library, founded in 1452 by Domenico Malatesta Novello, brother of the prince of Rimini, containing 4000 MSS., many of them executed by order of the founder, and afterwards employed by the erudite Aldus Manutius in the preparation of his celebrated editions of the classics.

On an eminence, $1/2$ M. distant, stands the handsome church of **S. Maria del Monte*, a work of *Bramante*, and a Benedictine monastery. Productive sulphur-mines in the vicinity, towards the S.

The line crosses the stream *Pisciatello*, the upper part of which, termed *Urgone*, is identical with the river *Rubicon* of the ancients, the boundary between Italia proper and the Province of Gallia Cisalpina, and memorable for its passage by Cæsar at the commencement of the civil war between him and Pompey, B. C. 49.

The most recent investigations tend to show that the Rubicon has entirely abandoned its ancient course. It appears originally to have fallen into the Fiumicino, farther S., whilst at the present day its upper portion (Urgone) unites with the *Pisciatello*. Most of the towns and villages in this district have in turn laid claim to the distinction of possessing the Rubicon within their territory. Nor did they rest satisfied with a mere literary feud in order to gain the object of their ambition. An action involving this question was instituted at Rome, and in 1756 the 'Rota' decided in favour of the claim of the *Uso* (p. 256), beyond the small town of *Savignano*, and near *S. Arcangelo* (birthplace of Pope Clement XIV. Ganganelli, in 1705). On the road between Cesena and Savignano stands a column bearing a decree of the Roman senate, threatening to punish those who should without authority trespass beyond the Rubicon. Montesquieu regarded this as genuine, but it is unquestionably one of several spurious monuments erected at different places during the continuance of the Rubicon controversy.

The line now crosses the *Uso*, and then the *Marecchia*.

Rimini *(*Tre Re e Posta, Aquila d'Oro*, both in the Corso; *Trattoria d'Europa* in the Piazza Cavour; *Caffè della Speranza* in the Piazza Giulio Cesare; **Rail. Restaur.*), beautifully situated near the Adriatic at the mouth of the Ausa and Marecchia, with 33,000 (town alone 16,000) inhab., is sometimes visited as a sea-bathing place (pleasant walk of 1 M. to the sea). Silk and fish are the staple commodities here. The modern, as well as the ancient edifices of Rimini deserve a visit.

Rimini, the ancient *Ariminum*, a town of the Umbrians, became a Roman colony in B. C. 269, and was extended and embellished by Cæsar and Augustus. During the Exarchate it was the most N. of the *Pentapolis Maritima*, or 'Five Maritime Cities', which were under the jurisdiction of one president. The other four were *Pesaro, Fano, Sinigaglia*, and *Ancona*. In 260 Ariminum became an episcopal see, and in 359 a Council against Arianism was held here. The town afterwards belonged to the Lombards. In 1200 it was given by Otho IV. to the Malatesta, who were at first vicegerents of the emperor, but subsequently hereditary princes. In 1503 they surrendered the town to the Venetians, from whom it was finally wrested by the Pope. The insurrections which broke out here in 1845 and 1853 were quelled, but the town at last threw off the papal yoke in 1860.

The broad road leading from the station enters the gate, beyond which it is termed Via Principe Umberto. After a walk of about 4 min. the visitor should diverge to the l. by the Via al Tempio Malatestiano, which soon leads to the principal church of

*S. *Francesco (Duomo, Tempio dei Malatesta)*, erected in the 14th cent. in the Ital. Gothic style, but magnificently remodelled in 1420 by *Sigismundo Malatesta* from designs by *Leo Battista Alberti* in accordance with the then prevailing classical style. On the coping round the church are the arms of the Malatesta and several other families connected with them. The seven vaults of the S. side contain the sarcophagi of the poets, philosophers, orators, and warriors whom Sigismund Malatesta, the brave and illustrious enemy of Pius II., entertained at his court.

The Interior, destitute of aisles, has an open roof and a series of spacious lateral chapels. To the r. of the entrance is the monument of Sigismund (d. 1468). On the r. between the 1st and 2nd chapels is the entrance to the Chapel of the Relics (which the sacristan opens), containing a fresco by *Pietro della Francesca* ('Pietri de Burgo opus 1481') representing Sigismund Malatesta kneeling before his tutelary saint St. Sigismund, king of Hungary. — The 2nd Chapel on the r., that of S. Michele, contains the tomb of Isotta (d. 1450), the wife of Sigismund. — The marble reliefs on the next chapel del S. Sagramento, are ascribed to *Ghiberti*. — The 1st Chapel on the l., restored in 1868, was destined by Sigismund Malatesta for the reception of his ancestors and descendants, as the inscription on the sarcophagus on the l. records.

From the small piazza in front of the church, the Via Patara leads S. to the Piazza Giulio Cesare, the ancient forum. A stone *Pedestal* here bears an inscription of 1855, according to which Cæsar harangued his army from it after the passage of the Rubicon. Near it is a small chapel erected on the spot where St. Antony once preached, and another on the canal where the saint is said to have preached to the fishes because the people refused to hear him. — The Corso d'Augusto, which crosses this piazza, leads to the l. to the Porta Romana, and to the r. to the Piazza Cavour and the bridge of Augustus.

The *Porta Romana is a triumphal arch of travertine of simple design, erected to Augustus to commemorate the restoration of the roads, as the inscription informs us. Above are medallion figures, on the inside Jupiter and Minerva, on the outside Neptune and Venus. — Near the Cappuccini are the supposed remains of an *Amphitheatre* (to which the Via dell' Anfiteatro, the second side-street of the Corso from the Porta Romana, leads).

In the Piazza Cavour is the *Palazzo del Comune*, containing an altar-piece by *Dom. Ghirlandajo*, and a Pietà by *Giov. Bellini* (painted about 1470). In front of it rises a bronze *Statue of Pope Paul V*. (inscription on the pedestal obliterated). Beyond the *Teatro Vittorio Emanuele*, erected in 1857, is the ancient *Palace of the Malatesta*, now a prison, and in a very dilapidated condition. Their arms are still to be seen over the entrance.

From the history of the Malatestas Dante derived the touching episode of 'Francesca da Rimini' (Inferno V, 121), which Byron has translated with such a masterly hand.

The *Library* in the Via Gambalunga, which diverges from the Piazza Cavour to the E., founded in 1617 by the jurist Gambalunga, contains 23,100 vols. and MSS., and a few Roman antiquities and inscriptions.

The church of *S. Girolamo* contains a *picture of the saint by *Guercino*.

At the end of the Corso is the five-arched **Ponte d'Augusto*, the highest of the bridges by which the *Marecchia* (ancient *Ariminus*) is crossed at Rimini, and one of the finest ancient structures of the kind. It crosses to the Borgo S. Giuliano, where the Via Æmilia united with the Via Flaminia which led to Rome. Here too is situated the church of

S. Giuliano, with altar-piece by *Paolo Veronese*, and an ancient picture by *Lattanzio della Marca*.

In the *Castel di S. Leo*, 18 M. to the W. of Rimini, the notorious *Cagliostro* (Giuseppe Balsamo, born 1743 at Palermo) died in confinement in 1794. From S. Leo a bridle-path, much frequented by fishermen, leads to *Florence* by *Camaldoli* and *Vallombrosa*, traversing picturesque ravines.

A somewhat shorter excursion may be made to the ancient republic of **San Marino**, the smallest in the world, said to have been founded in an inaccessible wilderness by St. Marinus at the time of the persecutions of the Christians under Diocletian. This diminutive state braved all the storms of mediæval warfare and even the ambition of Napoleon. It retained its ancient constitution till 1847, when its senate was converted into a chamber of deputies. The precipitous rock in a bleak district, on which the town (1000 inhab.) is situated, is reached by one road only, viz. that from Rimini. The village of *Borgo* at the base is the residence of the wealthier inhabitants. A cavern, through which a perpetual current of cold air passes, is an object of curiosity. The celebrated epigraphist and numismatist *Bartolommeo Borghesi*, born at Savignano in 1781, was from 1821 until his death on April 16th, 1860, a resident at S. Marino, where he arranged and described his admirable collections and received visits from foreign savants.

Beyond Rimini the line skirts the coast, passes *S. Martino* and *S. Lorenzo*, crosses the streams *Marano* and *Conca* (the Crustumium rapax of Lucan), and reaches stat. *La Cattolica*, so called from having been the residence of the Rom. Cath. bishops during the Council of Rimini in 359. The train crosses the *Tavollo* and passes the *Villa Vittoria*, situated on the l. side of the road to Rimini, the residence of Queen Caroline of England when Princess of Wales. Then across the *Foglia* (ancient *Isaurus* or *Pisaurus*) to

Pesăro *(Leone d'Oro; Italia; Caffè Nazionale* and *della Piazza)*, the ancient *Pisaurum*, once the capital of the province of Pesaro which was united with that of Urbino, and formerly appertaining to the Pentapolis Maritima (19,900 inhab.). A Roman colony was established here B. C. 184, which was afterwards destroyed by Totilas, but rebuilt by Belisarius. During the middle ages Pesaro was successively ruled over by the Malatesta, the Sforza, and the della Rovere, dukes of Urbino, under whom, especially through the influence of Lucrezia d'Este, it became a cradle of art and literature, and was visited by *Bernardo* and *Torquato Tasso*. In 1631 it was at length united to the States of the Church.

Pesaro was the birthplace of the celebrated composer *Gioacchino Rossini* (b. 1789, d. at Paris 1868), the 'swan of Pesaro' as he has been termed. Two of his admirers, Baron Salamanca of Madrid and M. Delahaute of Paris, have erected a statue to him (in bronze), on the r. of the egress from the station (visible also from the train).

The palace of the dukes of Urbino, with a magnificent hall, is now the seat of the authorities. In front of it are marble statues of *Rossini* and *Perticari*.

The Foglia is crossed by a bridge of Roman origin.

Among the churches may be mentioned: *S. Francesco*, with a *Coronation of the Virgin by *Giovanni Bellini; S. Cassiano*, with a St. Barbara by *Simone da Pesaro; S. Giovanni de' Riformati*, with a badly restored altar-piece by *Guercino*.

The *Biblioteca Olivieri* contains 13,000 vols. and 600 MSS., among which are several memorials of the golden era of Pesaro under the dukes, letters and observations of Tasso, etc. Adjacent to it is a small *Museum of Antiquities*. The *Ospizio degli Incurabili* possesses a fine collection of Majolica; in the *Palazzo Astico* are the *Marmora Pisaurensia*, described by Giordani in 1738. The principal treasures of art of which Pesaro formerly boasted have long since been transferred to Rome and Paris. The figs of Pesaro are highly esteemed.

Near Pesaro is *Monte S. Bartolo*, where the Roman tragic dramatist L. Attius is said to be interred; beyond it *L'Imperiale*, a villa erected by Leonora Gonzaga, and adorned with frescoes by *Raffaele del Colle*, once a favourite residence of the dukes, and praised by Bernardo Tasso, but sadly neglected since the last century. In the vicinity is the church of the *Girola-*

mitani, with a damaged picture of S. Jerome by *Giovanni Santi*. One of the finest prospects in the environs is obtained from an eminence behind the monastery.

An Excursion to Urbino may most easily be accomplished from Pesaro. Diligence daily at 5 a. m. from Urbino to Pesaro in 5—6 hrs., returning on the arrival of the afternoon trains. The road leads through the valley of the *Foglia*, which falls into the sea at Pesaro, to *Montecchio*, and then gradually ascends by the brook which falls into the Foglia.

Urbino (*Italia*, tolerable), the ancient *Urbinum Metaurense*, deriving its name from the neighbouring Metaurus, lies on an abrupt cliff, surrounded by barren mountains. The town (15,000 inhab.) boasts of a university with as many professors as students. Its monuments and historical associations are interesting.

In the 13th cent. the town came into the possession of the *Montefeltro* family, and under *Federigo Montefeltro* and his son *Guidobaldo* in the 15th cent. attained to such prosperity as entirely to eclipse the neighbouring courts of the Malatestas at Rimini and the Sforzas at Pesaro. *Federigo Montefeltro*, who distinguished himself as a condottiere in the feuds of the 15th cent., in 1474 married his daughter to *Giovanni della Rovere*, a nephew of Sixtus IV., and was in consequence created duke of Urbino. In this capacity he acquired a well-merited reputation as a patron of science and art, and Urbino was styled the 'Italian Athens'. His example was followed by his son *Guidobaldo I.*, zealously seconded by his duchess, the beautiful and accomplished *Elisabetta Gonzaga*. Guidobaldo was expelled in 1497 by *Caesar Borgia*, but after the death of Alexander VI. returned in triumph to Urbino, where he was visited during three festive days by his relative *Julius II.*, who now became pope (1503—13), and was on his route to Bologna. On this occasion the latter became acquainted with the youthful *Raphael Santi*, who (born March 28th, 1483, at Urbino) at first studied under the guidance of his father, the master *Giovanni Santi*, subsequently under the celebrated *Pietro Vanucci (Perugino)* at Perugia, and in 1504 went to Florence to perfect himself by the study of the admirable works of *Leonardo da Vinci* and *Michael Angelo Buonarotti*. On the death of Duke Guidobaldo in 1508, Julius II. summoned Raphael to Rome to decorate the Stanza della Segnatura with frescoes. Under Julius and his successor Leo X. Raphael acquired the reputation of the greatest painter of the day, and died April 6th, 1520. For the development of his genius, however, he was in a great measure indebted to the munificent patronage of the court of Urbino. Here Count *Balthasar Castiglione* wrote his 'Cortegiano', the ideal of a courtier; here, also, the erudite *Polydorus Vergilius* resided; and the artist *Federigo Baroccio*, who distinguished himself at Rome as a successful imitator of Raphael, was a native of Urbino (b. 1528), where he died in 1612. In 1626 the duchy was incorporated with the States of the Church, when Urban VIII. persuaded the last and childless duke *Francesco Maria II.* to abdicate.

The town still contains much that recals its pristine splendour. The *Ducal Palace*, erected by Federigo Montefeltro, was at that period regarded as the finest structure of the description in Italy, and is still an unrivalled specimen of the early Renaissance, remarkable for its symmetrical proportions and the rich decoration of its halls, windows, buttresses, chimneypieces (by *Francesco di Giorgio* and *Ambrogio Baroccio*, ancestor of the painter of that name) etc. On the stair the statue of Duke Frederick. The library of the palace and other collections were transferred to Rome. The corridors contain a considerable collection of well arranged inscriptions from Rome and the Umbrian municipia, commenced by the epigraphist *Fabretti*.

The *Cathedral* possesses good pictures of St. Sebastian and the Eucharist, by *Baroccio*, of St. Martin and Thomas à Becket, by *Timoteo della Vite*, and a portrait of the duke.

S. Francesco contains pictures by *Giovanni Santi*, a Madonna with St. John the Baptist, St. Sebastian, St. Jerome, and St. Francis, with three kneeling figures of the donors, members of the Buffi family (not of the family of Raphael, as was formerly believed); St. Rochus and Tobias by *Timoteo della Vite;* also monuments of the princes of Urbino.

S. Francesco di Paola, with two pictures of *Titian*, the Resurrection and Eucharist. — *S. Giuseppe*, with a *Madonna by *Timoteo della Vite*, and (in the oratorio) a copy of Raphael's Sposalizio by *Andrea Urbani*. — The *Oratorio of the Confraternità di S. Giovanni* is covered with paintings by *Lorenzo da S. Severino* and his brother, of the school of Giotto, History of the Virgin and John the Baptist. — The college near *S. Agata* contains an interesting picture by *Justus van Ghent*, a pupil of Van Eyck, of 1774. — In the church of **S. Bernardino*, 3/4 M. from the town, are the tombs of the dukes Federigo and Guidobaldo; in the sacristy 13 painted panels by *Antonio di Ferrieri* (1435), and the Dead Christ by *Giovanni Santi*.

Raphael's House is indicated by an inscription. On one of the walls is a Madonna with sleeping Child, long regarded as an early production of Raphael, but ascertained to have been executed by his father *Giovanni Santi*. It is intended to erect in his native town a monument worthy of the great master, for which purpose a committee has for some years existed.

In the *Theatre*, formerly celebrated for its decorations by *Girolamo Genga*, the first Italian comedy was performed. This was the Calandra of Cardinal *Bibbiena* (or rather *Bernardo Divizio* of Bibbiena in the Casentino, b. 1470, d. at Rome 1520), the friend of Pope Leo X. and patron of Raphael.

From the height occupied by the *Fortezza* an interesting *survey of the sterile chain of the Apennines may be made.

From Urbino a small diligence runs daily to *Fossombrone* in 3 hrs. The traveller may alight at the point where the road reaches the *Metaurus*, and visit the neighbouring *Furlo Pass on foot. A carr. may be procured at the village of *Acqualagna* (3½ M.) to convey the traveller back to Fossombrone. Communication between Fossombrone and *Fano* is kept up by vetturini, by the diligence from Perugia 3 times weekly, and by the corriere daily. The traveller bound for Rome may therefore easily accomplish an excursion to Urbino, either from Pesaro, or from Fossombrone.

From Pesaro to Ancona the line skirts the coast, occasionally approaching within a few yards of the sea, of which a pleasant view is afforded.

Fano *(Il Moro; Tre Re)*, the ancient *Fanum Fortunae*, is indebted for its origin to a temple of Fortune, a fact commemorated by a modern statue of Fortune on the public fountain. It afterwards became a prosperous place, and was celebrated as the birthplace of Vitruvius. It is now a pleasant little town, surrounded by ancient walls and a deep moat, and sometimes visited as a watering-place (less expensive than Rimini).

The principal attraction is the **Triumphal Arch of Augustus*, originally a structure of very simple design, to which an additional story was added in the 4th cent. when it was re-dedicated to Constantine.

Churches: **Cathedral of S. Fortunato;* in front of it are four recumbent lions which formerly supported the pillars of the portico. In the interior the chapel of S. Girolamo (2nd to the l.) contains a monument of the Rainalducci family; nearly opposite (4th to the r.) is a chapel adorned with 16 frescoes by *Domenichino*, once excellent, now disfigured by restorations. In the chapel of the sacristy, a Madonna with two saints, by *Lodovico Caracci*.

S. Maria Nuova possesses two fine paintings by *Pietro*

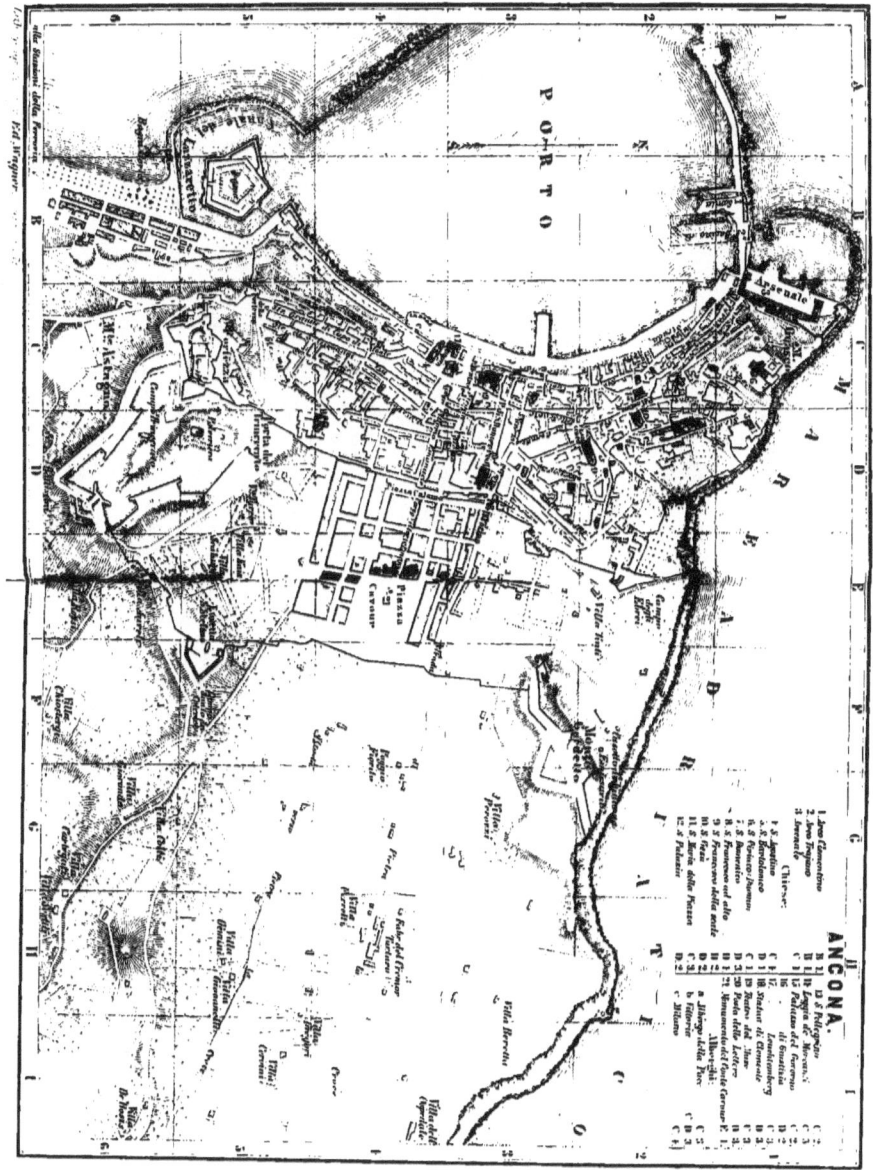

Perugino, one a Madonna, painted in 1497 for the Duranti family, with beautiful 'predella', the other the Annunciation.

S. Paterniano, dedicated to the first bishop of Fano, a handsome structure, possesses a Betrothal of the Virgin, by *Guercino*.

S. Pietro, an imposing and richly decorated church, is embellished with fine frescoes by *Viviani;* in the chapel of the Gabrielli an Annunciation by *Guido Reni*.

S. Francesco contains several monuments of the Malatesta of the 14th and 15th cent. (closed).

The *Collegio Folfi* contains David with the head of Goliath, by *Domenichino*, and copies of his frescoes in the cathedral.

The *Theatre*, decorated by *Bibiena*, once one of the most celebrated in Italy, has recently been re-erected. Pope Clement VIII. (Aldobrandini) was born at Fano in 1536. The first printing-press with Arabic types was established here in 1514 at the expense of Pope Julius II.

A good road leads from Fano by *Fossombrone* to *Urbino;* another over the *Furlo Pass* to *Fossato*, on the line from Ancona to Rome.

Beyond Fano the train crosses the broad and impetuous *Metauro*. the ancient *Metaurus*, celebrated for the defeat of Hasdrubal, B. C. 207; then the *Cessano*, near stat. *Marotto*, and reaches

Sinigaglia *(Locanda della Formica)*, the Roman *Sena Gallica*, a seaport-town with 23,000 inhab., a large proportion of whom are occupied in the fishing trade. The ancient town, belonging to the Galli Senones, was destroyed by Pompey during the civil war between Marius and Sulla. During the middle ages it was frequently devastated by fire and sword, so that the present aspect of the town is comparatively modern. The town is well known for its important *Fair*, held between July 20th and Aug. 8th, established 600 years ago, and once the most frequented in Italy. Sinigaglia was an episcopal diocese as early as the 4th cent. Pope *Pius IX*. (Giovanni Maria, Count Mastai-Feretti) was born here in 1790, and the celebrated singer *Angelica Catalani* in 1784 (d. at Paris, 1849).

Stat. *Case Bruciate;* fine view towards the S. of the promontory of Ancona, rising above the sea. A short distance farther, the train crosses the *Esino*. At stat. *Falconara* the line unites with the Ancona and Rome Railway.

45. Ancona and its Environs. Osimo. Loreto.

Hotels. La Pace (Pl. a), on the quay, D. $3^1/_2$, omnib. 1, facchino $^1/_2$ fr.; Vittoria (Pl. b), Strada Calamo, with *trattoria, R. 2 fr. — Europa, Via S. S. Annunziata; Milano (Pl. c), on the quay, close to the railway gate. — Caffè del Commercio at the theatre; Dorico, opp. the Loggia (p. 245); Garibaldi, Piazza Cavour. — *Birraria Glaenzer, with garden, Corso Vit. Emanuele.

Post Office (Pl. 20, open 8—6 o'clock), Strada Calamo. — *Telegr. Office* in the Via del Porto.

Fiacres. One-horse from station to town, incl. luggage 1, at night 1½ fr.; two-horse 1½ or 2 fr. — For 1 hr. 1½—2 fr., each additional ½ hr. 60—80 c. — Beyond the town 2 fr. 50 or 3 fr. 60 c. for 1 hr., each additional ½ hr. 1 fr. 15 or 1 fr. 70 c.

Steamboats of the Austr. Lloyd (office in the Piazza S. Maria) to Trieste once weekly in 20 hrs., to Athens in 6 days, comp. *Baedeker's S. Italy*. There are also Engl., French, and Ital. companies; agents *Burnas*, *Biby*, and *Levi*, all in the Via di Porto.

Railway to Foggia and Brindisi (Foggia-Naples) see *Baedeker's S. Italy*. First stations (p. 245) *Osimo*, *Loreto*, and *Porto Recanati*; thus far in 1—1¼ hr.; fares 3 fr. 10, 2 fr. 20, 1 fr. 50 c. — From Ancona to Foligno and Rome see *Baedeker's Central Italy*.

Ancona, the capital of a province, with 46,000 inhab. (of whom upwards of 6000 are Jews), and possessing an excellent harbour, is beautifully situated between the two promontories of *Monte Ciriaco* and *Monte Conero* or *Monte Guasco*. It has been a free harbour since 1732, a privilege it was permitted to retain when incorporated with the kingdom of Italy (the formalities of the douane must therefore be undergone when the town is quitted). Silk and oil are largely manufactured here. Ancona is celebrated for the beauty of its women.

Ancona is supposed to have been founded by Doric Greeks from Syracuse, whence termed *Dorica Ancon* (i. e. 'elbow', from the form of the promontory). It was subsequently a Roman colony, and was furnished by Trajan with an enlarged mole. In the middle ages it repeatedly recovered from the ravages of the Goths and others, and in 1532 came into the possession of Pope Clement VII. through the instrumentality of Gonzaga. Ancona is also frequently mentioned as a fortress in the annals of modern warfare. Thus in 1796 it was surrendered to the French, in 1799 to the Austrians, in 1805 to the French again; in 1815 it was ceded to the pope, to whom it belonged till 1860. In 1832-38 the citadel was garrisoned by the French (under the Perier ministry), in order to keep in check the Austrians, who were in possession of Bologna and the surrounding provinces. In 1849 the town was the scene of many excesses, and on June 18th was re-captured by the Austrians; on Sept. 20th, 1860, after the battle of Castelfidardo, it was finally occupied by the Italians.

On the old mole the marble *Triumphal Arch (Pl. 2), erected A. D. 112 by the Roman senate in honour of Trajan on the completion of the new wharf, as the inscription records, is still standing. It is one of the finest existing ancient works of this description. Traces of the bronze decorations with which it was once enriched are still distinguished.

The new wharf, constructed by Pope Clement XII., also boasts of a triumphal arch, from designs by *Vanvitelli*, but far inferior to that above mentioned. The harbour is defended by several forts.

The *Cathedral of S. Ciriaco (Pl. 6), dedicated to the first bishop of Ancona, stands on a lofty site, once occupied by the temple of Venus mentioned by Catullus (36, 13) and Juvenal (IV, 40), and contains the magnificent columns which once appertained to the ancient temple. The structure was begun in the 10th cent., the façade is of the 13th. The foremost columns of the beautiful Gothic portico rest on red lions. The octagonal dome is reputed the oldest in Italy. The crypt of the r. transept contains the *Sarcophagus of Titus Gorgonius, Prætor of Ancona, and other Christian antiquities; in the other transept are the tombs of St. Cyriacus, Marcellinus, and Liberius. — Within a house in the vicinity are scanty remains of a Roman amphitheatre. — The churches of *S. Francesco* (Pl. 9) and *S. Agostino* also possess Gothic porticoes. The Romanesque portico of *S. Maria della Piazza* (Pl. 11) is a still finer structure.

In the *Piazza Maggiore* or *di S. Domenico* stands a marble statue of Pope Clement XII. (Corsini, 1730—40), the greatest benefactor of the town. The *Loggia de' Mercanti* (Exchange), designed by Tibaldi, has a Moorish aspect.

The still unfinished *Corso Vittorio Emanuele* extends towards the E. from the piazza of the theatre, terminating in the spacious *Piazza Cavour*, which was embellished in 1868 with a colossal statue of the minister.

The height above the railway affords a pleasing survey of the town and harbour.

Excursions from Ancona. The Province of Ancona, the ancient *Picenum*, is a remarkably fertile district, replete with beautiful scenery. The Apennines send forth a series of parallel spurs towards the sea, forming a number of short, but picturesque valleys. The towns and villages are invariably situated conspicuously on the heights. To the W. the view is bounded by the *Central Apennines*, which here attain their greatest elevation in several continuous ranges, from the *Montagna della Sibilla* to the *Gran Sasso d'Italia*, and are covered with snow till July. Towards the E. glitters the broad Adriatic, on which numerous picturesque sails are visible in clear weather, a contrast which constitutes the principal charm of the views on the E. coast of Italy.

On the coast to the S. of Ancona, rises the ***Monte Conero** (1763 ft.), with a venerable Camaldulensian monastery, commanding a superb panorama. Distance about $9^1/_2$ M. A tolerable road skirting the heights on the coast is followed nearly to ($7^1/_2$ M.) *Sirolo* (2000 inhab.), and a path then ascends to the top of the hill in $^3/_4$ hr. A carr. (see p. 244) may be taken as far as the foot of the hill.

The Ancona-Foggia Railway (fares to Recanati see p. 244) penetrates the heights which surround Ancona by means of a tunnel. To the l. rises the Monte Conero (see above). First stat. (r.).

Osimo (*Albergo della Corona*, in the market-place; omnibus from the station to the town, 3 M. distant, 60 c.), the ancient *Auximum*, constituted a Roman colony B. C. 144, and mentioned by Cæsar, is now a small country-town (pop. 15,000), situated on a hill, in a naturally strong position. The greater part of the *Town Wall, dating from the 2nd cent. B. C., is still standing. A walk round it is recommended for the sake of the beautiful view it affords. The *Palazzo Pubblico* in the spacious *Piazza* contains inscriptions and statues of celebrated natives of the place, dating from the imperial period, barbarously mutilated on the occasion of the capture of the town in the 16th cent. One of the inscriptions mentions Pompey, who was settled for a time in Picenum. — From Osimo to Loreto in $1^1/_2$ hr. by carr. (one-horse 5 fr.).

Proceeding hence by railway, the traveller perceives (on the r.) *Castelfidardo*, where on Sept. 18th, 1860, the papal troops under Lamoricière were totally defeated by the Italians under Cialdini. Lamoricière fled with a few attendants to Ancona, where he was soon compelled to capitulate.

Loreto (*Campana*, or *Posta*, in the principal street; *Pace*; omnib. to the town 60 c.), situated on a hill at some distance from the line, and affording admirable *views of the sea, the Apennines, and the province of Ancona, is a celebrated resort of pilgrims (half a million annually).

The *Chiesa della Casa Santa* (or 'Church of the Holy House') is architecturally uninteresting. The handsome façade was erected under Sixtus V., a colossal statue of whom adorns the entrance flight of steps. Over the principal door is a life-size statue of the Madonna and Child, by *Girolamo Lombardo*, his sons, and his pupils; also three superb bronze- doors, executed under Pope Paul V., 1605—21, and worthy of comparison with those of Pisa and Florence. The campanile, designed by *Vanvitelli*, is a very lofty structure in a richly decorated style, surmounted by an octagonal pyramid. The principal bell, presented by Pope Leo X. in 1516, weighs 11 tons.

In the interior, l. of the entrance, a beautiful font, cast in bronze by *Tiburzio Vercelli* and *Giambattista Vitale*, and adorned with basreliefs and figures of Faith, Hope, Charity, and Fortitude. On the altars and in the chapels of the nave, *mosaics representing St. Francis of Assisi, by *Domenichino*, and the Archangel Michael, by *Guido Reni;* also a number of valuable pictures, frescoes and sculptures.

In the centre of the church rises the '*Casa Santa*', a simple brick-building, 13 ft. in height, 27˙ft. in length, and 12 ft. in width, surrounded by a lofty *Marble Sreen designed by *Bramante*, and executed by a number of the most celebrated masters (*Sansovino, Girolamo Lombardo, Giovanni da Bologna, Bandinelli*, etc.). It was commenced under Leo X., continued under Clemens VII. and completed under Paul III. The four sides are adorned with beautiful sculptures, reliefs, statues of prophets -and sibyls, etc.

W. Side. *Annunciation, by *Sansovino*, termed by Vasari 'una opera divina'; smaller representations by *Sangallo*, *Gir. Lombardo*, and *Gugl. della Porta.*

S. Side. *Nativity, by *Sansovino;* David and Goliath, Sibyls, Adoration of the Magi, by other masters.

E. Side. *Arrival of the Casa at Loreto, by *Niccolò Tribolo;* above it Death of the Virgin, by *Giambologna.*

N. Side. *Nativity of the Virgin, commenced by *Sansovino,* continued by *Baccio Bandinelli* and *Rafaele da Montelupo.* Basreliefs: *Nuptials of the Virgin, by the same masters.

This sumptuous and unparalleled structure with its embellishments cost an enormous sum, although a number of the masters piously declined remuneration.

In a niche of the interior is a small image of the Virgin and Child in cedar, painted black, attributed to St. Luke. It is richly adorned with jewels, the lustre of which is enhanced by silver lamps always kept burning. In 1798, it was carried off to Paris by the French.

In the l. Transept is the entrance to the *Treasury (open to the public on Sund. till 11. 30 a. m., at other times fee 1 fr.), which contains a number of valuable votive offerings and other curiosities, the gifts of monarchs and persons of rank. Several of the treasures disappeared at the time of the Peace of Tolentino (1797).

According to the legend, the house of the Virgin at Nazareth was an object of the highest veneration since 336, when the aged Empress Helena, mother of Constantine, made a pilgrimage thither, and caused a basilica to be erected over it. Owing to the incursions of the Saracens the basilica fell to decay, and after the loss of Ptolemais the *Casa Santa* was miraculously transplanted by the hands of angels to the coast of Dalmatia (the precise spot being between Fiume and Tersato), in 1291, where it remained undisturbed during three years. For some unknown reason, however, it was again removed by angels during the night, and deposited near Recanati, on the ground of a certain widow *Laureta* (whence the name *Loreto*). A church was erected over it, and a number of houses soon sprang up for the accommodation of the devout believers who flocked to the spot. In 1586 Pope Sixtus V. accorded to Loreto the privileges of a town.

Among the numerous illustrious pilgrims who have visited the spot Tasso may be mentioned. He alludes to this in the beautiful Canzone:

'Ecco fra le tempeste, e i fieri venti
Di questo grande e spazioso mare,
O santa Stella, il tuo splendor m'ha scorto,
Ch' illustra e scalda pur l'umane menti'.

The *Jesuits' College* and the *Palazzo Apostolico*, commenced in 1510 from Bramante's designs, are situated in the piazza in front of the church. The latter is an episcopal residence. Valuable pictures in the *Hall of the Princes:* *Titian*, Christ and the woman taken in adultery; *Vouet*, Last Supper; *Schidone*, St. Clara; *Guercino*, Descent from the Cross; *Ann. Caracci*, Nativity of Christ.

From Loreto railway in 20 min. to

Recanati, situated at some distance from the line, a fortified and important place in the middle ages. Municipal privileges were accorded to it by Emp. Frederick II. in 1229, the charter of which is shown at the *Palazzo Comunale*. The town is loftily situated and commands a number of charming views. The Cathedral of *S. Flaviano*, with Gothic porch, contains the monument of Gregory XII., of 1417. Several of the palaces merit notice, especially that of the *Leopardi*. The library and collections of the scholar and poet *Giacomo Leopardi* are shown here.

From Recanati the traveller may either return by Loreto to

the railway, or prolong his excursion to **Macerata**, a place of some importance (diligence thence to the station). The road thither passes the ruins of *Helvia Ricina*, after the destruction of which Recanati and Macerata sprang up. Remains of an amphitheatre, of a bridge,. etc. are observed close to the river *Potenza*.

46. From Bologna to Ravenna.

Railway in 3—3^1/$_2$ hrs.; fares 9 fr. 30, 7 fr. 40, 5 fr. 60 c.

From Bologna to *Castel Bolognese* see p. 234. The line to Ravenna here diverges to the E. — Stat. *Solarolo*, *Lugo* (where an important market is held in Sept.), *Bagnacavallo* (birthplace of the painter Ramenghi, 1484—1542, who is generally known by the name of his native town), *Russi*, *Godo*. Country flat and well cultivated.

Ravenna. [*Spada d'Oro, Strada del Monte, R. 2, D. 3, A. 1/2 fr.; Albergo d'Europa, or S. Marco, in the same street. Caffè in the Piazza Vittorio Emanuele. — *Fiacres*: per drive 1, at night 1^1/$_2$ fr., two-horse 1^1/$_2$ or 2 fr.; first hour 1^1/$_2$—2^1/$_2$ fr., each additional ^{1}/$_2$ hr. 75 c. or 1 fr. 25 c.; beyond the town 2 or 4 fr. per hr. — *Chief Attractions*: Baptistery (p. 250), Dante's Tomb (p. 251), S. Vitale (p. 252), S. Nazario e Celso (p. 253), S. Maria in Cosmedin (p. 253), S. Apollinare Nuovo (p. 254), S. Apollinare in Classe (p. 255)], a town of ancient origin, capital of a province till 1860, popul. 19,118, is situated in the plain between the rivers Lamone and Ronco (Rom. *Bedesis*), in a somewhat unhealthy locality.

The town was founded by the Pelasgi, but at an early period came into the possession of the Umbrians. Augustus constructed the Portus Classis and a canal, connected with the Po, round the S. side of the town, and appointed Ravenna the headquarters of the Adriatic fleet. The commerce of the place now became more considerable, and a new quarter between the town and the harbour (Cæsarea, a name which is perpetuated by the ruined church of *S. Lorenzo in Cesarea*) was erected. The harbour, however, having been gradually filled up by the deposits of the Po, Classis and Cæsarea fell to decay, whilst Ravenna continued to be the capital of the province Flaminia. As early as A. D. 44 it became an episcopal see, *St. Apollinaris*, a disciple of St. Peter, being the first bishop. The Emp. Honorius transferred his residence hither from Rome in 402 on account of the great strength of the place, and in 438 Ravenna became the seat of an archiepiscopal see. After the fall of the Western Empire the town was taken by the Herulian Odoacer, king of Italy, then in 493 by Theodoric the Great, king of the Ostrogoths, after which it once more attained much of its former splendour and was the residence of the Gothic kings till 552. It then became the seat of the exarch or governor of the Eastern Roman, or Greek Emperors, and continued under their sway until 752, when the Lombard Aistulph banished Eutychius the last exarch and took possession of the town. Shortly afterwards, however, Ravenna was retaken by Pepin, king of the Franks, and handed over to the pope, under whose rule it remained, excepting when his authority was disputed on several occasions by the Guelphs and Ghibellines. In 1275 the Polenta family, of whom honourable mention is made by Dante, obtained the supreme power. In 1318 Ravenna began to be governed by its own dukes; in 1440 it came into the possession of the Venetians, under whom its prosperity materially increased; in 1509 it was conquered by Pope Julius II., and belonged to the States of the Church till the treaty of Tolentino in 1797. It was,

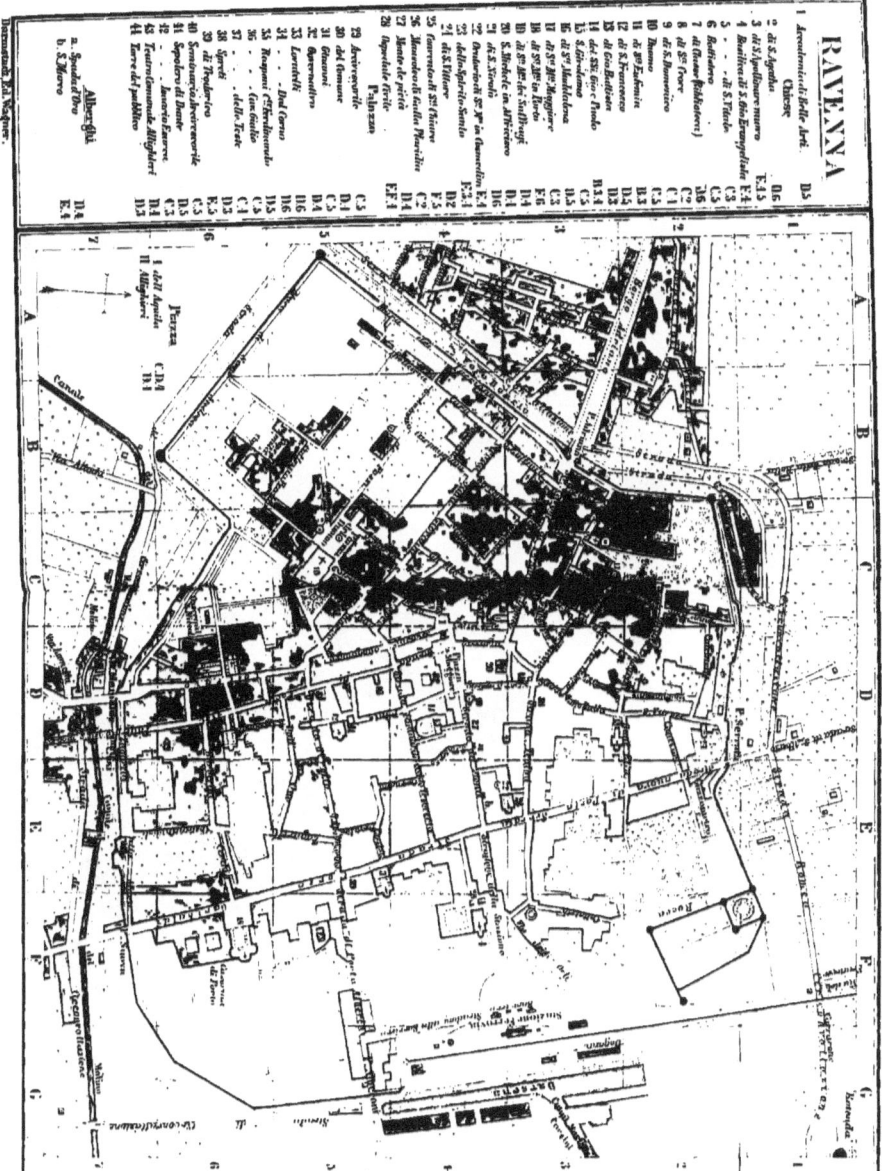

however, restored in 1815, but again severed from the papal dominions in 1860.

Those interested in the history of art are strongly recommended to visit Ravenna, as no other town in Italy contains such a number of monuments, most of them in good preservation, of the architecture, sculpture, and painting (mosaics) of the early part of the middle ages. (The traveller should inspect some of the numerous early Christian sarcophagi with which many of the streets are bordered.)

The circumference of the town is considerable (3 M.), but nearly one half of the area is occupied by gardens. It possesses six gates: W. the *Porta Adriana*, erected in 1585 on the site of the ancient Porta Aurea, E. the *P. Alberoni*, S. the *P. S. Mamante*, N. the *P. Nuova*, the *P. Sisi* of 1568, and the *P. Serrata*, closed by the Venetians, but re-opened by Julius II. and named *P. Giulia*.

Ravenna was originally a seaport, but is now nearly 5 M. distant from the sea. After the Porto Candiano had become choked up, the *Canale Naviglio* was constructed in 1737, in order to connect Ravenna with the sea, and is especially important for the communication with Chioggia and Venice. The present harbour of Ravenna is used for the coast-traffic only. Near it is the hut in which Garibaldi sought refuge in 1849 from his Austrian pursuers on his flight from Rome. His wife died during the flight and was interred here. (Steamboat to Trieste once weekly in 10—12 hrs.)

Lord Byron, who preferred Ravenna to all the other towns of Italy, and was influenced in some measure by his intimacy with the Countess Guiccioli, who was a member of the Gamba family of Ravenna, spent two years of his life here, during which he wrote several of his finest works; the 'Prophecy of Dante', 'Marino Faliero', the 'Two Foscari', 'Cain', 'Heaven and Earth', and the 'Vision of Judgment'. He resided at No. 225 Strada di Porta Sisi, near the Piazza S. Franscesco; the same house was afterwards occupied by Garibaldi, as a memorial-tablet records.

The *Piazza Maggiore*, in the centre of the town, which is said to correspond with the ancient Forum Senatorium, is adorned with two lofty granite columns erected by the Venetians in 1483, surmounted with statues of SS. Apollinaris and Vitalis, with bas-relief by *Pietro Lombardo;* also a statue of Pope Clement XII. (1738) and a colonnade of 8 columns of granite, said to belong to a basilica erected or restored by Theodoric. Beyond this Piazza is the

Piazzetta dell' Aquila, with a granite column crowned by an eagle, erected in 1609 to Cardinal Gaetani.

The Strada del Duomo leads direct hence to the **Cathedral** (Pl. 10) of *S. Orso*, or *Basilica Orsiana*, almost entirely re-erected by [Archb. Guiccioli in the 17th cent. on the site of a church of great antiquity. It consists of nave and aisles with transept, surmounted by a dome in the centre.

Interior. The chapel of the Madonna del Sudore in the r. transept contains the marble sarcophagi of SS. Barbatian and Reginald. The high altar contains a marble sarcophagus with the remains of 9 bishops, of a very early date. The silver crucifix is adorned wih figures executed in the 6th cent. At the back of the choir are several marble slabs with figures of animals, dating from the 6th cent., fragments of an ancient pulpit ('ambo'). The Sacristy contains the *Easter Calendar* from 532 to 626 and the °*Ivory Throne* of St. Maximian, with bas-reliefs of the 5th and 6th cent. representing the history of Joseph. In the lunette to the r. above the entrance of the sacristy °Elijah in the desert, fed by the angel, a fresco by *Guido Reni*. The chapel of the Holy Sacrament in the l. transept contains the °Falling of the Manna and Abraham and Melchisedech (?), by *Guido Reni*. The frescoes on the ceiling, Christ in glory, are by the pupils of G. Reni. In the l. aisle is the monument of the above-mentioned Archbishop Guiccioli.

The ***Baptistery** (Pl. 6) *(S. Giovanni in Fonte,* or *Battisterio degli Ortodossi),* adjoining the cathedral (entrance through the house of the curé), probably also founded by St. Ursus (d. 396) and dedicated to John the Baptist, is an octagonal structure, with series of arcades in the interior resting one above the other. The cupola is decorated with *mosaics of the 5th cent., the most ancient at Ravenna, representing the Baptism of Christ, and the 12 Apostles. The large font is of white marble (5th cent.). A niche contains an urn from the temple of Jupiter of Cæsarea (?). An ancient cross of metal on the roof dates from 688.

The *Archiepiscopal Palace* (Pl. 29), E. of the cathedral, possesses a chapel of the 5th cent. with mosaics etc., entirely in its original condition. In one of the halls ancient inscriptions are preserved. The episcopal *Archives* comprise about 25,000 documents on parchment.

On the r., at the commencement of the Strada di Classe leading to S. Mamante, the *Academy of the Fine Arts* (Pl. 1; visitors ring at the gate, 75 c.), containing an interesting collection of pictures, especially by masters of the place, such as a Crucifixion, Descent from the Cross, and several portraits by *Luca Longhi* (d. 1580); pictures by his son *Francesco;* then a Descent from the Cross by *Vasari;* Madonna and saints by *Cotignola;* a large ancient mosaic found near Classe. On the upper floor a collection of casts, among them a bust of St. Apollinaris by *Thorwaldsen;* *tombstone with recumbent statue of Guidarello Guidarelli, 'guerrier Ravennate', formerly in S. Francesco (fee 75 c.).

In the same street, No. 192, is the former Camaldulensian Monastery of **Classe** (Pl. 7), now occupied by the Collegio and the Academy. The *Library*, or *Biblioteca Comunale* (first floor), founded 1714 by the Abbate Caneti, contains upwards of 50,000 vols. and 700 MSS., among the latter the celebrated MS. of Aristophanes of the 10th cent., one of Dante of 1369, another by Pietro Dante, commentary of Benvenuto da Imola, prayer-book of Mary Stuart with miniatures, the visitors' book from the tomb of Dante (p. 252), the wooden coffin which contained the remains of the great poet, found in 1865 during researches instituted on the occasion of the 6th centenary of his birth, rare editions, such as the Decretals of Boniface VIII. of 1465, etc. There is also a small collection of objects in ivory and coins of the popes, the Medici, and the Malatesta, the golden ornaments of the helmet of King Odoacer, etc. (fee 75 c.). A number of Rom. inscriptions are built into the walls. — The old *Refectory*, which the custodian also shows, contains the Marriage at Cana, a fresco by *Luca* and *Francesco Longhi*, and some fine carving on the door. — The monastery-church of *S. Romualdo* is richly decorated with rare and beautiful marbles, and contains a ciborium of lapis lazuli etc.

S. Niccolò, built by Archb. Sergius in 768, contains numerous paintings by the Augustine monk *Padre Cesare Pronti* and by *Francesco da Cotignola*.

S. Agata (Pl. 2; entrance in the Via di Porta Sisi, between Nos. 96 and 97), dating from the 5th cent., consisting of nave and aisles with a vestibule in the interior, is embellished with fine columns of marble. — The *Palazzo Lovatelli del Corno* (Pl. 33), near the Porta Sisi, contains a few good pictures. — In the same street is Byron's house (p. 249).

S. Francesco (Pl. 12) is said to have been founded by St. Petrus Chrysologus about the year 450, on the site of a temple of Neptune, but is now entirely modernized. The aisles are separated from the nave by 22 columns of coloured marble; unsightly modern ceiling.

At the entrance are several ancient tombstones; r. that of Ostasio da Polenta of 1396; l. that of Enrico Alfieri, who died in 1405 as general of the Franciscans, a member of the same family as the poet of that name. R. the sarcophagus of the archbishop St. Liberius, of the 5th cent. The Cappella del Crocefisso, the 2nd on the r., contains two *columns of Greek marble with capitals by *Pietro Lombardi*.

Adjoining the church is *****Dante's Tomb** (Pl. 41, closed, keys at the town-hall; but it may be sufficiently well seen through the gate). The poet died at Ravenna, where he enjoyed the protection of Guido da Polenta, on Sept. 14th, 1321, at the age of 56, and was interred in the church of S. Francesco. In 1482 Bernardo Bembo, the Venetian governor (father of the celebrated Cardinal Bembo), caused the present mausoleum to be erected from designs by *Pietro Lombardi*, and it was subsequently restored in 1692 and 1780.

It is a square structure with a dome, embellished with medallions of Virgil, Brunetto Latini the poet's master, Can Grande della Scala, and Guido da Polenta his patron; opposite the entrance is a half-length relief of Dante, and below it a sarcophagus, a marble urn in which now contains the poet's remains (originally deposited in a wooden coffin, see above). It bears the epitaph attributed to Dante himself:

*Jura Monarchiae, Superos, Phlegethonta lacusque
Lustrando cecini, voluerunt fata quousque,
Sed quia pars cessit melioribus hospita castris,
Actoremque suum petiit felicior astris,
Hic claudor Dantes, patriis extorris ab oris,
Quem genuit parvi Florencia mater amoris.*

The visitors' book formerly kept here, now preserved at the library, contains the following beautiful lines of Dante written by Pope Pius IX. when here on a visit in 1857 (from Purg. XI, 100):

*Non è il mondan rumore altro che un fiato
Di vento ch'or va quinci ed or va quindi,
E muta nome, perchè muta lato.*

S. Michele in Affricisco, erected in the 16th cent., is now destroyed. The mosaics of the tribune and the old tower are still preserved.

Adjacent is **S. Domenico**, originally a basilica, founded by the exarchs and subsequently restored, adorned with works of *Niccolò Rondinello* of Ravenna, pupil of *Giovanni Bellini*.

****S. Vitale** (Pl. 5) was erected during the reign of Justinian by Archb. Ecclesius on the spot where S. Vitalis suffered martyrdom, and was consecrated by St. Maximian in 547. It is an imitation of the not much more ancient church of St. Sophia at Constantinople, and served in its turn as a model to Charlemagne for the cathedral of Aix-la-Chapelle. The church is octagonal, with a choir, three-sided on the exterior, and round in the interior, added to it on the E. side. The Interior, unfortunately marred by modern restoration, is divided by eight massive pillars into a central space with a passage around it. Between the pillars are semicircular niches with pairs of columns and arches, in two series, one above the other, over which rises the dome, constructed of earthen vessels. Each of the windows in the dome is divided by a mullion into two round-arched halves. The pavement has been raised more than 3 ft., and the street is 6 ft. above the former level.

The Choir is adorned with admirable *Mosaics, which are however inferior in excellence of style to those of earlier date in the baptistery (p. 250), as well as to those of S. Maria in Cosmedin (p. 251): Christ enthroned on the globe, angels at the sides, then St. Vitalis and Ecclesius with the church itself. Below, l. Emp. Justinian with S. Maximian, r. the Empress Theodora accompanied by the ladies of her court, both presenting offerings. On the triumphal arch are represented Jerusalem and Bethlehem. Above, at the sides, the 4 Evangelists sitting, Isaiah and Jeremiah standing, on the r. Moses as a shepherd, above which he is represented removing his sandals at the burning bush, on the l. he receives the Tables of the Law; on the r. in the central scene an altar with bread and wine; at the sides the blood-sacrifice of Abel and the bloodless offering of Melchisedech. L. in the centre a table at which the three angels are entertained by Abraham, Sarah at the door laughing, and sacrifice of Isaac. In the archway busts of Christ, the Apostles, and SS. Gervasius and Protasius. R. by the entrance of the choir an admirable *Greek Relief from a temple of Neptune; genii before the throne of Neptune with his shell and trident; opp. to it a modern copy. In the portico of the sacristy a *Roman Relief, the Apotheosis of the emperor; the goddess Roma is recognised sitting on the l., on the star above the forehead Julius Caesar, then Augustus and Claudius. Opp. are fragments of an early Christian sarcophagus, with Daniel in the lions' den, and the Raising of Lazarus.

To the N. at the back of the church is the monument of the exarch Isaac (d. 641), in a small receptacle a sarcophagus with Greek inscription, erected by his wife Susanna. Adjacent to it are several other ancient inscriptions.

The custodian of S. Vitale also keeps the key of

*S. Nazario e Celso, the *Mausoleum of Galla Placidia*, founded about 440 by that Empress, daughter of Theodosius the Great and mother of Valentinian III. The church is in the form of a Latin cross, 46 ft. long, 39 ft. broad, with a dome, and adorned throughout with beautiful mosaics (of the 5th cent.) representing the 4 Evangelists, prophets, the Good Shepherd, the Saviour with the gospels in his hand, stags at the spring, etc. The altar, constructed of transparent oriental alabaster, was formerly in S. Vitale; behind it is the large marble *Sarcophagus* of Galla Placidia (d. 450), formerly enriched with plates of silver. The Empress sitting on a throne was formerly to be seen in the interior, but her remains were destroyed in 1577 by the accidental ignition of the robes. On the r. of this monument is a marble sarcophagus decorated with Christian emblems, containing the remains of the Emp. Honorius, brother of Galla Placidia; l. that of Constantius III., her second husband (417) and father of Valentinian III.; at the sides of the entrance are two small sarcophagi containing the remains of the tutors of Valentinian and his sister Honoria. These are the sole monuments of the emperors of ancient Rome which still remain in their original position.

S. Giovanni Battista, with an ancient round tower, erected by Galla Placidia in 438 for her confessor St. Barbatian, was almost entirely remodelled in 1683. The columns of the interior belong to the original structure.

Towards the E. the Strada di Porta Serrata leads to the l. through a gate to the Rotonda (p. 255), and to the r. to the church of

S. Spirito, or *S. Teodoro*, erected by Theodoric for the Ar'an bishops, a basilica containing 12 columns of coloured marble. In the first chapel on the l. is a pulpit of the 6th cent. with ancient sculptures. — The custodian keeps also the key of the adjacent

***S. Maria in Cosmedin,** once the baptistery of S. Spirito. The octagonal dome was adorned with *mosaics in the 6th cent., when it became a Rom. Cath. church. On the dome the Baptism of Christ, surrounded by the 12 Apostles. The walls are covered with half obliterated frescoes of the last century. The present pavement is about 7 ft. above the original level.

S. Giovanni Evangelista, or *S. Giovanni della Sagra*, near the railway-station (Pl. 4; if closed, visitors knock at the door), erected in 444 by the Empress Galla Placidia in consequence of a vow made during a voyage from Constantinople, has also lost much of its interest, as well as its ancient mosaics, by alterations. Above the *Portal, constructed at the end of the 13th or commencement of 14th cent., are reliefs in allusion to the foundation of the church. Recent excavations prove that the court in front of the church once formed the atrium of the edifice.

The Interior, with clumsy barrel-vaulting, consists of nave and aisles borne by 24 antique columns. The vaulting of the 4th chapel is adorned with frescoes, ascribed to Giotto, of the four Evangelists, and the four fathers of the church SS. Gregory, Ambrose, Augustine, and Jerome. In the closed chapel l. of the choir are some remnants of old *mosaics, representing the storm at sea (see above) and Galla Placidia.

*S. Apollinare Nuovo (Pl. 3), a basilica erected about 500 by Theodoric as an Arian cathedral, was subsequently converted by the Archbishop S. Agnello into a Rom. Cath. place of worship. The Campanile on the r. of the W. portal exhibits the round shape peculiar to the Ravenna churches. The interior contains 24 marble columns brought from Constantinople; the walls of the nave are adorned with interesting *mosaics of 570, afterwards extensively restored: l. the town of Classis with the sea and ships, in the foreground 22 virgins with the Magi, worshipping the Infant Saviour and his mother; r. the city of Ravenna with the church of S. Vitalis and the palace of Theodoric, and 24 saints with wreaths receiving the blessing of Christ; above are apostles and saints; still higher, scenes from scriptural history. In the last chapel on the l. a portrait of Justinian in mosaic, formerly on the outside of the portal, and an ancient episcopal chair.

In the same street a few paces to the S. of S. Apollinare a few scanty remnants are left of the *Palace of Theodoric* (Pl. 39), in which the exarchs and the Lombard kings subsequently resided. They consist of a high wall surmounted by 8 small columns of marble bearing round arches, with a simple gateway below. The columns and treasures of art of this palace were removed to Germany by order of Charlemagne. R. of the principal door, in the wall is a porphyry vessel, probably once a bath, brought here in 1564, formerly supposed to have contained the ashes of Theodoric and to have stood on the summit of his monument.

Still farther on, by the Porta Nuova, is **S. Maria in Porto** (Pl. 18), erected in 1553 from the remnants of the Basilica S. Lorenzo in Cesarea, containing in the l. transept a very ancient marble figure of the Virgin in the Byzantine style, transferred hither from the church of S. Maria in Porto Fuori. In the 4th chapel on the l. the martyrdom of St. Mark; opp. to it, in the 4th chapel on the r., St. James by *Della Porta;* the paintings of the 5th chapels on the r. and l. are by *Franc. Longhi.* In the choir an old porphyry vase of admirable workmanship.

About $1/3$ M. from the Porta Serrata is situated the *Rotonda (S. Maria della Rotonda), the mausoleum of Thedoric the Great. In order to reach it, the traveller takes the road to the r. almost immediately after quitting the gate, and crosses the railway, beyond which the tomb is seen to the l., shaded by poplars (key at the house, 30 c.). It was probably erected by his daughter Amalasuntha (about 530). The structure is of decagonal shape with flat dome of 36 ft. in diameter, consisting of a single huge block of Istrian rock. The substructure with its ten arches is half under water; the upper part is approached by a double staircase of marble, added in 1780.

About $2^{1}/_{2}$ M. from the Porta Alberoni is the church of **S. Maria in Porto Fuori**, erected by Bishop Onesti (known as 'Il Peccatore'), in consequence of a vow made during a storm at sea in 1096, a basilica with open roof. The l. aisle contains the sarcophagus of the founder, of 1119. The choir and the two adjacent chapels contain ancient *Frescoes*, erroneously attributed to Giotto, scenes from the life of Mary and the Saviour, but unfortunately much damaged. This spot is supposed to have been the site of the old harbour, and the massive substructure of the clock-tower to have appertained to the lighthouse (faro). (A visit to this church may conveniently be combined with that of S. Apollinare.)

St. Appollinare in Classe. No traveller should quit Ravenna without making an excursion to this church, situated 3 M. from the Porta Nuova (carr. see p. 248). About $3/4$ M. from the gate a small marble column surmounted by a Greek cross *(la Crocetta)* marks the site of the ancient basilica of *S. Lorenzo in Cesarea*, the last remnant of the former town of *Caesarea* (p. 248), which was removed in 1553. $1/4$ M. farther, the Ponte Nuovo crosses the united rivers *Ronco* and *Montone*, the confluence is observed higher up. (Before the bridge is crossed, a path leads l. in 20 min. to the church of S. Maria in Porto, the lofty tower of which is seen from a distance.) The road then traverses marshy meadows to ***S. Apollinare in Classe***, erected in 534 by *Julianus Argentarius* on the site of a temple of Apollo, consecrated in 549, and restored in 1779. This is the most imposing of the basilicas of Ravenna which are still preserved. It consists of nave and aisles, with a vestibule at the W. end, and a round campanile (p. 254). The exterior exhibits traces of an attempt to relieve the surfaces of the walls with pilasters and arches. The spacious interior rests on 24 cipolline columns, and has an open roof. The walls are decorated with portraits of bishops and archbishops of Ravenna, an unbroken series of 126, from the first bishop St. Apollinaris, who suffered martyrdom in 74 under Vespasian, to the present archbishop.

The aisles each contain four marble sarcophagi of archbishops.

The crypt, a species of corridor in which the remains of St. Appollinaris once reposed, is now partially under water. Above it is the broad flight of steps leading to the 'tribuna' and the richly decorated high altar. The canopy of the latter is borne by four columns of black and white Oriental marble. The dome of the tribuna is adorned with well-preserved *mosaics of the 6th cent.: in the centre a large cross on a blue ground with gilded stars, at the sides Moses and Elias, beneath whom is St. Apollinaris preaching to his flock; below, on the r., the sacrifice of Melchisedech, on the l. Constantine and other Rom. emperors, among whom are the four archbishops SS. Ursicinus, Ursus, Severus, and Ecclesius. The arch of the choir is also embellished with mosaics: in the centre a bust of Christ, at the sides the emblems of the four evangelists, beneath them two flocks of sheep hastening to Christ from the towns of Jerusalem and Bethlehem.

The *Pine-Forest of Ravenna*, or *La Pineta*, probably the most venerable and extensive in Italy, and frequently extolled by *Dante*, *Boccaccio*, *Dryden*, *Byron*, and other poets, begins a short distance beyond the church of S. Apollinare, and extends for many miles along the road to Rimini, as far as *Cervia*. If the traveller prolong his excursion for 1½ hr. more, he may drive through the nearer extremity of the forest. (The whole excursion to S. Apollinare, the Pineta, and S. Maria Fuori occupies about 4 hrs. by carr.)

About 2 M. from Ravenna, on the bank of the Ronco, rises the *Colonna de' Francesi*, a memorial of the victory gained on April 11th, 1512, by the united armies of Louis XII. of France and the Duke of Ferrara (at which the poet Ariosto was present) over the Spanish troops and those of Pope Julius II. At the moment when the victory was decided, the brave *Gaston de Foix* fell; 20,000 dead were left on the field. Cardinal de' Medici, who a year later ascended the papal throne as Leo X., was taken prisoner on the occasion. The square column was erected in 1557 by Pietro Cesi, governor of the Romagna.

From Ravenna a road leads to (65 M.) *Ferrara* by *Alfonsine*, *Lavezzola*, *Argenta*, *Consandolo*, and *Fossanova*, traversing a flat, well-cultivated district, but destitute of interest.

A good road leads from Ravenna to *Rimini* (no diligence), skirting the coast, but seldom affording a view of the sea, which is concealed by sandhills. It traverses a monotonous, flat district, passing S. Apollinare in Classe, the pine-forest, *Cervia* (a small town in an unhealthy situation, an episcopal see, with salt-works in the vicinity), *Cesenatico*, *S. Martino*, a wooden bridge over the *Uso*, probably the *Rubicon* of the ancients (comp. p. 237), and *Celle*, altogether 33 M., a journey which may be accomplished by carr. in 5 hrs., a route recommended to parties of three or four travellers together in preference to the railway.

47. From Bologna to Florence.

Railway. Express in $4^1/_4$ hrs., 16 fr. 55 c. or 13 fr.; ord. trains from Bologna to Pistoja in 4 hrs., thence to Florence in $1^1/_2$ hr.; fares to Pistoja 11 fr. 80, 8 fr. 65, 6 fr. 50 c.; to Florence 13 fr. 80, 11 fr. 20, 8 fr. 40 c.

This line, which intersects the Tuscan Apennines in nearly a straight direction, is one of the most imposing structures of the kind in existence. Bridges, tunnels (45 in all), and galleries are traversed in uninterrupted succession. Beautiful views are obtained (generally to the l.) of the valleys and gorges of the Apennines, and farther on, of the luxuriant plains of Tuscany, the 'Garden of Italy'. Doubts, however, have frequently been entertained as to the solidity of these great structures, and much of the traffic between the Romagna and Tuscany is in consequence still carried on by means of the old roads across the Apennines from Forli and Faenza to Florence. A rival line is contemplated.

As far as Porretta the line ascends the valley of the *Reno*, which it crosses a short distance beyond Bologna. On an island in the Reno, not far from Bologna, the Second Triumvirate was determined on by Octavian, Antony, and Lepidus, to the proscriptions of which Cicero and others fell victims (comp. p. 218).

First stat. *Borgo Panigale;* then **Casalecchio,** where the mountainous valley of the Reno expands into the plain of the Po. Here on June 26th, 1402, the army of Giovanni Bentivoglio was defeated by Gian Galeazzo Visconti, and on May 21st, 1511, that of Pope Julius II. under the command of the Duke of Urbino, by the French. L., near stat. *Sasso*, the brook *Setta* falls into the Reno, from which a subterranean aqueduct, constructed by Augustus, leads to Bologna. The restoration of this channel, with a view to supply the town with better water, has recently been proposed. Next stat. **Marzabotto,** with modernized castle, visible from the train. Between this point and Pracchia there are 22 tunnels. At stat. *Vergato* the valley expands; then stat. *Riola;* l. rise the abrupt peaks of *Monte Ovolo* and *Monte Vigese;* a landslip from the latter destroyed the village of Vigo in 1851. On the l. bank of the Reno is the restored castle of *Savignano*, with picturesque environs; farther on, the village of **Porretta** *(*Locanda Nuova d'Italia; Palazzino)*, on the Reno, with mineral springs and baths, much frequented in summer. Beyond Porretta the line quits the valley of the Reno. Numerous tunnels are now passed through, and the culminating point of the line reached. Beyond stat. **Pracchia** the line gradually descends by means of a series of galleries; beyond stat. *Pitecchio* a view is at length revealed of the lovely and populous plain of Tuscany. A number of charming villas are next passed, and the train stops at **Pistoja** (p. 278).

From Pistoja to Florence see R. 51.

The old road, now disused, from Bologna to Florence ascends the valley of the *Savena* and passes *S. Rufilo, Pianoro, Filigare*, and *Pietramala* in a bleak district. About $^1/_2$ hr. E. from the latter are *I Fuochi*, or the burning mountain (Monte di Fo), the flames of which (produced by gas, as proved by Volta) produce a most striking effect, especially at night.

Similar, though less imposing, is the *Acqua Buja*, 1/4 hr. W. of Pietramala, with inflammable water-bubbles. From Pietramala an ascent of 1 hr. at the base of *Monte Beni* and the *Sasso di Castro* to *Covigliajo*, at a considerable elevation, with an inn (Posta); then 1 1/4 hr. more to *La Futa*, the culminating point of the road, about 3000 ft. above the sea-level, occasionally obstructed by snow in winter. Then a descent to *Monte Carelli*, beyond which another ridge of the Apennines is traversed, and the road finally descends to the valley of the *Sieve*, known as the *Val di Mugello*. The road to the r. leads to *Barberino* and thence to *Prato* (and *Pistoja*), that to the l. to *Florence*. About 2 M. before Cafaggiolo is reached, the road passes *Le Maschere*, now an inn, situated in the midst of most picturesque scenery, and affording views of the Apennines and the extensive valley of the Arno.

Cafaggiolo is a post stat. on the r. bank of the Sieve. Then *Fontebuona*, beyond which the road descends rapidly; somewhat to the l. is *Pratolino*, a villa of the former grand-dukes, situated in the woods. A castle once erected here by Buontalenti for Francesco de' Medici, son of Cosmo I., for the reception of his mistress Bianca Capello, has long since been destroyed. Almost the sole trace of its former splendour is the column of Apenninus, 60 ft. in height. The road now descends between villas and gardens, passing *Fiesole* (p. 329), to Florence, which is entered by the Porta S. Gallo.

48. From Genoa to Florence *(by sea)* by Leghorn, Pisa, and Empoli.

The Italian **Mail Steamers** (comp. p. 86) of the *Società Rubatino* and *Società Peirano* start daily at 11 p. m. from Genoa for Naples viâ Leghorn. The vessels of the French *Compagnie Fraissinet* leave on Mondays and Thursdays at 8 p. m., and those of the *Compagnie Valéry* on Mondays and Thursdays at 10 p. m. for Naples viâ Leghorn and Civitavecchia. The Messageries Impériales have discontinued touching at Genoa. Fares to Leghorn 32 fr. 50, 22 fr. 50 c.; tickets should be procured at the offices previous to the starting of the vessel. As some of these vessels are not entirely unexceptionable with regard to cleanliness, enquiries should be made beforehand on this head. — Boat to or from the steamer 1 fr. each pers. incl. luggage. — Travellers arriving at Genoa by sea, and intending to proceed thence by railway, avoid trouble and annoyance by at once booking their luggage for its destination, at the harbour, immediately after the custom-house examination. For this purpose a facchino of the douane (20 c.) should be employed, and not one of the unauthorized and importunate bystanders.

Leghorn, Ital. *Livorno*, French *Livourne*.

Arrival. The steamboats generally enter the inner harbour *(porto vecchio*, or *Mediceo)*, but occasionally do not proceed beyond the outer harbour *(porto nuovo)*. The tariff for disembarcation varies accordingly: from the Porto Nuovo each pers. 1 fr., with ordinary luggage 1 fr. 50 c., for each additional package 30 c.; from the Porto Vecchio each pers. 50 c., with luggage 1 fr.; children under 8 years free, over 8 at half-fares. These fares should be paid to the superintending official, and not to the boatmen. — Porterage into the town, or to the stat., each box 80, travelling-bag 40, hatbox 20 c., or for these three articles together 1 fr. (according to tariff).

Hotels. Victoria and **Washington**, on the harbour and canal, R. 3—5 fr., D. at 5 o'cl. 3 1/2 fr.; *Gran Bretagna with the Pension Suisse, near the harbour, Via Vittorio Emanuele 17, R. 2 fr. and upwards, D. 3 1/2 fr.; Hôtel du Nord, Hôtel d'Angleterre, both on the harbour; Iles Britanniques, 33 Via Vittor. Em.; *Robertson's Private Boarding House, comfortable. — Those acquainted with the language, or accompanied by Italians, will find some of the less pretending inns very tolerable and inexpensive; most of them have a trattoria, or restaurant, connected with them, in which meals are taken à la carte, and are situated in the Via Vittor. Emanuele, such as Giappone, Pergola, Luna, Ville de Turin, Roma, Patria, etc. — For a prolonged stay a private lodging is easily obtained.

Cafes. *Vittoria, Piazza d'Arme; *Posta, Via Vitt. Emanuele, opp. the post-office; Borsa, in the same street. — *Beer:* Meyer, Via Ricasoli. — *Restaurants:* Giappone, Fenice, Giardinetto, Pergola, all in the Via Vitt. Eman.; Ghiaccaio, Piazza d'Arme.

Post Office corner of the Corso Vitt. Eman. and Piazza Carlo Alberto. — *Telegraph Office* Via de' Lanzi 5.

Fiacres. Drive in the town 85 c., beyond the town 1 fr. 70 c.; per hour 1 fr. 70 c., each additional 1/2 hr. 60 c.; to or from the stat. 1 fr. At night, from 1 to 6 a. m., in the town 1 fr. 15 c., beyond the town 2 fr. 80 c.; per hr. 2 fr. 85 c.; to or from the stat. 1 fr. 80 c. — The services of the railway facchini at the stat. are gratuitous, but they generally receive a trifling fee.

Reading Room. Gabinetto Letterario e Scientifico, Piazza d'Arme 30, open the whole day, adm. 50 c.

Sea Baths. Casino e Bagni di Mare and dello Scoglio della Regina, both outside the Porta a Mare. Bath with boat and towel 1 fr.; season from the middle of June to August. — Warm Baths in the town, near S. Marco, in winter 1 fr. 40 c., in summer 1 fr.; also in the Via della Pace.

Consuls. English (Mr. *Macbean*) Via della Madonna 12; American, next door to the Victoria Hotel; Spanish, Piazza dei SS. Pietro e Paolo 7, visa for Rome 4 fr.; commissionaire who procures it 1 fr.; Prussian, Piazza dei Domenicani 6; Dutch, Via del Monte Vecchio 3; Russian, Via Ricasoli 5; French, Piazza Maria. — Belgian, Danish, Swedish, and other consuls also reside here.

Theatres. Regio Teatro degli Avvolorati, in the street of that name; Regio Teatro dei Floridi, Via S. Marco 9, etc.

English Church, resident chaplain.

Railway by *Pisa* and *Massa* to *La Spezia*, see R. 49. — To Rome by the *Maremme Line* in 10 hrs. — Steamboat-passengers touching at Leghorn generally have time for a short excursion to Pisa, for the sake of visiting the cathedral and Campo Santo.

Leghorn, a very insignificant place in the 16th cent. (in 1551 only 749 inhab.), is indebted for its size and importance to the Medicis, who invited hither the oppressed and discontented from all parts of the continent, such as Roman Catholics from England, Jews and Moors from Spain and Portugal, and merchants from Marseilles who were anxious to escape from the perils of civil war. Montesquieu consequently terms Leghorn 'the masterpiece of the dynasty of the Medicis'. Leghorn is a free harbour, and protected by fortifications. The rapidly increasing population is now 99,500 souls, exclusive of a fluctuating sea-faring community of upwards of 3000.

The town contains little to detain the traveller. It is a well built, thoroughly modern place. A few hours will suffice to explore it. The *Harbour* is a very busy spot, and extensive new works are now in progress. The inner harbour *(Porto Vecchio,* or *Mediceo)* is too shallow to admit vessels of large tonnage; the *Porto Nuovo* was therefore constructed during the present century, to the W. of the old harbour, and protected from the open sea by a semicircular mole. Picturesque glimpses are obtained hence of the sea with the islands Elba, Gorgona, and Capraja. An excursion by boat on the harbour will be found very pleasant in fine weather (1 fr. per hr., agreement necessary). By the harbour is the *Statue of the Grand Duke Ferdinand I., by *Giov. dell' Opera*, with 4 Turkish slaves in bronze by *Pietro Tacca*. On the pier, 500 yds. in length, rises the *Lighthouse*, erected by the Pisans in 1303, the platform of which affords a good survey of the town, harbour, and sea.

The town possesses well-paved streets and large and handsome squares. It is intersected by canals, and connected by a navigable canal with the *Arno*, the influx of which is 7 M. to the N. The *Corso Vittorio Emanuele* is the principal street. It leads from the harbour to the spacious *Piazza d'Arme*, in which the cathedral, the town-hall, and a small royal palace are situated. It proceeds thence to the *Piazza Carlo Alberto*, formerly termed *Piazza dei Principi*, adorned with colossal *Statues of the Grand Dukes Ferdinand III. and Leopold II.*, the last but one (d. 1824) and the last grand-duke of Tuscany. The original inscriptions on the former monument were superseded by others in 1860, which record the repudiation of the House of Lorraine and the annexation of Tuscany to the kingdom of Victor Emmanuel. — The water of Leghorn is bad, but this evil was greatly remedied by the construction of a conduit 5 M. in length, during the reign of Leopold II.

Walks. Pleasant grounds to the S., outside the Porta a Mare, and along the coast by the road to Ardenza; also in the *Giardino dei Bagni* (adm. 50 c., or by subscription) in the same neighbourhood, where a band plays every evening during the bathing-season (Caffè Ristoratore).

Railway from Leghorn to Pisa in 25 min., fares 2 fr., 1 fr. 50, 1 fr. 20 c.; from Pisa by Empoli to Florence in 2½ hrs., fares 7 fr. 80, 6 fr. 40 c., 5 fr.

The line crosses the Arno Canal and traverses flat meadow-land, intersected by canals and occasionally relieved by a few pines; to the r. a range of hills at some distance.

Pisa see p. 265.

The railway to Florence traverses a beautiful and fertile district on the l. bank of the Arno, running parallel to the high road as far as Montelupo. To the l. are the *Monti Pisani* (p. 272) with the ruined castle on the Verruca. Stat. *Navacchio*; then stat. *Cascina* on the Arno, where on the festival of S. Vittorio, July 28th, 1364, the Pisans sustained a defeat from the Florentines (in the vicinity are the hydraulic works employed in draining the *Lago di Bientina*). Next stat. *Pontedera*, a small town at the confluence of the *Era* and Arno, where the road through the beautiful valley of the Era to *Volterra* diverges (diligence 3 times weekly in 6 hrs., fare 5 fr.).

Next stations *La Rotta*, *S. Romano*, and *S. Pierino*. To the

l. in the distance the chain of the Apennines comes in view; r. on the height is **San Miniato dei Tedeschi**, a small town, elevated by Emp. Frederick II. in 1226 to the dignity of seat of the imperial governor. Francesco Sforza was born here. The *Cathedral*, dating from the 10th cent., was remodelled 1488, and decorated with statues in 1775. This town, like those of *Fiesole*, *Colle*, and *Volterra*, has the privilege of conferring the rank of nobility by an entry in its 'golden book'.

Stat. **Empoli** is a small town in a fertile district. In 1260, after the defeat of the Florentines on the Arbia, the Ghibellines proposed to transfer the seat of government hither and to raze Florence to the ground. This project, however, was strenuously opposed by the heroic Farinata degli Uberti, an incident beautifully recorded by Dante in the 10th canto of his Inferno. The town is a busy place with old houses and narrow streets, and a church of 1093, containing good pictures by Giotto, Jac. da Empoli, Cigoli, etc., and a fine Baptistery of 1447. A festival, celebrated here on Corpus Christi Day (Fête de Dieu), commemorates the ancient importance of the town.

Railway hence (S.) to Siena and Orvieto, see *Baedeker's Central Italy*.

The line follows the valley of the Arno, crosses the small river *Pesa*, and reaches *Montelupo*. The castle (Rocca) of this place, according to the historian Villani, was fortified by the Florentines in 1203 in order to keep in check the hostile *Capraja* on the opposite side. Hence the appellation Montelupo, 'mountain of the wolf', which was desirous of devouring the goat (capra). On the l., before Montelupo is reached, the traveller perceives the *Villa Ambrogiana*, erected by Ferdinand I. on the site of an ancient castle of the Ardinghelli, and surmounted by towers and pinnacles. Beyond Montelupo the line crosses the Arno, and slowly winds through the defile of the *Gonfolina*, through which the Arno flows. The heights are clad with rock-pines, below which the *pietra serena*, a kind of sandstone frequently employed in the construction of the palaces of Florence, is quarried. At the extremity of the Gonfolina the line crosses the *Ombrone*, which falls into the Arno, and traverses a vine-clad district to the old borough of *Signa*, with its grey towers and pinnacles, founded in 1377 by the Florentines to command the road at this point. This place, as well as the opp. village of *Lastra*, is celebrated for its straw-plait. The valley now expands, richly cultivated and resembling one continuous garden. Near stat. *S. Donnino* is *Brozzi*, with numerous villas which proclaim the proximity of the capital. The train now approaches the *Cascine*, the park of Florence, and enters the stat. near S. Maria Novella.

Florence see p. 282.

49. From Genoa to Pisa *(by land)* by La Spezia.

From Genoa to Chiavari (24 M.) railway in 1³/₄ hr., fare 4 fr., 2 fr. 80 c., 2 fr.; the continuation to La Spezia is in course of construction. Between Chiavari and La Spezia (45 M.) diligence 3 times daily, usually full and not recommended, in correspondence with the trains, in 9¹/₂ hrs.; fares during the day coupé 8, interior 7, banquette 6 fr., at night coupé 12, interior 10 fr.; one-horse carr. 25, two-horse 40 fr. — From Spezia to Pisa railway in 2³/₄ hrs., 7 fr. 50, 6 fr. 10, 4 fr. 65 c.

The line, opened in 1869, partly follows the direction of the high road, and skirts the coast, the *Riviera di Levante*, which affords views hardly inferior to those on the Riviera di Ponente (p. 94). The numerous promontories are penetrated by means of cuttings and tunnels, of which upwards of 30 are passed, many of them of considerable length. Stations *Sturla*, *Quinto*, *Nervi* (with lemon-groves), *Pieve di Sori, Recco, Camogli*, situated to the r. on the shore. Farther on, the promontory of *Sta. Margarita* is penetrated by a long tunnel; the line now skirts the *Bay of Rapallo* with its numerous villas. Stat. *S. Margarita*, r. on the coast; then *Rapallo*, a small seaport-town whence a considerable traffic in olive-oil is carried on, with the pilgrimage-church of the *Madonna di Montallegro*.

Chiavări (**Posta*, R. 1¹/₂, L. ¹/₂, A. ¹/₂ fr.; *Fenice*) is a small town (pop. 10,000), charmingly situated, possessing silk-manufactories and a handsome church.

Beyond it the high road passes a succession of picturesque villages.

Lavagna, with wharf for small vessels, is the ancestral seat of the Counts Fieschi. Here Sinibaldo de' Fieschi, professor of law at Bologna, and afterwards elevated to the papal throne as Pope Innocent IV. (1243—54), the powerful opponent of Emp. Frederick II., was born. Giov. Luigi de' Fieschi, well known in history as the conspirator against the power of the Doria family (1547) at Genoa, was also a native of Lavagna.

The road follows the coast and leads to *Sestri a Levante* (Albergo della Strada ferrata), picturesquely situated on a bay which is terminated by a promontory. It then ascends the beautifully wooded mountains in long windings, affording fine retrospects of the peninsula and valley (the village in the latter is *Casarza*). Farther on, the village of *Bracco* becomes visible on the l.; then to the r. the view is again disclosed of the sea, above which the road leads. The village on the coast below is *Moneglia*. Then a gradual ascent through a somewhat bleak district to the *Osteria Baracca* (2236 ft.), whence the road descends into a valley in which the village of *Baracca* lies. After a slight ascent the road next traverses a well cultivated district to *Pogliasca* (Europa) and *Borghetto* (Ville de Milan) in the valley of the impetuous *Vara*, an affluent of the *Magra* which falls into the sea near Sarzana and was the ancient frontier between Italy and Liguria, as the Rubicon on the E. formed the frontier of Gaul. The road skirts the broad, gravelly channel of the river for some distance, then diverges l. and enters a wooded tract, in which beautiful chestnuts predominate. Beyond Baracca the sea does not again come into view, until the last height before Spezia is attained, whence a magnificent prospect of the bay and the precipitous mountains of Carrara is enjoyed.

La Spezia (*Croce di Malta; Ville de Milan* (where Garibaldi resided during his captivity after the battle of Aspromonte), R. 3 fr., L. 75., A. 75 c. — Of the second cl. Albergo Nazionale, R. 2. A. and L. ³|₄ fr., in the principal street, and Gran Bretagna (commercial). — *Sea Baths* 50 c., indifferent, the best near the rail. stat. behind the Cappuccini. *Warm Baths* adjoining the 'Croce di Malta'), a small town with 11,000 inhab., is charmingly situated at the N. W. angle of the *Golfo della Spezia*, between two rocks crowned with forts. It possesses one of the best harbours in Europe, known and praised by the Romans as the *Portus Lunae*, and since 1861 the principal naval depôt of Italy. La Spezia is visited as a bathing-place in summer especially by the Genoese. Mild climate and rich vegetation.

Beautiful walks along the coast. Delightful excursion to *Porto Venere* on the W. side of the bay (two-horse carr. in 1½ hr. 10 fr.; boat, in the same time, with one rower 8. with two 10 fr.), on the site of the ancient *Portus Veneris*. A most charming prospect is enjoyed from the ruins of the church of *S. Pietro* rising above the sea, and supposed to occupy the site of the former temple of Venus. The opposite island of *Palmaria*, with a small fortress, is employed as a penal establishment for brigands. Pleasant excursions may also be made to the E. side of the bay, to the village of *Lerici* etc.

The Railway to Pisa passes through several tunnels and reaches stat. *Arcola*, with conspicuous campanile. Beyond the next tunnel the broad *Magra* is crossed. Then on the l. lies

Stat. **Sarzana** *(New-York; Lunigiana)*, Rom. *Sergiana* or *Luna Nova*, from its having superseded the ancient Luna, with the picturesque fortification of *Sarzanella*, constructed by *Castruccio Castracani*. In 1467 the place fell into the hands of the Florentines under Lorenzo de' Medici, from whom it was again wrested by Charles VIII. of France; it subsequently belonged to the Genoese, then to the Sardinians. Sarzana was the birthplace of Pope Nicholas V. (Tommaso Parentucelli, 1447—55), a great patron of learning, and the founder of the library of the Vatican The *Buonaparte* family is also said to have been settled in the Lunigiana, near Sarzana, before they transferred their residence to Corsica. The *Cathedral*, a good example of Italian Gothic, constructed of white marble, was commenced in 1355. The environs are very fertile. Among the mountains to the l.

the white rocks and gorges of the neighbouring marble-quarries are visible. To the r. a fine view of the Bay of La Spezia.

Between Sarzana and the next stat. Avenza are the ruins of *Luna*, situated on the coast. This old Etruscan town fell to decay under the Roman emperors, and was finally destroyed by the Arabians in 1016; its episcopal see was transferred in 1465 to Sarzana. The site of the ancient town is still marked by the ruins of an amphitheatre and circus. From the town of Luna the district derives its appellation of *La Lunigiana*.

Next stat. *Avenza*, a small town on the brook of that name, above which an old castle of Castruccio Castracani, of 1322, with its bold round towers and pinnacles, picturesquely rises. This was formerly the frontier town of the Duchy of Massa. On the coast to the r. is a small harbour for the shipment of the Carrara marble.

Branch Railway from Avenza in 12 min. to

Carrara (*Locanda Nazionale*, with the *Trattoria del Giardinetto*, in the principal street on the r., pranzo 2 fr.; travellers are cautioned not to spend the night here, as the mosquitoes are insufferable). A visit to the the celebrated and interesting quarries requires 3 hrs. at least. Guides demand 5 fr., but will generally reduce their charge to 2—3 fr.; for a mere superficial survey their services may be dispensed with. Leaving the station, the traveller turns to the r. and follows the street in a straight direction, past the theatre, to the Piazza, which is adorned with an over lite-size statue of the grand-duchess Maria Beatrice, erected in 1861. The bridge to the l. at the end of the piazza should then be crossed, and the road with deep ruts, ascending on the r. bank of the *Torano*, followed. At (1/4 M.) a group of houses a path diverges to the r. to extensive quarries of an inferior quality of marble, but the traveller continues to follow the road, passing numerous marble cutting and polishing premises. Beyond the village of *Torano*, round which the road leads, the first mines, recognisable by broad heaps of rubbish, are situated on both sides of the valley. The blocks are detached, drawn out by oxen, and rolled down the hill. The finer description is termed *marmo statuario*. About 400 mines with 6000 workmen are at present in operation. The hours of labour are from 5 a. m. to 2 or 3 p. m.; the forenoon is therefore the best time for a visit (a supply of copper coins should not be forgotten). A horn is blown as a signal when the rock is about to be blasted. The mines of *Monte Crestola* and *M. Sagro* yield the best and largest blocks. The mines of *Fantiscritti*, 3 M. from Carrara, were worked by the ancient Romans (see below).

The town of Carrara contains numerous studios of sculptors (*Lazzerini, Franchi, Pellicia, Bonanni*, etc.), some of which should be visited. Most of the inhabitants obtain their livelihood by working the marble. The following churches should also be inspected: *S. Andrea*, in a half Germanic style of the 13th cent., like the cathedral of Monza, possesses an interesting façade and good sculptures. *Madonna delle Grazie*, with sumptuous decorations in marble.

The *Accademia delle Belle Arti* contains a great number of copies from antiques, as well as works by sculptors of Carrara, and several Roman antiquities found in the mines of Fantiscritti (see above), e. g. a bas-relief of Jupiter with Bacchus etc.

Beyond Avenza the line next reaches

Stat. **Massa** (*Quattro Nazioni*), formerly capital of the Duchy of Massa-Carrara, with 10,000 inhab., pleasantly situated, surrounded by mountains. The *Palace* was once occupied by Napoleon's sister Elisa Bacciocchi (Duchess of Massa-Carrara). The

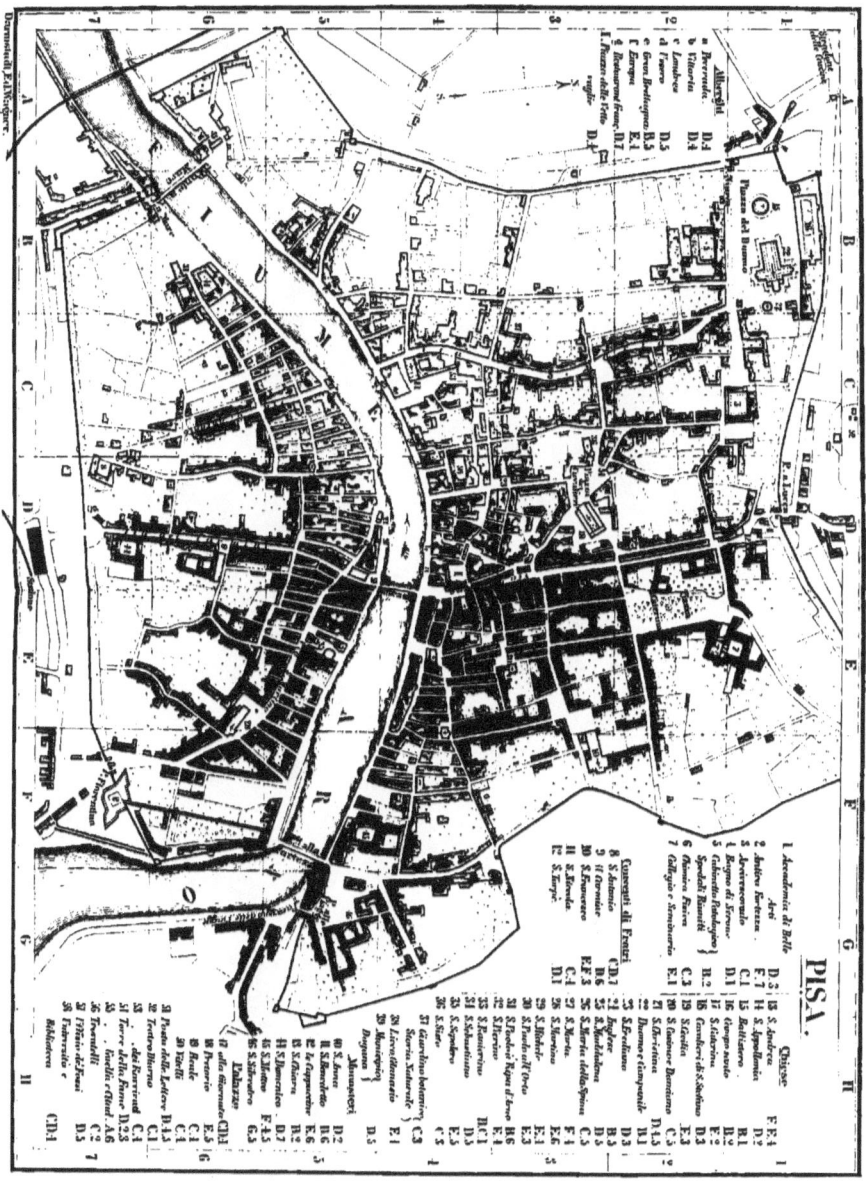

marble-quarries here are very valuable, rivalling those of Carrara.

The train traverses a fertile, well cultivated tract. L. the picturesque ruins of the old castle of *Montignoso*, on an abrupt height, soon become visible. Then stat. *Queceta*; about 3 M. to the l. lies the village of *Serravezza*, with marble-quarries, a place frequented as a summer-residence.

Pietrasanta *(Unione*, outside the gate towards Massa; *Europa)*, a small town surrounded by ancient walls, beautifully situated among gentle slopes, was besieged and taken in 1482 by the Florentines under Lorenzo de' Medici. The following churches deserve notice:

S. Martino (Il Duomo), commenced in the 13th cent., was altered and extended at various periods down to the 16th cent. Ancient font in the *Battisterio*. Bronzes by *Donatello*. Campanile of 1380.

S. Agostino, an unfinished Gothic structure of the 14th cent., contains a painting by *Taddeo Zacchia*, of 1519, and a fine altar by *Staggi*. The pinnacled *Town Hall* is situated in the Piazza, between these two churches. — Mines of quicksilver are worked in the vicinity.

Near stat. *Viareggio* (Albergo del Commercio), a small town on the coast, with sea-baths, the line enters the marshy plain of the *Serchio*, crosses the river beyond stat. *Torre di Lago*, and soon reaches the station of *Pisa*.

50. Pisa.

Arrival. The station of Pisa is at the S. extremity of the town. Those, therefore, who desire to visit the cathedral and its environs only, leave their luggage at the station, and, disregarding the importunities of the bystanders, proceed by fiacre (1 fr.) to the cathedral and Campo Santo.

Hotels. On the Lung' Arno, N. side: °Grand Hôtel Peverada, R. 3, L. 1 fr.; °Vittoria; °Gran Bretagna; Europa, by Ponte di Mezzo; Hôtel de Londres, near the station, D. 4½, R. 3½ fr.; °Hôtel de la Minerve, opposite the stat., R. 3, L. ½ fr., A. 70 c.; °Hôtel de la Ville, R. 2—3, D. 3 fr.; Ussero by the Lung' Arno, S. side. — La Pergola, Via del Borgo, near the Ponte di Mezzo, a small Italian inn.

Restaurants. Nettuno, in the Lung' Arno; Restaurant Français, near the station, both recommended.

Cafés. Ciardelli, Burchi, Ussero, all in the Lung' Arno, N. side.

Furnished Apartments in the Lung' Arno, 2—3 rooms 100—130 fr. per month; cheaper as the summer approaches.

Fiacres. One-horse per drive 45 c., two-h. 70 c., to and from the station 60 or 85 c., 1st hour 1 fr. 10 resp. 1 fr. 70., each additional hour 85 c. or 1 fr. 15 c.

Post Office on the l. bank of the river, below Ponte di Mezzo.

Physicians. Bartolini, Feroci, Fedeli, Burci.

Photographer. Huguet and Van Lint, Lung' Arno, below Ponte di Mezzo.

Baths. Bagni Ceccherini, Lung' Arno, N. side, near Ponte Mare.

English Church Service during the winter and spring.

Pisa, a quiet town with 50,000 inhab., situated 6 M. from

the sea on both banks of the Arno, is considered a good winter-residence for invalids, on account of the mildness and moisture of the atmosphere, while the heat in summer is very oppressive. The town, called *Pisae* by the ancients, once lay at the confluence of the Arnus and Auser (Serchio), of which the latter now has an estuary of its own.

In B. C. 180 Pisa became a Roman colony, Augustus gave it the name of *Colonia Julia Pisana*, and Hadrian and Antoninus Pius erected temples, theatres and triumphal arches here, all traces of which have long since disappeared. In the middle ages the town attained to considerable affluence by its commerce and maritime traffic, owing in a great measure to the crusades, and became a rival of Genoa and Venice. Sardinia, Corsica, Palermo and the Balearic Islands were once under the supremacy of Pisa; but these places were lost to it in succession, first owing to the defeat of the fleet under Ugolino, at Meloria, near Leghorn, by the Genoese, then in consequence of the unsuccessful wars with Lucca and Florence. Feuds of the nobles also tended materially to impair the resources of Pisa. After the assassination of *Pietro Gambacorti* in 1392 it came into the possession of the Visconti of Milan, and in 1406 into that of Florence, the fortunes of which it thenceforth shared. Pisa has produced more celebrated architects and sculptors than perhaps any other town in Italy. Of these the most distinguished were *Nicola Pisano* (about 1240) and his son *Giovanni Pisano*, *Andrea Pisano*, the pupil of the latter (about 1340), and his son *Nino Pisano*. The Pisan school of painting held a considerably inferior rank; fine works by *Buffalmacco*, *Bennozzo Gozzoli*, in the Campo Santo etc., are to be seen here, but these masters were not natives of the place. The *University* of Pisa, founded about 1340 by *Bonifacio della Gherardesca* and renewed by Cosmo I. in 1542, with a staff of 60 professors and attended by about 600 students, has educated a number of celebrated men at various periods. Here *Galileo*, who became professor of mathematics in 1610, first observed the oscillations of the pendulum, and paved the way for the subsequent discoveries which have rendered his name immortal. His *Statue*, by *Emilio Demi*, adorns the court of the university, having been erected 1839 to commemorate the *first* collection of the *Scienziati Italiani*. The University is also noted for the prominent part which it took in the events of 1848—59.

The busiest part of the town and chief resort of strangers is the **Lung' Arno** (especially the sheltered N. side), a broad and handsome quay extending along both banks of the river, which are connected by means of three bridges (besides that of the railway). At the W. end of the Lung' Arno rises the statue of Ferdinand I., a work of the school of *Giambologna*. The far-famed illumination *(La Luminara)* here takes place on June 17th, every three years; the Carnival is also celebrated here. The Lung' Arno with its prolongation outside the Porta alle Spiagge *(Passeggiata Nuova)* is much frequented in the evening. The inundation of the Arno in 1869 caused considerable damage here. Churches and buildings in the Lung' Arno worthy of note, see pp. 270, 271.

Of the sights of Pisa the most interesting is the ****Piazza del Duomo**, with the *Cathedral*, the *Leaning Tower*, the *Baptistery* and the *Campo Santo*, a group of buildings without parallel, situated outside the town and removed from its disturbing influences. Three hours at least are required to explore these structures; guide unnecessary.

*Il Duomo, erected after the great naval victory of the Pisans near Palermo (1063) by *Busketus* and *Rainaldus* in 1067—1103 in the Norman-Tuscan style, was consecrated by Pope Gelasius II. in 1118. It is a basilica with nave and double aisles, 292 ft. in length, with galleries over the aisles, intersected by a transept with aisles, and surmounted by an elliptical dome over the centre. This remarkably perfect edifice is constructed entirely of white marble, with black and coloured ornamentation. The most magnificent part is the façade, adorned with four different series of columns, one above another. The choir, too, presents an imposing appearance. The ancient bronze-gates were replaced in 1602 by the present doors, with representations of scriptural subjects, executed by *Mocchi*, *Tacca*, *Mora*, and others, from designs by *Giovanni da Bologna*.

The Interior (entered usually on the E. side, opposite the Campanile) is borne by 68 columns, many of which are of Greek and ancient Roman origin, having been captured by the Pisans in war. The nave has a richly gilded ceiling; the aisles are vaulted, and above them runs a triforium.

In 1596 the dome and the whole church, with the exception of the choir, were seriously injured by a conflagration, but were subsequently restored. Many traces of the restoration are observable, especially in the interior.

Nave. Most of the tombstones formerly here have been removed to the Campo Santo. A few still remain by the *W. Wall*, on the r. and l. of the principal entrance, among them that of Archb. Rinuccini (d. 1582), by *Tacca*, and that of Archb. Giuliano de' Medici (d. 1660). The designs of the 12 altars are attributed to *Mich. Angelo*, the execution to *Staggi da Pietra Santa*. The large altar-pieces are by *Lomi*, *Allori*, *Salimbeni*, and other masters of the 16th cent. — Pulpit adorned with lions and evangelists by *Nicola Pisano*. The swaying of the bronze lamp which hangs in the nave is said first to have suggested to Galileo the idea of the pendulum. On the last pillar of the nave on the r., St. Agnes, by *And. del Sarto*.

R. Transept: 1st altar on the r., Madonna, by *Pierino del Vaga* and *Sogliani*. Above the *Cappella di S. Ranieri*, which contains a sarcophagus by *Foggini*, is a Madonna in mosaic. A niche adjoining the chapel on the r. contains an ancient statue of Mars, commonly revered as St. Ephesus. The Madonna and Child which adorn the basin for holy water at the entrance were designed by *Mich. Angelo*.

The Choir contains finely carved stalls (prophets, landscapes, animals etc.). The high altar, overloaded with marble and lapis lazuli, dating from 1774, was restored in 1825. Above it, Christ on the Cross, by *Giambologna*. On the arch of the choir, angels by *Dom. Ghirlandajo*, unfortunately much retouched. The mosaics of the dome (Christ between Mary and John the Baptist) are by *Cimabue*. Of the pictures in the choir, SS. Margaret and Catharine on the r. in front of the high altar, and SS. Peter and John on the l. by *And. del Sarto* are worthy of inspection; beyond the high altar, *Abraham's Sacrifice, and Entombment by *Sodoma*. The capitals of the two columns on the r. and l., with representations of children, are by *Michael Angelo*.

L. Transept. Over the Cappella del SS. Sagramento, the Annunciation in mosaic. The altar, richly decorated with silver, was presented by Cosmo III.; behind it, Adam and Eve, a basrelief by *Mosca*.

The *Baptistery *(Il Battisterio),* commenced in 1153 by Dio-

tisalvi, but according to the inscriptions not completed till 1278, with Gothic additions of the 14th cent., is also entirely constructed of marble. It is a beautiful circular structure, surrounded by half columns below, and a gallery of smaller detached columns above, surmounted by a conical dome (179 ft. high, restored in 1856). It has four entrances; at those on the N. and E. are ancient sculptures in marble of the 12th cent. — The Interior rests on 8 columns and 4 pillars, above which there is a simple triforium; in the centre the octagonal *Font, with beautiful marble rosettes, and an admirable hexagonal *Pulpit, borne by 7 columns, with reliefs by *Nicola Pisano*, 1260: 1st, Annunciation and Nativity; 2nd, Adoration of the Magi; 3rd, Presentation in the Temple; 4th, Crucifixion; 5th, Last Judgment. A dome, restored in 1856, surmounts the structure, 179 ft. in height. Sculptures at the E. entrance represent the martyrdom of John the Baptist. Fine echo in the interior.

The *Campanile, or clock-tower, commenced by the architects *Bonanno of Pisa* and *William of Innsbruck* in 1174, and completed by *Tommaso Pisano* in 1350, rises in 8 different stories, which like the Baptistery are surrounded with half-columns and colonnades. Owing to its remarkable oblique position, 12 ft. out of the perpendicular (height 151 ft.), it is usually known as the Leaning Tower. Discussions have frequently arisen as to whether this peculiarity was intentional or accidental. The most probable solution is that the foundations settled during the progress of the structure, and that, to remedy the defect as much as possible, an attempt was made to give a vertical position to the upper portion. The *View from the platform, embracing the town and environs, the sea to the W., and the mountains N.E., is very beautiful; a good staircase of 294 steps leads to the top. Permission (for a party of not fewer than *three*, but if necessary the custodian will make up a party) is obtained at the town-hall. The tower contains 6 bells, the heaviest of which weighs 6 tons and is suspended on the side opposite the overhanging wall of the tower.

The *Campo Santo, or Burial Ground, was founded by Archb. Ubaldo, 1188—1200 (access daily; visitors knock at the door to the l., 1/2 fr. to the custodian on leaving). After the loss of the Holy Land the archbishop conveyed 53 ship-loads of earth hither from Mt. Calvary, in order that the dead might repose in holy ground. The structure which surrounds the churchyard was commenced in 1278 by order of the senators of the city, and completed in 1283 by *Giovanni Pisano*, in the Gothic-Tuscan style. It is 441 ft. in length, 145 ft. in width, and 48 ft. in height. Externally there are 43 flat arcades resting on 44 pilasters, the capitals adorned with figures. Over one of the two entrances is a marble canopy, with a Madonna by *Giovanni*

Pisano. In the interior it is a spacious hall, the open, pointed windows of which, with their beautiful tracery, 62 in number, look upon a green quadrangle. Three chapels adjoin the Campo; the oldest is r. of the entrance, in the centre of the E. side, with dome of later date. The walls are covered with *frescoes by painters of the oldest Tuscan school, beneath which is a collection of sculptures, partly Roman and Etruscan, partly mediæval. The latter are most important links in the history of the earliest Italian sculpture. The tombstones of those buried here form the pavement.

Paintings. To the r. of the chapel on the E. wall a Crucifixion, Resurrection, and Ascension by a follower of Giotto, supposed to be *Buffalmacco*.

On the *S. Wall:* *Triumph of Death, which fills with horror those who are devoted to earthly joys, but is welcome to the miserable and self-denying (on the l. an admirable equestrian group, who on their way to the chase are suddenly reminded by three open coffins of the transitoriness of human pleasures); the *Last Judgment (attitude of the Judge celebrated), attributed by Vasari to *Andrea Orcagna*, and Hell, the next picture, attributed by the same authority to *Bernardo*, Andrea's brother, have been pronounced by modern investigators not to be the works of these masters. Then the life (temptations and miracles) of the holy hermits in the Theban wilderness, by *Pietro Lorenzetti* of Siena. Between the two entrances, the life of St. Ranieri, the tutelary saint of Pisa: the upper scenes (delivery from a worldly life, journey to Palestine, victory over temptation, retirement to a monastery) probably painted by *Andrea da Firenze* and *Barnaba* about the year 1360, the lower and better executed scenes (return from Palestine, miracles, death, and removal of his body to the cathedral of Pisa) were painted by *Antonio Veniziano* about 1386. Then, above, scenes from the life of St. Ephysius (who as a Rom. general, fighting against the heathens, receives a flag of victory from the Archangel Michael, but is afterwards condemned and executed); below, scenes from the life of St. Potitus, admirably pourtrayed by *Spinello Aretino*, about 1390. Next the history of Job, by *Francesco da Volterra* (erroneously attributed to *Giotto*), begun in 1371, a vigorous work, but unfortunately in bad preservation.

On the W. wall no paintings of importance.

On the N. Wall the history of Genesis: first the Creation (God the Father holding the world in both hands, 'il mappamondo'); then in the upper series, Creation of man, the Fall, Expulsion from Paradise, Cain and Abel. Building of the ark, Deluge, and Sacrifice of Abraham, by *Pietro di Puccio* of Orvieto, about 1390 (attributed by Vasari to *Buffalmacco*). The lower series and all the following paintings on the N. wall are by *Benozzo Gozzoli* of Florence, 1469—85, °representations from the Old Testament, admirably executed 'a tempera': Noah's vintage and drunkenness (with the '*Vergognosa di Pisa*', or ashamed female spectator), the Curse of Ham, the Tower of Babel (with portraits of celebrities of that period, Cosmo de' Medici, his son Pietro, and his grandsons Lorenzo and Giuliano), the history of Abraham, Isaac, Jacob and Esau, Joseph, Moses and Aaron, Fall of the walls of Jericho, history of David, Solomon and the Queen of Sheba; this last much injured. Benozzo himself was interred below the history of Joseph.

Sculptures and Monuments: S. Side, in the l. corner inscriptions in honour of Caius and Lucius Cæsar, grandsons of Augustus. Roman sarcophagus with the rape of Proserpine; on it is placed a fine head of M. Agrippa in basalt. Column with mutilated statue of the Madonna, by *Nicola Pisano*. Fragment of a sarcophagus with fine Bacchanalian representation. R. of the entrance the monument of the oculist Andrea Vacca (d. 1826) by *Thorwaldsen*, Tobias curing his father's blindness. Madonna and Child with six saints, beneath them the history of Christ by *Tommaso Pisano*. Tombstone of Count Algarotti (d. 1764), erected by Frederick the Great. — W. End: Large ancient bath, subsequently used as a sarcophagus. Virgin and Child by *Giovanni Pisano* (mutilated). Monument of Emp. Henry VII. of Luxembourg, protector of Pisa which favoured the Ghibellines (d. 1313 at Buonconvento), workmanship in the style of the Pisan school. On the wall above, the chains of the ancient harbour of Pisa, captured by the Genoese in 1632; parts of them were given to the Florentines, who suspended them at the entrance of the Baptistery at Florence, but were restored to the Pisans in 1848; a second chain was restored to them by the Genoese in 1860. Two Roman sarcophagi with Etruscan cinerary urns placed on them; between them a group by *Giovanni Pisano*. Sarcophagus of Bishop Ricci (d. 1418), of the earlier Pisan school. Bust of Count Camillo Cavour, by *Dupré* of Florence. On a broken column, a marble vase with fine Bacchanalian representation.

N. Corridor: Mutilated relief of the Three Graces. Large Greek relief from a tomb. Virgin and Child by *Giovanni Pisano*. In the chapel an ancient Madonna, attributed to *Gaddi*. Beautiful head of a young Greek, perhaps Achilles. Head of Pluto. Sarcophagus with Bacchanalian representation, upon it the bust of Isotta of Rimini by *Mino da Fiesole*. Sarcophagus with the myth of Hippolytus and Phædra, from which Nicola Pisano copied several figures for his pulpit (p. 268); the remains of the Countess Beatrix (d. 1076), mother of the celebrated Mathilde, were subsequently deposited here. Sarcophagus with children gathering fruit. Several Egyptian antiquities. Bacchanalian sarcophagus with the myth of Actæon on the cover. Sitting statue, supposed to be the Emp. Henry VII., surrounded by four of his counsellors. Sarcophagus with the hunt of Meleager, another with battle of barbarians, a third with the 9 Muses.

E. End: Griffin in bronze with Coptic inscriptions. Sarcophagus of Ph. Dezio by *Staggi*. Statue of Leonardo Fibonacci by *G. Paganucci*. Monument of Count Mastiani, with the sitting statue of his inconsolable widow, by *Bartolini*. Etruscan altar with rams' heads at the corners. Monument of the singer Angelica Catalani (d. at Paris 1849), by *Costoli*. Statue of Nicola Pisano by *Salvini*. In the open space between the arcades two antique fountain-spouts. — A visit to the Campo Santo by moonlight is very impressive; previous notice must be given to the custodian.

Among the remaining churches the following deserve mention:

*S. Caterina, in the German-Tuscan style, erected about 1253, is situated in a beautiful square planted with trees and adorned with a statue of Peter Leopold, by *Pampaloni*. The church contains (l. by the door) the tombstone of Archbishop Simone Saltarelli by *Nino Pisano*, 1342; an altar (3rd l.) of St. Thomas Aquinas with the portrait of the saint by *Francesco Traini*, 1340; in the 1st chapel r. of the choir, a Madonna with Peter and Paul, by *Fra Bartolommeo* and his friend *Mariotto Albertinelli* (d. 1512).

S. Francesco possesses frescoes on the ceiling of the choir by *Taddeo Gaddi*, and cloisters with richly decorated columns and foliage.

*S. Maria della Spina (Pl. 26), so called from a fragment of the 'Crown of Thorns' preserved here, situated on the l. bank of the Arno, is a pretty church in the French-Gothic style, erected in 1230 by the senate and the noble families Gualandi and Gattosi, for sailors about to go to sea. It was enlarged in 1323, and adorned with admirable statues by *Giovanni Pisano* and *Nino*

Pisano. The key is kept at the opposite house (No. 22; visitors ring).

S. Michele in Borgo, in the Sotto-Borgo, near the Ponte di Mezzo, designed by *Nicola Pisano* (?), in the Gothic style of the 13th cent., with ancient crypt, is supposed to occupy the site of an old heathen temple.

S. Nicola, founded about the year 1000 by Count Hugo of Tuscany as a Benedictine Abbey, with obliquely placed *Campanile* containing an admirable winding staircase, was designed by *Nicola Pisano*.

***S. Paolo a Ripa d'Arno** (Pl. 31), on the l. bank of the Arno, not far from the Ponte a Mare, dating from the 12th cent., has a fine façade, embellished with three rows of columns, which are said to have served as a model for the façade of the cathedral. The interior is adorned with badly preserved frescoes of 1400.

S. Sisto, founded on the festival of S. Sisto (Aug. 6th) in 1089, to commemorate several victories of the Pisans, contains fine columns of granite in the interior. It frequently served as a place of assembly for the Council of Pisa, and is consequently still under the special protection of the town.

S. Stefano ai Cavalieri, begun from designs by *Vasari* in 1565, interior completed 1595, the façade designed by *Buontalenti*, is the church of the knights of the Order of St. Stephen. It contains Turkish trophies, and paintings of the battle of Lepanto (1571) and other victories, by *Cristoforo Allori, Jacopo da Empoli*, and others. On the 2nd altar to the l. a Nativity by *Bronzino:* '*Quem genuit adoravit*', a finely conceived work. Excellent organ.

The adjacent *Piazza dei Cavalieri*, formerly *degli Anziani*, was once the great central point of the Republic of Pisa. The *Palazzo de' Cavalieri*, adjoining the church, erected by *Vasari*, is now a school; above the door are busts of 6 masters of the order; in front of the building a marble statue of the Grand-Duke Cosmo, erected in 1596. Opposite once stood (till 1655) the ill-famed 'Tower of Hunger', or rather *Torre dei Gualandi alle sette Vie*, in which, in 1288, Archb. *Ruggieri degli Ubaldini* caused Count Ugolino dei Gerardeschi with his sons and nephews to be starved to death as a punishment for treason, as described by Dante in the 33rd canto of his *Inferno*.

Among the **Palaces** on the Lung'Arno the following should be inspected:

Palazzo Lanfreducci (now *Uppezinghi*), erected from designs of *Cosimo Pagliani*, with portions of a chain over the principal entrance and the enigmatical inscription '*Alla Giornata*'. It contains a small picture gallery; one of the works is 'Heavenly and Earthly Love' by *Guido Reni*.

**Pal. Agostini*, a fine Gothic brick structure of the 16th cent., the ground-floor of which is occupied by the *Caffè dell' Ussero*,

Loggia de' Banchi (Pl. 39), erected in 1605 by *Buontalenti* for Ferdinand I., is now a corn-exchange. — The handsome *Pal. Gambacorti* is now the custom-house (dogana).

Pal. Lanfranchi (now *Toscanelli*), attributed to *Mich. Angelo*, where Lord Byron resided for some time.

La Sapienza, the university, not far from the Lung'Arno, is a spacious structure of 1493, extended 1543, with a fine court, and a library containing among other curiosities the celebrated *Statuto di Pisa*, the basis of the ancient constitution. Connected with the university are the *Museum of Natural History*, founded 1590, containing specimens especially important in the ornithology and geology of Tuscany, and the *Botanical Garden* (both in the Via S. Maria), one of the oldest in Italy, founded 1544, organized in 1563 by the celebrated *Cesalpino*, and superseded by the present garden in 1595 under the directions of *Giuseppe Benincasa*.

The **Accademia delle belle Arti** (Via Frediano, No. 972), founded in 1812 by Napoleon, under the management of *Carlo Lasinio*, contains a collection, not yet arranged, of pictures of the earlier Pisan, Florentine, and other schools: Madonnas of the school of *Benozzo Gozzoli* and *Filippo Lippi*, beautiful *Madonna by *Sodoma* (formerly in S. Maria della Spina), cartoon by *Benozzo* of a picture, no longer extant, in the Campo Santo, representing the arrival of the Queen of Sheba at the court of Solomon; also an old German picture by *Rogier van der Weyde*, etc.

The *Archivio del Duomo* (formerly church of S. Felice) contains very ancient documents. A repository for the town-archives is now being prepared.

Of the ancient Pisa nothing remains except fragments of baths *(Bagni di Nerone)* near Porta Lucca. The house where they are to be seen is indicated by an inscription.

Environs. Outside the Porta Nuova, between the Maltraverso Canal and the r. bank of the Arno, about 1½ M. in the direction of the sea, is situated the **Cascine S. Rossore**, a farm founded by the Medici, with fine plantations of pines.

On the coast, about ¾ M. farther, lies **Il Gombo**, an unpretending sea-bathing place, commanding a beautiful view of the mountains of Viareggio and the Bay of Spezia (omnibus to the baths in summer from the Sotto-Borgo). Here the poet Shelley was drowned, July 7th, 1822; his friend Byron afterwards caused his remains to be burned, and the ashes deposited near the pyramid of Cestius at Rome.

The **Monti Pisani**, a range of hills to the E., are very picturesque; among them, about 6 M. from the town, in the *Valle dei Calci*, lies *La Certosa*, or Carthusian Abbey, a fine structure of the 14th cent. (1367), with church and cloisters, restored in 1814. To the r. above it is *La Verruca*, a mountain 1765 ft. above the sea-level, crowned with ruins of a castle of the 15th cent. and commanding a most delightful prospect.

About 3 M. S.W. of Pisa, on the old post-road to Leghorn, r. of the railway, in the direction of the Arno and opp. to S. Rossore, is situated the ancient basilica of ***S. Pietro in Grado**, erected before the year 1000, containing beautiful antique columns and capitals, occupying the spot, according to tradition, where St. Peter first landed in Italy. It was formerly

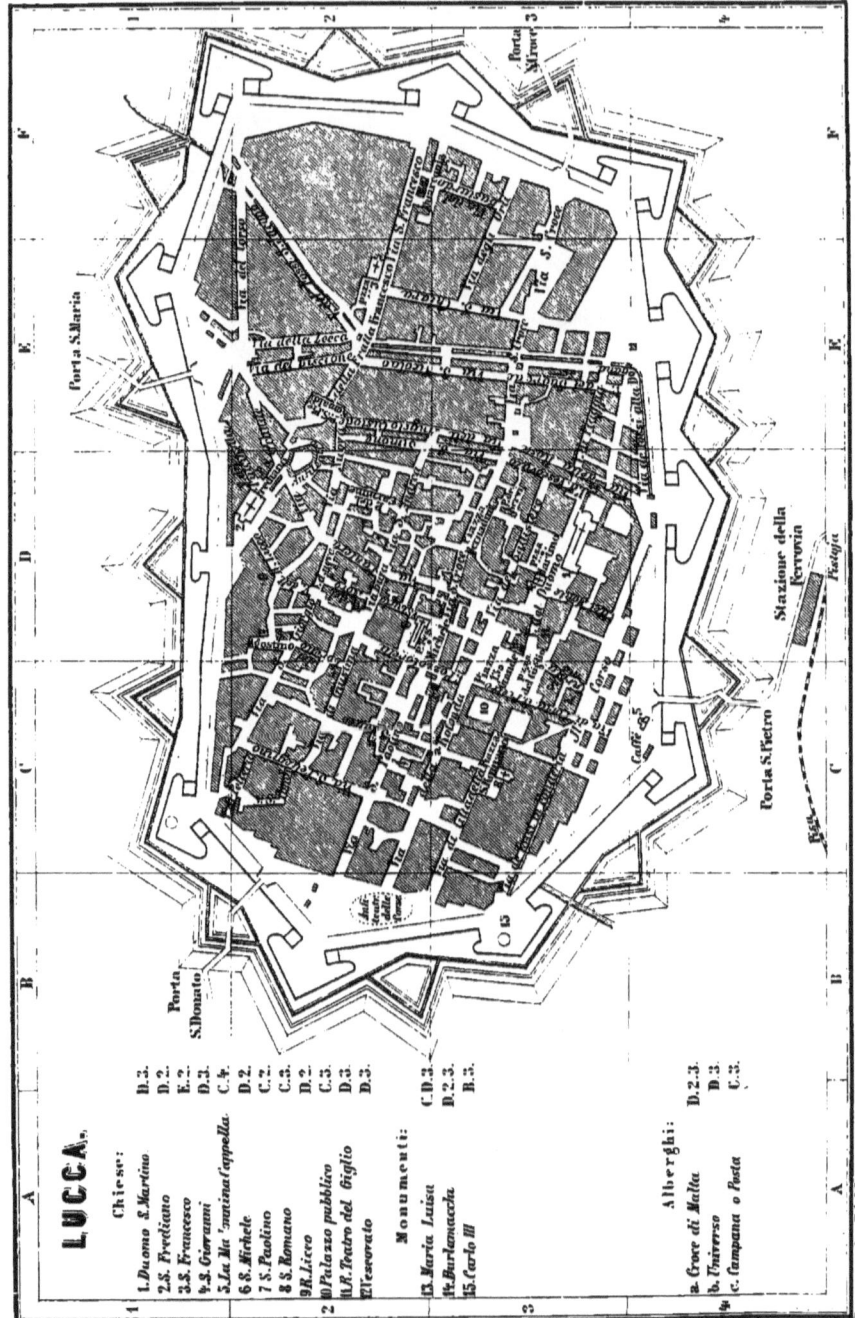

much frequented as a pilgrimage-church. The faded paintings in the interior are of the 14th cent. The ancient estuary of the Arno, with the harbour of Pisa, must once have been at this spot, before the present coast was formed by alluvial deposits.

One of the favourite excursions hence is to the *Baths of Pisa*, the *Bagni di S. Giuliano* (see below), which are reached in a few minutes by the Lucca line.

51. From Pisa to Florence by Lucca and Pistoja.

Railway in 4 hrs.; fares 9 fr. 70 c., 7 fr. 85 c., 6 fr.

The line intersects the fertile plain between the Arno and Serchio. First stat. *Bagni di San Giuliano*, at the base of the *Monti Pisani*, known to the ancients as *Aquae Calidae Pisanorum* (Plin. Hist. Nat. II., 103). *Il Pozzetto* is the warmest spring (104° Fahr.), *Bagno degli Ebrei* the coldest (82°). Twelve different baths are distinguished by the names of heathen divinities; there is also a bath for the poor, as well as the usual adjuncts of a watering-place. Many Roman antiquities have been found here.

At the following stat. *Rigoli* the line approaches the *Serchio*, the l. bank of which it traverses as far as the next stat. *Ripafratto*. It then describes a complete semicircle round the beautifully formed *Monte S. Giuliano*, which, as Dante says (Inferno, 33, 30), prevents the two towns of Pisa and Lucca from seeing each other.

Lucca (*Croce di Malta, Pl. a; **L'Universo*, Pl. b; *Campana* or *Posta*, Pl. c; *Trattoria Corona*, near the station, recommended), with 64,000 inhab., formerly the capital of the duchy of that name, is an antiquated place situated in a fertile plain, with well-preserved fortifications, and many interesting churches. '*Lucca l'industriosa*' is noted for its silk factories, a branch of industry introduced from Sicily in the 14th cent., and also for its woollen goods. The oriental *fez* is largely manufactured here and exported to the Levant.

The foundation of Lucca (Greek and Roman *Luca*) belongs to a very remote period. It first appertained to Liguria, afterwards to Etruria; under the Romans it subsequently became an important municipium. Here, in B. C. 56, *Julius Caesar*, at that period governor of Gaul, held a conference with Pompey and Crassus, with whom he had been associated since B. C. 60, in order to discuss a plan for the administration of the vast Roman empire for the ensuing five years. The splendour of Lucca at that period is still indicated by the remains of the Roman *Amphitheatre near *S. Frediano*. After the fall of the Roman Empire, Lucca belonged successively to the Goths, Lombards, and Franks, then became a duchy, and in the 12th cent. a republic. The feuds of the Guelphs and Ghibellines impaired the strength of the place so seriously that in 1314 it was compelled to succumb to *Uguccione della Faggiuola* of Arezzo, the warlike governor of Pisa, who is believed by some to be the deliverer promised to Italy by Dante (Inferno, I, 102). The poet resided with his friend Uguccione at Lucca in 1314, and there became enamoured of the youthful *Gentucca* (Purgatorio 24, 23), but he does not describe the inhabitants in very flattering terms (Inferno 21, 41). After the expulsion of Uguccione, Lucca fell in 1325 into the hands of the powerful *Castruccio Castrani degli Interminelli* of Lucca, who was also master of Pisa and Pistoja. On Sept. 23rd, 1325 he defeated the Florentines at *Altopascio*, and in 1327 was nominated imperial governor of Tuscany by Emp. Lewis the Bavarian. On his death in 1328 the power of Lucca declined; its next master was *Martino della Scala*; it subsequently came into the possession of Pisa, but in 1369 purchased its own freedom from Charles IV. for 300,000 fl. and remained independent till the invasion of the French in 1799. In 1805 Napoleon gave Lucca as a principality to his sister *Elisa Bacciocchi*; in 1814 it came into the possession of the dukes of Parma of the house of Bourbon, who in 1847 ceded it to Tuscany. — The greatest artist of whom Lucca boasts is *Matteo Cividali* (1440), whose principal works are in the cathedral.

Immediately on quitting the station, the traveller perceives within the ramparts the handsome

Cathedral of S. Martino (Pl. 1), erected in 1060—70 in the Romanesque style by Bishop *Anselmo Badagio* (afterwards Pope Alexander II.), remarkable for its sumptuous façade, added by *Giudetto* in 1204, and for its impressive choir. The vestibule contains sculptures of the beginning of the 13th cent. representing the history of St. Martin. Over the small door is St. Regulus on the r., and a Descent from the Cross on the l. by *Nicola Pisano* (1233). The interior, in the form of a Latin cross, with nave and aisles 136 paces in length, transept 70, and nave 44 paces in width, received various Gothic additions in the 14th cent., especially in the arches of the transept. The old frescoes on the vaulting were restored in 1858.

The stained glass in the side windows is modern, those in the choir by *Pandolfo di Ugolino da Pisa*. Services of the custodian unnecessary, except to show the pictures which are covered. 1st Altar on the r., Nativity by *Passignano*; 2nd, Adoration of the Magi, *F. Zucchero*; 3rd, Last Supper, *Tintoretto*; 4th, Crucifixion, *Passignano*; Pulpit by *Matteo Cividali* (1498). In the sacristy a Madonna with SS. Clement, Peter, Paul, and Sebastian, by *Dom. Ghirlandajo*. "*La Croce dei Pisani*, beautifully executed in 1350 by *Bettuccio Baroni*, in silver, gilded, originally belonged to the Pisans, but was carried off by the inhabitants of Lucca (not shown except by special permission, to be procured on the previous day). The r. Transept contains the beautiful marble *monument of Pietro da Nocetto, secretary of Pope Nicholas V., by *Matteo Cividali* (1472); by the same master, on the wall to the r., is the portrait of Count Domenico Bertini (1479); also in the Cappella del Sagramento (1st Chapel r. of the choir) two angels in an attitude of adoration and the altar of St. Regulus (r. of the choir), with St. Sebastian and John the Baptist and beautiful basreliefs. L. of the choir the 'Altar of Liberty', which Lucca recovered in 1369 from Emp. Charles IV. (inscription: *Christo liberatori atque divis tutelaribus*), with a Resurrection by *Giambologna* (1579). On the wall St. Petronilla, by *Daniele da Volterra*. In the following Cappella del Santuario, a Madonna with SS. Stephen and John by *Fra Bartolommeo* (1509). The marble decorations are by *Civitali*. The l. Transept contains the *sarcophagus of Ilaria del Carretto (d. 1405), by *Jacopo della Quercia* (1444). In the Nave is a small octagonal chapel of marble, partially gilded (*Il Tempietto), erected in 1484 by *M. Civitali*, and containing the *Volto Santo di Lucca*, an ancient crucifix in cedar-wood, said by tradition to have been made by *Nicodemus*, and to have been transferred in a miraculous manner from the Holy Land to Lucca in 782. It is shown publicly three times a year only, but may be inspected at any time by permission of the archbishop. In front of the entrance is suspended a candelabrum of solid gold, 24 lbs. in weight, presented by the inhabitants of Lucca in 1836, when the approach of the cholera was dreaded. On the opposite side a statue of St. Sebastian, also by *Civitali*. In the l. Aisle, 5th altar (from the entrance) Visitation of the Virgin, by *Jacopo Ligozzi*. Over the 2nd altar: the Presentation in the Temple, by *A. Bronzino*. L. of the entrance, Descent from the Cross, and St. Nicodemus carving the Volto Santo (see above), a fresco by *Cosimo Roselli*. On the pavement of the nave, inlaid work of coloured stones, representing Solomon's Judgment.

At the back of the cathedral is the small Chapel of *Sta. Maria della Rosa*, a remarkable Gothic structure of 1333.

The Bishops (since 1726 Archbishops) of Lucca enjoy special privileges and wear scarlet robes like those of the Cardinals; the 18 canons and 33 minor ecclesiastics also possess higher distinctions than those usually appertaining to their rank.

S. Giovanni (Pl. 4), near the cathedral, is a basilica of the 8th or 9th cent., with nave, aisles, and transept. The façade is modern with the exception of the portal, over which there is a relief of the Madonna with the Apostles of the 12th cent., and groups of animals on the r. and l. In the interior the coffered ceiling is supported by ten columns, of which the three fluted are probably ancient. In the l. aisle a monument to Giov. Farina (d. 1847). — Adjoining the l. transept is a venerable *Baptistery*, the roof of which was renewed during the Gothic period.

A few paces from this church, the traveller reaches the

*Piazza Maggiore *(Napoleone)*, with the Palazzo Pubblico, where in 1843 a handsome *Monument was erected to the Duchess Marie Louise, in recognition of the service rendered by her to the town by the erection (1823—32) of an aqueduct (worthy of inspection) of 459 arches. — The *Palazzo Pubblico* (Pl. 10), formerly *Ducale*, commenced in 1578 from designs by *Ammanati*, but still incomplete, contains a small and choice *Collection of Pictures*, most of them modern, by *Michele Ridolfi* (of Lucca, d. 1853), *Nocchi* (Aurora), *Giovanetti*, *Camuccini*, etc.

Not far from the Piazza Maggiore is the church of *S. Alessandro*, a simple structure completed before 1080, containing fine antique columns.

A short distance farther, at the end of the street diverging to the l. opposite the 'Croce di Malta' hotel, is situated *S. Romano* (Pl. 8), which existed as early as the 8th cent., but was remodelled in the 17th by *Vincenzo Buonamici*. It contains two excellent pictures by *Fra Bartolommeo*, the *Madonna della Misericordia, of 1515, and *God the Father with Mary Magdalene and St. Catharine of Siena, of 1509 (both covered). Behind the high altar the sarcophagus of St. Romanus, attributed to *Civitali*, 1490.

The traveller next proceeds to the venerable church of *S. Michele* (Pl. 6), founded in 764 by Teutprandus and his wife Gumpranda, with an over-decorated façade of 1188, rising high above the nave, and surmounted by an angel with brazen wings. The row of columns on the S. side was added in 1377. The 1st Chapel r. of the entrance contains a Madonna in Trono by

18*

Fra Filippo Lippi. — The *Palazzo Pretorio*, an edifice of the 16th cent., is also situated in the Piazza S. Michele. Opposite the N. portal of the church rises the statue of *S. Burlamacchi* (d. 1548), by Cambi, erected in 1833.

*S. *Frediano* (St. Frigidianus) (Pl. 2), a basilica of the 7th cent., on the N. side of the town, was founded by the Lombard kings Bertharic and Cunibert, in honour of an Irish saint of that name, who was bishop of Lucca in 560—78. The present façade was erected in the 12th cent. on the site of the former apse; the Ascension in mosaic with which it is adorned was restored in 1827. The nave was originally flanked with double aisles, the outer of which have been converted into two series of chapels. Most of the 22 columns are ancient.

The **Cappella di S. Agostino* (2nd to the l.) contains two old *frescoes by *Amico Aspertini*, pupil of Francia, judiciously retouched by *Michele Ridolfi*. On the ceiling God the Father, surrounded by angels, prophets and sibyls; in the lunette to the l. the Entombment; below it, to the l., an image of Christ found in the sea (*Volto Santo*, p. 274), drawn by two oxen, r. St. Augustine, baptized by St. Ambrosius at Milan. In the lunette on the wall on the r. St. Augustine instructing his pupils, and presenting them with the rules of his order; beneath, to the l., the Nativity and Adoration of the Magi; r. the miracles of S. Frediano, who checks an inundation of the sea. — In the Cappella del Sagramento (4th to the l.) an altar with reliefs by *Jacopo della Quercia* (1422), a Madonna with four saints. — Over the altar to the r. behind the pulpit is the *Coronation of Mary; below are king David and Solomon, St. Anselm and St. Augustine, by *Francesco Francia* (covered). At the foot of the picture are four scenes from the history of the Augustine Order. — The 2nd chapel on the r. from the entrance contains the tomb of St. Zita, the patroness of Lucca, mentioned by Dante (Inferno 21, 28); in the church, in front of the chapel, the ancient font, with unexplained representations by *Magister Robertus* (1151).

If the traveller now cross the Piazza S. Frediano which adjoins the church on the E., and turn either to the r. or l., he will reach an entrance to the *Piazza del Mercato* (Pl. D, 2), with remains of a Roman *Amphitheatre*, consisting of two series of arcades, each of 54 arches; the lowest rows of seats are covered with rubbish. Remnants of an ancient theatre are also shown near the church of *S. Maria di Corte Landini.*

S. Francesco (Pl. 3), a spacious edifice, erected in 1442, contains the monuments of the poet Giov. Guidiccioni (16th cent.) and the celebrated Castruccio Castracani (d. 1328), to the r. by the wall, between the 3rd and 4th altars.

Among the numerous charitable institutions of Lucca may be mentioned the *Deposito di Mendicità* (poor-house), established in the Italian-Gothic *Palazzo Borghi*, with lofty tower, erected in 1413 by *Paolo Guinigi*, chief of one of the most powerful families of Lucca. Among the *Libraries* the most remarkable are the *Archiepiscopal*, containing 20 valuable MSS. and 400 rare editions, the *Library of the Chapter* with about 500 MSS., the *Biblioteca Reale* with MSS. (amongst them Latin poems of Tasso, written by his own hand) and early specimens of printing. The *Archives* also contain several curiosities.

Those who have a few hours at their disposal should devote them to a *Walk round the ramparts, which afford a succession of pleasant views of the town with its numerous towers, and of the beautiful mountains in the vicinity. In the grounds on the N. side stands the monument of *Charles III. of Spain*, erected by his granddaughter the Duchess Marie Louise, in 1822. (Near it the Caffè di Marte).

The environs of Lucca are delightful and afford favourite sites for villas, many of which are let to strangers. They are generally well fitted up, but in summer hot and destitute of shade.

The stranger should visit the (3½ M.) royal *Villa di Marlia, surrounded by beautiful grounds, points of view, etc., resembling Marly at Paris (whence the name); also a Greek chapel with old paintings etc. (permission must be obtained at Lucca).

On the road to Viareggio, about 6 M. to the W., near the *Lake of Massaciuccoli*, are situated the Roman ruins known as the *Bagni di Nerone, with beautiful environs. The *Aqueduct* to the S. of Lucca, with its 459 arches, recalling the Campagna of Rome, is worthy of inspection.

The **Baths of Lucca**, known in the middle ages, about 12 M. distant from the town (diligence and omnibus several times daily in 2½ hrs., fare 3 fr.; carr. 15 fr.), are situated to the N. in a mountainous district, on the small river *Lima*. An excursion there and back may easily be accomplished in one day if Lucca be quitted at an early hour. The town is quitted by the Porta Sta. Maria. The road leads N. by the bank of the Serchio, the impetuous water of which is confined between lofty embankments. The road to the beautiful *Villa Marlia* (see above) diverges to the r. The Serchio is then crossed by the bridge of *Muriano*, decorated with figures of saints, and a charming hilly district is traversed. The road passes the villages of *Sesto*, *Val D'Ottavo*, and *Diecimo*, crosses the *Devil's Bridge*, said to have been constructed by Castruccio in 1322, and enters the valley of the *Lima*, on both banks of which roads lead to the baths. About 3 M. farther is the prosperous village of *Ponte a Serraglio*, with hotels (Europa; *Croce di Malta), post-office (letters arrive daily between June 1st and Sept. 30th from Lucca at 10 a. m. and are despatched at 4. 30 p. m.), casino, ball-rooms, etc. Here too the principal baths are situated. There are also warm springs at *Villa*, *Bernabò*, *Docce Basse*, *Bagni Caldi*, and *S. Giovanni* (85—130° Fahr.). Of these Bernabò (so called from a native of Pistoja who was restored to health here in the 16th cent.) is most recommended. The valley of the Lima is cool and well shaded, affording healthy and delightful quarters for the summer. Many beautiful excursions may be made among the neighbouring mountains, thus to the bridge *Della Maddalena*, to the village of *Lugliano*, to the old watch-tower *Bargilio*, affording a magnificent prospect in clear weather. The arrangements for the accommodation of visitors, pensions (5 fr. a day and upwards, children and servants one-half, at Pagnini's and others). carriages, horses, donkeys, shops, etc. resemble those of Interlaken, although on a smaller scale. Messrs. *Carina* and *Giorgi* are two of the principal physicians. The best and quietest apartments are at the *Bagni alla Villa* and the *Bagni Caldi*, the most cheerful at *Ponte a Serraglio*, which is the central point of the various establishments, and the usual evening resort of the visitors. The casino, or *Ridotti*, stands on an eminence in the vicinity. Near it is the *Nuovo Ospedale*, erected by the Russian Prince Nicholas Demidoff.

The railway from Lucca to Pistoja at first traverses the plain to the E.; at a short distance to the S. lies the *Lago di Bientina* (p. 260). Stat. *Porcari;* then *Altopascio*, where the line turns to the N. Next stat. *Pescia* (Posta), a small town, situated about 1½ M. to the N. on the river of that name, which the railway now crosses, in a delightful district, where the silk-culture and several paper-manufactories flourish. The *Cathedral* of Pescia possesses remains of an ancient façade, and a fine monument of Baldassare Turrini by *Raffaele da Montelupo*, a pupil of Michael Angelo.

Hence to Pistoja the district continues to be most attractive. Stat. *Borgo a Bugiano*, then *Monte Catini*. Here, on Aug. 29th, 1315, Ugguccione della Faggiuola, the Ghibelline prince of Pisa and Lucca, defeated the Florentines. The warm baths *(Bagni di Monti Catini)* in the vicinity, furnished by the former Grand Duke Leopold I. with bath-establishment and other conveniences, attract a considerable number of visitors.

The line intersects the rich valley of the *Nievole*. Stat. *Pieve a Nievole;* r. *Monsummano* on a conical eminence, with warm springs. By the next stat. *Serravalle*, an important frontier-fortress during the wars between Lucca and Pistoja, the line crosses the watershed between the Nievole and *Ombrone*, both affluents of the Arno. On an eminence near the Ombrone, in a fertile district, is situated the ancient town of

Pistoja ("Albergo di Londra, outside the town, on the way to the stat.; Globo, Posta, both in the Piazza Cino; Caffè del Globo. *Fiacres:* One-horse per drive 60 c., two-horse 80 c., 1st hour 1 fr. 40, two-horse 1 fr. 70 c., each following hour 1 fr., two-horse 1 fr. 30 c.), Rom. *Pistoria*, near which, B. C. 62, Catiline was defeated and slain, in the middle ages the focus of the fiercest struggles between the Guelphs and Ghibellines. In the year 1300 the *Cancellieri* and *Panciatichi*, or *Black* and *White* parties, mentioned by Dante (Inferno 24, 143), who afterwards extended their operations to Florence and influenced the fortunes of the poet himself, were formed here. Pistoja was the birthplace of the celebrated jurist and poet *Cino* (1270—1336), a contemporary of Dante, but unknown to him, and of the satirist *Niccolò Forteguerri* (1674—1735), author of the Ricciardetto. In the history of art the town also holds a prominent position owing to its valuable sculpture of the 12th—14th cent. The modern Pistoja possesses broad, well-built streets, 12,000 inhab., iron works of some extent, and gun-manufactories. Pistols are said to have been invented here and to derive their name from Pistoja.

If the traveller follow the Via Cino, which comes from the rail. stat. and intersects the Corso Vitt. Emanuele at a right angle, as far as the Piazza Cino, and here turn to the r. into the Via Cavour, he will soon reach the old Romanesque church of *S. Giovanni Fuoricivitas (Evangelista)*, erected about 1160, with a façade decorated in the Pisan fashion with rows of columns. *Gruamons*, whose name is inscribed above the relief of the Last

Supper on the architrave of the side-entrance, was perhaps the architect. The *Pulpit*, adorned with 10 reliefs on three sides, is of the school of *Nicola Pisano*, about 1270. Interesting basin for the holy water, borne by three female figures, by *Giovanni Pisano*. The Visitation of Mary, a life-size group in terracotta, by *Andrea della Robbia*. The sacristy contains a fine picture of the time of *Giotto*, representing the Virgin with Evangelists and Saints.

The Via S. Matteo, the third side-street beyond S. Giovanni which diverges from the Via Cavour to the l., leads to the *Piazza*, to the r. in which rises the

*Cathedral of S. Jacopo, founded at an early period, and extended in the 13th cent. from designs by *Nicola Pisano* (?). The tribuna was added in 1599 by *Jacopo Lafri*. In the vestibule are faded frescoes by *Giovanni Pistojese*. Over the principal entrance a good bas-relief in terracotta (Madonna surrounded by angels) by *Andrea della Robbia*.

The Interior, sadly marred by alterations, and restored with little taste in 1838—39, consists of nave and aisles borne by 16 columns and 3 buttresses.

By the wall of the entrance is the °Font, adorned with a large relief representing the Baptism of Christ, and four smaller ones, by *Andrea Ferrucci da Fiesole*. To the r. of the entrance is the °Monument of Cino da Pistoja (d. 1336), attributed by Vasari to *Andrea Pisano*. The bas-relief represents Cino instructing 9 pupils, among them Petrarch, who afterwards composed a sonnet on his master's death, calling on the women to mourn for Cino as the poet of Love. The female figure is thought to be Selvaggia Vergiolesi, the wife or mistress of Cino. Above is the statue of Cino, surrounded by 6 smaller figures (of which the female figure is perhaps symbolical of Jurisprudence). The inscription of 1614 refers to Cino as a jurist only: *Cino eximio juris interpreti Bartholi praeceptori dignissimo populus Pistoj. civi suo b. m. fecit.* — L. of the entrance the Monument of Cardinal Fortiguerra, with the bust and high reliefs, by *Verrocchio* (1474) and *Lorenzetto*. — The Cappella del Sagramento (l. of the choir) contains a Madonna with St. John and St. Zeno by *Lorenzo di Credi*, presented by Ferdinand de' Medici (1598). High relief bust of Bishop Donato de' Medici by *A. Rossetini* (1475). Over the high altar a Resurrection by *Angelo Bronzino*. Beautifully inlaid choir stalls, attributed to *Vitoni* (1500). In the Cappella S. Jacopo (r. of the choir) a richly decorated altar and canopy (covered); in a niche over the altar a sitting statue of St. James, surrounded by apostles and prophets, wrought in silver by *Giglio Pisano* (1349 —53). In front of the altar is a large silver tablet with 15 reliefs of subjects from the Old Testament, by *Andrea di Jacopo d'Ognabene* (1316) of Pistoja; the silver tablets at the sides by *Piero da Firenze* (1357) and *Leonardo di Ser Giovanni*, pupil of Orcagna (1366). About 446 lbs. of silver are said to have been employed in the execution of this work of art. In 1293 this altar was pillaged by Vanni Fucci, who is accordingly placed by Dante (Inferno 24, 139) in the infernal regions. The Crypt, borne by six columns, is also modernized.

The campanile was originally a fortified tower, termed Torre del Podestà, and still bears the arms of the former governors of the town. *Giovanni Pisano* adapted the tower to its present purpose and added the three series of arches.

Opposite to the cathedral is situated the octagonal *Baptistery of *San Giovanni Rotondo*, erected in 1337 by **Andrea Pisano** in the Italian Gothic style, with sculptures and a handsome pulpit on the exterior. The large font is of earlier origin than the building itself and probably dates from 1256.

Adjacent is the *Palazzo Pretorio*, formerly *del Podestà*, with additions of 1367—77, now the seat of the tribunal. The court (cortile) is surrounded by handsome arcades, adorned with numerous armorial bearings of the Podestà's, remarkable for the admirable Gothic style of the drawing, restored in 1844. To the l. of the entrance are the stone table, and seats of the ancient court of judicature, bearing the inscription of 1507:

> *Hic locus odit, amat, punit, conservat, honorat,*
> *Nequitiam, leges, crimina, jura, probos.*

The piazza is adorned with a Statue of *Forteguerri* (see p. 278), erected in 1863. Opposite to the Pal. Pretorio is the *Palazzo della Comunità* (degli Anziani), erected in the Ital. Gothic style 1294—1385, with a vestibule, now the Municipio.

The Via Ripa della Comunità leads hence to the l., and the first street diverging from it to the l. brings the traveller to the *Ospedale del Ceppo*, erected in 1277, but subsequently remodelled, embellished with a *frieze with reliefs in terracotta, representing the works of mercy, erected in 1525—85 by *Giovanni*, *Luca*, and *Girolamo della Robbia*, one of the finest productions of these masters. — The traveller should now pass the Ospedale by the Via delle Pappe to the l., which leads to a small planted piazza, then follow the Via del Carmine to the l.; the first side-street to the r. will then bring him to

S. Andrea, a very ancient edifice, and probably formerly the cathedral. On the architrave of the entrance are sculptures of 1186, representing the Adoration of the Magi with the inscription: *Fecit hoc opus Gruamons magister bon. et Adod frater ejus.* These masters were natives of Pistoja, where they executed several other works. The narrow nave and aisles are supported by 12 columns and 2 pillars The *Pulpit* by *Giovanni da Pisa*, 1298—1381, a hexagon with reliefs from the Old Testament on five sides, is a copy of that executed by his father at Pisa, to which it is preferred by Cicognara.

Of the other churches may be mentioned:

S. Bartolommeo in Pantano, an early structure in the Lombard style, with sculptures by *Rodolfino* (1167) on the façade, representing the Mission of the apostles, and a pulpit by *Guido da Como* (1250), borne by lions.

S. Domenico, in the Corso Vitt. Eman., erected in 1380, contains the monument of the jurist Filippo Lazari (d. 1412), by *Bernardo di Matteo Fiorentino*, 1464. The *Cappella Rospigliosi* is adorned with monuments of the family of that name, and the miracle of S. Carlo Borromeo, by *Jacopo da Empoli*, St. Dominicus receiving the rosary, by *Angelo Bronzino*, and St. Sebastian by *R. Ghirlandajo*. Adoration of the Magi and Crucifixion with saints. The Virgin and Thomas Aquinas, by *Fra Paolo Pistojese*. The cloisters were decorated with paintings by *Sebastiano Veronese* and others, 1596.

S. Francesco al Prato, an Italian Gothic building of 1294, possesses some good paintings by *Bronzino* and other masters. The hall of the chapter is decorated with frescoes of scenes from the life of St. Francis, attributed by Vasari to *Puccio Capanna* (about 1400).

S. Maria dell' Umiltà, a few paces beyond the Piazza Cino (p. 279) to the l., with a bare façade, was erected in 1494 by *Ventura Vitoni*, pupil of Bramante; dome of 1509 by *Vasari*, in the Renaissance style, of symmetrical proportions; frescoes and paintings of the interior by the same master and others.

Among the *Palaces* may be mentioned *Palazzo Panciatichi*, near S. Giovanni Evangelista, and *Pal. Cancellieri*, recalling by their names the deadly feuds of the middle ages. The families of these names, as well as the Rospigliósi, are still in existence at Pistoja.

Two *Libraries*, the *Fabbroniana* and *Fortiguerra*, founded by two cardinals born at Pistoja, contain a number of valuable works. In the *Accademia delle Scienze*, the *Casa Bracciolini* and *Casa Tolommei*, several pictures and curiosities are preserved. — The *Villa Puccini, 1 M. to the N. of Pistoja, possesses beautiful gardens and works of art by Pampaloni etc.

Railway from Pistoja to Bologna see R. 47.

The Line to Florence intersects a rich tract at the base of the Apennines. Stat. *S. Piero*. L. the picturesque castle of *Monte Murlo* comes into view; near it, July 31st, 1535, the Florentine republicans, under Baccio Valori and Filippo Strozzi, succumbed to the superior power of the Grand Duke Cosmo de' Medici. The castle, in the style of the 13th cent., is the property of the Counts della Gherardesca, descendants of the illfated Ugolino, whose death in the 'Tower of Hunger' at Pisa (1284) is depicted in thrilling terms by Dante (Inferno C. 33). Monte Murlo deserves a visit, which may easily be accomplished on foot from San Piero, and the walk may advantageously be prolonged to Prato ($4^1/_2$ M.).

Prato *(Posta)*, a well-built town with 35,000 inhab., on the *Bisenzio*, with beautiful environs, is an industrial place, strawplait being one of the staple commodities; it also enjoys a high reputation for the excellence of its bread. It formerly appertained to Florence, the fortunes of which it shared throughout the whole of the middle ages. In 1512 the town was taken by storm by the Spaniards under Cardona. The cathedral with its adjuncts is the principal point of attraction.

Il Duomo, commenced in the 12th cent., completed by *Giovanni Pisano* in the 14th, is a structure in the Tuscan Gothic style, with façade of 1450, the gallery of which was adorned by *Donatello* with sculptures. From this gallery the highly revered *Sacra Cintola*, or 'girdle of the Virgin' which is preserved in the cathedral, is periodically exhibited to the people. Over the principal entrance a Madonna with SS. Stephen and Lawrence in terracotta, by *Luca della Robbia*.

By the principal entrance the Virgin delivering the girdle to St. Thomas, by *Rhidolfo Ghirlandajo*, the guardian angel by *Carlo Dici*. In the interior: *Cappella della Cintola, adorned with mural paintings by *Agnolo Gaddi* (1395), from the life of the Virgin, and her statue on the altar, by *Giovanni Pisano*. In the choir, at the back of the high altar, are the *histories of John the Baptist and St. Stephen by *Fra Filippo*; r. the *Death of St. Bernard, by the same master. Fine round *pulpit, resting on sphinxes and snakes, by *Mino da Fiesole*, adorned with admirable reliefs. — The campanile, in the Lombard style, is by *Giovanni Pisano*.

Madonna delle Carceri, erected in 1492 by *Giuliano da San Gallo*, is in the form of a Greek cross, surmounted by a dome, containing a fine altar by *Antonio da San Gallo*, brother of the architect. — *S. Domenico*, of the 13th cent., possesses paintings by *Fra Filippo*. — *S. Francesco* contains (in the hall of the Chapter) mural paintings by *Niccolò Petri*.

The *Palazzo della Comunità* and the *Casa del Cancelliere* contain paintings by *Filippo Lippi*.

About 2 M. to the N. W. of the stat. rise the hills of *Monteferrato*, which those who have leisure should visit. A short distance farther is *Figline*, with serpentine-quarries, yielding the stone known as Verde di Prato, which has been employed in architecture for centuries. About 8 M. farther are the copper-smelting works of *La Briglia*, successfully carried on by English proprietors.

Beyond Prato the train proceeds to stat. *Calenzano*, *Sesto* (l. is *La Doccia*, a villa of the Marchese Ginori, with porcelain manufactory, at the base of *Monte Morello*, p. 286), *Castello* (near it is *La Petraja*, a royal villa, celebrated flower-gardens, p. 329), *Rifredi*, and *Florence*.

52. Florence.

Arrival. There are two railway-stations at Florence: 1. *Stazione Centrale* (Pl. C, 2, 3) for all the railways, where omnibuses from most of the hotels meet every train (1—1½ fr.); fiacre 1 fr., at night 1½ fr., each box 50, travelling-bag 25 c., trifling gratuity to railway porter. 2. *Stazione Porta Croce* (Pl. G, 4), where the trains of the Roman line stop, too far from the middle of the town for most travellers.

Hotels. In the Lung' Arno, best situation: *Italia (Pl. a, formerly Palazzo Murat), *Hôtel de la Paix (Pl. c), *New York (Pl. b), Hôtel de la Ville (Pl. i), *Gran Bretagna; charges in all: R. 3, L. 1, A 1, D. 5, omnibus 1½, pension 10 fr.; Vittoria (Pl. k), Arno (Pl. m), Washington (Pl. l), these three a degree less expensive. — In the new quarter near the Cascine: *Universo, Corso Vitt. Emanuele; Corona d'Italia, Via Palestro; Anglo-American, Via Garibaldi 7; *Pension Thuillier (Pl. s), Via Garibaldi 5, quiet, 8 fr. per diem. — In the Via Tornabuoni: Hôtel du Nord; H. de l'Europe; 'H. Suisse (Pl. r) R. from 2½, D. 4 fr., patronized by French visitors; near it, Ville de

FLORENCE. *52. Route.* 283

Paris, with restaurant, Via della Spada 3; Pensione Inglese, Via del Sole 6; Pensione Americana, Via Vigna Nuova; *Leone Bianco, Via Vigna Nuova, in the Ital. style, unpretending. — The following hotels, situated near the Piazza della Signoria, between the Cathedral on the N. and the Arno on the S., are of moderate pretensions, but conveniently placed: Hôtel Central, Albergo del Parlamento (visited by deputies to the Ital. parliament), both in the Via dei Leoni, at the back of the Palazzo Vecchio. Then, in the Ital. style: *Luna (Pl. n), R. 2½, L. ½, A. ½ fr.; Rossini, corner of Via Ghibellina and V. Proconsolo; Patria, Fenice, and Stella d'Italia, in the Via Calzajoli, indifferent; Porta Rossa, R. 2½, A. ¾, L. ¾ fr., Via Porta Rossa, between V. Calzajoli and V. Tornabuoni; *Hôtel de Genève, Via Porta S. Maria, a short distance N. of the Ponte Vecchio; Fontana, Via Castellani 3; S. Marco, Via dei Saponaj. R. from 1½ fr., for those of moderate requirements. — Near the central station: La Nazione, of the first class, H. et Pension d'Angleterre, Città di Milano, all in the Via Cerretani; *Bonciani, Via Panzani 21, the nearest to the station (with restaur.); Roma, of the first class, Piazza S. Maria Novella 7; Isole Britanniche (*Alb. Scarpa*), in the same Piazza; new hotel in the Via della Scala 42; in the same street the H. et Pension dell'Alleanza, of less pretension.

Hôtels Garnis and **Private Apartments.** Casa Nardini, Borgo SS. Apostoli No. 17, second floor, R. (several looking to the Lung-Arno) 1½ fr. per diem. No. 5 in the same street, Casa Santi. Similar establishments, recognisable by the notices or placards, are situated in the Lung-Arno, Piazza della Signoria, near the cathedral, Piazza S. Maria Novella, Piazza Pitti, etc. In winter, which is the 'season' at Florence, two rooms with every convenience cost on an average 60 fr. per month, attendance about 5 fr.; in summer 40—50 fr. The pleasantest situation in winter is the sunny side of the Lung-Arno. The other quarters of the town on the r. side of the Arno (environs of the cathedral, Via dei Cerretani, Piazza S. Maria Novella, Via Cavour, Piazza dell' Independenza, etc.), as well as the Piazza Pitti, may also be mentioned as healthy and agreeable situations. The quarter of the town on the l. bank of the Arno, especially in the vicinity of the river, is considered less healthy. In winter it is most important to secure rooms with a S. aspect, which is almost indispensable for health, as well as comfort in Italy, where brilliant sunshine so often strongly contrasts with bitterly cold winds. The Lung-Arno is almost deserted in summer on account of the exhalations and the swarms of gnats and mosquitoes, and a N. aspect is preferred. The heat in July and August is generally most oppressive, and for these months quarters should be sought for in one of the numerous villas charmingly situated on the neighbouring heights. Information respecting houses to be let in whole or in part may be obtained at the offices of the commission-agents.

Restaurants, most frequented at the dinner-hour, 5—7 o'clock: *Doney, D. 7 fr., or à la carte, Via Tornabuoni 16; *Café de Paris, Via Cerretani (D. at 4 or 5 fr., or à la carte); *La Toscana, Via Calzajoli; *Luna (Pl. n), Caffè delle Alpi, D. at 5. 30 p. m. 2½ fr., in the Piazza S. Maria Maggiore, near the Via Cerretani; Melini, Ital. wine-house, see below; Rossini, Fenice, Patria, Stella, see above; Antiche Carrozze, Borgo SS. Apostoli, near the Ponte Vecchio, and Leon Bianco (see above), D. at 5 o'cl. 2 fr. 20 c., both good although unpretending; Porta Rossa and degli Artisti, in the Via Porta Rossa; Ville de Paris, Via della Spada 3; Barile, see below. — Dinners à la carte (2—4 fr., bread 10, wine about 60 c.) are more common than tables d'hôte.

Cafés, a few only with seats in the open air: *C. de Paris (see above); *Doney, Via Tornabuoni 14; Parlamento, at the back of the Pal. Vecchio; Flora, Via del Proconsolo; Gloria Italiana and Piccolo Elvetico, in the Piazza del Duomo; Risorti, Via Cavour; Ferruccio and Wital, Via Porta S. Maria, N. of the Ponte Vecchio. — Usual charges: cup of coffee 20—30, glass of ice 30 c., light Florence beer 50 c. per bottle, beefsteak for déjeûner ¾—1 fr., etc. — An atmosphere of tobacco-smoke generally pervades these cafés, which are less inviting than those in many other Italian towns. — Strangers are frequently assailed in the cafés by hawkers of photographs etc., who often sell their wares at one-third or one half of the price at first demanded. The well known 'Fioraje', or flower-girls, are also importunate intruders (5 c).

Confectioners. *Castelmur, Stuppani, both in the Via Calzajoli; *Doney, *Giacosa, both in the Via Tornabuoni.

Wines. Good Ital. at Melini's (see above); Barile (Ital. 'osteria'), Via dei Cerchi 10, near Piaz. della Signoria. A 'fiasco' is usually ordered, but the quantity actually consumed only is paid for.

Beer at the *Birraria of *Gilli* and *Letta*, in the Piaz. della Signoria, Viennese beer 35 c. per glass; Birraria Cornelio, Via Canto de Nelli 9, not far from S. Lorenzo.

Ambassadors. English, Via dei Buoni 2 (Pal. Orlandini); American, Via Maggio 7; Spanish, Pal. Guadagni, outside the Porta al Prato; Austrian, Via S. Apollonia 8; Russian, Via Ghibellina 77. There are also French, Prussian, Belgian, and other legations, but their addresses are less likely to be useful than the above, and need not be here enumerated.

Reading Room. Vieusseux, Piazza S. Trinità, 8. a. m. to 10 p. m., adm. 50 c., per month 7, quarter 14 fr.; Vanni, Via Tornabuoni, near S. Gaetano, less expensive.

Post Office in the Uffizi, open daily from 8 a. m. to 10 p. m.; six deliveries of letters daily; postage within the city 5 c. — *Telegraph Office* in the Palazzo Riccardi, Via dei Ginori 2.

Fiacres stand in the Piaz. S. Trinità, Piazza della Signoria, near the cathedral, etc. Each driver is bound to carry a 'tariffa'. *Within the city* ('cinta daziaria'): per drive one-h. 80 c., two-h. 1 fr.; per hr. 1 fr. 60 c., or 2 fr.; at night (1—6 a. m.) 1 fr. or 1 fr. 25 c. per drive, 2 fr. or 2 fr. 50 c. per hr.; box 50, travelling-bag 25 c. — *Beyond the gates:* first $1/2$ hr. 2, at night $2^1/_2$ fr., each additional $1/_2$ hr. 1 or $1^1/_2$ fr.

Omnibuses from Piaz. della Signoria (some also from Piaz. del Duomo) to all the gates of the city 10 c., on Sund. and holidays 15 c.

Physicians. *Drs.* Levier, Piazza Pitti; Kirch, Via Tornabuoni 7; v. Coelln, Via del Sole 14. — *Dentists:* Dunn, Piazza S. Maria Novella; Campani, Piazza della Signoria.

Druggists. English, Roberts, Via Tornabuoni 17; Groves, Borgo Ognissanti 15.

Baths. Peppini, Via SS. Apostoli No. 16, near S. Trinità; Papini, Via Vigna Nuova 19, and Corso Vitt. Emanuele 17b; also in the Via di Parione 28, at the back of the Palaz. Corsini.

Theatres. *Della Pergola (Pl. 104), erected in 1638, remodelled in 1857, Via della Pergola 12, for operas and ballet, seats for upwards of 2000 pers., representations during a few months only in the year, adm. 3 fr.; *Pagliano or Cherubini (Pl. 103), Via Ghibellina 81, adm. $1^1/_2$ fr.; Niccolini (Pl. 101), Ital. and French comedy, Via Ricasoli 8; Delle Loggie, generally French comedy, Via dei Neri (Loggie del Grano); Nazionale (Pl. 100), Via dei Cerchi; Alfieri (Pl. 97), Via Pietra Piana; Rossini (Pl. 98), formerly *Borgognissanti*, and several others. — *Open-air Theatres:* Goldoni (Pl. 99); Politeama (Pl. 105), Corso Vitt. Emanuele, near the Cascine, operas, ballet, farces, and sometimes a circus. Principe Umberto (Pl. 106), Piaz. Azeglio; Arena Nazionale, in the Via Nazionale, and Nuova Arena al Parterre, both outside the Porta S. Gallo.

Booksellers. Goodban, Piazza S. Trinità, for English, French and Italian literature, also photographs and engravings; Bettini, for Italian literature, Via Tornabuoni; Loescher, principally for German literature, Via Tornabuoni. Brecker, Via Maggio 15, with circulating library. Berletti, Via de' Banchi, circul. musical library. — Pianos may be hired of Ducci, Via Tornabuoni, Piazza Antinori.

Photographers. Goodban, see above; Alinari, Via Nazionale 8, a very attractive establishment; Bernoud, Via dell' Oriuolo 51, shop Via del Proconsolo 20.

Shops. The best are in the Via Calzajoli and Via Tornabuoni. Alabaster-wares etc. in the Lung-Arno. In shops where the prices are not fixed, the price demanded is almost invariably one-third or one-half in excess of the real value of the article. A polite offer by the purchaser of what he believes to be an adequate price will generally be attended with the desired result. This pernicious system is unfortunately almost universally prevalent in Italy.

Bankers. Du Fresne, Via di Corso 2; Fenzi and Co., Piazza della Signoria. — *Money Changers:* Via Calzajoli 9, Via Cerretani, Borgognissanti 15, etc.

English Church Service. *English Church*, Via Maglio, behind S. Marco; *English Chapel*, Palazzo Rinuccini 31. — *Presbyterian Service*, Lung-Arno Guicciardini 9.

Railways. (1). To Bologna by Pistoja see R. 47. — (2). To Pisa by Pistoja and Lucca see R. 51. — (3). To Pisa and Leghorn by Empoli see R. 48. — (4). By Empoli to Siena and Orvieto. — (5). To Arezzo and Perugia 3 times daily in $4^1/_2$—$6^1/_2$ hrs.

To Rome three different routes: 1st. By Arezzo, Cortona, Perugia, Foligno, Terni, and Narni ($232^1/_2$ M.), by railway in 12—16 hrs.; 2nd. Railway to Orvieto in 7 hrs., thence by diligence in 18 hrs.; 3rd. By Leghorn and Civitavecchia along the coast (Maremme Line), $271^1/_4$ M., in 14 hrs. — Those who prefer to perform the journey between Leghorn and Civitavecchia by sea may also procure through-tickets at Florence. The offices of the steamboat-companies *Fraissinet*, *Valéry*, and *Rubatino* are in the Piazza della Signoria; that of the *Messageries Impériales* in the same square, corner of the Via della Farina; that of the *Società Peirano*, Piazza S. Margherita, adjoining the Badia. It is, however, perhaps more satisfactory to procure the steamboat-ticket after arriving at Leghorn (comp. p. 258).

From Florence to *Forli* (p. 235) Corriere daily at 3 p. m., Diligence on Tuesd., Thursd., and Sat. at 3 a. m.; coupé 15, intérieur 12 fr.; from Forli to Ravenna (corresponding with these conveyances), 4 or 3 fr. Starting-point Via dei Leoni 25. — From Florence to *Faenza* (p. 235) Corriere daily at 3 p. m.; Diligence on Tuesd. and Sat. at 4 a. m., in 12 hrs.; coupé 15, intérieur 12 fr.; starting-point Locanda della Cervia, Via de' Cardinali, near the Via Calzajoli.

Diary. *Churches* generally open the whole day except from $12^1/_2$ to 2 or 3 p. m.

**Accademia delle Belle Arti*, daily exc. Sund. 9—3 o'cl., p. 308.

Bargello, see Museo Nazionale.

Biblioteca Laurenziana, daily exc. Sund. and holidays 9—3, vacation from Oct. 1st to Nov. 12th, p. 313.

Bibl. Marucelliana, daily exc. Sund. 10—2, p. 311.

Bibl. Nazionale, daily exc. Sund. and festivals, in summer 9—5, in winter 9—4, p. 298.

Bibl. Riccardiana, daily exc. Sund. 9—3; vacation from Aug. 20th to Nov. 12th.

**Boboli, Garden*, daily from morning till evening by permission, which must be applied for before 3 p. m.; open to the public on Sund. forenoon; p. 322.

Galleria Berte, daily 10—3, frequently not accessible, p. 306.

Gal. Buonarotti, Mond. and Thursd. 9—3, p. 316.

Gal. Corsini, Tuesd., Thursd., and Sat. 10—3, p. 315.

***Gal. Pitti*, daily 9—3, Sund. and festivals 10—3, Mond. 12—3, p. 318.

**Gal. Strozzi*, Mondays (unless a festival) 11—1, p. 316.

***Gal. degli Uffizi*, daily 9—3, Sund. and festivals 10—3, Mond. 12—3, p. 291.

**S. Lorenzo*, new sacristy and chapel of the princes, daily 8—12 and 3—$4^1/_2$ o'cl., p. 312.

Museum, Egyptian, daily till 3 p. m., p. 317.

**Mus. di S. Marco*, Oct. 1st to March 31st 9—3, Apr. 1st to Sept 30st 10—4; on Sund. gratis, at other times 1 fr.; p. 307.

**Mus. Nazionale*, daily 10—4, 1 fr., on Sund. gratis, p. 302.

Mus. di Storia Naturale, Tuesd., Thursd., and Sat. 10—4; strangers admitted daily on application; p. 323.

Zoological Garden daily, adm. 50 c., Sund. forenoon 25 c., p. 328.

Principal Attractions: Piazza della Signoria with the Palazzo Vecchio and the Loggia dei Lanzi (p. 290); Galleria degli Uffizi (p. 291); Piazza del Duomo with the Baptistery and the Cathedral (p. 300); the churches of S. Croce (p. 304), S. Lorenzo (p. 311), S. Maria Novella (p. 313), S. Marco (p. 307); the Accademia delle belle Arti (p. 308); the Pal. Pitti with the picture-gallery (p. 319) and the Boboli Garden (p. 322); the views from S. Miniato (p. 325), from Bello Sguardo (p. 327) and from the heights of Fiesole (p. 329). — A stay of 4—6 days will not suffice for more than a very superficial survey of the sights of Florence.

Florence, the capital of the kingdom of Italy since 1864, formerly capital of the Grand Duchy of Tuscany, ranks with Rome, Naples, and Venice as one of the most attractive towns in Italy. Whilst in ancient times Rome was the grand centre of Italian development, the modern metropolis has since the middle ages superseded it as the focus of intellectual activity. The modern Italian language and literature have emanated almost exclusively from Florence, and here too the fine arts have attained the zenith of their glory. An amazing profusion of treasures of art, such as exists in no other locality within so narrow limits, reminiscences of a history of profound significance for the whole of Europe, perpetuated by numerous and imposing monuments, and finally the delightful environs of the city combine to render Florence one of the most interesting and attractive places in the world.

Florence, Italian *Firenze*, formerly *Fiorenza*, from the Latin *Florentia*, justly entitled 'la bella', is situated on both banks of the *Arno*, an insignificant stream except in rainy weather, in a charming valley of moderate width, picturesquely enclosed by the Apennines, the highest summit of the spurs of which (*Monte Morello*, about 3000 ft.) rises to the N. On the S. the heights rise more immediately from the river, on the N. they are 3—4 M. distant, whilst towards the N.W., in the direction of Prato and Pistoja the valley expands considerably. Sudden transitions of temperature frequently occur, and are trying to those in delicate health. The most agreeable months here are April, May, and the first half of June, September, October and November. In the depth of winter and the early spring bitterly cold winds often prevail; in July and August the heat is generally most oppressive. On the whole, however, Florence is considered a healthy place, especially since the introduction of sanitary improvements with regard to the supply of water, extra-mural interment, etc., which have been effected in consequence of the ravages of the cholera in 1854 and 1855.

Since 1864, when Florence superseded Turin as the capital of Italy, the city has undergone great improvements, having laid aside the character of a quiet provincial town, and assumed that of a busy and populous metropolis. The rapidity with which its precincts have been extended in every direction (p. 289) afford the best proof of its prosperity. As early as the 15th cent.

Florence contained 90,000 inhab., in 1859 about 112,000, and now 143,000. The Florentines have ever been noted for the vigour of their reasoning powers and for their preeminence in artistic talents, and even at the present day their superiority over the Genoese and the inhabitants of other towns of Lombardy is apparent from their manners and their dress.

Florence does not lay claim to very great antiquity. It was probably founded by the Romans in the first century B. C., under Sulla, and, as ancient records and some scanty ruins indicate, must at an early period have attained to considerable prosperity, owing to its highly favourable situation. The town was devasted by the incursions of the barbarian hordes during the dark ages, but revived about the commencement of the 11th cent. In 1010 the Florentines conquered the ancient town of Fiesole, aided the Pisans in their contests with Lucca and Genoa, and took an active part in the feud which broke out about this period between the Guelphs and Ghibellines, the town generally supporting the cause of the pope against the imperial party. The most powerful families in the town, such as the Buondelmonti, were on the side of the Guelphs, in opposition to whom the Uberti for a brief period held the supremacy under Emperor Frederick II. After that monarch's death (1250), however, the Guelphs returned, and in 1283 a species of republic was constituted by the twelve guilds of the citizens, under twelve presidents (priori), the nobility being excluded. About the year 1300 the party struggles again burst forth between the same rival families, under the new names of the *Whites* and the *Blacks* (p. 278), in which the Guelphs (Neri) were eventually victorious, and the Whites, among whom was the poet *Dante Allighieri*, banished. King Robert of Naples then sent Count *Walter de Brienne*, Duke of Athens, to Florence as governor, and his authority for a time repressed the civic broils; but in 1343 he was expelled by the people, and a turbulent and lawless period of 70 years ensued, during which the power of the wealthy commercial family of the *Medici* gradually developed itself. The real founder of their dynasty was *Giovanni de' Medici* (d. 1428). His son *Cosmo* was overcome by the Albizzi in 1433, but after an exile of one year returned as the 'liberator of his country', and resumed the reins of government with almost princely magnificence. He was succeeded by his son *Pietro* in 1464, and in 1465 by his grandson *Lorenzo*, surnamed *Il Magnifico*, who, as a statesman, scholar, and patron of art and science, attained the highest celebrity. The conspiracy of the Pazzi (1478), to which his brother *Giuliano* fell a victim, did not avail to undermine the power of this prince, but proved successful against his feeble son and successor *Pietro II.*, who was banished in 1494, with his brothers *Giovanni* (afterwards Pope Leo X.) and *Giuliano*. Their property was confiscated, and Charles VIII. of France now occupied Florence, where *Hieronymus Savonarola*, the celebrated prior of S. Marco, soon exercised his despotic sway, which was terminated in 1498 by his death at the stake. The intermediate supremacy of the Gonfaloniere *Pietro Soderini* now followed, but in 1512 the partisans of the Medici compelled him to abdicate, and recalled the brothers *Giuliano* and *Giovanni*. The former soon resigned his authorithy, the latter became pope, and they were succeeded by *Lorenzo*, a natural son of Pietro II., and the first of the illegitimate line of the Medicis. The family was, however, again banished in 1527, but Emp. Charles V., who had married his daughter to *Alessandro Medici*, attacked the town and took it in 1530 after a siege of eleven months, during which Michael Angelo, as engineer on the side of the republic, and his brave partisan Ferruccio greatly distinguished themselves. The emperor then constituted Alessandro hereditary sovereign of Florence. The assassination of the latter, perpetrated by his own cousin Lorenzo, Jan. 7th, 1537, did not conduce to the re-establishment of the republic. He was succeeded by *Cosmo I.* (1537—64), who entirely suppressed all political liberty in the city, but to some extent revived the fame of the Medici by his liberal patronage of art of every kind. (He was the founder of the Accademia delle Belle Arti.) His successor *Fran-*

cesco Maria assumed the title of 'Granduca' of Tuscany in 1567. In 1737 the Medici family became extinct by the death of *Giovanni Gaston*. The Emperor Charles VI. then presented Tuscany to Duke *Francis Stephen of Lorraine* (Lorena), husband of his daughter Maria Theresa, who himself became emperor in 1745 as Francis I. He was succeeded in Tuscany in 1766 by his second son *Leopold*, and the latter, becoming emperor in 1790, was followed by his second son *Ferdinand III.*, who was expelled from his dominions by the storms of the Revolution at the commencement of the present century. Tuscany is indebted to these princes of the house of Lorraine for a number of excellent institutions and reforms. On the termination of the Napoleonic kingdom of Etruria in 1814 the Grand Duke Ferdinand III. returned, and was succeeded in 1824 by his son *Leopold II.*, uncle of Victor Emmanuel, and last Duke of Tuscany. He was compelled by the Revolution of 1849 to take refuge in flight, and was finally banished in consequence of the events of 1859. In accordance with a popular resolution passed on March 15th, 1860, Tuscany became a portion of the Kingdom of Italy then in process of organisation.

The proud position occupied by Florence in the history of art and science was first established by *Dante Allighieri*, born here in 1265, author of the 'Divine Comedy', and the great founder of the modern Italian language. In 1302 he was banished with his party, and in 1321 died at Ravenna. *Giovanni Boccacio*, the first expounder of the illustrious Dante, and celebrated for his 'Decamerone', which served as a model for the 'Canterbury Tales' of Chaucer, also lived at Florence. *Macchiavelli*, *Guicciardini*, *Galileo*, and many other eminent men of letters and science were also natives of this city. About the close of the 12th cent. *Arnolfo di Cambio*, builder of the cathedral, the tower of which was erected by *Giotto* in 1334, then *Andrea di Cione*, surnamed *Orcagna*, renowned for his Loggia dei Lanzi (1374), and 40 years later *Filippo Brunellesco*, constructor of the dome of the cathedral, attained a high reputation here as architects. In the plastic art Pisa took precedence of Florence in the 13th cent. (*Nicola* and *Giovanni Pisano*; in the 14th cent. *Andrea Pisano*), but *Giotto*, *Luca della Robbia*, and *Lorenzo Ghiberti* in the 14th and 15th cent. contributed greatly to enhance the lustre of Florentine art. In the 16th cent. all these masters were surpassed by *Michael Angelo Buonarotti*, and at a very recent period *Pampaloni*, *Bartolini*, *Dupré* have highly distinguished themselves.

Florence also lays claim to the highest rank in the art of painting, the founder of which in Italy, *Giovanni Cimabue*, was born here about the year 1240. A new era in the art was introduced by *Giotto di Bondone*, born 1276 at Vespignano near Florence, who first ventured to deviate from traditional and stereotype forms, devoted his energies to a faithful study of nature, and advocated unfettered scope of the imagination. His new maxims were instrumental in imparting a new impulse to art throughout an entire century, whilst his contemporary and friend Dante awakened the slumbering powers of the language and poetical imagination of Italy. In Giotto's footsteps followed *Taddeo Gaddi*, *Giottino*, *Andrea di Cione*, *Spinello Aretino*, *Antonio Veneziano*, and others, until in the 15th cent. a more pleasing imitation of nature was introduced by *Masaccio* and *Fra Filippo Lippi*. The pious *Fra Giovanni Angelico da Fiesole* (about 1450) strove to impart an expression and charm of sublimity to his compositions, whilst *Domenico Ghirlandajo* and *Benozzo Gozzoli* (d. 1485) adhered more closely to nature. The culminating point of art was attained by *Leonardo da Vinci*, who was born at Florence in 1452 (d. 1519), and his great rival *Michael Angelo Buonarotti* (1474—1563), a pupil in his capacity as painter of Ghirlandajo, but whose principal works are not at Florence; then by *Fra Bartolommeo* (1469—1517) and *Andrea Vannucchi*, surnamed *del Sarto* (1488—1530), painters who held themselves aloof from the influence of other schools. Subsequent artists who attained to distinction in the 16th and 17th cent. were *Ridolfo Ghirlandajo*, then *Giorgio Vasari*, author of the biography of preceding artists, *Angelo Bronzino*, *Cristoforo Allori*, *Carlo Dolci*, etc. The period of the highest development of art is coincident with that of the revival of science; this was the epoch of the Renaissance, or new birth of antiquity, the glory of which its admirers strove to reawaken in poetry and eloquence, as well as in art and science. Florence under the Medicis in the 15th cent. was the great focus of this aim, the principal results of which emanated hence, exercising a marked influence on the whole of Italy, as well as the rest of Europe.

Florence is situated on both banks of the *Arno*, but by far the greater part of the city lies on the r. bank. On the latter, to the N. of the Ponte Vecchio, at some distance from the river, was situated the Roman town of Florentia, which however was extended at an early period in the middle ages to the opposite bank of the Arno. The walls of the city, which have recently been almost entirely removed, were constructed at the same time as the cathedral, between 1285 and 1388. The ancient *Gates* however have been spared, of which the following are the most interesting: *Porta alla Croce* (Pl. G, 5), erected in 1284, with frescoes by Ghirlandajo; *Porta S. Gallo* (Pl. F, 2), erected in 1330, also adorned with frescoes by Ghirlandajo; *Porta Romana* (Pl. A, 6), erected in 1328 by Jacopo Orcagna. The *New Quarters* of the town are at the W. end, on the r. bank of the Arno, extending as far as the Cascine (p. 328), and here the best hotels and the residences of English, American, and other visitors are situated. A number of broad new streets have also been constructed on the site of the old fortifications, to the N. and E. of the Porta S. Gallo, extending as far as the Arno, and not yet entirely completed.

Bridges. The oldest of the six bridges which connect the banks of the Arno is the *Ponte alle Grazie*, constructed 1235, with a chapel of 1471, and restored 1835, the scene in 1283 of the union effected between the Guelphs and Ghibellines. The *Ponte Vecchio* said to have existed as early as the Roman period, reconstructed, after its repeated demolition, by Taddeo Gaddi in 1362, consists of three arches, over which a gallery is carried to connect the Pitti Palace and the Uffizi with the Palazzo Vecchio. *Ponte S. Trinità*, erected soon after 1567 in a substantial and handsome style by Bartolommeo Ammanati, is embellished with statues representing the four seasons. *Ponte alla Carraja*, originally constructed 1218, destroyed together with the Ponte Vecchio by an inundation in 1333, restored 1337, was finally renewed in 1559 by Ammanati by order of Cosmo I.

The river is bordered on both sides by broad and handsome quays, termed the *Lung' Arno*, of which the different parts are the *Lung' Arno Corsini*, the *Lung' Arno Soderini*, *Lung' Arno Nuovo*, etc. The busiest streets are the *Via Tornabuoni* (Pl. C, 4) and the *Via Calzajuoli* (Pl. D, 4).

The city possesses 87 churches and a number of grand old houses and palaces which bear testimony to its ancient prestige. The following piazzas deserve mention: *Piazza della Signoria, P. dell' Annunziata, P. di S. Croce, P. del Duomo, P. di S. Maria Novella, P. dell' Indipendenza* (Pl. D, E, 2), the *P. d'Azeglio*

(Pl. F, 4), not entirely completed, and the *Piazza Savonarola* (Pl. G, 2, 3), now in course of construction.

The ***Piazza della Signoria** (Pl. D, 4, 5), once the forum of the republic, and the scene of its most momentous transactions, is still the principal focus of public life. Here, too, in 1498, Savonarola and two other monks of his order, the Italian precursors of the Reformation, were burned at the stake. In this piazza is situated the ***Palazzo Vecchio** (Pl. 88), originally the seat of the 'Signoria', or government of the republic, and subsequently the residence of Cosmo I., erected 1298 by *Arnolfo di Cambio*, and subsequently considerably altered and furnished with a lofty tower. On the frieze are seen the armorial bearings of the Tuscan towns and halfway up is an inscription recording the popular resolutions passed on March 15th, 1860. At the entrance are *Michael Angelo's* celebrated *David, placed here in 1504 (the injury to the left arm was sustained during the disturbances which resulted in the second banishment of the Medicis in 1527), and Hercules and Cacus by his rival *Baccio Bandinelli*. Beyond these are two insignificant statues by *Bandinelli* and *Rossi*. The court is by *Michelozzi*; the fountain-figure, a boy with a fish, by *Verocchio*. The *Great Hall* in the interior, constructed under the directions of Savonarola in 1495, was to have been decorated with frescoes from the celebrated cartoons of the 'Cavalry Skirmish' by Leonardo and the 'Bathing Soldiers' by Michael Angelo (1504). The walls are now adorned with frescoes by *Vasari*, illustrative of the history of the city. The hall has recently been fitted up for the sessions of the Italian parliament, and divided into compartments, the woodwork of which however is removable. Most of the marble sculptures formerly here are now in the Bargello (p. 303). The palace is also the residence of the minister of the exterior. — At the N. corner of the edifice is the brazen lion known as *Il Marzocco;* l. is the **Great Fountain* with Neptune and Tritons, erected by *Bartolommeo Ammanati* under Cosmo I., adjacent to the equestrian statue of Cosmo by *Giovanni da Bologna*, 1594.

The ***Loggia dei Lanzi** (or *dell' Orcagna*) (Pl. 53), erected 1375 by *Andrea di Cione (Orcagna)*, derives its appellation from the spearsmen, or 'lancers', who acted as guards here in the reign of Cosmo I. One of the lions by the flight of steps is antique, the other by *Flaminio Vacca*. Beneath the arches to the r. is the *Rape of the Sabines, a group in marble executed by *Giovanni da Bologna* in 1583; l. *Perseus with the head of the Medusa, in bronze, by *Benvenuto Cellini*, by whom the statuettes and basreliefs of the pedestal were also executed; behind it the *Rape of Polyxena, a large group in marble by *Fedi*, erected in 1866. In the centre a *Warrior supporting a dead man, usually supposed to represent Ajax with the body of Patroclus, a copy of a Greek work; by the wall at the back are 6 large draped female statues, of which the third to the l. represents the so-called *Thusnelda, from Trajan's Forum at Rome. Judith with the head of Holofernes, in bronze, by *Donatello*. Hercules slaying the Centaur Nessus, by *Giovanni da Bologna*.

To the l. behind the equestrian statue is the *Palazzo Uyuccioni* (Pl. 87), erected in 1550, from designs variously attributed to *Raphael*, *Michael Angelo* and *Palladio*. The new palazzo in course of construction opposite to the Pal. Vecchio occupies the site of an ancient edifice, which according to tradition was partially erected by Pisan captives in 1364.

Between the Pal. Vecchio and the Loggia de' Lanzi begins the *Portico degli Uffizi* (Pl. 86), erected 1560—74 by *Giorgio Vasari*, the internal niches of which are adorned with *Marble Statues* of celebrated Tuscans. The names of the characters represented and of the respective sculptors are engraved on the bases. They are as follows, beginning on the l.: Andrea Orcagna; behind it on the sides of the first door, Cosmo, 'pater patriæ', and Lorenzo 'il magnifico'; then Nicola Pisano, Giotto, Donatello, Leo Batt. Alberti, Leonardo da Vinci, Michael Angelo, Dante, Petrarch, Boccaccio, Macchiavelli, Guicciardini, Vespucci, Galileo, Pier Antonio Micheli, Franc. Redi, Paolo Mascagni, Andrea Cesalpino, S. Antonio, Ricorso, Guido Aretino, and Benvenuto Cellini; in the external niches, towards the Arno, Francesco Ferrucci (p. 287), Giovanni delle Bande Nere (p. 311), Piero Capponi, and Farinata degli Uberti. Opposite the first mentioned statues are the *Post Office* and the *Mint (La Zecca)* (Pl. 96), a structure of 1361, containing a fine collection of the ancient and modern coins of Siena and Florence.

The traveller coming from the Piazza della Signoria enters by the second door to the l. under this portico, and ascends by a staircase of 126 steps to the **Galleria degli Uffizi** (open daily 9—3, Sundays and festivals 10—3 o'clock only; no fees). The gallery originated with the Medici collections, to which numerous additions were made by the Lorraine family, and it is now one of the best in the world, both in extent and value. A few of the finest objects only in this vast collection are here enumerated. The stranger whose time admits of a brief visit only should first walk through the corridors, in order to become acquainted with their topography, and then return to the *Tribuna, the gem of the whole gallery. Permission to copy is easily obtained by addressing a written application to the directors. The position of many of the best pictures is occasionally altered, but is sufficiently indicated by the number of copyists who surround them. (Catalogues at the entrance, 3½ fr.)

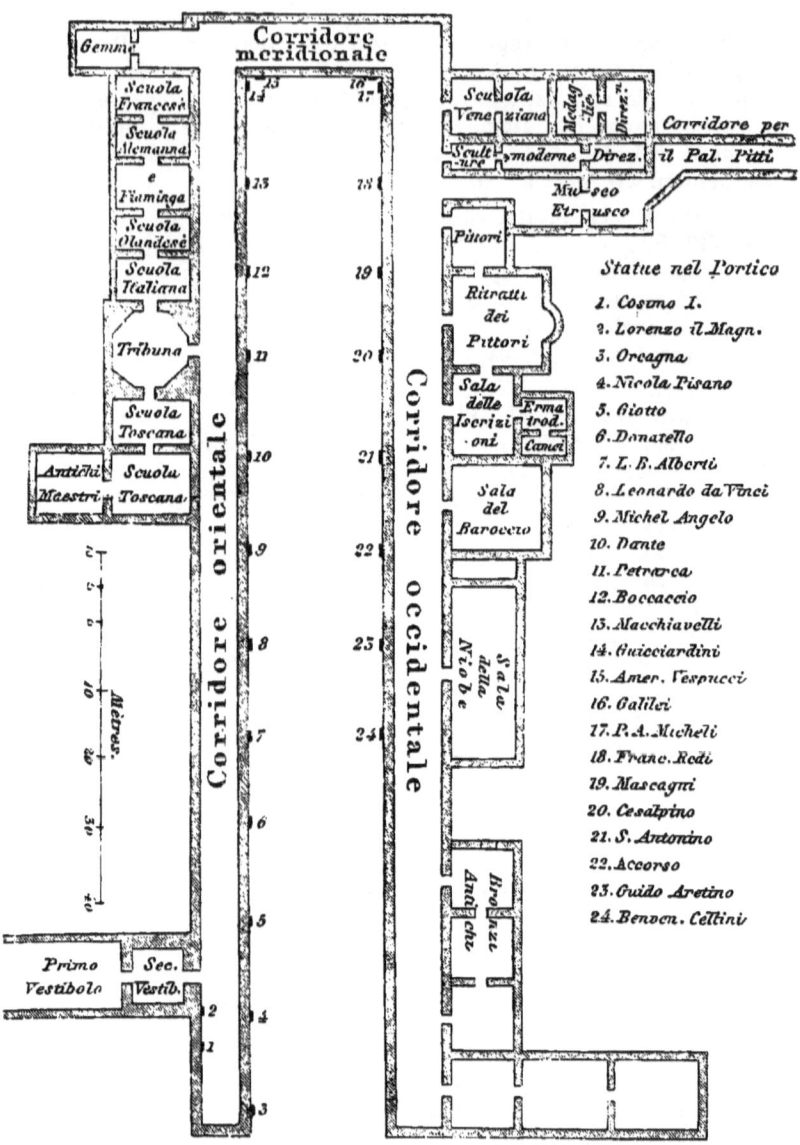

First Vestibule: Busts of members of the Medici family. Bronze statues of Mars and Silenus, the latter with the infant Bacchus in his arms, a copy of the original antique at Rome. Various Roman reliefs with representations of processions and sacrifices.

Second Vestibule: Two pillars with trophies in relief; busts of Cybele and Jupiter. A horse, *two dogs, and a *wild boar, all antiques.

E. Corridor, 530 ft. in length, adorned with mythological ceiling-paintings by *Bernardino Poccetti:* on the upper part of the walls are 534 portraits of princes and great men, commenced under Cosmo I. and constantly increased. On either side are exhibited ant. busts, statues, and sarcophagi, above which are pictures. The visitor proceeding to the r. from the entrance and commencing at the end should observe the following objects.

Ancient Sculptures in Marble: 35. Agrippina sitting; 39. Sarcophagus with representations from the life of a Roman; 38. Hercules slaying Nessus (almost entirely modern); 41, 47, 48. Busts of Cæsar (with bronze head), Augustus, and Agrippa; 75. Beautiful statue of an Athlete (the 14th of those so designated), which has recently been discovered to be a copy of the celebrated Doryphorus of Polycletes. Also a collection of Roman sarcophagi (Rape of Proserpine, Labours of Hercules, Hunt of Meleager, Apollo and the Muses, etc.) and a number of Roman portraits-heads. At the end a sarcophagus with the fall of Phaëton and the Heliades.

Pictures: 2. *Cimabue*, St. Cecilia; *6. *Giotto*, Christ on the Mt. of Olives; 9. *Simone* and *Lippi Memmi* (of Siena), Annunciation with lateral pictures (S. Giulietta and S. Ansano); 12. *Pietro Laureati* (of Siena), Hermit saints of the wilderness of Thebes; *17. *Fra Angelico da Fiesole*, Tabernacle with gold ground, on the exterior St. Mark and St. Peter, on the interior St. Mark, John the Baptist and Madonna with the Child, surrounded by angels playing on instruments; *24. *Lor. di Credi*, Madonna, worshipping the Child; *25. *Botticelli*, Madonna; 36. *Luca Signorelli*, Holy Family; 39. *Botticelli*, Birth of Venus.

S. Connecting Passage, with similar decorations and contents, of which the following three antiques merit special notice: *138. Thornextractor; 127. Round altar with bas-reliefs, representing the Sacrifice of Iphigenia, bearing the name of Cleomenes; 146. Nymph extracting a thorn (*Venere della Spina*).

W. Corridor, of the same length as that on the E., adorned with frescoes representing the rise of art, and with portraits of celebrated Florentines. R. and l. of the entrance statues of Marsyas. The pictures are comparatively unimportant, but at the end there are several fine sculptures: *380. Bacchus, an early work of *Michael Angelo;* in the centre an antique altar from Rome, dedicated to the Lares; 389. *Sansovino*, Bacchus; 388. Unfinished statue of Apollo by the same master; 383. *Benedetto da Majano*, John the Baptist; 384. *Donatello*, John the Baptist; 387. *Donatello*, David; 385. *Baccio Bandinelli*, Copy of the Laocoon group.

Returning hence, and passing through the second door l. of the entrance, the visitor next enters the octagonal

** *Tribuna*.

Here the master pieces of ancient sculpture and modern painting are combined so as to form a magnificent and almost unparalleled collection. The hall was constructed by *Bernardo Buontalenti;* the decorations are by *Bernardino Poccetti.* In the centre are placed five very celebrated marble sculptures: *Satyr playing on the cymbal, restored by *Michael Angelo*. The group of the *Wrestlers, found with that of the Children of Niobe. The *Medici Venus, found in the 16th cent. in the villa of Hadrian near Tivoli, brought to Florence in 1680, under Cosmo III.; the Greek inscription designates *Cleomenes*, son of Apollodorus, as the master. The *Grinder, supposed to be a Scythian from the group of Marsyas who is being flayed, found at Rome in the 16th cent. The Apollino, or young Apollo, of the school of *Praxiteles*.

Paintings, beginning on the l.: *1131. *Raphael*, Pope Julius II.; 1132. *Correggio* (?), Head of John the Baptist; 1133. *A. Caracci*, Bacchante; **1129. *Raphael*, Madonna with the goldfinch (del Cardinello); 1130. *Fra Bartolommeo*, Job; *1127. *Raphael*, The youthful John; 1128. *Van Dyck*, Emp. Charles V.; *1125. *Raphael* (?), Madonna at the well; 1126. *Fra Bartolommeo*, Isaiah; *1123. *Raphael*, The Fornarnia (?); 1124. *Franc. Francia*, Portrait. Over the door: 1122. *Perugino*, Madonna with SS. John and Sebastian; *1120. *Raphael*, Female Portrait; 1121. *Mantegna*, Elisabeth of Mantua; *1118. *Correggio*, Repose during the Flight to Egypt; 1119. *Baroccio*, Duke Francis Maria II. of Urbino; 1116. *Titian*, A Prelate; *1117. *Titian*, Venus; 1114. *Guercino*, Sibyl of Samos; 1115. *Van Dyck*, Jean de Montfort;

1113. *Guido Reni*, Madonna; 1111. *Mantegna*, Altar-piece, representing the Adoration of the Magi, the Circumcision and the Resurrection; 1112. *A. del Sarto*, Madonna with SS. John and Francis; 1110. *Orazio Alfani*, Holy Family; 1109. *Domenichino*, Cardinal Agucchia; 1107. *Daniele da Volterra*, Massacre of the Innocents; *1108. *Titian*, Venus; 1106. *G. Lanfranchi*, St. Peter; 1104. *Spagnoletto*, St. Jerome; 1105. *Schidone*, Holy Family. Over the door: 1145. *Lod. Caracci*, Rebecca and Eleazar; 1143. *Lucas of Leyden*, Crucified Christ; 1144. *Giulio Romano*, Madonna; *1141. *A. Dürer*, Adoration of the Magi; 1142. *Cranach*, Adam; *1139. *Michael Angelo*, Holy Family; 1140. *Rubens*, Venus and Minerva contending for a youth; 1137. *Guercino*, Endymion; 1138. *Cranach*, Eve; 1134. *Correggio*, Madonna; 1135. *Luini*, Herodias with the head of the Baptist; 1136. *Paolo Veronese*, Holy Family.

The door l. (when approached from the corridor) leads from the Tribuna to the

Tuscan School.

1st Saloon: 1146. *Lor. di Credi*, Annunciation; 1147. *Andrea del Sarto*, Portrait of himself; 1152. *Fra Bartolommeo*, God the Father; 1159. *Leonardo da Vinci* (?), Head of the Medusa; *1161. *Fra Bartolommeo*, Nativity and Circumcision of Christ; 1163. *Lor. di Credi*, Portrait of Verocchio; 1167. *Masaccio*, Portrait of an old man; 1179. *Fra Filippo Lippi*, St. Augustine; 1184. *Fra Angelico*, Death of the Virgin. — 2nd Saloon: 1252. *Leonardo da Vinci*, Adoration of the Magi (unfinished); 1257. *Filippino Lippi*, Adoration of the Magi, with portraits of the Medici; *1259. *Albertinelli*, Visit of Mary to Elisabeth; *1265. *Fra Bartolommeo*, Virgin with the protecting saint of Florence (in chiaroscuro); 1268. *Filippino Lippi*, Madonna with saints; 1271. *Bronzino*, Christ in Hades; 1275. *Ridolfo del Ghirlandajo*, St. Zenobius, bishop of Florence, resuscitating a dead man; 1277. Same master, Transference of the remains of St. Zenobius to the cathedral; *1279. *Sodoma*, St. Sebastian; 1284. *Pontormo*, Venus (designed by Michael Angelo).

Saloon of the Ancient Masters.

Pictures by *Alessandro Botticelli*, *Lorenzo di Credi*, *Beato Angelico* (*1290. Coronation of the Virgin), *Luca Signorelli* (*1291. Holy Family), *Domenico del Ghirlandajo*, *Benozzo Gozzoli*, *Fra Filippo Lippi*, etc.

The visitor now returns through the Tribuna to the

Venetian and Lombard School.

R. 1403. *Massari*, Madonna; 1064. *Canaletto*, Palace of the Doges at Venice; 1068. *P. Veronese*, Head as a study; 1074. *Francesco Solimena*, Diana and Callisto; 1077. *Canaletto*, The Grand Canal at Venice; 1094. *Albano*, Rape of Europa; 990. *Albano*, Venus with Cupids; 995. *Dosso Dossi*, Murder of the Innocents; 998. *Guido Reni*, Madonna with Jesus and John; 1000. *P. Veronese*, Madonna; 1001. *Parmeggianino*, Madonna; 1002. *Titian*, Madonna; 1003. and 1005. *Salvator Rosa*, Landscapes; 1007. *A. Caracci*, Madonna; 1011. *Cignani*, Madonna; 1012. *Salvator Rosa*, Landscape; 1016. *Correggio*, Head as a study; 1019. *Palma Vecchio*, Madonna; 1031. *Caravaggio*, Head of the Medusa; 1037. *Palma Vecchio*, Jesus at Emmaus.

Dutch School.

R. *922. *Rembrandt*, Interior of a house; 926. *Gerard Dow*, Apple-woman; 934. *Schalken*, Seamstress; 941. *F. Mieris*, Woman asleep; 952. *Mieris*, Wooing; 954. *Mieris*, The drinkers; 955. *Brouwer*, Tavern-scene; 958. *Terburg*, Lady drinking; 960. *Paulyn*, Miser; 965. *Heemskerk*, Card-players; 968. *Schalken*, Pietas; *972. *Metzu*, Lady and hunter; 976. *F. Mieris*, Portrait of himself; 977. *Jan Steen*, Violin-player; 979. *Rembrandt*, Landscape; 854. *Mieris*, Quack; *973. *Ostade*, Man with a lantern; *882. *Ruysdael*, Landscape with cloudy sky; 888. *Slingeland*, Children blowing soap-bubbles; 891. *Heyden*, Town-hall of Amsterdam; *897. *Berkeyden*, Cathedral of Haarlem.

Flemish and German School.

1st Saloon: r. *812. *Rubens*, Venus and Adonis; 810. *Rubens*, Silenus; 838. *Cranach*, Luther; 839. *Holbein*, Portrait; 845. *Cranach*, Electors John and Frederick of Saxony; 847. *Cranach*, Luther and Melanchthon; 848. *Claude Lorrain*, Sea-landscape with the Villa Medici at Rome; 777. *Dürer*, St. James the Great; 783. *Van Dyck*, Madonna; 784. *Holbein*, Zwingli; *786. *G. Dow*, Schoolmaster; 799. *Holbein*, Sir Thomas More; 800. *Schalken*, Girl with a candle. — In the 2nd Saloon eight pictures from the lives of SS. Peter and Paul, by *Johann Schäuffelin* of Nuremberg. R. 744. *Nic. Frumenti* (German School), Tabernacle with the Raising of Lazarus; 742. *D. Teniers senr.*, Alchemist; 698. *Van der Goos*, Madonna; 760. *Teniers junr.*, Love-scene; *703. *Memling*, Madonna; 705. *Teniers junr.*, Physician; 706. *Teniers junr.*, St. Peter weeping.

French School.

This saloon contains numerous battle-pieces, by *Bourguignon* and others, and a beautifully inlaid table. R. 679. and 689. Portraits of the poet Vittorio Alfieri and the Countess of Albany (b. 1763, d. at Florence 1824), by *Fabre de Montpellier*, with two autographs by Alfieri on the back; 693. *Poussin*, Venus and Adonis (a sketch); 674. *Larguillière*, Rousseau; 672. *Grimoux*, Young pilgrim; 667. *Clouet*, Francis I. on horseback.

Then to the l. in the corridor is the

Cabinet of the Gems

(generally closed since a theft committed in 1860; application should be made to one of the custodians). This saloon contains four columns of oriental alabaster and four of verde antico; in the six cabinets are preserved upwards of 400 gems and precious stones, once the property of the Medici. In the 1st cabinet on the r. a vessel of lapis lazuli; two basreliefs in gold on a ground of jaspar, by *Giovanni da Bologna*. 2nd: Two vessels of onyx; casket of rock-crystal with representation from the life of Christ, executed by *Valerio Belli* for Pope Clement VII.; *portrait of the grand-duke Cosmo III., in Florentine mosaic, of 1619; three bas-reliefs in gold on a ground of jaspar, by *Giovanni da Bologna*; two vases of rock-crystal. 3rd: Cover of a crystal vase, in enamelled gold, executed for Diana of Poitiers. The glass-cabinets by the window contain golden trinkets of ancient Etruscan workmanship. 4th: Venus and Cupid in porphyry. 5th: Bas-relief of gold and jewels, representing the Piazza della Signoria, by *Giovanni da Bologna*. 6th: Vase of rock-crystal, by *Benvenuto Cellini*.

*Two Saloons of the Venetian School.

1st Saloon: r. 576. *Titian*, Portrait of Sansovino; 583. *Giov. Bellini*, Pietà; 589. *Paolo Veronese*, Martyrdom of St. Justina; 590. *Titian*, Madonna; *596. *P. Veronese*, Esther in presence of Ahasuerus; 595. *Jacopo da Ponte*, surnamed *Bassano*, Portraits of the painter's family; *599, 605. *Titian*, Portraits of the Duke and Duchess of Urbino. — 2nd Saloon: r. 609. *Titian*, Battle between Venetians and Imperial troops; 613. *Paris Bordone*, Portrait; 614. *Titian*, Giovanni de' Medici (father of Cosmo I.); 616. *Pordenone*, Paul struck by lightning; 617. *Tintoretto*, Marriage of Cana (a copy); *618. *Titian*, Madonna (a study); *622. *Giorgione*, Maltese knight; 623. *Palma Vecchio*, Madonna; 625. *Titian*, Madonna; **626. *Titian*, 'Flora'; 628. *Bonifazio*, Last Supper; 633. *Titian*, Madonna; *636. *P. Veronese*, Crucifixion; 638. *Tintoretto*, Sansovino; *648. *Titian*, Catharina Cornaro, Queen of Cyprus.

Two Corridors with Sculptures of the Tuscan School.

I. 347—351. Five bas-reliefs in marble representing the history of St. Giovanni Gualberto of the monastery of S. Salvi near Florence, by *Benedetto da Rovezzano*. 352. Tomb-relief of the wife of Fr. Tornabuoni, by *Verocchio*. II. *Ten bas-reliefs with singing choristers, by *Luca della Robbia*, originally destined to embellish the organ in the cathedral. Another, but inferior relief, 373. dancing children, by *Donatello*, was executed for the same purpose. 374. Virgin (unfinished), by *Michael Angelo*. 362. *Fides. by *Matteo Cicitali*. Over the door: Mask of a satyr, an early work of *Michael Angelo*.

Beyond this is the Office of the Director; also the Collection of Coins, accessible by special permission only.

Etruscan Museum,
Drawings, Passage to the Pitti Palace.

A stair descends to the 1st Saloon, containing painted vases, most of them found in Tuscany, a few from S. Italy. In the centre is the celebrated *François (or *Peleus*) *Vase*, so called from a Frenchman of that name who discovered it in a tomb near Chiusi in 1845, and unrivalled in size and richness of decoration (marriage of Peleus, Calydonian hunt, Return of Theseus from Crete, Battle of the centaurs, etc.), and bearing ancient Greek inscriptions attached to the different representations, beneath which are the names of the artists *Clitias* and *Ergotimos*. The vases exhibited in the cabinets by the walls are less important. — 2nd Saloon: Vases destined for religious and domestic purposes, of many different forms, black and without representations; also a few terracottas. — A stair descends hence to a long Corridor which leads over the Ponte Vecchio to the Palazzo Pitti, a walk of nearly 10 min. Here a number of Etruscan cinerary urns, with representations in relief and inscriptions, are preserved. Also an admirable collection of *Drawings, founded by Cardinal Leopold de Medici, and afterwards considerably extended, so that it now comprises about 28,000. All those which are exposed to view are furnished with the names of the masters. Very interesting those of (l.) *Dürer* and *Rubens*, (r.) *Fra Bartolommeo*, **Raphael, Michael Angelo* and *del Sarto*. — Then a number of portraits of the Medici in tapestry.

Two Saloons of the Painters.

The walls are covered with portraits of the most celebrated painters of all nations from the 15th cent. to the present time, painted by themselves and furnished with the names. The 1st Saloon contains the old masters; on the r. wall and half of the l. are those of Central Italy, on the other walls those of N. Italy, on the side by which the room is entered those of foreign countries. The most celebrated names here are **Leonardo da Vinci, Raphael, Michael Angelo, Pietro Perugino, Andrea del Sarto, Masaccio* (or *Filippino Lippi?*), *Giulio Romano;* Venetian School, *Titian, Paolo Veronese, Tintoretto, Palma Vecchio;* Bolognese School, the two *Caracci, Guercino, Guido Reni.* Also **Albert Dürer, Lucas van Leyden, Holbein, Rubens, Van Dyck, Rembrandt, Gerard Dow.* In the centre a large *Marble Vase of Greek workmanship, known as 'The Medicean Vase', with sculpturing representing the Sacrifice of Iphigenia. In a niche opp. the entrance the statue of Card. Leopold de' Medici, the founder of this collection of portraits. In the 2nd Saloon modern masters: *Angelica Kauffmann, Mad. le Brun, Raphael Mengs, Reynolds, Overbeck, Canova, Winterhalter, Ingres.*

Cabinet of Inscriptions.

The walls are covered with a number of ancient Greek and Latin inscriptions, most of them from Rome, arranged in 12 classes according to their subjects (the gods and their priests, the consuls, dramas, military events, private affairs, etc.). There are also some fine Statues: *268. Bacchus and Ampelus; *263. Mercury; *266. Venus Urania; *265. Venus Genetrix; 264. Priestess (head new). L. of the door of the next room an interesting relief representing the Elements. Also a number of cinerary urns and busts with (sometimes fictitious) inscriptions.

Cabinet of the Hermaphrodite.

*306. Hermaphrodite reclining on a panther's skin. On either side of the door, 307. and 324. torsos of Bacchus, one of basalt, the other of Parian marble; 308. Ganymede with the eagle; 311. Pan and hermaphrodite, both restored by *Benvenuto Cellini;* 310. The infant Hercules strangling two snakes; 315. Torso of a Faun; *318. Head of the dying Alexander; 323. Cupid and Psyche.

A door in this cabinet leads to the (generally closed)

Cabinet of the Cameos.

The cases 1st—4th contain the antique cameos, 5th—6th the modern; 7th—10th the ancient cut stones, 11th and 12th the modern. In the 1st case,

l. of the entrance, a cameo, with the *Sacrifice of Antoninus Pius, is remarkable for its size: Cupid riding on a lion, with the name of the artist (Protarchos). Among the modern cameos in the 12th case, in the middle opp. the door, is one with a portrait of Savonarola. Also a number of works in Niello (engraving on silver), e. g. Coronation of the Virgin by *Maso Finiguerra*; also in ivory. By the wall opp. the window: Cast of Dante's features taken after death, 1321, presented in 1865 by Marchese Torriani.

Saloon of Baroccio.

By the walls and in the centre four tables of Florentine mosaic. That in the centre, executed 1613—18 by *Jacopo Antelli*, from *Ligozzo's* design, alone cost 40,000 ducats (nearly 20,000 *l.*). The following pictures are the most interesting: r. 154. *Bronzino*, Portrait; 157. *Honthorst*, Infant Jesus adored by angels; 158. *Bronzino*, Descent from the Cross; *162. *Guido Reni*, Sibyl; 163. *Sustermans*, Galileo; *169. *Baroccio*, The Virgin interceding with the Saviour (Madonna del Popolo); 171. *A. Caracci*, Industrious ape; *180. *Rubens*, Helena Forman, his second wife; 186. *Carlo Dolci*, Magdalene; *190. *Honthorst*, Adoration of the Shepherds; *191. *Sassoferrato*, Madonna dei Dolori; 195. *Caravaggio*, The tribute-money; 196. *Van Dyck*, Margaret of Lorraine; 197. *Rubens*, Elisabeth Brand, his first wife; 203. *Guido Reni*, Bradamante and Fiordaspina (from Ariosto's Orlando Furioso); 208. *Baroccio*, St. Francis receiving the stigmata; 210. *Velasquez*, Philip IV. of Spain on horseback; *216. *Rubens*, Bacchanalian; 220. *Snyders*, Boar-hunt.

*Saloon of Niobe,

constructed 1779, and so named from the far-famed ancient group of the *Children of Niobe, seven sons and seven daughters (slain by Apollo and Diana), whose position indicates that they once adorned the pediment of a temple (probably of Apollo), the unfortunate mother occupying the centre of the group, with her slain and expiring children on either side. These statues, which appear to have been copied from a work by *Scopas* or *Praxiteles*, were found at Rome in 1583 and placed by Cardinal Ferdinand de' Medici in his villa on the Monte Pincio (now the property of the French Academy), whence they were subsequently transferred to Florence. Various opinions prevail with regard to the proper arrangement of the group. Among the paintings are: r. 139. *Sustermans*, the Florentine Senate swearing allegiance to the young Grandduke Ferdinand II.; 140. *Rubens*, Henri IV. at the battle of Ivry; 144. *Van Dyck*, Rubens' Mother (?); 147. *Rubens*, Entry of Henri IV.ʳ into Paris; 148. *Honthorst*, Supper; 152. *Honthorst*, Fortuneteller.

Two Cabinets of Ancient Bronzes.

In the 1st Cabinet, in the centre, under glass, ancient armour in bronze and vessels, found in 1863 near Orvieto; by the walls bronze heads, found in the sea near Leghorn, among them, on the r. wall, Sophocles and Homer; *423. Over life-size statue ('Orator'), with Etruscan inscription, found near the Trasimene Lake; 425. Minerva, found near Arezzo; 427. Chimera (as described by Homer in the 6th Bk. of the Iliad: a lion and goat, with tail of a serpent), found at Arezzo; in front of it a tripod; colossal horse's head; two inscriptions on bronze tablets. The 2nd Cabinet contains in the centre a *Bronze Statuette of a youth ('L' Idolino'), found at Pesaro, with handsome pedestal (15th cent.). The cases by the walls contain a number of small bronzes, some of them statuettes, others articles of domestic use, candelabra, lamps, metal mirrors, helmets, spurs, horse-bits, etc.; also Christian anticaglias (diptychon of the consul Basilius).

Galleria Feroni

(closed), bequeathed by the proprietor of that name to the city in 1850, and transferred hither from the Palazzo Feroni (Pl. 66) a few years ago. It contains few objects of great merit, and is not yet finally arranged. On the wall r. of the entrance: *D. Teniers*, Interior of a butcher's shop and tavern; *Carlo Dolci* (?), Madonna; on the l., *Schidone*, Madonna and Child.

In the following rooms (likewise closed) a collection of Etruscan antiquities is about to be arranged.

The first floor of the edifice contains the *Biblioteca Nazionale* (open daily except on Sundays and festivals, in summer 9—5, in winter 9—4 o'clock, entrance by the 8th door from the piazza), which has been formed since 1860 by the union of the grand-ducal library, formerly in the Pitti Palace, and the still more extensive Biblioteca Magliabecchiana. The latter, founded by *Antonio Magliabecchi*, a jeweller of Florence, has been dedicated to the use of the public since 1747. The present library contains about 200,000 vols and 8000 MSS., comprising the most important works from the literature of other nations. There are also several very rare impressions: the first printed Homer, Florence 1488; Cicero ad Familiares, Venice 1469; Dante, Florence 1481. Every facility is afforded for the use of the library; to the r. at the end of the great reading-saloon is the room containing the catalogues. — The staircase to the r. of the library leads to the *Central-Archives of the state, arranged by *Bonaini*, one of the most imposing collections of this description. Some of the apartments here are fitted up for the sessions of the Italian senate.

Quitting the Uffizi, the stranger should now cross the Piazza della Signoria, and turning to the l., proceed by the handsome *Via dei Calzajoli* towards the *Piazza del Duomo*.

To the l. on the way thither is the church of ***Or San Michele** (Pl. 31), the square form of which still proves its original destination as a corn-hall *(Horreum Sancti Michaelis)* erected by *Arnolfo* in 1284, and converted into a church at the expense of the guild of weavers by *Taddeo Gaddi* in 1337, and *Andrea Orcagna* in 1343. The structure is in the Gothic style, richly adorned internally and externally with sculptures. On the E. side, towards the Via Calzajoli, (r.) St. Luke, by *Giovanni da Bologna*; Christ and St. Thomas, by *Andrea del Verocchio*. (l.) John the Baptist, by *Ghiberti;* beneath, eagles on bales of wool. Then, as the spectator proceeds farther l., on the S. side (r.) St. John, by *Baccio da Montelupo*. The adjacent canopy formerly protected a Madonna by *Mino da Fiesole* (at present in the interior of the church, p. 299), now St. George by *Donatello*, which was originally destined for the vacant niche to the N.; (l.) St. James by *Nanni d'Antonio di Banco*. St. Mark, by *Donatello*. On the W. façade, statues of (r.) St. Eligius, by *Nanni di Banco*, beneath it a relief with a farrier; St. Stephen, by *Lorenzo Ghiberti*; (l.) St. Matthew, by the same master, or perhaps by *Michelozzo*. On the N. side (r.) an empty niche (see above). Four saints by *Nanni di Banco*, with relief representing a sculptor's studio. (l.) St. Philip, by the same. St. Peter, by *Donatello*. The coloured medallions in bas-relief below the niches are by *Luca della Robbia*.

In the Interior, consisting of two naves separated by two

pillars, to the r. the fine *High Altar (Ciborium)*, a celebrated work of *Andrea Orcagna*, executed in marble and precious stones, with numerous reliefs from sacred history; beneath it is preserved the miracle working image of the Virgin. At the side-altar under the organ a marble group of the Holy Family, by *Francesco da S. Gallo;* N. side Madonna and Child, by *Mino da Fiesole* (p. 298).

Opposite the church (on the r.) is the *Oratorio of S. Carlo Borromeo* (Pl. 6), constructed 1284 by *Arnolfo*, but considerably altered in 1616, for its present destination.

The Via dei Calzajoli, before its extension, contained the ancient towers of the *Adimari*, *Medici*, and *Visdomini*. The stranger next reaches the (r.) entrance to the *Bazaar* (Pl. 40), and passes a number of attractive shops, etc. The streets to the l. lead to the busy and animated *Market*, where meat, vegetables, fish, etc. are sold, and which extends as far as the Piazza Strozzi (Pl. C, 4).

On the l. at the extremity of the Via Calzajoli is the oratory **Bigallo** (Pl. 45), an edifice erected in 1248 for charitable purposes, now an orphan-asylum. Over the arcades (N.) are three small statues (Virgin and two Saints), by *Andrea* or *Nicola Pisano*, and two almost obliterated frescoes from the legend of St. Peter the Martyr. The chapel, now archives of the orphan asylum, contains a Madonna by *Alberto Arnoldi*, 1363.

Opposite is the *Church of St. John the Baptist*, *Il **Battistero** (Pl. 5), one of the most ancient structures in the city, originally erected in the 6th cent. on the site of a Roman temple (probably that of Mars), and subsequently renewed at various periods, e. g. in 1293 by *Arnolfo;* from this period too dates the remarkably chaste marble work with which the exterior is covered. The structure is octagonal, 87 ft. in diameter, and surmounted by a dome. It originally served as a cathedral, but has been used as a baptistery since 1128, and in the 14th and 15th cent. was furnished with its three celebrated *Bronze Doors.

The oldest of these is on the S. side, opposite the Bigallo, completed by *Andrea Pisano* in 1330 after 22 years of labour. The representations are from the life of St. John. The bronze decorations at the sides are by *Lorenzo Ghiberti* and his son *Vittorio* (about 1446); above is the Beheading of John the Baptist by *Vincenzo Danti*.

The *Second Door, towards the cathedral, executed by *Lorenzo Ghiberti* (1428—42) is a marvel of art, representing ten different scenes from scripture history: 1. Creation and Expulsion from Paradise; 2. Cain slaying his brother and Adam tilling the field; 3. Noah after the Flood, and his intoxication; 4. Abraham and the angels, and Sacrifice of Isaac; 5. Esau and Jacob; 6. Joseph and his brethren; 7. Promulgation of the Law on Mt. Sinai; 8. The Walls of Jericho; 9. Battle against the Ammonites; 10. The Queen of Sheba. This is the door which Michael Angelo pronounced worthy of forming the entrance to Paradise. The bronze decorations at the sides are also by *Ghiberti;* over the door the *Baptism of Christ, by *Andrea Sansovino*, the angels by *Spinacci*. The two porphyry columns were presented by the Pisans (in 1200) in recognition of the assistance rendered them by the Florentines against Lucca in the expedition to Majorca in 1117. The chain of the harbour of Pisa, carried off by the Florentines in 1362, was formerly suspended here, but has been recently restored to the Pisans and is preserved in the Campo Santo.

The Third Door (N.) is also by *Ghiberti* (1403—27). It represents in 28 sections the history of Christ, the Apostles and Fathers down to St. Augustine. Many rival artists are said to have competed for the honour of undertaking this work, of whom the principal were *Ghiberti*, *Brunellesco* (in the Bargello, p. 303), *Jacopo della Fonte*, *Simone da Colle*, and probably also *Donatello*, but the preference was given to *Ghiberti*. Above the door the Preaching of St. John by *Fr. Rustici* (supposed to have been designed by Leonardo da Vinci).

In the Interior of the baptistery are a number of statues and pictures of subordinate importance. The dome and small choirs are adorned with old *mosaics by *Andrea Tafi*, *Apollonio Greco*, *Jacopo da Turrita*, *Domenico Ghirlandajo*, *Taddeo* and *Agnolo Gaddi*, *Alessio Baldovinetti*, *Lippo Lippi* etc., which however are not recognisable except on very bright days. On the pavement ancient mosaics with the zodiac and inscriptions. R. of the high altar the tomb of Pope John XXIII. (d. 1419), who was deposed by the Council of Constance, the recumbent bronze statue by *Donatello*. On the festival of St. John an altar of massive silver with a cross of the same metal are placed here, adorned with bas-reliefs from the life of the Baptist, by *Maso Finiguerra*, *Antonio da Pollajuolo*, *Maestro Cione*, *Verocchio*, and others. The altar contains 325 lbs. of silver, the cross 141 lbs. In front of the church is a column of speckled marble (cipollino), erected in 1330 to commemorate the removal of the remains of St. Zenobius.

The *Cathedral (Pl. 8), *Il Duomo*, or *La Cattedrale di S. Maria del Fiore*, so called from the lily which figures in the arms of Florence, was erected 1298—1474 on the site of the earlier church of St. Reparata by *Arnolfo di Cambio*, *Giotto*, *Taddeo Gaddi*, *Andrea Orcagna*, and *Lorenzo di Filippo*. The dome was added 1421—36 by *Filippo Brunellesco*; its height (298 ft., with the lantern 354 ft.) exceeds that of the domes of St. Peter and the Pantheon at Rome (ascent see p. 301). The church, a grand example of Italian Gothic, 555 ft. in length, 340 ft. (across the transepts) in breadth, is one of the most admired in Italy. The façade had already been commenced by Arnolfo, but his successor *Giotto* designed a new and more imposing plan (of which copies still exist, e. g. in the cloisters of S. Croce and S. Marco), and executed one half of it himself. In 1586 this work was demolished with a view to replacing it by a new façade, designed by *Buontalenti*, *Dosio*, *Cigoli*, and others, a project which however was not carried out. The cathedral (like S. Croce, S. Lorenzo, etc.) consequently remained destitute of a façade, a defect which it was sought to remedy by supplying its place with frescoes, but these have long since disappeared. In April, 1860, Victor Emanuel laid the foundation-stone of a new façade. The workmanship of the marble-clad walls is excellent and chaste. The two side-entrances and the chapels are sparingly ornamented. The grand proportions of the interior are most impressive, although the walls present a somewhat bald appearance. The choir, instead of being at the extremity of the church, is appropriately placed under the dome.

Interior. On the entrance-wall old frescoes by *Paolo Uccello* (4 prophets), and the Coronation of the Virgin in mosaic, by *Gaddo Gaddi;* at the sides frescoes (angels) by *Santi di Tito*, restored 1842. — The design of the coloured mosaic pavement is attributed to *Baccio d'Agnolo Buonarotti* and *Francesco da S. Gallo.*

R. Aisle. Monument of Filippo Brunellesco with his portrait in marble, by his pupil *Buggiano.* Monument of Gianozzo Manetti, attributed to *Donatello.* (r.) Bust of Giotto by *Benedetto da Majano;* (l.) by the pillar a fine receptacle for consecrated water by *Arnolfo* or *Giotto.* (r.) Monument of Pietro Farnese by *Jacopo Orcagna.* Bust of the learned Marsilius Ficinus, by *A. Ferrucci.* Over the following door (r.) the Mausoleum of Antonio Orso, Bishop of Florence, by *Andrea Pisano.* By the pillar of the dome, towards the nave, St. Matthew, statue by *Vincenzo de' Rossi*, opposite to it St. James, by *Giacopo da Sansovino.*

R. Transept: r. St. Philip, l. St. James the Great, by *Giovanni Bandini.* Each of the 4 side-chapels is adorned with two saints, painted al fresco by *Lorenzo di Bicci.* The stained glass windows are said to have been executed at Lübeck in 1434 by the Florentine *Domenico Livi da Gambassi*, from designs by *Ghiberti* and *Donatello.* — Over the door of the sacristy a bas-relief (Ascension) by *Luca della Robbia.*

In the Nave, E. side, statues of (r.) St. John, (l.) St. Peter by *Benedetto da Rovezzano.* Beneath the altar of the Tribuna (or chapel) of St. Zenobius is the shrine containing the relics of the saint, in bronze, by *Lorenzo Ghiberti.* Last Supper on a golden ground, painted a tempera by *Giovanni Balducci.*

The octagonal Choir, constructed of marble from designs by *Giuliano di Baccio d'Agnolo*, is adorned with basreliefs by *Bandinelli* and *Giovanni dell' Opera.* Behind the high altar an unfinished group (Entombment) by *Michael Angelo.* The paintings in the octagonal dome, commenced 1572 by *Vasari* and continued by *Federigo Zuccheri* (prophets etc.) are not easily distinguished.

Bronze door of the N. Sacristy by *Luca della Robbia.* Above it a basrelief in terracotta (Resurrection), by the same master. In this sacristy Lorenzo de' Medici sought refuge in 1478, on the outbreak of the conspiracy of the Pazzi, to which his brother Julian fell a victim.

L. Transept. The Tribuna della S. Croce contains statues of St. Andrew and St. Thomas by *Andrea Ferrucci.* In the chapels frescoes by *Lorenzo di Bicci.* The 10 stained glass windows are by *Lor. Ghiberti.* In the centre of the tribune is a rounded piece of marble covered with wooden planks, placed here about the year 1450 by the celebrated mathematician *Paolo Toscanelli* of Florence, the sun shining on which through an aperture in the lantern of the dome indicates the point when it passes the meridian. In 1755 *P. Leonardo Ximenes* added a graduated dial in order to admit of more accurate observations, as an inscription on one of the pillars of the dome records.

L. Aisle. By the side-door is a *portrait of Dante, with a view of Florence and a representation from the 'Divine Comedy', painted on wood by *Domenico di Michelino* in 1465 by command of the republic. Then Arnolfo, with the design for the cathedral, medallion in high relief by *Bartolini* (1483). Statue of the secretary of state Poggio Bracciolini, by *Donatello.*

The Ascent of the Dome (p. 300) is strongly recommended, both for the sake of obtaining an idea of its construction, and for the *view (more extensive than from the Campanile, see below). Entrance by a door in the r. aisle (opened by the sacristan; attendant 1 fr.); easy ascent of 463 steps to the upper gallery, whence the adventurous may clamber up a ladder of 57 steps more to the cross on the summit.

The ***Campanile,** or bell-tower, commenced by *Giotto* in 1334 and completed by his successor *Taddeo Gaddi*, a square structure in the style of the cathedral, 293 ft. in height, recently restored, is regarded as one of the finest works of the kind in existence. The tower consists of four stories, the lowest of which is richly decorated with reliefs and statues. On the W. side are statues of the 4 Evangelists by *Donatello* (*St. Matthew, the finest) and *Giovanni de' Rossi*; on the S., four prophets by *Andrea Pisano* and *Giottino*; on the E., four saints by *Donatello* and *Niccolò Aretino*; on the N., four sibyls by *Luca della Robbia* and *Nanni di Bartolo*. Beneath these are bas-reliefs designed by *Giotto*, executed by *Andrea Pisano* and *Luca della Robbia:* the 7 cardinal virtues, 7 works of mercy, 7 beatitudes and 7 sacraments; in the lower series is represented the development of mankind from the Creation to the climax of Greek science. It is ascended by a good staircase of 414 steps (fee 1 fr. for 1—2 pers.). Beautiful view from the top, embracing the valley in which the city extends, the neighbouring heights, studded with villas and richly cultivated, and the mountains to the N., S., and E. At the summit are seen the pillars on which, according to Giotto's plan. a spire of 100 ft. was to have risen, but the project was abandoned by Gaddi.

Opp. the S. side of the Campanile is the *Church of the Misericordia (Pl. 27), founded in 1244, belonging to the long established order of brothers of charity, who, garbed in their black robes, with cowls covering the head and leaving apertures for the eyes only, are frequently encountered in the streets whilst engaged in their missions of mercy. It contains a Madonna by *Andrea del Sarto*, and other pictures, amongst them the Plague of 1348 by *Lodovico da Cigoli*.

Opposite the campanile is the *Canonry (Casa dei Canonici)*, erected 1827 by *Gaetano Baccani*, with the statues of *Arnolfo di Cambio*, constructor of the cathedral, and *Filippo Brunellesco*, both by *Luigi Pampaloni* (1830). In one of the following houses (No. 29) is immured the *Sasso di Dante*, a stone on which the great poet is said to have been wont to sit on summer evenings.

Quitting the Piazza della Signoria the stranger crosses the *Piazza S. Firenze* to the l., passing the church of that name, and reaches the *Palazzo del Podestà*, commonly known as *Il Bargello (Pl. 39), erected about the year 1250 by *Arnolfo* for the *Podestà*, or chief magistrate of the Republic. This imposing structure, which had since the 16th cent. been employed as a prison, and was consequently totally disfigured in the interior, was restored on the occasion of the Dante Exhibition in 1865, and destined for the new *National Museum, illustrative of the history of Italian culture and art in mediæval and modern times. Part of the collection, which is still in course of formation, belongs to the state, and part to private individuals. It contains several admirable works, such as the Renaissance bronzes formerly in the Uffizi. The inspector *Cav. Cavalcaselle* is well known as the author of a new history of Italian painting. Entrance from the Via Ghibellina, daily 10—4 o'cl. 1 fr., on Sund. gratis.

The visitor first enters the picturesque *Court*, embellished with the armorial bearings of the former Podestà's. — The *Ground Floor* contains (to the r.) a collection of weapons. — A handsome stair ascends to the first floor. The *Vestibule* contains a bell cast by *Bartolommeo Pisano* in 1228. *I. Saloon.* Sculptures in marble, most of them from the Palazzo Vecchio: *Baccio Bandinelli*, Grand-duke Cosmo I.; *Bandinelli*, Adam and Eve; *Vincenzo del Rossi*, a series of sculptures representing the combats of Hercules; *Giambologna*, Virtue triumphant; adjoining it, **Michael Angelo's* Dying Adonis; *M. Angelo*, 'Victory', an old man fettered by a youth, unfinished, perhaps destined for the monument of Julius II. at Rome; *M. Angelo*, Bust of Brutus, also unfinished. — *II. Saloon:* ancient furniture. — *III. Saloon:* fine collection of fayence, formerly in the Uffizi; the objects specially worthy of notice are in the glass-cabinets in the middle, many of them from paintings by Raphael, and once the property of the della Rovere family. — *IV. Saloon*, originally a chapel, then for centuries an unwholesome prison, adorned with *frescoes by *Giotto:* on the window-wall Paradise, with a portrait of Dante as a youth (beneath it a Madonna and St. Jerome by *Ghirlandajo*); on the entrance-wall, almost obliterated, the Infernal regions; at the side, the history of Mary Magdalene, much damaged. *V. Saloon:* carving in ivory, statuettes, etc., in the centre a cabinet with fine specimens of glass of the 16th cent. (The door on the l. in this saloon leads to the second floor, see below.) — *VI. Saloon* (and the 7th contain): bronzes from the Uffizi. In the centre: *Donatello*, David; by the walls, anatomical statuettes in wax and bronze by *Luigi Cigoli*; small fountain-figure by *Valerio Cioli;* on the wall above it, a bas-relief representing a dog, by *Benv. Cellini;* Juno, by *Giambologna* (?). — *VII. Saloon.* In the centre: *Donatello*, figure of a child; *Giambologna, celebrated Mercury; *Andr. Verocchio*, David. By the walls: 1. *Benv. Cellini*, Colossal busts of the grand-duke Cosmo I. in bronze; *Benv. Cellini*, Model in wax and bronze for Perseus (p. 290). Opposite the entrance-wall: Abraham's Sacrifice by *Lor. Ghiberti*, and the same by *Fil. Brunellesco*, specimens produced in their competition for the execution of the gates of the baptistery (p. 299). Under these: *Lor. Vecchietta* (d. 1482), recumbent statue in bronze; then Thetis, Venus, Vulcan, several well-executed birds, and a bust of Mich. Angelo, all of the *School of Giambologna;* also a number of small copies of celebrated sculptures. — The visitor now returns to the 5th Saloon and ascends to the upper story. *1st Room.* On the walls interesting frescoes by *Andr. del Castagno* (about 1450), transferred to canvas, the most remarkable being eight portrait-figures (e. g. Dante, Petrarch, Boccaccio, etc.), formerly in the Villa Pandolfini at Legnaia; also a collection of furniture, seals, and a beautiful 'angel musician', a statuette in marble by *Nicola Pisano* (?). — *2nd Room.* Terra cottas by *Luca della Robbia* and his school. — The cabinet beyond this contains handsome old furniture, the property of private persons. — A *Cabinet* adjoining the 1st Room contains two **Stained-glass Windows*, representing the Nativity and the Adoration of the Magi, the latter with the armorial bearings of Leo X., from designs by *Luca Signorelli*, or one of his pupils (beginning of 16th cent.); they were formerly in the cathedral at Cortona, and have been described by Vasari. — On the r. and l. of this cabinet are two rooms containing weapons, curious ecclesiastical vestments, etc., most of which are private property.

Opposite, in the Via del Proconsolo, is the church of **La Badia** (Pl. 4), erected 1625 by *Segaloni*, on the site of an earlier structure of the 13th cent. by *Arnolfo*, containing the *Monument of Bernardo Guigni by *Mino da Fiesole*, and a Madonna by *Fra Filippo Lippi*.

Following the Via Ghibellina from the Bargello, the traveller reaches a building on the r., part of which is occupied by the Teatro Pagliano (Pl. 103). In the entrance to it (No. 83 in the street), a lunette of the first stair is adorned with a *Fresco* of the middle of the 14th cent., representing the 'Expulsion of the Duke of Athens (p. 287) from Florence on the festival of St. Anne, 1343', interesting on account of the view it contains of the Palazzo Vecchio. The lunette, which is closed, is opened on application to the custodian of the theatre (50 c.).

In the ***Piazza S. Croce** (Pl. E, 5), one of the largest in Florence, with which many reminiscences from the earlier history of the city are connected, stands ***Dante's Monument** (Pl. 85), by *Pazzi*, inaugurated with great solemnity, on the 600th anniversary of the birth of the poet, May 14th, 1865, a statue 18 ft. in height on a pedestal 22 ft. high, the corners of which are adorned with four shield-bearing lions; round the pedestal below are the arms of the principal cities of Italy.

To the r. is the *Palazzo dell' Antella* (now *del Borgo*) (Pl. 58), with façade decorated with frescoes and constructed 1620, within the short space of 27 days, by *Giovanni da S. Giovanni* and five or six other masters.

The church of ***S. Croce** (Pl. 7), a cruciform basilica borne by columns, was commenced in 1294, from a design by *Arnolfo di Cambio*, on the site of a former church of the Franciscans, completed 1442, and consecrated by Cardinal Bessarion in presence of Pope Eugene IV. The front alone remained uncompleted, but the old design of *Simone Pollajuolo*, surnamed *Cronaca* was at length rescued from oblivion, and the foundation-stone of the new façade laid by Pope Pius IX. in 1857. The work was skilfully executed by the architect *Nicolo Matas* and consecrated in 1863. It harmonizes well with Arnolfo's structure, and with its rich decorations in light marble combines the advantages of ancient and modern architecture. The *Interior*, consisting of nave and aisles 460 ft. in length, and of equal breadth (26 ft.) and height (61 ft.), with a transept 41 ft. in width, and open roof, rests on 14 octagonal pillars at considerable intervals, and produces an impressive effect, enhanced by its numerous monuments of celebrated men. This church may be termed the Pantheon of modern Italy, and is moreover rendered extremely interesting by the frescoes of Giotto which were discovered within the last twenty years under the white-wash. In 1566 *Giorgio Vasari*, by order of Cosmo I., made several alterations in the altars, which however hardly accord with the simple dignity of the interior.

R. Aisle. At the entrance, small honorary monument to *Manin*, with portrait-bust (his tomb at S. Mark's at Venice, p. 193). *Tomb of Michael Angelo whose remains repose beneath (d. at Rome, 1563), erected 1570, the bust by *Battista Lorenzi*, the sculptures and painting by *Giovanni dell' Opera*, *Valerio Cioli* and *Lorenzi*. Honorary monument to Dante (interred at Ravenna, p. 251), by *Stefano Ricci*, erected 1829. *Alfieri, by *Canova* (erected by the Countess of Albany). *Marble pulpit, l. by the pillar, with 5 reliefs, by *Benedetto da Majano*. Macchiavelli (d. 1527), by *Innocenzo Spinazzi*, erected 1787, with inscription: *Tanto nomini nullum par elogium.* The learned Lanzi. Leonardo Bruni (d. 1444), surnamed Aretino from his birthplace, above it a Madonna, bas-relief by *Andr. Verocchio*. The naturalist Micheli; Leopoldo Nobili; opposite, in front of the pillar towards the nave, Vincenzo Alberti (minister of Leopold I.), by *Emilio Santarelli*.

R. Transept. At the corner: Monument of Principe Neri Corsini (d. 1859) by *Fantachiotti*, recently erected. The (closed) chapel of the Castellani (del S. Sagramento) is adorned with frescoes by *Starnina* and *Taddeo Gaddi*. Over the altar a Last Supper, by *Vasari*. *Monument of the Countess of Albany (d. 1824), widow of the young Pretender, by *Luigi Giovannozzi*, the two angels and bas-relief by *Santarelli*. Farther on, Cappella Baronzelli, now Giugni, with frescoes by *Taddeo Gaddi*. Over the altar a marble group by *Bandinelli*. Altar-piece, *Coronation of the Virgin, with saints and angels, by *Giotto*. — The door of the corridor leading to the sacristy is next reached; at the end of the corridor the chapel of the Medicis, with bas-reliefs by *Luca della Robbia*, and marble ciborium by *Mino da Fiesole*. *Madonna on the throne, with 10 saints, by *Giotto*. Sacristy with old pictures of the school of *Giotto* etc. — The chapel r. in the church on leaving the corridor contains *frescoes by *Giovanni di S. Giovanni*. — The 3rd chapel belongs to the Buonaparte family; monuments of Carlotta Buonaparte and of Julia Clary-Buonaparte, by *Bartolini*. In the 4th chapel *God the Father with the Madonna, St. Roch, and St. Sebastian, attributed to *Andrea del Sarto*; the *frescoes on the walls, representing the history of (r.) John the Baptist, and (l.) St. John the Evangelist, are among the finest of *Giotto's* works. The Cappella Bardi (the 5th) also contains *frescoes by him from the life of St. Francis of Assisi; the altar-piece (covered) represents the same saint, taken from life by Cimabue.

The Choir is adorned with frescoes by *Agnolo Gaddi* (middle of the 14th cent.), representing the legend of the Finding of the Cross, and on the ceiling the four Evangelists and saints. The high altar was executed from a design by *Vasari*.

L. Transept. In the 3rd chapel modern frescoes in the lunette, oil-paintings at the sides, by *Luigi Sabatelli* and his sons, representing the Miracles of St. Antony etc. In the 4th chapel frescoes by *Bernardo Daddi* (insignificant) and Madonna with saints, of the school of *Luca della Robbia*. In the 5th chapel frescoes by *Giottino*, Conversion of the Emp. Constantine and Miracles of St. Sylvester; monument of Uberto de' Bardi, with portrait by *Giottino*. The Niccolini chapel, in the N. E. corner of the transept (closed) was constructed by *Antonio Dosio*; it contains no objects of interest. — In the following chapel a monument of the architect Alessandro Galilei, by *Ticciati*; crucifix by *Donatello*. — In the side-chapel the monument of Princess Sophia Czartoryska, by *Bartolini*. — Farther on, monument of the composer L. Cherubini (born at Florence 1760, d. 1842) by *Fantacchiotti*, erected in 1859.

L. Aisle. Tomb of the engraver Raphael Morghen (d. 1833), by *Fantacchiotti*. On the opp. pillar the monument of the celebrated architect Leo Battista Alberti, erected by the last of his family, a group by *Bartolini*, the master's last work, and unfinished. Carlo Marzuppini, by *Desiderio da Settignano*. Vittorio Fossombroni (minister, d. 1844), by *Bartolini*. Angelo Tavanti (minister, d. 1781). Giovanni Lami (d. 1770), by *Spinazzi*. On the pillar Pietà, a painting by *Angelo Bronzino*. Monument of the jurist Pompeo Signorini (d. 1812), by *Stefano Ricci*. *Galileo Galilei, by *Giulio Foggini*. Over the altar next to the entrance a Descent from the Cross, by *A. Bronzino*. Adjoining it is the monument of the naturalist Targioni Tozzetti.

The central S. door, by the monument of Leonardo Bruni, leads to the *Cloisters*, which contain old monuments of the families of Alamanni, Pazzi, della Torre, etc., and modern ones by *Costoli, Santarelli, Bartolini*, and *Pampaloni*. Here on the l. is the **Chapel of the Pazzi* (visitors descend the steps, gate opened by the sacristan, 30 c.), erected by *Filippo Brunellesco*, containing numerous terracottas by *Luca della Robbia*. Nearly opposite to it, on the other side of the cloisters, is the ancient Refectory, now a carpenter's work shop (entrance by the large door), adorned with frescoes of the Last Supper and scenes from the life of St. Francis, ascribed to *Giotto*. The Inquisition, which was abolished by Duke Peter Leopold, once held its sessions here.

No. 9 in the *Via dei Malcontenti*, which passes the church of S. Croce on the N. side, is the **Palazzo Berte** (Pl. 60), containing a valuable collection of pictures, formerly in the *Palazzo Guadagni* near S. Spirito (accessible if the proprietor is residing here 10—3, fee 1 fr.). The 3rd Room contains the most important works: *Tintoretto*, Portrait; *Salvator Rosa*, *Sermon on the Jordan and *Baptism of Christ.

Quitting the Piazza del Duomo, the Via de' Servi passes the stately *Palazzo Manelli* (formerly *Ricci*, then *Riccardi*) (Pl. 74), erected by *Buontalenti* in 1565, and leads to the handsome ***Piazza della SS. Annunziata,** with two handsome *Fountains by *Pietro Tacca*, and the equestrian *Statue of the grand-duke Ferdinand I., by *Giovanni da Bologna* (his last, but not best work; he died 1608, upwards of 80 years of age), erected in 1608, and cast of metal captured from the Turks; the pedestal was adorned in 1640, under Ferdinand II. On the r. side of the piazza rises the ***Spedale degli Innocenti**, or *Foundling Hospital* (Pl. 92), erected 1421 from the designs of *Brunellesco* and his pupil *Francesco della Luna;* charmingly executed infants in swaddling clothes between the arches, by *Luca della Robbia*. Frescoes beneath the portico by *Poccetti;* the busts of the four Medicis, Cosmo I., Francesco I., Ferdinando I. and Cosmo II., by *Sermei*, pupil of Giovanni da Bologna. L. in the court, over the door leading to the church, an *Annunciation by *Luca della Robbia*. The *Church* of the Foundling Hospital (restored 1786) contains an altar-piece, the *Adoration of the Magi, by *Domenico Ghirlandajo* (1488). — Opposite to the Spedale is the hall of the brotherhood *Servi di S. Maria*, similar in style to the hospital, erected by *Antonio da S. Gallo*. — At the E. extremity of the piazza rises the old church of

***SS. Annunziata** *(Basilica Parrochiale e Convento della Santissima Annunziata Servi di Maria)* (Pl. 2), founded in 1250, but frequently altered and redecorated at subsequent periods. Handsome portico with three doors; that on the W. leads to the monastery and the cloisters, that in the centre to the church, the third to the chapel of the Pucci, founded 1300, restored 1615, which contains a St. Sebastian by *Antonio da Pollajuolo* (accessible only by special permission of the family). Over the central door a mosaic by *David del Ghirlandajo*, representing the Annunciation.

A species of entrance-court, which is first entered, is adorned with *Frescoes by *Andrea del Sarto* and his pupils. R. the Assumption, by *Rosso Fiorentino*; Visitation, by *Pontormo*; Nuptials of Mary, by *Franciabigio*; *Nativity of Mary, by *Andrea del Sarto*; *Arrival of the Magi, by the same master. Farther on, l. of the entrance, Nativity, by *Baldovinetti*; Investiture of S. Filippo, by *Cosimo Roselli*; *S. Filippo giving his garment to a sick man, by *Andrea del Sarto*; monument and bust of Andrea, by *G. Caccini*; *Gambler struck by lightning and S. Filippo, by *Andrea del Sarto*; *Cure of a man possessed with an evil spirit, *Death of S. Filippo and miracles wrought by his robes, both by *Andrea del Sarto*.

The Interior consisting of nave without aisles, transepts, two series of chapels, and surmounted by a dome, is adorned with a large ceiling-painting of the Annunciation, by *Ciro Ferri* (1670). The 4th chapel on the r. contains the monument of the engraver Giovita Garavaglia (d. 1835), by *Lorenzo Nencini*. Over an altar in the S. transept a Pietà by *Baccio Bandinelli*, who is buried beneath it with his wife. The great rotunda of the choir, designed by *Leo Battista Alberti*, adorned with frescoes by *Volterrano* (1688) and *Ulivelli*, is peculiar. The 5th choir-chapel contains a crucifix and reliefs by *Giovanni da Bologna*, with the monument of that master; in the 6th chapel a Resurrection by *Bronzino*; in the 7th a *Madonna with saints, by *Pietro Perugino*. In the 1st chapel of the nave, after the choir is quitted: Assumption, by *Pietro Perugino* (or *Albertinelli?*). In the 3rd chapel the Last Judgment, copied from Michael Angelo's picture at Rome by *Alessandro Allori*. Frescoes by the same. A chapel in the nave, to the l. of the entrance, covered with a species of canopy, erected by *Piero de' Medici* from *Michelozzi's* design, and sumptuously decorated with silver and gold by subsequent princes, contains a 'miraculous' picture of the Virgin behind the altar, a fresco of the 13th cent., highly revered. Over the altar a Head of the Saviour, by *Andrea del Sarto*.

A door in the N. transept leads to the *Cloisters*; over it is a *fresco by *Andrea del Sarto*, the Madonna del Sacco. Adjacent is the monument of the Falconieri, founders of the church. On the same side is the entrance to the chapel of the guild of painters (*Compagnia di S. Luca*), adorned with paintings by *G. Vasari*, *Fra Paolino da Pistoja*, etc.

The *Via della Sapienza* leads hence to the *Piazza di S. Marco*. Here is situated the church of **S. Marco**, erected in 1290, consisting of a nave with flat ceiling and a dome above the choir.

Interior. Over the central door Christ, painted a tempera on a gold ground, by *Giotto*. R. wall. 1st altar: St. Thomas Aquinas before the Crucified, by *Santi di Tito*. 2nd altar: Madonna with saints, by *Fra Bartolommeo della Porta*. 3rd altar: Madonna and two saints, a mosaic of the Roman school. — In the vestibule of the sacristy a statue of the Risen Christ, by *Antonio Novelli*. In the sacristy a recumbent statue of St. Antony in bronze, by *Portigiani*. Annunciation by *Fra Bartolommeo* (?). Adjoining the choir l. the chapel of Prince Stanislaus Poniatowsky (d. 1833), containing pictures by *Santi di Tito* etc. — Then the Chapel of St. Antony (who was once a monk in this monastery); architecture and statue of the saint, by *Giovanni da Bologna*. Frescoes on either side of the entrance with the funeral obsequies of St. Antony, by *Passignani*. In the picture on the l., members of the Medici family are represented as supporting the Canopy in the procession; statues of SS. Philip, John, Thomas Aquinas, Antonine the Abbot, Eberhard, and Dominicus, by *Francavilla*, the bas-relief by *Portigiani*; over the altar, Conversion of Matthew by *Poppi* (r.), and Healing of the leper by *Naldini* (l.). This church contains the tombs of the celebrated scholar *Johannes Picus di Mirandola*, who died in 1494 at the age of 31, and the equally distinguished *Angelus Politianus* (d. 1494), who was a monk of this monastery (between the 2nd and 3rd altars of the l. wall).

Adjacent to the church is the entrance to the once far-famed ***Monastery of S. Marco**, now suppressed, having been opened to the public on Oct. 1st, 1869, as the *Museo Fiorentino di*

S. Marco (daily, from Oct. 1st to March 31st, 9—3, from Apr. 1st to Sept. 30th 10—4 o'clock; Sund. gratis, at other times 1 fr.). The building was originally occupied by 'Silvestrine' monks, but was transferred under Cosmo 'pater patriae' to the Dominicans, who were favoured by the Medicis. In 1436—43 it was restored in a handsome style from designs by *Michelozzo*, and shortly afterwards decorated by *Fra Giovanni Angelico da Fiesole* (b. 1387, d. 1455) with tho e charming frescoes which to this day constitute an unrivalled model of profound and devoted piety. The painter *Fra Bartolommeo della Porta* (1469—1517) and the powerful preacher *Girolamo Savonarola* (burned at the stake in 1498, see p. 287) were also once inmates of this monastery.

The *Cloisters*, which are entered immediately from the street (formerly from the sacristy of the church, p. 307), are partially decorated with frescoes of the 18th cent., but the latter are far surpassed by the numerous and excellent works of the earlier masters. Among these the following deserve special notice: on the principal wall, nearly opposite the entrance, *Christ on the Cross, with St. Dominic; over the door to the sacristy, *St. Peter the Martyr, indicating the rule of silence peculiar to the order by placing his hand on his mouth; over another door, St. Dominic with the scourge; over the entrance to the 'foresteria', or apartments devoted to hospitality, Christ as a pilgrim welcomed by two Dominican monks — all by *Fra Angelico*. Near the approach to the upper floor (in the first cloister): Christ on the Cross, with two disciples, by *Fra Bartolommeo*. The adjoining door on the r. leads to the *Small Refectory*, containing a *Last Supper by *Dom. del Ghirlandajo*, and also to the *Upper Floor*, the corridor of which and the adjacent cells are adorned with a succession of frescoes by Fra Angelico and partly by his pupils. In the *Corridor:* Annunciation, Christ on the Cross with St. Dominic, and an Enthroned Madonna with saints. In the *Cells:* *Coronation of the Madonna by Christ and saints, *Adoration of the Magi, the two Maries at the Sepulchre, etc. Opposite the staircase is a cell containing reminiscences of St. Antonine. The last cells on the l. in the passage were once occupied by *Savonarola*, where a copy of an old picture representing his execution (original at the Pal. Corsini, p. 315), autographs, etc. perpetuate his memory. On the r. of the staircase is the *Library*, the arrangement of which is incomplete. Glass-cases in the middle contain a number of books of the Gospels with miniatures, most of them by *Fra Benedetto*, the brother of Angelico. On the other side of the passage are two cells, containing three smaller *panel pictures by *Fra Angelico* which formerly decorated relic-caskets in S. Maria Novella. An adjacent room contains the flags and colours of all the towns and corporations which were represented at the Dante festival in 1865. — The visitor now descends again to the cloisters, and by the next door to the l. enters the *Chapter Hall*, adorned with *Christ crucified between the thieves, and a group of saints below, all over life-size, by *Fra Angelico*. The door in the corner of the cloisters leads to the *Large Refectory*, one wall of which is embellished with the 'Providenza' (the brethren assembled at table and receiving food from two angels) by *Fra Bartolommeo*, and a Crucifixion.

The *Accademia della Crusca*, founded in 1582 to maintain the purity of the Italian language, and established in part of this building, is publishing a large dictionary of the language, and occasionally holds public sessions.

On the l., as the Via Ricasoli is entered from the Via della Sapienza, is (No. 52) the entrance of the **Academy of the Fine Arts** (Pl. 37) (open 9—3 o'clock daily, except Sundays).

The Entrance Hall contains four bas-reliefs in terracotta, by *Luca della Robbia*, and busts of great painters, in plaster. Hence to the r. through a room with casts of modern sculptures to the

Saloon of the Great Pictures.

This collection, in point of value the third in Florence (ranking after those of the Uffizi and the Pitti), is especially instructive owing to its chronological arrangement. It commences with: 1. Byzantine Magdalene; 2. Madonna, by *Cimabue*; 3. St. Humilitas of Faenza, by *Buffalmacco*; 4.—13. Ten scenes from the life of St. Francis, by *Giotto*; thus leading by progressive steps to the culminating point of the art. Of the 124 pictures exhibited here, the following merit special examination: 15. *Giotto*, Madonna with angels; 18.—29. Twelve small scenes from the life of Christ, by the same; 30. *Fra Lorenzo di Firenze*, Annunciation, with SS. Catharine, Antony, Paul, and Francis. Above: 31. *Taddeo Gaddi*, Entombment; *32. *Gentile da Fabriano*, Adoration of the Magi, an excellent picture of 1423; *34. *Fra Angelico*, Descent from the Cross; 36. *Masaccio*, Madonna with angels; 37. *Andrea del Castagno*, Penitent Magdalene; 40. *Filippo Lippi*, Madonna with saints; 43. *Andrea del Verocchio*, Baptism of Christ, the first angel in which on the l. was painted by *Leonardo da Vinci*, a pupil of this master; 46. *Alessandro Botticelli*, Madonna with several saints, and 47. Coronation of the Virgin; 50. *Domenico Ghirlandajo*, Nativity; 51. *Lorenzo di Credi*, Nativity (his finest work); 53. *Pietro Perugino*, Christ on the Mt. of Olives; 55. Assumption of the Virgin, with SS. Michael, Giovanni Gualberto, Dominicus, and Bernard, brought from Vallombrosa, painted in 1500; 56. Christ on the Cross, both by *Perugino*; 57. Descent from the Cross, the upper half by *Filippo Lippi*, the lower by *Pietro Perugino*; 58. *Perugino*, Dead Christ on the knees of Mary; 59. *Andrea del Sarto*, Four saints; 62. Two angels by the same; 65. *Fra Bartolommeo*, Madonna with Jesus, St. Catharine, and other saints; 66. Mary appearing to St. Bernard, by the same; 67. *Raffaelino del Garbo*, Resurrection; 69. Dead Christ, Madonna, Mary Magdalene and other saints, designed by *Fra Bartolommeo*, executed by his pupil *Fra Paolino da Pistoja*; 68. *Fra Bartolommeo*, St. Vincent; 70. *Mariotto Albertinelli*, Holy Trinity (under this picture is the entrance to the saloon with the works of the students); 71. *Fra Paolino da Pistoja*, Madonna presenting St. Thomas with her girdle; 72. *Mariotto Albertinelli*, Madonna with Jesus and 4 saints; 73. Annunciation, by the same. 1510; 75. *Francesco Granacci*, Madonna and 4 saints; 78. *Fra Bartolommeo*, Five heads of saints (that in the centre supposed to be Savonarola, next to him a Carthusian monk with his finger on his mouth). Under the window, 79. Bronze bust of Michael Angelo; 82. *Fra Bartolommeo*, Five saints; 88. *Angelo Bronzino*, Portrait of Cosmo de' Medici; 89. *Alessandro Allori*, A lady of the Medici family; 92. *Angelo Bronzino*, The two Maries with the body of Christ; 93. *Alessandro Allori*, Annunciation; 97. *Francesco Morandini*, Crucifixion; 100. *Santi di Tito*, Dead Christ in the arms of Mary; *99. *Carlo Dolci*, God the Father; 103. *Matteo Rosselli*, Adoration of the Magi.

The following rooms, entered in another direction, are usually closed, but between 9 and 3 o'clock the custodians are bound to admit visitors (fee optional). Through the library of the Academy another vestibule is reached (from the street No. 50), then the

Saloon of the Ancient Pictures,

containing 60 pictures, most of them by unknown masters of the Tuscan school of the 14th and 15th cent., uninteresting to the non-professional. Adjacent is the

Saloon of the Small Pictures,

with 71 works of the 14th—17th cent., most of them excellent: 3. Ascension and Annunciation, attributed to *Giotto*; 8. *Fra Angelico*, Miracle wrought by SS. Cosmus and Damianus; 11. and 24. Life of Christ in 8 pictures and 35 sections, by the same; 12. *Fra Filippo Lippi*, Madonna adoring the Saviour; 13. *Lorenzo di Credi*, Nativity; 16. *Fra Angelico*, History of five martyrs; *18. *Perugino* (or *Raphael?*), Two portraits of monks; 19. *Fra Angelico*, Six representations from the legends of the saints; 20. Madonna with the Infant Jesus, above it the Trinity, by the same; 27. *Carlo Dolci*, Portrait of Fra Angelico; 28. *Fra Bartolommeo*, Hieronymus Savonarola as S. Pietro Martire; *Fra Angelico*: 36. Coronation of the Virgin; 38. Passion, below it the Adoration of the Magi; 40. Entombment; 41. Last Judgment, with numerous figures; 49. St. Thomas Aquinas with his pupils; 50. Albertus Magnus teaching theology.

Saloon of the Designs (Cartoni).

A number of the original designs of the most celebrated masters are preserved here: 1. *Fra Bartolommeo*, St. Peter; 2. Madonna (della Gatta), copy from *Raphael*; 4. *Fra Bartolommeo*, St. Paul; 5. Madonna, attributed to *Raphael*; 6. *Correggio*, Madonna; 8. Mary Magdalene, 10. St. Jerome, 11. St. Catharine of Siena, all by *Fra Bartolommeo*; 17. *Andrea del Sarto*, Madonna (in the Palazzo Panciatichi, p. 311); 21. Madonna (del velo), attributed to *Raphael*; 18. Madonna, 22. St. Dominicus, by *Fra Bartolommeo*.

In a straight direction from the entrance (No. 49) a court is reached, where several bas-reliefs by *Luca della Robbia* are preserved; colossal horse's head from the Monte Cavallo in Rome; original model of the Rape of the Sabine women, by *Giovanni da Bologna;* St. Matthew, just commenced, by *Michael Angelo*, etc. Then to the r. through a passage with reliefs in plaster, at the extremity of which is the *Gallery of Statues*, a rich collection of casts of the most celebrated sculptures in Europe. In the court is a small chapel with a *fresco by *Giovanni da S. Giovanni*, representing the Flight into Egypt, transferred hither in 1788 from the garden of the Palazzo della Crocetta. — The *Saloon of Architecture* contains designs by the most celebrated architects. Finally several other apartments containing drawings, pictures, casts, etc. by modern artists.

The custodian of the Academy also keeps the keys of the **Cloisters of the Recollets**, or barefooted monks *(Chiostro della Compagnia dello Scalzo)*, Via Cavour 69, opposite the church of S. Marco, adorned with admirable *frescoes from the history of John the Baptist, painted in grisaille by *Andr. del Sarto.* — Adjacent is the *Casino Mediceo* (now *Dogana*, Pl. 51), remodelled in 1570 by *Buontalenti*, where Lorenzo il Magnifico, and after him Giuliano de' Medici, preserved a great number of the treasures of art which were subsequently transferred by Cosmo I. to the gallery of the Uffizi.

In the vicinity (Via Ricasoli), in the apartments of the former monastery of *S. Niccolò*, is the Government Manufactory of *Florentine Mosaics* (lavori in pietra dura), established here since 1797. This work, consisting of inlaid coloured stones, has enjoyed a great reputation since the 16th cent.

To the l., at the commencement of the Via Cavour, is the ***Palazzo Riccardi** (Pl. 83), the ancient *Palace of the Medici*, which has been in the possession of the government since 1814. It was erected about 1434 under Cosmo, the 'father of his country', by *Michelozzi*, and was celebrated as a seat of art and science, where the Greek refugees first met with a hospitable reception. Lorenzo il Magnifico was born here in 1448, as well as his sons Pietro, Giovanni, and Giuliano. The illegitimate Medici, Julius, Hippolytus, and Alexander subsequently resided here, and this family continued in possession of the palace until it was sold by the grand-duke Ferdinand II. to the Marchese Gabriello Riccardi, who considerably extended it, enclosing within its precincts the *Strada del Traditore*, where on Jan. 7th, 1537, Duke Alexander was assassinated by Lorenzino de' Medici. An imposing gateway leads to a vestibule and court, where ancient busts, statues, sarcophagi, Greek and Latin inscriptions from Rome, etc. were placed by the Marchese Riccardi in 1719. The four windows of the ground-floor were designed by *Michael Angelo*. The second court contains the statue of Duke Alexander. Three staircases ascend to the upper floors, occupied by the *Biblioteca Riccardiana* and the offices of the minister of the interior. The library, founded by the Riccardi, and purchased by the state in 1812, comprises 23,000 vols. and 3500 MSS., including several by *Dante*, *Petrarch*, *Macchiavelli*, *Galileo*, ancient diptychs, etc. Admission 9—3 o'cl. daily, except Sundays (vacation Aug. 10th to Nov. 12th). — The private *Chapel* of the Medici, also on the upper floor (opened on application by the custodian of the Academy, 50 c.) is embellished with frescoes by *Benozzo Gozzoli*, representing the history of the Magi, with numerous portraits of the Medici. In the *Gallery* adjoining the library are frescoes (vicissitudes of human life) painted by *Luca Giordano* in 1683.

In this street are also the palaces of the *Panciatichi* (by *Carlo Fontana*, about 1700; Pl. 76), *Covoni* (formerly *Capponi*, by *G. Silvani*, about 1660), *Pestellini* (formerly *Naldini*; Pl. 79), *Pucci* (formerly *Ughi*, recently altered by *Bonaiuti*; Pl. 82), *Poniatowski* (1740; Pl. 81) and *Bartolommei* (formerly *Cappoli e Medici*, by *Gherardo Silvani*; Pl. 59), all structures of considerable pretension. Also the *Biblioteca Marucelliana* (Pl. 43), founded in 1703 by *Francesco Marucelli* (near S. Marco, open every week-day 10—2).

Opposite the palace of the Medici, in the Via delle Cantonelle, is situated the church of *S. Giovannino degli Scolopi* (appertaining to the Padri delle Scuole Pie), erected 1352, remodelled 1580 by B. Ammanati, completed 1661 by *Alfonso Parigi*. The scientific institutions of the city are established here, comprising a library, observatory, etc. The church possesses frescoes and pictures by *Allori*, *Bronzino*, *Santi di Tito*, etc.

Immediately adjacent in the **Piazza S. Lorenzo**, with the church of that name, is the *Base di S. Lorenzo*, by *Baccio Bandinelli*, adorned with sculptures (Giovanni delle Bande Nere, father of the first Cosmo, triumphing over his enemies). In 1850 the monument was restored and furnished with a statue of Giovanni, as the inscription records.

*S. Lorenzo (Pl. 17), founded 390, consecrated by St. Ambrose in 393, is one of the most ancient churches in Italy. In 1423 it was burned down, and subsequently re-erected by the Medicis in the late Romanesque style, from the designs of *Filippo Brunellesco*. After his death it was completed (with the exception of the façade) by *Donatello* and *Michael Angelo*. The latter erected the sacristy and the Laurentian Library. The cloisters were constructed by *Brunellesco*. The church, which has recently

been sumptuously restored, consists of nave and aisles with transept, surmounted by a dome; at the sides are chapels in the form of niches. The edifice rests in the interior upon 14 lofty Corinthian columns and 2 pillars.

At the end of the r. Aisle the monument of the painter Benvenuti (d. 1844) by *Thorwaldsen*. Bas-reliefs on the two pulpits by *Donatello* and his pupil *Bertoldo*. — R. Transept, side-chapel r., on the r., Nativity, by *Cosimo Rosetti*. Over the altar of the chapel a figure of the Virgin, erected in 1856 to commemorate the cessation of the cholera in 1855.

From the N. side of the r. transept the New Sacristy is entered to the l., the Chapel of the Princes to the r. In the church, at the foot of the high altar, is the simple tomb of Cosmo de' Medici, surnamed 'Pater Patriae' (d. 1464). In the 2nd chapel l. of the choir the monument of a Countess Moltke, by *Dupré*, erected 1864. — The Old Sacristy was erected by *Filippo Brunellesco*, with bronze doors, bas-reliefs, and statues of the 4 Evangelists (beneath the dome), all by *Donatello*. L. of the entrance the monument of Giovanni and Pietro de' Medici, by *Andrea del Verocchio*. In the centre the marble monument of Giovanni Averardo de' Medici and his wife Piccarda Bueri, by *Donatello*. In the 2nd chapel an Annunciation, by *Fra Filippo Lippi*. — In the l. Aisle the Martyrdom of St. Lawrence, a large fresco by *Angelo Bronzino*. The adjoining door leads to the cloisters and the library (p. 313). In the following chapel, St. Sebastian, by *Jacopo da Empoli*.

The ****New Sacristy** (*Sagrestia Nuova*, open 8—12 and 3—4¹|₂ o'clock), entered from the r. transept of the church (see above), a chapel of admirable proportions, adorned with two series of Corinthian pilasters one above the other, constructed by Michael Angelo in 1523—29, contains the celebrated ***Monuments of the Medicis**, executed by *Michael Angelo* by order of Pope Clement VIII. (Giulio de' Medici, 1523—34), and unquestionably the chef d'œuvre of the master. R. the mausoleum of Giuliano de' Medici, Duke of Nemours, brother of Pope Leo X. and younger son of Lorenzo il Magnifico (d. 1516). Above is the figure of the duke in a sitting posture; over his tomb are the *statues of Day and Night, master-pieces of Michael Angelo, the latter especially admired. A contemporary poet, Giovanni Battista Strozzi, wrote upon it the lines:

La Notte, che tu vedi in si dolci atti
Dormire, fu da un Angelo scolpita
In questo sasso, e perchè dorme ha vita;
Destala, se nol credi, e parleratti.

Michael Angelo, in allusion to the suppression of liberty (by Alessandro de' Medici 1530, see p. 287) answered:

Grato m' è 'l sonno e più l'esser di sasso;
Mentre che 'l danno e la vergogna dura
Non veder, non sentir m' è gran ventura;
Però non mi destar; deh! parla basso!

Opposite is the statue of Lorenzo de' Medici, Duke of Urbino, grandson of Lorenzo il Magnifico, d. 1518, represented in profound meditation (hence termed *il pensiero*); beneath it his tomb with *statues of Evening, and Dawn (*Crepusculo e Aurora*), also by *Michael Angelo*, erected by order of Pope Clement VII. (Giulio de' Medici, 1523—34). Lorenzo was father of Catharine de' Medici, queen of Henry II., and mother of Charles IX. of France, and of the first duke of Florence Alexander de' Medici, who was assassinated on Jan. 7th, 1537, by his cousin Lorenzo. Opposite to the altar in the centre, is an unfinished *Madonna, by *Michael Angelo*, and the statue of *St. Cosmo*, by *Fra Giovanni Angiolo da Montorsoli*. At the back of the altar the tomb of the grand-duke Ferdinand III. (d. 1824).

The **Chapel of the Princes** (*Cappella dei Principi*, open daily 8—12 and 3—4¹|₂ o'clock, fee 30—50 c.), the burial-chapel of the grand dukes of the Medici family, was constructed in 1604 by *Matteo Nigetti*, by order of the grand-duke Ferdinand I. (designed by *Giovanni de' Medici*). It is octagonal in form, covered by a dome, and gorgeously decorated with marble and valuable *mosaics in stone. The paintings in the dome (Creation, Fall, Death of Adam, Sacrifice of Noah, Nativity, Death and Resurrection, Last Judgment) are by *Pietro Benvenuti*. In six niches below are the granite sarcophagi of the princes, some of them with gilded bronze statues, from Cosmo I. (see p. 287) to Cosmo III. (d. 1723, whose son Giov. Gaston was the last of the family, d. 1737). On the coping round the chapel are placed the armorial bearings of 16 Tuscan towns in stone-mosaic. — On the construction and decoration of this chapel a sum of 22 million lire (about 900,000 *l*.) was expended by the Medici family from their private resources.

In the cloisters, l. of the church of S. Lorenzo, is the entrance to the celebrated **Biblioteca Laurenziana** (Pl. 41), founded by Cosmo in 1444, extended by Lorenzo de' Medici, transferred by Cosmo I. to this edifice which was erected in 1571, and subsequently augmented by the purchase of new works and the bequest of the libraries of *Gaddi*, *Strozzi*, *Redi*, and Count *Angiolo d'Elzi* of Siena. It contains a collection of the rarest old editions of the Greek and Latin classic authors, but its principal treasure consists of about 8000 MSS. in different languages. Access daily 9—3 o'clock, except Sundays and festivals (vacation Oct. 1st to Nov. 12th, custodian's fee $1/2$—1 fr.). The building was commenced in 1524 according to the design of *Michael Angelo*, and completed in 1571 by *Vasari*; the rotunda, containing the Biblioteca Delciana, was erected in 1841, from *Pasquale Poccianti's* design.

The wooden ceiling of the Library was executed by *Tasso* and *Carota*, from *Michael Angelo's* designs. The latter also furnished the design for the 88 'Plutei' to which the MSS. are attached. Among these is a number of codices of rare value: Virgil of the 4th or 5 cent.; Tacitus, two MSS. of the 10th and 11th cent., the older brought from Germany, and the sole copy containing the first 5 books of the Annals. The Pandects, of the 6th or 7th cent., carried off from Amalfi by the Pisans in 1135, the oldest existing MS. of this collection, on which the study of Roman Law almost entirely hinges. Most important MS. of Æschylus. Cicero's Epistles ad Familiares, written by Petrarch. Petrarch's Canzone, with portraits of Petrarch and Laura. MSS. and letters of Dante. Decamerone of Boccaccio. MSS. of Alfieri. Document of the Council of Florence 1439. Maps of Ptolemæus, miniatures, etc. Catalogues of Oriental MSS. by Lewis Assemann and Bandini, continued by Furia.

Hence by the Via del Giglio to the *Piazza S. Maria Novella*, where festivals and games were frequently celebrated in former times. The principal of these, instituted in the reign of Cosmo I. in 1563, took place on the eve of the festival of St. John, and consisted of a race of four four-horse chariots, termed *Prasina* (green), *Russata* (red), *Veneta* (blue), and *Alba* (white), resembling those of the ancient Romans. Two obelisks of marble, of 1608, standing on brazen tortoises, by *Giambologna*, served as goals.

The church of ***S. Maria Novella** (Pl. 25), commenced in 1278 on the site of an earlier edifice, from designs by the monks *Sisto* and *Ristoro*, and completed in 1371, was furnished with a beautiful marble façade, designed by *Leo Battista Alberti*, in 1456—1470. A quadrant and two concentric meridians which are seen here were constructed by *P. Ignazio Danti* in 1572. The walled up pointed arcades of black and white marble which adjoin the church on the r., were originally constructed from designs by *Brunellesco*, but were frequently altered at subsequent periods, and have recently been restored. The interior, a Latin cross with pointed vaulting, consists of nave and aisles resting on 12 pillars, to which chapels were afterwards added by *Vasari* and others.

Entrance Wall: over the central door, a crucifix of the school of *Giotto*; on the r. the Trinity with the Virgin and St. John, one of the best works of *Masaccio*. — The altar-pieces in the r. Aisle are of the 17th cent. — In the r. Transept, to the r. by the steps, is the Gothic monument of the Patriarch Joseph of Constantinople (d. 1440), who had come to the great Council of 1439, which was first held at Ferrara in 1438, and afterwards at Florence, by Pope Eugene IV. and the Greek Emp. John VII. (Palæologus) with a view to the union of the Western and Eastern churches. A union was resolved on, but never carried out. — The steps may now be ascended to the Cappella Rucellai, which contains a large Madonna, one of *Cimabue's* best productions. — R. of the choir the Chapel of Filippino Strozzi, with his monument by *Benedetto da Majano*, and frescoes by *Filippino Lippi* (1486), the Miracles of SS. John and Philip. — In the Choir *Frescoes by *Domenico Ghirlandajo*, r. the history of John the Baptist, l. that of Mary, each in 7 sections. The first picture to the r., representing Zacharias in the Temple, contains among the people portraits of contemporaries of the painter, members of the Platonic Academy founded by Lorenzo il Magnifico: Angelo Poliziano, raising his hand, Marsilius Ficinus, translator of Plato, garbed as a canon; Gentile de' Becchi, Bishop of Arezzo; the erudite Cristoforo Landino, Commentator of Dante, Horace, and Virgil; the Tornabuoni, founders of the chapel. — The Chapel l. of the choir, by *Giuliano da S. Gallo*, contains the celebrated wooden crucifix of *Brunellesco*, which gave rise to the rivalry between him and his friend Donatello. — The following Gaddi Chapel, by *Antonio Bosio*, is adorned with the Raising of the daughter of Jairus by *A. Bronzino*, and bas-reliefs by *Bandini*. — The Strozzi Chapel in the l. transept, to which a stair ascends, contains *frescoes with numerous figures; opposite the entrance the Last Judgment, l. Paradise, by *Andrea Orcagna*; Hell (r.), by his brother *Bernardo*; altar-piece, finished 1357, by *Andrea*. — The next door, in the corner, leads to the sacristy, the most interesting object in which is a *fountain by *Luca della Robbia*, a magnificent work of its kind. — The altar-pieces in the l. Aisle are of the 17th and 18th cent.

On the W. side of the church are the ancient Cloisters, termed *Il Chiostro Vecchio*, or *Verde*, adorned with frescoes by *Paolo Uccello*, painted in grisaille, or terra verde. R. in the cloisters is the Cappella degli Spagnuoli, commenced 1320, with frescoes of *Giotto*'s school (erroneously attributed to *Taddeo Gaddi* and *Simone Memmi*), on the wall over the altar the Passion, on the ceiling the Resurrection, Ascension, Descent of the Holy Ghost, Christ and the doubting Peter on the water. On the E. side (r.) the Church militant and triumphant, the pope and emperor on the throne, surrounded by their counsellors and illustrious men, such as Petrarch with Laura, Boccaccio, Cimabue etc. On the W. side (l.) Thomas Aquinas in his professorial capacity, surrounded by angels, prophets, and saints, in his hand an open book; at his feet the discomfited heretics Arius, Sabellius, and Averrhoës. In the niches 14 figures representing virtues and sciences. The Great Cloisters, the largest at Florence, with frescoes by *Cigoli*, *Allori*, *Santi di Tito*, *Poccetti*, and others are adjacent to the above.

The Laboratory of the monastery (Spezeria, entrance in the Via della Scala), celebrated for the perfumes and liqueurs prepared in it, especially that of Alkermes, contains a room (formerly a chapel) decorated with frescoes of the 14th cent. (the Passion), probably by *Spinello Aretino*.

The *Railway Station* (Pl. C, 2, 3) is in the vicinity of this church.

The Via de' Fossi leads hence to the *Piazza del Ponte alla*

Carraja, then r. to the broad street (formerly a suburb) of **Borgo Ognissanti**, where horse-races (corso dei barberi) have for centuries taken place. A small *Theatre* is situated here, and a short distance farther, in the *Piazza Manin*, the *Monastery* and *Church of the Minorites di S. Salvadore d' Ognissanti* (Pl. 30), erected 1554, remodelled 1627, the façade by *Matteo Nigetti*, with *lunette by *Luca della Robbia*, representing the Coronation of Mary. In the interior, consisting of a nave and transept with flat ceiling, St. Augustine, al fresco, by *A. Botticelli*, Madonna with saints by *Santi di Tito*, St. Jerome, al fresco, by *Domenico Ghirlandajo*. A chapel in the l. transept approached by steps contains a crucifix by *Giotto*. Adjacent is the entrance to the sacristy, adorned with frescoes by *Giovanni da S. Giovanni*, *Ligozzi*, and *Ferrucci*.

The street next leads (termed in its prolongation *Via del Prato*) to the *Porta al Prato*, whence the *Cascine* (p. 328) are reached to the l.; they may also be reached by entering the *Lung-Arno Nuovo*, by the Piazza Manin, and either following this street, or the *Corso Vittorio Emanuele*, passing the *Politeama* (p. 284) and leading to the *Nuova Barriera* (comp. p. 328).

Turning l. from the Borgo Ognissanti to the *Ponte S. Trinità*, the traveller will perceive (Lung-Arno Corsini, No. 10) the **Palazzo Corsini** (Pl. 66), erected, or at least remodelled, in 1656, from designs by *Silvani* and *Ferri* (magnificent staircase by the latter). It contains a valuable picture-gallery (open on Tuesd., Thursd. and Sat. 10—3 o'cl.; entrance at the back, Via di Parione 7; porter 1/2—1 fr.; catalogues for the use of visitors), in 12 different apartments. **Raphael's* cartoon of the picture of Julius II. at the Uffizi (p. 293), several works by *Palma Vecchio*, *Paolo Veronese*, *Giulio Romano*, and *Seb. del Piombo*, and a few Dutch masters should be noticed. — By the Ponte S. Trinità is the *Palazzo Fontebuoni* (Lung-Arno, No. 2) (Pl. 67), formerly *Gianfigliazzi*, where Alfieri resided and died Oct. 9th, 1803. Then the *Casino dei Nobili*, an aristocratic rendezvous and seat of the Jockey Club. — The imposing **Palazzo Spini**, once the seat of this ancient family, a structure groundlessly attributed to *Arnolfo di Cambio*, is now the town-hall (*Palazzo della Comunità*, Pl. 64). — Adjoining it is the old *Palazzo Buondelmonti* (Pl. 59), formerly *Scali*, where since 1820 the reading-rooms of Vieusseux (p. 284) have been established. On the opposite side of the street are the church and monastery of **S. Trinità** (Pl. 35), erected about 1250, altered in 1570 by *Buontalenti*.

The interior consists of nave and aisles with transept, and is flanked with chapels at the sides and adjoining the high altar. The 4th Chapel on the r. contains the Annunciation by the Camaldulensian monk *Don Lorenzo*; the *Cappella de' Sassetti, the second on the r. from the high altar, is adorned with frescoes from the life of St. Francis by *Dom. Ghirlandajo*; beneath are the founders of the picture, Francesco Sassetti and his wife Nera Corsi. The sibyls on the ceiling are by the same artist.

In front of the church lies the *Piazza S. Trinità*, adorned with a column of granite from the Baths of Caracalla at Rome, erected here in 1563, and furnished with an inscription in honour of the grand-duke Cosmo I. in 1569. On the summit is placed a statue of Justice in porphyry, by Francesco Ferrucci, added in 1581.

Farther on in the Via Tornabuoni is situated the *Palazzo Strozzi (Pl. 84), erected in 1489 by *Benedetto da Majano* for the celebrated Filippo Strozzi, and presenting an example of the Florentine palatial style in its most perfect development. It possesses three imposing façades (that towards the Via Tornabuoni is 120 ft. in width, and 98 ft. in height), constructed in huge 'bossages', and a handsome court added by *Cronaca*. The lanterns and flag-holders are among the finest specimens of Italian iron-work of the 15th cent. The upper floor of the edifice contains a fine picture-gallery (open on Mondays 11—1 o'cl., closed on festivals), consisting chiefly of works of the Florentine school, by *Giotto*, *Andr. del Sarto*, *Allori*, *Bronzino* (portrait of Filippo Strozzi), *La Puttina di Tiziano by *Titian*, Pope Paul III. by *Paolo Veronese*, etc.

In the vicinity, Via Vigna Nuova 20, is the *Palazzo Rucellai*, erected about 1460 by *Leo Batt. Alberti*, who for the first time here employed a combination of rustica and pilasters.

The house in which *Dante* was born in 1265 (Pl. 46), recently restored, is in the Via S. Martino (formerly Via Riccarda) No. 2, not far from the Piazza della Signoria; that of *Amerigo Vespucci* near the church of S. Giovanni di Dio, in the Borgo Ognissanti. *Macchiavelli's* house (Pl. 48) is No. 16 in the Via dei Guicciardini, beyond the Ponte Vecchio. Next door (No. 17) (Pl. 72) is the *Palazzo Guicciardini* (1482—1541). *Galileo's* house (Pl. 47) is Via della Costa, No. 13, near the Boboli Garden and the Belvedere fortification. The house of *Bianca Capello*, wife of Francis I., and well known for the romantic vicissitudes of her history, is also worthy of notice; Via Maggio 26, erected 1566. The traveller interested in historical research should observe the numerous memorial-tablets immured in various places, recording important events in the annals of Florence.

The **House of Michael Angelo** (Pl. 49) is in the Via Ghibellina, corner of Via Buonarroti No. 49, not far from S. Croce. In the 17th cent. a descendant of his family here founded a collection of pictures and antiquities, which the last of the Buonarroti bequeathed to the city. It merits a visit chiefly on account of the designs and other reminiscences of Michael Angelo (admission Mondays and Thursdays, 10—3 o'clock, a trifling fee expected; on other days by payment of a fee).

The *Ante-Chamber* contains a few terracottas by the *della Robbia* and fragments of antiques; No. 34, on the r. near the door, is a two-edged sword with the arms of the Buonaroti. — On the l. a room with paintings and drawings: 92. *Venet. School*, Death of Lucrezia; 95. *Bugiardini* (?), Mich. Angelo in a turban; 97. *Marcello Venusti* (pupil of Mich. Angelo), M. Angelo as an old man; 99. *Cristofano Allori*, Mich. Angelo as a young man; then a number of drawings by *M. Angelo:* 117. Design for the façade of S. Lorenzo (p. 311), 121. Small sketch of the 'Last Judgment', 124. Madonna and Child. — On the r. of the ante-room, *I. Saloon:* 57. Sitting statue of Mich. Angelo, executed by *Ant. Novelli* in 1620; on the walls scenes from the life of M. Angelo; 55. Madonna and Child, with St. John and other saints, a painting, 56. Battle of Hercules and the Centaurs, a relief, both by *M. Angelo*. — *II. Saloon:* Portraits of the ancestors of M. Angelo by *Pietro da Cortona, Domenico Pugliani*, etc.; 70. Bust of the grandson of M. Angelo, the founder of this gallery. In the adjoining cabinet: 71. *Jac. Pontormo*, Vittoria Colonna (?). — *III. Saloon*, the chapel, decorated with frescoes of saints etc.; 80, 74. Marble busts of the last proprietor and his wife; 75. Descent from the Cross, plaster model of a basrelief, and 76. Madonna and Child, a basrelief in marble, both by *M. Angelo*; *82. Bust of M. Angelo in bronze, from a cast taken after death by *Giambologna*. — *IV. Saloon*, the studio: in the cabinets *models by M. Angelo in wax and clay, of David, the Crucified, etc.; on the walls are portraits of celebrated Florentines and other Italians by *Rosselli* and *Cecco* (beginning of 17th cent.). — The last *Cabinet* (closed) contains two vols. of autographs, letters, and poems by M. Angelo.

The Via Faenza leads from the centre of the city to the fortress of *S. Giovanni Battista*, usually termed *Fortezza da Basso*, erected by Cosmo I. in 1534. The refectory of the suppressed monastery of **S. Onofrio** in this street (No. 57) contains a *fresco of the Last Supper (Cenacolo, date 1545), discovered 1845, attributed, but without sufficient foundation, to *Raphael*. In the same building is *Rosellini's* **Egyptian Museum** (Pl. 54), to which the Egyptian antiquities of the Uffizi have also been transferred. The Refectory and Museum are open daily till 3 p. m. (at a later hour, fee 50 c.).

L. *Bank of the Arno*. About one-fourth part of the city lies on this bank. A short distance to the r. beyond the Ponte alla Carraja are situated the piazza and church **del Carmine** (Pl. 22). The latter was consecrated in 1422, but entirely burned down in 1781, and re-erected within the following ten years. Among the portions which escaped destruction is the *Brancacci Chapel in the r. transept, embellished in 1423—28 by *Masaccio*, and after him by *Filippino Lippi* with highly interesting frescoes from the history of the Apostles, especially from that of St. Peter (modern investigation has proved that those formerly attributed to Masolino were executed by Masaccio). Those by *Masaccio* are: on the pillars of the *Entrance*, above, on the r. the Fall, on the l. the *Expulsion from Paradise. *L. Wall:* above, *Peter taking the piece of money from the fish's mouth; below Raising of Eutychus, and Peter enthroned (the latter finished by Lippi). *Wall of the Altar:* above, *Peter preaching, and baptizing; below, Peter healing the sick, and distributing alms. *R. Wall:* above, Healing the cripples, and Raising of Tabitha. — The following are by *Filippino Lippi*: on the r. wall, below, the Crucifixion of Peter, and Peter and Paul before the proconsul;

on the entrance pillars, below, on the l. Peter in prison, on the r. his release. — The choir contains the tomb of Pietro Soderini, by *Benedetto da Rovezzano*, 1513, restored 1780. The Corsini chapel, l. in the transept, contains the tomb of St. Andr. Corsini, Bishop of Fiesole, and three large reliefs in marble by *Foggini*, in celebration of the praises of the saint; painting in the dome by *Luca Giordano*. In the sacristy (entered from the r. transept) frescoes from the history of St. Cecilia (discovered 1858), perhaps by *Spinello Aretino*. The cloisters of the monastery (entrance r., adjoining the church) contain a *Madonna with the Child and the 4 Evangelists, attributed to *Giotto*. — The adjacent building, formerly a Carmelite monastery, is now a barrack. The old Refectory, with the Last Supper by *Dom. Ghirlandajo*, is no longer accessible.

In the Piazza S. Spirito is situated the imposing *Palazzo Guadagni* (Pl. 71), erected by *Cronaca*.

The church of ***S. Spirito** (Pl. 33), a basilica with nave and aisles in the form of a Latin cross, surmounted by a dome, and flanked with 38 chapels, was designed by *Filippo Brunellesco*, and commenced in 1433, but having been destroyed by fire was not finished till 1481. Its noble proportions, particularly in the interior which is borne by 31 Corinthian columns and 4 pillars, render it one of the most attractive structures in Florence. The Campanile, erected by *Baccio d'Agnolo* (d. 1543), deserves inspection.

R. Aisle. 2nd Chapel: Pietà, a group in marble, copy from Michael Angelo (original in St. Peter's at Rome), by *Nanni di Baccio Bigio*. 8th Chapel: Archangel Raphael with Tobias, group by *G. Baratta*. — R. Transept. 11th chapel: Madonna by *Donatello*. 13th chapel: Madonna with SS. Nicholas and Catharine, by *Filippo Lippi*. — The Choir with screen of marble and bronze, was constructed 1599—1608 by *Michelozzi*, the high altar with canopy by *Caccini* and *Silvani*. — In the S. E. corner-chapel of the N. arm of the nave four saints on gold ground, by *Giotto* (?); in the following chapel Madonna and saints by *Botticelli*. L. Transept: l. Trinity, school of *Perugino*. L. Aisle: 2nd chapel, Madonna with four saints, by *Pietro Perugino*. In the Sacristy a saint healing the sick, by *Allori*. — Farther on, St. Anna, Madonna and saints, by *Ridolfo del Ghirlandajo*. 2nd chapel from the entrance Christ, a statue, copy from Michael Angelo (in S. Maria sopra Minerva at Rome), by *Taddeo Landini*.

The First Cloisters, erected by *Alfonso Parigi* (entrance by the sacristy, see above) are adorned with frescoes by *Perugino*, *Ulivelli*, *Baldi*, and *Cascetti*, representing saints of the Augustine order. — The Second Cloisters are by *Ammanati* (1564), the paintings by *Poccetti*. — Part of the monastery is now occupied by the military.

The ***Palazzo Pitti** (Pl. 80), situated on an eminence, and visible from many parts of the city, was designed and begun by *Brunellesco*, by order of Luca Pitti, the powerful opponent of the Medici, but owing to the decline of his prosperity (after 1466) remained uncompleted. In 1559 it was sold by his great-grandson to Eleonora, consort of the grand-duke Cosmo, and foundress of the Boboli Garden. The edifice was then completed by *Bartolommeo Amanati*, by the addition of the wings and the handsome court. In the 18th cent. the two projecting lateral halls were added, and thus arose the present palace, an edifice unrivalled in its simple grandeur. The central structure is 350 ft. in breadth and 122 ft. in height. Behind the court the garden (p. 322) ascends the hill. Since the 16th cent. the Pitti Palace has been the residence of the reigning sovereign, and is now that of Victor Emmanuel. The upper floor of the l. wing (entrance in the corner by the guardhouse, or from the Uffizi by the connecting gallery, see p. 296) contains a **Collection of upwards of 500 *Pictures* of the old masters, most of them excellent, formerly the property of Cardinal Leopold and Carlo de' Medici, and the Grand-duke Ferdinand II. (admission daily 9—3 o'clock, on Sundays and festivals 10—3, Mondays 12—3; no fees).

An insignificant staircase (on the 1st floor is the ingress from the Uffizi, see above) leads to a corridor containing a beautiful vase of porphyry, a copy of that preserved in the museum of Berlin, and a large porcelain vase from Sèvres. This corridor leads to the gallery, which extends through a suite of splendid saloons, adorned with allegorical ceiling-paintings whence their names are derived. They are sumptuously fitted up with marble and mosaic tables and velvet-covered seats, and heated in winter. Each saloon is provided with a list of the pictures it contains. Permission to copy is readily granted, if a written application be made to the director.

The six principal saloons are first visited; the entrance was formerly at the opposite extremity, so that the numbers of the pictures, as enumerated below, are now in the reverse order (catalogue 2 fr. 50 c.).

Saloon of the Iliad,

so termed from the subject of the frescoes by *Luigi Sabatelli*. It contains four tables of variegated marble and four vases of nero antico; in the centre a group in marble by *Bartolini*, Madonna and Child with St. John. R. of the entrance door: 236. *Bassano*, The Saviour in the house of Martha; 235. *Rubens*, Holy Family; 230. *Parmigianino*, Madonna with angels (Madonna del collo lungo); 229. Female portrait, attributed to *Raphael*; 228. *Titian*, Head of the Saviour; 227. *Carlo Dolci*, St. Martha; *225. *A. del Sarto*, Assumption; 222. *Giorgione*, Female portrait; 220. *A. Caracci*, Christ with saints; 219. *Pietro Perugino*, Mary and John adoring the Child; 218. *Salvator Rosa*, A warrior; 217. *Carlo Dolci*, St. John; 216. *Paolo Veronese*, Daniel Barbaro; 214. *F. Baroccio*, Copy of the Madonna del S. Girolamo, of Correggio; 213. *Carlo Dolci*, Moses; 212. *Bronzino*, Cosmo I.; 208. *Fra Bartolommeo*, Madonna del Trono; 207. *Leonardo da Vinci* (?), Portrait of a goldsmith; 206. *Bronzino*, Francesco I. de' Medici; 201. *Titian*, Ippolito de' Medici; 200. *Titian*, Philipp II. of Spain; 198. *Velasquez*, Portrait; 197. *Guido Reni*, Caritas; 196. *Paolo Veronese*, St. Benedict and other saints; 195. *Giacomo Francia*, Portrait; 194. *Paris Bordone*, St. George; 191. *A. del Sarto*, Assumption of the Virgin; 190. *Sustermans*, Portrait of the son of Frederick III. of Denmark; 188. *Salvator Rosa*, Portrait of himself; 186. *Paolo Veronese*, Baptism of Christ; 185. *Giorgione*, Concert of 3 persons; 184. *Andrea del Sarto*, Portrait of himself.

Saloon of Saturn.

R. of the entrance door: 182. *Pontormo*, Martyrdom of 40 Saints; 181. *Salvator Rosa*, Portrait of a poet; 179. *Sebastiano del Piombo*, Martyrdom of St. Agatha; 178. *Guido Reni*, Cleopatra; 176. *Domenichino*, Mary Magdalene; 175. *Albano*, Holy Family; *174. *Raphael*, Vision of Ezekiel; 173. *Albano*, Christ appearing to Mary; 172. *A. del Sarto*, Disputa della Trinità; *171. *Raphael*, Tommaso Fedra Inghirani; 168. *Guercino*, St. Peter; 167. *Giulio Romano*, Dance of Apollo and the Muses; **165. *Raphael*, Madonna del Baldachino; 164. *Pietro Perugino*, Entombment; 163. *A. del Sarto*, Annunciation; 161. *Giorgione*, Finding of Moses; 160. *Van Dyck*, Virgin; *159.

320   *Route 52.*   FLORENCE.   *Palazzo Pitti.*

Fra Bartolommeo, Risen Christ among the 4 Evangelists; *158. *Raphael*, Cardinal Bibbiena; *157. *Lorenzo Lotto*, Three periods of life; 154. *Carlo Dolci*, John the Baptist asleep; 153. *Correggio*, Head of a child; 152. *Schiavone*, Cain slaying his brother; *151. *Raphael*, Pope Julius II.; *150. *Van Dyck*, Charles I. of England and his queen Henrietta of France; 149. *Pontormo*, Ippolito de' Medici; 148. *Dosso Dossi*, Bambocciata; 147. *Giorgione*, Nymph pursued by a satyr.

Saloon of Jupiter.

In the centre Clio, writing on a shield wreathed with laurel the names of Montebello, Palestro, and S. Martino, a statue in marble by *V. Gonsani*. R. of the entrance door: *140. *L. da Vinci*, Portrait; *139. *Rubens*, Holy Family; 136. *Paolo Veronese*, The Saviour parting from his mother; 135. *Salvator Rosa*, Battle; 134. *Paolo Veronese*, The women at the Sepulchre; *133. *Salvator Rosa*, Battle (the figure on the l., below the shield, with the word Sarò, is the painter's portrait); 132. *Crespi*, Holy Family, 131. *Tintoretto*, Vincenzo Zeno; 130. *Bassano*, Portrait of a woman; 129. *Mazzolini*, The adulteress; 127, 128. *Morone*, Portraits; 125. *Fra Bartolommeo*, St. Mark; 124. *A. del Sarto*, Annunciation; *123. *A. del Sarto*, Madonna in Gloria with four saints; 122. *Garofalo*, Sibyl divulging to Augustus the mystery of the Incarnation; 118. *Andrea del Sarto*, Portraits of himself and his wife; 117. *Spagnoletto*, Portrait of Simone Paganucci; 113. *Michael Angelo*, The Fates; 112. *Borgognone*, Battle-piece; 111. *Salvator Rosa*, Conspiracy of Catiline; 110. *Titian*, Bacchanalian; 109. *Paris Bordone*, Female portrait; 108. *Paolo Veronese*, Portrait. — 4th wall: 141. *Rubens*, Nymphs attacked by Satyrs.

Saloon of Mars.

R. of the entrance door: 103. *Guercino*, Moses; 102. *Luini*, Magdalene; 101. *Baroccio*, Christ; 100. *Guido Reni*, Rebecca at the well; 99. *Guercino*, St. Sebastian; 97. *And. del Sarto*, Annunciation; *96. *C. Allori*, Judith; 95. *Allori*, Abraham's Sacrifice; *94. *Raphael*, Holy Family, termed Madonna dell' Impannata; 93. *Rubens*, St. Francis; 92. *Titian*, Portrait; 91. *Carlo Dolci*, Peter weeping; 90. *Cigoli*, Ecce Homo; 89. *Paris Bordone*, Repose during the Flight to Egypt; 87, 88. *A. del Sarto*, History of Joseph; 86. *Rubens*, Mars going forth to war; 85. *Rubens*, Rubens with his brother and the scholars Lipsius and Grotius; 84. *Palma Vecchio*, Holy Family; 83. *Titian*, Luigi Cornaro; *82. *Van Dyck*, Cardinal Giulio Bentivoglio; *81. *A. del Sarto*, Holy Family; 80. *Titian*, Andreas Vesalius (the physician); **79. *Raphael*, Madonna della Seggiola; 76. *Van der Werff*, Duke of Marlborough; 104. *Luca Giordano*, Conception. — 4th wall: 106. Portrait of Galileo, school of *Sustermans*.

Saloon of Apollo.

R. of the entrance: *67. *Titian*, Magdalene; 66. *And. del Sarto*, Portrait of himself; *64. *Fra Bartolommeo*, Pietà; 62. *And. del Sarto*, Madonna; *Raphael*, Leo X. and the cardinals de' Medici and de' Rossi; **61. *Raphael*, Angiolo Doni, friend of the master (Nos. 59. and 61. belonged to the family till 1758, when they were transferred to Avignon, where they were purchased in 1826 for the Gallery for the sum of 5000 scudi); *60. *Rembrandt*, Portrait of himself; **59. *Raphael*, Portrait of Maddalena Strozzi Doni; *58. *And. del Sarto*, Descent from the Cross; 57. *Giulio Romano*, Copy of Raphael's Madonna della Lucertola; 56. *Murillo*, Holy Family; 54. *Titian*, Pietro Aretino; 52. *Pordenone*, Holy Family; 51. *Cigoli*, Descent from the Cross; 50. *Guercino*, Peter raising Tabitha; 49. *Tiberio Titi*, Leopoldo de' Medici as a child; 47. *Guido Reni*, Bacchus; 42. *P. Perugino*, Mary Magdalene; 41. *Cristoforo Allori*, Hospitality of St. Julian; **40. *Murillo*, Madonna; 39. *Angelo Bronzino*, Holy Family; 38. *Palma Vecchio*, Christ at Emmaus; 37. *Paolo Veronese*, Portrait of his wife; 36. *Girolamo da Carpi*, Archbishop Bartolini Salimbeni; 35. Bishop Girolamo Argentino, school of Morone. — 4th wall: 71. *Carlo Maratta*, S. Filippo Neri.

Saloon of Venus.

R. of the entrance: 23. *Rustichino*, Death of Magdalene; 21. *Pietro da Cortona*, Saints praying; 20. *L. Cranach*, Adam; **18. *Titian*, Portrait (La

Palazzo Pitti.   FLORENCE.   *52. Route.* **321**

Bella di Tiziano); *17. *Titian*, Betrothal of St. Catharine; 16. *Rembrandt*, Old man; 15. *Salvator Rosa*, Sea-piece; *14. *Rubens*, Landscape; *9. *Rubens*, Landscape, Ulysses on the island of the Phæaci; 8. *Guercino*, Apollo and Marsyas; 7. *Pourbus*, Portrait; 5. *Garofalo*, St. James; 4. *Salvator Rosa*, Harbour at sunset; 3. *Tintoretto*, Cupid, Venus, and Vulcan; 2. *Salvator Rosa*, Falsehood with a mask; 1. *A. Dürer*, Eve.

Visitors return hence to the Saloon of the Iliad, and thence enter the

Saloon of the Education of Jupiter.

Ceiling-paintings by *Catani*. 241. *Clovio*, Descent from the Cross; 244. *Fr. Pourbus*, Portrait; 246. *Garofalo*, Gipsy; *248. *Tintoretto*, Descent from the Cross; 252. *Holbein*, Claude Lorrain, Duc de Guise; 254. *Palma Vecchio*, Holy Family; 255. *Van der Helst*, Portrait; *256. *Fra Bartolommeo*, Holy Family; 257. *Paris Bordone*, Sibyl prophecying to Augustus; 259. *Correggio*, Christ (a copy); 264. *Tintoretto*, Resurrection; 265. *And. del Sarto*, John the Baptist; **266. *Raphael*, 'Madonna del Granduca'; 267, 268. *Paolo Veronese*, Portraits of children; 269. *P. Veronese*, Presentation in the Temple; 270. *Carlo Dolci*, Martyrdom of St. Andrew; 277. *Bronzino*, Don Garzia de' Medici. — Hence l. into the

Sala della Stufa.

The frescoes illustrating the golden, silver, brazen, and iron ages are by *Pietro da Cortona*, ceiling-paintings by *Matteo Rosselli*, 1622. Here are preserved four small antique statues, in marble, and a column of green porphyry, bearing a small porcelain vase with the portrait of Napoleon I., and two statues in bronze (Cain and Abel), copied by *Papi* in 1849 from the marble statues executed by *Dupré* for the Duke of Leuchtenberg.

Returning hence and traversing a passage, the visitor perceives on the l. a small *Bath-room*, most tastefully fitted up, with pavement of modern Florentine mosaic, and four small statues of Venus by *Giovanni Insom* and *Salvatore Bongiovanni*.

Saloon of Ulysses.

Ceiling-painting by *Gaspero Martellini*, representing the return of Odysseus, an allusion to the restoration of the grand-duke Ferdinand III. after the revolution. No. 288. *Carlo Dolci*, Jesus on the Mount of Olives; 289. *Ligozzi*, Madonna appearing to St. Francis; 297. *Paris Bordone*, Pope Paul III.; 305. *C. Allori*, St. John in the wilderness; 306. *Salvator Rosa*, Landscape; 307. *A. del Sarto*, Madonna and saints; 311. *Titian*, Duke Alphonso I. of Ferrara; 312. *Salvator Rosa*, Landscape on the coast; 313. *Tintoretto*, Madonna; 316. *Carlo Dolci*, Portrait; *320. *A. Caracci*, Small landscape; *324. *Rubens*, Duke of Buckingham; 325. *Carlo Dolci*, Madonna and the Infant Jesus, two miniatures. — Handsome Cabinet (stipo) of ebony, inlaid with coloured wood and ivory; in the centre a large porcelain vase.

Saloon of Prometheus,

with paintings by *Giuseppe Colignon*. In the centre a magnificent round table of modern mosaic, executed for the London Exhibition of 1851, but not sent thither, value 30,000 *l*. — No. 337. *Scipio Gaetano*, Ferdinand I. de' Medici; 338. *Fra Filippo Lippi*, Madonna with saints; 339. *Tintoretto*, Portrait; 340. Madonna with two saints, school of *Perugino;* *341. *Pinturicchio*, Adoration of the Magi; 345. *Baldassare Peruzzi*, Holy Family; 346. *F. Zuccheri*, Mary Magdalene, on marble; 347. *Filippino Lippi*, Holy Family; 348. *Botticelli*, Holy Family; 353. *Botticelli*, Portrait of the 'Beautiful Simonetta', the mistress of Giuliano de' Medici, who died at an early age and whose praises were sung by the poets Pulci and Poliziano; 354. *L. di Credi*, Holy Family; 355. *Luca Signorelli*, Holy Family; 358. *Dom. Ghirlandajo*, Adoration of the Magi; 362. *Jacopo Boattieri*, Holy Family; 365. *Albertinelli*, Holy Family; *373. *Fra Angelico da Fiesole*, Madonna with saints, a winged picture over the door; 377. *Fra Bartolommeo*, Ecce Homo; 379. *J. da Pontormo*, Adoration of the Magi; 384. *A. Pollajuolo*, St. Sebastian; 388. *Filippino Lippi*, Death of Lucretia. — Hence to the

Galleria Poccetti,
which derives its name from the ceiling-paintings by *Bernardino Poccetti*. Two tables of oriental alabaster and one of malachite. *Bust of Napoleon I., by *Canova*. Nos. 481, 485. Portraits by *Sustermanns*; 490. *Guercino*, St. Sebastian; 494, 495. *Titian*, Portraits.

Returning to the Prometheus Saloon, the visitor next enters a **Corridor**, on the walls of which are 6 marble mosaics, two of which represent the Pantheon and the tomb of Cæcilia Metella at Rome, the other four the different arts; then a number of *miniature portraits, and four stands with valuable drinking cups, objects in ivory, etc.

Saloon of Justice.

Ceiling-painting by *Fedi*. In the centre a handsome cabinet, purchased in Germany by Ferdinand II. No. 389. *Tintoretto*, A sculptor; 398. *Artemisia Gentileschi*, Judith; 399. *Salviati*, Patience; 401. *Sustermanns*, The canon Pandolfo Ricasoli; 403. *Bronzino*, Grand-duke Cosmo I.; 404. *Carlo Dolci*, Vittoria della Rovere; 405. *Bonifazio Bembo*, Christ in the Temple; 400. *Carlo Dolci*, St. Dominicus praying; 408. *Peter Lely*, Oliver Cromwell (a genuine portrait, sent by the Protector to the grand-duke Ferdinand II.).

Saloon of Flora.

Ceiling-painting by *Marini*, decorations by *Landi*. In the centre *Venus by *Canova*. No. 415. *Sustermans*, Grand-duke Ferdinand II. de' Medici; 416, 421. *Gaspard Poussin*, Landscapes; 423. *Titian*, Adoration of the Shepherds; 430. *Cigoli*, Madonna; 436. *Gaspard Poussin*, Landscape; 437. *Van Dyck*, Repose during the Flight into Egypt; 438. *Ruthard*, Stag attacked by tigers.

Saloon of the Children (Sala de' Putti).

Frescoes by *Marini*, decorations by *Rabujati*. 451. *Rachel Ruysch*, Fruit; *453. *Salvator Rosa*, Landscape; 465. *Ruisdael*, Landscape; *470. *Salvator Rosa*, Landscape, with Diogenes throwing away his drinking-cup ('*la foresta dei filosofi*'); 476. *And. del Sarto*, Holy Family; 480. *A. Caracci*, Nymph with satyrs.

The *Biblioteca Palatina*, founded by Ferdinand III. for his private use, is now united with the Magliabecchiana, together forming the *Biblioteca Nazionale* (p. 298). The ground-floor of the palace contains several rooms with good *Modern Works of Art*, historical pictures by *Bezzuoli* and *Sabatelli*, statues by *Bartolini* (Carità), *Ricci* (Innocence), etc. (Application for admission is made to the porter at the entrance.) Also the *Treasury* (l. in the second court, accessible 10—3 o'clock, fee $1/2$ fr.), containing the royal plate, and many interesting specimens of ancient and modern goldsmiths' work. In the cases to the l. are works by *Benvenuto Cellini*. R. a crucifix of bronze by *Giovanni da Bologna*, opposite it a crucifixion by *Tacca*. Cruet-stand of lapis-lazuli etc.

The ***Boboli Garden** [entrance by the Palazzo Pitti, l. wing; open to the public on Sundays and Thursdays; access on other days gratis by applying (before 3 p. m.) to the *Prefetto del Palazzo* (in the court behind the principal gate of the palace, 1st door to the l.), from whom a permission valid for several weeks or months may be obtained] surrounds the palace and extends in terraces up the hill. It was laid out by *Tribolo* in 1500, under Cosmo I., and extended by *Buontalenti*, and commands a succession of charming *views of Florence with its palaces and churches, among which the Palazzo Vecchio, the dome and campanile of the cathedral, and the tower of the Badia are most conspicuous. The long walks, bordered with evergreens, and the terraces, adorned with vases and statues, attract numerous pleasure-seekers on Sundays and holidays.

On entering (see above, and comp. the plan of Florence) the visitor first perceives in a straight direction a grotto with four statues, modelled by *Michael Angelo* for the monument of Pope Julius II.; in the centre the Rape of Helen, a new group by *Vincenzo de' Rossi*. At the entrance to the grotto, Apollo and Ceres, statues by *Bandinelli*. The principal path next leads to an open space termed the *Amphitheatre*, formerly employed for festivities of the court; r. a handsome fountain, l. an Egyptian obelisk (brought hither from Rome) and an ancient basin of red marble. Then an ascent to the Basin of Neptune, adorned with a statue of the god by *Stoldo Lorenzi*; then, higher up, the statue of Abbondanza, commenced by *Giovanni da Bologna*, finished by *Tacca* (fine view hence). To the r. in the vicinity a small casino (closed on public days; access on other days by applying to the gardener, 30 c.), commanding a charming and uninterrupted view.

Above the garden is the *Fortezza di Belvedere*, constructed 1590 by *Buontalenti* by command of Ferdinand I. Near it the closed gate of S. Giorgio. From the Abbondanza a path towards to W. leads to an open grassplot, also affording a fine view, whence the visitor about to leave the garden may descent direct. Towards the S. a beautiful avenue, adorned with numerous statues (copies of old works, as well as modern originals), descends to a charming Basin (*la vasca dell' isolotto*), enlivened by swans and other water-fowl. In the centre, on an island planted with flowers, rises a fountain surmounted by a colossal statue of Oceanus, by *Giovanni da Bologna*. The surrounding walks are embellished principally with 'genre' works. A path leads from this basin in a straight direction to a grass-plot with two columns of granite, and thence to the Porta Romana, which however is usually closed; in the vicinity several ancient sarcophagi. To the r. of the Oceanus basin a broad path, parallel with the palace, is reached, by which the principal entrance may be regained. Another issue, near a fountain with Bacchus on the lion, leads into the Via Romana.

To the l. is the Botanical Garden, to inspect which permission is obtained at the Museo Naturale.

Near the Pitti Palace. Via Romana 19, is the *Museum of the Natural Sciences *(Museo di Fisica e di Storia Naturale)* (Pl. 55) (open Tues., Thurs., Saturd. 10—3, to strangers daily accessible with permission of the secretary), established by Leopold I. in the palace of the Torrigiani purchased by him, and greatly augmented at subsequent periods. The public museum is on the second floor; the mineralogical, geological, and palæontological collections occupy 9, the zoological 13 rooms. Then an admirable anatomical collection in 12 rooms, consisting chiefly of models in wax, prepared by *Clemente Susini* and his successors *Calenzuoli* and *Calamai*.

On the first floor is situated the **Tribuna of Galileo*, inaugurated in 1840, on the occasion of the assembly at Florence of the principal scholars of Italy, constructed by *Giuseppe Martelli*, and adorned with paintings by *Giuseppe Bezzuoli*, *Luigi Sabatelli*, etc., illustrating the history of Galileo, Volta and other naturalists; also a statue of Galileo by *Costoli*, and numerous busts of celebrated men, and mosaics in the pavement, designed by *Sa-*

batelli, executed by *Giov. Batt. Silvestri*. By the walls are six cabinets containing instruments from the time of Galileo downwards. This structure, with its decorations, is alone said to have cost 40,000 *l*.

Popular Festivals: *Festival of John the Baptist* (June 24th). On the eve of this day fireworks are exhibited on the Ponte alla Carraja, and horse-races take place from the Porta al Prato to the Piazza S. Croce. On the day itself high mass is celebrated at the cathedral; then a carriage-race in the Piazza S. Maria Novella; in the evening, music, and illumination of the cathedral and the vicinity of the Piazza della Signoria. *Easter Sunday*: Lo Scoppio del Carro, a vehicle with small cannon which are fired in front of the cathedral. *Holy Thursday*: washing of feet at the Pitti Palace. *Ascension:* festivities in the Cascine. S. *Annunziata*, in August, and other church festivals.

53. Environs of Florence.

The heights surrounding Florence afford a series of charming views of the city and the neighbouring country; some of the edifices erected on them also deserve notice. Those whose sojourn is of some duration will find ample scope for excursions in all directions. The principal points are here enumerated.

The new *Crescent* erected on the E. side of the city on the site of the former fortifications, is continued to the l. bank of the Arno by means of the upper *Ponte di Ferro* (Pl. F, 6), and ascends gradually to the new *Piazza Michele Angelo*, situated below S. Miniato (see below). The road then describes a long curve, skirting the hills, towards the S. *(Strada dei Colli)*, and descends in windings to the Porta Romana (Pl. A, 6). It commands several striking views of the town, and affords a pleasant drive of $1-1^1/_2$ hr. (carr. see p. 284).

a. San Miniato, with its façade of light marble, on the height E. of Florence, is a conspicuous object from many different points. It may be reached by carriage or on foot in less than $^1/_2$ hr. The road to it cannot be mistaken: the church is visible on the height as soon as the *Porta S. Miniato* is passed (Pl. D, 6). Ascending the cypress-planted road, the traveller first reaches the Franciscan monastery of *S. Salvadore del Monte*, with a church erected by *Cronaca*, the simple and chaste proportions of which were deservedly praised by Michael Angelo, who termed it 'la bella villanella'.

A few minutes more will bring the traveller to the closed entrance of the Hill of S. Miniato (accessible daily, on Sundays and festivals till noon only; porter 10 c., for opening the church and sacristy 50 c.), which together with the church is employed as a burial-ground.

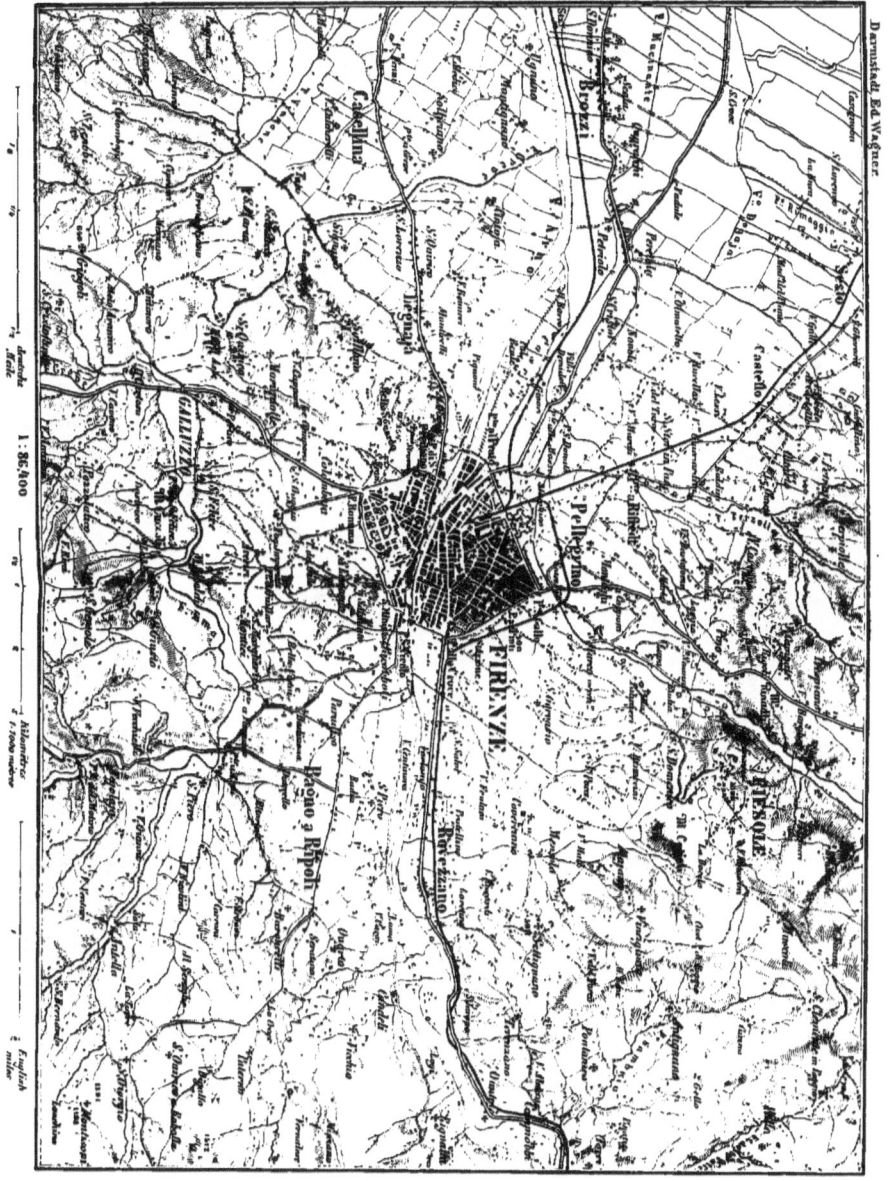

The church of *S. Miniato al Monte, founded by Bishop Hildebrand of Florence in 1013, on the site of an earlier structure, is a basilica of admirable proportions with nave and aisles, without a transept, and may in many respects be termed a truly classical edifice. The elegantly incrusted *Façade* dates f.om the 12th, the mosaics with which it is adorned from the 13th cent. The tower was restored by *Baccio d'Agnolo* in 1519. The *Interior*, recently restored, rests on 12 columns of white, and 4 handsome pillars of greenish grey marble, and has an open roof. The choir with its simple apse is raised by a spacious crypt beneath.

Aisles. On the wall on the r. Enthroned Madonna and saints, on the l. a Madonna with saints and a Crucifixion, of the beginning of the 15th cent. — In the nave, between the flights of steps (16) ascending to the choir, is a chapel constructed in 1446 by Piero de' Medici from a design by *Michelozzo*. In the l. aisle is the *Chapel of S. Giacomo, constructed by *Antonio Rossellini*, containing the monument of Cardinal Jacopo of Portugal (d. 1459); ceiling adorned in a masterly manner by *Luca della Robbia*. — The *Crypt*, to which a flight of 7 steps descends, rests on four columns and two pillars, prolonged in the choir above, and also on 28 smaller columns of graceful form, some of them ancient. Beneath the altar here is the tomb of S. Miniato. — The front-wall of the crypt, the screen of the choir, and the pulpit present beautiful specimens of incrusted marble-works. The upper part of the *Apse* is adorned with a mosaic of S. Miniato before the Saviour, executed in 1297, recently restored. The 5 windows under the arches are closed with semi-transparent slabs of marble. Over an altar on the r. the portrait of S. Giovanni Gualberto, the saint of Vallombrosa (attributed to *Giotto*), who, on meeting the murderer of his brother at the foot of this hill, was besought by him for mercy in the name of the Crucified. The haughty noble, touched with pity, not only spared his enemy, but resolved thenceforward to devote himself to a life of piety. He became a monk in this monastery, and afterwards founded the celebrated monastery of Vallombrosa. — On the S. side of the choir is the *Sacristy* (closed), erected 1387 in the Gothic style, adorned with *frescoes from the life of St. Benedict (his youth, ordination at Subiaco, miracles, etc.) by *Spinello Aretino*. Beneath them, admirable inlaid work in wood.

The beautiful mosaic pavement, which according to the inscription was executed in 1207, also deserves inspection.

The piazza in front of the church commands a charming view of Florence and its environs (afternoon-light most favourable): on the height to the r. Fiesole, then the city itself with S. Croce, the cathedral, S. Lorenzo, the Palazzo Vecchio, S. Maria Novella, and the Lung' Arno; to the l. hills studded with villas, the Fortezza del Belvedere, Bello Sguardo, and Villa Giramonti. In 1529 *Michael Angelo*, as the engineer of the republic, fortified this eminence with works which are still partially preserved, and here conducted the defence of the city during eleven months against the Imperial troops (p. 287).

b. **Poggio Imperiale.** Immediately to the l., outside the Porta Romana, through which the high road to Siena and Rome issues, the new Strada dei Colli, mentioned p. 324, commences. To the r. of it a fine avenue of lofty cypresses, evergreen oaks, and larches, embellished with a few statues, leads in 20 min. to the

Villa Poggio Imperiale. It was thus named and almost entirely fitted up by Magdalen of Austria, wife of Cosmo II., and afterwards adorned with various works of art, which were removed in 1860. The handsome edifice is now employed as an educational establishment, conducted by nuns, and consequently no longer accessible.

At Poggio Imperiale the road divides: that to the *right* (and after $1/2$ M. to the r. again) leads to *Galuzzo* and the *Certosa* (see below); that to the *left* (soon passing a group of houses, following the Via del Pian Giullari, and ascending the height, where at a bifurcation of the road, a bye-road in a straight direction is to be followed) leads to the **Torre del Gallo**, which owes its name to a family of that name (according to others, to its conspicuous weather-cock). From this tower *Galileo* is said to have made his most important astronomical observations. Fine panorama from the summit (fee $1/2$ fr.).

Returning hence to the carriage-road, the traveller turns to the l. by a road affording picturesque views and leading to the height of S. Miniato. The road to the r. passes ($1/4$ hr.) several houses and villas, among which is the **Villa of Galileo**, marked by a bust and inscription, where the great astronomer passed the last years of his life (1631—42), latterly deprived of sight and surrounded by a few faithful friends. Here he was visited by his illustrious contemporary Milton. — The road diverging to the r. a short distance beyond this villa leads direct to the ($2^1/4$ M.) Val d'Ema and the Certosa (see below).

A short distance hence, near the church of *S. Margherita a Montici*, stands the villa where *Francesco Guicciardini* wrote his history of Italy. Here too, on Aug. 12th, 1530, the Florentines who had been betrayed by their general Malatesta, signed the articles by which the city was surrendered to the imperial troops, thus becoming subject to the rule of the Medici. From that event the house derives its name *Villa della Bugia*.

c. **La Certosa** in the *Val d'Ema* is 3 M. distant by the high road from Porta Romana (carriage 6 fr., viâ Poggio Imperiale or Torre del Gallo see above). To the r., as the height beyond the gate is ascended, rises the church of *S. Gaggio;* farther on is the village of *Galuzzo*, beyond which the brook *Ema* is soon reached (l. on the height a nunnery). On an eminence, clothed with cypresses and olive-trees, at the confluence of this brook with the *Greve*, rises the imposing Carthusian Monastery (Certosa), in appearance resembling a mediæval fortress. After crossing the Ema the traveller reaches a gateway (generally closed) with a statue of S. Lorenzo, by which the garden is entered. The principal approach however diverges to the r. on the height, farther on. The monastery, which is approaching dissolution and contains but few inmates, was erected in 1341 by the Florentine

Nicola Acciaioli, from a design by *Orcagna*. The po.ter (1—2 pers. 1 fr.; visitors are usually admitted without difficulty, although special permission from the minister of the interior is nominally required), shows the church or rather the series of chapels of which it consists. The most valuable pictures are a St. Francis, by *Cigoli*, and Trinity by *Giotto*; in the lower chapel are the tombstones of the Acciaioli, among them one by *Donatello*. Some of the empty cells, which enclose the building like pinnacles, command picturesque views, especially through the valley of the Ema towards Prato and the Apennines. The rooms occupied for several months by Pius VI., when banished from Rome by the French, are also shown.

    d. **Bello Sguardo,** to the S. of Florence, easily recognised by its small pavilion with a red roof, is celebrated for the delightful prospect it commands. The traveller should on no account fail to visit it. The route cannot be mistaken. From Porta Romana the town-wall must be followed to the r. and the second road to the l. taken. This first leads to an open space with the small church of *S. Francesco di Paola*, which contains the monument of Benozzo Federighi, bishop of Fiesole, by *Luca della Robbia*. The carriage-road (fiacre there and back see p. 284), is then followed in a straight direction, and on the height, where it divides, the road to the l. is taken (a few paces beyond this point the road to the Monte Oliveto diverges to the r., see below). At the next bifurcation a side-path to the l. is followed, which in a few minutes leads to the **Bello Sguardo (visi.ors ring at the small gate on the r. near the corner, fee 2—3 soldi on leaving). The view embraces Florence, with the Pitti Palace, S. Croce, the Palazzo Vecchio, Or S. Michele, the cathedral, S. Lorenzo, S. Maria Novella, etc.; r. on the height S. Miniato, opposite the spectator lies Fiesole, l. the populous valley of the Arno, over which tower the distant Apennines. The view is seen to the best advantage towards sunset. — In the vicinity is the *Villa degli Albizzi*, with a bust of Galileo and an inscription to the memory of that illustrious astronomer, who frequently resided here and cultivated the garden with his own hands.

    The first road to the r. beyond the Bello Sguardo leads r. to *Monte Oliveto*. Those, who wish to visit the Bello Sguardo from the Porta S. Frediano follow the city-wall to the l. and take the first road to the r., leading to the above-mentioned church of S. Francesco.

    e. **Monte Oliveto.** About $1/3$ M. beyond the Porta S. Frediano (Pl. A, 3) the 'Via di Monte Oliveto' diverges to the l. from the Leghorn road, and reaches the entrance to the garden of the monastery after $1/2$ M. (a gate marked No. 5; key to obtain access to the point of view, next door, No. 6, 2—3 soldi). A slight eminence here planted with cypresses commands an admirable *prospect: N.W. the beautiful valley of Florence, with Prato and Pistoja, enclosed by mountains, over which rises one of the peaks of the marble-mountains of Carrara; N.E. lies Florence, then Fiesole with the numerous villas which deck its heights; E. the Fortezza di Belvedere and S. Miniato; in the background the barren mountain-chain of the Casentino. Towards the S. the view is excluded by the intervening heights.

The monastery-buildings are now employed as a military hospital. Between the Bello Sguardo and Monte Oliveto is situated the *Badia di S. Bartolommeo di Monte Oliveto*, erected 1334, adorned with frescoes by *Poccetti;* in the refectory an Annunciation by *Dom. Ghirlandajo*. The garden is also visited for the sake of the view it commands of Florence and the environs.

From the suburb of *S. Frediano* a suspension-bridge (5 c.) leads to the *Cascine*.

f. The **Cascine**, or park of Florence, lies to the W., beginning near the *Barriera Nuova* (in the Piazza Vitt. Emanuele, Pl. A, 2), and extends for about 2 M. in length, but is of moderate breadth, being bounded by the Arno and the Mugnone. It affords delightful and refreshing walks to the traveller fatigued with sight-seeing. The name is derived from a farm to which it belongs. It is a favourite rendezvous of the fashionable world in the afternoon. — Outside the town, immediately to the l., is a small café; opposite which, to the r., is a notice indicating the entrance to the *Zoological Garden* (adm. 50 c., Sund. forenoon 25 c.), founded in 1860 on the occasion of the exhibition at Florence. About the middle of the Cascine is a large open space (where a military band plays several times weekly), surrounded by several country-houses (*Casino delle Cascine*, a café belonging to Doney's hotel, p. 283), a gay and fashionable resort towards sunset. Beyond this spot the park is comparatively deserted. About 1 M. farther the extremity of the Cascine is reached.

On the road to Pistoja, about $^3/_4$ M. from the Porta al Prato, is situated the **Villa Demidoff**, the property of a Russian millionnaire who was created a prince by the former grand-duke of Tuscany, containing valuable collections of modern pictures, arms etc., and surrounded by gardens and hot-houses. Admission on Mondays and Thursdays (not always granted) on application by letter to the secretary of the prince.

About $1^1/_2$ M. from the Villa Demidoff, r. beyond *Ponte a Rifredi* (railway-station, see p. 282), and in the vicinity of the ancient church of *S. Stefano in Pane*, lies the **Villa Careggi**, property of the grand-dukes till 1780, then that of the Orsi family, erected by *Michelozzi* for the first Cosmo, who here terminated his brilliant career in 1464. Here, too, was once established the *Platonic Academy*, of which Marsilius Ficinus, Picus of Mirandola, Angelus Politianus, Christophorus Landinus and many others of the greatest men of that period were members. Lorenzo il Magnifico, grandson of Cosmo, also died at Careggi (1492). Fine view of the environs. A few frescoes by *Pontormo* and *Bronzino* and a series of portraits are reminiscences of the history of this edifice.

Farther W. is the **Villa della Petraia**, possessing delightful gardens, erected by *Buontalenti*, and adorned with paintings by *Andrea del Sarto* and *Daniele da Volterra*, celebrated as the seat of the Brunelleschi who in 1364 so strenuously opposed the adverse faction under Hawkswood. The villa, which is now fitted up as a royal residence, is most conveniently reached from the railway-station *Castello* (p. 282). Near it is the *Villa Quarto*, with beautiful gardens, formerly the property of the Medicis, now that of Prince Demidoff.

From railway-stat. *Sesto* (p. 282) a visit may be paid to the great porcelain-manufactory *della Doccia*, the property of Marchese Ginori, who possesses a villa here.

g. **Fiēsole**, on the height to the N. of Florence, is 3 M. distant (carr. 7—8 fr., see p. 284). In the open space by the *Porta S. Gallo* (Pl. F, 2), where a Triumphal Arch of no artistic merit, erected in 1738, commemorates the entry of the grand-duke Francis II., the traveller turns to the r. within the new 'Cinta Daziaria' (boundary of imposts) to the gate (opened within the last few years). Beyond the gate he follows the l. bank of the *Mugnone*, an insignificant stream, which however in rainy weather sometimes causes great devastation, to (1 M.) *Villa Palmieri*, the property of the ex-ducal family, the terrace of which crosses the road by a bridge. Boccaccio makes this the residence of the narrators in his Decamerone during the plague in 1348. The road then ascends rapidly between garden-walls, and reaches (1 M.) the church of *S. Domenico di Fiesole*, in the former monastery of which *Fra Angelico*, the celebrated painter of saints, lived before his removal to S. Marco at Florence; the choir of the church contains a Madonna with saints, painted by him. (Opposite the church the 'Via della Badia' diverges to the l., see p. 330). The road divides here: the old road to the l. leads past the *Villa Mozzi*, once a favourite residence of Lorenzo il Magnifico, reaching the height in 20 min.; the new road to the r. winds gradually upwards, passing several pretty villas, finally skirting the S. side of the ancient Etruscan wall of Fiesole. This excellent road is principally indebted for its construction to the *Golden Book* of Fiesole. This venerable volume enjoys the privilege of ennobling those whose names are inscribed on its pages, and, when the Fiesolans were desirous of constructing the road, their 'golden book' distributed its favours extensively among the Florentines and others, in return for a substantial equivalent.

Fiēsole (Trattoria l'Aurora, terrace with superb view; *Locanda Firenze*), Lat. *Faesulae*, is an ancient Etruscan town, the Cyclopean walls of which are still partially preserved (especially on the N. side). It was for a long period more powerful than its rival Florence, to the jealousy of which it at last fell a victim in 1010 (p. 287). The town, the seat of a bishop, but now of no importance, contains 11,500 inhab. (incl. the environs), who like most of the natives of this district are engaged in straw-plaiting (purchasers of their wares should as a rule give only half the price demanded).

On the height the traveller enters the spacious *Piazza of Fiesole*, and perceives immediately opposite to him the *Cathedral*, commenced in 1028 by Bishop Jacopo Bavaro, shortly after the destruction of the ancient Faesulae by the Florentines, but not completed till a much later date. It is a basilica of poor exterior, consisting of nave and aisles with a transept, and a spacious crypt beneath the choir. The chapel r. of the choir contains the *monument of Bishop Salutati (d. 1462), by *Mino da Fiesole*, opposite to which is a *bas-relief by the same master, representing the Madonna with St. Remigius and St. Leonhard, in the foreground the Infant Christ, and John the Baptist with a beggar.

Opposite the cathedral at the W. side of the piazza are the *Episcopal Palace* and the *Seminary*. On the E. side of the piazza is the *Palazzo del Pretorio*, of the 13th cent., bearing the arms of the magistrates (podestà). Adjacent to it is the venerable church of *S. Maria Primerana*, dating from the 10th cent., containing a tabernacle in terracotta of the school of *L. della Robbia*. — A farm at the back of the cathedral contains scanty remnants of an ancient *Theatre*.

The site of the old Acropolis of Faesulae is occupied by a *Franciscan Monastery*, to which the street ascending to the W. opposite the cathedral leads. On the r., a little below the monastery, rises the venerable church of *S. Alessandro*, with 12 antique columns of cipollino, probably occupying the site of a heathen temple. The plateau in front of it commands a beautiful and extensive *view of the valley of Florence, bounded on the S. by several ranges of hills, on the E. by the mountain-chain of the Casentino, on the W. by the heights of Monte Albano, beyond which the mountains of Carrara stand prominently forth.

Those whom time permits should ascend the eminence a short distance E. of Fiesole, which rises to a greater height than the Franciscan monastery and commands an uninterrupted panorama.

On the way back the traveller should visit the ***Badia di Fiesole**, 1/4 M. to the W. of S. Domenico di Fiesole (p. 329), a monastery founded in 1028, occupied first by Benedictine, afterwards by Augustine monks. It was remodelled by *Brunellesco* in 1462, by order of the elder Cosmo de' Medici, and forms a remarkably attractive pile of buildings. The church, with a transept, but destitute of aisles, is covered with barrel-vaulting, and is of noble proportions throughout. That part of the façade which is decorated with black and white marble belongs to the older structure, and is coeval with S. Miniato (p. 325). In the interior are several tombstones of the celebrated families of the Salviati, Marucelli, Doni, etc., who once resided in the neighbouring villas. The Refectory is adorned with a fresco by *Giovanni di S. Giovanni*, representing angels ministering to Christ in the wilderness, remarkable for the animation of the style. The monastery, which was highly favoured by the Medicis, was frequently the residence of members of the 'Platonic Academy' (p. 328). Picus of Mirandola here worked at his exposition of Genesis. After the suppression of the monastery (1778), the printing-office of the learned *Francesco Inghirami*, where a number of important works were published, was established here. — The road back to Florence descends, skirts the r. bank of the Mugnone, and leads the whole way to the city between lofty garden-walls.

h. About ³/₄ M. from the *Porta alla Croce* at Florence, l. of the high road, are situated the remains of the monastery of **S. Salvi**, of the order of Vallombrosa, and mentioned as early as 1084, where in 1312 Emp. Henry VII. established his headquarters during the siege of Florence. A *fresco here by *And. del Sarto*, representing the Last Supper, is still well preserved. The traveller may prolong his walk hence in the valley of the Arno as far as *Compiobbi*, a station on the line from Florence to Arezzo, and return to Florence by the last train.

i. **Vallombrosa.** A visit to this celebrated monastery may be accomplished from Florence in one day; it is advisable, however, to start on the previous evening and pass the night at S. Pelago (see below). It the traveller intends to include the Casentino Valley and the monasteries of Camaldoli and Alvernia in the excursion, three days will be required.

The train from Florence to Arezzo should be taken as far as *Pontassieve* (in 55 min.). From the central station near S. Maria Novella the train performs the circuit of the city, and stops at the station near *Porta alla Croce*, which may be more conveniently situated for some travellers than the principal station. It then skirts the r. bank of the Arno. The valley soon contracts. Stat. *Compiobbi*, a small village, lies in a richly cultivated district, above which rise barren heights. Stat. *Pontassieve* (Italia; Vapore, both very poor inns; carriages to Pelago 5—6 fr.), a small village at the confluence of the *Sieve* and Arno, formerly derived some importance from its situation on the high road leading through the valley of the Sieve and over the Apennines to Forli.

Quitting the railway-station, the traveller follows the broad road to the r., which after a few hundred paces crosses the Sieve. At (3 M.) the point where the road divides for the third time, the traveller should descend to the r., and proceed to ($2^1/_4$ M.) the village of *Pelăgo* (Locanda al Buon Cuore, R., B., and D. 5 fr., but previous agreement necessary; mule to Vallombrosa 5 fr.). The road continues practicable for carriages as far as the former monastery-farm of *Paterno* ($3^3/_4$ M. from Pelago, one-horse carr. 5 fr.), now a royal agricultural institution, or even as far as the village of *Tosi*, $1^1/_2$ M. farther. Those who make the excursion in one day need not go by Pelago, but may proceed direct from Pontassieve to Paterno and Tosi. The rugged and stony path ascends hence to the l. by a chapel (carriage-road projected), traverses meadows, underwood, and pine forest, and about halfway up the Pratomagno mountain reaches

Vallombrosa (2980 ft.), situated in a shaded and sequestered spot. The monastery was founded about 1050 by *S. Giovanni Gualberto*, scion of a wealthy and powerful family of Florence, who after a career of youthful profligacy resolved to devote the remainder of his life to the most austere acts of penance. His brother Hugo having fallen by the knife of an assassin, Gualberto was bound by the customs of that age to follow the bloody law of retaliation. Descending one Good Friday from the church of S. Miniato (p. 325) near Florence, accompanied by armed followers, he suddenly encountered the guilty object of his vengeance at a narrow part of the road. The latter fell at his feet and implored for mercy. The knight, suddenly moved by a generous impulse, forgave his enemy, and resolved for ever to renounce the world and its passions. He accordingly retired to the cloister of S. Miniato; but deeming the discipline there too lax, he betook himself to this lonely spot and founded Vallombrosa. The monastery, which had acquired extensive landed property and considerable wealth in the course of ages, has recently been suppressed by the Italian government. The present extensive buildings, together with the church, erected 1638, are now occupied by the *Istituto Forestale*, or a royal school of forestry, opened in Aug. 1869, with 3—4 teachers and 30—40 pupils. Small osteria outside the walls.

Il Paradisino, or *Le Cette*, a smaller cloister situated on a rock, $1/_4$ hr. to the l. above the monastery, and now uninhabited, commands an admirable survey of the latter, which lies 266 ft. below, and of the broad valley of the Arno as far as Florence, half of the dome of which is visible behind a hill. The horizon is bounded by the marble-hills of Carrara.

Another pretty point of view is situated $1^1/_4$ M. to the S. of the monastery. The path leads to the l. of the inn, and immediately beyond it passes a spring (to the r. below the path), then traverses the wood, and reaches a projecting rock commanding an extensive view of the valley of the Arno.

The summit of the *Pratomagno commands an extensive prospect; the ascent from Vallombrosa (guide 2 fr.) occupies 1 hr. The path traverses dense pine-forest, then dwarfed beech-underwood, and finally green pastures. The culminating point of the chain is crossed, and the sinuosities of the mountains followed by a winding path for some distance. The scenery of the Apennines is characterised by wild and bleak slopes and narrow ridges, intersected by profound gorges. Fine grained grauwacke (macigno), varied occasionally by grauwacke-slate or the more recent clayslate, forms the principal mass of this group. The vegetation is scanty and monotonous, insects and birds are rare, water seldom visible.

The view from the summit, which is 5323 ft. above the sealevel, is obstructed on the N. and S. by peaks of equal altitude. E. lies the green Casentino Valley, drained by an impetuous brook, the water of which is praised by Dante (Inf. 30, 64), and bounded on the N. E. by the lofty Monte Falterona (where the Arno rises), a buttress of the principal chain of the Apennines. W. the fertile and richly cultivated valley of the Arno stretches as far as the dome of the cathedral of Florence, beyond which the blue Mediterranean is visible in the extreme distance. Above the towers of Florence rise the indented peaks of the mountains of Carrara and other summits, among which the Monte Cimone (6907 ft.), the loftiest of the N. Apennines, is most conspicuous.

From the Pratomagno a steep path descends through woods and ravines (1½ hr.), skirting the brook *Solano*, traversing green meadows and stony slopes overgrown with thistles, then through underwood of beeches and chestnuts, past *Cetica* and several other mountain-villages to the picturesque market-town of *S. Niccolò*, commanded by the ancient fort of that name, and situated at the confluence of the Solano and Arno, where the fertile Casentino expands. The river is crossed by a wooden bridge, beyond which a good road leads to the r., passing the ancient church of *Campaldino*, where in a sanguinary conflict, June 11th, 1289, Dante distinguished himself as an intrepid horseman, and aided his Guelph countrymen to crush the might of Arezzo and the Tuscan Ghibellines. The next place of importance is *Poppi* (p. 334).

k. **Camaldoli** and **Alvernia**. An attractive excursion may be undertaken from Vallombrosa to the *Casentino*, or upper valley of the Arno, a district which affords an insight into the scenery of the Apennines. The carriage-road from Pontassieve (p. 331) to the Casentino crosses the *Consuma Pass*, about 9 M. distant. The expedition is, however, especially suitable for pedestrians. From Vallombrosa a bridle-path (guide necessary, 2 fr.) traverses the brow of the hills, affording a succession of fine views, and leading in 2 hrs. to the *Osteria della Consuma*, the inn of a small mountain-village. If a carriage can be procured here, the traveller should drive to *Bibbiena* (15 M.), or at least to *Prato-*

vecchio (10 M.). The road traverses the lonely height of the *Monte Consuma* for 3 M., after which a view of the valley of the Arno is gradually disclosed. About 6 M. farther, near the extensive ruins of the castle of *Romena*, the road divides; that to the l. leads to *Pratovecchio*, a short distance farther, and beyond it to *Stia*. From Pratovecchio pedestrians may proceed by *Moggiona* (poor inn) to *Camaldoli* in 3 hrs. The road to the r. leads by *Castel S. Niccolò* (p. 333) to **Poppi**, capital of the valley, situated on a hill rising above the Arno, the old castle of which with lofty tower, erected 1274, has long been visible to the traveller. Passing *Ponte a Poppi*, a few houses at the foot of the hill, **Bibbiena** is next reached, 3 M. farther, birthplace (in 1470) of Bernardo Divizio, afterwards Cardinal Bibbiena, the patron of Raphael. From Bibbiena Camaldoli is reached by *Soci* and *Partina* in 3 hrs., Alvernia by the valley of the *Corsalone* in 2 hrs. The direct footpath between the monasteries may be traversed in 4 hrs. Pedestrians may therefore reach Camaldoli in one day from Vallombrosa by Consuma and Pratovecchio, and on the following day proceed thence by Alvernia to Bibbiena.

The ancient abbey of **Camaldoli** lies in a grassy valley surrounded by forest. It was founded about the year 1000 by St. Romuald, but frequently destroyed by fire and devastated by war, in consequence of which the church was re-erected in 1523, and again in 1772. It has recently been suppressed by the Italian government, like all the other monasteries in Italy. The environs are wild and beautiful. A zigzag path ascends rapidly ($3/4$ hr.) to the *Sacro Eremo*, a second monastery with hermitages, founded by St. Romuald in 1046. The name of the place is said to be derived from Campus Maldoli, in consequence of a pious Count Maldolus, the last proprietor, having presented it to his friend St. Romuald. From this spot the reputation of the order for austere discipline, sanctity, and erudition extended throughout the whole of Italy, although the number of their cloisters was never great. Camaldoli lost its valuable library and many treasures of art owing to the rapacity of the French in 1808. In 1814 the monastery was restored.

The *views from the narrow mountain-ridge at the back of Camaldoli, especially from the summit which is not planted with trees, termed the *Prato al Soglio, are very extensive and beautiful. To the N.E. the houses of Forli may be distinguished, still farther the situation of Ravenna, and in the extreme distance the glittering Adriatic; W. the chain of the Pratomagno and the green dales of Vallombrosa, the lower valley of the Arno as far as the Maremme of Pisa and Leghorn, and beyond them the Mediterranean. The spectator here stands on one of the summits of the 'back-bone of Italy', whence innumerable mountains and valleys, as well as the two different seas, are visible.

The source of the Arno (4250 ft.) on the *Falterona* may be visited hence, and the excursion may be extended to the summit of the mountain by those whose energies are unimpaired. Dante, who in the 14th canto of the Purgatorio describes the course of the Arno, accompanying it from its source to Arezzo and Florence with bitter complaints of the swine of the Casentino, the dogs of Arezzo, the wolves of Florence, and the foxes of Pisa, perhaps visited the Monte Falterona in person. Travellers generally proceed from Camaldoli on mules or donkeys to **Alvernia**. The S. height is ascended as far as the chapel of St. Romuald; then r. a descent to *Moggiona*, beyond which the path turns to the l., traversing a long and fatiguing succession of gorges and slopes; the path at the base of the mountains is therefore preferable. The market-town of *Soci* in the valley of the *Archiano* is first reached, then the profound valley of the *Corsalone*; beyond it a blunted cone rises, on which the path ascends in windings to a stony plain with marshy meadows. Above this rises the abrupt sandstone mass of the *Vernia*, to a height of 850 ft. On its S.W. slope, one-third of the way up, and 3906 ft. above the sea-level, is seen a wall with small windows, the oldest part of the monastery, built in 1218 by St. Francis of Assisi. The church is of 1264. In 1472 a conflagration entirely destroyed the monastery. Beautiful forests are situated in the vicinity, from the openings in which imposing mountain-views are often enjoyed. One of the grandest points is the *°Penna della Vernia*, or ridge of the Vernia, also known simply as *l'Apennino*, 4790 ft. above the sea, 'the rugged rock between the sources of the Tiber and Arno', as it is called by Dante (Paradiso II. 106). To the E. are seen the lofty *Sassi di Simone*, the mountains which bound the Tuscan Romagna in the direction of the republic of San Marino; N.E. the sources of the Tiber are situated behind the *Fumajolo*.

Near the monastery are the *Luoghi Santi*, a number of grottoes and rock-hewn chambers in which St. Francis once lived. The church contains no pictures worthy of mention, but several excellent reliefs in terracotta, especially an *°Annunciation by *Luca della Robbia*.

To the S., not far from the monastery, is situated the ruined castle of *Chiusi*, occupying the site of the ancient *Clusium Novum*, where Lodovico Buonarotti, father of Michael Angelo, once held the office of Podestà. The great master himself was born March 6th, 1475, at *Caprese*, in the valley of the *Singerna* in the vicinity, but in 1476 his parents removed to *Settignano*, in the vicinity of the quarries.

The traveller is recommended to return from Bibbiena to Florence by Arezzo (diligence daily in 3 hrs.; one-horse carr. 10 fr.). The road follows the l. bank of the Arno, passing several small villages, quits the river at *Giovi*, and entering the rich *Val di Chiana* leads to **Arezzo** (** Le Chiavi d'Oro*), stat. on the line Florence-Perugia-Rome (to Florence railway in 2½—3½ hrs.; fares 8 fr. 70, 7 fr. 15, 5 fr. 55 c.). Arezzo, and thence to Perugia, etc. see *Baedeker's Central Italy*.

54. Corsica.

Steamboats between the mainland and Corsica: *a*. Valery Co. once weekly from Marseilles to Ajaccio, fares 30 and 20 fr., to Bastia and Calvi also once weekly; *b*. From Nice fortnightly to Ajaccio, also to Bastia; *c*. From Leghorn 3 times weekly to Bastia in 6 hrs., fares 16 and 13 fr. (incl. fee for embarcation). Also once weekly from Ajaccio to Porto Torres in Sardinia in 7 hrs. Embarcation 1 fr.; breakfast and dinner 8 fr. in the first, 6 fr. in the second cabin. — Diligence-communication between Ajaccio and Bastia and all the principal places in the island.

Corsica (French *La Corse*), situated between 43° and 41° 21′ N. Latitude, 55 M. distant from Italy and 110 M. from France, and separated from Sardinia by the Strait of Bonifazio, 9 M. in width, possesses an area of 3365 sq. M. and a population of 259,861 souls. A broad mountain-chain, terminating towards the N. in the Capo Corso, consisting of grey granite and limestone formations, occupies almost the entire island. On the W. it rises abruptly from the sea, forming a number of bold promontories and deeply indented bays. On the E. side, towards Italy, the alluvial deposits have been more abundant, and have formed a level coast of some breadth. The vast altitude attained by the mountains within a comparatively small space (e. g. Monte d'Oro 8690 ft., Monte Rotondo 9053 ft.) imparts a wild and imposing character to the scenery. Nine-tenths of the entire area of the island are uncultivated, whilst the mountains for the most part are clothed with magnificent forests. The Flora of the island is remarkable for its rare luxuriance and diversity, comprising specimens of almost every species of plant found on the shores of the Mediterranean. The timber of Corsica was highly esteemed by the ancients, and still supplies most of the French and Italian dockyards. Its mineral wealth, however, is far inferior to that of Sardinia.

The character of the natives, notwithstanding the levelling and equalizing effects of advancing civilisation, corresponds with the wild aspect of their country, and, at least in the more remote districts, still preserves many of those features described by the ancients as peculiar to these islanders. Their insatiable thirst for revenge *(vendetta)*, formerly one of the chief causes of the depopulation of the island, has never been thoroughly eradicated, although the authorities have adopted the most rigorous measures to counteract the evil. The perpetrators of these dark deeds withdraw themselves from the arm of justice and retire as outlaws *(banditi)* to the mountains, where, hunted like wild beasts by a corps of gensdarmes constituted for this express purpose, they frequently protract their miserable existence for many years. At the same time this revengeful ferocity is to a certain extent compensated for by bravery, love of freedom, simplicity of manners, and hospitality, virtues which usually characterize a vigorous and primitive race. Their ballads, too, and especially their dirges *(vocĕri)*, are replete with poetical pathos. Moreover, few countries of similar extent have produced more illustrious characters, or witnessed more thrilling achievements, than those recorded in the annals of Corsica.

The situation and climate of the island are Italian, as was also its history down to the year 1768. Since the commencement of the present century its union with France has been still more closely cemented by its connection with the family of Napoleon. It now forms the 86th Department of the Empire, the capital of which is Ajaccio, and is divided into 5 Arrondissements: Ajaccio, Bastia, Calvi, Corte, and Sartona. Italian is still the language of the natives, but French is employed for all official purposes and is spoken by all the educated classes.

The great attractions of Corsica are its beautiful scenery and its interesting historical associations, for it can boast of no antiquities or treasures of art. A visit to the island is now easily and expeditiously accomplished. A week suffices for the ordinary traveller to become acquainted with Ajaccio, Corte (ascent of Monte Rotondo), and Bastia. Those, however, who desire a more thorough insight into the resources of the country and the character of the natives will encounter serious difficulties, which introductions to inhabitants of the island will best enable them to overcome.

Corsica, like its sister-island Sardinia, which was peopled by the same race, never attained to a high degree of civilisation in ancient times. The entire island is depicted as having been a wild and impenetrable forest, of very evil reputation. Its possession was nevertheless keenly contested by the great naval powers of ancient times. The Phocæans, banished from Asia by the Persians, founded the town of Alalia (afterwards Aleria) on the E. coast, at the mouth of the Tavignano, B. C. 556. After a great naval battle in 536, however, they were compelled by the allied Etruscans and Carthaginians to abandon their settlement and migrate to Massilia (Marseilles). The island then became subject to the Etruscans, and subsequently to the Carthaginians, from whom it was wrested by the Romans in 237. Under Marius and Sulla the colonies of Aleria and Mariana were established on the E. coast, but were both subsequently destroyed. The island was frequently employed as a place of banishment; thus the philosopher Seneca spent 8 years here during the reign of the Emp. Claudius. His account of the country and its inhabitants is by no means flattering, and the Corsicans occasionally declare that 'Seneca era un birbone'. The following lines written by him are to this day partially true:

'Prima est ulcisci lex, altera vivere raptu,
Tertia mentiri, quarta negare deos'.

After the fall of the Western Empire Corsica frequently changed masters; the Vandals, Byzantines, Ostrogoths, Franks, and Saracens rapidly succeeded each other in its possession. In 1070 the Pisans, and in 1348 the Genoese obtained the supremacy, which the latter retained till the 18th cent.

Their oppressive sway, however, gave rise to a long series of conspiracies and insurrections, in many of which a number of remarkable characters and bold adventurers distinguished themselves. Thus Arrigo della Rocca, Vincentello d'Istria, and Giampolo da Leca in the 14th and 15th cent., and Renuccio della Rocca and Sampiero di Bastelica (killed on Jan. 17th, 1567) in the 16th. Finally, in 1729, the universal disaffection to Genoa began to assume a more serious aspect, notwithstanding the efforts made by the Republic to stifle it with the aid of German auxiliaries. The last of a long succession of adventurers was a Baron Theodore Neuhof, son of a Westphalian noble, who landed on March 12th, 1736, at Aleria, near the mouth of the Tavignano, attended by a number of followers, and provided with warlike equipments. He was shortly afterwards proclaimed king of Corsica, under the title of Theodore I., but his success was short-lived, for the Genoese were assisted by the French. Theodore returned twice subsequently to Corsica, but was ultimately compelled to seek an asylum in London, where he died in obscurity in 1756. Meanwhile the Corsicans, under the command (subsequently to 1755) of the heroic Pasquale Paoli (born in 1724 at Stretta, a village among the mountains S.W. of Bastia; died in London in 1807), fought so successfully against the Genoese, that the latter lost the entire island with the exception of Bastia. By the Treaty of Compiègne in 1763 Genoa ceded Corsica to the French, who however were still strenuously opposed by Paoli and other leaders, and were unable thoroughly to assert their supremacy until 1774. After the French Revolution Paoli returned from England to Corsica, after an exile of 20 years, and became president of the island. Internal dissensions, however, again springing up, the English were invited by Paoli to his aid, and in 1794, under Hood, conquered the island. In 1796 they were compelled to abandon their conquest, and since that period Corsica has belonged to France.

Ajaccio.

Hôtel de France, in the Place d'Armes, at the corner of the Rue du Marché, R. 1½, Pension 6½ fr. per diem, déjeûner at 10, dinner at 5. 30 o'clock. **Hôtel du Nord**, Rue du Marché. — *Cafés:* Roi Jérôme, Napoléon, and Solferino in the Rue du Marché. — *Private rooms* 40 fr. per month (without attendance).

Banker: *M. Bozzo*, Boulevart Roi Jérôme.

Steamboats to Marseilles on Tuesdays at 10 a. m., to Nice every alternate Saturday.

Diligence daily to Bastia (p. 343), Sartona, and Vico. Office in the Cours Napoléon. *Post Office* in the same street.

Ajaccio (pronounced Ajassu in French), with 14,558 inhab., was founded by the Genoese in 1492, and constituted the capital of the island in 1811 by Napoleon, at the request of his mother Letitia. It is most beautifully situated in an extensive bay, which extends N. to the *Punta della Parata*, near the *Isole Sanguinarie*, and S. to the *Capo di Muro*, whilst the background is formed by imposing mountains, often covered with a snowy mantle until late in the summer. The town presents a somewhat deserted aspect, although great improvements have taken place of late years. The mildness of the climate attracts a number of invalids as winter-residents (about 150 in number, chiefly English and Germans).

The broad *Place* and *Rue du Marché*, one of the principal streets in the town, adorned with a fountain and a marble statue of Napoleon I., leads from the harbour to the *Place d'Armes*. To the r. in the Place du Marché, at the point where the *Boule-*

vart *Roi Jérôme* diverges, is situated the *Hôtel de Ville*, with a library on the ground-floor. On the first floor is the *Reception Hall, adorned with busts and pictures illustrative of the history of the family of Napoleon.

The *Rue Fesch*, the next street to the r., leads to the *Collége Fesch*, which contains a large collection of pictures, most of them copies, and casts (admission gratis on Sundays, 12—4 o'clock; at other times by payment of a fee), bequeathed to the town by Cardinal Fesch, and augmented by gifts from the Emperor. The court contains a statue of the cardinal in bronze.

Adjoining the college is the new and handsome *Chapelle Fesch*, to which the monuments of Letitia Ramolino, the mother of Napoleon (d. Feb. 2nd, 1836, in her palace at Rome), and of Cardinal Fesch (d. at Rome, 1839), her half-brother, have been recently transferred from the cathedral (p. 339).

By the street to the l. opposite to the fountain, then by the third transverse street to the r., the stranger reaches the small *Place Letizia*, where the house in which Napoleon was born is situated (the concierge lives opposite, fee 1 fr.). It is preserved in its original condition, but presents nothing remarkable beyond its historical association. A small room, with two windows, a cupboard in the wall, and a marble chimney-piece, is pointed out as that in which Napoleon was born (Aug. 15th, 1769).

The family of Buonaparte appears to have emigrated in the 16th cent. from Sarzana in Tuscany, perhaps with the powerful Malaspinas, to Corsica. Messire Francesco Buonaparte, the eldest of the family, died at Ajaccio, in 1567. Napoleon's father, Carlo Maria Buonaparte, born at Ajaccio, March 29th, 1746, was educated at a school founded by Paoli at Corte, and subsequently studied law at Pisa. He then became an advocate at Ajaccio, where he enjoyed considerable popularity, but was soon appointed by Paoli his secretary at Corte. After the disastrous battle of Ponte Nuovo, May 9th, 1769, in consequence of which Corsica lost its independence to France, Carlo fled with his young wife Letitia Ramolino to the Monte Rotondo. He shortly afterwards returned to Ajaccio, where the French General Marbeuf, the conqueror of Corsica, accorded him protection, and where, about two months later, Napoleon was born. In 1777 Carlo was appointed deputy of the nobility for Corsica, and travelled viâ Florence to Paris. He died at Montpellier in February, 1785. Napoleon, then 16 years of age, having quitted the school at Brienne two years previously, was studying at the École Militaire at Paris. The letter of condolence which he wrote to his mother on the occasion is still extant. During his visits to Ajaccio his favourite retreat was Milelli, a small country-house in the neighbourhood. After the storming of the Bastille in 1789 and the great succeeding crisis, Napoleon with his elder brother Joseph warmly espoused the popular cause at Ajaccio. He then repaired to Marseilles to welcome Paoli on his return from exile, and the latter prophesied on this occasion that a great destiny was in store for the youth. In 1791 Napoleon obtained the command of the newly constituted Corsican batallions, and in this capacity practically commenced his military career. In 1792, Paoli, dissatisfied with the proceedings of Napoleon, sent him to S. Bonifazio, to join the expedition against Sardinia. This, however, proved an utter failure, and on January 22th, 1793, Napoleon narrowly escaped being slain by insurgents. Shortly afterwards he broke off his connection with Paoli and was compelled to quit Corsica with his family. During the zenith of his power the Emperor evinced little partiality for his native island, which he visited for the last time on September 29th, 1799, on his return from Egypt. During his exile in the island of St. Helena, however, his thoughts appear frequently to have reverted to Corsica. 'What reminiscences Corsica has left to me!' he was frequently heard to exclaim; 'I still think with pleasure of its mountains and its beautiful scenery; I still remember the fragrance which it exhales.' Antommarchi, Napoleon's physician in St. Helena, and the priest Vignale, who performed the last offices of religion, were Corsicans, and shared the fate of their illustrious compatriot.

The *Cathedral*, dating from the Genoese period, where Napoleon was baptized on July 22nd, 1771, formerly contained the monuments already mentioned.

The *Place d'Armes* is adorned with a bronze statue of the great Emperor, his looks turned towards the sea in the direction of France, surrounded by his four brothers Joseph, Lucien, Louis, and Jerome. The inscription records that the monument was erected by 'grateful Corsica' by voluntary subscription, and inaugurated in 1865.

In the Cours Napoléon, which diverges opposite this Place, is situated the palace of the *Pozzo di Borgo*, one of the most distinguished Corsican families. Carlo Andrea Pozzo di Borgo, born on March 8th, 1768, an early friend of Napoleon, a democrat and adherent of Paoli, afterwards became the Emperor's bitterest enemy. He subsequently became a Russian counsellor of state, and in 1802 was created a count and appointed ambassador, in which capacity he indefatigably devoted his energies to opposing his ambitious countryman. He proved a great benefactor to Corsica, which he frequently visited. He died at Paris in 1842. His nephew, the heir to his extensive property, afterwards fell a victim to Corsican revenge.

The Cours Napoléon terminates in the high road to Bastia. To the r., outside the gate, is the monument of *General Abbatucci*, a Corsican who fell in 1796, whilst defending the town of Huningue. This road affords a pleasant and cheerful promenade. Adjoining it is the Botanical Garden which merits a visit.

The road on the N. side of the bay, passing the new *Hospice Eugénie*, although destitute of shade, also affords a charming walk. The gardens here contain numerous family burialplaces and chapels.

From Ajaccio to S. Bonifacio, and to Bastia by the E. Coast.

The carriage-road from Ajaccio to Calvi (p. 344) is not yet entirely completed. Diligence as far as Vico. — From Ajaccio to Bonifacio by the road 85 M.; diligence daily to Sartena, 52 M. distant.

The fortress of **Bonifacio** (3589 ft.) is picturesquely situated on a prominent and lofty rock. It possesses high and dilapidated houses, of the Pisan and Genoese periods, and narrow, unattractive streets. The principal street is termed *Piazza Doria*. The town was founded in 883 by the Tuscan Marquis Bonifazio, after a naval victory over the Saracens. *Il Torrione*, a large tower of that remote date, is still extant. Bonifacio subsequently came into the possession of the Pisans, then into that of the Genoese, by whom it was treated with marked favour. In return for this partiality this town, as well as Calvi, remained inviolably faithful to Genoa, as was proved in 1420 by its memorable defence against King Alphonso I. of Arragon. In 1541 the Emp. Charles V., on his return from the expedition against Algiers, paid a visit to Bonifacio. The house of Filippo Cataccioli, in which the Emperor lodged, is still pointed out. The town once boasted of 20 churches, of which the cathedral of *S. Maria del Fico*, the handsome Gothic church of *S. Domenico*, with numerous tombstones of Templar knights and Genoese nobles, and the small church of *S. Francesco* (with a spring, the only one which the town possesses) now alone remain.

A stone bench above the Marina of Bonifacio, by the old gate of the fortress, near the small chapel of *S. Rocco*, commands a charming *view, especially by evening-light, of the strait, which separates Corsica from Sardinia. On the opposite coast the town of *Lunga Sardo*, with its lighthouse, is visible; farther distant, a series of watch-towers on the shore may be distinguished; on the l. lies the island of *S. Maddalena*. On the coast below Bonifacio are situated three beautiful and imposing *Grottoes*, which visitors explore by boat.

The distance from Bonifacio to Bastia is 92¹/₂ M. The E. coast of Corsica is somewhat bleak and desolate. The road leads past the bay of *S. Manza* to (16¹/₄ M.) *Porto Vecchio*, the only good harbour constructed by the Genoese, and supposed to occupy the site of the ancient Portus Syracusanorum. Hence to the mouth of the *Tavignano* (no bridge) 44¹/₂ M., where, near the lake of *Diana*, the ancient town of *Aleria* was situated. Fragments of masonry and vaulting, and remnants of a circus are still to be seen. Coins, vases, and inscriptions have also been found here. The modern Aleria consists of the Genoese castle and a small group of houses only, for this coast, owing to the want of cultivation, is marshy and unhealthy. Here, on March 12th, 1736, the adventurer Neuhof landed from an English vessel, and on April 15th was crowned king, a dignity he enjoyed for a very brief period. On the heights, 16 M. farther N., lies *Cervione*, where Neuhof once held his court. The river *Golo*, often nearly dry in summer, is next crossed. In the extensive plain at its mouth, on the l. bank, once lay *Mariana*, the Roman colony founded by Marius, the remains of which are visible on the shore, 3 M. from the road. The ruins of a beautiful chapel, and of a church termed *La Canonica*, a basilica of noble proportions, in the Pisan style, are situated here.

From Ajaccio to Bastia.

95 M. Diligence daily in 20 hrs., usually starting at 11 a. m., and halting for dinner at Vivario at 7 p. m. (dinner at Corte on the return-journey). The service is well performed, and horses are changed frequently. Intérieur 16, coupé 24 fr.; from Ajaccio to Corte 12 and 18 fr. — Omnibus from Corte to Bastia daily at 6 a. m. in 8—10 hrs.

The road traverses the well cultivated plain of *Campoloro* (i. e. *Campo dell' Oro*), which extends to the S. half of the bay of Ajaccio, and is watered by the *Gravone*. The road follows the stream and ascends. The scenery gradually becomes more attractive, magnificent forests clothe the slopes, and several beautiful retrospects are enjoyed. Beyond *Bogognano* (25 M. from Ajaccio) the Gravone is quitted, and a mountain, 3672 ft. high, traversed. On the N. towers the *Monte d'Oro*, a few hundred feet lower than Monte Rotondo (p. 342), but of more imposing proportions; on the S. rises the *Monte Renoso*. The road next traverses the great forest of *Vizzarona*, and descends rapidly to the pleasant mountain-village of *Vivario*. It then turns N. and skirts the base of the Monte Rotondo, leading through a wooded and well-cultivated tract, past the villages of *Serraggio*, *Capo Vecchio*, *S. Pietro*, and *Corte*. Pursuing the same direction, the road next reaches the *Golo*, the principal river of the island, at *Ponte alla Leccia*, 12$^1/_2$ M. from Corte.

A road leads hence to Calvi, 46$^1/_4$ M. distant, to which a diligence runs. It proceeds to the E. by Morosaglia and Porta, and descends to the coast. *Porta* was the birthplace (1775) of Marshal Sebastiani (d. at Paris in 1851), father of the Duchess of Praslin, who was murdered by her husband in 1847. Several miles higher up lies the Canton *Rostino*, or *Morosaglia*, the native place of the Paoli family. A dilapidated cottage is still pointed out in the hamlet of Stretta, as that in which Pasquale Paoli was born in 1724. His father Hyacinth was a physician and poet, and at the same time leader of the Corsicans; his mother Dionysia Valentina was a native of the neighbouring *Pontenuovo*. Anecdotes of his noble and heroic character are still current in this district; his memory is also perpetuated by a school, established in an old monastery at Morosaglia with funds bequeathed by him for the purpose. An apartment in the same monastery was once occupied by Pasquale Paoli as his study, and here his elder brother Clement, once a general, afterwards a monk, died in 1793. The latter, who distinguished himself at the battle of Borgo, on the river Golo (see below), in 1768, was endowed with the same noble and heroic disposition as his brother.

The road to Bastia follows the r. bank of the Golo, which it crosses at (5 M.) *Pontenuovo*. Here, on May 9th, 1769, the decisive battle was fought, by which the subjugation of Corsica was effected. The Golo is followed as far as the point where the road unites with that from Bonifazio (p. 339).

A road leads S. from the river to (4$^3/_4$ M.) the village of *Vescovato*, situated among mountains and forests of chestnuts, and containing the house of Pietro Filippini, the Corsican historian of the 16th cent. His work was republished at Pisa in 1827, having been edited by the learned Gregori at the instance of the Corsican Pozzo di Borgo. Here also is situated the château of Count Matteo Buttafuoco (now the property of the family of Marshal Sebastiani), who when a young French officer invited Rousseau to Vescovato, in consequence of the following passage in his 'Contrat Social' alluding to the Corsicans: 'The vigour and perseverance with which these brave people have succeeded in gaining and defending their liberty merit for them that some wise man should teach them how to preserve it. I have a certain presentiment that this island will one day cause astonishment to the whole of Europe'. The latter prediction was fulfilled 20 years after Rousseau's death (1778), although in a very different manner from that which the philosopher had in view.

The road now leads direct to the N.; the coast-district is flat and full of lagoons. To the l. on the hill lies *Borgo*, where the French were defeated by Clement Paoli, Oct. 1st, 1768.

Corte and the Monte Rotondo.

Corte (**Hôtel de l'Europe*, with two cafés and the diligence-office, at the extremity of the town towards Bastia; déjeûner at 11, dîner at 6 o'clock), with 5754 inhab., a sous-préfecture and capital of an Arrondissement, lies on the *Tavignano*, surrounded by mountains. It is commanded by a lofty citadel, which rendered it an important and keenly-contested point in the wars of former centuries. In Paoli's time it was the central point of his democratic government. His study, with window-shutters lined with cork, by way of additional precaution, and the council-chambers are still shown at the *Palazzo di Corte*. An university, printing-office, and newspaper were also established here by Paoli. The Corsican parliament of that period held its sessions at the neighbouring Franciscan monastery. Marble-quarries are worked in the vicinity.

The *Place Paoli*, the principal square, is embellished with a bronze statue of the noble-minded patriot, erected in 1854. Two or three hundred Arabian shikhs and cadis from Algiers, who took an active part in the late insurrections, are incarcerated in the citadel here.

The **Monte Rotondo** is most conveniently ascended from Corte. The night after the ascent may be spent in one of the uninviting chalets at the base, or the traveller may prefer to return to Corte on the same day. In the latter case a journey of 14 hrs. at least, partly on horseback, partly on foot, must be reckoned upon. Guide and mule about 20 fr. A supply of provisions necessary. The ascent is not easily accomplished except in the summer months. At an early hour the traveller ascends the valley of the wild *Restonica*, which here falls into the Tavignano after a course of 35 M. A broad and wooded dale is at first traversed, beyond which the path becomes a mere shepherd's track. Pine and larch forest afford shade, whilst bleak open tracts and sequestered chalets, some of them 5000 ft. above the sea-level, are also occasionally passed. After a ride of 3 hrs., the *Rota del Dragone*, a grotto in the rocks affording shelter to 200 sheep and goats, recalling Homer's description of the Cave of Polyphemus, is attained. The *Co di Mazzo*, the last shepherds' station, inhabited only during the summer, is reached after 2 hrs. more. These rude hovels, beautifully situated on one of the lower buttresses of the Monte Rotondo, afford shelter for the night in case of necessity (milk and cheese only to be had). Then across several rocky ridges in 2 hrs. more to the *Trigione*, the last spur of the Rotondo, a wilderness of blocks of granite. The crater-shaped, snow-capped summit is visible hence; below it lies the small and clear *Lago di Monte Rotondo*; in the foreground, green pastures. Fields of snow and ice, rising from the lake, must be laboriously traversed (2 hrs.) before the summit (9053 ft.) is attained. A magnificent *Panorama is here enjoyed. The spectator surveys the greater part of the island; N. the Capo Corso; W. the bays of Porto, Sagona and Ajaccio; E. the blue Mediterranean, with the islands of Monte Cristo, Pianosa, Capraia, and Elba, and the mainland of Italy; then the white Alpes Maritimes, extending from Toulon and Nice to Genoa. Corsica itself resembles a vast rocky relief-map; its principal mountain-chains, with their rivers and valleys, are distinctly recognisable. Towards the

S., however, the view is obstructed by the broad and massive Monte d'Oro. In the neighbourhood of the summit lie a number of desolate valleys, in most of which small lakes are situated. Their discharge descends to form the Restonica. The descent may be made on the side next to the *Lago di Pozzolo*, where the dark rocky pyramid of the *Frate* (monk) rises. Violets and forget-me-not (here popularly termed the 'marvellous flower of the mountains') grow abundantly in the rocky clefts on the banks of the lake. The muffro, or mufflone, the wild horned sheep of Corsica, of a dark brown colour, with silky hair, browses on these lofty summits. Bandits (i. e. outlaws, those under a ban) are also occasionally encountered, but these unfortunate outcasts seldom or never molest strangers (comp. p. 336). The huts of Co di Mazzo may now be regained in 3 hrs., and Corte in 4—5 hrs. more.

Bastia.

*Hôtel de l'Europe, Rue de l'Intendance, 6 fr. per diem; Hôtels de France and d'Italie in the Boulevart de Paoli. — Restaurant de la Paix, in the Boulevart; Café Univers Guitton.

Diligences daily to Ajaccio, to Luri and Rogliano on the Capo Corso, and to S. Fiorenzo and Balagna.

Steamboat Offices: Valery Co. (to Nice), near the harbour; Vapori Italiani (to Leghorn), in the Boulevart.

Bastia, with 21,535 inhab., the busiest commercial place in the island, and till 1811 its capital, was founded in 1380 by the Genoese and defended by a strong castle (whence the name of the town, signifying 'bastion'). The cathedral of *S. Giovanni Battista* contains several ancient tombs. In *S. Croce* rich decorations in marble. The former college of the Jesuits contains a library of 30,000 vols. and natural history collections. The Promenade on the coast is embellished with a marble statue of Napoleon. The inscription mentions Corsica, in consequence of its connection with Napoleon, as '*quasi gentium principatu donatam.*' (!)

The old town with the citadel rises above the more modern quarter situated near the harbour. Beautiful walk along the coast towards the N., where a number of easily attained heights afford a variety of fine views of the sea and coast.

From Bastia to Capo Corso, S. Fiorenzo, and Calvi.

A very attractive excursion may be made to the long and narrow peninsula in which the *Serra Mts.* rise, culminating in the Monte Alticcione and Monte Stello (5000 ft.), and terminating in the Capo Corso (*Promontorium Sacrum*) on the N. Beautiful valleys descend from these mountains on the E. and W. A good road leads along the coast from Bastia, passing several ancient watch-towers of the Pisans and Genoese, and affording a view of the picturesque islands of Elba, Capraia, and Monte Cristo. At *Brando* there is a *Stalactite Cavern*, surrounded by pleasant gardens. *Luri* possesses a charming valley, watered by several streams, and producing a luxuriant growth of grapes, oranges and lemons. The Serra is then crossed to *Pino* on the W. side, with villas and beautiful gardens. At the extremity of the promontory, to the N. beyond *Rogliano* and *Ersa*, rises a lighthouse. An ancient, half-ruined circular structure near it is popularly, but groundlessly termed the 'Tower of Seneca'.

A road leads from Bastia across the Serra to the (13³/₄ M.) small seaport of **S. Fiorenzo**, charmingly situated on the bay of that name on the W. side of the island, and commanded by a fort. In the neighbouring low ground formerly lay the mediæval town of *Nebbio*, the ruined cathedral of which *(S. Maria Assunta)*, of the 12th cent., stands on an eminence. The road proceeds hence in the vicinity of the sea, crosses the small river *Ostriconi*, and reaches the small, but thriving seaport-town of *Isola Rossa*, founded in 1758 by Pasquale Paoli, notwithstanding the war in which he was then engaged with Genoa. Its appellation is derived from three red cliffs rising from the sea in front of the harbour. The environs are delightful; the view from the *Monte S. Reparata*, surmounted by a deserted church, is especially beautiful by evening-light.

The road then leads to *Algajola*, a deserted old town on the coast, with marble quarries in the vicinity. During the Genoese period it was fortified, and formed the central point of the fertile district of *Balagna*. The loftily situated village of *Lumio*, farther on, with its orange-plantations and hedges of cactus, commands a beautiful view of the valley and the town of Calvi (43 M. from S. Fiorenzo), an important and fortified place during the Genoese period, noted for its faithful adherence to the Republic, and in 1794 bravely defended against the English by the French commandant Casabianca. The natives of the place maintain that Columbus was born here, and that the name still exists. Traces of the English bombardment are still observable. The principal church contains the tombs of the Baglioni family, who bore the surname Libertà, from having distinguished themselves in the 15th and 16th cent. The environs of Calvi are marshy. Charming view of the bay, with the promontory of *Rivellata*, and of the rocky mountains of *Calenzana*, to the E. of the town.

A diligence runs from *Calvi*, traversing the beautiful and fruitful valley of the *Balagna* (where the powerful Malaspina family dwelt for centuries), enclosed by lofty mountains, to *Novella*, the last village, then through narrow rocky ravines to *Ponte alla Leccia* in the valley of the Golo, where the high road from Bastia to Ajaccio is reached.

INDEX.

Abano 179.
S. Abbondio 129. 134.
Acqua Buja 258.
Acqualagna 242.
Acquanegra 155.
Acqui 146.
Adda, the 49. 55. etc.
Adelsberg 68.
Adige, the 53. 164. etc.
Adria 180.
Adriatic, the 216. 237. etc.
Aemilia, Via 216.
S. Agăta 138.
Agay 27.
Agedincum 2.
S. Agnese 99.
Agno, the 135.
Agram 67.
Agums 53.
Ajaccio 337.
Aigle 35.
Aiguebelle 31.
Aigues Mortes 18.
Ain, the 6. 29.
Ainay 8.
Airan 18.
Airolo 42.
Aix 21.
Aix-les-Bains 30.
Alà 63.
Alais 18.
Alassio 96.
Alba 109.
Albaredo, Monte 81.
Albarine, the 29.
Albenga 96.
S. Alberto 235.
Albesio 123.
Albigaunum 96.
Albĭnen 36.
Albissola 95.
Albizzate 131.
Aleria 340.
Alessandria 145.
Alfonsine 256.
Algabi Gallery, the 37.
Algajola 344.
Aloxe 4.
Alpes Maritimes, the 108.
Alpienbach, the 37.
Alpines, the 16.
Alseno 217.
Alserio, Lago 122.
Alticcione, Monte 343.
Altinum 213.

Altopascio 277.
Altorf 40.
Alvernia 334.
Ambérieux 29.
Ambrogiana. Villa 261.
S. Ambrogio (near Modena) 218.
— (near Turin) 33.
— (near Varese) 136.
St. Amour 6.
Amstäg 41.
Ancona 243.
Ancone, the 80.
Andeer 47.
Andermatt 42.
Andes 171.
St. André, Grotto of 105.
— château 105.
St. Andrea del Lido, island 216.
Anemo 235.
Angera 141.
Anges, Baie des 103.
Annōne 86.
—, Lago d' 124.
Antibes 28.
Antipolis 28.
S. Antonio 56.
—, Cantoniera 42.
Anzasca Valley 37.
Aosta 83.
Apennines, the 84. 145. 335. etc.
Aposa, the 226.
Aprica 161.
—, Passo d' 161.
Aquae Allobrogum or
— *Gratianae* 30.
— *Patavinae* 179.
— *Sextiae* 21.
— *Statielae* 146.
Aquileia 215.
Arausio 12.
Arbedo 44. 51.
Arc, the 31.
S. Arcangelo 237.
Archiano, the 334.
Arco 62.
Arcola 263.
Arcole 172.
Arcs, Les 27.
Arda, the 217.
Ardo, the 214.
Ardon 35.
Arelate 19.

Arena-Po 84.
Arenzano 95.
Arezzo 335.
Argegno 126.
Argenta 256.
Ariminum 237.
Arlberg, the 52.
Arles 19.
Armançon, the 2.
Armeno 143.
Arno, the 260. 286. etc.
Arola 144.
Arona 141.
Arquà 180.
Arquata 146.
Ascona 138.
Asiago 61.
Asigliano 110.
Aspremont, the 105.
Assenza 151.
Assina, Vall' 122.
Asso 122.
Asti 86.
Astico, the 61.
Ateste 180.
Athenaeum 8.
Atlitzgraben, the Obere and Untere 65.
Atzwang 59.
Aubagne 26.
Auer 59.
Augusta Praetoria Salassorum 83.
— *Taurinorum* 73.
Ausa, the 237.
Auxerre 2.
Auximum 245.
Avenio 14.
Avenza 264.
Averser Rhein, the 47.
Avigliana 33.
Avignon 14.
Avio 63.
Avisio, the 60.
Axenberg, the 40.
Axenstein 40.
Azi, Mont d' 30.

Bacchiglione, the 173.
Bacher Mts., the 66.
Badagnano 85.
Badelwand, the 65.
Baden 64.
Bagnacavallo 248.
Bagni 179.

Bagni Caldi 277.
— di S. Giuliano 274.
— di Lucca 277.
— di Nerone 277.
Bagnolo 155. 171.
Bagneau 27.
Balagna 344.
Baldichiēri 86.
Baldo Monte 63. 154.
Balerno 132.
Bâle 5.
Balferin, the 36.
Balino 154.
Balzola 110.
Bandol 26.
Bar 28.
Baracca 262.
Baradello, Castello 122.
Barbentane 16.
Barberino 258.
Bard 33. 81.
Bard, Fort 81.
Bardolino 154.
Bardonnêche 32.
Bärenburg, the 47.
Bargilio 277.
Barni 122.
Baro, Monte 130.
Barrasso 131.
S. Bartŏlo 70.
—, Monte 240.
S. Bartolommeo', Monte 152.
Bassano 61.
Bastia 343.
Bâtie, chât. 30.
Battaglia 180.
—, Canale di 179.
Raveno 38. 139.
Beaucaire 16.
Beaulieu 106.
Beaune 4.
Beauregard, chât. 12.
Beckenried 40.
Bédarrides 13.
Bedretto, Val 42.
Belbo, the 109.
Belfort 5.
Belgiojoso 154.
Belgirate 141.
Bella, Isola 130.
Bellaggio 126.
—, the Punta di 128.
Bellano 129.
Bellegarde 29.
Bellinzago 145.
Bellinzona 44.
Belluno 214.
Benacus, Lacus 151.
S. Benedetto 171. 236.
Beni, Monte 258.
Berceau, the 99.
Bergamasco 109.

Bergamo 149.
Bergeggi, promont. 95.
Berici, Monti 172. 174.
Berisal 36.
Bernabò 277.
St. Bernard, the Great 83.
S. Bernardino Pass, the 50.
S. Bernardino 50.
Bernina, the 56.
Berre 21.
Bertinoro 236.
Besançon 5.
Beseno, castle 62.
Bevera, the 107.
Beverin, Piz 46.
Bex 35.
Bezzecca 154.
S. Biagio, Isola di 152.
Bianco Canal, the 180.
Biandrone, Lago di 131.
Biasca 43.
Bibbiena 334.
Biella 110.
Bientina, Lago di 260.
Bietschhorn, the 36.
Binago 131.
Binasco 147.
Bironico 44.
Bisbino, Monte 125.
Bisenzio, the 281.
Bissone 133.
Bistriza, the 68.
Biturrita 13,
Blaisy-Bas 3.
Blegno, Val 43.
Blumau 59.
Boara 180.
Bobbio 85.
Bodio 43.
Boesio, the 131.
Bogliaco 153.
Bogognano 340.
Bois-le-Roi 1.
Boletto 144.
Bolladore 56.
Bologna 225.
 *Accademia delle Belle Arti 231.
 Archives 231.
 Arciginnasio 228.
 *S.Bartolommeo di Porta Ravegnana 232.
 Biblioteca comun. 228.
 *S. Cecilia 230.
 *Certosa 233.
 Collegio di Spagna 233.
 *S. Domenico 229.
 S. Giacōmo Maggiore 229.
 *S. Giovanni in Monte 230.
 Library 231.

Bologna:
 *Madonna di S. Luca 234.
 S.Martino Maggiore 230.
 *S. Michele in Bosco 233.
 La Montagnola 233.
 Museum of Antiquities 231.
 Palazzo Arcivescovile 230.
 *— Baciocchi 232.
 — Bargellini 232.
 — Bentivoglio 232.
 — Bevilacqua Vincenzi 233.
 — Fava 233.
 *— della Mercanzia 232.
 *— Pepòli 233.
 — del Podestà 227.
 — Pubblico 227.
 — Tanari 233.
 — Zambeccari di S. Paŏlo 233.
 *— Zampieri 233.
 *S. Petronio 228.
 *Piazza Vittorio Emanuele 227.
 S. Pietro 230.
 Portico de' Banchi 228.
 *S. Stefano 229.
 Torre Asinelli 232.
 Torre Garisenda 232.
 *University 230.
 *S. Vitale ed Agricola 230.
Bolzanēto 146.
Bolzāno 111.
Bolzano s. Bozen.
Bonaduz 46.
S. Bonifacio 172.
Bonifacio (Cors.) 339.
Bononia 226.
Bonowicz, château 67.
Borbone, the 86.
Bordighera 97.
Borghetto 262.
Borgio 96.
Borgo 61.
— (Corsica) 341.
— a Bugiano 278.
— S. Dalmazzo 107.
— San Donnino 217.
— Lavezzaro 145.
— S. Martino 110.
— Panigale 257.
— Sesia 144.
— Ticino 145.
— Vercelli 110.
— Vico 125.
Borgoforte 171.
Borgomanero 111.
Borigli, the 99.
Bormida, the 146.
Bormio 55.

INDEX. 347

Borromean Islands, the 139.
Boruniza, the 68.
Bosaro 180.
Bourg 29
Bourg St. Andéol 12.
Bourget, Lac du 30.
Bourgogne, the Canal de 2.
Bouveret 34.
Bozen 59.
Bozzolo 172.
Brà 109.
Bracco 262.
Bramans d'Essillon 32.
Brandizzo 110.
Brando 343.
Branzoll 59.
Brauglio, the 55.
Braus, Col di 107.
Brè 135.
—, Monte 135.
Bregaglia, Val 49.
Breglio 107.
Brenner 57.
Brennersee, the 57.
Brenno, the 43.
Breno 160.
Brenta, the 61. 174.
Brescia 155.
Bressana 149.
Bressanone 58.
Bresse, the 29.
Briançon 80.
Brianza, the 121.
Brieg 36.
Brienno 126.
Briglia, La 282.
Briona 144.
Brione, Monte 153.
Brionian Islands, the 70.
Brissago 138.
Brixen 58.
Brixener Klause, the 58.
Broteaux, les 7.
Brou, Church of 29.
Brouis, Col di 107.
Brozzi 261.
Bruck 65.
Brunn 64.
Brunnen 40.
Brunnsee, château 66.
Bruno 109.
Brunoy 1.
Buccione 143.
Buche di Vela 62.
Buffalora, the 50.
Buochs 39.
—, Lake of 39.
Buon-Consiglio, castle 60.
Buràno 212.
Burgeis 53.
Bürgenstock, the 39.
Bürglen 41.

Busalla 146.
Busto Arsizio 142.
Buttier, the 83.
Buttrio 215.

Cabbe 99.
Cabbiolo 50.
Cabillonum 4.
Cadempino 45.
Cadenabbia 126.
Cadenazzo 44.
Caesarea 248.
Cafaggiolo 258.
Cagne 28.
Cairo 146.
Calamandrana 109.
Calanda, the 45.
Calcababbio 149.
Calcaccia, the 43.
Calceranica 61.
Calci, Valle dei 272.
Caldiero 172.
Caldonazzo 61.
Calenzana 344.
Calenzano 282.
Calliano 62.
Caltignaga 111.
Calūso 81.
Calvaggione, Mte. 132.
Calvi 344.
Calvo, Monte 105.
Cama 50.
Camaldoli 334.
Camargue, the 21.
Cambiàno 86.
Camerlata 122.
Camignone 159.
Camnago 122.
Camoghè, Monte 44.
Camogli 262.
Camonica, Val 160.
Campaldino 333.
Campi 154.
Campitello 172.
Campo (Lake of Como) 126.
— (Lake of Garda) 154.
— Dolcino 48.
— Formio 214.
Campoloro 340.
Camporciero, Val di 82.
Camporosso 99.
Canaria Valley, the 42.
Candelo 110.
Canelli 109.
Canněro 138.
Cannes 27.
Cannet 28.
Canobbio 138.
Canonica, La 340.
Canossa 218.
Canova 46.
Cantalupo 109.
Cantone, Isòla del 146.

Canzo 122.
Caorso 163.
Capella Mts., the 71.
Capo d'Istria 70. 216.
— Nero 97.
— Verde 97.
— Vecchio 340.
Capo di Ponte (near Belluno) 214.
— (Val Camonica) 160.
Capolago 132.
Capraja 261.
Caprese 335.
Caprino, Monte 135.
Carate 125.
Caravaggio 162.
Carelli, Monte 258.
Carema 81.
Careno 126.
Cariguano 109.
Carlotta, Villa 127.
Carmagnola 109.
Carnian Alps, the 67.
Carona 135.
Carpentoracte 13.
Carpentras 13.
Carpi 171.
Carrara 264.
Carsaniga 121.
Carso, the 68.
Casalbuttano 162.
Casale 110.
Casalecchio 257.
Casaletto 162.
Casalmaggiore 172.
Casalpusterlengo 155. 216.
Casarsa 214.
Casarza 262.
Cascina 260.
Case Bruciate 243.
Casentino, Valley 333.
Caslino 122.
Cassano 123. 149.
St. Cassien 28.
Cassina 132.
Cassis 26.
Cassone 154.
Castagnole 109.
Castagnovizza 215.
Casteggio 84.
Castel Arquato 217.
— Bolognese 234.
— S. Giovanni 84.
— Guelfo 217.
— S. Leo 239.
— Maggiore 184.
— S. Pietro 234.
— S. Niccolo 334.
Castelfidardo 246.
Castelfranco (Romagna) 218.
— (Venetia) 61.
Castellaro 99.

INDEX.

Castellatsch 47.
Castelletto 154.
Castello 154. 282.
Castellone 162.
Castellucchio 172.
Castelnuovo 109. 151.
Castiglione 172.
S. Caterina 55.
Catini, Monte 278.
Cattajo, castle 179.
Cattolica, La 239.
Cava 149.
Cava Tigozzi 155.
Cavaller Maggiore 109.
Cavo Tassone, Canal 184.
Cazzanore 123.
Celle 95. 256.
Cembra, Val 60.
Cemenelium 104.
Ceneda 214.
Cenère, Monte 44.
Cenis, Mont 32.
Centallo 108.
Cento 184.
Centre, the Canal du 4.
Ceppina 55.
Ceraino 63.
Ceresio, the Lago 132.
Ceriale 96.
Cerro 86.
Certosa di Bologna 233.
— di Pavia 147.
— di Pisa 272.
— di Val d'Ema 326.
— di Val Pésio 108.
Ceruso, the 95.
Cervia 256.
Cervione 340.
Cervo 96.
Cesanne 80.
Cesena 236.
Cesenatico 256.
Cessano, the 243.
Cesson 1.
Cetica 333.
Cette 19.
—, Le 332.
Cézy 2.
Chablis 2.
Chagny 4.
Challant, Val de 82.
Chalon-sur-Saône 4.
St. Chamas 21.
Chambave 82.
Chambéry 30.
Chambre, La 31.
Chamousset 31.
Champorcher, Val 82.
Charenton 1.
Charmettes, Les 30.
Chasse 10.
Chat, Mont du 30.
Châteauneuf 12.

Château Neuf (Nice) 105.
Châtillon (near Aosta) 82.
— (Savoy) 30.
Châtillon-sur-Seine 3.
Chauve, Mont 105.
Chegino 143
Chernex 34.
Chevalier, Mont 28.
Chiana, Val di 335.
Chiasso 132.
—, Ponte 132.
Chiavari 262.
Chiavenna 49.
—, the 163.
Chiese, the 151.
Chignin, chât. 30.
Chignolo 155.
Chillon, castle of 34.
Chioggia 213.
Chiusa di Verona 63.
Chiusi 335.
Chivasso 81. 110.
Chur 45.
Churburg, the 53.
Cicognolo 172.
Cilli 66.
Cimella or
Cimiès 104.
Cimone, Monte 225. 333.
Ciotat, La 26.
Ciraun 47.
Ciriaco, Monte 244.
Cisano 154.
Cittanova 70.
Cittiglio 131.
Civate 124.
Civenna 122.
Civiasco 144.
Cividale 215.
Cividate 160.
Clarens 34.
Claro 43.
Clastidium 84.
Claudia Celleia 66.
Clavenna 49.
Clusium Novum 335.
Coccaglio 150.
Cocina 153.
Cocquio 131.
Codogno 155. 216.
Codroipo 214.
Cogoleto 95.
Coire 45.
Colico 49. 130.
Collonges 29.
Colma, Col di 144.
Colombano, Monte 55.
Colombier, the 29.
Colonges 34.
Colorno 172.
Comabbio, Lago di 131.
Comacina, Isola 126.
Combs-la-Ville 1.

Comerio 131.
Como 122.
—, the Lake of 124.
Compiobbi 331.
Conca, the 289.
Conegliano 214.
Conero, Monte 245.
Confinale, Monte 55.
Coni 108.
Consandolo 256.
Consuma Pass, the 333.
Coppa, the 84.
Corciago 37.
Corenno 129.
Corgoloin 4.
Cormons 215.
Corniche, Route de la 99.
Cornigliano 95.
Cornio, Col di 108.
Corno, the 214.
— dei tre Signori 54.
Correggio 218.
Corsalone, the 334.
Corsica 335.
Corso, Capo 343.
Corte 341.
Cortèno 161.
Corteolona 155.
Corticella 184.
Cosciago 131.
St. Côme 4.
Costigliole 109.
Côte d'Or, the 3. 4.
Côte Rôtie, La 11.
Cottian Alps, the 73.
Courmayeur 83.
Courthézon 13.
Covelo 61.
Covigliajo 258.
Crau, the plain of 21.
Crédo, Tunnel du 29.
Crema 162.
Cremeo 50.
Cremia 129.
Cremona 162.
Cremusina, La 43.
Cresciano 43.
Crestola, Monte 264.
Creuzot 4.
Crevola 37.
Cribiaschina, the 43.
Cristallo, Monte 54.
Croce 136.
—, Capo della 96.
—, Santa- 214.
Crocetta, La 218.
Crocione, Monte 127. 136.
Croisette, Cap de la 28.
Croisière, La 12.
Croix Rousse, La 6.
Crostolo, the 217.
Crussol 11.
Cucciago 122.

INDEX. 349

Cularo 11.
Culoz 29.
Cumano 154.
Cuneo 108.
Curone, the 83.
—, Ponte 83.
Curtalone 172.
Curver, Piz 46.
Custozza 63. 169.
Cuvio, Val 131.
St. Cyr 26.

Dala, the Ravine of the 35.
Daila 70.
S. Dalmazzo 107.
—, Abbey 107.
S. Damiano 86.
Darfo 160.
Dazio Grande 43.
Dertona 83.
Dervio 129.
Desago 135.
Desenzano 152.
Desio 121.
Devil's Bridge, the 41.
Diana, lake of 340.
Diano Castello 96.
— Marino 96.
Diavolo, Ponte del 56.
Diecimo 277.
Dijon 3.
Disentis 46.
Disgrazia, Monte della 57.
Divazze 68.
Divēria, the 37.
Docce Basse 277.
Doccia, La, Villa 329. 289.
Doire, the 81 82 etc.
Dolce Acqua 99.
Dolo 174.
Domaso 130.
Domegliarà 63.
Domleschg 46.
Domo d'Ossöla 37.
Donat 47.
Dongo 129.
Donnaz 81.
S. Donnino 261.
Donzères 12.
Dora Baltea, the 81. 83. etc.
— Riparia, the 33. 110. etc.
Dorio 129.
Dos Trento 60.
Dossobuono 169.
Doubs, the 5.
Draguignan 27.
Drappo 107.
Drau, the 66.
Drena, Castello di 62.
Drò 62.

Drôme, the 11.
Druentia 16.
Duggia, Val 144.
Duino 215.
Durance, the 16. 80.

Ecluse, Fort de l' 39.
Edolo 161.
Eggenberg, castle 65.
Egna 59.
Ehrenhausen 66.
Eichberg 65.
Einshorn, the 47.
Eisack, the 58. 59.
S. Elena, island 216.
Ema, the 326.
Empoli 261.
Ems 45.
Endoume 25.
Enguiso 154.
Enza, the 217.
Epierre 31.
Eporedia 81.
Era, the 260.
Erba 123.
Ersa 343.
Ermitage, the 11.
Erstfelden 41.
Escarène 107.
Esino, the 243.
L'Estaque 21.
Este 180.
Estérel, Mont d' 27.
Estressin 10.
St. Etienne-du-Bois 6.
L'Etoile 12.
Etsch, the 53 etc.
Euganean Mts., the 179.
Eza 100.

Faenza 235.
Faesulae 330.
Faido 43.
Falconara 243.
Falterona, Monte 333.
Fano 242.
Fautiscritti 264.
Fara 144.
Fardün, castle 47.
Fariolo or Feriolo 38. 139.
Fasana 70.
Faventia 235.
Felizzano 86.
Felsberg 45.
Felsina 226.
Fenestrelle 80.
Fenis, castle 82.
Feriolo or Fariolo 38. 139.
Ferrara 180.
Ferrera 33.
— Valley, the 47.
Feysin 10.

Fiave 154.
Fidentia Julia 217.
Ficsole 329.
Figline 282.
Filigare 257.
Finale 96.
Finstermünz 53.
Fiora 40.
S. Fiorenzo 344.
Fiorio, Villa 153.
Firenze 282.
Firenzuola 217.
Fitznau 39.
Fiumalbo 225.
Fiume 71.
Fiume Latte 128.
Fivizzano 218.
Flamboin 2.
Florence 282.
 *Accademia delle Belle Arti 308.
 *SS. Annunziata 306.
 *Archives 298.
 Badia 305.
 Bargello 302.
 Base di S. Lorenzo 311.
 *Battistero 299.
 Bazaar 299.
 *Bello Sguardo 327.
 Biblioteca Laurenziana 313.
 — Magliabecchiana 298.
 — Marucelliana 311.
 — Nazionale 298.
 — Riccardiana 311.
 Bigallo 299.
 *Boboli Garden, the 322.
 Borgo Ognissanti 315.
 Botanic Garden 323.
 *Campanile 300.
 Bridges 289.
 Canonry 302.
 S. Carlo Borromeo 299.
 Carmine, Mad. del 317.
 Cascine 328.
 Casino Mediceo 310.
 — dei Nobili 315.
 *Cathedral 300.
 *S. Croce 304.
 *Dante's Statue 304.
 Dogana 310.
 Egyptian Museum 316.
 Fortezza da Basso 317.
 — di Belvedere 323.
 FoundlingHospital 306.
 S. Francesco di Paola 327.
 Gates 289.
 *S. Giovanni Battista 299.
 S. Giovannino degli Scolopi 311.
 House of Bianca Capello 316.

Florence:
  House of Dante 316.
  — — Galileo 316.
  — — Macchiavelli 316.
  — — Michael Angelo 316.
  — — Amerigo Vespucci 316.
  *Loggia dei Lanzi 290.
  *S. Lorenzo 311.
  Madonna del Carmine 317.
  S. Marco 307.
  *—, Monastery 307.
  *S. Maria Novella 311.
  S. Miniato 325.
  Mint, the 291.
  *Misericordia 302.
  Monte Oliveto 327.
  Mosaics, manufact. of 310.
  *Museo di Storia Naturale 323.
  — Nazionale 302.
  S. Niccolò 310.
  Ognissanti 311.
  S. Onofrio 316.
  *Or S. Michele 298.
  Palazzo dell' Antella 304.
  — Bartolommei 311.
  — Berte 306.
  — Buondelmonti 315.
  — Corsini 315.
  — Covoni 311.
  — Fontebuoni 315.
  — Guadagni 318.
  — Guicciardini 316.
  — Manelli 306.
  — Panciatichi 311.
  — Pestellini 311.
  *— Pitti 318.
  — del Podestà 302.
  — Poniatowski 311.
  — Pucci 311.
  *— Riccardi 310.
  — Rucellai 316.
  — Spini 315.
  — Strozzi 316.
  *— Uguccioni 290.
  *— Vecchio 290.
  *Piazza S. S. Annunziata 306.
  *— S. Croce 304.
  — del Duomo 298.
  — S. Lorenzo 311.
  — S. Maria Novella 313.
  *— della Signoria 289.
  — S. Trinità 316.
  Post Office 291.
  Recollets, cloisters of the 310.

Florence:
  S. Salvatore del Monte 324.
  S. Salvi 331.
  Sasso di Dante 302.
  *Spedale degli Innocenti 306.
  *S. Spirito 318.
  Theatres 284.
  *Tribuna del Galileo 323.
  S. Trinità 315.
  *Uffizi, Galleria degli 291.
  Zoolog. Garden 328.
  Zecca, La 291.
St. Florentin 2.
Flüelen 40.
Foglia, the 240.
St. Fons 10.
Fons Aponi 179.
Fontainebleau 1.
Fontaines 4.
Fontana 107.
Fontana fredda 217.
Fontebuona 258.
Forli 235.
Forlimpopoli 236.
Formigine 222.
Fornasette 135.
Forum Alieni 180.
  — *Cornelii* 234.
  — *Julii* 27. 215.
  — *Licini* 124.
  — *Livii* 235.
  — *Popilii* 236.
Fossano 108.
Fossanova 256.
Fossato 243.
Fossombrone 242.
Fourneau 31.
Fourvières 7.
Foux, La 18.
Fragenstein, castle 51.
Franzdorf 67.
Franzensfeste 58.
Franzenshöhe 54.
Frati, Isola dei 152.
Freienfeld 58.
Fréjus 27.
—, Col de 32.
Fressinone, the 37.
Friaul 214.
Frodolfo, the 55.
Fröhlichsburg 53.
Frohnleiten 65.
Frontière, La 32.
Frugarolo 146.
Fuentes, castle 49.
Fumajolo, the 335.
Fuochi, the 257.
Furlo Pass, the 242.
Fürstenburg, castle 53.

Furva, Val 55.
Futa, La 258.

Galbiga, Monte 136.
Gallarate 141.
Galleno 161.
Gallicra 184.
Gallinaria, Isola 96.
Galuzzo 326.
Gaudria 132. 136.
Ganterthal, the 36.
Gard, Pont du 18.
Garda 154.
— Lake of 151.
Garde, La 26.
Gargnano 153.
Garibaldi, Fort 188.
Garlate, Lago di 130.
Garzeno 129.
Gavia, the 55.
Gavirate 131.
Gazza, Monte 62.
Gazzate 131.
Gemonio 131.
Generoso, Monte 132.
Geneva 6. 29.
—, Lake of 34.
Genoa 86.
  Accademia delle Belle Arti 90.
  *Acqua Sola 93.
  S. Ambrogio 90.
  *SS. Annunziata 91.
  Arsenal 89.
  *Cathedral 90.
  Dogana 89.
  Exchange 90.
  Fortifications 88.
  *Harbour 89.
  *S. Lorenzo 90.
  *S. Maria di Carignano 88.
  S. Matteo 90.
  Municipio 91.
  Palazzo Balbi 92.
  *— Brignole 91.
  — of Columbus 92.
  *— Doria 92.
  — Ducale 90.
  — Marcello Durazzo 91.
  *— Pallavicini 91.
  — Reale 92.
  — Rosso 91.
  -- della Scala 91.
  — Spinola 93.
  Ponte Carignano 89.
  Statue of Columbus 92.
  Teatro Carlo Felice 90.
  Town Hall 90.
  University 92.
  Villa Negro 93.
  *— Pallavicini 93.

Gère, the 10.
St. Germain, chât. 29. 82.
S. Germano 110.
Gersau 40.
Gessens, Phare de 30.
Gesso, the 108.
Ghiffa 138.
S. Giacŏmo (Bernardino) 50.
— (near Chiavenna) 48.
Giaglione 33.
Giandola 107.
Giarole 110.
Ginistrella, Monte 144.
Gionnero, Monte s. Monte Generoso.
S. Giorgio 85. 184.
Giornico 43.
S. Giovanni on the Adriatic 215.
— (Lake of Garda 154.
— (near Nice) 106.
—, Castel 84.
—, Island (Lake of Como) 126.
— — (Lago Maggiore) 139.
S. Giovanni Manzano 215.
Giovi 335.
—, Galleria dei 146.
Gittana 129.
Giudicaria 154.
S. Giuliano 83.
—, Monte 273.
S. Giuliano, Bagni di 273.
S. Giulio, Isola 143.
Glanum 16.
Gleichenberg 66.
Glion 34.
Gloggnitz 64.
Glurns 53.
Godo 248.
Coito 151. 172.
Golo, the 340. 341.
Golzano 155.
Gomagoi 54.
Gombo, Il 272.
Gondo 37.
Gonfolina, the 261.
Gorbio 99.
Gorizia 215.
Gorlago 150.
Gorner Grat, the 36.
Görz 215.
Gorzone Canal, the 180.
Göschenen 41.
Gossensass 58.
Gösting 65,
Gotschakogel, the 65.
St. Gotthard, the 42.
Gozzano 111.
Graïan Alps, the 73.

Graisivaudan, Valley of 30.
Gran Sasso d'Italia 245.
Grand' Croix, La 32.
Grandes Roches, Les 34.
Granges 35.
Granier, Mont 30.
Grasse 28.
Grasstein 58.
Gratianopolis 11.
Gratz 65.
Gravedōna 129.
Gravellona 38.
Graveson 16.
Gravone, the 341.
Grenoble 11. 30.
Greve, the 326.
Gries 57.
Grigna, Monte 129.
Grignan, château 12.
Grignano 68.
Grigno 61.
Grimaldi 98.
Grivelli, château 138.
Grödenerbach, the 59.
Grono 50.
Grosotto 56.
Grumello 150.
Guardia, Monte 218.
Guasco, Monte 244.
Guastalla 171.
Guelfo, Castel 217.
Guglielmo, Monte 160.
Guidizzolo 151. 172.
Guillotière, la 6.
Guinzano 147.

Haimingen 52.
Haute-Combe, Abbey 30.
Heidersee, the 33.
Heinzenberg, the 46.
Helvia Ricina 248.
Héricourt 5.
Hinterrhein 50.
Hoch Finstermünz 53.
Hoch-Realt 46.
Hohenems, castle 45.
Hohen-Rhätien, castle 46.
St. Honorat 28.
Hôpitaux, Les 29.
Hospenthal 42.
St. Hospice 106.
Hrastnig 67.
Hyères 26.
—, the Islands of 27.

Idria 67.
If, Château d' 25.
S. Ilario 217.
Imola 235.
L'Imperiale 240.
Inust 52.

Incino 124.
Incisa 109.
Induna 136.
Inn, the 51.
Innsbruck 51. 57.
Intelvi Valley, the 126.
Intra 139.
Intschi 41.
Inverigo 121.
Isaurus 240.
Isel, hill 57.
Iselle 37.
Iseo 159.
—, Lago d' 159.
Isera 62.
Isère, the 11. 30.
Isola 48.
— Bella 139.
— del Cantone 146.
— dei Frati 152.
— Gallinara 96.
— Madre 140.
— Rossa 344.
— dei Pescatori or
— Superiore 140.
Isoletto, rock 154.
Isonzo, the 215.
Ivano, château 61.
Ivrea 81.
Ivry 1.

St. Jean 106.
St. Jean de Maurienne 31.
Joigny 2.
Jorio, Passo 129.
St. Joseph, monastery 66.
Jouan, Golfe 28.
Joviniacum 2.
Julian Alps, the 67. 216.
St. Julien 31.
Jumeaux, the 82.
Juvalta, castle 46.

Kainach, the 66.
Kaltwasser Glacier, the 36.
Kapella Mts., the 71.
Kapfenberg 65.
Karlsdorf 66.
Karst, the 68.
Katzis 46.
Kaunserthal, the 52.
Kindberg 65.
Klamm 65.
Klausen 58.
Klein-Stübing 65.
Klus, the 41.
Kollmann 59.
Königswand, the 54.
Kranichsfeld 66.
Krieglach 65.
Kronburg, ruins 52.
Kurtatsch 59.
Küssnacht (Lake of Lucerne) 39.

352 INDEX.

Labeck, castle 66.
Lacus Benācus 151.
— *Larius* 124.
— *Sebinus* 159.
— *Verbanus* 137.
Ladis 52.
Lagarina, Val 62.
Laggersberg, the 52.
Laglio 126.
Lago Inferiore 169.
— Maggiore 137.
— Superiore 169.
Lagueglia 96.
Laguno, the 190.
Laibach 67.
Laibach, the 67.
Laisse, the 30.
Lambro, the 121. 122.
Lamone, the 235.
Lancenigo 214.
Landeck 52.
Landskron, castle 65.
Lans-le-Bourg 32.
Lanza, the 131.
Larius, Lacus 124.
La Roche 2.
Lasnigo 122.
Lastra 261.
Laudegg, castle 52.
Laus Pompeia 216.
Lausanne 33.
Lavagna 262.
Lavaux 34.
Lavedo, promontory 126.
Laveno 138.
Lavezzola 256.
Lavino 218.
Lavis 60.
Laxenburg 64.
S. Lazaro 217.
Lazise 154.
Lecchio, Isola 152.
Leccia, Ponte alla 341
Lecco 130.
—, the Lake of 130.
Ledro, Lago di 154.
Ledro Valley, the 154.
Leghorn 258.
Legnano 142.
Legnoncino, Monte 129.
Legnone, Monte 129. 130.
Leibnitz 66.
Lenno 124.
S. Leo, Castello di 239.
Leobersdorf 64.
S. Léonard 35.
Lerici 263.
Lerins, Iles 28.
Lesa 141.
Lesecce 68.
Leuk 35.
Leuzumo 154.
Lévant, Ile du 27.

Levante, Riviera di 262.
Leventina, the 43.
Levico 61.
Leyment 6.
Leytha Mts., the 64.
Lezzeno 126.
Liciniforum 124.
Liechtenstein, castle 64.
Lierna 130.
Lieusaint 1.
Lima, the 277.
Limito 149.
Limone (Lake of Garda) 153.
— (Col di Tenda) 108.
Limonta 130.
Lira, the 41. 48.
L'Isle-sur-le-Doubs 5.
L'Isle-sur-Sorgue 16.
Littai 67.
Livenza, the 214.
Livorno 258.
Livron 12.
Lizerne, the 35.
Lizzana 62.
Loano 96.
Locarno 138.
Locate 147.
Lodi 216.
Loëche 35.
Loing, the 3
Loitsch 67.
Lomellina, the 149.
Lonato 151.
Lonigo 172.
Lons-le-Saulnier 6.
Loppio, Lake of 154.
S. Lorenzo 96. 239.
Loreto 246.
S. Loretto 160.
Loriol 12.
Lostallo 50.
Loveno 128.
Lovera 56.
Lovēre 160.
Luc, Le 27.
Lucca 273.
—, the Baths of 277.
Lucciago, Madonna di 143.
Lucendro, Lake of 42.
Lucerne 38.
—, the Lake of 39.
S. Lucia 63. 151.
Lucino 131.
Lucmānier, the 46.
Lueg, castle 57.
Lugano 133.
—, the Lake of 132.
Lugdunum 6.
Lugliano 277.
Lugo 248.
Luinate 131.

Luino 138.
Lumino 51.
Lumio 344.
Luna 264.
Lunel 18.
Lunga Sardo 340.
Lunigiana, La 264.
Lurate 131.
Luri 343.
Luserna, Torre 80.
Lyons 6.
Lysbach, the 81.

Maccagno 138.
Maccaron, Mont 105.
Macerata 248.
Macon 5.
Macra, the 108.
Madatschspitz, the 54.
Maddalena, La 108.
—, island 340.
Madeleine, la 106.
Maderno 153.
Madesimo, the 48.
Madonna degli Angeli 108.
— di Caravaggio 162.
— di Gallivaggio 48.
— della Guardia 146.
— di Lucciago 143.
— di S. Martino 127.
— di Montallegro 262.
— del Monte (near Varese) 136.
— — (near Vicenza) 174.
— d'Oropa 110.
— Pilone 109.
— del Sasso (Lago Maggiore) 138.
— — (Lake of Orta) 143.
— di Tirano 56. 161.
—, Val 145.
Madre, Isōla 140.
Madrera, Val 130.
Magadino 51. 138.
Magenta 111.
Magerbach 52.
Maggia, the 138.
Maggiore, Lago 137.
—, Monte 70.
Magliaso 135.
Magnan, the 103. 106.
Magra, the 262. 263.
Magreglio 122.
Maira, the 49.
Majoria, castle 35.
Malamocco 190.
Malain 3.
Malcesine 154.
Malcro, the 56.
Malghera, Fort 174.
Malgrate 124. 130.
Malgue, La 26.

INDEX.

Malnate 131.
Malon, the 110.
Mals 53.
St. Mammès 2.
Mandello 130.
Manerba 152.
Manerbio 155.
Mantua 169.
S. Manza 340.
Marano 174.
—, the 239.
Marburg 66.
Marcaria 172.
Marchirolo 131.
S. Marco (Simplon) 37.
— (Tyrol) 63.
Maremme, the 259.
Marecchia, river 237. 239.
Marengo 146.
S. Margarita 262.
S. Margherita a Montici 326.
Margreid 59.
Ste. Marguerite 28.
S. Maria, Monastery (near Claro) 43.
— (Stelvio) 54.
— Assunta 184.
— delle Grazie 172.
— Maddalena 180.
— della Salute 44.
Mariana 340.
Ste. Marie 21.
Marienberg, Abbey 53.
Marignano 216.
S. Marino 239.
Marne, the 1.
Maroggia 133.
Marone 160.
Marotto 243.
Marseilles 22.
Martigny 35.
St. Martin 33.
St. Martin, Pont 81.
Martino, Capo 98.
S. Martino (Lake of Lugano) 133.
— (near Rimini) 239. 256.
— (on the Ticino) 111.
— (near Verona) 172.
— d'Albaro, promontory 89.
—, Madonna di 127.
—, il Sasso 127.
Martinswand, the 51.
Marzabotto 257.
Maschere, le 258.
Masein 46.
Masino 143.
Masnago 131: 136.
Masone 37.
Massa 204.
Massaciuccoli, Lago di 277.

Massilia 22.
S. Massimo 168.
Masuccio, Piz 56.
Matarello 62.
Matrey 57.
Matterjoch, the 82.
Maures, Mont. des 26.
St. Maurice 35.
S. Maurizio 218.
—, Monte 123.
Maurizio, Porto 96.
Mediolanum 111.
Meina 141.
Melano 133.
Mele, Capo delle 96.
Melegnano 216.
Melide 133.
Mella, the 155.
Melun 1.
Melzo 149.
Menaggio 128.
Mendrisio 132.
Mentone 98.
Mesocco 50.
Mestre 174. 213.
Metaurus 242. 243.
Meursault 4.
Mezz-Isola 159.
Mezzo, Lago di 169.
Mezzo Lago 154.
— Lombardo 60.
— Tedesco 60.
Mezzola, Lago di 49.
St. Michel 31.
St. Michel, Piz 46.
S. Michele 172.
— della Chiusa 33.
— Lombardo 60. 161.
Migiandone 37.
Milan 111.
 S. Alessandro 116.
 °S. Ambrogio 116.
 °Arco della Pace 119.
 Arena 119.
 Biblioteca Ambrosiana 119.
 °Brera 117.
 S. Carlo Borromeo 116.
 Castle 119.
 °Cathedral 113.
 Cavour's Statue 120.
 °Galleria Vitt. Emanuele 115.
 Giardino Pubblico 120.
 °S. Lorenzo 116.
 S. Maria di S. Celso 117.
 °S. Maria delle Grazie 117.
 S. Mauricio 117.
 Museo Civico 120.
 Ospedale Maggiore 119.
 Palazzo Ciani 117.
 — Litta 117.

Milan:
 Palazzo Marino 117.
 — Reale 115.
 — Saporiti 117.
 Piazza del Duomo 115.
 Teatro della Scala 112.
Mils 52.
Mincio, the 151. 154.
S. Miniato 325.
— dei Tedeschi 261.
Miradolo 155.
Miramar, château 68. 70.
Mirandola 171. 234.
Mischäbel, the 36.
Mitterdorf 65.
Mittersee, the 53.
Mittewald 58.
Modane 32.
Modene 222.
Mödling 64.
Moësa, the 44. 50.
Moësola, Lago 50.
Moggiona 334.
Moglia 171.
Mogliano 213.
Molaret 33.
Molina 154.
Moltrasio 125.
Momo 111.
Monaco 100.
Monate, Lago di 131.
Moncalieri 85.
Mondatsch, the 54.
Mondragon 12.
Moneglia 262.
Monfalcone 215.
Moniga 152.
Mons Pessulus 18.
Monselice 180.
Monsummano 278.
Montagna 56.
— (Heinzenberg) 46.
Montalban, Fort 100.
Montaldo, Castle 81.
Montanaro 81. 172.
Montario, castle 172.
Montbard 3.
Montbéliard 5.
Mont Cenis 32.
Montboron, promont. 105.
Monte S. Bartolo 240.
— Carelli 258.
— Carlo 99.
— Carmelo 96.
— Catini 278.
— Maggiore 70.
— Murlo 281.
— Oliveto 327.
— Santo 215.
Montebello (Piedmont) 84.
— (near Vicenza) 172.
Montecchio 217. 241.
Montechiaro 172.

BAEDEKER. Italy I. 2nd Edit.   23

Monteferrato 282.
Montegrotta 179.
Montélimart 12.
Montelupo 261.
Montereau 2.
Monterey 28.
Monterone, Monte s.
Monte Motterone.
Montgeron 1.
Monti Pisani 272.
Monticelli 109. 163.
Montignoso 265.
Montjovet 82.
—, Defile of 82.
Montmajour 21.
Montmélian 31.
Montmorot, chât. 6.
Montone, the 235. 255.
Montorfano, the 128.
—, monast. 150.
Montpellier 18.
Montreux 34.
Monza 120.
Morbegno 57.
Morcote 136.
Morello, Monte 282.
Moret 2.
Morgozzolo, Monte s.
Monte Motterone.
Mori 63.
Morignone 56.
Mornas 12.
Morosaglia 341.
Morschach 40.
Mortola 98.
Mortara 145.
Motta, La 161.
Motta S. Damiano 154.
Motterone, Monte 142.
Mougins 28.
Mozzecane 169.
Mugello, Val di 258.
Muggia 70.
Mugnone, the 329.
Mulhouse 5.
Muotta, the 40.
Mur, the 65.
Murano 212.
Muriano 277.
Murlo, Monte 281.
Muro, Capo di 337.
Mürz, the 65.
Mürzzuschlag 65.
Muslone 153.
Musocco 142.
Musotto 109.
Musso 129.
Mustina 222.
Muy, Le 27.
Muzzano, Lake of 135.
Mythen, the 40.
Mythenstein, the 40.

Nabrësina 68. 215.
Nago 154.
Napoule, Golfe de la 27.
Nasen, the 39.
Nauders 53.
Navacchio 260.
Naviglio Adigetto 180.
— Grande 111. 113.
— della Martesana 113.
— di Pavia 113. 147.
S. Nazzaro 163.
Nebbio 344.
Nejve 109.
Nemausus 17.
Nerone, Bagni di 277.
Nervi 262.
Nesso 126.
Neu-Habsburg, ruins 39.
Neumarkt 59.
Neusiedler See, the 64.
Neustadt 64.
Neustift 58.
Nevers 4.
Nice 100.
St. Nicholas 36.
S. Niccolò (near Piacenza) 84.
— (Casentino) 333.
Nievole, the 278.
Nîmes 16.
Nivolet, Dent de 30.
Nizza 100.
Nizza di Monferrato 109.
Noce, the 60.
Noli 95.
Nolla, the 46.
Non, Val di 60. 161.
Nonantola 222.
Nonsberg, the 161.
Notre-Dame de la Garde 25.
— — des Neiges, chapel 33.
Novalesa 33.
Novara 110.
Novella 344.
Novi (near Alessandria) 146.
— (near Modena) 171.
Nuits-sous-Ravières 3.
Nure, the 85. 163.
Nure, Ponte 217.
Nus 82.

Obercilli 66.
Oberlaibach 67.
Obladis 52.
Oedenburg 64.
Oetzthal, the 52.
Oggebbio 138.
Oglio, the 150. 155 etc.
Olbia 23.
Olcio 130.

Oldesc 153.
Oleggio 145.
Olgiate 131.
Olgirate, Lago d' 130.
Olimpino, Monte 132.
Olivone 46.
Ollioule, the 26.
Ollioules St. Nazaire 26.
Ollon St. Triphon 35.
Olmeneta 155. 162.
Olona, the 112. 131.
Ombrone, the 261. 278.
Omegna 143.
Oneglia 96.
Onno 130.
Ora 59.
Orange 12.
Orco, the 110.
Orlando, Torre d' 217.
Ornavasso 37.
Oro, Monte d' 341.
Orsera 70.
Orta 143.
—, Lago d' 143.
Ortenstein 46.
Ortler, the 54.
Osimo 245.
Osogna 43.
Ospedaletto 150. 155.
Ossöla, Val d' 37.
Ostriconi, the 344.
Ouche, the 3.
Ouchy 34.
Oulx 32.
Oviglio 109.
Ovolo, Monte 257.

Padernione 62.
Padova or
Padua 175.
Paglione or Paillon, the 103.
Palazzolo 150.
Palestrina 190.
Pallanza 139.
Palmaria 263.
Paltaus, castle 58.
Palud, La 12.
Pambio 134.
Panaro, the 218. 222.
S. Paolo, islet 159.
Papia 148.
Parabiago 142.
Parata, Punta della 337.
Parè 130.
Parenzo 70.
— river 172. 219.
Parona 63.
Partina 334.
Pas-des-Lanciers 21.
Pasbles 106.
Paspels 46.
Patavum 175.

INDEX.

Paterno 332.
Patsch 57.
Paullo 225.
Pavia 148.
Paviole 180.
Pazzallo 134.
Pedenos 55.
—, Val 55.
Peggau 65.
Pegli 94.
Pelago 332.
Pella 143.
Pellino, the 144.
Pendolasco 56.
Pentapolis maritima 237.
Penzano 124.
St. Peray 11.
Pergine 61.
Peri 63.
Pernegg 65.
Perosa 80.
Perrache 9.
Pertengo 110.
Pesa, the 261.
Pesaro 240.
Pescantina 63.
Pescatori, Isola dei 140.
Peschiera 151. 154.
— d'Iseo 159.
Pescia 278.
Pésio, Val 108.
— —, Certosa di 108.
Pessione 86.
St. Peter 68.
Petersberg, the 52.
Petraja, La 329.
Pfannberg, castle 65.
Pflersch-Thal, the 58.
Pfunds 52.
Pfyn 35.
Piacenza 84.
Piadena 172.
Pianazzo 48.
Pianello 129.
Piano, Lago del 136.
Piano del Tivano 126.
Pianoro 257.
Pianzano 214.
Piave 214.
— river 61. 214.
Picenum 245.
Piè di Castello 62.
S. Pier d'Arena 95. 146.
S. Pierino 260.
S. Piero 281.
St. Pierre-d'Albigny 31.
Pierrelatte 12.
Pietas Julia 71.
Pietolo 171.
Pietra 96.
Pietra Murata 62.
Pietramala 257.
Pietrasanta 265.

S. Pietro 161.
— in Casale 184.
Pieve 154.
— di Cento 184.
— a Nievole 278.
— a Pelago 225.
— di Sori 262.
Pignerol 80.
Pilat, Mont 11.
Pilatus, the 39.
Pinerolo 80.
Pineta, La 256.
Pino 343.
Piolenc 12.
Piottino, Monte 43.
Piovere 153.
Pioverna, the 129.
Pipet, Mont 10.
Pirano 70. 216.
Pisa 265.
  Academy 272.
  Archives 272.
  °Baptistery 267.
  Bagni di Nerone 272.
  °Botan. Garden 272.
  °Campanile 268.
  °Campo Santo 268.
  °S. Caterina 270.
  °Duomo 267.
  S. Francesco 270.
  Lung-Arno 266.
  S. Maria della Spina 270.
  S. Michele in Borgo 271.
  Nat. Hist. Museum 272.
  S. Nicola 271.
  Palaces 271.
  S. Paolo a Ripa d'Arno 271.
  °°Piazza del Duomo 266.
  °S. Pietro in Grado 272.
  Sapienza 272.
  S. Sisto 271.
  S. Stefano ai Cavalieri 271.
Pisa, the Baths of 273.
Pisaurum 240.
Pisciatello, the 237.
Pisogne 160.
Pissevache, the 35.
Pistoja 278.
Pitecchio 257.
Piumegna, the 43.
Pizzighettone 155.
Pizzigone, Monte 144.
Pizzo, Monte 160.
Pizzocolo, Mte. 153.
Plaisance 84.
Plan de l'Aiguille 10.
Platteinkogl, the 52.
Plessur, the 45.
Pliniana, Villa 125.
Po, the 79. 85 etc.
Po di Primaro 184. 235.

Poggio Imperiale, Villa 325.
Poggio Renatico 184.
Pogliasca 262.
Polk, the 68.
Pojana 174.
Pola 70.
Polcevēra, the 146.
Polenta 236.
Polesella 180.
Polleggio 43.
S. Polo 85.
Pöltschach 66.
Ponal, Fall of the 153.
St. Pons, monastery 105.
Ponsas, castle 11.
Pont d'Ain 29.
Pont St. Esprit 12.
Pont St. Martin 81.
Pont-de-Veyle 29.
Pontassieve 331.
Ponte di Brenta 174.
— Chiasso 132.
— Curone 83.
— alla Leccia 344.
— S. Marco 151.
— Nure 217.
— a Poppi 334.
— a Rifredi 328.
— a Serraglio 277.
— Tresa 135.
Pontedecimo 146.
Pontedera 260.
Pontelagoscuro 180.
Pontenuovo 341.
Pontevico 155.
Pontigny 2.
Pontlatzer Brücke, the 52.
Ponzana 110.
Poppi 334.
Porcari 277.
Pordenone 214.
Porlezza 136.
Porquerolles 27.
Porretta 257.
Porta 341.
Portcros 27.
Porto 136.
— S. Benedetto 171.
— Maurizio 96.
— Valtravaglia 138.
— Vecchio 340.
— Venere 263.
Portus Lunae 263.
Poschiavino, the 56.
Possagno 61.
Pössnitz 66.
Postojna 68.
Potenza 248.
Pötschach 64.
Pozzolengo 151.
Pozzolo, Lago di 343.
Pozzuolo 83.

23*

Prà 96.
Pracchia 257.
Prad 53.
Pragerhof 66.
Pranzo 153.
Prato 281.
Prato al Soglio 334.
Pratolino 258.
Pratomagno, the 333.
Pratovecchio 333.
Praz, la 31.
Preganziolo 213.
Premosello 37.
Premstätten 66.
Pressura, Monte 54.
Prestanek 68.
Pricutta, Mte. 32.
Primaro, Po di 184.
S. Primo, Monte 122.
Primolano 61.
Privas 12.
Promontorium Sacrum 343.
Prosecco 68.
Provaglio 159.
Prutz 52.
Pugieu 29.
Pusiano 124.
—, Lago di 122. 124.
Pyrimont 29.

Quaderna 234.
Quarnero Bay, the 71.
Quarsano 126.
Quart, castle 82.
Queceta 265.
St. Quentin 18.
Quinto 262.

Rabenstein, castle 65.
Racconigi 109.
Raetionicum 129.
St. Rambert 11.
St. Rambert-de-Joux 29.
Rapallo 262.
St. Raphael 27.
Rarek 68.
Raron 86.
Ratonneau 21.
Raut-Glacier, the 37.
Ravenna 248.
 Academy 250.
 St. Agata 251.
 *S. Apollinare in Classe 255.
 *S. Apollinare Nuovo 254.
 Archives 250.
 *Baptistery 250.
 Biblioteca Comunale 250.
 Cathedral 249.
 Classe 250.

Ravenna:
 Colonna de' Francesi 256.
 *Dante's Tomb 251.
 S. Domenico 252.
 S. Francesco 251.
 S. Giovanni Battista 253.
 S. Giovanni Evangelista 254.
 Library 250.
 S. Lorenzo in Cesarea 255.
 S. Maria in Cosmedin 253.
 — in Porto 254.
 — in Porto Fuori 255.
 *— della Rotonda 255.
 S. Michele in Affricisco 252.
 *S. Nazario e Celso 253.
 S. Niccolò 251.
 Palace of Theodoric 254.
 Palazzo Arcivescovile 250.
 *Piazza Maggiore 249.
 Piazzetta dell' Aquila 249.
 Pineta, La 256.
 S. Romualdo 251.
 *Rotonda, the 255.
 S. Spirito 253.
 *S. Vitale 252.
Raxalp, the 64.
Realta 46.
Rebbio 131.
Recanati 247.
Recca, the 215.
Recco 262.
Recoaro 174.
Reggio 217.
Regoledo 129.
Reichenau 45.
Reichenauer Thal 64.
Reifenstein, castle 58.
Reka 71.
S. Remigio, promont. 139.
S. Remo 97.
Remoulins 18.
St. Remy 16.
Reno, the 218. 257.
Renoso, Monte 340.
S. Reparata, Monte 344.
Reschen 53.
— -Scheideck, the 53.
Resegone, Monte 122.
Restonica, the 342.
Reuss, the 38. 40.
Reyzousse, the 29.
Rezzano 85.
Rezzato 151.
Rezzonica, Villa 61.

Rezzonico 129.
Rhäzüns 46.
Rhegium Lepidi 217.
Rhein, the Averser- 47.
— Hinter- 45.
— Vorder- 45.
Rheinwaldthal, the 47. 50.
Rhò 111. 142.
Rhone, the 7. 10 etc
—, la Perte du 29.
—, the Petit 21.
Riddes 35.
Ried 52.
Rietberg 46.
Rifredi 282.
Rigi, the 39.
Riglio, the 163.
Riguli 273.
Rimini 237.
Riola 257.
Ripafratto 273.
Ritorto, the 124.
Riva (Lake of Como) 49.
— (Lake of Garda) 153.
—, Lago di 49.
Riva di Palanzo 123.
Rivarolo 146.
Rivellata, promont. 344.
Riviera, the 43.
— di Levante 262.
— di Ponente 94.
Rivoli 63.
Robecco 155.
Robillante 108.
Roccabruna 99.
Rocca S. Casciano 236.
Rocchetta Pass, the 60.
S. Rocco 160.
Roche-de-Glun 11.
Roche taillée, the 11.
Rochemelon, the 33.
Roffla Gorge, the 47.
Rogliano 343.
Rognac 21.
Rogoredo 147. 216.
Rohitsch, Baths of 66.
Roja, the 97. 107.
Romagna, the 216.
Romagnano 144.
S. Romano 260.
Romena 334.
Roncaglia 163.
Ronco (Apennines) 236.
— (Lago Maggiore) 138.
Ronco, the 236.
Rongellen 47.
Roquebrune 27.
Roquefavour 21.
Roquemaure 13.
Rossillon 29.
S. Rossore 272.
Rostino 341.
Rothenbrunn 46.

INDEX. 357

Rothenfluh, the 39.
Rotonda, Villa 174.
Rotondo, Monte 342.
Rotta, La 260.
Rotunda, the 121.
Route de Grenoble 30.
Roverbella 169.
Roveredo (Bernardino)50.
— (Tyrol) 62.
Rovigno 70.
Rovigo 180.
Rovio 132.
Rubico 61.
Rubicone, the 237.
Rubiera 218.
Rubio 61.
S. Ruffio 257.
Russi 248.
Rütli, the 40.
Rutzbach, the 57.

Saasgrat, the 36.
Sabbionetta 172.
Sacile 214.
Sacro Monte, the (near Orta) 143.
— (near Varallo) 144.
— (Calmaldoli) 334.
Sagor 67.
Sagro, Monte 264.
Sala 126.
Salassins, Pont des 82.
Sale Marazzino 160.
Sallenche, the 35.
Salloch 67.
Salò 152.
Salon 21.
Salorino 132.
Salurn 59.
Salute, la 138.
Saluzzo 109.
Saluzzola 110.
S. Salvadore, Monte 134.
S. Salvi 331.
Salvore 70. 216.
Samoggia 218.
Sanguinarie, Isole 337.
Sann, the 67.
Sansobbia, the 95.
Santerno, the 234.
Santhià 110.
Santo, Monte 215.
Saône, the 4.
Saorgio 107.
Sapis 236.
Sarca, the 62.
Sarca, Val 62.
Sarchè, Le 62. 154.
Sardagna 62.
Sarnico 159.
Sarns 58.
Sarnthal, the 59.
Sartirana 145.

Sarzana 263.
Sarzanella 263.
Sassalbo 218.
Sassella 57.
Sasso 257.
Sasso di Castro 258.
— Rancio, il 129.
— del Ferro, the 139.
Sassuola 225.
Sau, the 67.
Sava 67.
Save, the 67.
Savena, the 226. 257.
Savigliano 108.
Savignano 237. 257.
Savio, the 236.
Savona 95.
Saxon, Baths of 35.
Scandiano 218.
Scanupia, Monte 61.
Scarena 107.
Schächenthal, the 41.
Schamser Thal, the 47.
Schelleberg 58.
Schleglmühl 64.
Schluderns 53.
Schneeberg, the 64.
Schöllenen, the 41.
Schwarzau, the 64.
Schwyz 40.
Scrivia, the 83. 146.
Seben, monastery 58.
Sebenstein, castle 64.
Secchia, the 218. 222.
Seckau, castle 66.
Secugnago 216.
Seelisberg 40.
Segusio 33.
Scillon 29.
Sella Lake, the 42.
Semmering 65.
—, the 64.
Sempione 37.
Sena Gallica 243.
Senio, the 234.
Sens 2. 3.
Serbelloni, Villa 127.
Serchio, the 265.
Seregno 121.
Sérézin 10.
Sergiana 263.
Seriate 150.
Serio, the 150.
Sermione, promont. 152.
Sernio 56.
Serra 225.
—, la, Pass 56.
Serra Mts., the 343.
Serraggio 340.
Serraglio 171.
Serravalle (Apennines) 146.
— (Tyrol) 63.

Serravalle (Tuscany)278.
Serravezza 265.
Serves 11.
Servola 70.
Sesia, the 110. 143.
—, Val 144.
Sessame, Valle 47.
Sessana 68.
Sesto 120. 277.
Sesto Calende 141.
Sestri a Levante 262.
— a Ponente 95.
Setta, brook 257.
Sette Comuni, the 61.
Settignano 335.
Settimo 110.
Settimo-Vittone 81.
Sevron, the 6.
Seyne, La 26.
Seyssel 29.
Sibilla, Mont. della 245.
Siegmundsried 52.
Sierre 35.
Sieve, the 258. 331.
Signa 261.
Silaro, the 234.
Silinen 41.
Sill, the 57.
Silz 52.
Simone, the Sassi di 335.
Simpeln or Simplon 37.
— Pass, the 36.
Singerna, the 335.
Sinigaglia 243.
Sinnus 234.
Sion 35.
Sirolo 245.
Siviano 159.
Sizzano 144.
Soave, castle 172.
Soazza 50.
Soci 334.
Solano, the 333.
Solarolo 248.
Solbiate 131.
Sole, Val di 161.
Solero 86.
Solferino 63. 151.
Solman, the 6.
Somma 141.
Somma Campagna 151.
Sommariva, Villa s. V. Carlotta.
Soncino 163.
Sondrio 56.
Sonzino 163.
Sopra Villa 123.
Soresina 162.
Sorgue, the 16.
Sorgues 13.
Sornico 130.
Sospello 107.

358 INDEX.

Speluga 48.
Spezia, La 263.
Spielfeld 66.
Spinetta 83.
Splügen 48.
Splügen Pass, the 48.
Spondinig 53.
Spotorno 95.
Sprechenstein, castle 58.
Spressiano 214.
Stafflach 57.
Staffora, the 83.
Stalvedro, Stretto di 42.
Stams 51.
Stanghella 180.
Stans 39.
Starkenbach 52.
Staziona 161.
S. Stefano 97. 216.
S. Stefano Belbo 109.
— in Pane 329.
Steinach 57.
Steinbrücken 67.
Stello, Monte 343.
Stelvio 53.
Stelvio Pass, the 54.
Stenico 154.
Sterzing 58.
Stia 334.
Stilfs 53.
Stoechades 27.
Strambino 81.
Strasbourg 5.
Strassengel, church of 65.
Stresa 140.
Stretta 341.
Strona, the 38.
Stubaythal, the 57.
Stura, the 108. 110 etc.
Sturla 262.
Succursale di Torino 110.
Sugana, Val 61.
Sulden Glacier, the 54.
Suldenthal, the 54.
Sulzano 160.
Sulzberg, the 161.
Suna 139.
Surettahorn, the 48.
Susa 33.
Susten 36.
Suvers 48.

Taggia 97.
Tagliamento, the 214.
Tagstein 46.
Tain 11.
Talfer, the 59.
Tambohorn, the 48.
Tanlay 2.
Tanăro, the 86. 109. 145.
Tarascon 16.
Taro, the 217.
Tartsch 53.

Tassone, Cavo, Canal 184.
Tauroeis 23.
Tavazzano 216.
Tavernelle 172.
Tavignano, the 340. 341.
Tavollo, the 239.
Tavordo 136.
Teglio 56. 161.
Telfs 51.
Tell's Platte 40.
Tellina, Val 56. 161.
Tenay 29.
Tenda 107.
—, Col di 108.
Tenno 153.
Teplitz 67.
Tergeste 69.
Terglou, the 67.
Terlago 62.
Termignon 32.
Ternitz 64.
Tersăto, castle 71.
Tesino, the 61. 154.
Tessin s. Ticino.
Thalie, the 4.
Thermae Pannonicae 64.
Thomery 2.
Thusis 46.
Ticino, the 51. 137 etc.
—, the Canton of 133. 138.
Ticinum 148.
Tignale 153.
Timavo, the 215.
Timavus 215.
Tirano 56. 161.
—, Madonna di 56. 161.
Titan, Ile du 27.
Tivano, Piano del 126.
Toblino, castle 62.
Toblino, Lake of 62.
Toccia or
Toce s. Tosa.
Tomiliasca 46.
Tonale, Monte 161.
Tonnerre 21.
Torano, the 264.
Torbole, the 154.
Torcello 212.
Torno 125.
Torrazza di Verolan 110.
Torre-Beretti 145. 149.
— del Gallo 326.
— di Lago 265.
— Luserna 80.
— d'Orlando 217.
— di Vezio 128.
Torretta 105.
—, castle 105.
Torri 154.
Torri, Le 163.
Torrigia 126.
Tortona 83.
Tosa, the 37. 137.

Toscolano 153.
Tösens 52.
Tosi 332.
Toulon 26.
Tour, La 80.
Tourbillon, castle 35.
Tournanche, Val 82.
Tournon 11.
Tournus 4.
Tourtemagne 36.
Tovo 56.
Trafoi 54.
Tramin 59.
Tratta, Monte 154.
Trautson, château 57.
Tre Croci 136.
Trebbia, the 84.
Trebbo 218.
Trebia 84.
Trecate 111.
Treib 40.
Tremelone, island 154.
Tremezzina, the 126.
Tremezzo 126.
Tremŏla, Val 42.
Tremōsine 153.
Trent 60.
Tresa, the 135. 137.
Tresenda 56. 161.
Tresero, Piz 55.
Treviglio 149.
Treviso 213.
Trezzo 130.
Tridentum 60.
Trient, the Gorge du 35.
Trieste 68.
Triffail 67.
Trigione, the 342.
Trinità, La 107.
Trinquetaille 19.
Trivella, castle 107.
Tropaea Augusti 99.
Trostburg, castle 59.
Trufarello 85. 109.
Tschingel Glacier, the 36.
Tschürgant, the 52.
Tüffer, Markt 67.
Turbia 99.
Turin 72.
  Accademia delle Belle Arti 77.
  *Armoury 74.
  Arsenal 77.
  Botanic Garden 79.
  *Campo Santo 80.
  Capuchin Monastery 79.
  Cathedral 78.
  *Cemetery 80.
  Consolata, La 79.
  Corpus Domini 78·
  Giardino Pubblico 79.
  Giardino Reale 74.
  Gran Madre di Dio 79.

Turin:
  S. Massimo 78.
  °Monuments 75. 77.
  Museo Lapidario 77.
  Museum of Antiquities 76.
  Nat. Hist. Museum 76.
  Palazzo dell' Accademia delle Scienze 75.
  — Carignano 74.
  — Madama 74.
  - Reale 74.
  Picture Gallery 76.
  Polytechn. School 79.
  Protestant Church 79.
  °Superga 80.
  Synagogue 79.
  Valentino, the 79.
  °Via di Po 73.
  Zoolog. Garden 74.
Turr, La 47.
Turtman 36.

Udine 214.
Umago 70.
Umbrail, Piz 55.
Unterau 58.
Urbano, Forte 218.
Urbino 241.
Urgbach, the 52.
Urgone, the 237.
Uri, the Bay of 40.
Urner Loch, the 41.
Urseren 42.
—, the Valley of 42.
Uso, river 237. 256.

Vaise 7.
Val Madonna 145.
— d'Ottavo 277.
— Rhein 47. 50.
— Travaglia 138.
Valais, the Canton of 35.
Valcarès, Etang de 21.
Valdieri, Baths of 108.
Valence 11.
St. Valentin auf d. Heide 53.
Valenza 145.
Valeria, castle 35.
Vallauris 28.
Valle 145.
Valle dei Calci 272.
St. Vallier 11.
Vallombrosa 331.
Valmara, the 127.
Vals, château de 11.
Valserine Viaduct, the 29.
Valstagna 61.
Val Tellina, the 56. 161.
Valtravaglia 138.
Vanoise, Mont 32.
Vaprio 162.

Var, the 28.
Vara, the 262.
Varallo 144.
Varallo-Pombia 145.
Varazze 95.
Varen 36.
Varenna 128.
Varese 131.
—, Lago di 131.
Varigotti 96.
Varrone, the 129. 153.
Vaucluse 16.
Vedeggio, the 44.
Velleia 85.
Vence 28.
Venda, Monte 179.
Venice 184.
  °Accademia delle Belle Arti 199.
  SS. Apostoli 201.
  Archaeolog. Museum 197.
  Archives 202.
  °Arsenal 199.
  Botan. Garden 212.
  Bridge of Sighs 198.
  °Cà d'Oro 211.
  °Campanile 194.
  Campo di Marte 212.
  Clock Tower 194.
  Corte del Remer 211.
  S. Crisostomo 201.
  Dogana di Mare 208.
  Fondaco de' Tedeschi 211.
  °— de' Turchi 211.
  S. Francesco della Vigna 201.
  °°Frari 202.
  Gesuiti 203.
  Giardino Papadopoli 212.
  Giardini Pubblici 212.
  °S. Giorgio Maggiore 203.
  °°SS. Giovanni e Paolo 203.
  S. Giuliano 205.
  °°Grand Canal 208.
  Lagune, the 190.
  S. Lazzaro 205.
  °Library 195.
  Lido 212.
  °°St. Marco 192.
  S. Maria Formosa 205.
  — de' Miracoli 205.
  — dell' Orto 205.
  °— della Salute 206.
  — Zobenigo 206.
  Merceria, the 195.
  Murazzi 190.
  Museo Civico 211.
  Palazzo Balbi 210.
  — Barbarigo 210.

Venice:
  Palazzo Battagia 211.
  °— Bembo 210.
  — Bernardo 210.
  — de' Camerlinghi 211.
  °— Cavalli 209.
  °— Contarini-Fasan 209.
  — Contarini delle Figure 210.
  — Contarini degli Scrigni 210.
  °— Corner della Cà Grande 209.
  — Corner della Regina 211.
  °— Corner-Spinelli 210.
  — Correr 211.
  — Dandolo 210.
  — Dario-Angarani 208.
  °°— Ducale (of the Doges) 195.
  — Emo-Treves 209.
  — Erizzo 211.
  °— Farsetti 210.
  — Ferro 209.
  — Fini 209.
  °— Foscari 210.
  — Giustiniani 209.
  — Giustinian-Lolin 209.
  — Grassi 209.
  °— Grimani 210.
  — Grimani della Vida 211.
  — Labia 212.
  °— Loredan 210.
  — Manfrin 212.
  — Mangilli-Valmarana 211.
  — Manin 210.
  — Manzoni-Angarani 209.
  — Michieli dalle Colonne 211.
  — Mocenigo 210.
  — Moro-Lin 210.
  — Da Mula 209.
  — Persico 210.
  — Pesaro 211.
  — Pisani 210.
  °— Rezzonico 209.
  — Sagredo 211.
  — Tiepolo-Stürmer 210.
  — Tiepolo-Zucchelli 209.
  — Tron 211.
  °°— Vendramin - Calergi 211.
  — Venier 209.
  — Zichy-Esterhazy 209.
  S. Pantaleone 206.
  °Piazza of St. Mark 191.
  Piazzetta, the 195.
  S. Pietro di Castello 206.

360 INDEX.

Venice:
  Piombi, the 198.
  *Ponte di Rialto 211.
  Ponte de' Sospiri 198.
  Pozzi, the 198.
  Procuratie 191.
  Railway Station 184. 212.
  *Redentore 206.
  Riva degli Schiavoni 198.
  S. Rocco 207.
  *S. Salvadore 207.
  Scala dei Giganti 196.
  Scalzi 207.
  Scuola di S. Marco 204.
  *S. Sebastiano 207.
  Seminario Patriarcale 208.
  S. Simeone Piccolo 208.
  *Statue of Colleoni 204.
  *S. Stefano 208.
  Theatres 187.
  Torre dell' Orologio 194.
  *S. Zaccaria 208.
  Zecca 195.
Venere, Porto 263.
Ventimiglia 97.
Ventoux, Mont 12. 16.
Verbanus, Lacus 137.
Vercelli 110.
Vergato 257.
Vergiate 141.
Vermanagna, the 108.
Vernayaz 35.
Vernex 34.
Vernia, the 335.
Verola Nuova 155.
Verona 163.
  *Amphitheatre 164.
  *S. Anastasia 165.
  Campo Santo 168.
  Cappella de' Pellegrini 166.
  Castello S. Pietro 168.
  — Vecchio 166.
  Cathedral 166.
  Dante's Statue 165.
  S. Fermo Maggiore 167.
  Giardino Giusti 168.
  S. Giorgio 166.
  S. Giovanni in Fonte 166.
  Loggia, la 165.
  S. Maria Antica 165.
  Museo Civico 168.
  — Lapidario 164.
  Palazzo del Consiglio 165.
  — Pompei 168.
  Piazza Brà 164.
  — delle Erbe 164.
  *— dei Signori 165.

Verona:
  S. Pietro Martire 166.
  Ponte di Castello 166.
  — delle Navi 168.
  Porta de' Borsari 164.
  — Stuppa 166.
  Roman Theatre 168.
  Tomb of Juliet 167.
  *Tombs of the Scaligers 165.
  *S. Zenone 166.
Verona, La Chiusa di 63.
Verrex 82.
Verruca, La 272.
Verruca, the (Trent) 60.
Vescovato 341.
Vesontio 5.
Vespolate 145.
Vevay 34.
Veyle, the 29.
Veytaux 34.
Vezia 45.
Vezzano 62.
Via Aemilia 216.
  — *Flaminia* 216.
Via Mala, the 46.
Viareggio 265.
Vicenza 173.
Vico 123.
Vidauban 27.
Viège 36.
Vienne 10.
Vieux-Mont-Ferrand 29.
Vigese, Monte 257.
Vigevano 145.
S. Vigilio 152. 154.
Vignola 222.
Vigo 257.
Vigolo 62.
Villa 277.
Villa Amalia 123.
  — degli Albizzi 327.
  — Ambrogiana 261.
  — Antongina 126.
  — Balbianello 126.
  — della Bugia 326.
  — Calderara 130.
  — Caréggi 328.
  — Carlotta 127.
  — Clary 105.
  — Colobiano 125.
  — Demidoff 328.
  — Doccia 329.
  — Enderlin 134.
  — d'Este 125.
  — Faroni s. V. Taverna.
  — Fiorio 153.
  — Frizzoni 127.
  — Gaggi s. V. Antongina.
  — Galbiati 126.
  — del Galileo 326.
  — Giulia 128.
  — Lasquez 130.

Villa Manfrini 213.
  — Marchino 134.
  — Marlia 277.
  — Melzi 127.
  — Mozzi 329.
  — Mylius 128.
  — Napoli 125.
  — Negro 93.
  — Odescalchi s. V. Raimondi.
  — Paldi 128.
  — Pallavicini 93.
  — Palmieri 329.
  — Passalacqua 125.
  — Pasta 125.
  — Petraia 328.
  — Pizzo 125.
  — Pliniana 125.
  — Poggio Imperiale 325.
  — Pratolino 258.
  — Prina 139.
  — Quarto 329.
  — Raimondi 125.
  — Rezzonica 61.
  — Rotonda 174.
  — Serbelloni 127.
  — Smith 105.
  — Sommariva s. V. Carlotea.
  — Taglioni 125.
  — Tanzina 134.
  — Taverna 125.
  — Trubetzkoi 125.
  — Vasalli 134.
  — Vigoni 128.
  — Vittoria 240.
Villafranca (near Asti) 86.
  — (near Nice) 105.
  — (near Verona) 169.
Villamaggiore 147.
Villanuova (near Asti) 86.
  — (near Verona) 172.
Villastellone 109.
Villefranche (near Aosta) 82.
  — (near Nice) 105.
Villeneuve (Lake of Geneva) 34.
  — St. Georges 1.
St. Vincent 82.
Vintschgau, the 53.
Visgnola 130.
Viso, Monte 108.
Visp or
Vispach 36.
Vitrolles 21.
S. Vittore 51. 172.
Vittoria 107.
Vittuone 111.
Vivario 340.
Viviers 12.
Vizzarona 340.
Voghera 83.

Voglans 30.
Vogogna 37.
Volta 151.
Volterra 260.
Voltri 95.
Voragine 95.
Vöslau 64.
Voujacourt 5.
Vuache, Mont the 29.

Wäggis 39.
Waidbruck 59.
Waldensian Valleys, the 80.

Wartenstein, castle 64.
Wasen 41.
Wattingen 41.
Weinzettelwand, the 65.
Weisseneck, castle 66.
Welfenstein, castle 58.
Wildon, castle 66.
Wiltau, Abbey 57.
Wippthal, the 58.
Worms s. Bormio.
Wytenstein, the 40.

Yères, the 1.

Yonne, the 2.

Zams 52.
Zanelli, Canal 235.
Zapporthorn, the 48.
Zebru, Monte 54.
Zenna 127.
S. Zeno 155.
Zermatt 36. 82.
Zibio, Monte 225.
Zillis 47.
Zirknitzer See, the 68.
Zirl 51.
Zufallspitz, the 54.

www.ingramcontent.com/pod-product-compliance
Lightning Source LLC
Chambersburg PA
CBHW030322020526
44117CB00030B/379